FOOD SCIENCE

SECOND EDITION

some other AVI books

Food Technology and Engineering

TECHNOLOGY OF WINE MAKING, 3RD EDITION *Amerine, Berg and Cruess*
DAIRY LIPIDS AND LIPID METABOLISM *Brink and Kritchevsky*
FUNDAMENTALS OF FOOD ENGINEERING, 2ND EDITION *Charm*
THE TECHNOLOGY OF FOOD PRESERVATION, 3RD EDITION *Desrosier*
ECONOMICS OF FOOD PROCESSING *Greig*
PRINCIPLES OF PACKAGE DEVELOPMENT *Griffin and Sacharow*
DRYING OF MILK AND MILK PRODUCTS *Hall and Hedrick*
FOOD PROCESSING OPERATIONS, VOLS. 1, 2, AND 3 *Joslyn and Heid*
QUALITY CONTROL FOR THE FOOD INDUSTRY, 3RD EDITION *Kramer and Twigg*
BAKERY TECHNOLOGY AND ENGINEERING, 2ND EDITION *Matz*
CEREAL TECHNOLOGY *Matz*
BREAD SCIENCE AND TECHNOLOGY *Pomeranz and Shellenberger*
SOYBEANS: CHEMISTRY AND TECHNOLOGY, VOL. 1 *Smith and Circle*
THE FREEZING PRESERVATION OF FOODS, 4TH EDITION, VOLS. 1, 2, 3, AND 4
Tressler, Van Arsdel and Copley
FOOD DEHYDRATION, 2ND EDITION, VOLS. 1 AND 2 *Van Arsdel, Copley
and Morgan*
FOOD OILS AND THEIR USES *Weiss*

Food Chemistry and Microbiology

MICROBIOLOGY OF FOOD FERMENTATIONS *Pederson*
FOOD ENZYMES *Schultz*
PROTEINS AND THEIR REACTIONS *Schultz and Anglemier*
CARBOHYDRATES AND THEIR ROLES *Schultz, Cain and Wrolstad*
CHEMISTRY AND PHYSIOLOGY OF FLAVORS *Schultz, Day and Libbey*
LIPIDS AND THEIR OXIDATION *Schultz, Day and Sinnhuber*
PRACTICAL FOOD MICROBIOLOGY AND TECHNOLOGY, 2ND EDITION *Weiser,
Mountney and Gould*
FUNDAMENTALS OF DAIRY CHEMISTRY *Webb and Johnson*

Nutrition

MILESTONES IN NUTRITION *Goldblith*
NUTRITIONAL EVALUATION OF FOOD PROCESSING *Harris and Von Loesecke*
PROTEINS AS HUMAN FOOD *Lawrie*
PROGRESS IN HUMAN NUTRITION, VOL. 1 *Margen*

FOOD SCIENCE

SECOND EDITION

by NORMAN N. POTTER, Ph.D.

Professor of Food Science,
Cornell University, Ithaca, New York

Formerly, Manager, Food Technology,
American Machine and Foundry Company,
Springdale, Conn.

Formerly, Assistant Head, Cereal Chemistry
Division, The Fleischmann Laboratories,
Stamford, Conn.

WESTPORT, CONNECTICUT

THE AVI PUBLISHING COMPANY, INC.

1973

Library of Congress Catalog Card Number: 73-79374
ISBN-0-87055-140-X

Printed in the United States of America

Dedicated to

My parents, sons, and dear wife, Adele

Preface to the Second Edition

Since the First Edition of *Food Science* was published in 1968 it has enjoyed wide circulation in the United States and in several other countries and has been accepted as a textbook in many colleges and universities. It also has been translated into Japanese and Spanish. This response has encouraged me to adhere to the objectives set forth in the preface to the First Edition and to largely retain the original format in revising the volume.

The field of Food Science and Food Technology, like so much else in today's rapidly changing world, has been racing forward at a pace that leaves most of us humbled in the attempt to keep up. In preparing this revision I have endeavored to update, and, where appropriate, expand the original material to keep the book current. Many sections have been added or modified to bring in new subject material broadly ranging from aspects of intermediate moisture food technology and winemaking, to concerns over food waste control, the safety of food additives, and uncertainties of the green revolution. A new chapter on improving nutritional quality and nutritional labeling also has been added. But these additions, in most instances, have purposely been kept short so as not to exceed book length still appropriate to a single volume.

Since the First Edition of this book, many useful suggestions have been received that have helped in preparing the revision and I acknowledge these with sincere appreciation. I further wish to thank Mrs. Barbara I. Lynch for outstanding secretarial help, Dr. Donald K. Tressler and Mr. John J. O'Neil for their assistance with the manuscript, and Cornell University for continuing to provide encouragement for this kind of undertaking.

NORMAN N. POTTER
Ithaca, New York

January 1973

Preface to the First Edition

This book is written primarily for those who have received no previous instruction in the field of Food Science. Its purpose is to introduce and to survey the complex and fascinating interrelationships between properties of food raw materials and their methods of handling and manufacture into an almost unlimited number of useful products.

The literature of Food Science and Food Technology is extensive in its detailed treatment of specific commodities, unit operations, and control methods. This provides the advanced student and seasoned professional with a wealth of excellent reference material generally quite adequate to their particular needs. Much of this literature, however, presupposes a basic training in Food Science or a related discipline. Thus it does not address itself to the needs for insight and appreciation of the broad scope of Food Science by new students considering this field as a career opportunity, or to the needs of professionals in allied fields that today service the food industry in countless capacities.

It would be difficult to select a major field with greater impact upon our everyday lives, upon the economic and political fortunes of nations, and indeed upon the near future of the world itself than the field of Food Science. Yet the terms Food Science and Food Scientist are but vaguely understood by the majority of people who could fairly well describe the realm and activities of chemists, physicists, electronic engineers, and molecular biologists.

The field of Food Science employs professionals from each of the above disciplines, and from at least a score more of the time-honored sciences and technologies. Food Science today teams together such specialists as the physicist, mathemetician, and rheologist to study the extensibility and extrusion properties of bread dough; the microbiologist, nutritionist, and toxicologist to investigate the safety of a processed spread; the microwave engineer, packaging engineer, and statistician to define a quality controlled high speed unit process; and the oceanographer, demographer, and political scientist to determine the feasibility of a new source of food for narrowing the widening gap between world food production and an exploding population. Today this gap is wider than ever before in history and contributes to such current statistics as a projected mortality rate in India alone of some 50 million children from malnutrition or starvation over the next ten years. The world food shortage has been termed the greatest challenge that mankind ever has been called upon to face. The incorrect image of a Food Scientist dressed in white standing over a large kettle armed with a stirring paddle cannot be expected to attract students of the caliber that is essential to cope with such sober problems now and in the immediate years ahead.

But Food Science is also a study in contrasts. While more than half the world's people go hungry, in the United States there are to be found some 8,000 food items on supermarket shelves. The degree of sophistication built into many of them by Food Scientists may be criticized in some instances on the grounds that such effort may better be put into studies on nutrition, preservation, and production of foodstuffs essential to life in less fortunate regions of the world. However, it is evident that the luxury of this new product proliferation could only follow upon the fulfillment of more basic food needs through mastery of the fundamental principles underlying Food Science and the application of Food Technology.

The food industry in the United States and in other highly developed countries is in a dynamic state of change, with many of the traditional methods of production, processing, and control giving way to more efficient and less costly techniques. In less developed areas of the world, food industries are evolving which will first utilize to a great extent the basic technology from which further innovations can stem, but the process is slow and one can only grossly estimate the countless millions that are expected to starve in the course of this evolution.

An introductory text on Food Science should recognize these contrasts and the rapid rate of change that is taking place in Food Science and applied technology, and at the same time not overlook the common fundamental principles upon which all are based. This is attempted in the current book.

In preparing the text the author was fully aware of the futility of any attempt to cover thoroughly in a single volume a body of knowledge so broad as is encompassed by the term Food Science, even in an introductory fashion. The masterful work prepared by a group of specialists and edited by Professor Morris B. Jacobs, entitled "The Chemistry and Technology of Food and Food Products" required three volumes. But unfortunately good technical books unlike good wines do not improve with age, and the last printing of this authoritative work was made in 1951. More recently the series of texts of the Avi Publishing Company have done much to gather and update the knowledge of various segments of Food Science and food industry practice. These works, and others too numerous to cite here, have been drawn upon heavily in the gathering of representative material for this book. The many publications of the U. S. Department of Agriculture and the Quartermaster Food and Container Institute for the Armed Forces, now incorporated into the U.S. Army Natick Laboratories, Army Material Command, also have been found invaluable, as have the journals of the Institute of Food Technologists, and such publications as *Food Engineering* and *Food Processing-Marketing*, to name but a few.

The author further wishes to acknowledge with gratitude the many industrial companies and other sources that have permitted reproduction of photographs and illustrative material used throughout this book.

Special appreciation is here expressed to the many reviewers who have examined and commented on the various chapters, and particularly to Dr. Donald K. Tressler and Mr. John J. O'Neil for their many helpful suggestions during the preparation of the manuscript.

Finally I am indebted to Mrs. Mary Kuss for typing and outstanding secretarial help, to Cornell University for allowing the time for this undertaking, and to Professor Robert F. Holland, Head of the Food Science Department at Cornell, for his continued encouragement.

NORMAN N. POTTER
Ithaca, New York

June 1968

Contents

xiii

CHAPTER 1

Introduction: Defining Food Science

It is appropriate for the introduction to a beginning book on Food Science to attempt to define the meaning of the term Food Science. This is not easy to do in a fashion that would satisfy a majority of professionals in the field.

Up to about 20 yr ago the vast majority of scientists, technologists, and production personnel in the food field did not receive formal training in Food Science as it has come to be recognized today. This was because very few colleges and universities offered a total curriculum leading to a degree in Food Science. Rather, many of these institutions, including the Land Grant Colleges, were organized according to specialty along commodity lines. Thus the food industry today, as well as governmental and academic institutions, are made up largely of persons who received their original technical training in Dairy Science, Meat Science, Cereal Chemistry, Pomology, Vegetable Crops, Horticulture, etc. Many others were trained as specialists in the basic sciences and applied fields of Chemistry, Physics, Microbiology, Statistics, and Engineering. This has had many advantages generally associated with specialization. It also has resulted in certain limitations, especially for commodity oriented individuals in segments of the food industry undergoing rapid technological change.

PREPARATION FOR FOOD SCIENCE

Often the views of industry and the academic community differ with respect to a definition of the term Food Scientist, and what should constitute appropriate formal training. Similarly, the major schools offering a Food Science degree have not yet reached full agreement in this regard. In 1966, the Council Committee on Education of the Institute of Food Technologists adopted a set of minimum standards for an undergraduate curriculum in Food Science. These standards, offered as a guide to curricula development provide an insight to what Food Science is coming to mean.

Recommended course work to have been completed at the high school level includes 4 yr of college-preparatory Mathematics permitting the student to enter a college-level course in Analytical Geometry and Calculus, 1 yr each of Biology and Chemistry with an additional year of Physics desirable, at least 2 yr of a foreign language, 4 yr of English, and at least 2 yr of Social Sciences.

At the college level proposed standards include a solid core of required lecture and laboratory courses equivalent to the following:

(1) Food Chemistry (1 semester or 4 credits) covering the basic composition, structure, and properties of food and the chemistry of changes occurring during processing and utilization.
(2) Food Analysis (1 semester or 4 credits) covering the principles, methods, and techniques of quantitative physical and chemical analyses of foods and food products, the analyses to be related to the standards and regulations pertaining to food processing.
(3) Food Microbiology (1 semester or 4 credits) including the relationship of habitat to the occurrence of microorganisms on foods; microbiological action in relation to food spoilage and food manufacture; physical, chemical, and biological destruction of microorganisms in foods; methods for microbiological examination of foodstuffs; and public health and sanitation bacteriology.
(4) Food Engineering (2 or 3 semesters equal to 8 or 9 credits) covering engineering concepts and unit operations applicable to food processing. Principles would include mechanics, fluid mechanics, transfer and rate processes, and process control instrumentation. Unit operations would include fluid flow, heat transfer, evaporation, drying, extraction, distillation, filtration, mixing, and material handling.
(5) Food Processing (2 semesters or 8 credits) dealing with the general characteristics of food raw materials; harvesting, assembling, and receiving of raw materials; methods of food preservation; processing objectives including factors influencing food acceptability and preferences; packaging; and water, waste disposal, and sanitation.
(6) Other courses related to Food Science and Technology to strengthen knowledge in areas of interest for either professional or graduate work.

To the above has since been added appropriate course work to give the student a good understanding of human nutrition.

Required courses in fields other than Food Science, many of which are necessary as prerequisites to the above material, include English, Mathematics, Statistics, Physics, Biology, Microbiology, Humanities, and Chemistry including General Chemistry, Quantitative Analysis, and Organic Chemistry.

To complete the usual 120-semester hour requirement for the undergraduate degree, the Institute of Food Technologists advises that the student further elect courses from a complementary discipline and develop a sequence that will lead to greater competence in an area of special interest. This can serve as a base for a subsequent graduate program. Such areas could be Chemistry, Engineering, Microbiology, Nutrition, Economics or Business. Courses in Physical Chemistry, Biochemistry, Genetics, world feeding problems, and computer science also are recommended where they can be fitted in.

The above minimum requirements would provide a sound undergraduate training for the field of Food Science. But the student completing such a curriculum could not yet rightly be called a Food Scientist. The terms Food Scientist and Food Technologist are often used interchangeably and confuse some. The same Council Committee suggests that the term Food

Technologist be used to describe those with a B.S. degree and the term Food Scientist be reserved primarily for those who acquire an M.S. or Ph.D. degree. In the words of the Committee, "The primary difference in these types of preparation is that the food technologist is concerned with the acquistion of knowledge and its professional application. The food scientist has much of the same preparation but he acquires additional knowledge and skills that will enable him to develop new knowledge of a more basic nature. The additional preparation of the food scientist is concerned with developing research competence." It can be added that the graduate curriculum through additional courses also generally provides the Food Scientist with a second area of specialization and competence which may be commodity oriented or represent enlargement of any of the above or related subject areas.

ACTIVITIES OF FOOD SCIENTISTS

The preparation requirements for Food Science still fall short of an adequate definition of Food Science. Some would say that Food Science covers all aspects of food raw material production, handling, processing, distribution, marketing, and final consumption. Others would choose to limit Food Science to the properties of food materials and their relation to processing and wholesomeness. The latter view imposes serious limitations if it fails to recognize that the properties of food materials can be greatly influenced by such factors of raw material production as amount of rainfall, type of soil, degree of soil fertilization, plant and animal genetic characteristics, methods of harvest and slaughter, and so on. At the other end, not to encompass such determinants of consumption as cultural and religious dictates and psychological acceptance factors, would be to ignore the end use for which a product is produced. Unfortunately, this has been all too common in the past. Psychology and sociology prove important in an affluent society where there is much to choose between in the selection of purchased foods, as well as in the less fortunate areas of the world where customs and taboos often are responsible for malnutrition although there may be no shortage of essential nutrients.

Where definitions can be restrictive, more on the scope of current Food Science can be illustrated by way of examples.

It has been estimated that nearly two billion people do not have enough to eat and that perhaps as many as 10,000 die every day for either the lack of enough food or enough protein and vitamins to prevent malnutrition (Fig. 1). Many Food Scientists are attempting to develop cheap sources of protein sufficiently palatable to be used to supplement the diets of the poor, which in extreme cases can produce in children an advanced state of protein deficiency known as kwashiorkor. Dried milk in sufficient quantities will supply the needed protein but is relatively expensive, especially when

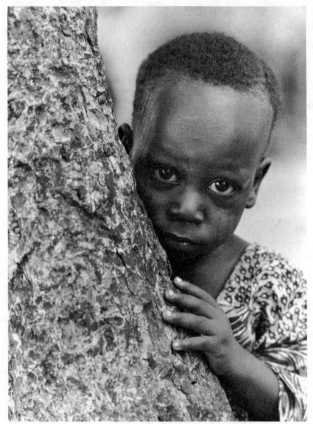

FAO Photo by C. Bavagnoli

FIG. 1. WORLD FOOD SHORTAGES ARE THE GREATEST CHALLENGE
OF THIS CENTURY

it must be exported to needy regions of consumption. Fish "flour" prepared from whole fish of species not commonly eaten, is a cheaper source of protein. So also is Incaparina, a cereal formulation containing about 28% protein and prepared from a mixture of maize, sorghum, and cottenseed flour. Incaparina and similar type products, originally developed to utilize highly nutritious low cost crops grown in Central and South America, can be made largely from ingredients available in many countries where the diet is deficient in protein (Fig. 2). A protein rich dairy product has been developed from ingredients readily available in India. Called Miltone, it contains peanut protein, hydrolyzed starch syrup, and cow or buffalo milk. Food Scientists of some petroleum companies also are trying to produce cheap food by growing microorganisms on petroleum wastes, but this work is still in the experimental stage. Among problems to overcome is cost of

HOW MUCH PROTEIN WILL 1 PESO BUY?

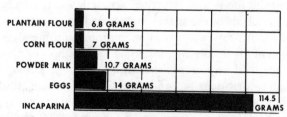

PLANTAIN FLOUR 6.8 GRAMS
CORN FLOUR 7 GRAMS
POWDER MILK 10.7 GRAMS
EGGS 14 GRAMS
INCAPARINA 114.5 GRAMS

Copyright © (1964) by Institute of Food Technologists from Dr. H. W. Bruins

FIG. 2. RELATIVE COST OF PROTEIN FROM INCAPARINA AND
OTHER FOODS

refining petroleum to remove the potentially carcinogenic compound benz-pyrene.

A knowledge of Food Science is required for the feeding of men under extremely adverse conditions (Fig. 3). The astronaut adds a small quantity of room temperature water from a water gun to dehydrated meat and gravy in a special pouch, then kneads the container and consumes the food through a tube. The special problems he faces are limited space, limited weight of refrigeration and cooking equipment permitted, special dietary requirements dictated by the stress and physical inactivity of his mission, and weightlessness. Weightlessness is the reason for the feeding tube. Any crumbs or liquid that might get loose in the space craft would float and become a hazardous nuisance. If one wishes to note the still more exotic,

Courtesy of Food Engineering

FIG. 3. MEAL OF POT ROAST AND GRAVY BEING RECONSTITUTED
BY ASTRONAUT

to save weight of food carried into space there even have been devised highly compressed foods with structural strength and these may be used as construction materials of the space craft. A leading aircraft company holds such a patent. It is proposed that at an appropriate time after landing the pilot can augment his rations by consuming parts of his craft.

Food Science is of importance to military feeding. Among the requirements are high caloric density, compactness, ease of reconstitution (that is, solubility when water is added), long term storage stability at elevated temperatures, packaging in easy opening containers that are light in weight and do not have hard sharp edges that can bruise a soldier in action (this usually means flexible foil and plastic), and above all nutrition combined with palatability. To develop foods with these properties requires the greatest skills of the Food Scientist. One such food is the compressed bar of freeze-dried peas (Fig. 4).

Courtesy of U.S. Army Natick Laboratories

Fig. 4. Compressed Freeze-Dried Peas and Their Rehydrated Counterpart

Food Science is involved in the making of foods that look and taste like meat but are made from soybean proteins. If soybean proteins are dissolved in alkali they form a sticky liquid. This liquid may be extruded through tiny holes and then recoagulated in an acid bath in the form of fibers. The fibers then can be spun into ropes with texture approaching the fibrous texture of chicken or beef muscle tissue. The fabricated tissue then can be interlaced with fats, food flavorings, and food colors. Products are almost indistinguishable from chicken meat, fish, ham, or beef. The products also may be dehydrated, compressed, or otherwise processed (Fig. 5). Meat-like products for vegetarians, for patients with special dietary restrictions such

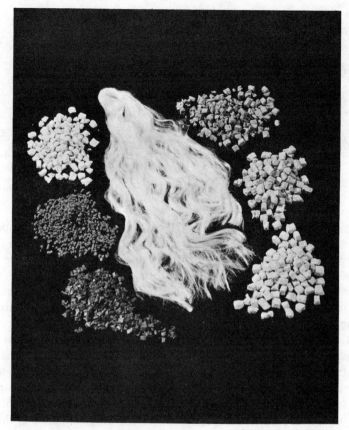

Courtesy of Food Engineering

FIG. 5. SOY PROTEIN FIBERS AND SIMULATED MEAT PRODUCTS MADE FROM THEM

as controlled levels of fat, and for numerous other food uses are now available commercially from several manufacturers. The "bacon" chips to be found in some brands of peanut butter are thus fabricated from soybean proteins. A meat-like texture, with blandness that permits flavoring for individual tastes, also has been produced from skim milk. By adding calcium chloride to the milk a curd is formed, which after cutting into appropriate pieces may be fried in hot oil to yield meat-like snacks high in milk protein.

Food scientists today are involved in the development of the widest range of fabricated foods and food analogs that challenge conventional natural products. Besides simulated meat and milk products, a novel method for preparing synthetic caviar has recently been disclosed by Russian scientists. It involves mixing a suspension of protein with gelatin, dispersing the suspension into a water immiscible liquid to form jellylike beadlets, and

FIG. 6. THE ANDREI ZAKHAROV, FLAGSHIP OF THE SOVIET CRAB-FISHING FLOTILLA

firming the beadlets with a tanning agent. The protein-gelatin suspension may be colored and flavored to produce beadlets closely resembling the natural eggs of sturgeon, salmon, and other fish.

Food Science is involved in the operation of fishing vessels that are floating factories (Fig. 6). Facilities include automatic separators for small and large fish, mechanized fish cooling tanks, automatic oil extractors, ice making equipment, complete canning factories, equipment for preparing fish fillets and cakes, and equipment for dehydrating fish and preparing dried fish meal. The reason for this factory approach is to prevent bacterial spoilage and to minimize protein and fat losses that otherwise would limit how long a fishing vessel could remain at sea. These factories can remain at sea for two months or more and range as much as 4000 miles from their home base. The Japanese and Russians have been most active in this kind of development.

Food Science is required to perfect controlled atmosphere storage of fruits and vegetables. Fruits such as apples, after they are harvested, still have living respiring systems. They continue to mature and ripen. They require oxygen from the air for this continued respiration which ultimately results in softening and breakdown of the apple tissue. It has long been known that if the air is depleted of much of its oxygen and is enriched in carbon dioxide then respiration is markedly slowed down. For some fruits the best atmosphere is one that contains about 3% of oxygen and about 2 to 5% of carbon dioxide, the rest being nitrogen. Such atmospheres are produced commercially by automatic generators which sample the atmosphere continuously and readjust it as needed. Refrigerated warehouses using controlled atmosphere storage now permit year round sale of apples (Fig. 7) which was not possible due to storage deterioration before this innovation. Controlled atmospheres low in oxygen also are currently being used to preserve lettuce quality during refrigerated truck transport and to reduce

Courtesy of Dr. R. M. Smock, Cornell University

FIG. 7. APPLES IN EXCELLENT CONDITION AFTER ONE YEAR OF
CONTROLLED-ATMOSPHERE STORAGE

spoilage of strawberries during air shipment. In the latter case storage compartment air is displaced by carbon dioxide from the sublimation of dry ice.

Food Science aids in perfecting mechanical harvesting to replace a shortage of labor. However, mechanical harvesting demands special characteristics to be bred into fruits and vegetables by geneticists. It requires that these products develop and ripen in the field uniformly so that at the time of picking the majority of the product is ready for the mechanical picker which cannot distinguish and leave unripened product behind. It requires that fruit release from the branch readily and be especially resistant to easy bruising by the machine. One interesting approach to mechanical harvesting by U.S. Dept. of Agr. scientists involves application of electric current to the branches of an orange tree to reverse the natural direction of sap flow and facilitate spontaneous fruit droppage from the branches for easy collection.

Food Science includes quick freezing of delicate tissues with liquid nitrogen and other low temperature (cryogenic) liquids. When fruits and vegetables are frozen, ice crystals form within and between the cells which make up the pulpy tissue. If freezing is slow large ice crystals form which can rupture the cell walls. When such a product is thawed the pulp becomes soft and mushy and liquid drains from the tissue. Tomato is particularly susceptible. Under very rapid freezing conditions, as may be obtained with liquid nitrogen at $-320°$ F, minute crystals are formed and the cellular structure is frozen before it can be ruptured. The product on thawing far better retains its original appearance and texture. Nevertheless, even with such rapid freezing only selected types of tomatoes are satisfactory and can withstand the treatment. However, less fragile frozen plant and animal foods of increasing variety owe their current commercial excellence to cryogenic freezing.

Food Science aids in the prevention of outbreaks of food poisoning through the judicious application of food preservation methods. The food industry today has a miraculous record of preventing such mishaps when it is considered that billions of cans, jars, and pouches of food materials are consumed annually. Occasionally, however, this excellent record is broken by a limited outbreak in which persons succumb to toxic food. This was the case in 1963 with mildly smoked fish vacuum packed in plastic pouches. The fish was preserved by heat and smoking, but not sufficiently to destroy the spores of the anaerobic bacterium *Clostridium botulinum.* Then a vacuum was drawn removing air from the pouches and the pouches were sealed. In transit and storage, refrigeration failed, the spores grew and toxin was produced. Finally, the fish was consumed without further heating. This chain of events proved lethal. Had the fish been completely sterilized to destroy the spores, or had air been left in the package to discourage growth of this anaerobic organism, or had the fish been cooked before eating which would have destroyed the toxin, most probably the outbreak would not have occurred. Certainly there is nothing wrong with plastic pouches, vacuum packaging, or smoked fish provided the principles of bacteriology and food science are carefully followed. Frequently these principles incorporate a margin of safety even in the event of refrigeration failure. Two additional incidents involving *Clostridium botulinum* toxin in canned soups occurred in 1971. Both were traced to insufficient heat processing in the manufacture of the canned products. In one case, a death resulted and the company has been forced out of business. In the other, prompt recall of widely distributed suspect cans and an intensive study of processing conditions leading to an adjusted process corrected further danger, but not without a financial loss of several million dollars.

Food Science enables packers to tenderize beef. The application of tenderizing enzyme-salt mixtures to the surface of meat cuts is common household practice. One new product concept (Fig. 8) is that tenderizing proteolytic enzymes be sprayed onto the meat surface. However, a practice now commercial has gone further. Proteolytic enzymes are injected into the animal shortly before it is slaughtered and the pumping action of the heart is depended upon to circulate the tenderizer throughout the tissues. When the animal is slaughtered and the meat cuts are prepared they are more tender then they otherwise would be.

Food scientists are studying the modification of beef muscle composition

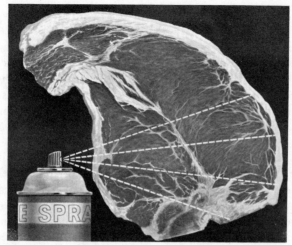

Courtesy of Rohm and Haas Co.

FIG. 8.   ONE OF SEVERAL METHODS OF APPLYING PROTEOLYTIC
ENZYMES TO TENDERIZE MEAT

and properties through special feeding practices. The Japanese are producing beef of exceptionally high quality by the inclusion of beer in the ration, together with controlled exercise. In the United States and other countries it has become common commercial practice to use the hormone diethylstilbestrol as a feed adjunct to stimulate animal growth and reduce feed costs. Stilbestrol has additional slight effects of increasing moisture, protein, and ash, and decreasing fat levels of beef muscle. Similar findings have been reported for lamb. On the other hand, diethylstilbestrol has come under attack as a possible health hazard, since under certain conditions it can cause cancer in mice and in humans. Its continued use will depend upon proof of safety in meat as consumed.

Food scientists are also studying the production of milk by cows fed minimum synthetic diets, and the organoleptic and functional properties of this milk. It has long been known that many of the nutritional requirements of cows are met by microbial synthesis of complex compounds in the cow's rumen from simpler materials. Recent Finnish work has shown that cows can maintain high levels of milk production on minimum rations containing purified carbohydrate and no protein, the nitrogen source being supplied by inexpensive urea and ammonium salts. Milk from cows thus fed is quite normal in gross composition, amino acid constitution of its protein, flavor properties, and functional characteristics. These findings are of particular significance since they provide a means for converting low value cellulosic materials such as forest products and low cost nitrogen compounds into valuable animal protein of a kind that is highly acceptable to man.

Food scientists are working on the production of flavors by specific enzyme systems acting on basic raw material substrates. Studies currently in progress involve the addition of segments of food plant tissues from fruits, vegetables, and spices, as sources of the enzymes, to solutions of sugars and salts. Following incubation under controlled conditions the solutions are assayed for flavor compounds. This work is in the very early stages of investigation.

Food scientists are also studying the removal of ions from liquid foods through the combined use of permselective membranes and electric current, a process known as electrodialysis. Special membranes can be made to allow passage of cations but restrict movement of anions. Others permit movement of anions but hold back cations. Such membranes can be assembled into compartmented "stacks" which are connected to the anode and cathode of an electric circuit. Ions in liquids passing through the compartments tend to migrate to the poles of opposite charge provided they are not rejected by a specific permselective membrane. By proper choice of membranes and stack construction certain anions, cations, or combinations of both may be removed from food liquids. In this fashion tart fruit juices are being deacidified, and cheese whey as well as protein-rich liquid from pressed fish tissue are being desalted to produce commercial food ingredients.

Food scientsts operate computer controlled automatic bakeries, ice cream plants, frankfurter manufacturing facilities, and margarine plants. All formulas are calculated in advance and the metering of ingredients to mixers, ovens, freezers, and other equipment is controlled by punch cards or computer tapes. Based on daily changes in the cost of formula ingredients, ratios of ingredients as well as operating conditions can be altered by changing punch cards. However, behind this automation is the skill of the formulator, food scientist, and the quality control laboratory. Figure 9 shows baked cakes emerging from the ovens traveling to the blast freezers in such an automated bakery.

Food scientists establish international food standards to promote and facilitate world trade and at the same time uphold high standards with respect to wholesomeness and value of foods purchased between nations. Standards generally must cover ingredient composition, microbiological purity, and subjective quality factors that often are not universally agreed upon. Wherever possible, standards also must not be discriminatory against one nation or another. This sometimes poses highly perplexing problems. Many countries would agree that Cheddar cheese to be called by this name should be made from cow's milk and contain a moisture content of not

FIG. 9.   VIEW OF THE EXIT END OF A MODERN AUTOMATED, CONTINUOUS
OVEN

more than 39%. In India, however, much of the milk comes from the buffalo. Further, cheese of this type made from buffalo milk is of poor texture unless somewhat more moisture is retained. Thus, an international standard upholding cow's milk as the raw material source, and a maximum of 39% moisture, could be to the disadvantage of India were she to decide to manufacture such a product for export. Similar type problems are currently being studied on the widest variety of food items by international expert committees.

These examples are cited simply to begin the orientation process that will lead to an appreciation of the vast scope of Food Science. Almost limitless other examples might have been chosen from such areas as: food preservation by irradiation; freeze concentration to remove water without loss of volatiles; sterilization or pasteurization of liquid foods without heat, e.g., removal of bacteria with microporous membranes; low calorie food formulation without sugar and the subsequent requirements for texture replenishment due to the omission of this functional ingredient; the use of chemical additives to enhance the physical, chemical, and nutritional properties of foods; the detection of pesticides and chemicals in foods at nanogram levels; and quick cooking methods using infrared, dielectric, or microwave energy.

All of these areas, and a great many more referred to in subsequent chapters provide daily problems for the Food Scientist. Together they help convey a better understanding of the term Food Science than can a simple definition.

BIBLIOGRAPHY

AMERICAN MEAT INSTITUTE FOUNDATION. 1960. The Science of Meat and Meat Products. Cooper Freeman & Co., San Francisco, Calif.

ANDERSON, O. E., JR. 1953. Refrigeration in America. Princeton Univ. Press, Princeton, N. J.

ANON. 1966. IFT Council adopts undergraduate curriculum minimum standards. Food Technol. 20, 1567–1569.

BAKER, E. A., and FOSKETT, D. J. 1958. Bibliography of Food. Academic Press, New York.

BLANCK, F. C. (Editor) 1955. Handbook of Food and Agriculture. Reinhold Publishing Corp., New York.

BORGSTROM, G. (Editor) 1961–1965. Fish as Food, Vols. 1, 2, 3, and 4. Academic Press, New York.

BORGSTROM, G. 1965. The Hungry Planet: The Modern World at the Edge of Famine. Macmillan Co., New York.

BORGSTROM, G. 1968. Principles of Food Science, Vols. 1 and 2. Macmillan Co., New York.

CRUESS, W. V. 1958. Commercial Fruit and Vegetable Products. McGraw-Hill Book Co., New York.

DESROSIER, N. W. 1961. Attack on Starvation Avi Publishing Co., Westport, Conn.

DESROSIER, N. W. 1970. The Technology of Food Preservation, 3rd Edition. Avi Publishing Co., Westport, Conn.

HARRIS, R. S., and VON LOESECKE, H. (Editors) 1960. Nutritional Evaluation of Food Processing. Reprinted in 1971 by Avi Publishing Co., Westport, Conn.

IFT COUNCIL COMMITTEE ON EDUCATION. 1969. Recommendations on subject matter outlines for food oriented courses proposed in the minimum standards for undergraduate education in food science and technology. Food Technol. 23, 307–311.

JACOBS, M. B. (Editor) 1951. The Chemistry and Technology of Food and Food Products, Vols. 1, 2, and 3. Interscience Publishers, New York.

JOSLYN, M. A., and HEID, J. L. (Editors) 1963. Food Processing Operations, Vols. 1, 2, and 3. Avi Publishing Co., Westport, Conn.

KRAMER, A., and TWIGG, B. A. 1970. Quality Control for the Food Industry, 3rd Edition, Vol. 1. Avi Publishing Co., Westport, Conn.

MATZ, S. A. (Editor) 1959. The Chemistry and Technology of Cereals as Food and Feed. Avi Publishing Co., Westport, Conn. (Out of print.)

MATZ, S. A. 1969. Cereal Science. Avi Publishing Co., Westport, Conn.

MATZ, S. A. 1970. Cereal Technology. Avi Publishing Co., Westport, Conn.

MEYER, L. H. 1960. Food Chemistry. Reinhold Publishing Corp., New York.

PARKER, M. E., HARVEY, E. H., and STATELER, E. S. 1953–1954. Elements of Food Engineering, Vols. 1, 2, and 3. Reinhold Publishing Corp., New York.

PYKE, M. 1964. Food Science and Technology. John Murray, London.

TRESSLER, D. K., VAN ARSDEL, W. B., and COPLEY, M. J. (Editors) 1968. The Freezing Preservation of Foods, Vols. 1, 2, 3, and 4. Avi Publishing Co., Westport, Conn.

TRESSLER, D. K., and JOSLYN, M. A. (Editors) 1971. Fruit and Vegetable Juice Processing Technology, 2nd Edition. Avi Publishing Co., Westport, Conn.

U.S. DEPT. AGR. 1959. Food, The Yearbook of Agriculture. U.S. Dept. Agr.

U.S. DEPT. AGR. 1966. Protecting Our Food, The Yearbook of Agriculture. U.S. Dept. Agr.

WEBB, B. H., and JOHNSON, A. H. (Editors) 1965. Fundamentals of Dairy Chemistry. Avi Publishing Co., Westport, Conn.

WIEGAND, E. H. 1960. The food technologist—his training. Food Technol. 14, 473–476.

CHAPTER 2

Magnitude, Division, and Interdependent Activities
of the Food Industry

AN IDEA OF SIZE

The food industry is very large. This is so regardless of the criteria we use to measure it. Some perspective of the United States food industry is in order for general interest and because an appreciation for the size and division of this industry must influence judgements the student of food science ultimately will be called upon to make.

The U.S. food industry employs more than one-seventh of the working population. This is greater than the combined number employed in the steel, automobile, chemical manufacturing, communications, public utilities, and all mining operations. The food industry produces, processes, transports, and distributes our foodstuffs. Approximately seven million farmers, orchardmen, cattlemen, fishermen and others are involved in the production of the raw materials that must be subsequently handled. As the chain of activities proceeds, some 120,000 farm marketing people are engaged in such functions as produce buying, cattle fattening, creamery and grain elevator operations, and warehouse management. Food processing operations to convert commodities into the canned, frozen, dehydrated, fermented, formulated, and otherwise modified forms consumers demand utilize approximately another 1.7 million people. Transportation of foodstuffs by rail, truck, water, and air involve about 600,000 transport workers. Wholesale distribution functions to stock retail outlets are estimated to employ 300,000 people. Retail distribution, including private stores, chain stores, and supermarkets accounts for the labors of an additional 1.7 million people. Restaurants, drive-ins, cafeterias in hospitals, plants, and schools, vending machines, airline feeding, and other food service operations utilize about two million people. Technically trained personnel serving the food industry in state, federal, and industrial positions of research, development, and quality control number some 25,000.

On the basis of sales, the food industry is the Nation's largest industry. In 1965, consumers spent $85 billion on food. Today, the figure is about $120 billion and going up. This is about 16% of total disposable income. Incidentally, in the United States food is the world's greatest bargain. Nowhere else can people feed themselves on slightly less than one-sixth of their annual income. This was not always the case and certainly is not representative of less developed parts of the world where the majority of man's labor may be required for food.

The abundance in the United States is not due to more people, animals, and land on today's farms, but is the result of increased efficiency in agricultural operations through science and technology. Since 1920, crop-land has not increased but production per acre has gone up sharply, and total numbers of livestock have changed very little but production per animal has had a steady rise. This increased production results from greater use of fertilizers, agricultural chemicals, animal and plant genetic improvements, and farm mechanization. Each year more food for more people is being produced by fewer farmers. Thus, in 1940 one farmer supplied the food for about 12 people, in 1960 one farmer supported about 28 people, and it is projected that by 1975 one farmer will be able to pro-duce the food required by 50 people.

This has not been without negative consequences, namely the produc-tion of great quantities of food surpluses, and its effect on prices in past years. This has been alleviated by subsidizing farmers to limit their plant-ing and production of certain commodities, by exporting to less developed areas of the world, and by seeking new manufacturing and processing methods to convert surplus foods into new forms that create consumer demands and new markets. Examples of the latter are conversion of surplus wheat into bulgur—a form of boiled wheat that can be dehydrated and consumed as a cereal, or peeled wheat which acquires the appearance and some of the eating qualities of rice. Further examples are the con-version of perishable commodities such as sweet potatoes, apples, and fruit juices to more stable dehydrated forms, either for export or for use in other manufactured foods.

The food abundance in the United States is not restricted to quantity but includes quality, variety, and convenience. Figure 10 indicates the way food was sold in big cities in the early 1900's. Fresh produce under-went heavy spoilage; variety was lacking; what variety there was, was seasonal; and the consequences of unsanitary handling were all too com-mon. In contrast, today's supermarkets stock about 8,000 items, and the battle is for shelf space and preferred position. This is largely the work of the food processor who may manufacture a basic food in 20 or more forms to entice the food purchaser. This gives rise to such problems as the need for multiple daily deliveries. At the present time on weekends, in some supermarkets the shortage of storage space is so great that 3 or 4 deliveries of cartons of fluid milk may be required daily. The concentra-tion processes for orange juice, evaporated milk, the newer 3:1 sterile concentrated milk, and other high-moisture foods, originally developed as preservation processes and to lower costs of bulk transportation, in the future may find their greatest impetus from shortage of display space.

Courtesy of U. S. Dept. of Agr.

FIG. 10.   BIG CITY MARKETING OF FOOD IN THE EARLY 1900's

This picture makes it easy to understand the interesting and perhaps surprising statistics on food packaging requirements. For packaging and shipping, the food industry in recent years has been consuming approximately 84% of all metal cans, 76% of all glass containers, 68% of all flexible packaging materials, 47% of folding paper boxes, 41% of aluminum foil, and 27% of all corrugated and fiber boxes.

DIVISION OF THE FOOD INDUSTRY

The division of the food industry may be made in various ways. One of the simplest is to divide the segments of the industry into the functions of raw material acquisition, manufacture, and distribution (Fig. 11). Under such a division the technologies of farming, orchard management, and fishing include plant and animal variety selection, their cultivation and growth, their harvest and slaughter, and the storage and handling of the raw materials to be further processed. Manufacturing functions include the numerous unit operations and processes that many consider to be the core of Food Technology. Distribution becomes involved in product form, weight and bulk, storage requirements and storage stability, and in product attributes conducive to product sales. But this overall division is artificial and the segments flow into one another. The food

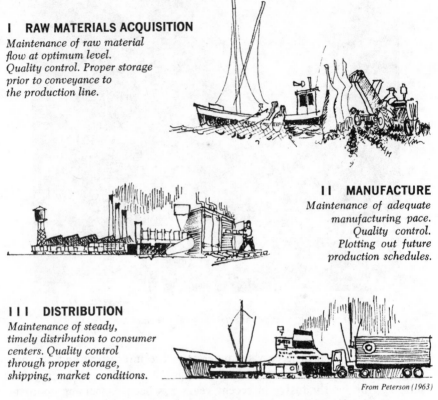

I RAW MATERIALS ACQUISITION
*Maintenance of raw material
flow at optimum level.
Quality control. Proper storage
prior to conveyance to
the production line.*

II MANUFACTURE
*Maintenance of adequate
manufacturing pace.
Quality control.
Plotting out future
production schedules.*

III DISTRIBUTION
*Maintenance of steady,
timely distribution to consumer
centers. Quality control
through proper storage,
shipping, market conditions.*

From Peterson (1963)

FIG. 11.   DIVISIONS AND FUNCTIONS IN THE FOOD INDUSTRY

industry is so geared that there is a highly planned organization and rhythm to the functions of the segments. In a well developed food industry this involves planning and scheduling of all phases to eliminate or at least minimize both shortages and surpluses between farmer, manufacturer, and distributor. Thus it is common for large companies to own and manage farms or plantations, processing and distribution facilities, and even the ultimate outlets for sale of their manufactured products to ensure smoothest operation and highest profits.

If the industry is divided according to function, then it is sometimes helpful to understand the relative dollar value of the different functions. However, this is not simple because there are great differences between products, as analyses of the percentage of the consumer's dollar spent for production, processing, transportation, and selling of different foods has shown. Currently, in the case of beef, the greatest cost is in farm production and the smallest cost is in processing and packaging. In contrast, for canned tomatoes the biggest cost is in processing and packaging, and farm production represents next to the smallest cost.

A more common way of dividing the food industry is along major product lines. This is done in Table 1, which also gives the fraction of the

TABLE 1

CONSUMERS' RELATIVE EXPENDITURES FOR
VARIOUS FOODS CONSUMED AT HOME, 1971[1]

Food Group	%
Meats	29.6
Dairy products	18.1
Poultry	4.0
Eggs	3.2
Bakery and cereal products	15.4
Fresh fruits	4.2
Fresh vegetables	6.7
Processed fruits and vegetables	10.6
Fats and oils	3.6
Miscellaneous products	4.6
Total	100.0

[1]Adapted from U.S. Dept. Agr. (1971A).

consumer dollar spent in the major food categories. Of the consumer dollar spent for foods consumed at home in 1971, about 30¢ went for meat products, about 22¢ for fresh and processed fruits and vegetables, about 18¢ for dairy products, about 15¢ for bakery and cereal products, and so on. This does not necessarily reflect the poundage or per capita consumption of each of the food categories since the cost of a pound of each food differs greatly.

The order of magnitude of the poundage of food produced can be estimated from government data on U.S. farm production in *National Food Situation*. Major commodities in 1970 included approximately 83 billion pounds of wheat, over 60 billion pounds of corn for human food and a great deal more for animal feed, about 25 billion pounds of fresh and processed fruit, about 33 billion pounds of vegetables, over 36 billion pounds of meat as carcass weight, about 11 billion pounds of poultry, and the enormous figure of about 117 billion pounds of fluid milk.

However, food is not necessarily consumed in the form in which it is produced. Of the 117 billion pounds of milk produced, less than half was directly consumed as fluid milk. Approximately $\frac{1}{4}$ went into the manufacture of butter, about $\frac{1}{5}$ into cheese, about $\frac{1}{8}$ into ice cream and other frozen desserts, and so on. Since the yield is only about 4 lb of butter per 100 lb of milk, and about 10 lb of cheese per 100 lb of milk, this amounted to some 1.1 billion pounds of butter, and approximately 2.2 billion pounds of cheese.

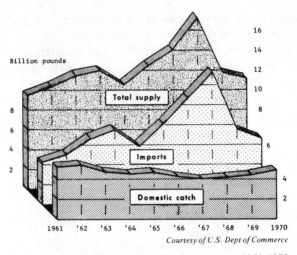

Billion pounds

Total supply

Imports

Domestic catch

1961   '62   '63   '64   '65   '66   '67   '68   '69   1970

Courtesy of U.S. Dept of Commerce

FIG. 12. U.S. SUPPLY OF FISHERY PRODUCTS, 1961–1970
(ROUND-WEIGHT BASIS)

What has been happening in recent years with respect to the U.S. supply of fishery products is indicated in Fig. 12. During the decade of the sixties, most of the U.S. fish supply has been imported. In 1970, the domestic catch was approximately 5 billion pounds and imports accounted for approximately another 6.5 billion pounds. Of the supply less than half goes for human food. The majority of this is canned, and lesser amounts are sold in fresh, frozen, salted, and smoked form. The remainder has gone into pet foods, fishery by-products largely for animal feed, and into waste. Fish meal, formerly considered a by-product, has received much attention in laboratories and in the popular press, particularly within the last 10 yr because of its potentially high protein value and the great quantity that can be derived from the sea. This makes fish meal a potentially important food source to help meet the protein requirements of the world's population explosion. However, the crude fish meals and fish concentrates had to be converted to a wholesome and palatable form suitable for human consumption, with such attributes as low bacterial count, high protein quality, bland taste so that they could be incorporated into other food recipes, storage stability, and low cost. These properties are now characteristic of a product known as fish flour, being manufactured in limited amounts in several countries. To be economical, fish flour for several years was made from the whole fish including heads, tails, and entrails, and so its acceptance has been slow on aesthetic grounds. But modern processing yields a wholesome product which is now accepted as an item of commerce by the U.S. Food and Drug Administration. In more recent years, fish flour made from eviscerated fish also has appeared on the market.

Since everything about the food industry is big, it is to be expected that the number and size of food processing plants are large. Currently the estimated number of sizeable (employees in excess of 20) food processing plants in the United States is about 30,000. The trend is for this number to become smaller and the plants themselves to become larger. This continues to concern some legislators who point out monopolistic tendencies in the food industry. In Table 2 the trend to concentration in recent years is in-

TABLE 2

PERCENTAGE OF BUSINESS ACCOUNTED FOR BY
THE FOUR LARGEST FIRMS [1]

Branch of Industry	Year	%
Commercial meat production	1964	29
Young chicken slaughter (federally inspected)	1964	18
Turkey slaughter (federally inspected)	1964	24
Fluid milk	1963	23
Ice cream and ices	1963	37
Fruit and vegetable canning	1963	24
Fruit and vegetable freezing	1963	24
Flour milling	1965	24
Baking	1963	23
Breakfast cereals	1964	85
Crackers and cookies	1964	62
Food retailing (food stores)	1963	18

[1] From Report of the National Commission on Food Marketing, 1966.

dicated by the percentage of U.S. business accounted for by the four largest food companies in specific branches of the food industry. Outstanding have been breakfast cereals with 85%, and crackers and cookies with 62% of the business going to the four largest firms in these areas. Similarly, 37% of the ice cream business, and 29% of the meat business went to the four largest firms.

Currently in the United States, about 1 out of every 5 dollars spent on food represents food eaten away from home. This has been the situation since at least 1960. Actually, the quantity of food consumed outside of the home is only about $\frac{1}{10}$ that eaten at home, the dollar ratio representing higher outside prices. This food away from home is consumed in restaurants, industrial and school cafeterias, hospitals, airplanes, and through vending and other outlets. These types of food service have their own specific requirements for ease of preparation and serving speed, providing new challenges and opportunities for convenience food manufacturers, suppliers of packaging materials, makers of quick cooking and reconstituting equipment, catering establishments, and an ever-increasing variety of carry-out and fast-food franchise chains.

Regarding international trade, food imports outside of coffee, tea, cocoa, sugar, and a few additional products are not of major significance in the U.S. food economy; and food exports, amounting to about $7 billion in 1970, have been relatively limited, largely due to a world trade situation that has not been conducive to a growing food export business. An exception to this has been the exportation of large quantities of cereal grains and legumes, as well as surplus commodities such as wheat and dried milk to famine stricken areas. Also, there is presently a growing demand for U.S. food processing and packaging equipment throughout the world.

By no means have limited food exports meant restriction of American food industry activities to within the United States. Most major American food companies have vigorous international divisions with manufacturing facilities in many parts of the world. The tendency to manufacture and sell outside of the United States is increasing greatly. Such American companies as General Foods, CPC International, H. J. Heinz, Borden, Campbell Soup, Standard Brands, Kraftco, Coca-Cola, Pepsico, Del Monte, Swift, Beatrice Foods, Quaker Oats, Ralston Purina, and General Mills, to list but a few, have extensive overseas operations. Their overseas plants are often larger and more modern than many of their U.S. counterparts (Fig. 13).

Courtesy of Food Engineering

FIG. 13.   COCA-COLA BOTTLING PLANT IN ESSEN, GERMANY

When these companies go into food production in different countries they do not simply build a plant and resume operations as in the United States. Experience has shown that often they must modify well-known products to suit local tastes of the consumers. Even the most popular soft drink formulations may vary in certain parts of the world. Another problem facing companies entering operations in a new country is related to available food ingredients. In some countries, the food producer may not import certain essential or important ingredients, but must utilize local ingredients such as wheat or cocoa. These may differ substantially from equivalent ingredients used in the United States and thus require extensive reformulation and process changes to achieve acceptable quality. This is further aggravated by local food laws which often prohibit the use of specific food acidifiers, preservatives, or food colors that are permitted in the United States.

Another factor relative to the size and division of the food industry is that this industry, in the broader sense, is not made up just of producing, processing, and food distribution companies. There are the many companies in allied industries that are deeply involved in food research and serving the food industry. These are the companies that produce the non-food commodities that are essential to the success of the food industry. A good example is the packaging industry. Such companies as United States Steel make the steel and tin-plate for the billions of cans used for food each year. They have worked for years on the corrosive effects and interactions of different foods with the metals used in the manufacture of cans. They have supported extensive research on heating processes such as aseptic canning, where modification in the gage of the metal for cans may be indicated because pressure retorting is not employed. The same is true of the leading aluminum companies in the development of aluminum cans, aluminum dishes, and foil for food use.

The study of can closure, can closure machines, and heat transfer into cans for sterilization, has continuously kept food scientists and engineers busy in such organizations as American Can Co. and Continental Can Co. These and numerous other companies also do extensive research and development in food packaging in glass, paper, and plastic. Tinted glass that screens out ultraviolet rays and thus protects light sensitive foods, and plastic films that have maximum moisture barriers and resistance to heating and freezing are studied by food scientists in these companies. The chemical manufacturers such as Pfizer, Allied Chemical, DuPont, Merck, and others figure heavily in the food industry by supplying many of the acidulants, preservatives, enzymes, stabilizers, and other chemicals used in foods. All of these must be functional, and fully satisfy specifications of safety set down by the Food & Drug Administration. DuPont, for example, is the leading manufacturer of gases used in food aerosol cans.

The food machinery manufacturers, often the prime innovators of new food processing methods and systems, are the people who develop the pasteurizers and irradiators, the microwave ovens and the infrared cookers, the freeze-drying systems and the liquid nitrogen freezers.

All of these, and many many more companies in the allied industries work directly with food.

INTERDEPENDENT ACTIVITIES

As has been stated, the production of specific foods in a highly advanced and organized food industry is a systematic and rhythmic process. The food manufacturer does not simply decide to produce 10 million pounds of margarine and then casually do so. If he did, he might find himself at one end unable to procure the necessary vegetable oils at a competitive price, and at the other without a ready and adequate outlet for his product. These factors alone could make him unsuccessful in the highly competitive food field, where often fractions of a cent per pound or per package make the difference between economic success or failure. Throughout all of his production, manufacturing, and distribution operations, these fractions of cents per unit of food product are carefully controlled along with the quality aspects of his product. Since the food industry is a low mark-up high volume industry, and numbers like several hundred thousand units per day—such as quarts of milk or loaves of bread—are common for a single plant, losses of fractions of a cent per unit anywhere along the chain from farmer to consumer can mean losses to the food producer of hundreds of thousands of dollars per year. To gain insight into the overall process it is well to trace the technology of typical food products, not in the detail of subsequent chapters, but with sufficient examples to illustrate the food production method. Two such products, which differ substantially, are bread and frozen orange juice concentrate.

Bread Producing Operations

Bread is made principally from wheat, and there are numerous botanical species and varieties of wheat. There are spring and winter wheats, which define the season following planting. Spring wheat is planted as soon as the winter ground softens and becomes dry. Winter wheat is planted in the fall, to permit development of a root system before winter dormancy, which gives the wheat an early start with the coming of spring. There also are the terms soft wheat and hard wheat. Soft wheat is low in protein, yields a "weak" flour, and is better suited to the manufacture of cakes and cookies. Hard wheat is higher in protein, yields a "strong" flour and is used in breadmaking. We say "strong" flour because the higher protein content yields a strong elastic dough, so necessary to hold the carbon dioxide produced by yeast, and other leavening gases.

Wheat to produce bread must first be ground into flour, and this milling process is based on the structure of the wheat kernel. In making flour we are interested in removing the outer layers of the wheat kernel known as the bran, and the lower portion or germ which is high in fat, and then recovering the starchy, proteinaceous central portion, the endosperm. The composition of wheat will vary greatly (Table 3), for example the protein content may range anywhere from 7 to 18%, and so the composition of flour made from wheat will vary greatly.

The miller carries out the following steps: (1) receives and stores the wheat; (2) cleans the wheat of soil and weed seeds; (3) tempers or conditions the wheat (adjusts moisture for best milling); (4) mills wheat into flour and its by-products; (5) blends batches of flour for desired properties; and (6) stores the finished product.

TABLE 3

APPROXIMATE COMPOSITION OF WHEAT [1]

| | Composition Range | |
Determination	Low	High
	%	%
Protein (N × 5.7)	7.0	18.0
Mineral matter (ash)	1.5	2.0
Lipids (fat)	1.5	2.0
Starch	60.0	68.0
Cellulose (fiber)	2.0	2.5
Moisture	8.0	18.0

[1] From Shellenberger (1959).

The actual milling is done with a roller mill equipped with several sets of rollers. The first rollers are called break rollers since they break open the kernel. These are followed by sifters which remove endosperm from bran and germ. Subsequent rollers are set closer together and are called reduction rolls since they grind still finer. These too are followed by sifters to separate the ground endosperm or flour.

The breadmaking properties of flour and dough will depend upon such characteristics as flour moisture; protein, ash, fiber, and fat contents; particle size; and the gluten protein quality. The elasticity and film-forming property of dough after flour is kneaded with water, essential for gas retention and an open structure in the baked loaf, is seen in Fig. 14. This well-developed dough is directly dependent upon the farmer's selection of wheat varieties, his growing practices, and the proper degree of ripening prior to harvest. The miller's practices, in turn, influence dough properties through flour particle size, moisture content, degree of germ removal, extent of starch granule rupture and gluten damage during milling, and proper blending of flour fractions.

At the bakery the breadmaking process begins. Flour held in huge bulk bins is conveyed pneumatically to a mixer where it is blended with the remaining bread formula ingredients. A typical white bread formula is seen in Table 4. The dough is kneaded and dumped into troughs and the troughs are placed in a fermentation room with controlled temperature

Courtesy of Dr. H. H. Schopmeyer

Fig. 14.   Film-Forming Property of Well-Developed Dough

and humidity to permit the yeast to develop flavor and leaven the dough (Fig. 15 and 16).

After several hours of fermentation, the dough troughs are hoisted and emptied into dough divider machines. These dividers cut the dough into one-pound pieces. The fermented dough structure is sponge-like and very fragile. Dividing causes a cut surface on each dough piece which allows gas to escape, and so to seal the cut surface the pieces are put through a rounder.

However, this further punishes the dough piece and knocks gas from it, and so the rounded pieces are given another chance to rise in what is

Table 4

TYPICAL STRAIGHT DOUGH FORMULA
FOR WHITE PAN BREAD[1]

Ingredient	Flour Basis, %
Flour	100
Water	65 (variable)
Yeast	2
Yeast food	0.25 to 0.50
Malt	0.5
Salt	2
Sugar	6
Skim milk solids	6
Shortening	4
Enrichment tablet[2]	—

[1]From Rumsey (1959).
[2]Enrichment tablets are supplied with vitamin and mineral content suitable to bring the finished bread up to federal requirements for enriched bread.

Courtesy of Baker Perkins Co.

FIG. 15. HORIZONTAL BATCH MIXER FOR BREAD DOUGH

known as an overhead dough proofer. But now the rounded pieces of dough are the wrong shape to fit into loaf pans, and so the dough pieces next are passed through a sheeter-molder. This flattens the dough piece and then rolls it into an elongated shape. From here the dough pieces are dropped into baking pans. The arrangement of the rounder, overhead dough proofer, and sheeter-molder, proceeding from right to left is seen in Fig. 17.

Once again the action of the sheeter-molder punishes the dough by knocking out leavening gases, and so the pans are placed on racks to give the dough a further recovery time prior to actual baking. The pans then go to the baking ovens. After about a 20-min bake they emerge to be depanned and the loaves cooled.

The cooled loaves, which may require as much as 90 min of cooling, emerge from overhead carriers to the slicing and wrapping machines. Cooling is necessary to permit efficient slicing and to prevent moisture from forming under the bread wrappings. From here the bread goes by truck to the grocery and supermarket.

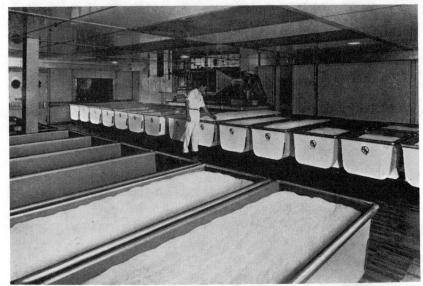

Courtesy of Union Steel Products Co.

FIG. 16. TYPICAL BREAD DOUGH FERMENTATION ROOM OF WHOLESALE BAKERY

Courtesy of Baker Perkins Co.

FIG. 17. ARRANGEMENT OF DOUGH MAKE-UP EQUIPMENT INCLUDING ROUNDER, OVERHEAD PROOFER, AND SHEETER-MOLDER

This cumbersome series of events is the way nearly all commercial bread was made until very recent years. It is easy to understand from this why food scientists and equipment engineers have obtained hundreds of patents in an attempt to simplify the breadmaking process. The most successful of these is the continuous breadmaking process with equipment such as is shown in Fig. 18. This equipment replaces 6 of the former

Courtesy of American Machine and Foundry Co.

Fig. 18. Continuous Breadmaking System Showing Components for Automatic Dough Mixing, Extrusion, Dividing, and Panning

machines, reduces the breadmaking process from about 8 hr to about 2, and provides additional substantial savings in labor. In brief, the system utilizes a liquid fermentation step to produce an active leavening and flavor-contributing brew. This brew is pumped and continuously combined with flour enroute to a high speed mixer which develops the dough. The mixer also is a continuous extruder with direct cut-off of dough pieces into moving pans. Currently about half of the bread in the United States is being made by such a system.

In the course of bringing bread to the supermarket shelf a number of inspections and checks are made to protect the consumer. First there is the U.S. federal grading of wheat quality, then there are the miller's quality control tests, then the federal Standards of Identity, defining acceptable bread formulas. Next there are the Food and Drug Administration standards for approved chemicals in the bread. There are the bakery's quality control tests which are supplemented by periodic FDA inspections of the sanitary conditions of the bakery. Finally there are check-ups at the bakery and in the supermarket by state and local inspectors to ensure honest weight of the baked loaf.

Frozen Orange Juice Concentrate

This is the product that has largely replaced fresh orange juice in the United States. It is purchased from the supermarket freezer generally in 6-oz cans. After thawing, three additional cans of water are added to make 24 oz of single strength orange juice. This product has revolutionized the citrus industry since its introduction in 1945. It met with almost immediate acceptance by the consumer and now its production far exceeds that of other forms of orange juice, grapefruit juice, and all other blended fruit juices combined.

Its production really begins about a year in advance, when processors contract with orange grove managers to purchase their next year's crop and thus ensure themselves of an adequate supply of raw materials. Then there is grave concern over the possibility of frost, as has occurred in Florida several times in the past ten years. If one drives through the orange groves of Florida on a cold day in winter, it is common to see burning smudge pots and large windmill-like blowers to circulate warm air between the orange trees, since cold weather and frost not only damage the oranges but kill the trees.

There are several varieties of oranges used for juice, the best known of them bearing such names as Homosassa, Parson Brown, Hamlin, Jaffa, Pineapple, and the most popular, the Valencia. These varieties differ in their growing season, resistance to frost, and in the flavor, color, and acidity of the juice and in other respects.

The anatomy of the orange is a most important consideration, and based on this structure is the design of machines used to obtain the juice (Fig. 19). The peel of an orange consists of an outer colored portion—the flavedo, and an inner white spongy layer—the albedo. Beneath the albedo are the pulpy orange segments containing the juice and the pits. These segments are separated by fibrous membranes. In the center is a pithy core around which most of the seeds are concentrated. The pith and membranes are referred to as "rag."

The flavedo contains orange peel oil which is desired in the juice in limited amounts. The albedo, rag, pulp, and seeds contain bitter components which produce bitter juice if the orange is excessively squeezed. The different parts of the orange contain volatile flavor compounds, sugars, enzymes, acids, proteins, fats, pigments, and vitamins. The mixture of these ending up in the juice depends upon the variety of orange, the growing conditions, the degree of ripeness, and the method of squeezing

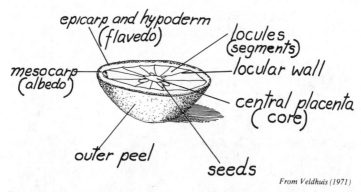

epicarp and hypoderm
(flavedo)

locules
(segments)

mesocarp
(albedo)

locular wall

central placenta
(core)

outer peel

seeds

From Veldhuis (1971)

FIG. 19. STRUCTURE OF THE ORANGE DETERMINES DESIGN OF EQUIP-
MENT TO OBTAIN THE JUICE

or extracting the juice. The flavor, color, nutritional value, and the storage stability of the juice depend upon this mixture of components in the juice. There are federal and state regulations concerning the maturity of fruit that may be harvested since degree of maturity affects the solids content and the acidity of the juice.

Truckloads of oranges arriving at the processing plant pass through washing troughs and a sizing and grading room. Damaged and moldy fruit are rejected.

The whole fruit next goes to the line of citrus juice extractors. The extractors are ingenious machines that are designed to take advantage of the structure of the orange. A closeup of the extractors indicates how they function (Fig. 20). The oranges drop into individual cups and radial fingers come down on them causing the peel to be split. Then a cylindrical knife comes up and cuts a plug out of the bottom of the fruit. The juice is then squeezed through the hole from this plug. The plug and the peel are pushed upward and ejected as waste. The machine is so designed that during the squeezing, oil from the peel runs down the outside of the fruit to be collected separately from the juice. If all the oil were allowed into the juice it would be too aromatic and bitter.

The juice stream containing some pits and minor amounts of pulp then goes to screens for their removal.

Juices differing in acidity and flavor may then be blended and sweetened by the addition of sugar if this is desired and permitted by law. In the past, Florida law prohibited sugar addition, although it is permitted in California provided the juice is appropriately labelled.

Juice at this point contains considerable air and oxygen. Oxygen will cause destruction of vitamin C, loss of color, and loss of flavor, so the juice is next passed through a vacuum deaerator to remove air and oxygen.

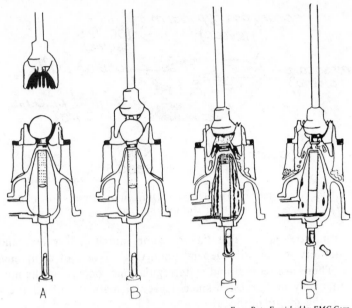

From Data Furnished by FMC Corp.

FIG. 20.   OPERATION OF FMC IN-LINE JUICE EXTRACTOR

Photo by M. K. Veldhuis

FIG. 21.   MODERN LOW-TEMPERATURE ORANGE JUICE CONCENTRATOR

The juice is still very perishable due to microorganisms and to natural enzymes. It therefore is next passed through a pasteurizer of the heated tube type. The juice is now ready for concentration.

Natural orange juice contains about 10.5% solids. If we are to make a 4:1 concentrate the solids must be raised to 42% and this is done in a low temperature vacuum evaporator such as seen in Fig. 21. However, when orange juice is concentrated some of the flavor constituents boil away. Therefore, it is common practice to over-concentrate to about 55% solids and then add back fresh single-strength orange juice to the desired 42% solids. The fresh juice in this way adds flavor to the concentrated juice. Some peel oil also may be added to enhance flavor.

The concentrated orange juice is now ready to be frozen, and this may be done by first slush-freezing the concentrate by passing it through tubular type heat exchangers (Fig. 22). The cold concentrated juice slush is then filled into cans, sealed, and passed through a freezer tunnel and

Photo by Votator Div., Chemetron Corp.

FIG. 22.   VOTATOR TYPE HEAT EXCHANGER FOR SLUSH-FREEZING
CONCENTRATED JUICE PRIOR TO FILLING INTO CANS

solidly frozen. The cans are finally shipped in refrigerated trucks to the frozen food cabinet of the supermarket.

The number of processing steps to produce bread or frozen orange juice concentrate is by no means excessive as far as manufactured food products go. There are scores of products such as beer, instant coffee, cheese, peanut butter, and table–ready meats, for example, that are equally involved in their manufacture. All require critical raw material selections and manipulations, specific temperatures and holding times, and rigorous quality control tests to ensure wholesomeness and a competitive position in the marketplace.

BIBLIOGRAPHY

ANON. 1966. Food from farmer to consumer. Rept. Natl. Commission on Food Marketing, Washington, D.C.

BARTON, G. T. 1966. Our food abundance. *In* Protecting Our Food—The Yearbook of Agriculture 1966. U.S. Dept. Agr.

FOOD ENGINEERING STAFF. 1963. World food manufacture. *In* Food Technology the World Over, Vol. 1. M. S. Peterson, and D. K. Tressler (Editors). Avi Publishing Co., Westport, Conn.

GREIG, W. S. 1971. Economics of Food Processing. Avi Publishing Co., Westport, Conn.

HADSELL, R. M. 1971. Food processing: search for growth. Chem. Eng. News *49*, No. 34, 17–23, 26–27.

HAMPE, E. C., JR., and WITTENBERG, M. 1964. The Lifeline of America, Development of the Food Industry. McGraw-Hill Book Co., New York.

JUDGE, E. E. 1971. The Almanac of the Canning, Freezing, Preserving Industries. E. E. Judge, Westminster, Md.

LARSEN, R. A. 1970. Milling. *In* Cereal Technology. S. A. Matz (Editor). Avi Publishing Co., Westport, Conn.

MATZ, S. A. 1972. Bakery Technology and Engineering, 2nd Edition. Avi Publishing Co., Westport, Conn.

PETERSON, M. S. 1963. Factors contributing to the development of today's food industry. *In* Food Technology the World Over, Vol. 1. M. S. Peterson, and D. K. Tressler (Editors). Avi Publishing Co., Westport, Conn.

PETERSON, M. S., and TRESSLER, D. K. 1963, 1965. Food Technology the World Over, Vols. 1 and 2. Avi Publishing Co., Westport, Conn.

POMERANZ, Y., and SHELLENBERGER, J. A. 1971. Bread Science and Technology. Avi Publishing Co., Westport, Conn.

REYNOLDS, J. E. 1966. Industry: Profit and protection. *In* Protecting Our Food. The Yearbook of Agriculture 1966. U.S. Dept. Agr.

RUMSEY, L. A. 1959. Commercial baking procedures. *In* The Chemistry and Technology of Cereals as Food and Feed, S. A. Matz (Editor). Avi Publishing Co., Westport, Conn.

SHELLENBERGER, J. A. 1969. Wheat. *In* Cereal Science. S. A. Matz (Editor). Avi Publishing Co., Westport, Conn.

TRESSLER, D. K. 1963. United States. *In* Food Technology the World Over, Vol. 1. M. S. Peterson, and D. K. Tressler (Editors). Avi Publishing Co., Westport, Conn.

TRESSLER, D. K., and JOSLYN, M. A. (Editors). 1971. Fruit and Vegetable Juice Processing Technology, 2nd Edition. Avi Publishing Co., Westport, Conn.

U.S. DEPT. AGR. 1954. Marketing, The Yearbook of Agriculture. U.S. Dept. Agr.

U.S. DEPT. AGR. 1962. After a Hundred Years, The Yearbook of Agriculture. U.S. Dept. Agr.

U.S. DEPT. AGR. Agricultural Statistics. U.S. Dept. Agr.

U.S. Dept. Agr.   1966.   Protecting Our Food, The Yearbook of Agriculture. U.S. Dept. Agr.

U.S. Dept. Agr.   1971A.   Marketing and Transportation Situation, August. U.S. Dept. Agr.

U.S. Dept. Agr.   1971B.   National Food Situation. U.S. Dept. Agr.

Veldhuis, M. K.   1971.   Orange and tangerine juices. *In* Fruit and Vegetable Juice Processing Technology, 2nd Edition. D. K. Tressler, and M. A. Joslyn (Editors) Avi Publishing Co., Westport, Conn.

CHAPTER 3

Constituents of Foods: Properties and Significance

INTRODUCTION

There probably is nothing more central to the study of food science than a knowledge of the constituents of foods and their properties. The constituents of foods and their behavior is fundamental to all phases of food science and technology—food spoilage and food preservation, the methods of food processing and food manufacture, food cooking and preparation, and nutrition. The advanced student of food science, grounded in the basic disciplines of organic chemistry, physical chemistry, and biochemistry, can visualize the properties and reactions between food constituents on a molecular basis. The beginning student is not yet so equipped. This chapter, therefore, will be more concerned with some of the general properties of the major food constituents, and how these underlie certain practices of food science and technology.

Food is composed of three main groups of constituents, carbohydrates, proteins, and fats, and derivatives of these. In addition, there is a group of inorganic mineral components, and a diverse group of organic substances present in comparatively small proportions; these include such substances as the vitamins, enzymes, emulsifiers, acids, oxidants, antioxidants, pigments, and flavors. There also is the ever present and very important constituent, water. These constituents are so arranged in different foods as to give them their structure, texture, flavor, color, and nutritive value.

The above constituents occur in foods naturally. Sometimes we are not satisfied with the structure, texture, flavor, color, nutritive value, or keeping quality of foods, and so we add other materials to foods. These may be natural or synthetic.

THE CARBOHYDRATES

Important members of this class of compounds are the sugars, dextrins, starches, celluloses, hemicelluloses, pectins, and certain gums. Chemically, the carbohydrates contain only the elements carbon, hydrogen, and oxygen. One of the simplest carbohydrates is the six carbon sugar glucose. Glucose and other simple sugars form ring structures of the following form:

α-D-glucose   α-D-mannose   α-D-galactose

These simple sugars each contain 6 carbon atoms, 12 hydrogen atoms, and 6 oxygen atoms. The differences are in the positions of oxygen and hydrogen around the ring. These differences in arrangement of the elements are sufficient to make a difference in the solubility, sweetness, rates of fermentation by microorganisms, and other properties of these sugars.

Two glucose units may be linked together with the splitting out of a molecule of water. The result is the formation of a molecule of a disaccharide, in this case maltose:

maltose

Common disaccharides formed in similar fashion are sucrose or cane sugar from glucose and fructose (a five membered ring), maltose or malt sugar from two molecules of glucose, and lactose or milk sugar from glucose and galactose. These disaccharides also differ from one another in solubility, sweetness, susceptibility to fermentation, and other properties.

A larger number of glucose units may be linked together in polymer fashion to form polysaccharides. One such polysaccharide is amylose, an important component of plant starches:

amylose (1,4′ α-linked glucose units)

In like manner, the chain of glucose units linked together slightly differently forms cellulose.

Thus the simple sugars are the building blocks of the more complex polysaccharides, which progress from the disaccharides and trisaccharides, to the dextrins which are intermediate in chain length, on up to the starches, celluloses, and hemicelluloses; molecules of which may contain several hundred or more simple sugar units. Chemical derivatives of the simple sugars linked together in chain form likewise yield the pectins and carbohydrate gums.

Just as the disaccharides, dextrins, starches, celluloses, hemicelluloses, pectins, and carbohydrate gums, are built up of simple sugars, or their derivatives, so they can be broken down or hydrolyzed into progressively smaller units, including their simple sugars. Such breakdown in the case of amylose, a straight chain fraction of starch, or amylopectin, a branched chain fraction (Fig. 23), can thus yield dextrins of varying intermediate chain length, the disaccharide maltose, and the simple monosaccharide glucose. This breakdown or digestion can be accomplished with acid, or by specific enzymes, which are biological catalysts. Microorganisms, germinating grain, and man possess various such enzymes.

The chemically reactive groups of sugars are the —OH or hydroxyl groups around the ring structure, and upon opening of the ring the $-C\diagdown_{H}^{\diagup O}$ or aldehyde group and the $-C\diagdown^{\diagup O}$ or ketone group. Sugars that possess free aldehyde or ketone groups are known as reducing sugars. All monosaccharides are reducing sugars. Where two or more monosaccharides are linked together through their aldehyde or ketone groups so that these reducing groups are not free we have nonreducing sugars. The disaccharide maltose is a reducing sugar. The disaccharide sucrose is a nonreducing sugar. Reducing sugars particularly can react with other food constituents, such as the amino acids of proteins, to form compounds that affect the color, flavor, and other properties of foods. In like fashion, the reactive groups of long chain sugar polymers can combine in a cross-linking fashion. In this case the long chains can align and form fibers, films and three-dimensional gel-like networks. This is the basis for relatively new technology in the production of edible films from starch as a potential packaging material.

Carbohydrates play a major role in biological systems and in foods. They are produced by the process of photosynthesis in green plants. They may serve as structural components as in the case of cellulose, they may be stored as energy reserves as in the case of starch in plants and liver glycogen in animals, they may function as essential components of nucleic acids as in the case of ribose, and as components of vitamins such as the

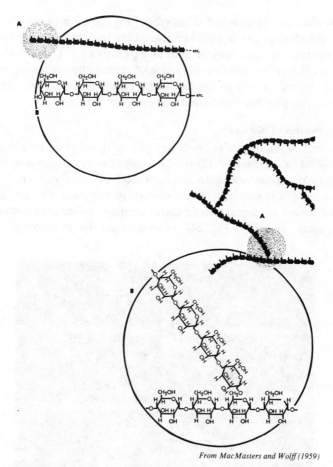

From MacMasters and Wolff (1959)

FIG. 23. STRAIGHT CHAIN AMYLOSE AND BRANCHED CHAIN
AMYLOPECTIN FRACTIONS OF STARCH

ribose of riboflavin. Carbohydrates can be oxidized to furnish energy, and glucose in the blood is a ready source of energy for animals. Fermentation of carbohydrates by yeast and other microorganisms can yield carbon dioxide, alcohol, organic acids, and a host of other compounds.

Some Properties of Sugars

Such sugars as glucose, fructose, maltose, sucrose, and lactose all share the following characteristics in varying degrees: (1) they have sweetness and are usually used for their sweetness; (2) they are soluble in water and readily form syrups; (3) when water is evaporated from their solutions they form crystals, and this is the way sucrose is recovered from sugar cane juice; (4) they supply energy for nutrition; (5) they are readily fermented by microorganisms; (6) in high concentration they prevent the growth of microorganisms, so they may be used as a preservative; (7) on heating they darken in color or caramelize; (8) some of them combine with proteins to give dark colors, known as the browning reaction; and (9) in addition to sweetness, they give body and mouth feel to solutions.

Some Properties of Starches

The starches important in foods are primarily of plant origin: (1) they are not sweet but are bland; (2) they are not readily soluble in cold water; (3) they form pastes and gels in hot water; (4) they provide a reserve energy source in plants and supply energy in nutrition; (5) they occur in seeds and tubers as characteristic starch granules (such granules from different sources are seen in Fig. 24) (when a suspension of starch granules in

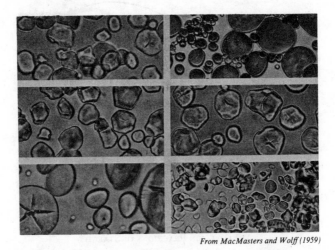

From MacMasters and Wolff (1959)

FIG. 24. UNGELATINIZED STARCH GRANULES

water is heated the granules swell or gelatinize; this adds viscosity to the suspension and finally a paste is formed; on cooling this paste can form a gel); (6) their viscosity is used to thicken foods; (7) their gels are used in puddings; (8) their gels can be modified by sugar or acid; (9) their pastes and gels can revert or retrograde back to the insoluble form on freezing or ageing, causing food defects; and (10) partial breakdown of starches yields dextrins (the dextrins, intermediate in chain length between the starches and sugars, exhibit properties that also are intermediate between these two classes of materials).

In recent years much has been learned about modifying the properties of natural starches by physical and chemical means. This has greatly increased the range of uses for starch as a food ingredient, especially with respect to controlling the texture of food systems and permitting the manufacture of food items that require minimum heating to achieve desired viscosity.

Modification techniques include reduction of a starch's viscosity by chemically or enzymatically breaking the molecules at the glucosidic linkages or by oxidation of some of the hydroxyl groups. The swelling properties of starch heated in water also can be slowed down by cross-linking reagents that react with hydroxyl groups on adjacent starch molecules to form chemical bridges between linear chains. Such cross-linked starch also has a lesser tendency to break down in viscosity in acid foods and at high temperatures as in cooking and canning. Starch further may be modified by reacting its hydroxyl groups with a range of reagents that form ester, ether, acetal, and other derivatives. A major effect of this type of modification is to interfere with the tendency of linear molecules to associate or retrograde to the insoluble form on freezing and ageing. Starch granules also may be precooked to produce a starch that will swell in cold water.

Some Properties of Celluloses and Hemicelluloses

These carbohydrate polymers are relatively resistant to breakdown: (1) they are abundant in the plant kingdom and act primarily as supporting structures in the plant tissues; (2) they are insoluble in cold and hot water; (3) they are not digested by man and so do not yield energy in his nutrition; (4) they can be broken down to glucose units by certain enzymes and

Courtesy of R. D. Preston

FIG. 25. CELLULOSE FIBERS IN PLANT CELL WALL, ELECTRON MICROGRAPH X 15,000

microorganisms; (5) the long cellulose chains may be held together in bundles forming fibers as in cotton and flax (cellulose fibers in the cell wall of a plant are seen in Fig. 25) (this is what contributes stringiness to celery, and what often is ruptured by the growth of ice crystals when vegetables such as lettuce are frozen); (6) the fiber in food which produces necessary roughage is cellulose; and (7) the hard parts of coffee beans and nut shells contain cellulose and hemicellulose.

Some Properties of Pectins and Carbohydrate Gums

These sugar derivatives, usually present in plants in lesser amounts than the previously cited carbohydrates, exhibit the following: (1) like the starches and celluloses, pectins are made up of chains of repeating units (but the units are sugar acids rather than simple sugars); (2) pectins are common in fruits and vegetables and are gum-like (they are found in and between cell walls and help hold the plant cells together); (3) pectins are soluble in water, especially hot water; (4) pectins in colloidal solution contribute viscosity to tomato paste and stabilize the fine particles in orange juice from settling out; (5) pectins in solution form gels when sugar and acid are added and this is the basis of jelly manufacture; (6) other carbohydrate gums from plants include gum arabic, gum karaya, and gum tragacanth (from seaweeds come the gums agar-agar, and carageenan); and (7) in addition to their natural occurrence, pectins and gums are added to foods as thickeners and stabilizers.

THE PROTEINS

The molecules of proteins are made up principally of carbon, hydrogen, oxygen, and nitrogen. Most proteins also contain some sulfur and traces of phosphorus and other elements.

The proteins are found in plants and animals, they are essential to all life. In animals they help form supporting and protective structures such as cartilage, skin, nails, hair, and muscle. They are major constituents of the enzymes and antibodies, and of body fluids such as blood, milk, and egg white.

Like the carbohydrates, the proteins are built up of smaller units, the amino acids. These amino acids are polymerized to form long chains. Typical amino acids have the following chemical formulas:

$$\begin{array}{c} CH_3 \\ \diagdown \\ CH_3 \diagup \end{array} CHCH_2\underset{\underset{NH_2}{|}}{C}HCOOH \qquad CH_2CH_2CH_2CH_2\underset{\underset{NH_2}{|}}{C}HCOOH$$

$$\underset{NH_2}{|}$$

leucine   lysine

$$\begin{array}{c} CH_3CH_2 \\ \diagdown \\ CH_3 \diagup \end{array} CHCHCOOH \\ \qquad\qquad | \\ \qquad\qquad NH_2$$

isoleucine

$$\begin{array}{c} CH_3 \\ \diagdown \\ CH_3 \diagup \end{array} CHCHCOOH \\ \qquad\qquad | \\ \qquad\qquad NH_2$$

valine

Amino acids have the $-NH_2$ or amino group, and the $-COOH$ or carboxyl group attached to the same adjacent carbon atom. These groups are chemically active and can combine with acids, bases, and a wide range of other reagents. The amino and carboxyl groups themselves are basic and acidic, respectively, and the amino group of one amino acid readily combines with the carboxyl group of another. The result is the splitting out of a molecule of water and the formation of the peptide bond which has the following chemical representation:

$$\begin{array}{ccccccc} & H & & O & & | & \\ H_2N - & C & - & C & - N - & C & -COOH \\ & | & & & H & H & \end{array}$$

In this case, where two amino acids have reacted we have produced a dipeptide, with the peptide bond at the center. The remaining free amino and carboxyl groups at the ends, in like fashion can react with other amino acids forming polypeptides. These and other reactive groups on the chains of different amino acids can enter into a wide range of reactions with many other food constituents.

There are presently recognized 20 different amino acids that make up human tissues, blood proteins, hormones, and enzymes. Eight of these are designated essential amino acids since they cannot be synthesized by man at an adequate rate to sustain growth and health and must be supplied as such by the foods consumed. The remaining amino acids also are necessary for health but can be synthesized by man from other amino acids and nitrogenous compounds and so are designated as nonessential. The essential amino acids include leucine, isoleucine, lysine, methionine, phenylalanine, threonine, tryptophan, and valine. To this list of eight is added histidine to meet the demands of growth during childhood. The remaining nonessential amino acids are alanine, arginine, aspartic acid, cysteine, cystine, glutamic acid, glycine, hydroxyproline, proline, serine, and tyrosine. The list of essential amino acids differs somewhat for other animal species.

The complexity of amino acid polymerization to form protein chains is indicated in Fig. 26 for the protein of human hemoglobin. There is enormous opportunity for variation between proteins. This variation arises from combinations of different amino acids, from differences in sequence of amino acids within a chain, and from differences in the shapes the chains assume. That is whether they are straight, coiled, or folded. These differences are largely responsible for the differences in the taste and texture of chicken muscle, beef muscle, and milk curd.

The protein chains also can be oriented parallel to one another like the strands of a rope as in wool, hair, and the fibrous tissue of chicken breast. Or they can be randomly tangled like a tangled bunch of string. Thus proteins taken from different foods such as egg, milk, and meat may have a very similar chemical analysis as to C, H, O, and N, and even with respect to their particular amino acids, yet contribute remarkably different structures to the foods containing them.

Further, the complex and subtle configuration of a protein can be readily changed, not only by chemical agents but by physical means. Thus a given protein can exist in solution and be converted to a gel or precipitate. This happens to egg white when it is coagulated by heat. Or the process can be reversed and go from a precipitate to a gel or solution as in the case of dissolving animal hoofs with acid or alkali to make glue. This has already been referred to in the case of producing texturized foods from soybean protein.

When the organized molecular or spatial configuration of a protein is disorganized we say the protein is denatured. This can be done with heat, chemicals, excessive stirring of protein solutions, and with acid and alkali.

These changes in the food proteins are easily recognized in practice. When meat is heated the protein chains shrink and so steak shrinks on cooking. When milk is coagulated by acid and heat, protein precipitates, giving us cheese curd. If the heat or acid is excessive, the precipitated curd shrinks and becomes tough and rubbery.

Protein solutions can form films and this is why egg white can be whipped. The films hold entrapped air, but if you overwhip you denature the protein, the films break, and the foam collapses.

Like the carbohydrate polymers, proteins can be broken down to yield intermediates of various sizes and properties. This can be accomplished with acids, alkalis, and enzymes. The products of protein degradation in order of decreasing size and complexity are: protein, proteoses, peptones, polypeptides, peptides, amino acids, NH_3, and elemental nitrogen. In addition, highly odorous compounds may result in the course of decomposition such as mercaptans, skatole, putrescine, and H_2S.

Controlled cheese ripening involves a desirable degree of protein breakdown. Putrefaction of meat is the result of excessive protein breakdown accompanying other changes. The deliberate and unavoidable changes in proteins during food processing and handling are among the most in-

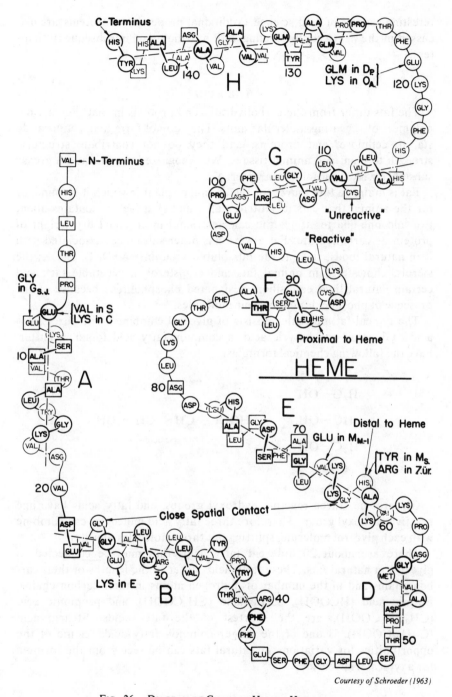

Courtesy of Schroeder (1963)

Fig. 26.   Diagram of Chain of Human Hemoglobin

teresting aspects of food science. Additional properties of proteins are discussed in the next chapter dealing with nutrition, and in subsequent chapters.

THE FATS

The fats differ from the carbohydrates and proteins in that they are not polymers of repeating molecular units. They do not form long chains as do starch, cellulose, and proteins, and they do not contribute structural strength to plant and animal tissues. We recognize fat as a smooth greasy substance which is insoluble in water.

Fat is mainly a fuel source for the animal or plant in which it is found, or for the animal that eats it. Nutritionally, and as a fuel, it contains about two and one-quarter times the calories found in an equal dry weight of protein or carbohydrate. Fat always has other substances associated with it in natural foods, such as the fat soluble vitamins A, D, E, and K; the sterols, cholesterol in animal fats and ergosterol in vegetable fats; and certain natural lipid emulsifiers designated phospholipids because of the presence of phosphoric acid in their molecules.

The typical fat molecule consists of glycerol combined with three fatty acids. Glycerol, and butyric acid, a common fatty acid found in butter, have the following chemical formulas:

$$H_2C-OH$$
$$HC-OH \qquad HOOC-CH_2-CH_2-CH_3$$
$$H_2C-OH \qquad\qquad \text{butyric acid}$$
$$\text{glycerol}$$

Glycerol has three reactive hydroxyl groups, and fatty acids have one reactive carboxyl group. Therefore three fatty acid molecules can combine with each glycerol molecule, splitting out three molecules of water.

There are about 20 different fatty acids that may be connected to glycerol in natural fats. These fatty acids differ in the lengths of their carbon chains and in the number of hydrogen atoms in their carbon chains. Formic acid (HCOOH), acetic acid (CH_3COOH), and propionic acid (CH_3CH_2COOH), are the shortest of the fatty acids. Stearic acid ($C_{17}H_{35}COOH$), is one of the longer common fatty acids. Some of the opportunities for variations in natural fats can be seen from the formula for a typical triglyceride:

$$H_2C-O-C\overset{O}{\underset{}{\diagdown}}(CH_2)_{10}-CH_3$$
$$HC-O-C\overset{O}{\underset{}{\diagdown}}(CH_2)_{16}-CH_3$$
$$H_2C-O-C\overset{O}{\underset{}{\diagdown}}(CH_2)_7-CH=CH-(CH_2)_7-CH_3$$

In this case the fatty acids reacting with glycerol from top to bottom are lauric acid, stearic acid, and oleic acid, with carbon chain lengths of 12, 18, and 18, respectively. Stearic and oleic acids, although of similar chain length, differ with respect to the number of hydrogen atoms in their chains. Stearic acid is said to be saturated with respect to hydrogen. Oleic acid with two less hydrogen atoms is said to be unsaturated. Another 18 carbon unsaturated fatty acid with 4 less hydrogen atoms and 2 points of unsaturation is linoleic acid. This unsaturated fatty acid is a dietary essential for health.

Fat molecules can differ with respect to the chain lengths of their fatty acids, the degree of unsaturation of their fatty acids, the position of specific fatty acids with respect to the three carbon atoms of glycerol, orientation in the chains of unsaturated fatty acids to produce spatial variations within these chains, and in still other ways.

Fat molecules need not have all of the three hydroxyl groups of glycerol reacted with fatty acids as in a triglyceride. When two are reacted the molecule is known as a diglyceride, and when glycerol combines with only one fatty acid molecule we have a monoglyceride. Diglycerides and monoglycerides have special emulsifying properties.

Natural fats are not made up of one type of fat molecule but are mixtures of many fat molecules, which may vary by any of the mechanisms indicated above. This complexity of fat chemistry today is well understood to the point where fats of very special properties are custom produced and blended for specific food uses.

The chemical variations in fats lead to widely different functional, nutritional, and keeping quality properties. The melting points of different fats are an example of this functional variation. The longer fatty acids yield harder fats, and the shorter fatty acids contribute to softer fats. Unsaturation of the fatty acids also contributes to softer fats. An oil is simply a fat that is liquid at room temperature. This is the basis of making solid fats from liquid oils. Hydrogen is added to saturate highly unsaturated fatty acids, and the process is known as hydrogenation. More will be said about changes in fat consistency in the chapter on fats and oils.

Some additional properties of fats important in food technology are the following:

(1) They gradually soften on heating, that is they do not have a sharp melting point.

(2) When heated further they first begin to smoke, then they flash, and then they burn. The temperatures at which these occur are known as the smoke point, the flash point, and the fire point. This is important in commercial frying operations.

(3) Fats may become rancid when they are oxidized or when the fatty acids are liberated from glycerol by enzymes.

(4) Fats form emulsions with water and air. Fat globules may be suspended in a large amount of water as in milk or cream, or water droplets may be suspended in a large amount of fat as in butter. Air may be trapped as an emulsion in fat as in butter-cream icing or in whipped butter (see Fig. 27).

(5) Fat is a lubricant in foods—that is, butter makes the swallowing of bread easier.

(6) Fat has shortening power—that is, it interlaces between protein and starch structures and makes them tear apart easily and short rather than allow them to stretch long. In this way fat tenderizes meat as well as baked goods.

ADDITIONAL FOOD CONSTITUENTS

While the carbohydrates, proteins, and fats often are referred to as the major food constituents due to their presence in foods in substantial

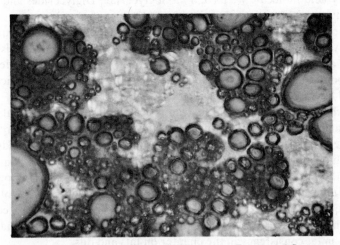

FIG. 27. PHOTOMICROGRAPH OF COMPOUND EMULSION SHOWING FAT ENCIRCLING AIR BUBBLES AND THE FAT SUSPENDED IN A CONTINUOUS WATER PHASE

amounts, there are other groups of substances in foods which play an important role, out of proportion to their relatively small concentration in foods.

These include the natural emulsifiers, acids, oxidants, antioxidants, enzymes, pigments, flavors, vitamins, and minerals. Water also must not be overlooked.

Natural Emulsifiers

Materials that keep fat globules dispersed in water or water droplets dispersed in fat are emulsifiers. Without emulsifiers mayonnaise would separate into water and oil layers. The mayonnaise emulsion is stabilized by the presence of egg yolk, but the active ingredients in egg yolk stabilizing the emulsion are phospholipids, the best known of which is lecithin. There are many lecithins differing in their fatty acid contents. Chemically, a typical lecithin would have the following formula:

$$H_2C-OOC-C_{17}H_{33}$$
$$HC-OOC-C_{17}H_{31}$$

$$H_2C-O-\overset{\overset{\displaystyle O}{\|}}{\underset{\underset{\displaystyle O_-}{|}}{P}}-O-CH_2CH_2\overset{+}{N(CH_3)_3}$$

Lecithins are structurally like fats but contain phosphoric acid. Most important, they have an electrically charged or polar end (the + and − at the bottom) and a noncharged or nonpolar end at the top. The polar end of this and similar molecules is water-loving or hydrophilic and wants to be dissolved in water. The uncharged or nonpolar end is fat-loving or hydrophobic and wants to be dissolved in fat or oil. The result in a water-oil mixture is that the emulsifier dissolves part of itself in water and the other part in oil. If the oil is shaken in an excess of water the oil will form small droplets. Then the nonpolar ends of lecithin molecules orient themselves within the fat droplets and the polar ends stick out from the surface of the droplets into the water phase. This has the effect of surrounding the oil droplets with an electrically charged surface. Such droplets repel one another rather than having a tendency to coalesce and separate as an oil layer. The emulsion is thus stabilized. Such phenomena are common in foods containing oil and water. Lecithin and other phospholipid emulsifiers are present in animal and plant tissues and in egg, milk, and blood. Without them we could not have stable mayonnaise, margarine, or salad dressings. The mono- and diglycerides mentioned earlier also are highly effective emulsifiers.

Emulsifiers belong to a broader group of chemicals known as surface active agents, designated as such because they exert their effects largely at surfaces. Today a large number of natural and synthetic emulsifiers and emulsifier blends suitable for food use are available. Selection is based largely upon the type of food system to be emulsified. With water and oil one can have oil-in-water or water-in-oil emulsions. In an oil-in-water emulsion, water is the continuous phase and oil is the dispersed or discontinuous phase; mayonnaise is an example of this type of emulsion. In a water-in-oil emulsion, oil is the continuous phase and water is the dispersed phase; margarine is an example. Generally the phase present in greater amount becomes the continuous phase of the food system. In choosing an effective emulsifier for a manufactured food, oil-in-water emulsions are best stabilized with emulsifiers that have a high degree of water solubility (along with some oil solubility), while water-in-oil emulsions are best prepared with emulsifiers having considerable oil solubility and lesser water solubility.

Organic Acids

Fruits contain natural acids, such as citric acid of oranges and lemons, malic acid of apples, and tartaric acid of grapes. These acids give the fruits tartness and slow down bacterial spoilage.

We deliberately ferment some foods with desirable bacteria to produce acids and thus give the food flavor and keeping quality. Examples are fermentation of cabbage to produce lactic acid and yield sauerkraut and fermentation of apple juice to produce first alcohol and then acetic acid to obtain vinegar. In the manufacture of cheese a bacterial starter culture is added to milk to produce lactic acid. This aids in curd formation, and in the subsequent preservation of the curd against undesirable bacterial spoilage.

Besides imparting flavor and aiding in food preservation, organic acids have a wide range of textural effects in food systems due to their reactions with proteins, starches, pectins, gums, and other food constituents. The rubbery or crumbly condition of Cheddar cheese depends largely upon acid concentration and pH, as does the stretchability of bread dough, the firmness of puddings, the viscosity of sugar syrups, the spreadability of jellies and jams, and the mouth feel of certain beverages. Organic acids also influence the colors of foods since many plant and animal pigments are natural pH indicators. With respect to bacterial spoilage, a most important contribution of organic acids is in lowering a food's pH. Under anaerobic conditions and above a pH of 4.5 *Clostridium botulinum* can grow and produce lethal toxin. This hazard is absent from foods high in organic acids resulting in a pH below 4.5.

Oxidants and Antioxidants

Certain food constituents are adversely affected by oxygen in the air. This is so of fats, oils, and certain oily flavor compounds which may become rancid on excessive exposure to air. Carotene which yields vitamin A, and ascorbic acid which is vitamin C, also are diminished in vitamin activity by oxygen.

Oxygen is an oxidant, it causes oxidation of the above materials. Oxygen is always present in and around foods, though it may be minimized by nitrogen or vacuum packaging.

Certain metals such as copper and iron are strong promoters or catalysts of oxidation. This is one of the reasons why copper and iron have largely been replaced in food processing equipment by stainless steel. Many natural foods, however, contain traces of copper and iron but they also contain antioxidants.

An antioxidant, as the term implies, tends to prevent oxidation. Natural antioxidants present in foods include lecithin (which also is an emulsifier), vitamin E, and certain sulfur-containing amino acids. However, the most effective antioxidants are synthetic chemicals approved by the Food and Drug Administration for addition to foods. These will be considered in a later chapter on food additives.

Enzymes

The deeper one goes into the life sciences, the more will be said about enzymes. Enzymes are biological catalysts that promote the widest variety of biochemical reactions. Amylase found in saliva promotes digestion or breakdown of starch in the mouth. Pepsin found in gastric juice promotes digestion of protein. Lipase found in liver promotes breakdown of fats. These are all enzymes.

There are literally thousands of different enzymes found in bacteria, yeasts, molds, plants, and animals. Even after the plant is harvested or the animal is killed most of their enzymes continue to promote their specific chemical reactions.

The food we harvest, process, and consume contains a great number of active enzymes. Enzymes are large protein molecules which like other catalysts need to be present in only minute amounts to be effective.

One theory of enzyme action is diagramatically illustrated in Fig. 28.

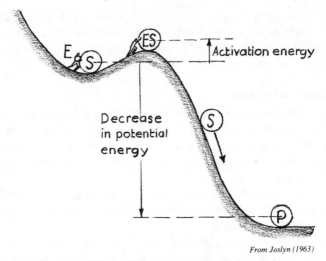

From Joslyn (1963)

FIG. 28.   DIAGRAMATIC ILLUSTRATION OF THEORY OF ENZYME
ACTION

Enzymes have the ability to lower the activation energies of specific substrates. They do this by temporarily combining with the substrate to form
an enzyme-substrate complex which is less stable than the substrate alone.
This lowering of activation energy overcomes the resistance to reaction.
The substrate thus excited plunges to a still lower energy level by forming
new products of reaction. In the course of reaction the enzyme is released
unchanged. The release of the enzyme so that it can continue to act explains why enzymes are effective in such trace amounts.

The reactions catalyzed by a few enzymes of microbial origin are indicated in Table 5. Some properties of enzymes important to the food
scientist are the following: (1) in living fruits and vegetables enzymes control the reactions associated with ripening; (2) after harvest, unless destroyed by heat, chemicals, or some other means, enzymes continue the
ripening process, in many cases to the point of spoilage—such as soft
melons and overripe bananas; (3) because enzymes enter into a vast
number of biochemical reactions in foods, they may be responsible for
changes in food flavor, color, texture, and nutritional properties; (4) the
heating processes in food manufacturing are designed not only to destroy
microorganisms but also to inactivate food enzymes and thereby extend
the storage stability of foods; (5) when microorganisms are added to foods
for fermentation purposes we really are interested in the enzymes the
microorganisms produce; and (6) enzymes also can be extracted from
biological materials and purified to a high degree. Such commercial en-

TABLE 5

EXAMPLES OF EXTRACELLULAR HYDROLYTIC ENZYMES [1]

Enzyme	Substrate	Catabolic Products
Esterases		
lipases	glycerides (fats)	glycerol + fatty acids
phosphatases		
lecithinase	lecithin	choline + H_3PO_4 + fat
Carbohydrases		
fructosidases	sucrose	fructose + glucose
alpha glucosidases	maltose	glucose
(maltase)		
beta glucosidases	cellobiose	glucose
(cellobiase)		
beta galactosidases	lactose	galactose + glucose
(lactase)		
amylase	starch	maltose
cellulase	cellulose	cellobiose
cytase	. . . .	simple sugars
Nitrogen carrying compounds		
proteinases	proteins	polypeptides
polypeptidases	proteins	amino acids
desamidases		
urease	urea	CO_2 + NH_3
asparaginase	asparagin	aspartic acid + NH_3
deaminases	amino acids	NH_3 + organic acids

[1] From Weiser *et al.* (1971).

zyme preparations may be added to foods to break down starch, tenderize meat, clarify wines, coagulate milk protein, and produce many other desirable changes. Some of these additional changes are indicated in Table 6.

Pigments and Colors

One of the most pleasing attributes of a food is its color, and there is much to be said for the statement, "we also eat with our eyes."

Foods may acquire their color from any of several sources. One major source is the natural plant and animal pigments. Chlorophyll which gives the green color to lettuce and peas, carotene giving the orange color to carrots and corn, lycopene contributing to the red of tomatoes and watermelons, anthocyanins contributing purple to beets and blueberries, and oxymyoglobin giving the red color to meats are examples.

These natural pigments are highly susceptible to chemical change—as in fruit ripening and meat ageing. They also are sensitive to chemical and physical effects during food processing. Excessive heat alters virtually all natural food pigments. Chopping and grinding also generally changes food colors. This is because many of the plant and animal pigments are organized in tissue cells and pigment bodies, such as the chloroplasts which contain green chlorophyll. When these cells are broken by grinding and chopping the pigments leach out and are partially destroyed on contact with air.

TABLE 6

SOME COMMERCIAL ENZYMES AND THEIR APPLICATION [1]

Type	Typical Use
Carbohydrases	production of invert sugar in confectionery industry; production of corn syrups from starch; conversion of cereal starches into fermentable sugars in malting, brewing, distillery, baking industry; clarification of beverages and syrups containing fruit starches.
Proteases	chill-proofing of beers and related products; tenderizing meat; production of animal and plant protein hydrolyzates.
Pectinases	clarification of fruit juices; removal of excess pectins from juices such as apple juice before concentration; increase of yield of juice from grapes and other products; clarification of wines; dewatering of fruit and vegetable wastes before drying.
Glucose oxidase —Catalase	removal of glucose from egg white before drying; removal of molecular oxygen dissolved or present at the surface of products wrapped or sealed in hermetic containers.
Glucosidases	liberation of essential oils from precursors such as those present in bitter almonds, etc.; destruction of naturally occurring bitter principles such as those occurring in olives and the bitter principle glycosides in cucurbitaceae (cucumber and related family).
Flavor enzymes (flavorases)	restoration and enrichment of flavor by the addition of enzymes capable of converting organic sulfur compounds into the particular volatile sulfur compounds responsible for flavor in garlic and onions, e.g., conversion of alliin of garlic into garlic oil by alliianase; conversion of sulfur containing flavor precursors of cabbage and related spices (watercress, mustard, radish) by enzyme preparations from related rich natural sources of enzymes; addition of enzyme preparations from mustard seeds to rehydrated blanched dehydrated cabbage to restore flavor; production of natural banana flavor in sterilized banana puree and dehydrated bananas by naturally occurring banana flavor enzyme; improvement in flavor of canned foods by an enzyme preparation from fresh corn.
Lipases	improvement in whipping quality of dried egg white and flavor production in cheese and chocolate.
Cellulase	mashing of grain and brewing, clarification and extraction of fruit juices, tenderization of vegetables.

[1] From Joslyn (1963B).

Not all food color comes from true plant and animal pigments. A second source of color comes from the action of heat on sugars. This is referred to as caramelizing. Examples involving caramelization are darkening of maple sugar on heating, the color on toasting bread, and the brown color of caramel candy.

Thirdly, dark colors result from certain chemical interactions between sugars and proteins referred to as the browning reaction or the Maillard reaction. In this case an amino group from a protein combines with an aldehyde or ketone group of a reducing sugar to produce a brown color— an example is the darkening of dried milk on long storage.

There also are the complex color changes when a wide variety of organic chemicals present in foods come in contact with air. Examples are the darkening of a cut surface of an apple and the brown color of tea from tea tannins. These oxidations generally are intensified by the presence of metal ions.

In many foods and in cooking, final color is the result of a combination of several of the above, which adds to the complexity of the field of food color.

Not to be overlooked is the intentional coloring of food by the addition of natural or synthetic colors as in the coloring of gelatin desserts, or the addition of vegetable dyes to Cheddar cheese to make it orange.

Flavors

If food color is complex, then the occurrence and changes that take place in food flavors are perhaps even more complex.

In coffee alone there have been reported over 600 constituents that contribute to the flavor and aroma, although the contribution of many of them may be quite small. These organic chemicals are highly sensitive to air, heat, and interaction with one another—and the flavor and aroma of coffee, milk, cooked meats, and most foods is in a constant state of change—generally becoming less desirable as the food is handled, processed, and stored. There are exceptions, of course, as in the improvement of flavor when cheese is ripened, wine is aged, or meat is aged.

It is important to recognize and appreciate that good flavor often has a regional and cultural basis for acceptance. Not only do many orientals prize the flavors of 100-yr eggs and sauces made from rotted fish, but in the United States different blends of coffee are favored in the South and in the North, and sour cream is not as popular in the Midwest as in the East.

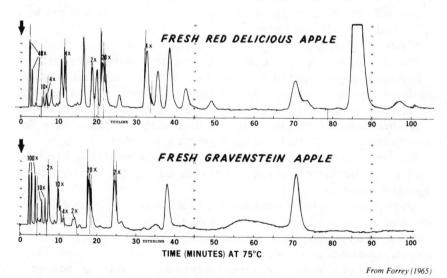

From Forrey (1965)

FIG. 29.   VAPOR ANALYSIS BY GAS CHROMATOGRAPHY OF APPLE VOLATILES

The chemistry of flavor is beyond the scope of this book. Much progress has been made in this area in recent years from use of advanced analytical methods such as gas chromatography. In this case aroma compounds are separated from one another on the basis of relative volatility from a special column through which gas is passed. Each different compound gives a specific peak on a recording chart. The peaks corresponding to aroma compounds obtained from two kinds of apples are seen in Fig. 29. While such methods are highly sensitive, for many flavor and aroma compounds they are not quite as sensitive as the human nose and tongue. Furthermore, the instrumental approach doesn't tell whether a flavor is liked or disliked. In these cases subjective methods of study are used. These employ various kinds of taste panels. Because the results are subjective, conclusions are generally based on the judgments of several people making up the panel.

Vitamins and Minerals

These constituents of foods, important out of proportion to the small amounts in which they are present, are discussed in the next chapter on the nutrients of food.

Water

A remaining constituent of foods is water. Water is present in most natural foods to the extent of 70% of their weight or greater. Fruits and vegetables may contain 90 and even 95% water. Cooked meat from which some of the water has been driven off will still contain about 60% water. Water will greatly affect the texture of foods—a raisin is a dehydrated grape, and a prune, a dried plum.

Water will greatly affect the keeping qualities of food which is one reason we remove it from foods, either partially as in evaporation and concentration, or nearly completely as in true food dehydration. When we freeze foods we also are removing water as such, since water is most active in foods in its liquid form. As a liquid in foods it is the solvent for numerous food chemicals and thus promotes chemical reactions between the dissolved constituents. It also is necessary for microbial growth.

The other reason we remove water from food (in addition to preservation) is to reduce the weight and bulk of the food and thus save on packaging and shipping costs.

A great deal of food science and food technology can be described in terms of the manipulation of water content of the food; its removal, its freezing, its emulsification, and its addition in the case of dissolving or reconstituting dehydrated foods.

Water will exist in foods in various ways—as free water in the case of tomato juice, as droplets of emulsified water in the case of butter, as water tied up in colloidal gels in gelatin desserts, as a thin layer of adsorbed water on the surface of solids often contributing to caking as in dried milk, and as chemically bound water of hydration as in some sugar crystals.

Some of these bound water forms are extremely difficult to remove from foods even by drying, and many dehydrated foods with as little as 2 to 3% residual water have their storage stability seriously shortened.

Close control of final water content is essential in the production of numerous foods, and as little as 1 to 2% of *excess* water can result in such common defects as molding of wheat, bread crusts becoming tough and rubbery, soggy potato chips, and caking of salt and sugar. Many skills in food processing involve the removal of these slight excesses of water without simultaneously damaging the other food constituents. On the other hand, even where a dehydrated product is involved, it is possible to remove too much water. In some cases the storage stability of a dehydrated item is enhanced by leaving a trace of moisture, equivalent to a monomolecular layer of water, to coat all internal and external surfaces. This monomolecular layer of water then may serve as a barrier between atmospheric oxygen and sensitive fatty constituents in the food which otherwise would be more easily oxidized.

It is obvious that the purity of water used in foods or associated with the manufacture of foods is of utmost importance. It is less obvious, however, that suitable drinking water from a municipal water supply may not be of adequate purity for certain food uses. This is particularly important in the manufacture of carbonated beverages, as will be discussed in a later chapter.

BIBLIOGRAPHY

ANON. 1955. Use of Sugars and Other Carbohydrates in the Food Industry. Advances in Chemistry Series No. 12. American Chemical Society, Washington, D.C.

BRAVERMAN, J. B. S. 1963. Introduction to The Biochemistry of Foods. Elsevier Publishing Co., Amsterdam, London, New York.

ESKIN, N. A. M., HENDERSON, H. M., and TOWNSEND, R. J. 1971. Biochemistry of Foods. Academic Press, New York.

FORREY, R. R. 1965. Private Communication. U. S. Dept. Agr., WURDD, Albany, Calif.

FOX, B. A., and CAMERON, A. G. 1970. Food Science a Chemical Approach. Univ. London Press, London.

FURIA, T. E. (Editor) 1972. Handbook of Food Additives, 2nd Edition. Chemical Rubber Co., Cleveland.

GLICKSMAN, M. 1969. Gum Technology in the Food Industry. Academic Press, New York.

HOOVER, W. J. 1964. Corn sweeteners. *In* Food Processing Operations, Vol. 3. M. A. Joslyn, and J. L. Heid (Editors). Avi Publishing Co., Westport, Conn.

JOSLYN, M. A. 1963A. Enzymes in food processing. *In* Food Processing Operations, Vol. 2. M. A. Joslyn, and J. L. Heid (Editors). Avi Publishing Co., Westport, Conn.

JOSLYN, M. A. 1963B. Water in food processing. *In* Food Processing Operations, Vol. 1. M. A. Joslyn, and J. L. Heid (Editors). Avi Publishing Co., Westport, Conn.

JOSLYN, M. A. (Editor) 1970. Methods in Food Analysis. Academic Press, New York.

KELLY, N. 1964. Sugar. *In* Food Processing Operations, Vol. 3. M. A. Joslyn, and J. L. Heid (Editors). Avi Publishing Co., Westport, Conn.

LLOYD, R. L. 1964. Starches in food processing. *In* Food Processing Operations, Vol. 3. M. A. Joslyn, and J. L. Heid (Editors). Avi Publishing Co., Westport, Conn.

MACKINNEY, G. and LITTLE, A. C. 1962. Color of Foods. Avi Publishing Co., Westport, Conn.

MACMASTERS, M. M., and WOLFF, I. A. 1959. Characteristics of cereal starches. *In* The Chemistry and Technology of Cereals as Food and Feed. S. A. Matz (Editor). Avi Publishing Co., Westport, Conn.

MATZ, S. A. 1962. Food Texture. Avi Publishing Co., Westport, Conn.

MATZ, S. A. 1965. Water in Foods. Avi Publishing Co., Westport, Conn.

MERORY, J. 1960. Food Flavorings—Composition, Manufacture, and Use. Avi Publishing Co., Westport, Conn.

MEYER, L. H. 1960. Food Chemistry. Reinhold Publishing Corp. New York.

NICKERSON, J. T. R. 1963. Preservatives and antioxidants. *In* Food Processing Operations, Vol. 2. M. A. Joslyn, and J. L. Heid (Editors). Avi Publishing Co., Westport, Conn.

PEARSON, D. 1971. The Chemical Analysis of Foods. Chemical Publishing Co., New York.

POMERANZ, Y., and MELOAN, C. E. 1971. Food Analysis: Theory and Practice. Avi Publishing Co., Westport, Conn.

SCHROEDER, W. A. 1963. The hemoglobins. Ann. Rev. Biochem. *32,* 301–320.

SCHULTZ, H. W. (Editor) 1960. Food Enzymes. Avi Publishing Co., Westport, Conn.

SCHULTZ, H. W., and ANGLEMIER, A. F. (Editors) 1964. Symposium on Foods: Proteins and Their Reactions. Avi Publishing Co., Westport, Conn.

SCHULTZ, H. W., DAY, E. A., and LIBBEY, L. M. (Editors) 1967. Symposium on Foods: The Chemistry and Physiology of Flavors. Avi Publishing Co., Westport, Conn.

SCHULTZ, H. W., DAY, E. A., and SINNHUBER, M. S. (Editors) 1962. Symposium on Foods: Lipids and Their Oxidation. Avi Publishing Co., Westport, Conn.

SWISHER, H. E., and SWISHER, L. H. 1963. Use of acids in food processing. *In* Food Processing Operations, Vol. 2. M. A. Joslyn, and J. L. Heid (Editors). Avi Publishing Co., Westport, Conn.

WEISER, H. H., MOUNTNEY, G. J., and GOULD, W. A. 1971. Practical Food Microbiology and Technology, 2nd Edition. Avi Publishing Co., Westport, Conn.

WEISS, T. J. 1963. Fats and oils. *In* Food Processing Operations, Vol. 2. M. A. Joslyn, and J. L. Heid (Editors). Avi Publishing Co., Westport, Conn.

WEISS, T. J. 1970. Food Oils and Their Uses. Avi Publishing Co., Westport, Conn.

CHAPTER 4

Nutritive Aspects of Food Constituents

INTRODUCTION

Man's body is made up of the nutrients he eats, somewhat rearranged, but still very largely recognizable. In addition to providing the substance for building and maintaining the body, the energy for all of the body's functions comes from the food consumed.

The food scientist must consider the nutritive aspects of food from two broad points of view: first, what nutrients do foods contain and what are man's requirements for these; and second, what are the relative stabilities of these nutrients and how are they affected by food processing and handling. The science of Nutrition, concerned with these broad areas, additionally deals with the physiological and biochemical phenomena of food utilization as related to health.

The nutrients of food, which must be supplied by the diet to produce and maintain optimum health, belong to the broad groups of carbohydrates, proteins, fats, vitamins, and minerals. Water, not generally classified as a nutrient, once again must not be overlooked, for no nutrient in short supply will bring the body's machinery to so quick a halt as water.

FOOD AND ENERGY

The major sources of energy for man and animals are carbohydrates, fats, and proteins. These nutrients have additional specific functions, but their conversions to yield energy are of fundamental importance. The energy value of foods is measured in heat units called Calories.

Calories

A calorie, spelled with a small "c" and often referred to as a small calorie, is the amount of heat required to raise the temperature of one gram of water one degree centigrade (from 14.5° to 15.5°C). A Calorie, spelled with a large C, is the amount of heat required to raise the temperature of a kilogram of water one degree centigrade or a gram of water 1,000° centigrade. This latter large Calorie is the unit commonly used in expressing energy values of foods.

The total potential energy of foods and food components is determined by actually burning the food in a steel bomb calorimeter under oxygen pressure. The bomb, and water that it is immersed in, rise in temperature, and this temperature rise is directly related to the gross energy content of

59

the food. Like other fuels, a gram of the dry matter from different foods yields different amounts of Calories.

The total potential energy of the food as determined by calorimetry may not be quite equal to the energy that can be derived from it by the animal or human. If the food or food constituent is not totally digestible, or if the food is not completely oxidized within the body, then its caloric value in metabolism will be less than its theoretical total energy content.

Not all carbohydrates (apart from their relative utilization in the body) yield equal amounts of energy when burned in a calorimeter. This also is true of fats and proteins. A fat that chemically is more highly oxidized than another will yield less energy on further combustion in a calorimeter than a corresponding unoxidized fat. Nevertheless, common averages from calorimeter studies in Calories per gram generally are given as 4.1 for carbohydrates, 9.5 for fats, and 5.7 for proteins.

Carbohydrates such as sugars and starches which generally are about 98% digested and fully oxidized by man provide man with about 4 Cal per gm. Most fats generally digested to the extent of 95%, yield man 9 Cal per gm. Proteins, due to incomplete digestion and oxidation, generally also yield an energy equivalent of 4 Cal per gm. Thus on an equal weight basis fat is generally two and one-quarter times as caloric as protein or carbohydrate. These simple relationships permit approximate calculations of the caloric values of foods when compositions are known.

The need for Calories is to satisfy the body's energy requirements for production of body heat, synthesis of body tissue, and performance of work. The greater part of the food we consume goes to satisfy these energy requirements. When the body performs little work then a greater proportion of this energy is conserved and stored in the form of fat. Likewise, when energy demands on the body exceed the intake of Calories then fat and other tissues are oxidized to provide this energy and the body loses weight. An excess intake of about one-third of an ounce of butter or margarine daily can result in the deposition of about seven pounds of fat in a year. This can be counteracted by walking approximately an additional mile and a half daily.

Comprehensive Calorie charts on common foods are readily available and are not included here, although the Calorie content for a few representative foods are given in the more general Table 7, which also includes the contents of other nutrients in these foods. While the Calorie contents of foods are relatively fixed, man's caloric requirements vary widely, depending upon such factors as physical activity, climatic conditions, weight, age, sex, and individual metabolic differences. Table 8 gives daily dietary allowances for each of the major nutrients, and for Calories, recommended by the Food and Nutrition Board, National Academy of Sciences—National

TABLE 7

APPROXIMATE VALUES FOR MAJOR NUTRIENTS AND CALORIES OF COMMON FOODS[1]

| Food | Serving | Calories | Protein Gm | Calcium Mg | Iron Mg | Vitamins | | | | | | Water % |
						A IU	C Mg	D IU	Thiamine Mcg	Riboflavin Mcg	Niacin Mg	
Apple, raw	1 large	117	0.6	12	0.6	180	9	0	80	60	0.4	85
Banana, raw	1 large	176	2.4	16	1.2	860	20	0	80	100	1.4	76
Beans, green, cooked	1 cup	27	1.8	45	0.9	830	18	0	90	120	0.6	92
Beef, round, cooked	3.2 ounces	214	24.7	10	3.1	0	0	0	74	202	5.1	55
Bread, white, enriched	1 slice	63	2.0	18	0.4	0	0	0	60	40	0.5	36
Broccoli, cooked	2/3 cup	29	3.3	130	1.3	3,400	74	0	70	150	0.8	90
Butter	1 tablespoon	100	0.1	33	0.0	460	0	5	tr.	tr.	tr.	16
Cabbage, cooked	1/2 cup	20	1.2	39	0.4	75	27	0	40	40	0.3	92
Carrots, raw	1 cup shredded	42	1.2	39	0.8	12,000	6	0	60	60	0.5	88
Cheese, Cheddar American	1 ounce	113	7.1	206	0.3	400	0	0	10	120	tr.	36
Chicken, fried	1/2 breast	232	26.8	19	1.3	460	0	0	67	101	10.2	53
Egg, boiled	1 medium	77	6.1	26	1.3	550	0	27	40	130	tr.	74
Liver, beef, fried	1 slice	86	8.8	4	2.9	18,700	10	19	90	1,300	5.1	57
Margarine, fortified	1 tablespoon	101	0.1	3	0.0	460	0	2	0	0	0.0	16
Milk, whole, cow's	6 ounces	124	6.4	216	0.2	293	2	4	73	311	0.2	87
Oatmeal, cooked	1 cup	148	5.4	21	1.7	0	0	0	220	50	0.4	85
Orange, whole	1 medium	68	1.4	50	0.6	285	74	0	120	45	0.3	86
Pork, shoulder, roasted	2 slices	320	19.2	9	2.0	0	0	0	592	144	3.2	43
Tomatoes, raw	1 large	40	2.0	22	1.2	2,200	46	0	120	80	1.0	94
Potatoes, white, baked	1 medium	98	2.4	13	0.8	20	17	0	110	50	1.4	75
Rice, white, cooked	1 cup	201	4.2	13	0.5	0	0	0	20	10	0.7	71
Sugar, white, granulated	1 tablespoon	48	0.0	0	0.0	0	0	0	0	0	0.0	tr.

[1] Adapted from Anon. (1966).

TABLE 8

FOOD AND NUTRITION BOARD, NATIONAL ACADEMY OF SCIENCES—NATIONAL RESEARCH COUNCIL RECOMMENDED DAILY DIETARY ALLOWANCES,[1] REVISED 1968
Designed for the maintenance of good nutrition of practically all healthy people in the U.S.A.

	Age[2] Years From Up to	Weight Kg	Weight (Lb)	Height Cm	Height (In.)	Kcalories	Protein Gm	Fat Soluble Vitamins Vitamin A Activity I.U.	Vitamin D I.U.	Vitamin E Activity I.U.
Infants	0–⅙	4	9	55	22	kg × 120	kg × 2.2[3]	1500	400	5
	⅙–½	7	15	63	25	kg × 110	kg × 2.0[3]	1500	400	5
	½–1	9	20	72	28	kg × 100	kg × 1.8[3]	1500	400	5
Children	1–2	12	26	81	32	1100	25	2000	400	10
	2–3	14	31	91	36	1250	25	2000	400	10
	3–4	16	35	100	39	1400	30	2500	400	10
	4–6	19	42	110	43	1600	30	2500	400	10
	6–8	23	51	121	48	2000	35	3500	400	15
	8–10	28	62	131	52	2200	40	3500	400	15
Males	10–12	35	77	140	55	2500	45	4500	400	20
	12–14	43	95	151	59	2700	50	5000	400	20
	14–18	59	130	170	67	3000	60	5000	400	25
	18–22	67	147	175	69	2800	60	5000	400	30
	22–35	70	154	175	69	2800	65	5000	...	30
	35–55	70	154	173	68	2600	65	5000	...	30
	55–75+	70	154	171	67	2400	65	5000	...	30
Females	10–12	35	77	142	56	2250	50	4500	400	20
	12–14	44	97	154	61	2300	50	5000	400	20
	14–16	52	114	157	62	2400	55	5000	400	25
	16–18	54	119	160	63	2300	55	5000	400	25
	18–22	58	128	163	64	2000	55	5000	400	25
	22–35	58	128	163	64	2000	55	5000	...	25
	35–55	58	128	160	63	1850	55	5000	...	25
	55–75+	58	128	157	62	1700	55	5000	...	25
Pregnancy						+200	65	6000	400	30
Lactation						+1000	75	8000	400	30

[1]The allowance levels are intended to cover individual variations among most normal persons as they live in the United States under usual environmental stresses. The recommended allowances can be attained with a variety of common foods, providing other nutrients for which human requirements have been less well defined.

[2]Entries on lines for age range 22–35 years represent the reference man and woman at age 22. All other entires represent allowances for the midpoint of the specified age range.

[3]Assumes protein equivalent to human milk. For proteins not 100 per cent utilized factors should be increased proportionately.

	Water Soluble Vitamins						Minerals					
Ascorbic Acid Mg	Folacin[4] Mg	Niacin Mg Equiv[5]	Riboflavin Mg	Thiamine Mg	Vitamin B$_6$ Mg	Vitamin B$_{12}$ µg	Calcium Gm	Phosphorus Gm	Iodine µg	Iron Mg	Magnesium Mg	
35	0.05	5	0.4	0.2	0.2	1.0	0.4	0.2	25	6	40	Infants
35	0.05	7	0.5	0.4	0.3	1.5	0.5	0.4	40	10	60	
35	0.1	8	0.6	0.5	0.4	2.0	0.6	0.5	45	15	70	
40	0.1	8	0.6	0.6	0.5	2.0	0.7	0.7	55	15	100	Children
40	0.2	8	0.7	0.6	0.6	2.5	0.8	0.8	60	15	150	
40	0.2	9	0.8	0.7	0.7	3	0.8	0.8	70	10	200	
40	0.2	11	0.9	0.8	0.9	4	0.8	0.8	80	10	200	
40	0.2	13	1.1	1.0	1.0	4	0.9	0.9	100	10	250	
40	0.3	15	1.2	1.1	1.2	5	1.0	1.0	110	10	250	
40	0.4	17	1.3	1.3	1.4	5	1.2	1.2	125	10	300	Males
45	0.4	18	1.4	1.4	1.6	5	1.4	1.4	135	18	350	
55	0.4	20	1.5	1.5	1.8	5	1.4	1.4	150	18	400	
60	0.4	18	1.6	1.4	2.0	5	0.8	0.8	140	10	400	
60	0.4	18	1.7	1.4	2.0	5	0.8	0.8	140	10	350	
60	0.4	17	1.7	1.3	2.0	5	0.8	0.8	125	10	350	
60	0.4	14	1.7	1.2	2.0	6	0.8	0.8	110	10	350	
40	0.4	15	1.3	1.1	1.4	5	1.2	1.2	110	18	300	Females
45	0.4	15	1.4	1.2	1.6	5	1.3	1.3	115	18	350	
50	0.4	16	1.4	1.2	1.8	5	1.3	1.3	120	18	350	
50	0.4	15	1.5	1.2	2.0	5	1.3	1.3	115	18	350	
55	0.4	13	1.5	1.0	2.0	5	0.8	0.8	100	18	350	
55	0.4	13	1.5	1.0	2.0	5	0.8	0.8	100	18	300	
55	0.4	13	1.5	1.0	2.0	5	0.8	0.8	90	18	300	
55	0.4	13	1.5	1.0	2.0	6	0.8	0.8	80	10	300	
60	0.8	15	1.8	+0.1	2.5	8	+0.4	+0.4	125	18	450	Pregnancy
60	0.5	20	2.0	+0.5	2.5	6	+0.5	+0.5	150	18	450	Lactation

[4]The folacin allowances refer to dietary sources as determined by *Lactobacillus casei* assay. Pure forms of folacin may be effective in doses less than 1/4 of the RDA.

[5]Niacin equivalents include dietary sources of the vitamin itself plus 1 mg equivalent for each 60 mg of dietary tryptophan.

Research Council. Especially depending upon physical activity, an adult male's daily Calorie requirement can range from about 2,500 to 5,000. If he is a lumberjack and needs 5,000 Cal per day, he must eat some fat since man's stomach is not large enough to hold this many Calories from carbohydrates and proteins alone, consumed at normal mealtimes. Such high Calorie requirements are not listed in Table 8 since these recommended daily dietary allowances are intended to cover most normal persons as they live in the United States under usual work and environmental stresses.

While fats are the most concentrated source of food Calories, carbohydrates are the cheapest source and proteins the most expensive. It generally is agreed that quite apart from the other nutritional demands of the body, and except for very young children and the aged, a daily intake of less than about 2,000 Cal represents severe dietary insufficiency. It is one of the sad contrasts of our time that while about two-thirds of the world's people go hungry (Fig 30), in the United States and certain other countries obesity from excess Calories is the major nutritional disease.

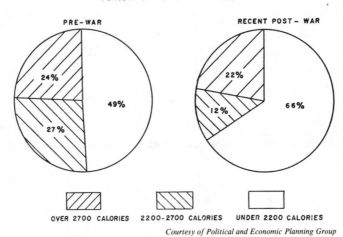

PERCENT OF TOTAL POPULATION

PRE-WAR   RECENT POST – WAR

24%   49%   27%   22%   12%   66%

OVER 2700 CALORIES   2200-2700 CALORIES   UNDER 2200 CALORIES

Courtesy of Political and Economic Planning Group

FIG. 30.   CALORIE LEVEL GENERALLY AVAILABLE TO THE WORLD POPULATION, PRE- AND POST-WORLD WAR II

ADDITIONAL ROLES OF CARBOHYDRATES, PROTEINS, AND FATS IN NUTRITION

The carbohydrates, proteins, and fats in many ways are interrelated and interconvertible in animal metabolism. Actually, beyond their contribution as an economical source of Calories, the body has no specific nutritional requirement for carbohydrates. That is, the body can derive its energy and carbon requirements from the proteins and fats, and also can synthesize blood glucose, liver glycogen, the ribose sugar components of nucleic acids, and other carbohydrates from proteins and fats.

On the other hand, carbohydrates from the foods consumed help the body use fat efficiently. They do this by supplying an organic acid formed as an intermediate in the oxidation of carbohydrates. This organic acid is required for the complete oxidation of fat to CO_2 and water.

Carbohydrates also exert a protein-sparing effect. When carbohydrates are depleted in the animal body and the animal needs additional energy it gets this energy by oxidizing fats and proteins. In the case of proteins, this energy requirement is thus satisfied at the expense of the body's requirement for proteins and amino acids as components of body tissues, enzymes, antibodies, and other essential nitrogen-containing substances. However, if carbohydrates are supplied, the body oxidizes them for energy in preference to protein and thus the protein is spared. In similar fashion, fats can exert a protein sparing effect.

The role of carbohydrates such as cellulose and hemicellulose in providing fiber and bulk is essential to a healthy condition of the intestine. In addition, the microflora of the intestine is much influenced by the nature of carbohydrates in the diet. When these carbohydrates are comparatively slow to dissolve, as in the case of starch and lactose, they remain in the intestinal tract for longer periods than the more highly soluble sugars. In this case they serve as readily available nutrients for growth of microorganisms that synthesize several vitamins of the B complex. On the other hand, the slow rate of absorption of lactose from the intestine can cause diarrhea in adults consuming excessive amounts of this sugar.

The roles of protein in supplying the nitrogenous matter for the synthesis of body tissues and other constituents of life, and in providing those essential amino acids that the body cannot itself synthesize have been mentioned. The true comparative value of different proteins depends upon their different amino acid compositions, especially their contents of the essential amino acids. In a mixture, a poor protein lacking certain essential amino acids can be supplemented by a good protein containing the missing amino acids to produce nutritional adequacy, but both should be given at the same feeding, since the body has a very limited protein storage capacity and all amino acids are needed for daily protein synthesis.

The amount of protein required daily, which beyond early childhood may range from about 40 to 80 gm (Table 8), depends upon the body demand—the demand being greatest during growth, pregnancy, and lactation.

One of the severest needs for protein on a world population basis is in infants after weaning and in young children. Protein shortage or protein

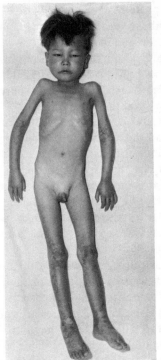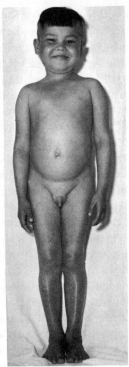

Courtesy of Scrimshaw and Bressani

FIG. 31.   PROTEIN DEFICIENCY DISEASE AND ITS CORRECTION IN
SAME CHILD BY IMPROVED DIET

malnutrition (Fig. 31) can be dramatically reversed by proper diet. However, in many instances where adequate protein and proper diet are withheld too long, recovery is not complete and mental as well as physical damage can persist throughout life.

Plant proteins generally are not as good as animal proteins, because certain essential amino acids are lacking. Thus, for example, most varieties of wheat, rice, and corn lack lysine; corn also lacks tryptophan; threonine is missing in rice. However, supplementation of incomplete plant proteins with the missing essential amino acids either in the form of synthetic compounds or as protein concentrates from natural sources such as soybeans can result in totally adequate protein. Much of this is now being practiced to improve world food resources.

In addition to supplying Calories for energy, fats supply polyunsaturated fatty acids, at least one of which, linoleic acid, is termed an essential fatty acid. As in the case of the essential amino acids, linoleic acid is called an essential fatty acid because animals cannot adequately synthesize it and so it must be supplied by the diet as such. In rats and in human infants absence of linoleic acid interferes with normal growth rates and results in skin disorders. Two other polyunsaturated fatty acids, linolenic acid and arachidonic acid, sometimes also are listed as essential fatty acids. However, since the body can convert linoleic acid to arachidonic acid and since linolenic acid can only partially replace linoleic acid, the newer literature regards only linoleic acid as an essential fatty acid. Good sources of linoleic acid include grain and seed oils, fats from nuts, and fats from poultry. Linoleic and other unsaturated fatty acids when present in high proportion of dietary fats can lower blood cholesterol levels under certain dietary conditions, more will be said about this shortly.

Vitamins A, D, E, and K are fat-soluble and so are to be found associated with the fat fractions of natural foods. Additionally, phospholipids which are organic esters of fatty acids and also contain phosphoric acid and usually a nitrogenous base, are partially soluble in fats. The emulsifying properties of lecithin have previously been mentioned. Lecithin, cephalin, and other phospholipids are found in brain, nerve, liver, kidney, heart, blood, and other tissues in addition to their presence in egg yolk. Because of their strong affinity for water they facilitate the passage of fats in and out of the cells and probably play a role in fat absorption from the intestine and the transport of fats from the liver.

PROTEIN QUALITY

It previously was stated that the true comparative value of different proteins depends upon their different amino acid compositions, especially their contents of the essential amino acids leucine, isoleucine, lysine, methionine, phenylalanine, threonine, tryptophan, and valine, plus histidine to meet the demands of growth during childhood. While this statement is essentially true it requires some further consideration.

Protein quality, or nutritional value of a protein, is meaningful only in terms of the usefulness of the protein for specific vital purposes such as growth, replacement of metabolic losses and damaged tissue, reproduction, lactation, and general well-being. The usefulness of a protein may differ for several of these functions. Further, a measure of usefulness of a protein based on chemical analysis of its amino acid makeup is complicated by a number of factors. These include accuracy of the analytical method under conditions that can preclude the detection of one or another amino acid or cause its destruction, availability and digestibility of the protein from foods that may not be readily broken down by digestive enzymes or absorbed through the intestine, and factors contributing to unpalatability of the protein-containing food.

These objections to chemical analysis of amino acid content are not encountered when a biological method such as an animal feeding study is used to measure protein quality. However, in this case a different set of obstacles are encountered. One of the most obvious is how closely results obtained with animals apply to man. Even where questions of digestibility and vital response are ruled out the palatability factor between species must be considered in arriving at a valid measure of the nutritional usefulness of a protein source. Notwithstanding these difficulties, research has shown that results obtained with young rats generally are applicable to man, and feeding tests under controlled conditions are far more easily carried out on rats than with man. Such tests may be run under a variety of experimental conditions which then influence the interpretations that may be given the nutritional findings.

Several test methods using the rat have been developed and result in specific terms that the food scientist encounters in the area of protein evaluation. One of the commonest methods involves measurement of weight gain of rats per gram of protein eaten. This is known as Protein Efficiency Ratio (PER). One of its principal limitations is that results depend upon the amount of food eaten, which can give an erroneous picture if the food is unpalatable. The modification known as Net Protein Retention (NPR) improves upon this. If two groups of animals are used and one is placed on the test protein diet and the other is placed on a protein-free diet then the weight loss of the protein-free group can be compared with the weight gain of the protein-receiving group. Properly controlled, the test becomes independent of food intake. Another measure is the proportion of absorbed nitrogen that is retained in the body for maintenance and/or growth. This is known as Biological Value (BV). It requires measurement of protein consumed and the fraction that is excreted in the urine and feces. Since Biological Value measures percentage of the absorbed nitrogen that is retained it does not account for the digestibility of the protein. Digestibility (D) also can be measured and is the proportion of consumed food nitrogen that is absorbed. When Biological Value is corrected for the Digestibility factor we get the proportion of nitrogen intake that is retained and this is termed Net Protein Utilization (NPU), which is BV × D. Since the nutritive value of a protein food involves both quality and quantity of protein contained, still another measure employs Net Protein Utilization multiplied by the amount of protein in the food—this is known as Net Protein Value. These are but a few of the approaches to measure protein usefulness.

The complexity of the assessment of protein quality and usefulness has come into special focus in recent years, especially with respect to developing high protein foods and supplements to correct nutritional deficiencies in underdeveloped regions of the world. Here the importance of field studies with human subjects under real life conditions has been repeatedly observed. Many new foods of excellent protein content measured by sophisticated laboratory procedures have failed in their purpose because of poor palatability, having been manufactured in a nonfamiliar physical form, or having been presented in a manner in conflict with accepted custom or demeaning of social status. A second area where indices of protein usefulness are of current concern has to do with food labeling. Presently in most countries there are inadequate legal definitions of what is meant by such terms as "high protein food," "protein rich," or "high protein quality," although guidelines are gradually being evolved. For a more detailed discussion of such problems the reader is referred to the section on Nutritional Labeling in Chapter 24.

ATHEROSCLEROSIS

Presently in the United States, cardiovascular diseases cause about one million deaths annually and the incidence of heart disease is greater than in any other country of the world. There are several types of heart disease but atherosclerosis and coronary thrombosis have been receiving major attention. Atherosclerosis is a disease characterized by deposition of a fatty material on the walls of the arteries. This material consists essentially of cholesterol, triglyceride fats, fibrous tissue, and red blood cells. As the deposit continues to build it restricts blood flow through the artery. When the coronary artery is involved, heart attack and death may follow. Coronary thrombosis, on the other hand, refers to the presence of a blood clot in the coronary artery that blocks the normal flow of blood to the heart. Thus, atherosclerosis can contribute to a coronary thrombosis by narrowing the lumen of the coronary artery so that a clot is more likely to exert blockage.

Besides diet, many factors appear to be associated with the occurrence of atherosclerosis. Among them are obesity, hypertension, diabetes, sedentary living, cigarette smoking, and high blood cholesterol levels. The latter may be caused by diet or be of hereditary origin. While diet does appear to be involved, it must be emphasized that its relative importance in contributing to atherosclerosis is not entirely clear. Since cholesterol, a sterol found in all animal tissues, eggs, milk, and other foods of animal origin is a component of the atherosclerotic deposit it is reasonable to hypothesize that foods high in cholesterol can contribute to atherosclerosis. Such foods can increase the level of cholesterol in the blood. But other components of diet also can result in high levels of blood cholesterol and this is especially true of large quantities of saturated fats and of sugars. Further, some investigators find that high levels of blood triglycerides correlate even more closely with coronary disease than do high levels of blood cholesterol. High levels of blood triglycerides also result from the consumption of large quantities of saturated fats and sugars. While consumption of large quantities of saturated fats can increase levels of both cholesterol and triglycerides in the blood, liberal quantities of polyunsaturated vegetable oils tend to decrease blood cholesterol.

The above considerations have influenced the thinking of many doctors and nutritionists. Until more is learned many are advocating a diet not overly rich in fats and sugars, and the substitution of polyunsaturated vegetable oils for at least part of the saturated animal fats. A reduction in quantity of foods high in cholesterol also is being recommended by some.

All of this has had an influence upon manufacturers of certain foods. Research currently is in progress to lower the cholesterol content of eggs and dairy products. Margarines and other fatty foods are available that have been manufactured with a high concentration of vegetable oils rich in polyunsaturated fatty acids. Such products are said to have a high polyunsaturated to saturated fat ratio or high P/S ratio. Because the complex interrelationships between heart disease and diet have not yet been fully explained, the Food and Drug Administration has been most cautious in regulating promotional claims for such products.

THE VITAMINS

Vitamins are defined as organic materials which must be supplied to an animal in small amounts other than essential amino acids or fatty acids. If the body could synthesize a vitamin then it would not have to be supplied as such and according to the above definition would not fall in the vitamin category. An exception to this is vitamin D, the only major vitamin the human body is known to be capable of manufacturing. Under certain circumstances, however, vitamin D may not be able to be synthesized in adequate amount and then it too must be supplied by diet or as a dietary supplement if life and health are to be sustained. Vitamins function in enzyme systems which facilitate the metabolism of proteins, carbohydrates, and fats, but there is growing evidence that their roles in maintaining health may extend yet further.

The vitamins are conveniently divided into two major groups, those that are fat-soluble and those that are water-soluble.

Fat-soluble vitamins are A, D, E, and K. Their absorption by the body depends upon the normal absorption of fat from the diet. Water-soluble vitamins include vitamin C, and the several members of the vitamin B complex.

Vitamin A

This vitamin is found as such only in animal materials—meat, milk, eggs, and the like. Plants contain no vitamin A but contain its precursor, beta-carotene. Man and other animals need either vitamin A or beta-carotene which they easily convert to vitamin A. Beta-carotene is found in the orange and yellow vegetables as well as the green leafy vegetables.

A deficiency of vitamin A leads to night blindness, failure of normal bone growth in the young, and diseases of membranes of the nose, throat, and eyes.

The chief food sources of vitamin A or its precursor beta-carotene, are liver, fish oils, dairy products, carrots, squash, sweet potatoes, and other green leafy vegetables. There is a recommended allowance of 5,000 IU (International Units) of vitamin A per day for adults. The recommended allowance is increased during pregnancy and lactation. This amount is easily supplied by a varied diet. The IU is a standardized measure of a vitamin's biological activity. In this case one IU corresponds to 0.3 gamma of pure crystalline vitamin A or 0.6 gamma of pure beta-carotene, which are equivalent. A gamma is one millionth of a gram. Today vitamin A and beta-carotene are made synthetically, as are other vitamins.

Vitamin D

Vitamin D is formed in the skin of man and animals by activation of sterols by ultraviolet light from the sun, or by ultraviolet activation of sterols artificially. Such sterols as cholesterol and ergosterol are involved. Cholesterol is found in and under the skin of animals. Irradiated ergosterol from yeast has served as a vitamin D source for addition to milk and other foods.

Shortage of vitamin D results in bone defects, the principal one being rickets. This shortage may occur when exposure to the sun is limited, as in winter when the skin is largely covered by clothing.

Most foods are low in vitamin D, although good sources are liver, fish oils, dairy products, and eggs. In children, 400 IU of vitamin D per day is considered optimum, and this is the basis of fortifying milk with added vitamin D at the level of 400 IU per qt.

Vitamin E

This vitamin, also known as alpha-tocopherol, is an antisterility factor in rats, and is essential for normal muscle tone in dogs and other animals, but its significance for man is still controversial. Vitamin E is a strong antioxidant and it may function as such in human metabolism. Diets excessive in polyunsaturated fats can lead to the formation of peroxidized fatty acids that may reach harmful levels. There is growing evidence that vitamin E can prevent this. Further, vitamin E may play a role in slowing down the aging process. Because of its antioxidant properties, vitamin E also is able to spare carotene and vitamin A from oxidative destruction.

Good sources of vitamin E are vegetable oils, but vitamin E deficiency under practical conditions of human nutrition is rare.

Vitamin K

Vitamin K is essential for normal blood clotting. Its deficiency generally parallels liver disease where fat absorption is abnormal. It also can be deficient in infants. This is prevented by giving pregnant mothers doses of vitamin K, and later giving infants vitamin K with their formulas. Good sources of vitamin K are green vegetables such as spinach and cabbage.

Vitamin C

Vitamin C is the antiscurvy vitamin. Its deficiency causes fragile capillary walls, easy bleeding of gums, loosening of teeth, and bone joint diseases.

Vitamin C, also known as ascorbic acid, is easily destroyed by oxidation especially at high temperatures, and is the vitamin most easily lost during food processing, storage, and cooking.

Recommended daily allowance in the United States for the adult male is 60 mg. In Great Britain and Canada, the same recommended daily allowance has been 30 mg. This is true with other vitamin and nutrient recommendations—there is not yet complete international agreement.

Excellent sources of vitamin C are citrus fruits, tomatoes, cabbage, and green peppers. Potatoes also are a fair source (although the content of vitamin C is relatively low) because we consume large quantities of potatoes. Milk, cereals, and meats are poor sources.

Two of the more recent claims for vitamin C have to do with removing high levels of cholesterol from the blood of rats, and preventing colds in humans. The significance of the rat studies in relation to cholesterol levels in the blood of humans has not yet been established. With regard to vitamin C for avoiding common colds, a very high level of one or more grams of vitamin C taken daily in the form of tablets has been advocated by some. At the present time, however, this is still an unproven theory not supported by the medical profession or the FDA.

Vitamins of the B Complex Group

This group contains thiamine, riboflavin, niacin, pyridoxine, pantothenic acid, folic acid, vitamin B_{12}, biotin, and choline.

All members of this group generally are found in the same principal food sources—such as liver, yeast, and the bran of cereal grains. All are required for essential metabolic activities and several function as parts of active enzymes. Absence of a particular B vitamin results in a specific deficiency disease.

Thiamine or Vitamin B₁

This was the first of the B vitamins to be recognized. The deficiency disease is beriberi and it is common where polished rice is a major dietary item, such as in the Far East. Fortification of rice or white bread with thiamine corrects this disease.

Important to the food technologist is the sensitivity of thiamine to SO_2, a common food preservative chemical, and to sulfite salts. Sulfur dioxide destroys the vitamin activity of thiamine and so where a particular food is a major source of thiamine it never should be preserved with SO_2, and this is prohibited by the Food and Drug Administration and the meat inspection laws. The recommended adult daily allowance for thiamine is about 1.4 mg. Best sources are wheat germ, whole cereals containing bran, liver, pork, yeast, and egg yolk. Thiamine is stable to heat in acid foods but less so in neutral foods and this is taken into account in food processing.

Recommended daily allowances for thiamine and other vitamins not only differ for children and adults, for different physiological states, and for different levels of physical activity, but a distinction also must be made between recommended levels and minimum acceptable levels. As given in Table 8, recommended levels provide a substantial margin of safety, and may be as much as five times the minimum levels required to sustain life.

Riboflavin or Vitamin B₂

Riboflavin is the yellow-green pigment of skim milk and whey.

Deficiency in man generally results in skin conditions, such as cracking of skin at the corners of the mouth. Recommended daily allowance for adult males is 1.7 mg. Liver, milk, and eggs are good sources. Meats and green leafy vegetables are fair sources of riboflavin.

Riboflavin is quite resistant to heat but very sensitive to light and this is why brown milk bottles have seen limited use in the past. Paper cartons which protect milk from light are more practical.

Niacin or Nicotinic Acid

This vitamin also is referred to as nicotinamide in the United Kingdom. It is not to be confused with nicotine from tobacco. A deficiency of niacin produces the disease known as pellagra in man. This can be cured by feeding niacin or by feeding the essential amino acid tryptophan from which niacin can be made in the body. Humans need about 17 mg of niacin per day and good sources are yeast, meat, fish, and poultry. Recently it was found that roasting of coffee beans increased niacin content about 25-fold making coffee a potentially significant source of this vitamin.

Pyridoxine or Vitamin B$_6$

While essential in man's diet for specific enzyme action and normal metabolism, a deficiency of this vitamin does not show a well-recognized disease. Vitamin B$_6$ is widely distributed in foodstuffs—best sources being muscle meat, liver, green vegetables, and grain cereals with bran.

Pantothenic Acid

This member of the B vitamin complex is widespread in foods and so there is a rarity of clear-cut deficiency disease in man. But a deficiency may appear in experimental animals on limited diets or in malnourished victims, such as war prisoners. In this case there is a general lowering in the state of well-being of the individual with signs of depression, less resistance to infection, and possibly less tolerance to stress. The human requirement for this vitamin is not well established but is believed to be about 5 mg per day. This is easily supplied in a normal diet.

Vitamin B$_{12}$ and Folic Acid

Vitamin B$_{12}$ is the anti-pernicious anemia factor and folic acid is a related vitamin also essential to prevent certain kinds of anemias. Neither vitamin B$_{12}$ nor folic acid are single substances but consist of closely related compounds with similar activity.

Vitamin B$_{12}$ is the largest vitamin molecule and contains cobalt in its structure, giving rise to one of the essential requirements for the mineral cobalt in nutrition.

Vitamin B$_{12}$ and folic acid are synthesized by bacteria and molds and are commercial by-products of antibiotic production. Good natural sources of these vitamins are liver, meats, and seafoods. Quantitative human requirements for these vitamins are not well known but are believed to be of the order of fractions of a milligram daily.

Additional Factors

There are several additional materials which are water-soluble and are generally listed with the vitamins of the B complex, although they are usually referred to as growth factors rather than vitamins in the strict sense. Such materials include biotin, inositol, para-amino benzoic acid, and choline. These factors seldom are in short supply when the diet is adequate to supply the other B vitamins. Further, several of the growth factors are produced by the normal microflora of the intestine.

MINERALS

Calcium and Phosphorus

Calcium and phosphorus are the minerals our foods must supply in greatest amounts. Deficiencies result chiefly in bone and teeth diseases. Calcium also is necessary for clotting of the blood, for the function of certain enzymes, and for control of fluids through cell membranes. Phosphorus is an essential part of every living cell. It is involved in the enzyme-controlled energy yielding reactions of metabolism. Phosphorus also helps control the acid-alkaline reaction of the blood. Highest requirements for calcium and phosphorus are for the young, and for pregnant and nursing mothers.

Important not only is the intake of these minerals but the percentage that is absorbed into the blood stream. Calcium and phosphorus can combine and precipitate one another and so they actually interfere with the effective absorption of one another. Oxalates in foods like rhubarb also can precipitate calcium and make it unavailable for nutritional purposes. Milk and dairy products are excellent sources of calcium and phosphorus and in normal diets there is seldom any deficiency. Vitamin D is essential for absorption of calcium from the intestinal tract, and lactose also is effective in promoting this absorption. This makes milk, especially milk fortified with vitamin D, a particularly valuable source of calcium.

Magnesium and Manganese

These two minerals are essential to enzyme function and normal metabolism. Magnesium also promotes proper calcification of bone. Deficiency diseases from shortages of these minerals are more common in farm and experimental animals which may have a restricted diet. Man's diet is generally adequate in magnesium and manganese.

Cobalt

As mentioned, cobalt is a part of vitamin B_{12}. However, cobalt will not replace the need for vitamin B_{12} in man.

Iron and Copper

Iron is required as a component of blood hemoglobin and copper aids in utilization of iron. The need for iron is related to the rate of growth and to blood loss.

Sodium and Chlorine

Sodium and chloride are the chief extracellular ions of the body. Great losses occur in sodium and chlorine during loss of body fluids, such as perspiration during exercise, and these must be replaced to prevent weakness, nausea, and muscle cramps. Under normal conditions man's daily intake from food of about ten grams of salt is more than adequate to meet his needs. Vegetables are relatively low in salt and so vegetarians and grass eating animals generally need salt supplementation to their diets.

Potassium

Potassium is found in all body cells. Potassium is essential for life—but rarely limiting even in the most meager diets.

Iodine

Iodine is an essential part of the thyroid hormone and is essential for the prevention of goiter in man. There is never a shortage of iodine where salt water fish are eaten. Central United States and parts of South America, away from the ocean, are short of indigenous iodine. Today the common use of iodized salt corrects the deficiency.

Fluorine

The fluoride ion is required for the development of sound teeth with resistance to tooth decay. Diets of growing children appear to be low in fluorine since supplementation of water with about 1 ppm reduces incidence of tooth decay. No other dietary requirement for fluorine is well documented. There are still other mineral requirements which diet must supply in at least trace amounts—but normal diets easily provide these.

WATER

About 60%, by weight, of a person's body is water. A normal person experiences symptoms of dehydration when about 5 to 10% of his body weight is lost as water and not soon replaced. Long before this are the experiences of thirst, weakness, and mental confusion. If the state of dehydration progresses further the skin and lips lose elasticity, the cheeks become pale and the eyeballs sunken, the volume of urine decreases, and ultimately respiration ceases. Under certain conditions a person may survive without food for about five weeks but can seldom live without water for more than a few days.

The need for water exists at the molecular level, the cellular level, and at the metabolic and functional levels. Water is the major solvent for the organic and inorganic chemicals involved in the biochemical reactions that are essential to life. Water is the principal medium that transports nutrients via body fluids to cell walls and through membranes. Water is the medium that carries nitrogenous waste products from the cells for ultimate elimination. The evaporation of water from the skin is one important mechanism for controlling and maintaining normal body temperature, essential for controlled rate of metabolic reactions and physical comfort of the individual.

The quantitative requirement for water is directly related to the sum of water losses from the body. These include losses from excretion and elimination of body wastes, perspiration, and respiration. Any factors that increase the rates of these processes, such as exercise, excitation, elevated temperature, or low relative humidity also increase the need for water replenishment.

A normal adult may consume 400 qt of water or more a year. About an equal amount is obtained from food. Given sufficient water, or water in excess, the body closely regulates its water content. Except in unusual cases of deprivation or illness, the body seldom suffers from a deficiency of water in the sense that there may be a deficiency of other essential nutrients. This is because, unlike many of the other nutrients, a decrease in body water causes almost immediate discomfort, driving the individual to correct the shortage.

STABILITY OF NUTRIENTS

One of the principal responsibilities of the food scientist and food technologist is to preserve food nutrients through all phases of food acquisition, processing, storage, and preparation. The key is in the specific sensitivities of the various nutrients, the principles of which are illustrated in Table 9. This shows the stability of vitamins, essential amino acids, and minerals to acid, air, light, and heat, and gives an indication of possible cooking losses. Vitamin A is highly sensitive to acid, air, light and heat; vitamin C to alkalinity, air, light and heat; vitamin D to alkalinity, air, light and heat; thiamine to alkalinity, air, and heat in alkaline solutions; etc. Because of these sensitivities, cooking losses of some essential nutrients may be in excess of 75%. In modern food processing operations, however, losses are seldom in excess of 25%.

Where nutrient losses are unavoidably excessive the law permits restoration or enrichment by the add-back of vital nutrients. This is the case in the enrichment of flour and the enrichment of white bread (Table 10). The standards for enrichment of food products are in a state of periodic revision as knowledge of nutrition increases.

The ultimate nutritive value of a food results from the sum total of losses incurred throughout its history—from farmer to consumer. Nutrient value begins with genetics of the plant and animal. The farmland fertilization program affects tissue composition of plants and animals consuming these plants. The weather and degree of maturity at harvest affect tissue composition. Storage conditions before processing affect vitamins and other

TABLE 9

STABILITY OF NUTRIENTS [1]

Nutrient	Neutral pH 7	Acid <pH 7	Alkaline >pH 7	Air or Oxygen	Light	Heat	Cooking Losses, Range %
Vitamins							
Vitamin A	S	U	S	U	U	U	0–40
Ascorbic acid (C)	U	S	U	U	U	U	0–100
Biotin	S	S	S	S	S	U	0–60
Carotenes (pro-A)	S	U	S	U	U	U	0–30
Choline	S	S	S	U	S	S	0–5
Cobalamin (B$_{12}$)	S	S	S	U	U	S	0–10
Vitamin D	S		U	U	U	U	0–40
Essential fatty acids	S	S	U	U	U	S	0–10
Folic acid	U	U	S	U	U	U	0–100
Inositol	S	S	S	S	S	U	0–95
Vitamin K	S	U	U	S	U	S	0–5
Niacin (PP)	S	S	S	S	S	S	0–75
Pantothenic acid	S	U	U	S	S	U	0–50
p-Amino benzoic acid	S	S	S	U	S	S	0–5
Vitamin B$_6$	S	S	S	S	U	U	0–40
Riboflavin (B$_2$)	S	S	U	S	U	U	0–75
Thiamine (B$_1$)	U	S	U	U	S	U	0–80
Tocopherols (E)	S	S	S	U	U	U	0–55
Essential amino acids							
Isoleucine	S	S	S	S	S	S	0–10
Leucine	S	S	S	S	S	S	0–10
Lysine	S	S	S	S	S	U	0–40
Methionine	S	S	S	S	S	S	0–10
Phenylalanine	S	S	S	S	S	S	0–5
Threonine	S	U	U	S	S	U	0–20
Tryptophan	S	U	S	S	U	S	0–15
Valine	S	S	S	S	S	S	0–10
Mineral Salts	S	S	S	S	S	S	0–3

S　=　stable (no important destruction).
U　=　unstable (significant destruction).
[1] From Harris and Von Loesecke (1960).

nutrients. Washing, trimming, and heat treatments affect nutrient content. Canning, evaporating, drying, and freezing alter nutritional values, and the choices of times and temperatures in these operations frequently must be balanced between good bacterial destruction and minimum nutrient destruction. Packaging and subsequent storage affect nutrients. One of the most important factors is the final preparation of the food in the home and the restaurant—the steam table can destroy much of what has been preserved through all prior manipulations.

The interaction between processing methods and nutrient retention is fundamental to the study of food science, and much more will be said about it in subsequent chapters. One is justified in asking where all this leaves us, and what of the claims that are commonly heard that our foods are being destroyed nutritionally. Some general conclusions appear clear. In the

TABLE 10

FEDERAL STANDARDS FOR FLOUR [1] AND BREAD [2] ENRICHMENT

	Flour		Bread	
	Minimum Mg/Lb	Maximum Mg/Lb	Minimum Mg/Lb	Maximum Mg/Lb
Thiamine	2.0	2.5	1.1	1.8
Riboflavin	1.2	1.5	0.7	1.6
Niacin	16.0	20.0	10.0	15.0
Iron	13.0	16.5	8.0	12.5
Calcium [3]	500	625	300	800
Vitamin D [3] (USP units)	250	1,000	150	750

[1] Anon. (1941).
[2] Anon. (1952).
[3] Optional ingredients.

United States today, except among the very poor, diets can be more varied, more convenient, more nutritious, and more economical than they have been anywhere else in the world ever before in history. It must be added, however, that good nutrition depends upon sensible food choices by an intelligent and well-informed public. In the United States today, and in other affluent societies, there is growing evidence that eating habits are changing to accommodate a faster pace of life, and with this change nutrition often suffers. This is especially true where traditional mealtimes are being replaced by quick and frequent snacking. Further, traditional foods are increasingly being replaced by less familiar, highly processed counterparts, leaving even the conscientious homemaker confused about the nutritional attributes of new products. This has resulted in considerable interest on the part of consumers, government, and the food processing industry in meaningful nutritional labeling of processed foods. For a detailed discussion of the many parameters of nutritional labeling the reader is referred to this subject in Chap. 24. It further may be said that in the United States today, and in other affluent societies, there probably is far more health danger from overeating than from undernourishment. In less fortunate parts of the world, basic Calories and proteins are in short supply as populations are increasing, and this may be the biggest problem the world has to face in the next 50 yr.

BIBLIOGRAPHY

AALSMEER, W. C., MITRA, K., SIMPSON, I. A., and OBANDO, M. 1954. Rice Enrichment in the Philippines. FAO Nutritional Studies *12*. FAO, Rome.
ALBRITTON, E. C. 1954. Standard Values in Nutrition and Metabolism. W. B. Saunders Co., Philadelphia.
ANON. 1941. Flour enriched. Federal Register *6*, 2579–2580.
ANON. 1952. Bread and rolls. Federal Register *17*, 4462.
ANON. 1966. Nutrition. *In* The World Book Encyclopedia *14*, 466–470. Field Enterprises Educational Corp., Chicago.

BENDER, A. E.   1967.   Dietetic Foods. Chemical Publishing Co., New York.

BOURNE, G. H.   1960–1964.   World Review of Nutrition and Dietetics, Vols. 1, 2, 3, 4, and 5. Hafner Publishing Co., London.

BYRD, O. E.   1955.   Nutrition Sourcebook. Stanford University Press, Stanford, Calif.

CAMERON, E. J., PILCHER, R. W., and CLIFCORN, L. E.   1955.   Retention of Nutrients During Canning. Natl. Canners Assoc., Washington, D.C.

DESROSIER, N. W.   1961.   Attack on Starvation. Avi Publishing Co., Westport, Conn.

FLECK, H., and MUNVES, E.   1962.   Introduction to Nutrition. Macmillan Co., New York.

FOOD and AGRICULTURE ORGANIZATION.   1969.   Manual on Food and Nutrition Policy. FAO, United Nations, Rome.

FOOD and AGRICULTURE ORGANIZATION.   1970.   Amino Acid Content of Foods and Biological Data on Proteins. FAO, United Nations, Rome.

HARRIS, R. S., and VON LOESECKE, S. B. (Editors)   1960.   Nutritional Evaluation of Food Processing. Reprinted in 1971 by Avi Publishing Co., Westport, Conn.

HORWITZ, A.   1961.   Food and protection of health. Federation Proc. 20, No. 1, Part 3, Suppl. No. 7, 398–403.

KING, C. G.   1962.   Trends in the nutritional use of lipids. In Symposium on Foods: Lipids and Their Oxidation. H. W. Schultz, E. A. Day, and R. O. Sinnhuber (Editors). Avi Publishing Co., Westport, Conn.

LAWRIE, R. A. (Editor)   1970.   Proteins as Human Food. Avi Publishing Co., Westport, Conn.

MARGEN, S. (Editor)   1971.   Progress in Human Nutrition, Vol. 1. Avi Publishing Co., Westport, Conn.

MORRISON, A. B.   1964.   Some aspects of the nutritive value of proteins. In Symposium on Foods: Proteins and Their Reactions, H. W. Schultz, and A. F. Anglemier (Editors). Avi Publishing Co., Westport, Conn.

NATIONAL ACADEMY OF SCIENCES—NATIONAL RESEARCH COUNCIL.   1959.   Evaluation of protein nutrition. Natl. Res. Council Publ. 711, Washington, D.C.

NATIONAL ACADEMY OF SCIENCES—NATIONAL RESEARCH COUNCIL.   1968.   Recommended Dietary Allowances. Natl. Res. Council Publ. 1694, Washington, D.C.

NUTRITION FOUNDATION.   1969.   Food, Science, and Society. Nutrition Foundation, New York.

ROBINSON, C. H.   1967.   Proudfit-Robinson's Normal and Therapeutic Nutrition. Macmillan Co., New York.

SCHWEIGERT, B. S., and PAYNE, B. J.   1956.   A summary of the nutrient content of meat. Bull. 30, Am. Meat Inst. Found., Chicago.

SCRIMSHAW, N. S., and BRESSANI, R.   1961.   Vegetable protein mixtures for human consumption. Federation Proc. 20, No. 1, Part 3, Suppl. No. 7, 80–89.

SEBRELL, W. H., JR., and HARRIS, R. S.   1954.   The Vitamins. Academic Press, New York.

U.S. DEPT. AGR.   1959.   Food, The Yearbook of Agriculture. U.S. Dept. Agr.

WATT, B. K., and MERRILL, A. L.   1963.   Composition of Foods—Raw, Processed, Prepared. Agriculture Handbook 8. U.S. Dept. Agr.

CHAPTER 5

Unit Operations of the Food Industry

INTRODUCTION

The number of different food products and the operations and steps involved in their production are indeed very great. Further, each manufacturer of a particular product introduces departures in methods and equipment from the traditional and established technology for that product, and processes are in a continual state of evolution. The food scientist and technologist would soon experience great frustration if there were not unifying principles and a systematic approach to the study of these operations.

THE UNIT OPERATION APPROACH

The involved processes of the food industry can be divided into rather common operations which we call unit operations. This also is true for the chemical engineer, who divides the operations of the complex chemical industry into unit operations. Examples of unit operations common to many food products, and previously listed by Parker *et al.* (1952) in *Elements of Food Engineering* are seen in Table 11.

TABLE 11

MAJOR UNIT OPERATIONS OF THE FOOD INDUSTRY [1]

1. Cleaning	8. Forming
2. Coating	9. Heat exchanging
3. Controlling	10. Materials handling
4. Decorating	11. Mixing
5. Disintegrating	12. Packaging
6. Drying	13. Pumping
7. Evaporating	14. Separating

[1] From Parker *et al.* (1952).

These operations are given alphabetically, not in the order of natural sequence or importance. It is to be appreciated that heat exchanging or heating, for example, is common to liquid and dry food products, to such diverse operations as pasteurizing milk, sterilizing foods in cans, roasting peanuts, and baking bread. Thus the unit operation of heat exchanging can be further broken down into many subheadings. The unit operation of mixing so broken down would include agitating, beating, blending, diffusing, dispersing, emulsifying, homogenizing, kneading, stirring, whipping, and working.

We may want to mix to beat in air as in making an egg white foam, or to blend dry ingredients as in preparing a ton of dry cake mix. Or we may wish to mix to emulsify as in the case of mayonnaise, or to homogenize to prevent fat separation in milk. We may wish to mix and develop a bread dough, which requires stretching and folding referred to as kneading.

Food processing is the selection and combination of unit operations into unit processes and more complex total processes.

Common Unit Operations

Materials Handling.—This includes such varied operations as hand and mechanical harvesting on the farm, refrigerated trucking of perishable produce over great distances, box car transportation of live cattle, and pneumatic conveying of flour from rail car to bakery storage bins.

Throughout such operations emphasis must be given to maintaining sanitary conditions, minimizing product losses (including weight loss of livestock), maintaining raw material quality such as vitamin content and physical appearance of fruits and vegetables, minimizing bacterial growth as with proper refrigeration, and timing all transfers and deliveries so as to minimize hold-up time which can be costly as well as detrimental to product quality.

The movement of produce from farm to processing plant, and of raw materials through the plant may take many forms. One of the newer methods of refrigerated trucking is illustrated in Fig. 32. Liquid nitrogen is carried in a tank on the truck and metered by a control valve as required to maintain a desired temperature for preserving perishable produce in transit. The nitrogen not only keeps the food cold but displaces air and so minimizes deterioration from oxygen.

Oranges are moved by truck trailers carrying 45,000 lb of fruit each. At the juice plant the oranges will be graded and washed. There is a limit to the size the trucks may be and the length of time the fruit may be held. This is because fruits and vegetables are alive, respire, and can cause the temperature of a batch to rise to the point where complete spoilage may occur.

Bulk dry sugar is delivered to confectionery and other types of food plants (Fig. 33). The sugar is pumped from the truck to storage bins by a pneumatic lift system. Storage must not be for a period of time nor at a temperature and humidity which will allow the sugar to cake. Transfer of sugar in the plant must avoid dusting and the buildup of static electricity to prevent possible explosion of the highly combustible sugar particles. This is also true in handling finely divided flour.

The use of a wide variety of screw conveyors, bucket conveyors, belt conveyors, and vibratory conveyors in food plants needs no elaboration

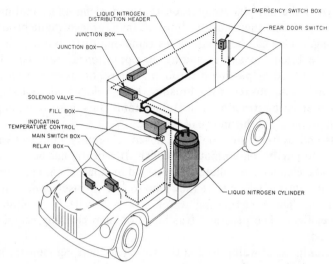

Courtesy of Linde Div., Union Carbide Corp.

FIG. 32. LIQUID NITROGEN REFRIGERATION SYSTEM FOR DELIVERY
TRUCK

From Kelly (1964)

FIG. 33. DELIVERY AND PNEUMATIC CONVEYANCE OF DRY SUGAR TO
STORAGE AT CONFECTIONERY PLANT

here beyond the obvious recognition that conveying and handling equipment for eggs in the shell must be different than for less fragile products.

Cleaning.—This can be as simple as removing dirt from egg shells with an abrasive brush, to as demanding an operation as removing bacteria from a liquid food by passing it through a microporous membrane. Cleaning can be accomplished with brushes, high velocity air, steam, water, vacuum, magnetic attraction of metal contaminants, and so on, depending upon the product and the nature of the dirt.

Clams and oysters commonly are hosed to remove mud and soil. This does little to purify contaminated shellfish. It recently has been found possible to take clams from polluted waters and incubate them in recirculating sterile water during which time they tend to free themselves of contaminating bacteria. The recirculating water is kept sterile by treatment with ultraviolet light. The practical feasibility of such cleaning remains to be determined.

The cleanliness of water used in the soft drink bottling industry must exceed many of the standards found adequate for drinking water. If a high degree of carbonation is to be achieved in the bottled drink then the water used in making the drink must be remarkably free of dust particles, colloidal particles, and certain inorganic salts, since these minimize carbon dioxide solubility and promote excessive escape of gas bubbles from the drink. To adequately clean this water may require that city water receive such additional treatments as controlled chemical flocculation of suspended matter, sand filtration, carbon purification, microfiltration, and deaeration. This is no longer the unit operation of cleaning but a total cleaning process.

Eviscerating poultry can be considered a cleaning operation. The incised bird generally is hung by the feet and the entrails are removed by a rather laborious hand operation. This still is common in the industry today. However, there are newer more economical methods being adopted, such as removing viscera with a tube under vacuum much as a vacuum cleaner removes dirt.

Then there are the cleaning methods dictated by surface characteristics of the product. Because pineapples have an irregular surface and soil particles can lodge in crevices, it would be hard to beat the scrubbing action of high pressure water jets.

Separating.—This unit operation can involve separating a solid from a solid as in the peeling of potatoes or the shelling of nuts. It can involve separating a solid from a liquid as in the many types of filtration, or a liquid from a solid as in pressing juice from a fruit. It might involve the separation of a liquid from a liquid as in centrifuging oil from water. Or it might involve removing a gas from a solid or a liquid as in vacuum removal of air from canned food in vacuum canning.

One of the commonest forms of separating in the food industry is the hand sorting and grading of individual units as in the case of vegetables and fruits. However, today there are many mechanical and electronic sorting devices to separate good from bad. Difference in color can be detected with a photocell and off-color products rejected. This can be done at enormous speeds with automatic rejection of discolored or moldy nuts or kernels of grain that flow past the photocell. In this case the food particles may individually pass through a light beam that activates a jet of air to blow the item from the main stream when an off-color changes the character of reflected or transmitted light. Light shining through eggs can detect blood spots and automatically reject such eggs. Automatic separation according to size is easily accomplished by passing fruits or vegetables over different size screens, holes, or slits.

The skins of fruits and vegetables may be separated using a lye peeler as seen in Fig. 34. Peaches, apricots, and the like are passed through a heated

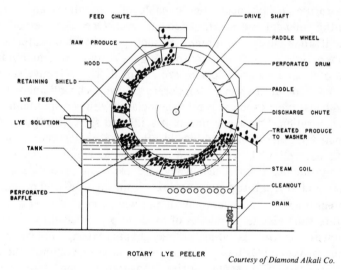

ROTARY LYE PEELER

Courtesy of Diamond Alkali Co.

FIG. 34.   FRUIT AND VEGETABLE LYE PEELER

lye solution. The lye or caustic softens the skin to where it can be easily slipped from the fruit by gentle action of mechanical fingers or by jets of water. Differences in density of the fruit and skin can then be used to float away the removed skin.

A novel approach to the separating of shells from nutmeats has recently been patented. In this method the nuts in their shells are dipped into an iron-containing solution which coats the shells but does not penetrate to the nutmeats. The nuts are subsequently broken and the shells are easily separated by conveying the nutmeats and shells past magnets.

Corn oil is separated from corn kernels. First the germ portion of the corn is separated from the rest of the kernel by milling. Then the oil is separated from the germ by applying high pressure to the germ in an oil press. Similarly, pressure is used to squeeze oil out of peanuts, soybeans, and cottonseeds. The last traces of oil can be removed from the pressed cake by the use of fat solvents. There then remains the separation of the oil from the solvent. All of this is done in the edible oil industry.

Further, there is the separation of salt from sea water, or sugar from sugar cane juice by the process of crystallization. Here evaporation of some of the water causes supersaturation of the solutions and crystals form. Since crystals are quite pure, this is also a purification process. The crystals are then separated from the suspending liquid by centrifuging.

Among newer methods of separation have been developed several sophisticated techniques involving manufactured membranes with tailormade porosities or permeabilities capable of separations and fractionations at the colloidal and macromolecular level. One such method, known as ultrafiltration, uses membranes of such porosity that water and low molecular weight salts, acids, and bases pass through the membrane but larger protein and sugar molecules are retained. This selective separation process, carried out at ambient temperatures, avoids heat damage to sensitive food constituents such as is often associated with elevated temperature water evaporation. Further, removal of acids and salts with the water prevents their concentration which would otherwise be detrimental to sensitive retained solids. Ultrafiltration processes currently are recovering protein and lactose from cheese whey and are being used to concentrate egg white, and to separate protein extracts from soybeans and peanuts.

Disintegrating.—This covers any of the wide range of operations that are used to subdivide large masses of foods into smaller units or particles. It may involve cutting, grinding, pulping, homogenizing, and so on. While the dicing of vegetables today is done on automatic machines, the cutting of meat still largely represents a time consuming, hand labor operation. This is because skill is required to separate specific cuts of meat, and the value of cuts can be sharply reduced by a sloppy job. However, automatic knives with a "brain" are being researched and developed. This work is based on the property of muscle, fat, and bone to absorb energy differently, and this difference can be adapted to direct knives electronically. In one possible approach, an energy beam can precede a mechanical knife. As the beam moves from flesh to bone and its absorption changes, the beam can signal the knife to change direction.

Disintegrating by grinding as in the case of preparing hamburger or hash (Fig. 35) always is associated with heating of the product due to frictional effects. This unwanted heating can be damaging to the food product. It can partially denature proteins or it can give burned flavors to ground coffee. Some kind of cooling is therefore required. In the case of meat this sometimes is done by grinding the meat in frozen form. Dry ice can be added to the meat or other food to chill it. Dry ice is used rather than regular ice since regular ice would melt and water the food but dry ice goes off as carbon dioxide and so does not change the composition of the food.

Homogenizing produces disintegration of fat globules in milk or cream from large globules and clusters into minute globules. The smaller fat globules then remain evenly distributed throughout the milk or cream with less tendency to coalesce and separate from the water phase of the milk. Disintegrating the fat globule is done by forcing the milk or cream under high pressure through a valve with very small openings. There are many

Courtesy of Rietz Manufacturing Co.

FIG. 35. REDUCING FROZEN MEAT TO HASH PARTICLES

ways to homogenize, including the use of ultrasonic energy to disintegrate fat globules or break up particles.

Pumping.—One of the commonest operations in the food industry is the moving of liquids and solids from one processing step to another by pumping. There are many kinds of pumps and the choice depends upon the character of the food to be moved (Fig. 36). One common type is a rotary gear pump (see external gear pump in Fig. 36). The inner gears rotate sucking food into the pump housing and subsequently squeezing food out of the pump housing. For reasons of mechanical efficiency, with this type of pump close clearances between the gears and housing are essential. It should be obvious that while such a pump would be effective for moving liquids and pastes, it would chew up chunk-type foods reducing them to

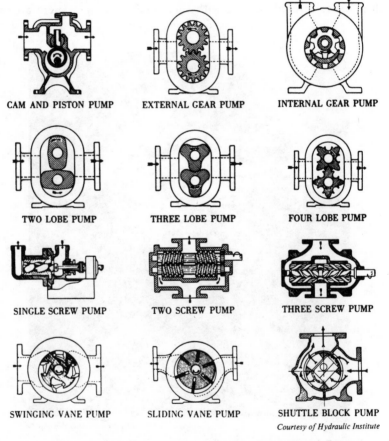

CAM AND PISTON PUMP   EXTERNAL GEAR PUMP   INTERNAL GEAR PUMP

TWO LOBE PUMP   THREE LOBE PUMP   FOUR LOBE PUMP

SINGLE SCREW PUMP   TWO SCREW PUMP   THREE SCREW PUMP

SWINGING VANE PUMP   SLIDING VANE PUMP   SHUTTLE BLOCK PUMP

Courtesy of Hydraulic Institute

FIG. 36. VARIOUS TYPES OF ROTARY POSITIVE DISPLACEMENT PUMPS

purées. Actually pumps sometimes are used to do just this, but generally disintegration is a change that can best be controlled with specialized equipment other than pumps, and pumps should be chosen primarily for their pumping efficiency. When we have a food with large pieces and want to maintain the form of the pieces without disintegration we may use a pump of the single screw type (Fig. 36). Such pumps are also called progressing cavity pumps and can be selected for large clearances of the cavities between the turning center rotor and the housing. The food is gently propelled from large clearance to large clearance by the screw-like action of the turning rotor. Food pieces such as corn kernels, grapes, and even small shrimp can be pumped without physical damage. In the gear type pump these would be ground up.

An essential feature for all food pumps is ease of disassembly for thorough cleaning. Today's sanitary stainless steel pumps in many cases can be easily disassembled in a short time.

Mixing.—Like pumps, there are scores of kinds of mixers, depending upon the materials to be mixed. One may wish to mix solids with solids, liquids with liquids, liquids with solids, gases with liquids, and so on.

For simple mixing of dry ingredients such as the components that make up a baking powder we might use a conical blender. The bowl has a tumbling action and this may be continued for 10 or 20 min until the mixture is made homogenous.

If we are preparing a dry cake mix we must cut the shortening into the flour, sugar, and other dry ingredients in order to produce a fluffy homogenous dry mix. We may use a ribbon blender which is a horizontal trough with one of several types of mixing elements rotating within it. The efficiency of the mixing job depends upon the choice of the mixing element. Three types of ribbon-like elements suitable for cutting in shortening are seen in Fig. 37.

For mixing solids into liquids to dissolve them, as in preparing a salt or sugar solution, we may use a propeller type agitator mounted within a stainless steel vat. There are a great number of propeller, turbine, and paddle types available for this kind of mixing.

All types of mixers do some work on the material being mixed and produce some degree of temperature rise. It is often desirable to minimize this temperature rise. However, mixers are also chosen to do special kinds of work on heavy viscous materials while they are being mixed. These mixers may have arms which knead dough, or paddles and arms which work butter as in a butter churn. These working mixers are designed with precise geometries to maximize efficiency and minimize horsepower requirements to achieve the mixing-working operation.

Still other mixers are designed to beat air into a product while it is being

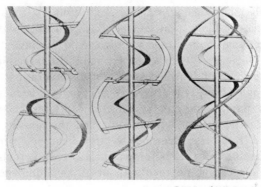

FIG. 37. PRECISELY DESIGNED MIXING ELEMENTS DETERMINE EFFICIENCY OF RIBBON BLENDER

mixed. The mixer-beater found in ice cream freezers is an example (Fig. 38).

As the ice cream mix is being frozen within the freezer bowl, the beating element, or dasher, turns within the bowl. It not only keeps the freezing mass moving to speed freezing and make freezing more uniform, but it beats air into the product to give the desired volume increase, or overrun, necessary for proper texture.

Heat Exchanging: *Heating.*—We heat foods for many different reasons. Some foods are heated to destroy microorganisms and preserve the food, as in pasteurized milk and canned peas. Others we heat to drive off moisture and develop flavors, as in the case of roasting coffee and toasting cereals. Still others are heated to make them more tender and more palatable as

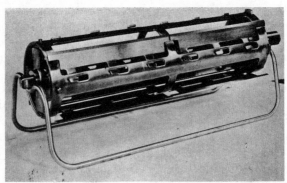

FIG. 38. MIXER-BEATER ELEMENT OF CONTINUOUS ICE CREAM FREEZER

in cooking operations. Some food ingredients, such as soybean meal, are heated to inactivate natural toxic substances that they may contain. Foods are heated by conduction, convection, radiation, or a combination of these.

Most foods are sensitive to heat, and prolonged heat causes burned flavors, dark colors, and loss of nutritional value. It therefore is desirable to heat such foods rapidly and then to cool them. Rapid heating is facilitated if the food is given maximum contact with the heating source. This may be accomplished by dividing the food into thin layers in contact with heated plates as in the plate type heat exchanger used to pasteurize milk (Fig. 39). The milk flows across one side of the plates while hot water heats the other side. The same equipment can be used for quick cooling with cold water or brine instead of hot water. This type of heater can be used only with liquid foods.

A jacketed tank or kettle with steam circulated in the jacket is another

Courtesy of De Laval Separator Co.

FIG. 39. PLATE TYPE HEAT EXCHANGER

very popular means of heating liquid foods. It will also heat foods with suspended solids like vegetable soup. The soup is kept in motion with a mixer propeller for uniform heating and to minimize burning onto the kettle wall.

For sterilizing foods in cans, entirely different heaters are used. The cans must be heated above the boiling point of water to achieve sterility in non-acid foods, and so large pressure cookers or retorts are used (Fig. 40). We employ steam under pressure for the high temperature needed, and the retort is of heavy construction to withstand this pressure. Another type of retort employs mechanical agitation for better convection of heat within

Courtesy of The Foxboro Co.

FIG. 40. STEAM RETORT FOR PROCESSING CANNED FOODS

the individual cans. The outside of the cans is heated by conduction from the steam.

For roasting coffee beans or nuts many kinds of heaters have been used. In one popular type the beans or nuts move from overhead hoppers into cylindrical vessels which turn and keep the beans in constant motion for even heating. The vessels may be heated within by circulating heated air, or with radiant heat from the vessel walls the exterior of which can be heated by contact with hot air, gas flame, or steam. In some instances this type of roaster is replaced with tunnel ovens in which the coffee beans or nuts pass on moving belts, or are vibrated beneath radiating infrared rods or bulbs. Whatever the method, precise control of temperature is essential for proper roasting.

Foods may be heated or cooked using toasters, direct injection of steam, direct contact with flame, electronic energy as in microwave cookers, and so on, and all of these are currently used in the food industry. Such processes as baking, frying, most food concentration, food dehydration, and various kinds of package closure all employ the unit operation of heating.

Cooling.—While heating is the addition of heat energy to foods, cooling is the subtraction of heat energy. This may be done to the degree where food is chilled to refrigerator temperature, or beyond this range to where the food is frozen. Primarily we refrigerate and freeze foods to prolong their keeping quality. But there are some foods which owe their entire character to the frozen state. A prime example is ice cream.

We cool a great deal of milk and cream by passing them in thin layers through heat exchangers of the type shown in Fig. 39, or by allowing the liquids to run down over the surface of a hinged leaf cooler. Within the leaves are pipes through which cold water or refrigerant is pumped.

Thirty-pound cans of liquid egg are commonly frozen solid in an air blast freezer or sharp freezer room maintained at about $-15°$ F. The cans are spaced to allow the cold air, which is circulated by fans and blowers, to get between them and speed the freezing operation (Fig. 41). In similar fashion, fruits such as apple slices, berries, and cherries are frozen. Frozen eggs and fruits in this form go mainly to bakeries for use after thawing. Thawing will be done by the unit operations of heating or disintegrating.

There are many kinds of commercial air blast freezers which automatically freeze peas, beans, and other vegetables as individual pieces. In one type the peas are loaded on trays which are automatically moved upward through a cold air blast. After freezing, the peas are dislodged from the trays automatically and the peas are conveyed under cold air to packaging equipment. The trays return to a position under the pea hopper to receive additional product and the cycle is repeated. Freezing of canned or pack-

Courtesy of Frick Co.

FIG. 41. COMMON METHOD OF FREEZING EGGS AND FRUIT IN
THIRTY POUND CANS

aged foods may be by direct immersion in a refrigerant. Here the cans may be agitated as they pass through the refrigerant within a vat, cylindrical shell, or tube. Agitation increases the efficiency of heat transfer.

The value of quick freezing to food quality will be discussed more fully in a later chapter. The advantages of quick freezing have led to the recent use of liquid nitrogen with its extremely low temperature of $-320°$ F. Food plants are currently installing large liquid nitrogen tanks (Fig. 42) and pumping the liquid nitrogen to freezers as well as spraying it directly onto foods to be frozen. Delicate products such as mushrooms which can not be frozen and retain as high quality by the older conventional methods are prepared commercially by this method.

Evaporating.—Evaporation in the food industry is used principally to concentrate foods by the removal of water. It is also used to recover desirable food volatiles and to remove undesirable volatiles.

The simplest kind of evaporation is when the sun evaporates water from sea water and leaves behind salt, as is done commercially. The next most

Courtesy Air Reduction Co.

FIG. 42. LIQUID NITROGEN INSTALLATION OUTSIDE OF FOOD PROCESSING PLANT

simple kind of evaporation is when a heated kettle is used to boil water from a sugar syrup and thus concentrate it, as is common in some kinds of candymaking. However, this requires considerable heat for a long period of time, which might be satisfactory for some kinds of candy, but would cause heat damage to such products as milk or orange juice if an attempt was made to concentrate them this way.

All liquids boil at lower temperatures under reduced pressure and this is the key to modern evaporation. If a heated kettle is enclosed and connected to a vacuum pump one has a simple vacuum evaporator. Such evaporators are being used to remove water from sugar cane press juice in the early stages of crystalline sugar production.

Evaporators differ widely in their design and can be connected in series as is the triple stage evaporator of Fig. 43. In this case progressively higher

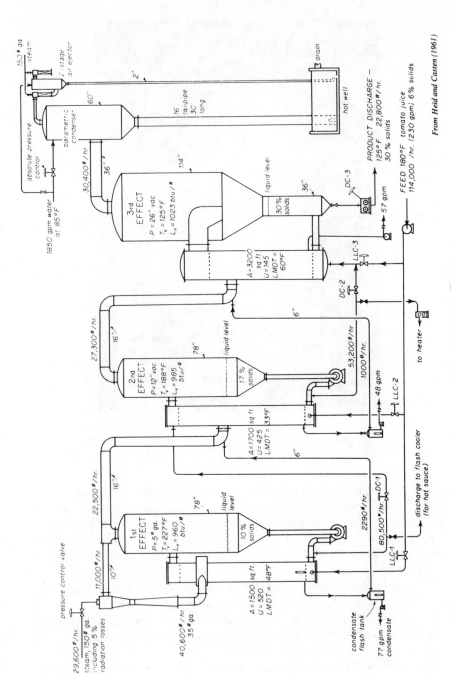

FIG. 43. DIAGRAM OF TRIPLE EFFECT EVAPORATOR

From Heid and Casten (1961)

degrees of vacuum are maintained in the subsequent stages through which the liquid food passes. Regardless of design, however, a principal objective of vacuum evaporators is to remove water at a relatively low temperature and thus not heat damage the food. Multiple stage evaporators can easily remove water at 120° F, and some are designed to boil off water at temperatures as low as 80° F.

Drying.—In drying the object also is to remove water with minimum damage to the food. While evaporators will concentrate foods 2- or 3-fold, driers will take foods very close to total dryness—that is to 97 or 98% solids. Driers are used to prepare such well known products as dried milk

Photo Courtesy Swenson Evaporator Co.

FIG. 44.   LOWER PORTION OF SPRAY DRYING TOWER FOR LIQUID
FOOD PRODUCTS

powder, and instant coffee. While food traditionally has been dried to preserve it from spoilage and to reduce its weight and bulk, some foods are dried as convenience items and for their novelty appeal; an example is freeze-dried bananas or freeze-dried ice cream for cereals. Drying as well as several of the other unit operations are treated in subsequent specific chapters, and so only a few brief comments are needed here.

We may dry liquid foods such as milk and we may dry solid foods, that is, foods in chunk form like shrimp or steak. It is generally much easier to dry liquid foods because these are easier to subdivide, either as a spray or a film, and in a subdivided form the moisture can be more quickly removed since it has less distance to travel to get out of the food mass.

Subdivision of a liquid is the principle behind the widely used spray drier (Fig. 44). Liquid food such as milk, coffee, or eggs is pumped into the top of the large tower, at which point the liquid is atomized by a spray nozzle or equivalent device. At the same time heated air is introduced to the tower. The heated air in contact with the fine droplets of food dry the droplets and dehydrated particles fall to the bottom of the tower and are drawn off into collectors. The moisture removed during drying is exhausted separately. Most commercially dried liquid foods are made this way.

Drying by subdividing food as a thin film is commonly done on a drum or roller drier of the kind illustrated in Fig. 45. The drum is heated by steam

From Feustel et al. (1964)

FIG. 45. SHEETS OF DEHYDRATED POTATO COMING OFF COMMERCIAL DRUM DRIER

from within, and the applied layer of food flashes off its moisture upon contact with the heated drum. The dried food is then mechanically scraped from the drum with long knives. Mashed potatoes, tomato purée, and several milk products frequently are dried this way.

Small food pieces such as peas and diced onions can be dried by moving them through a long tunnel-oven, and many types are in use. However, overheating and scorching in the course of water removal may give poor quality products in the case of particularly sensitive foods. For chunk foods a milder method is vacuum-freeze drying. There are many kinds of vacuum-freeze driers. In all types the food pieces first are frozen and then dehydrated under vacuum from the frozen state. The ice does not melt but under the conditions of high vacuum goes off directly as gaseous water vapor, a condition known as sublimation. This very low temperature drying protects all food quality attributes such as texture, color, flavor, and vitamins. Freeze drying is by no means restricted in its use to solid and particulate foods. Brewed coffee and quality juice products are dehydrated by freeze drying.

Forming.—Hamburger patties are formed by gently compacting ground beef into disc shape in various types of patty making machines which apply controlled pressure to the beef within an appropriate form. Excessive pressure is avoided or the hamburger will be overly tough after cooking. Uniform pressure is essential or patties will vary in weight. Pressure extrusion through dies of various shapes forms doughs into spaghetti and other pasta shapes for subsequent oven drying.

In the confectionery industry, besides pressure extrusion, candies are formed by depositing fondants, chocolate, and jellies into appropriate molds where they cool and harden. Here edible release agents may be sprayed on the mold to help separate the hardened confection. Other confections and food tablets may be formed from powdered ingredients by the application of intense pressure in specially designed tableting machines. Sometimes, as in the case of malted milk tablets, an edible binding agent is required to hold the malted milk powder together. When the powders are high in certain sugars or other thermoplastic food constituents an additional binding agent is not required. Here high pressure during tablet forming produces heat which melts some of the sugar or other thermoplastic material which then on cooling helps fuse the powdered mass together. This is one way to form fruit juice tablets from dehydrated fruit juice crystals. Some tablet forming machines also may employ additional heat beyond that generated by pressure.

Forming is an important unit operation in the breakfast cereal and snack food industries. The characteristic shapes of several popular breakfast cereals are the result of pressure extrusion through meticulously designed dies, together with adherence to precisely controlled operating conditions of temperature, pressure, dough consistency, cut off, and other variables. One special kind of forming is known as extrusion cooking. In this case a formulated dough or mash is extruded under high pressure with or without supplemental heat. The heat, largely from pressure, causes gelatinization of starch and other cooking effects while the material is forced through the extruder. In some cases pressure and temperature are so regulated that the food rises in temperature above that required to boil water. Then when the shaped food emerges from the extrusion cooker the heated water rapidly boils as pressure is relieved at the exit nozzle. This causes puffing of the formed piece. Such formed and puffed items may then receive additional oven drying.

Further examples of forming include the shaping of butter and margarine bars, the pressing of cheese curd into various shapes, the many manipulations given to bread dough to produce variety breads, and the shaping of sausage products in natural and artificial flexible casings.

Controlling.—With all of these and several additional unit operations combined into complex processing operations there have to be ways of measuring and controlling them to obtain the desired food product quality. Controlling may be considered a unit operation in itself. Its tools are valves, thermometers, scales, thermostats, and a wide variety of other components and instruments to measure and adjust such essential factors as temperature, pressure, fluid flow, acidity, specific gravity, weight, viscosity, humidity, time, liquid level, and so on.

Figure 46 shows a retort commonly used in the canning industry for processing food in glass jars. It is equipped to heat jars of food to the proper sterilization temperature, hold them for the required time, and then cool them. It has controls for steam flow, steam pressure, air pressure, water temperature, water level, and holding time. These controls can be manually operated or can be designed for automatic operation. In modern food plants most instrumentation and controls are automatic, and the plant operator or supervisor controls the process from a distance at a central panel board.

Packaging.—Food is packaged primarily to protect it. Depending upon the sensitivity of the food this can mean protection from microbial contamination, physical dirt, insect invasion, light, moisture pickup, flavor pickup, moisture loss, flavor loss, and so on.

Today, foods are packaged in metal cans, glass and plastic bottles, paper, a wide variety of plastic and metallic films, and combinations of these. Packaging is done by continuous automatic machines sometimes at speeds of 1,000 units per min. Many items formerly filled into rigid containers of metal and glass are being increasingly packaged in flexible and formable packaging materials, and filling and capping machines are being joined by

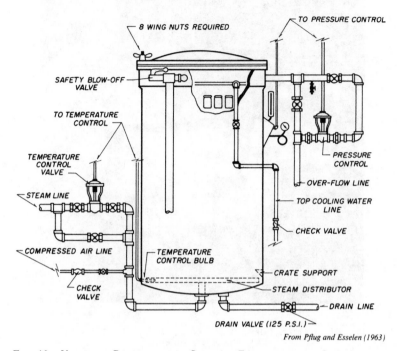

From Pflug and Esselen (1963)

FIG. 46. VERTICAL RETORT WITH SEVERAL ELEMENTS FOR CONTROL OF PROCESSING

more sophisticated systems. Much of the consumer milk supply has been packaged in paper cartons for several years. More recently equipment such as seen in Fig. 47 has been adapted to packaging potato salad, soups, cole slaw, and other viscous products into plastic coated paper cartons of the gallon size. Containers are automatically formed from stacked paper flats, volumetrically filled, and sealed by passing the upper flaps through heated jaws which melt the plastic coating and thus provide adhesion. Such packages are easy to open and easy to dispose of, making them particularly attractive to the restaurant trade.

Other machines form pouches from rolls of plastic film, fill them, and seal them. This is the way many popular boil-in-bag items are packaged. Still more complete systems (Fig. 48) form the container from roll stock film, fill the container to exact weight, draw a vacuum on the package to remove oxygen, back flush the package with inert nitrogen gas, seal the package, and finally stack the packages into cardboard cartons. This is the way some dessert powders and dehydrated soups are commonly packaged.

The container forming step is not limited to the use of paper flats or films of various materials. Some of the newer food packaging concepts

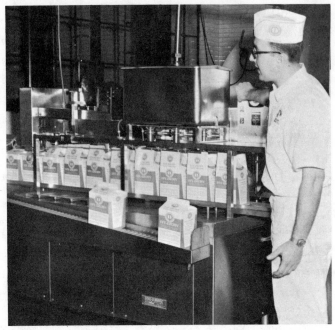

FIG. 47. CARTON FORMING, FILLING, AND SEALING MACHINE FOR VISCOUS FOODS

FIG. 48. AUTOMATIC PACKAGING EQUIPMENT FOR DRY SOUP MIX

utilize machines that start with plastic resins in granular form, melt these, and blow-mold or otherwise form rigid or semi-rigid containers for immediate filling and sealing. Two advantages of such a system are the savings of space in food plants that otherwise would have to store great numbers of empty containers, and the in-line production of virtually sterile containers, since the heat to melt the plastic resins also kills microorganisms.

The food scientist is not a mechanical engineer and doesn't design or build such machines. However, the specifications for suitable packaging materials, the product moisture when packaged, the maximum allowable oxygen in the package, the degree of protection of the product from light and odor penetration through the package—these and other requirements of the food, determined by the food scientist, define the kind of packaging and the parameters within which packaging systems may be designed.

Unit Operations May Overlap

The division or grouping of food processing steps into unit operations is not perfect and there can be overlapping. For example, filtering bacteria out of beer might logically be considered cleaning or it might be considered separating. Moving milk to a cheese vat might be viewed as pumping or it might be considered materials handling. Milling grain to yield flour might be considered disintegrating or separating, although actually it is both of these unit operations—disintegrating followed by separating.

Some overlapping does not seriously detract from the value of the unit operations concept. This concept permits one to think in an orderly fashion. What is more, some food texts and most food equipment catalogs are divided by unit operations. One may have the problem of blending fragile olive slices into sausage meat emulsion with minimum breakage as in the manufacture of certain table-ready meats, or of incorporating a whip improver into commercial liquid egg white without foaming the white. Applicable available equipment generally will not be found in reference sources under food commodity headings, but will be grouped in the mixing sections of equipment and engineering references.

If one considers any total food process, such as the manufacture of bread or frozen orange juice concentrate briefly described earlier, it is seen that the process is always a series of unit operations performed in a logical sequence. In modern food processing these operations are so connected as to commonly permit smooth, continuous, automatically controlled production.

BIBLIOGRAPHY

BRENNAN, J. G., BUTTERS, J. R., COWELL, N. D., and LILLY, A. E. V. 1969. Food Engineering Operations. Elsevier Publishing Co., Amsterdam.

CHARM, S. E. 1971. Fundamentals of Food Engineering, 2nd Edition. Avi Publishing Co., Westport, Conn.

CLARKE, R. J. 1957. Process Engineering in the Food Industries. Heywood, London.

EARLE, R. L. 1966. Unit Operations in Food Processing. Pergamon Press, Oxford.

FARRALL, A. W. 1963. Engineering for Dairy and Food Products. John Wiley & Sons, New York.

FOUST, A. S. et al. 1959. Principles of Unit Operations. John Wiley & Sons, New York.

FUESTEL, I. C., HENDEL, C. E., and MARCEL, E. J. 1964. Potatoes. In Food Dehydration, Vol. 2. W. B. Van Arsdel, and M. J. Copley (Editors). Avi Publishing Co., Westport, Conn.

HALL, C. W., FARRALL, A. W., and RIPPEN, A. L. 1971. Encyclopedia of Food Engineering. Avi Publishing Co., Westport, Conn.

HAWTHORN, J., and LEITCH, J. M. (Editors) 1962. Recent Advances in Food Science, Vol. 2. Butterworths, London.

HEID, J. L., and CASTEN, J. W. 1961. Vacuum concentration of fruit and vegetable juices. In Fruit and Vegetable Juice Processing Technology. D. K. Tressler, and M. A. Joslyn (Editors). Avi Publishing Co., Westport, Conn.

KELLY, N. 1964. Sugar. In Food Processing Operations, Vol. 3. M. A. Joslyn, and J. J. Heid (Editors). Avi Publishing Co., Westport, Conn.

MCCABE, W. L., and SMITH, J. C. 1956. Unit Operations of Chemical Engineering. McGraw-Hill Book Co., New York.

PARKER, M. E., HARVEY, E. H., and STATELER, E. S. 1952. Elements of Food Engineering, Vols. 1, 2, and 3. Reinhold Publishing Corp., New York.

PERRY, J. H. (Editor) 1963. Chemical Engineers Handbook, 4th Edition. McGraw-Hill Book Co., New York.

PFLUG, I. J., and ESSELEN, W. B. 1963. Food processing by heat sterilization. In Food Processing Operations, Vol. 2. M. A. Joslyn, and J. L. Heid (Editors). Avi Publishing Co., Westport, Conn.

VAN ARSDEL, W. B., COPLEY, M. J., and MORGAN, A. I., JR. (Editors) 1973. Food Dehydration, 2nd Edition, Vol. 1 and 2. Avi Publishing Co., Westport, Conn.

CHAPTER 6

Quality Factors and How They Are Measured

INTRODUCTION

From a practical standpoint, beyond one's nutritional needs, the foods people choose and the amounts they eat depend largely on quality.

In the modern supermarket there are often several brands of the same food commodity. Ultimately the consumer decides on the brand of choice based on relative quality and price. Price and quality need not go together, but the manufacturer knows that his greatest competitive advantage is superior quality and with it he generally can get a higher price or can sell a larger quantity.

This is illustrated in the grades and prices of canned whole tomatoes (Fig. 49). Here the nutrient value of the different grades is quite the same for all practical purposes, yet the price can vary as much as three-fold depending upon quality. This is why processors will go to great extremes to control quality. Quality has been defined as degree of excellence. We might also say that quality is the composite of characteristics that have significance and make for acceptability.

When we select foods and when we eat, we use all of our physical senses. We use our sense of sight, touch, smell, taste, and even hearing. The snap of a potato chip, the crackle of a breakfast cereal, and the crunch of celery are textural characteristics, but we also hear them. We eat with our eyes, fingers, tongue, palate, teeth, nose, and ears and quality measuring devices have been developed that take most of these into account. The Proctor Strain Gage Tenderometer (Fig. 50) was actually fitted with false teeth to simulate the cutting-grinding actions of chewing while measuring the resistance of foods to physical forces.

Food quality detectable by our senses can be broken down into three main catagories, as was done by Kramer and Twigg (1970) in their excellent book *Quality Control for the Food Industry, Vol 1, Fundamentals*. These categories are appearance factors, textural factors, and flavor factors (Table 12).

Appearance factors include such properties as size, shape, wholeness, different forms of damage, gloss, transparency, color, consistency, and so on.

Textural factors include hand feel and mouth feel of firmness, softness, juiciness, chewiness, grittiness, and the like.

Flavor factors include both taste and odor; sweet, salty, sour, bitter,

Quality   Relative Price

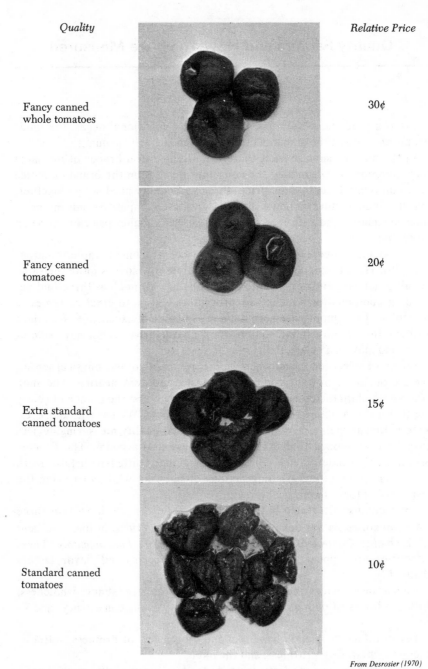

Fancy canned   30¢
whole tomatoes

Fancy canned   20¢
tomatoes

Extra standard   15¢
canned tomatoes

Standard canned   10¢
tomatoes

From Desrosier (1970)

FIG. 49.   QUALITY AND RELATIVE PRICE OF CANNED TOMATOES

From Kramer (1963)

FIG. 50.   PROCTOR STRAIN GAGE TENDEROMETER

fragrant, acid, burnt, and so on. Flavor and aroma are largely subjective, hard to accurately measure, and generally difficult to get a group of people to agree on. There are hundreds of descriptive terms that have been invented to describe flavor, depending on the type of food. Expert tea tasters have a language all of their own, and it is passed down to members of their guild from generation to generation.

Since we generally experience the properties of foods in the order of (1) their appearance, (2) their texture, and (3) their flavor, it is logical to discuss quality factors in this order now.

TABLE 12

SOME QUALITY CHARACTERISTICS [1]

Appearance Factors (eye appeal judged by sense of sight)
  size, shape, wholeness, pattern
  defects: damage, bruising, extraneous matter, specks, sediment
  spectral: gloss, transparency, turbidity, color (lightness, chroma, hue)
  consistency: viscosity, gel, flow, spread (these characteristics may also be apparent to the sense of touch)
Kinesthetic Factors (hand and mouth feel, judged by sense of touch)
  hand feel: firmness, softness, juiciness
  mouth feel: chewiness, fibrousness, grittiness, mealiness, stickiness
Flavor Factors (judged by sense of taste and smell)
  odor: fragrant, acid, burnt, goaty, etc.
  taste: sweet, sour, salty, bitter, etc.
  off-flavor: enzymatic, physiological, chemical, contaminated, overcooked, stale, etc.

[1] From Kramer (1963).

APPEARANCE FACTORS

In addition to size, shape, and wholeness, pattern might refer to the way olives are laid out in a jar or sardines in a can. Wholeness refers to degree of whole and broken pieces; the price of canned pineapple goes down from the whole pineapple rings, to pineapple chunks, to pineapple bits. Appearance also encompasses the positive and negative aspects of properly molded blue-veined cheeses, and the defect of moldy bread; as well as the quality attribute of ground vanilla bean specks in vanilla ice cream, and the defect of specks and sediment from extraneous matter. In the case of ice cream, while some manufacturers have added ground vanilla bean as a mark of highest quality, others have concluded that as often as not a less-sophisticated consumer misinterprets these specks and rejects the product.

Size and Shape

Size and shape are easily measured and are important factors in federal and state grade standards. Fruits and vegetables can be graded for size by the openings they will pass through (Fig. 51). Such simple devices were the forerunners of current high speed automatic separating and grading machines, although they are still used to some extent in field grading and in laboratory work. Size also can be approximated by weight after rough grading, for example, determining weight of a dozen eggs.

Shape may have more than visual importance, and the grades of certain types of pickles include the degree of curvature, which can be measured with a protractor (Fig. 52). Such curiosities can become quite important, especially in modern practices of replacing more and more hand labor by machine. When an engineer attempts to design a machine for automatically filling pickles into jars at high speeds he must consider that all pickles aren't shaped the same, and a machine concept that will dispense round objects like olives or cherries can be totally inadequate with irregularly shaped foods. Automatic kitchen and restaurant installations for rapid mass feeding have recently been developed. Some of the most difficult engineering problems were in designing equipment which would dispense odd-shaped pieces of fried chicken and shrimp into dishes moving on a conveyor belt.

Color and Gloss

Food color not only helps to determine quality, it can tell us many things. Color is commonly an index of ripeness or spoilage. Potatoes darken in color as they are fried—and we judge the endpoint of frying by color. The bleaching of dried tomato powder on storage can be indicative of too high an oxygen level in the headspace of the package, whereas the darkening

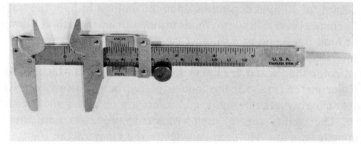

From Kramer (1963)

FIG. 51.   SIZE GRADING DEVICES FOR FRUITS AND VEGETABLES

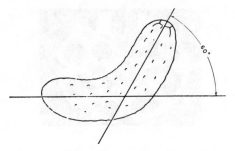

Courtesy of U. S. Dept. Agr.

Fig. 52.   Measurement of Curvature in Pickles

of dried tomato can reflect too high a final moisture level in the powder. The color of a food foam or batter varies with its density and can indicate a change in mixing efficiency. The surface color of chocolate is a clue to its storage history. These and many other types of color changes can be accurately measured in the laboratory and in the plant—all influence or reflect food quality.

If the food is a transparent liquid such as wine, beer, or grape juice, or if a colored extract can be obtained from the food, then various types of colorimeters or spectrophotometers can be used for color measurement. With these instruments a tube of the liquid is placed in a slot and light of selected wavelength is passed through the tube. This light will be differentially absorbed depending upon the color of the liquid and the intensity of this color. Two liquids of exactly the same color and intensity will transmit equal fractions of the light directed through them. If one of the liquids is a juice and the other is the same juice somewhat diluted with water, the latter sample will transmit a greater fraction of the incoming light and this will cause a proportionately greater deflection of a sensing needle on the instrument. Such an instrument can also measure the clarity or cloudiness of a liquid depending upon the amount of light the liquid lets pass. There are several other methods for measuring the color of liquids.

If the food is a liquid or a solid we can measure its color by comparing it to defined disks or colored tiles. These disks or tiles are available in hundreds of color shades and are defined by number. In the Macbeth-Munsell Disk Colorimeter (Fig. 53) the food is placed between two colored disks that most closely match its color, and colors are observed under controlled lighting. The quality control man keeps changing disks until the closest color match is made. He then can define the color of the food as being identical to the matching disk or falling between the two nearest disks. If one is working with tomatoes he would need only about ten disks with dif-

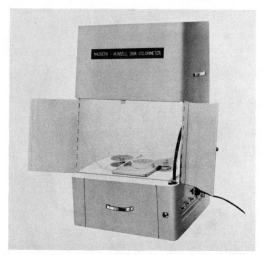

Courtesy of Macbeth Corp.

FIG. 53.   MACBETH-MUNSELL DISK COLORIMETER

ferent shades of red to cover the usual range of tomato color. The grade standards for tomatoes are based on such a method.

Color also can be measured much more precisely. Light reflected from a colored object can be divided into three components which have been termed value, hue, and chroma. Value refers to the lightness or darkness of the color; hue to the predominant wavelength which determines whether the color is red, green, or yellow; and chroma refers to the intensity of the color. The color of an object can be precisely defined in terms of numerical values of these three components. This is known as tri-stimulus colorimetry and is the basis for several color measuring instruments and systems of color notation. An instrument such as the Hunterlab Color and Color Difference Meter (Fig. 54) measures these chromaticity values of the surface of a food. Food samples having the same three numbers have the same color. These numbers vary with color in a systematic fashion that can be graphed to produce a chromaticity diagram (Fig. 55). The color chemist and quality control man can relate these numbers to color, and through changes in the numbers can follow gross or minute changes in product as may occur during ripening, processing, or storage. In similar fashion a quality control man can define color of a product and relate this information to distant plants to be matched at any future date. This is particularly useful where the food color is unstable making the forwarding of a standard sample unfeasible.

As with color, there are light measuring instruments which quantitatively

Courtesy of Hunter Associates Laboratory

FIG. 54.   HUNTERLAB COLOR AND COLOR-DIFFERENCE METER

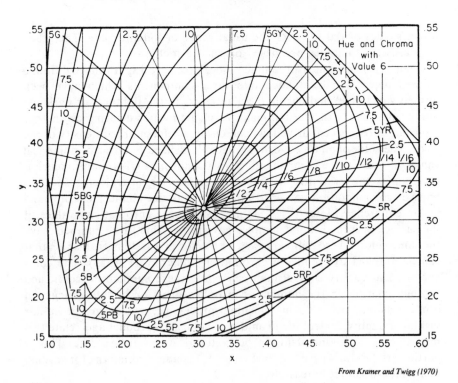

From Kramer and Twigg (1970)

FIG. 55.   ONE TYPE OF CHROMATICITY DIAGRAM

define the shine or gloss of a food surface—gloss is important to the attractiveness of gelatin desserts, buttered vegetables, and the like.

Consistency

While consistency may be considered a textural quality attribute, in many instances we can see consistency and so it also is another factor in food appearance. A chocolate syrup may be thin-bodied or thick and viscous. Similarly, a tomato sauce can be thick or thin. Consistency of such foods is measured by their resistance to flow.

This can be done by measuring the time it takes for the food to run through a small hole of a known diameter. The thicker the food the longer the time. Or one can measure the time it takes for more viscous foods to flow down an inclined plane as with the Bostwick Consistometer (Fig. 56).

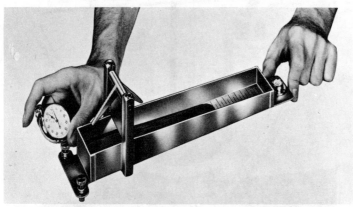

Courtesy of Central Scientific Co.

FIG. 56.   THE BOSTWICK CONSISTOMETER

This might be used for ketchup, honey, or sugar syrup. These last two devices for measuring consistency are called viscometers, since they measure viscosity which is one kind of consistency. There are several other types of viscometers using such principles as the resistance of the food to a falling weight such as a ball, and the time it takes the ball to travel a defined distance; and resistance to the rotation of a spindle, which can be measured by the power requirements of the motor or the amount of twist on a wire suspending the spindle.

TEXTURAL FACTORS

By texture we mean those qualities of food that we can feel either with the fingers, the tongue, the palate, or the teeth. The range of textures in foods is very great, and the departure from an expected texture is a quality defect.

We expect chewing gum to be chewy, crackers and potato chips to be crisp, and steak to be compressable and shearable between the teeth. The housewife squeezes melons and bread as a measure of freshness. In the laboratory we have more precise methods. However, the squeezing device in Fig. 57 gives only an approximation of freshness, since the reading also

Courtesy of G. Dalby

FIG. 57.   DALBY-HILL SQUEEZE-TESTER FOR BREAD

depends upon the stiffness of the wrapping and the looseness with which the bread slices are packed.

Measuring Texture

Food texture can be reduced to measurements of resistance to force (Fig. 58). If we squeeze food so that it remains as one piece, this is com-

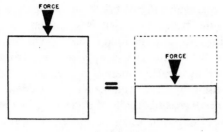

COMPRESSION

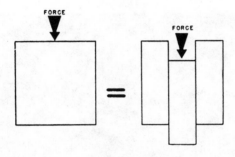

SHEARING

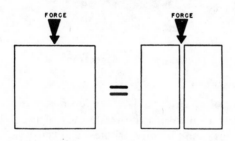

CUTTING

TENSILE STRENGTH

From Kramer and Twigg (1970)

FIG. 58.   PRINCIPLES OF TEXTURE MEASUREMENT

pression—as with the squeezing of bread. If we apply a force so that one part of the food slides past another, it is shearing—as in the chewing of gum. If the force goes through the food so as to divide it, we have cutting—as in cutting an apple. If the force is applied away from the material we have tearing or pulling apart, which is a measure of the food's tensile strength—as in pulling apart a muffin. When we chew a steak, what we call toughness or tenderness is really the yielding of the meat to a composite of all of these different kinds of forces. There are instruments to measure each kind of force, many with appropriate descriptive names.

The Succulometer (Fig. 59) uses compression to squeeze juice out of

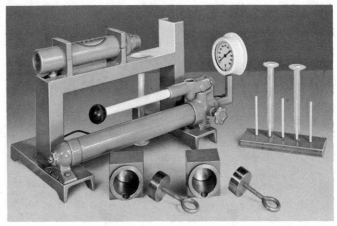

Courtesy of The United Co.

FIG. 59.   THE SUCCULOMETER

food as a measure of succulence. The Tenderometer (Fig. 60) applies compression and shear to measure the tenderness of peas. The Lee-Kramer Shear Press (Fig. 61) can measure firmness and crispness. This and similar instruments frequently are connected to a moving recording chart. The time-force curve traced on the chart gives a graphic representation of the rheological properties of the food item. Where an apple half might be tested, the tracing would show an initial high degree of force required to break the skin, and then a change in force as the compressing-shearing element enters and passes through the apple pulp.

Various forms of Penetrometers are in use. These generally measure the force required to move a plunger a fixed distance through a food material. A particular penetrometer used to measure gel strength is the Bloom Gelometer (Fig. 62). In this device, lead shot is automatically dropped into

Courtesy of FMC Corp.

FIG. 60.   THE TENDEROMETER

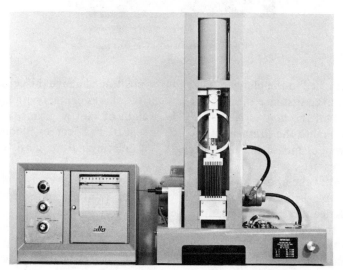

Courtesy of Allo Inc.

FIG. 61.   THE LEE-KRAMER SHEAR PRESS WITH RECORDER

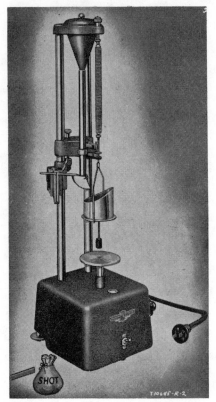

Courtesy of Precision Scientific Co.

FIG. 62. THE BLOOM GELOMETER

a cup attached to the plunger. The plunger positioned above the gel surface moves a fixed distance through the gel until it makes contact with a switch that cuts off the flow of lead shot. The weight of shot in grams, which is proportional to the firmness of the gel, is reported as degrees Bloom. This is one way of measuring the "strength" of gelatin and the consistency of gelatin desserts.

Several of the above methods for measuring texture obviously alter the food sample being tested so that it cannot be returned to a production batch. Since there are correlations between color and texture in some instances, there are applications where color may be used as an indication of acceptable texture. Under controlled conditions automatic color measurement may then be used as a nondestructive measure of texture, as has been applied in the case of evaluating the ripeness of certain fruits and vegetables moving along conveyor belts. Another nondestructive indication of texture is obtained by the experienced cheesemaker when he thumps the outside of a cheese and listens to the sound. This gives a rough indication of the degree of eye formation during ripening of Swiss cheese. One of the newer methods of nondestructive texture measurement makes use of sonic energy, which is absorbed to different extents depending upon the firmness of an object.

Texture Changes

The texture of foods is a natural attribute, and like the attributes of shape and color, texture does not remain constant. Water changes play a major role. Natural foods change on ageing. Texture of fresh fruit becomes soggy as the cell walls break down and the cells lose water. But as more water is lost from the fruit, it becomes dried out, tough, and chewy. This is desirable in the case of dried apricots, prunes and raisins. Bread and cake in the course of staling lose some water and this is a quality defect. Steaming the bread refreshes it somewhat by softening the texture. Crackers, cookies, and pretzels go the opposite way—they must be protected against moisture pickup that would soften texture.

Quite apart from the changes in texture of natural foods, there are the textural aspects of manufactured foods. Fat is a softener and a lubricant that the baker blends into a cake formula to tenderize the cake. Starch and numerous gums are thickeners, they increase viscosity. Protein in solution can be a thickener, but if the solution is heated and the protein coagulates it can form a rigid structure as in the case of cooked egg white or coagulated gluten in baked bread. Sugar affects texture differently depending upon its concentration. In dilute solution it adds body and mouth-feel to soft drinks. In concentrated solution it adds thickening and chewiness. In still higher concentrations it crystallizes and adds brittleness as in hard candies.

The food manufacturer not only can blend food constituents into an endless number of mixtures, but he may use countless food approved ingredients and chemicals to help modify texture.

FLAVOR FACTORS

We have said that flavor includes both taste and smell, is largely subjective and therefore hard to measure, and thus frequently leads to differences of opinion between judges of quality. This difference of opinion is quite honest and is to be expected for at least two reasons: (1) people differ in their sensitivity to detect different tastes and odors, and (2) even where they can detect them people differ in their preference.

Influence of Color and Texture on Flavor

There is another very important consideration when we try to judge flavor. Our opinion often is influenced by color and texture.

We associate such flavors as cherry, raspberry, and strawberry with the color red. Actually the natural flavor essences and the chemicals they contain are quite colorless. But in nature they occur in foods of typical color and so we associate orange flavor with the orange color, cherry flavor with red, lime flavor with green, chicken flavor with yellow, and beef flavor with brown.

We can prepare gelatin type desserts with no color and then inexperienced tasters may find it hard to distinguish lime from cherry. If we color the lime flavored item red and the cherry flavored item green then the challenge becomes still greater. Butter and margarine may be colored by the addition of a dye. Many consumers will agree that of two samples the yellow one has the stronger butter flavor, but this may not actually be the case. This is the reason "blind" testing is often employed in flavor evaluation; colored lighting being the means of masking out an influencing color.

Texture can be equally misleading. By thickening one of two identical samples of gravy with a tasteless starch or gum, many inexperienced tasters will judge the thicker sample to have the richer flavor. This can be entirely psychological. However, the dividing line between psychological and physiological is not always easy to draw. Our taste buds respond in a complex fashion not yet fully understood. Many chemicals can affect taste response to other compounds. It is entirely possible for texturizing substances to influence taste and flavor in a fashion that is not imaginary. Where a thickener might affect solubility or volatility of a flavor compound, its indirect influence on the nose or tongue could be very real.

Taste Panels

We can measure flavor in various ways depending upon our purpose. The use of gas chromatography to measure volatile materials has already been mentioned. Some flavor contributing substances can be measured chemically or physically with other instruments. Examples are salt, sugar, and acid. Salt concentration can be measured electrically by its effect upon the conductivity of a food solution. Sugar in solution can be measured by its effect upon refractive index. Acid can be measured by titration with alkali, or by potentiometric determination of hydrogen ion concentration as in determining pH (negative logarithm of the hydrogen ion concentration). All of these are largely research or quality control tools. When it comes to consumer quality acceptance there is still no substitute for measuring with people.

We may use individuals, but groups are better because differences of opinion average out. We may use trained individuals as is common in federal and state grading of agricultural products, such as butter and cheese. We may employ consumer preference groups—panels that are not specifically trained but can provide a good insight into what the customer generally will prefer. We can use panels of highly trained people who are selected

Courtesy of U. S. Dept. Agr.

FIG. 63.   TYPICAL TASTE PANEL ROOM WITH INDIVIDUAL BOOTHS

on the basis of their flavor sensitivity and trained to recognize attributes and defects of a particular product such as coffee or wine.

A typical taste panel room (Fig. 63) is provided with separate booths to isolate tasters so that they do not influence one another with conversation or by facial expressions. The booths may be equipped with colored lights when appropriate. The food sample is given to the taster through a closed window so the taster will not see how it was prepared and thus be influenced. The samples are coded with letters or numbers to avoid terms or brand names that might be influential.

The tasters are given an evaluation form of which there are many kinds. The one in Fig. 64 has columns for three samples with descriptive terms such as like definitely, like mildly, neither like nor dislike, dislike mildly, and dislike definitely. The taster checks his opinion for each sample and may make additional comments. The terms are given number rankings by the taste panel leader, such as 5 for like definitely down to 1 for dislike definitely. When all evaluation forms are complete, the taste panel leader tabulates and averages the results. A number ranking scale for flavor or for other quality factors is known as an hedonic scale.

Often taste panels are asked to choose between two samples in a preference test. Given just two samples a taster may choose one although he is really unable to distinguish between them. Given the same two samples again he might choose in reverse order quite by chance. To avoid this and gain more meaningful data on samples that are quite close in the attribute

Name	Product	Date
Sample No.	Sample No.	Sample No.

Like Definitely	Like Definitely	Like Definitely
Like Mildly	Like Mildly	Like Mildly
Neither Like Nor Dislike	Neither Like Nor Dislike	Neither Like Nor Dislike
Dislike Mildly	Dislike Mildly	Dislike Mildly
Dislike Definitely	Dislike Definitely	Dislike Definitely

Comments	Comments	Comments

From Kramer and Twigg (1970)

FIG. 64.   QUALITY EVALUATION FORM WITH HEDONIC SCALE

being studied, preference tests often involve three samples. In this case the taster may be given two samples that are identical and one that is different, all at the same time and appropriately coded. The taster is asked which two samples are similar and which sample is different, further, which is preferred. If the taster cannot correctly pick the odd sample then his preference loses significance. This is known as a triangle test. There are various ways of interpreting triangle tests and different kinds of preference tests, and statistical analysis of results is commonly employed.

The number of samples a taster can reliably judge at one sitting without his taste perception becoming dulled also is quite limited. This depends upon the product but generally is no more than about 4 or 5. Taste panel booths often are provided with facilities for rinsing the mouth between samples, or crackers may be offered to accomplish a similar effect.

Taste panels used in research, product development, and for purposes of evaluating new and competitive products are not restricted only to flavor. Texture, color, and many other quality factors can be meaningfully measured with this technique.

ADDITIONAL QUALITY FACTORS

Three very important kinds of quality factors which may not always be apparent by sensory observation are nutritional quality, sanitary quality, and keeping quality.

Nutritional quality frequently can be assessed by chemical or instrumental analyses for specific vitamins and other nutrients. In many cases this is not entirely adequate and animal feeding tests or equivalent biological tests must be used. Animal feeding tests are particularly common in evaluating new protein sources. In this case the interacting variables of protein level, amino acid composition, digestibility, and absorption of the amino acids all contribute to determine biological value. While the commercial feeding of livestock is done very largely on a nutritional quality basis, unfortunately most people do not choose their food on this basis.

Sanitary quality usually is measured by bacterial, yeast, mold, and insect fragment counts, as well as by sediment levels.

Keeping quality or storage stability is measured under storage and handling conditions that are set up to simulate or somewhat exceed the conditions the product is expected to encounter in normal distribution and use. Since normal storage tests may require a year or longer to be meaningful, it is common to design accelerated storage tests. These usually involve extremes of temperature, humidity, or other variables to show up developing quality defects in a shorter time. Accelerated storage tests must be chosen with considerable care since an extreme temperature or other variable frequently will alter the pattern of quality deterioration.

The major quality factors of appearance, texture, and flavor are referred to as organoleptic or sensory properties since they are perceived by the senses. There are hundreds of specific quality attributes unique to particular foods and sometimes they do not seem to make much sense, unless we accept the fact that they are traditional and people have become used to expecting them.

The head on a glass of beer is a quality factor, and its size, bubble structure, and foam stability, are all important quality attributes. But the slightest head foam at the top of a glass of wine or a cup of tea is a quality defect. A slight cloudiness or turbidity is desirable in orange juice and it is a quality attribute, but apple juice (at least in some parts of the country) must be crystal clear for highest quality. The quality of Swiss cheese is judged by the size, shape, gloss, and distribution of its eyes, but eyes in Cheddar cheese are a defect.

These and so many other quality attributes make our foods different and interesting; and in many cases the quality attribute which seems arbitrary really is associated with a more fundamental quality factor. The eyes in Swiss cheese are an indication of flavor through proper bacterial fermentation, and of proper cheese texture which was capable of holding the carbon dioxide formed during fermentation.

QUALITY STANDARDS

To help ensure food quality many types of quality standards have come into existence. These include research standards, trade standards, and various kinds of government standards.

Research standards are internal standards set up by a company to help ensure excellence of its products in a highly competitive market.

Trade standards generally are set up by members of an industry on a voluntary basis to assure at least minimum acceptable quality, and to prevent the lowering of standards of quality for the products of that industry.

Government standards are of many kinds. Some are mandatory, these are the standards that have been developed to protect our health and prevent deception of the consumer. More will be said about them in a later chapter. Other government standards known as Federal Grade Standards are largely optional and have been set up mainly to help producers, dealers, wholesalers, and retailers in marketing food products. The Federal Grade Standards provide a common language among producers, dealers, and consumers for trading purposes.

Federal Grade Standards

The Federal Grade Standards are standards of quality. They are administered by the Agricultural Marketing Service of the U.S. Dept. of Agr. To give meaning and uniformity to the standards, the U.S. Dept. of Agr. established an official system of food inspection and grading. Inspectors and graders are trained in the accepted quality factors and there are inspectors and graders for each major food catagory. Uniform grades of quality have been established for over a hundred foods, including meat, dairy, poultry, fruit, vegetable, and seafood products.

Taking meat products as an example, a federal meat grader will evaluate the overall quality of beef; taking into account such factors as shape of the animal carcass, quality and distribution of the exterior fat, age of the animal, firmness and texture of the flesh, including the fat marbling, and color of the lean meat. He will stamp the meat in such a repetitive way that the grade stamp will be present on all cuts even after the carcass is butchered for retail sale.

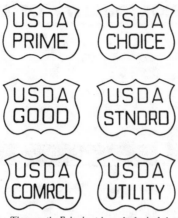

These are the Federal grade marks for beef that may be found in retail stores. Two other grades of beef—Cutter and Canner—are ordinarily used in processed meat products and are rarely, if ever, sold as cuts in retail stores.

Courtesy U. S. Dept. Agr.

FIG. 65.   FEDERAL GRADE MARKS FOR BEEF

The federal grade marks for beef will be found in retail stores as seen in Fig. 65. In order of decreasing quality they are Prime, Choice, Good, Standard, Commercial and Utility. These grade standards are quality standards, they do not reflect differences in wholesomeness, cleanliness, or freedom from disease. All meat must pass such inspection regardless of Federal Grade Standards.

In similar fashion other foods for which grade standards have been established are graded. Detailed brochures are published on each food, and quality control tests for the different quality factors are precisely defined. Liberal use of pictures is made where the quality factor is difficult to describe in words.

In the grading of eggs, for example, the freshness quality is fairly accurately measured by the visual condition of the egg white and the egg yolk (Fig. 66). A fresh egg has a high percentage of thick white next to the yolk and a small amount of thin white beyond the thick white. As the egg ages, the thick white breaks down and the proportion of the thick white to thin white decreases. Ultimately all of the white is thin watery white and no thick white will be seen. There is also flattening of the yolk with ageing and loss of freshness.

In similar fashion, quality defects of fruits and vegetables are defined (Fig. 67).

The grade standards for sweet potatoes consider the shape that yields "usable pieces" for processing. A usable piece means a segment of such

INTERIOR QUALITY OF EGGS
(Recommended standards for scoring the quality of broken-out eggs)

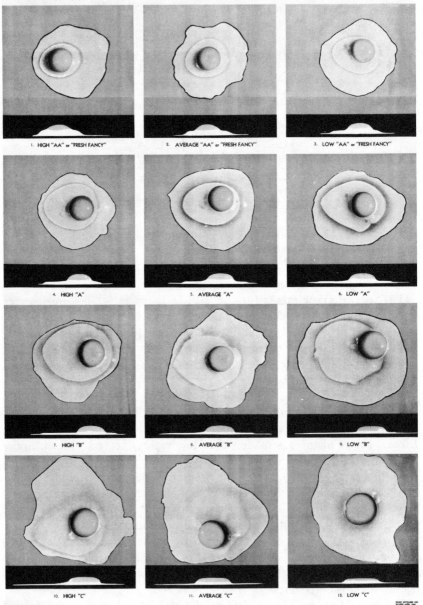

From U. S. Dept. Agr., Agriculture Handbook 75

FIG. 66.   CHANGES IN INTERIOR QUALITY OF EGGS ON AGEING

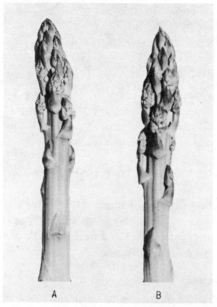

Courtesy of U. S. Dept. Agr.

FIG. 67. ASPARAGUS DEFECT: B SHOWS SLIGHT ADVANCED
DEVELOPMENT OF HEAD AND BRACTS

size and shape that it will be recognizable as a sweet potato after canning or freezing.

The quality attributes for fresh whole tomatoes such as ripeness, color, freedom from cracks and blemishes, size, etc., also include limited "puffiness." This is the amount of air void or open space between the tomato wall and the central pulp (Fig. 68).

Federal Grade Standards for shelled pecans include degree of shriveling, color of nut kernels, degree of chipping of nut halves, moldiness, decay, rancidity, broken shells, and so on.

Typically the final grade of a product is given after weighing each of the quality factors and giving each a numerical value. The values are then added up to give a total score. The Federal Grade Standard for canned concentrated orange juice allows 40 points for color, 40 points for flavor, and 20 points for absence of defects—which includes freedom from seeds, nonexcessive orange oil, proper reconstitution with water, doesn't settle out, etc. The relative importance given in Federal Grade Standards to different quality factors for a wide range of processed fruit and vegetable products is seen in Table 13.

Many kinds of score sheets are devised for special quality control pur-

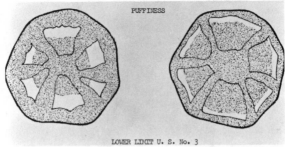

Courtesy of U. S. Dept. Agr.

FIG. 68.   THE DEFECT OF PUFFINESS IN TOMATOES

poses. The score sheets for quality control of military rations may include well over 100 quality factors, ranging from specific requirements for packaging materials to storage stability and performance of the packaged food under unique environmental conditions.

Planned Quality Control

Regardless of whether quality is to be maintained on agricultural raw materials or on manufactured food products, a systematic quality control program is essential. This program begins with customer specifications and market demand. What level of quality is demanded and can be produced for the price the customer can afford to pay? With these specifications agreed upon, appropriate testing methods and control stations can be set up. Control charts and corrective action where indicated will assure meeting the customer specifications.

In a food processing or food manufacturing plant, to meet quality specifications and market demands quality control testing must start with the raw materials. Acceptance sampling and testing of the raw materials will provide a basis for accepting or rejecting these raw materials and will give useful information on how to handle the material in order to obtain a finished product of the desired quality and shelf life. Quality control tests on the processed products through manufacturing, packaging, and even warehousing operations further guarantee that customer demands will be met.

The importance of the market demand aspect in establishing and striving to meet quality specifications cannot be overemphasized. While such factors as nutritional quality and sanitary quality ought not be permitted to vary from well established standards, organoleptic quality factors are by no means rigid. White eggs are preferred in New York but brown eggs are favored over white in Boston. Quality bread means different formulas, textures, and shapes in many markets of the United States and indeed all over the world.

TABLE 13

RELATIVE IMPORTANCE OF FACTORS INVOLVED IN U.S. DEPT. OF AGRICULTURE STANDARDS FOR PROCESSED FRUIT AND VEGETABLE PRODUCTS[1]

Product	Absence of Defects	Color	Flavor	Character	Consistency	Uniformity	Texture	Tenderness and Maturity	Clearness of Liquor
Apples	20	20	...	40	...	20 siz.	...	...	...
Apple butter	20	20	20	20 fin.	20	...	...	...	...
Apple juice	20	20	60	...	...	...	...	...	...
Apple sauce	20	20	20	20 fin.	20	...	...	...	...
Apricots	30	20	...	30	...	20 siz.	...	...	...
Asparagus	30	20	...	...	...	...	...	40	10
Green & wax beans	35	15	...	...	...	...	...	40	10
Dried beans	40	...	...	40	20	...	...	...	...
Lima beans	25	35	...	30	...	...	...	...	10
Beets	30	25	...	...	...	15	30	...	...
Berries	30	20	...	30	...	20	...	...	...
Blueberries	40	20	...	40	...	...	...	...	...
Carrots	30	25	...	...	shape	15 siz.	30	...	...
Cherries, sweet	30	30	...	20	...	20 siz.	...	...	...
Cherries, sour	30	20	...	30	...	20 pits	...	...	...
Corn, cream	20	10	20	...	20	...	...	30	...
Corn, whole	20	10	20	...	...	...	...	40	10
Cranberry sauce	20	20	20	...	40	...	...	...	...
Figs, kadota	30	20	...	35	...	15 siz.	...	...	...
Frozen apples	20	20	...	40	...	20	...	...	...
Fruit cocktail	20	20	...	20	...	20	...	...	20
Fruit jelly	...	20	40	...	40	...	...	...	...
Fruit preserv. (Jam)	20	20	40	...	20	...	...	...	...
Fruit salad	30	20	...	30	...	20 siz.	...	...	...
Grapefruit	20	20	...	20		(Wholeness 20)	(Drained Wt. 20)		
Grapefruit juice	40	20	40	...	...	...	...	...	...
Grape juice	20	40	40	...	...	...	...	...	...
Lemon juice	35	35	30	...	...	...	...	...	...
Mushroom	30	30	...	20	...	20 siz.	...	...	...
Olives, green	30	30	...	20	...	20 siz.	...	...	...
Olives, ripe	10	15	30	25	...	20	...	...	...
Orange juice	20	40	40	...	...	...	...	...	...
Orange juice con.	20	40	40	...	...	...	...	...	...
Orange marm.	20	20	40	...	20	...	...	...	...
Okra	20	15	15	...	...	10	...	35	5
Peaches	30	20	...	30	...	20 siz.	...	...	...
Peanut butter	30	20	30	...	20	...	...	...	...
Pears	30	20	...	30	...	20 siz.	...	...	...
Peas	30	10	...	...	...	...	...	50	10
Peas, field	40	20	...	40	...	...	...	...	...
Cucumber pick.	30	20	...	...	...	20	30	...	...
Pimientos	40	30	...	10	...	20 siz.	...	...	...
Pineapples	30	20	...	30	...	20	...	...	...
Pineapple juice	40	20	40	...	...	...	...	...	...
Plums	30	20	...	30	...	20 siz.	...	...	...
Potatoes, peeled	40	20	...	...	...	20	20	...	...
Prunes, dr.	30	20	...	35	...	15	...	...	...
Pumpkins & squash	30	20	...	20 fin.	30	...	...	...	...
Raspberries	20	25	...	35	...	20 siz.	...	...	...
Sauerkraut	10	15	45	15 crisp	...	...	...	...	15
Sauerkraut, bulk	10	15	45	15 crisp	...	...	...	...	15
Spinach	40	30	...	30	...	...	...	...	...
Sw. potatoes	40	20	...	20	...	20 siz.	...	...	...
Tomatoes	30	30	...	...		(Wholeness 20)	(Drained Wt. 20)		
Tomato juice	15	30	40	...	15	...	...	...	...
Tomato paste	40	60	...	...	...	...	...	...	...
Tomato pulp—pure	50	50	...	...	...	...	...	...	...
Tom. sauce-catsup	25	25	25	...	25	...	...	...	...
Chili sauce	20	20	20	20	20	...	...	...	...

[1] From Kramer and Twigg (1970).

BIBLIOGRAPHY

BAYTON, J. A. 1956. Statistical vs. psychological bias in consumer taste preference research. Trans. Mid-Atlantic Conf. Am. Soc. Quality Control. 23–28. 50 Church St., New York.

BOURNE, M. C. 1966. A classification of objective methods for measuring texture and consistency of foods. J. Food Sci. *31*, 1011–1015.

CAUL, J. F. 1957. The Profile Method of Flavor Analysis. *In* Advances in Food Research, Vol. 7. Academic Press, New York.

DANKER, W. H. (Editor) 1968. Basic Principles of Sensory Evaluation. Spec. Tech. Publ. *433*. Am. Soc. Testing Materials, Philadelphia.

DESROSIER, N. W. 1970. The Technology of Food Preservation, 3rd Edition. Avi Publishing Co., Westport, Conn.

GRANT, E. L. 1952. Statistical Quality Control, 2nd Edition. McGraw-Hill Book Co., New York.

GUNDERSON, F. L., GUNDERSON, H. W., and FERGUSON, E. R., JR. 1963. Food Standards and Definitions in the United States—A Guidebook. Academic Press, New York.

JUDGE, E. E. 1971. The Almanac of the Canning, Freezing, Preserving Industries. E. E. Judge, Westminster, Maryland.

KRAMER, A. 1952. The problem of developing grades and standards of quality. Food Drug Cosmetic Law J. *7*, 23–30.

KRAMER, A. 1963. Quality control: objectives, organization, methods, equipment. *In* Food Processing Operations, Vol. 1. M. A. Joslyn, and J. L. Heid (Editors). Avi Publishing Co., Westport, Conn.

KRAMER, A. 1969. The relevance of correlating objective and subjective data. Food Technol. *23*, 926–928.

KRAMER, A. and TWIGG, B. A. 1970. Quality Control for the Food Industry, Vol. 1, 3rd Edition. Avi Publishing Co., Westport, Conn.

LITTLE, A. D., INC. 1958. Flavor Research and Food Acceptance. Reinhold Publishing Corp., New York.

MACKINNEY, G., and CHICHESTER, C. O. 1954. The color problem in food. *In* Advances in Food Research, Vol. 7. Academic Press, New York.

MACKINNEY, G., and LITTLE, A. C. 1962. Color of Foods. Avi Publishing Co., Westport, Conn.

MATZ, S. A. 1962. Food Texture. Avi Publishing Co., Westport, Conn.

PERYAM, D. R., and PILGRIM, F. J. 1957. Hedonic scale method for measuring food preferences. Food Technol. *11*, No. 9, Insert, 9–14.

SCHULTZ, H. W., DAY, E. A., and LIBBEY, L. M. (Editors) 1967. Symposium on Foods: The Chemistry and Physiology of Flavors. Avi Publishing Co., Westport, Conn.

SCOTT-BLAIR, G. W. 1958. Rheology in food research. *In* Advances in Food Research, Vol. 8. Academic Press, New York.

SOUTHERLAND, F. L. 1960. Sanitation inspection program on processed fruits and vegetables and products thereof. Presented at Natl. Assoc. Frozen Food Packers Conv., March 6.

U.S. DEPT. AGR. 1953. U.S. Standards for Grades of Tomato Catsup. USDA Agr. Marketing Serv.

U.S. DEPT. AGR. 1955. U.S. Standards for Grades of Canned Peas. USDA Agr. Marketing Serv.

U.S. DEPT. AGR. 1958. Regulations governing inspection and certification of processed fruits and vegetables and related products. USDA Agr. Marketing Serv. SRA—AMS *155*.

U.S. DEPT. AGR. 1964. Egg Grading Manual. USDA Agr. Handbook *75*.

CHAPTER 7

Deteriorative Factors and Their Control

INTRODUCTION

From the moment food is harvested, gathered, caught, or slaughtered it undergoes progressive deterioration. Depending upon the food this deterioration may be very slow, as in the case of seeds or nuts, or it may be so rapid as to render the food virtually useless in a matter of hours.

Everything alive requires nourishment. Bacteria, yeasts, molds, insects, and rodents are in constant competition with man to consume his food supply. Further, the highly sensitive organic compounds of food, and the biochemical balance of these compounds, are subject to destruction by nearly every variable in our natural environment. Heat and cold, light, oxygen, moisture, dryness, the natural food enzymes themselves, and time—all tend to deteriorate foods.

In Fig. 69 boxes of harvested onions are waiting to be collected and moved to marketing channels. If they are not removed quickly and given proper storage and protection all of the work that went into their production will have been wasted. This is true for the majority of man's food.

The rapidity with which foods spoil if proper measures are not taken is indicated in Table 14. This gives the useful storage life of typical plant and animal tissues at 70°F. Animal flesh, fish, and poultry can become worthless in 1 to 2 days at room temperature. This is also true for several fruits and leafy vegetables, as it is for raw milk and many other natural products. Room temperature or field temperature can be much higher than 70°F during much of the year, and in some parts of the world throughout the year. At temperatures above 70°F food can become worthless in a matter of hours.

This has immediate significance in less developed areas as well as in the most highly advanced and organized societies. In less developed areas starvation has been known to occur in villages only 10 to 20 miles away from locations of a lush harvest because of spoilage. In highly advanced societies food production generally is centralized in areas where food can be most efficiently grown or processed. These areas in the United States can be two or three thousand miles away from a population center where the food will be consumed. Unless the deteriorative factors are controlled there would be no food for these population centers and indeed there could be no highly advanced society.

History has been made and wars won or lost over food deterioration

131

Courtesy of Purdue University

FIG. 69.   THESE ONIONS ARE AT THE MERCY OF THE ELEMENTS

and its control. Wars, and the need to provide food for armies thousands of miles from areas of food production, have always focused attention on the problems of food deterioration and this is still very true today. It is interesting to note that some of the most important advances in preventing food deterioration have been made in time of war.

At the close of the eighteenth century France was at war and Napoleon's armies were doing poorly on inadequate rations that frequently included spoiled meat and other unwholesome or unpalatable items. Similar problems, including elimination of scurvy, were facing the navy and merchant shipping. Prizes were offered as incentive to encourage development of useful methods of preserving food. From this came the discovery by Nicolas Appert that if food was sufficiently heated in a sealed container, and the container not opened, the food was preserved. Appert was

TABLE 14

USEFUL STORAGE LIFE OF PLANT AND ANIMAL TISSUES[1]

Food Product	Generalized Storage Life (Days), 70°F
Animal flesh	1–2
Fish	1–2
Poultry	1–2
Dried, salted, smoked meat and fish	360 and more
Fruits	1–7
Dried fruits	360 and more
Leafy vegetables	1–2
Root crops	7–20
Dried seeds	360 and more

[1]From Desrosier (1970).

awarded 12,000 francs and honored in 1809, and the world gained the art of food canning. It was not until the work of Pasteur, some 50 years later, that growth of microorganisms was shown to be the major cause of food spoilage; this provided an explanation for Appert's method of preservation.

The essence of food science may be said to be an understanding of the deteriorative factors and their control. Commonly, various degrees of preservation were accomplished long before an understanding of the principles involved were known; and many of the foods we prize today developed out of attempts to prevent deterioration and prolong storage life. One might not ordinarily think of butter as a means of preserving food, but long ago it was discovered that while milk deteriorated in a day or two, clumps of butter fat that formed when milk was agitated could be removed from the milk and would store for weeks or months. Similarly, cheese, smoked fish, dried fruits, and other valued foods had their beginnings in attempts to slow down the deteriorative processes.

MAJOR CAUSES OF FOOD DETERIORATION

The major causes of food deterioration include the following: (1) growth and activities of microorganisms, principally bacteria, yeasts, and molds; (2) activities of the natural food enzymes; (3) insects, parasites, and rodents; (4) temperature, both heat and cold; (5) moisture and dryness; (6) air, and more particularly oxygen; (7) light; and (8) time.

These factors are not isolated in nature. Bacteria, insects, and light, for example, can all be operating simultaneously to deteriorate food in the field or in a warehouse. Similarly, such factors as heat, moisture, and air will all affect the multiplication and activities of bacteria, as well as the chemical activities of the natural food enzymes.

At any one time, many forms of deterioration may take place, depending upon the food and environmental conditions. Total food preservation must eliminate or minimize all of these factors in a given food. Thus, for example, in the case of canned meats we sterilize the canned product to kill microorganisms and to destroy natural meat enzymes. We put the meat in a metal can which protects it from insects and rodents, as well as from light which could deteriorate its color and possibly its nutritive value. The can also protects the meat from drying out. Vacuum is applied, or the can is flushed with nitrogen to remove oxygen. The cans are stored in a cool room and the length of time the cans are held in supermarkets and in our homes is limited. In this case the preservative method takes into account all of the major factors in food deterioration. It is well to consider these factors individually.

Bacteria, Yeasts, and Molds

There are thousands of genera and species of microorganisms. Several hundred are associated in one way or another with food products. Not all cause food spoilage and many types are used in preserving foods, such as the lactic acid producing organisms of cheese, sauerkraut, and certain types of sausage. Others are used for alcohol production as in wine or beer-making, or for flavor production in other foods. However, except where these microorganisms are especially cultivated by selective inoculation, or by controlled conditions to favor their growth over the growth of less desirable types, microorganism multiplication on or in foods generally is the major cause of food deterioration.

Microorganisms capable of spoiling food are found everywhere—in the soil, water, and air; on the skins of cattle and the feathers of poultry; and within the intestines and all other cavities of the animal body. They are found on the skins and peels of fruits and vegetables, and on the hulls of grain and the shells of nuts. They are found on all food processing equipment that has not been sterilized, as well as on the hands, skin, and clothing of food handling personnel.

A most important point, however, is that microorganisms generally are not found within healthy living tissue—such as within the flesh of animals, or the flesh or juice of plants. But they are always present to invade the flesh of plants or animals through a break in the skin, or if the skin is weakened by disease or death. In this case they may digest the skin and penetrate through it to the tissue below.

Milk from a healthy cow is sterile as secreted, but becomes contaminated as it passes through the teat canals which are body cavities. Milk becomes further contaminated from dirt on the cow's hide, from the air, from dirty utensils, and so on.

Beef becomes contaminated when the animal is slaughtered and the protective skin is broken, especially during cutting.

Fruits, vegetables, grains, and nuts become contaminated when the skins or shells are broken or weakened. This is also true of healthy eggs. The inside of a healthy egg is sterile but the shell of the egg can be highly contaminated from passage through the chicken's body cavity at time of laying.

Bacteria are unicellular plants of many forms, although three principal shapes of the individual cells predominate (Fig. 70). These are the spherical shape represented by several forms of cocci, the rod shape of the bacilli, and spiral forms possessed by the spirilla and vibrios.

Many are motile by virtue of whip-like flagella. Others produce spores which are seed-like and remarkably resistant to heat, chemicals, and other adverse conditions (Fig. 71). Bacterial spores are far more

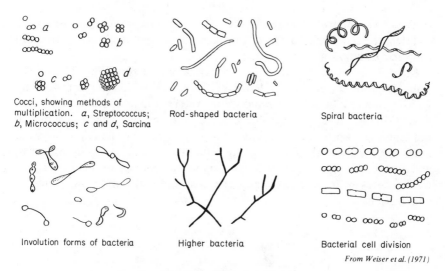

Cocci, showing methods of multiplication. *a*, Streptococcus; *b*, Micrococcus; *c* and *d*, Sarcina

Rod-shaped bacteria

Spiral bacteria

Involution forms of bacteria

Higher bacteria

Bacterial cell division

From Weiser et al. (1971)

FIG. 70.   MORPHOLOGY OF BACTERIA

resistant than yeast or mold spores, and more resistant to most processing conditions than natural food enzymes. Sterilization processes are aimed at these highly resistant bacterial spores.

All bacteria associated with foods are small. Most are of the order of one to a few microns in cell length and somewhat smaller than this in diameter. A micron is one-thousandth of a millimeter or one-twenty five thousandth of an inch. All can penetrate the smallest openings, many can pass through the natural pores of an egg shell once the natural bloom of the shell is worn or washed away.

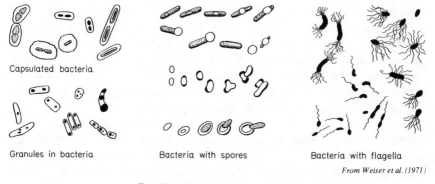

Capsulated bacteria

Granules in bacteria

Bacteria with spores

Bacteria with flagella

From Weiser et al. (1971)

FIG. 71.   BACTERIAL STRUCTURES

Yeasts are somewhat larger, of the order of 20 microns or so in individual cell length and about a third this size in diameter. Most yeasts are spherical or ellipsoidal.

Molds are still larger and more complex in structure (Fig. 72 and 73). They grow by a network of hair-like fibers called mycelia and send up fruiting bodies that produce mold spores referred to as conidia. The blackness of bread mold and the blue colored veins of blue cheese are due to the conidia, while beneath the fruiting heads the hair-like mycelia anchor the mold to the food. The mycelia are a micron or so in thickness, and like bacteria can penetrate the smallest opening; or in the case of weakened skin or shell can digest the skin and make their own route of penetration.

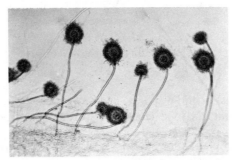

Courtesy Continental Can Co.

FIG. 72.   AN ASPERGILLUS MOLD (X 100) SHOWING MYCELIA AND CONIDIAL HEADS

The bacteria, yeasts, and molds will attack virtually all food constituents; some will ferment sugars and hydrolyze starches and cellulose, others will hydrolyze fats and produce rancidity, still others will digest proteins and produce putrid and ammonia-like odors. Some will form acid and make food sour, others will produce gas and make food foamy, some will form pigments and discolor foods, and a few will produce toxins and give rise to food poisoning. When food is contaminated under natural conditions, several types of organisms will be present together and contribute to a complex of simultaneous or sequential changes which may include acid, gas, putrifaction and discoloration.

Bacteria, yeasts, and molds like warm, moist conditions. Most bacteria multiply best at temperatures between 60° and 100°F and are termed mesophilic. Some will grow at temperatures down to the freezing point of water and are called psychrophilic or cold-loving. Others will grow at temperatures as high as 180°F and we call these thermo-

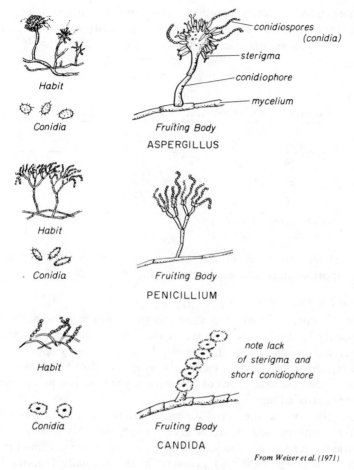

conidiospores
(conidia)

sterigma

conidiophore

Habit

mycelium

Conidia

Fruiting Body
ASPERGILLUS

Habit

Conidia

Fruiting Body
PENICILLIUM

Habit

note lack
of sterigma and
short conidiophore

Conidia

Fruiting Body
CANDIDA

From Weiser et al. (1971)

FIG. 73.   STRUCTURES OF SOME COMMON MOLDS

philic or heat-loving. The spores of many bacteria will survive prolonged exposure to boiling water and then multiply when the temperature is lowered.

Some bacteria and all molds require oxygen for growth and are called aerobic. Other bacteria will not grow unless all free oxygen is absent and are designated anaerobic.

Most important is the tremendous rate at which bacteria and other microorganisms can multiply. Bacteria multiply by cell division. One cell becomes 2, 2 become 4, and so on in exponential fashion. Under favorable conditions bacteria can double their numbers every 30 min. Under such conditions milk with an initial bacterial count of 100,000 or so per milliliter, which is not uncommon before pasteurization, if left standing at room temperature can reach a bacterial population of about 25 million in 24 hr, and an astronomical population of over 5 billion in 96 hr (Table 15).

TABLE 15

MULTIPLICATION OF BACTERIA IN MILK AT ROOM TEMPERATURE[1]

Storage Hours	Bacterial Count per Ml
0	137,000
24	24,674,000
48	639,885,000
72	2,407,083,000
96	5,346,667,000

[1] From Hammer and Babel (1957).

The above properties of bacteria, yeasts, and molds make them the most important cause of food deterioration.

Natural Food Enzymes

Just as microorganisms possess enzymes which ferment, rancidify, and putrify foods, healthy uninfected food plants and animals have their own enzyme complement, the activity of which largely survives harvest and slaughter. Cereal grains and seeds recovered after 60 years of storage still possessed the properties of respiration, germination, and growth—all enzyme controlled functions.

Not only can enzyme activity persist throughout the entire useful life of many natural and manufactured foods, but this activity often is intensified after harvest and slaughter. This is because enzymatic reactions are controlled and delicately balanced in the normally functional living plant and animal; but the balance is upset when the animal is killed or the plant removed from the field. Thus while pepsin helps digest protein in the animal intestine it does not digest the intestine itself in the healthy living animal. However, when the body defenses cease on slaughter, pepsin does contribute to proteolysis of the organs containing it. A great many similar "run away" enzymatic reactions can be cited in plants.

Unless these enzymes are inactivated by heat, chemicals, radiation, or some other means they continue to catalyze chemical reactions within foods. Some of these reactions if not allowed to go too far are highly desirable—like continued ripening of tomatoes after they are picked, and natural tenderizing of beef on ageing. But ripening and tenderizing beyond an optimum point becomes food deterioration; the weakened tissues fall subject to microbial infections and the deterioration reaches the point of rotting. This can happen in the field, supermarket, and home refrigerator, given sufficient time.

Insects, Parasites, and Rodents

Insects are particularly destructive to cereal grains and to fruits and vegetables. Both in the field and in storage it has been estimated that insects destroy 5 to 10% of the U.S. grain crop annually. In some parts of the world the figure may be in excess of 50%. The insect problem is not just one of how much an insect can eat, but when insects eat they damage the food and open it to bacterial, yeast, and mold infection. A small insect hole in a melon, not so bad in itself, can result in the total decay of the melon from bacterial invasion. Insects are generally controlled in grain, dried fruit, and spices by fumigation with such chemicals as methyl bromide, ethylene oxide, and propylene oxide. The use of these latter two fumigants frequently is prohibited with foods high in moisture because of the possible formation of toxic substances.

Insect eggs may persist, or be laid in the food after processing, as for example in flour. An interesting method of destroying insect eggs is to throw the flour with high impact against a hard surface as in a centrifuge-type machine known as an Entoleter (Fig. 74). The impact destroys the eggs. They remain in the flour but no further insect multiplication results.

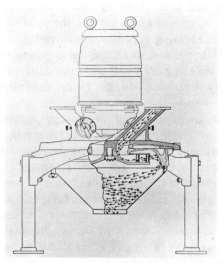

Courtesy of Safety Car Heating & Lighting Co., Inc.

FIG. 74.   ENTOLETER MACHINE CAPABLE OF DESTROYING INSECT
EGGS BY IMPACT

As for parasites, we need only mention here the trichinosis nematode which enters the hog from eating uncooked food wastes. The nematode penetrates the hog's intestines and finds its way into the pork. From pork that is not thoroughly cooked the live worm can infect man. It also is possible to destroy the nematode by controlled frozen storage which will be discussed in a later chapter. All pork and pork products are government inspected but as a further safeguard they should be thoroughly cooked before being consumed.

The problem with rodents too is not mainly the quantity of food they consume, but rather the filth with which they contaminate foods; rodent urine and droppings may harbor several kinds of disease causing bacteria.

Heat and Cold

Quite beyond their effects upon microorganisms, heat and cold can cause deterioration of food if not controlled.

Within the moderate temperature range over which food is handled, say 50° to 100° F, for every 18° F rise in temperature the rate of chemical reaction is approximately doubled. This includes the rates of many enzymatic as well as nonenzymatic reactions. Excessive heat of course denatures proteins, breaks emulsions, dries out foods by removing moisture, and destroys vitamins.

Uncontrolled cold also will deteriorate foods. Fruits and vegetables allowed to freeze and then thaw on the tree or vine will have their texture disrupted. Skins will crack leaving the food susceptible to attack by microorganisms. Freezing may also cause deterioration of liquid foods. If a bottle of milk is allowed to freeze the emulsion will be broken and fat will separate. Freezing also will denature milk protein and cause it to curdle. Carefully controlled freezing on the other hand need not cause these defects.

Cold damage to foods does not necessarily require the extreme of freezing. Many fruits and vegetables after harvest, like other living systems, have optimum temperature requirements. Held at common refrigeration temperatures of about 40° F several are weakened or killed and deteriorative processes follow. Table 16 gives a partial listing of damage done to some fruits and vegetables held cold but above the freezing point. The deteriorations include off-color development, surface pitting, and various forms of decay. Bananas, lemons, squash, and tomatoes are examples of products that should be held at temperatures no lower than about 50° F for maximum quality retention. This provides an exception to the somewhat inaccurate generalization that cold storage preserves all foods, and the colder the better.

TABLE 16

SEVERAL FRUITS AND VEGETABLES ARE DAMAGED
BY COLD TEMPERATURES ABOVE FREEZING ZONE [1]

Commodity	Approximate Lowest Safe Temperature, °F	Character of Injury When Stored Between 32°F and Safe Temperature
Apples		
certain varieties	34 to 36	internal browning, soggy breakdown.
Avocados	45	internal browning.
Bananas		
green or ripe	56	dull color when ripened.
Beans (snap)	45 to 50	pitting increasing on removal, russeting on removal.
Cranberries	34	low-temperature breakdown.
Cucumbers	45	pitting, water-soaked spots, decay.
Eggplants	45	pitting or bronzing, increasing on removal.
Grapefruit	45	scald, pitting, watery breakdown, internal browning.
Lemons	55 to 58	internal discoloration, pitting.
Limes	45	pitting.
Mangoes	50	internal discoloration.
Melons		
cantaloupes	45	pitting, surface decay.
Honey Dew	40 to 50	pitting, surface decay.
Casaba	40 to 50	pitting, surface decay.
Crenshaw and Persian	40 to 50	pitting, surface decay.
watermelons	36	pitting, objectionable flavor.
Okra	40	discoloration, water-soaked areas, pitting, decay.
Olives, fresh	45	internal browning.
Oranges, California	35 to 37	rind disorders.
Papayas	45	breakdown.
Peppers, sweet	45	pitting, discoloration near calyx.
Pineapples		
mature-green	45	dull green when ripened.
Potatoes		
Chippewa and Sebago	40	mahogany browning.
Squash, winter	50 to 55	decay.
Sweet potatoes	55	decay, pitting, internal discoloration.
Tomatoes		
mature-green	55	poor color when ripe; tendency to decay rapidly.
ripe	50	breakdown.

[1] From U.S. Dept. Agr., Agr. Handbook 66.

Moisture and Dryness

The gross changes in foods from excessive moisture pickup or loss need no further comment at this time. The requirement of moisture for chemical reactions and for microorganism growth also has been stated. It must be pointed out, however, that moisture need not be throughout the food to exert major effects.

Surface moisture resulting from slight changes in relative humidity can be a major cause of lumping and caking, as well as such surface defects as mottling, crystallization, and stickiness. The slightest amount of condensation on the surface of food can become a virtual swimming pool for the multiplication of bacteria or the growth of mold.

This condensation need not come from the outside. In a moisture-proof package, food materials such as fruits or vegetables can give off moisture from respiration and transpiration. This moisture is then trapped within the package and can support the growth of microorganisms. Nonliving foods in a moisture-proof package also can give up moisture and change the relative humidity of the package headspace. This moisture can then be recondensed on the surface of the food, particularly when storage temperature is permitted to decrease.

Air and Oxygen

Besides the destructive effects air and oxygen can have on vitamins (especially vitamins A and C), food colors, flavors, and other food constituents, oxygen is essential for good mold growth. All molds are aerobic and this is why they are found growing on the surface of foods and other substances or within cracks in these materials.

We exclude oxygen from foods by vacuum deaeration or inert gas purging in the course of processing, by vacuum packaging or by flushing containers with nitrogen or carbon dioxide, and in some instances by adding oxygen scavengers to foods and containers which promote residual trace oxygen removal through chemical reaction.

Light

It has already been indicated that some vitamins are destroyed by light, notably riboflavin, vitamin A, and vitamin C, and that light will deteriorate many food colors. Milk in bottles exposed to the sun develops "sunlight" flavor due to light induced fat oxidation and changes in the protein. Light-sensitive foods may be easily protected from light by impervious packaging.

Time

After slaughter, harvest, or food manufacture there is a time when the quality of food is at its peak, but this is only a transitory period. In many products this quality peak can be passed in the field in a day or two, or after harvest in a matter of hours. Fresh corn and peas are notable examples.

The growth of microorganisms, action of food enzymes, destruction by insects, effects of heat, cold, moisture, oxygen, and light, all progress with time. The longer the time the greater the destructive influences. This is not to say that certain cheeses, wines, whiskeys, and the like are not improved with ageing. But for the vast majority of foods time is an enemy and there is no substitute for freshness.

SOME PRINCIPLES OF FOOD PRESERVATION

In subsequent chapters several of the more important preservation methods are treated individually. It is well now to enlarge somewhat on some of the principles underlying control of food deterioration. These are the principles upon which food preservation methods are largely based.

If foods are to be kept only for short periods of time, then there are two very simple rules:

(1) Keep food alive as long as possible, in other words don't kill the animal or plant until just before it is to be eaten. A good example of this is keeping lobsters alive in a tank in a supermarket or restaurant—while alive (and healthy) they do not seriously deteriorate. This is also practiced with fish, poultry, fruits, and vetetables where possible. Unfortunately the possibilities are limited.

(2) If the food must be killed, then clean it, cover it, and cool it. However, cleaning, covering, and cooling will only delay deteriorative factors for a short time, for hours or perhaps at most for a few days. Microorganisms and natural food enzymes will not be destroyed or totally inactivated and so will take over very quickly.

For longer term practical preservation, as required for most of our food supply, further precautions are necessary. These are largely directed at inactivating or controlling microorganisms which are our principal cause of food spoilage.

CONTROL OF MICROORGANISMS

The most important means of controlling bacteria, yeasts, and molds are heat, cold, drying, acid, sugar, salt, smoke, air, chemicals, and radiations. Any one of these also can cause deterioration of foods and so it is a matter of balance; an amount of heat that will kill microorganisms but still leave the food largely undamaged, a dosage of radiation that will destroy bacterial spores but have minimum adverse effects upon food components. Indeed, the entire science of food preservation is one of compromise with respect to dosage or treatment.

Heat

Most bacteria, yeasts, and molds grow best in the temperature range of about 60°–100°F. Thermophiles will grow in the range of 150°–180°F. Most bacteria are killed in the range of 180°–200°F. But many bacterial spores are not destroyed even by boiling water at 212°F for 30 min. To ensure sterility, that is *total* destruction of microorganisms, we must go to a temperature of about 250°F (wet heat) and maintain this temperature for 15 min or longer. This is generally done with steam under pressure as in a laboratory autoclave or commercial retort. These and other temperature relations to microorganism life are seen in Table 17.

TABLE 17

TEMPERATURE RELATIONS TO BACTERIAL LIFE[1]

°F	Temperature Effects on Organisms
250	Steam temperature at 15 lb pressure kills all forms including spores in 15 to 20 min.
240	Steam temperature at 10 lb pressure kills all forms including spores in 30 to 40 min.
230	Steam temperature at 6 lb pressure kills all forms including spores in 60 to 80 min.
220	Steam temperature at 2 lb pressure.
212	Boiling temperature of pure water at sea level. Kills in vegetative stage quickly but not spores after long exposure.
200	Growing cells of bacteria, yeasts, and molds are usually killed (180° to
190	200°F).
180	
180	Thermophilic organisms grow in this range (150° to 180°F).
170	
160	
150	
170	Pasteurization of milk in 30 min kills all the important pathogenic bac-
160	teria as far as humans are concerned except the spore forming patho-
150	gens (140° to 170°F).
140	
100	Active growing range for most bacteria, yeast and molds (60° to 100°F).
98.6	
90.0	
80.0	
70.0	
60.0	
60	Growth retarded for most organisms (60°–50°F).
50	
50	Optimum growth of psychrophilic organisms (50° to 40°F).
40	
32	Freezing. Usually the growth of all organisms is stopped.
0	Bacteria preserved in a latent state.
−420	Many species of bacteria are not killed by the temperature of liquid hydrogen.

[1]From Weiser et al. (1971).

Commercial pressure retorts of the kind used in the canning industry operate at temperatures and for time intervals adequate to destroy the most resistant of bacterial spores within the canned food. Sterility or "commercial sterility" to be defined later on, is essential because the food may be stored in the can for a year or longer. Not all foods require the same amount of heat for sterilization.

When foods are high in acid, such as tomatoes or orange juice, one need not heat as severely because acid increases the killing power of heat. A temperature of 200°F for 15 min, for example, may be enough to gain sterility if sufficient acid is present. Safe temperatures and times for different foods have been well established and are published in handbooks used by the canning industry.

Another fundamental point on the use of heat and other means of preservation: it is not always necessary to kill all microorganisms and produce a sterile product. It may be necessary to employ only sufficient heat to destroy disease producing organisms in the food. This is done in the case of pasteurized milk. Most of the bacteria and all of the disease producing organisms that might be present in milk are destroyed by pasteurization at 145° F for 30 min, but the milk is not sterile. Nor need it be, since it will be held in a refrigerator and consumed generally within a few days. However, evaporated milk, which is intended to remain in a can at room temperature for months or even years must receive a greater heat treatment to ensure sterility or commercial sterility.

Cold

As stated before, most bacteria, yeasts, and molds grow best in the temperature range of 60°–100° F. Psychrophiles will grow down to 32° F, the freezing point of water, and below. At temperatures below 50° F, however, growth is slow and becomes slower the colder it gets (see Table 17). When the water in food is completely frozen there is no multiplication of microorganisms. But it must be pointed out that in some foods all of the water is not frozen until a temperature of 15° F or even lower is reached. This is because of dissolved sugars, salts, and other constituents, which depress the freezing point.

The slowing down of microbial activity with decreased temperatures is the basis behind refrigeration and freezing preservation. However, it is important to note that while cold temperatures will slow down microbial growth and activities, and may kill a certain fraction of the bacterial population, cold, including severe freezing, cannot be depended upon to kill all bacteria. This is illustrated by typical data in Table 18, where ice cream mix was inoculated with typhoid bacteria. In frozen storage the ice cream still retained over 600,000 live bacteria per milliliter after 1 yr. Not only do cold storage and freezing fail to sterilize foods, but when the

TABLE 18

EFFECT OF FREEZING ICE CREAM MIX ON TYPHOID BACILLI [1]

Samples Taken	Typhoid Bacilli per Ml of Ice Cream Mix
5 days old	51,000,000
20 days old	10,000,000
70 days old	2,200,000
342 days old	660,000
430 days old	51,000
648 days old	30,000
2 yr old	6,300
2 yr, 4 mo old	Viable typhoid bacilli

[1] From Weiser et al. (1971).

food is taken from cold storage and thawed, the surviving organisms often resume rapid growth since the food may have been somewhat damaged from the cold or frozen storage.

Drying

Microorganisms in a healthy growing state may contain in excess of 80% water. They get this water from the food in which they grow. If the water is removed from the food it also will transfer out of the bacterial cells and multiplication will stop. Partial drying will be less effective than total drying, though for some microorganisms partial drying as in concentration may be quite sufficient to arrest bacterial growth and multiplication. Bacteria and yeasts generally require more moisture than molds, and so molds often will be found growing on semi-dry foods where bacteria and yeasts find conditions unfavorable. Examples are mold growing on stale bread and partially dried fruits.

Slight differences in relative humidity within the room in which the food is held, or within the food package can make great differences in the rate of microorganism multiplication. In Fig. 75 meat was stored cold for 20 days at 75% and 95% relative humidity (RH). At each temperature of cold

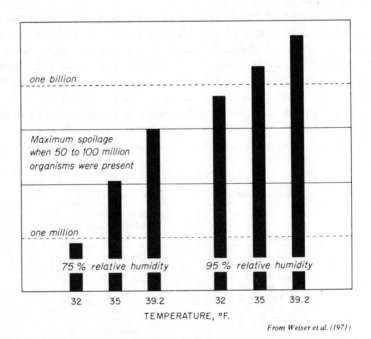

From Weiser et al. (1971)

FIG. 75. EFFECT OF RELATIVE HUMIDITY ON GROWTH OF MICRO-ORGANISMS IN MEAT STORED 20 DAYS

storage the higher humidity produced the higher population of micro-organisms.

Since microorganisms can live in one part of a food that may differ in moisture and other physical and chemical conditions from an area of the food inches away, we must be concerned with conditions in the "micro-environment" of the microorganisms. Thus it is common to refer to water conditions in terms of specific activity. The term "water activity" is related to relative humidity. Relative humidity is defined as the ratio of the partial pressure of water vapor in the air to the vapor pressure of pure water at the same temperature. Relative humidity refers to the atmosphere surrounding a material or solution. Water activity is a property of solutions, and is the ratio of vapor pressure of the solution compared with the vapor pressure of pure water at the same temperature. Under equilibrium conditions water activity equals RH/100. When we speak of moisture requirements of microorganisms we really mean water activity in their immediate environment, whether this be in solution, in a particle of food, or at a surface in contact with the atmosphere. At the usual temperatures permitting microbial growth, most bacteria require a water activity in the range of about 0.90 to 1.00. Some yeasts and molds grow slowly at a water activity down to as low as about 0.65. More will be said about water activity in Chap. 10, under the section entitled In-termediate Moisture Foods.

As stated previously, food is dried either partially or completely for several reasons, one of the most important is to preserve it against microbial spoilage. However, as was the case for freezing, partial or complete drying of food does not of itself necessarily kill all micro-organisms. It may actually preserve microorganisms as it preserves the food, and the dried food generally is far from sterile. While bacteria may not grow in the dried food, when the food is inadvertently remoistened or intentionally reconstituted, bacterial growth will resume unless the food is quickly consumed or held cold.

Acid

In sufficient strength acid denatures bacterial proteins much as it denatures food proteins and so microorganisms are sensitive to acid. Some are much more sensitive than others, and the acid produced by one organism during fermentation often will inhibit multiplication of another type of organism. This is one of the principles of controlled fermentation as a means of preserving foods against growth of proteolytic and other types of spoilage organisms.

Acid may be produced in foods by adding selected acid producing cultures, or acids may be added directly to foods as chemicals; examples are citric acid and phosphoric acid added to beverages, e.g., soda pop. Several foods such as tomatoes, citrus juices, and apples contain natural acidity. In each case the acid has varying degrees of preservative power. Much of this is due directly to the hydrogen-ion concentration which is expressed in terms of pH, but two acids producing the same food pH may not be equally preservative since the anions of certain acids also exert an effect. It also is well to recognize that the degree of acidity tolerable in foods from the standpoint of palatability is never sufficient in itself to ensure food sterility.

As mentioned earlier, acid combined with heat makes the heat more destructive to microorganisms. This is seen in Table 19 with respect to requirements for destruction of the spores of the anaerobic toxin producing *Clostridium botulinum.*

TABLE 19

TIME REQUIRED TO DESTROY THE VIABLE SPORES OF *Clostridium botulinum* IN DIFFERENT FOODS AND AT VARIOUS pH LEVELS[1]

Kind of Food	pH of Food	Temperature				
		194°F	203°F	212°F	221°F	226°F
		Minutes				
Hominy	6.95	600	495	345	34	10
Corn	6.45	555	465	255	30	15
Spinach	5.10	510	345	225	20	10
String beans	5.10	510	345	225	20	10
Pumpkin	4.21	195	120	45	15	10
Pears	3.75	135	75	30	10	5
Prunes	3.60	60	20	..	..	..

[1]From Weiser et al. (1971).

Sugar and Salt

We preserve fruits by placing them in a sugar syrup, and we preserve certain meat products by placing them in a salt brine. How does this work?

Bacteria, yeasts, and molds are contained by cell membranes. These membranes allow water to pass in and out of the cells. Active microorganisms may contain in excess of 80% water. When bacteria, yeasts, or molds are placed in a heavy sugar syrup or salt brine, water in the cells moves out through the membrane and into the concentrated syrup or brine. This is the well-known process of osmosis; in this case water moves from the cell with its 80% water content into the syrup or brine which may contain only 40 or 30% water. The tendency to equalize water concentration inside and outside the cell in this case causes a partial dehydration of the cell, referred to as plasmolysis, which interferes with microorganism multiplication. Quite the opposite can be accomplished by placing microorganisms in distilled water. In this case water can enter the cells and cause them to burst. This is known as plasmoptysis but it rarely occurs in food products. All of this is closely related to the water activity of solutions and foods. Solutions high in solute concentration have a high osmotic pressure and a low water activity. Dilute solutions are low in osmotic pressure and have a high water activity. The quantitative contribution of a specific solute to osmotic pressure and water activity depends upon the solute's molecular weight. An equal weight of a low

Courtesy Vilter Corp.

Fig. 76. Smoke is Combined with Other Preservatives in Various Sausage Products

molecular weight solute has a greater effect on increasing a solution's osmotic pressure and decreasing its water activity than the same weight of a high molecular weight solute.

Different organisms have various degrees of tolerance to osmosis and to sugar and salt. Yeasts and molds are more tolerant than most bacteria and this is why yeasts and molds often are found growing on high sugar or salt products, for example fruit jam, where bacteria are inhibited.

Smoke

As with most preservative methods, smoke was used long before the reasons for its effectiveness were understood. In preserving foods such as meats and fish with smoke, the preservative action generally comes from a combination of factors. Smoke contains preservative chemicals such as small amounts of formaldehyde and other materials from the burning of wood. These are unfavorable to microorganisms. But in addition smoke generally is associated with heat which helps kill microorganisms. This heat also tends to dry out the food somewhat, which further contributes to preservation. Smoking over a fire may be quite effective in preserving certain foods; on the other hand today smoke may be added merely to flavor foods, that is without heat from burning. In this case, the smoke may be a very poor preservative. In meat products such as seen in Fig. 76, smoke combined with other preservatives is used more for its flavor than for its preservative action.

Air

The differential requirements of microorganisms for oxygen and some of the means for removing air and oxygen have been cited. To control spoilage organisms that require air it is removed; for spoilage organisms that cannot tolerate it, air is provided. It is often fairly easy to exclude air from aerobes such as molds. Wax coating of cheeses, or oxygen impermeable skin-tight plastic films can be quite effective. Controlling strict anaerobes by providing air can be more difficult and dangerous, especially with large food pieces. This is because the center of the food piece can be under anaerobic conditions even if air is left in the headspace of a package. Further, some organisms consume oxygen and thus convert a formerly aerobic microenvironment into an anaerobic one favorable to other organisms. Thus in preserving food against *Clostridium botulinum*, measures in addition to inclusion of air generally are essential.

Chemicals

Many chemicals will kill microorganisms or stop their growth, but most of these are not permitted in foods. A few that are include sodium benzoate, sorbic acid, sodium and calcium propionate, ethyl formate, and sulfur dioxide; all in prescribed low levels, and only in certain foods.

The use of chemicals to control microorganisms, and for any other purpose in foods, is part of the broader consideration of permissible food additives, which will be dealt with in a later chapter. At the present time the Pure Food Law, administered by the Secretary of Health, Education, and Welfare through the Food and Drug Administration, regulates what chemicals may be used in foods, and the conditions of their use. New chemicals to be approved must undergo the most rigorous testing, and the burden of proof of safety resides with the producer or user of the chemical. The FDA also retains the right to reverse former decisions

From Weiser et al. (1971)

FIG. 77.   POULTRY STORAGE LIFE EXTENDED BY OXYTETRACYCLINE
DIP

and prohibit use of approved chemicals if new knowledge relative to safety warrants such action. The status of many chemicals may not be static at any given time. An interesting class of chemicals that illustrates this is the antibiotics.

Several antibiotics are effective in varying degrees against food spoilage organisms; among the more interesting have been penicillin, streptomycin, chlorotetracycline (aureomycin) and oxytetracycline, bacitracin, and subtilin. Of these, chlorotetracycline and oxytetracycline gained approval by the FDA for limited use as a preservative dip to extend the storage life of chilled uncooked poultry and fish (Fig. 77). Uncooked was stressed since subsequent normal cooking is capable of inactivating residual antibiotic that otherwise would remain on the skin or in the tissues. Inactivation was desirable because not all of the possible side effects of this chemical ingested by man were then or are now fully known. In 1967, after several years of limited commercial use, the FDA reconsidered all available evidence and disapproved the above use of these antibiotics on the grounds that they could possibly have long range undesirable effects, such as promoting resistant strains of bacteria through selection, and sometimes cause adverse physiological reactions in humans. Further, their use has been opposed on the grounds that they offered a substitute for good sanitary practice. Today in the United States no antibiotic may be added as a preservative to food to be directly consumed by humans, although antibiotics are permitted to be added to animal feeds and this is common practice.

Radiations

Microorganisms are inactivated to various degrees by different kinds of radiations. X-rays, microwaves, ultraviolet light radiation, and ionizing radiations are all kinds of electromagnetic radiations, differing in wavelength, that have been used to preserve food.

It can be said of all of these radiations that the doses required to completely sterilize most foods, and inactivate their natural enzymes,

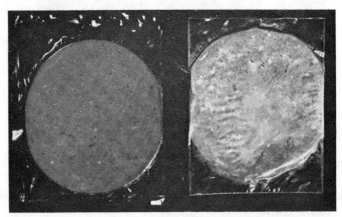

Courtesy of U. S. Army Natick Laboratories

FIG. 78. MEAT STORAGE LIFE EXTENDED BY IRRADIATION (LEFT: IRRADIATED; RIGHT: CONTROL)

are generally excessive or borderline from the standpoint of top food quality; and all may develop flavor, color, texture, or nutritional defects in a wide range of food materials. Less than sterilization doses appear more generally useful to extend product storage life.

By irradiated foods today is usually meant foods irradiated with ionizing radiations, as may be obtained from radioactive isotopes or electron accelerators. There is no significant temperature rise from this form of irradiation and so the term "cold sterilization" has been used. Figure 78 shows packaged irradiated and unirradiated meat after prolonged storage. The military especially has been interested in irradiation preservation of field rations. In recent years several foods had been approved for irradiation sterilization and irradiation pasteurization at specific doses in the United States and other countries. Safety of irradiated foods in the United States comes under the jurisdiction of the FDA much as in the case of chemical additives. In 1968, the FDA reversed prior decisions and prohibited the distribution of foods sterilized by irradiation. This action followed animal feeding test studies which indicated a possible health risk from the consumption of these foods. Food irradiation will be considered in more detail in a later chapter.

CONTROL OF ENZYMES AND OTHER FACTORS

Most of what has been said in this chapter regarding control of deteriorative factors has dealt specifically with microorganisms. This emphasis is justified because by far the greatest losses to the world's food supply are due to microorganisms. Further, preservation of foods against deterioration from natural food enzymes, probably the second greatest cause of spoilage, follow many of the same principles and methods that apply to preservation against microbial deterioration.

Just as microorganisms are controlled with heat, cold, drying, certain chemicals, and radiations, these are the principal means used to control and inactivate damaging natural food enzymes. Indeed, when foods are sterilized or pasteurized to inactivate microorganisms, natural food enzymes are simultaneously partially or completely destroyed. Likewise, when cold is employed to slow down microbial activity it also retards the activity of natural food enzymes.

What is important, however, is that some natural food enzymes may be more resistant to the effects of heat, cold, drying, radiations, and other means of preservation than some microorganisms. Thus a heat treatment or a radiation treatment may effectively destroy bacteria but leave certain damaging food enzymes largely intact to carry on food deterioration. Here few broad generalizations can be made and specific conditions for preservation must be selected in accordance with the unique spoilage patterns of individual foods. Nevertheless, in two general areas of preservation especially, irradiation and freezing, we frequently find that conditions which destroy or retard microorganism activity still leave enzymes functionally active.

As for preservation against such other factors as moisture, dryness, air, and light, protective packaging is usually employed to protect processed foods. Insects and rodents also are largely controlled by protective packaging combined with a high degree of sanitation.

BIBLIOGRAPHY

ALDRICH, D. G. (Editor) 1970. Research for the World Food Crisis. American Association for the Advancement of Science, Washington, D.C.

ANON. 1953. When in Doubt Throw It Out. Ohio Dept. of Health, Columbus.

DACK, G. M. 1956. Food Poisoning, 3rd Edition. University of Chicago Press, Chicago.

DESROSIER, N. W. 1970. The Technology of Food Preservation, 3rd Edition. Avi Publishing Co., Westport, Conn.

DESROSIER, N. W., and ROSENSTOCK, H. M. 1960. Radiation Technology in Food, Agriculture and Biology. Avi Publishing Co., Westport, Conn.

DYKSTRA, W. W. 1966. Damage by rodents and other wildlife. *In* Protecting Our Food— The Yearbook of Agriculture, 1966. U.S. Dept. Agr.

FOOD PROTECTION COMMITTEE. 1959. Principles and Procedures for Evaluating the Safety of Food Additives. Natl. Acad. Sci.—Natl. Res. Council Publ. *749,* Washington, D.C.

FRAZIER, W. C. 1967. Food Microbiology, 2nd Edition. McGraw-Hill Book Co., New York.

GOLDBERG, H. S. 1959. Antibiotics: Their Chemistry and Non-Medical Uses. Van Nostrand Reinhold Co., New York.

GOLDBLITH, S. A., JOSLYN, M. A., and NICKERSON, J. T. R. 1961. An Introduction to the Thermal Processing of Foods. Avi Publishing Co., Westport, Conn.

GRAY, W. D. 1959. The Relation of Fungi to Human Affairs. Henry Holt Co., New York.

HAMMER, B. W., and BABEL, F. J. 1957. Dairy Bacteriology, 4th Edition. John Wiley & Sons, New York.

HARDENBURG, R. E. 1966. Packaging and protection. *In* Protecting Our Food—The Yearbook of Agriculture, 1966. U.S. Dept. Agr.

HARRIS, K. L. 1946. Annotated bibliography of methods for the examination of foods for filth. J. Assoc. Offic. Agr. Chem. *24,* 201–210.

HOFFMANN, C. H., and HENDERSON, L. S. 1966. The fight against insects. *In* Protecting Our Food—The Yearbook of Agriculture, 1966. U.S. Dept. Agr.

JAY, J. M. 1970. Modern Food Microbiology. Van Nostrand Reinhold Co., New York.

LAMANNA, C., and MALLETTE, M. F. 1965. Basic Bacteriology—Its Biological and Chemical Background. Williams & Wilkins Co., Baltimore.

NORD, F. F. 1961. Advances in Enzymology 23. Interscience Publishers, New York.

NORRIS, J. R., and RIBBONS, D. W. (Editors) 1970. Methods in Microbiology, Vol. 3A. Academic Press, New York.

NUNHEIMER, T. D., and FABIAN, F. W. 1940. Influence of organic acids, sugars, and sodium chloride upon strains of food poisoning staphylococci. Am. J. Public Health *30,* 1040–1049.

OUGH, C. S., ROESSLER, E. B., and AMERINE, M. A. 1960. Effects of sulfur dioxide, temperature, time, and closures on the quality of bottled dry white table wines. Food Technol. *14,* 352–356.

RANGASWAMI, G. 1966. Agricultural Microbiology. Asia Publishing House, New York.

RANIERE, L. C. 1966. Weather and food. *In* Protecting Our Food—The Yearbook of Agriculture, 1966. U.S. Dept. Agr.

SCHULTZ, H. W. (Editor) 1960. Food Enzymes. Avi Publishing Co., Westport, Conn.

STAPLEY, J. H., and GAYNER, F. C. H. 1969. World Crop protection, Vol. 1. Chemical Rubber Co., Cleveland.

TANNER, F. W. 1944. The Microbiology of Foods. Garrard Press, Champaign, Ill.

THATCHER, F. S. 1958. Microbiological standards for foods. Food Technol. *12,* 117–122.

TRESSLER, D. K., VAN ARSDEL, W. B., and COPLEY, M. J. (Editors) 1968. The Freezing Preservation of Foods, Vols. 1, 2, 3, and 4. Avi Publishing Co., Westport, Conn.

Van Arsdel, W. B., Copley, M. J., and Morgan, A. I., Jr. (Editors)   1973.   Food dehydration, 2nd Edition, Vols. 1 and 2. Avi Publishing Co., Westport, Conn.
Weiser, H. H., Mountney, G. J., and Gould, W. A.   1971.   Practical Food Microbiology and Technology, 2nd Edition. Avi Publishing Co., Westport, Conn.
Wright, R. C., Rose, D. H., and Whiteman, T. M.   1954.   The commercial storage of fruits, vegetables, and florist and nursery stock. U.S. Dept. Agr. Handbook 66.

CHAPTER 8

Heat Preservation and Processing

INTRODUCTION

Of the various means for preserving foods the use of heat finds very wide application. The simple acts of cooking, frying, broiling, or otherwise heating our foods prior to consumption are forms of food preservation. In addition to making foods more tender and palatable, cooked foods will have a large proportion of their microorganism flora and natural enzymes destroyed, and so cooked foods generally can be held for several days provided they are protected from recontamination. Cooking generally will not sterilize a product, and so even if protected from recontamination food will spoil in a comparatively short period of time. This time is prolonged if the cooked foods are held refrigerated. These are common household practices.

Another feature of cooking is that it is usually the last treatment food receives prior to being consumed. The toxin that can be formed by *Clostridium botulinum* is destroyed by a ten-minute exposure to moist heat at 212° F. Properly processed commercial foods will be free of this toxin. Cooking provides a final measure of protection in those unfortunate cases where a processing slip-up does occur, or a faulty food container becomes contaminated. However, when we talk about heat preservation of food we generally mean those controlled processes that are performed commercially such as blanching, pasteurizing, and canning.

VARIOUS DEGREES OF PRESERVATION

It is necessary to recognize that there are various degrees of preservation by heating, and that our commercial heat preserved foods are not all sterile. A few terms must be identified and understood.

Sterilization

By sterilization we mean complete destruction of microorganisms. Because of the resistance of certain bacterial spores to heat, this frequently means a treatment of at least 250° F of wet heat for 15 min or its equivalent. It also means that every particle of the food must receive this heat treatment. If a can of food is to be *sterilized*, then immersing it into a 250° F pressure cooker or retort for the 15 min will not be sufficient. This is because of the relatively slow rate of heat transfer through the food in the can to the most distant point. Depending upon the size of the can, the effective time to achieve true sterility may be several hours. During this time there can be many changes in the food to depreciate its quality. Fortunately, many foods need not be completely sterile to be safe and have keeping quality.

Commercially Sterile

This term has been coined to describe the condition that exists in most of our canned and bottled products. "Commercially sterile" or the word "sterile" (in quotes), frequently seen in the literature, means that degree of sterility at which all pathogenic and toxin forming organisms have been destroyed, as well as all other types of organisms which if present could grow in the product and produce spoilage under normal handling and storage conditions. "Commercially sterilized" foods may contain a very small number of resistant bacterial spores, but these will not normally multiply in the food supply. However, if they were isolated from the food and given special environmental conditions they could be shown to be alive.

Our canned food supply which is "commercially sterile" generally has a shelf-life of two years or more. Even after longer periods, so-called deterioration generally is due to texture or flavor changes rather than to microorganism growth.

Pasteurized

By pasteurized we mean a comparatively low order of heat treatment, generally at temperatures below the boiling point of water. Pasteurized products, for example milk, will contain many living organisms—of the order of thousands per milliliter or per gram. However, pasteurization heat treatments are carefully chosen to destroy all *pathogenic* organisms that may be associated with the food. Pasteurized products, while safe from a disease-producing point of view, have only limited storage life due to multiplication of the surviving nonpathogenic organisms. Pasteurization frequently is combined with another means of preservation, and pasteurized foods generally must be stored under refrigeration. Pasteurized milk may be kept stored in a home refrigerator for a week or longer without developing significant off-flavors. Stored at room temperature however, pasteurized milk may spoil in a day or two.

Blanching

Blanching is a kind of pasteurization generally applied to fruits and vegetables primarily to inactivate natural food enzymes. This is common practice when such products are to be frozen, since frozen storage in itself would not completely arrest enzyme activity. Blanching, depending upon its severity also will destroy some microorganisms, as will pasteurization inactivate some enzymes. Sometimes the two terms are used interchangeably. It is probably better to reserve the term pasteurization to apply to those heat treatments which are designed specifically to destroy microorganisms.

DETERMINING HEAT TREATMENTS

Since heat sufficient to destroy microorganisms and food enzymes also generally affects other properties of foods adversely, it will be appreciated that in practice the mildest heat treatment that guarantees freedom from pathogens and toxins and produces the desired storage life will be the heat treatment of choice.

How then do we arrive at this heat treatment? In order to preserve foods by heat with safety, the following must be known:
(1) What time-temperature combination is required to inactivate the most heat resistant pathogens and spoilage organisms in our particular food.
(2) What are the heat penetration characteristics into our particular food, including the can or container of choice if it is packaged.

We must provide the heat treatment which will ensure that the remotest particle of food in a batch or within a container will receive a sufficient temperature, for a sufficient time, to inactivate both the most resistant pathogen and the most resistant spoilage organisms if we are to achieve sterility or "commercial sterility," and to inactivate the most heat resistant pathogen if pasteurization is our goal.

Different foods will support growth of different pathogens and different spoilage organisms and so our targets will vary depending upon the food to be heated.

HEAT RESISTANCE OF MICROORGANISMS

The most heat resistant pathogen we may expect in foods, especially those that are canned and will be held under anaerobic conditions, is *Clostridium botulinum.* However, there are nonpathogenic spore forming spoilage bacteria such as Putrefactive Anaerobe 3679 (PA 3679) and *Bacillus stearothermophilus* (FS 1518) which are even more heat resistant than *Cl. botulinum.* By targeting a heat treatment at inactivating these spoilage organisms we may be confident that *Cl. botulinum* and all other pathogens in the food will be destroyed.

Thermal Death Time Curves

Bacteria are killed by heat at a rate that is very nearly proportional to the number present in the system being heated. This is referred to as a logarithmic order of death, which means that under constant thermal conditions the same percentage of the bacterial population will be destroyed in a given time interval, regardless of the size of the surviving population. In other words, if a given temperature kills 90% of the population in one minute, 90% of the remaining population will be killed in the second minute, 90% of what is left will be killed in the third minute, and so on.

The logarithmic order of death also applies to bacterial spores, but the slope of the death curve will differ from that of vegetative cells, reflecting the greater heat resistance of spores. This is illustrated in Fig. 79 and 80.

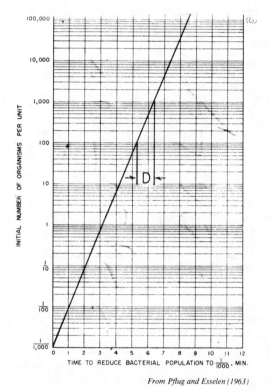

From Pflug and Esselen (1963)

FIG. 79. BACTERIAL DESTRUCTION RATE CURVE SHOWING LOGARITHMIC ORDER OF DEATH

Figure 79 also illustrates the concept of the "D value," which is defined as the time in minutes at a specified temperature required to destroy 90% of the organisms in a population. Thus the D value or decimal reduction time, decreases the surviving population by one log cycle. If a quantity of food in a can contained one million organisms and it received heat for a time equal to four *D* values then it would still contain 100 surviving organisms. If there were 100 such cans in a retort initially and the retort provided heat for a period equivalent to 7 *D* values, then it would be expected that the 100 cans with a total initial bacterial population of 100 million organisms would still contain 10 surviving organisms. Statistically these ten organisms should be distributed between the cans. Obviously, no can can have a fraction of an organism although the 100 cans will average 0.1 organism per can. In this case ten of the cans probably will have one organism each and could possibly ultimately spoil, while 90 of the cans would be sterile.

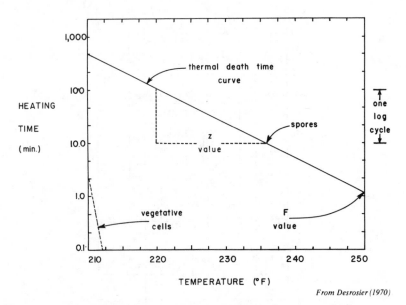

From Desrosier (1970)

FIG. 80. TYPICAL THERMAL DEATH CURVES FOR BACTERIAL SPORES AND
VEGETATIVE CELLS

Figure 80 illustrates two additional terms that are used in defining thermal death curves. These are the "*F* value" and the "*z* value." The *F* value is defined as the number of minutes required to destroy a stated number of organisms at a defined temperature, usually 250°F. The *z* value is the number of degrees Fahrenheit required for a specific thermal death curve to pass through one log cycle (change by a factor of ten). There is still another common term designated F_0 value or "sterilizing value." F_0 value is the time in minutes required to destroy a given number of organisms of a reference strain at a temperature of 250°F when the *z* value is 18°F. F_0 or sterilizing value, a common term in the canning industry, can be expressed by the equation:

$$F_0 = m \times \text{antilog} \frac{T - 250}{18}$$

where, m = minutes, and T = temperature in degrees Fahrenheit. The F_0 requirements for various foods differ and are a measure of the ease or difficulty with which these foods can be heat sterilized.

Thermal death curves have been determined experimentally for many important pathogens and food spoilage organisms. Two such curves for Putrefactive Anaerobe 3679 and *Bacillus stearothermophilus* (FS 1518) are seen in Fig. 81. They tell us how long it takes to kill these organisms (under defined conditions) at a chosen temperature. Thus, for example, we may use a temperature of 220° F, but it would take about 60 min at this temperature to kill a specified number of spores of PA 3679. On the other hand if we use a temperature of 250° F we can kill these spores in little over 1 min.

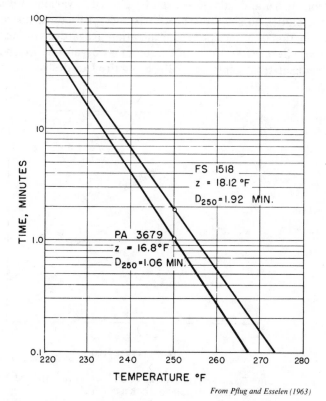

From Pflug and Esselen (1963)

FIG. 81.   THERMAL DEATH CURVES FOR PA3679 AND FS1518

The conditions that must be defined to make a thermal death curve meaningful and applicable to food processing are many. The requirement for a greater heat treatment the larger the initial microbial population, is inherent in the logarithmic order by which bacteria die. In addition, the sensitivities of microorganisms to heat (and therefore the characteristics of the thermal death curve) are markedly affected by the composition of the food in which the heating is done. It already has been pointed out that acid increases the killing power of heat. As will be enlarged upon shortly, many food constituents have an opposite effect upon heat sensitivity of microorganisms and protect them against heat. Thus, a thermal death curve established in a synthetic medium or in a given food is not necessarily applicable to a different food, and thermal death curves, where possible, are best established in the specific food for which a heat process is being designed.

Margin of Safety

Data from thermal death curves can be plotted in various ways. In Fig. 82 data are plotted to show the heat resistance of bacterial spore suspensions as a function of initial spore concentration. Regardless of the temperature chosen, the greater the number of microorganisms or spores, the greater the heat treatment that will be required to destroy them. Thus,

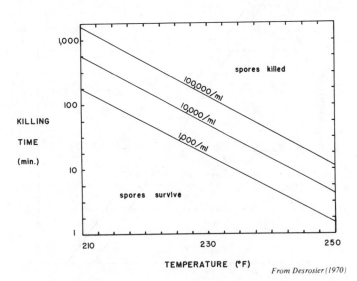

From Desrosier (1970)

FIG. 82. THE GREATER THE SPORE CONCENTRATION THE MORE HEAT REQUIRED TO KILL THEM

while a temperature of 250°F sterilizes a suspension containing 1,000 spores per milliliter in about 2 min, the same temperature would require about 10 min if the concentration of spores was 100,000 per ml.

We generally don't know how many organisms are present in a can of food to be commercially sterilized, or indeed which specific organism types are present. To provide a substantial margin of safety in low-acid foods we may assume that a highly heat-resistant spore former such as *Cl. botulinum* is present and that its population is large. From its thermal death curve established in the same food (or established in a medium giving no greater protection against heat destruction), we then take its D value at the temperature we choose to employ and heat for a time such that every particle of food in the can is exposed to this temperature for a period equal to 12 D values. This is sufficient to decrease any population of *Cl. botulinum* through 12 log cycles. Since even highly spoiled food rarely supports a bacterial population greater than a billion organisms per can, 12 D values will bring the microbial population of the can to a condition of sterility. Had a great number of such cans originally contained 1 billion *Cl. botulinum* organisms, then statistically, after a 12 D heat treatment, only 1 can in 1,000 would be expected to still harbor 1 living organism or spore, the other 999 cans would be sterile. Had the food contained 1 million organisms per can before heating (which is still unusually high) then the same 12 D heat treatment would be expected to render 999,999 cans out of 1 million sterile. Since the 12 D heat treatment also was based on destroying *Cl. botulinum*, it would be still more effective against less heat-resistant sporeformers and other far less heat-resistant nonsporeforming pathogens or spoilage organisms that might be present. When organisms still more heat-resistant than *Cl. botulinum* are chosen as targets for destruction then a heat treatment of less than 12 D values against these may be adequate. Thus, using Putrefactive Anaerobe 3679 (PA 3679) or *Bacillus stearothermophilus* (FS 1518) in low-acid foods, a 5 D heat treatment against these is considered essentially equal to a 12 D value against *Cl. botulinum* and quite sufficient to eliminate microbial spoilage and render the product pathogen-free. However, it should be stated that at the present time there is no general agreement on what theoretical number of survivors of different microorganisms is best for process calculations.

The heat treatments cited above, commonly employed in the canning industry for low-acid foods, would be excessive and unnecessary for acid foods. Acid foods are generally defined as foods having a pH of less than 4.5. Low-acid foods are those foods with a pH greater than 4.5. Table 20 gives the pH values for a number of foods, common spoilage agents associated with these foods, and an indication of the degree of heat processing

TABLE 20

CLASSIFICATION OF CANNED FOODS ON BASIS OF PROCESSING REQUIREMENTS[1]

Acidity Classification	pH Value	Food Item	Food Groups	Spoilage Agents	Heat and Processing Requirements
Low acid	7.0	lye hominy ripe olives, crabmeat, eggs, oysters, milk, corn, duck, chicken, codfish, beef, sardines	meat fish milk poultry	mesophilic spore-forming anaerobic bacteria	high temperature processing 240°–250°F
	6.0	corned beef, lima beans, peas, carrots, beets, asparagus, potatoes	vegetables	thermophiles naturally occurring enzymes in certain processes	
Medium acid	5.0	figs, tomato soup	soup		
	4.5	ravioli, pimientos	manufactured foods	lower limit for growth of *Cl. botulinum*	
Acid		potato salad tomatoes, pears, apricots, peaches, oranges	fruits	non-spore forming aciduric bacteria	boiling water processing (212°F)
	3.7	sauerkraut, pineapple, apple, strawberry, grapefruit	berries	acidic spore-forming bacteria	
High acid	3.0	pickles relish cranberry juice lemon juice	high acid foods (pickles) high acid-high solids foods (jam-jelly)	natural occurring enzymes yeasts molds	
	2.0	lime juice	very acid foods		

[1]From Desrosier (1970).

required for their treatment. With acid foods, in many cases temperatures at or below 212° F for a few minutes constitute adequate heat treatment.

Certain spices and food chemicals also combine with heat in killing microorganisms and so reduce the heat treatment that must be used. Still another factor in permitting lesser heat treatments to be used with acid foods is the sensitivity of *Cl. botulinum* to acid. *Clostridium botulinum* will not grow in foods with a pH below 4.5 (even at room temperature). There-fore such foods even if unheated would not constitute a health hazard from the standpoint of this heat-resistant organism.

THE PROBLEM OF HEAT TRANSFER

Even after we know the time and temperature required to destroy our target organisms from thermal death curves, and provide sufficient margin of safety, we are still far from a safe and reliable heat treatment. The problem now is how to ensure that every particle of food (within the con-tainer if the food is canned) receives the required heat treatment. This be-comes a problem of heat transfer, that is, heat penetration into and throughout the can or mass of food.

If cans are heated from the outside, as would be the case if they are submerged within a retort, the larger the can the longer it will take to heat the center portion of the can to any desired temperature. However, there are several other factors besides size and shape of the can that affect heat penetration into the food within the can. Principal among these factors is the nature and consistency of the food itself. This will determine, for example, whether heat will reach the center by straight conduction or will be speeded by some convection within the can.

Conduction and Convection Heating

Heat energy is transferred by conduction, convection, and radiation. In a retort as used in canning, conduction and convection are important. Conduction is the method of heating in which the heat moves from one particle to another by contact, in more or less straight lines. In the case of conduction the food does not move in the can and there is no circulation to stir hot food with cold food. Convection, on the other hand, is the method of heating which involves movement in the mass being heated. In natural convection the heated portion of food becomes lighter in den-sity and rises, this sets up circulation within the can. This circulation speeds temperature rise of the entire contents of the can. Forced convec-tion is when circulation is promoted mechanically.

It is easily visualized that a liquid food such as canned tomato juice can be readily set into convection heating motion in addition to the heating by conduction it receives through the can wall. On the other hand, a solid food such as corned beef hash is too viscous to circulate, and so it will be virtually completely heated by conduction through the can wall and through itself. A product containing free liquid and solid, such as a can of pears within a sugar syrup, will be intermediate and will rise in temperature from a combination of conduction and convection; conduction through the fruit and convection from the moving syrup. Convection heating is far more rapid than conduction heating and so, other things being equal, if cans of the three products were placed in the same retort, uniform complete heating would be expected to be reached first in the tomato juice, second in the canned pears, and last in the corned beef hash.

Cold Point in Food Masses

Where heat is applied from the outside, as in retorting, regardless of product the food nearest the can surfaces will reach sterilization temperature sooner than the food nearer the center of the can. The point in a can or mass of food which is last to reach the final heating temperature is designated the "cold point" within the can or mass.

It would be expected that in a can of solid food heated by conduction the cold point would be located in the very center of the can and this is so. In foods that undergo convection heating unless the cans are agitated the cold point is somewhat below the dead center of the can. If we are to ensure that commercial sterilization is achieved then we must allow sufficient time for the cold point of cans to reach the sterilization temperature and remain there for the required time interval to destroy our most resistant bacterial spores. If 12 D values are indicated and this corresponds, for example, to 250° F for 2.5 min in our particular system, then if we ensure that the cold point of cans receives 250° F for 2.5 min, or an equivalent heat treatment, we are assured that every other region within the can has been adequately heated.

Determining Process Time

We determine the time requirement of our retort to produce lethal temperature at the cold point with a heat sensing thermocouple. Figure 83 indicates proper placement of the thermocouple to measure temperature at the cold points in the case of canned foods that heat by conduction and natural convection. The cans with thermocouples are filled with the particular food under study, sealed, and placed in the retort. Figure 84 shows such cans with thermocouples attached in the retort waiting to be sterilized. We now admit steam to the retort and record temperature rise with time. In a particular retort filled with a given number of cans of specified size and contents it may require 30 to 40 min for the cold point of cans to reach

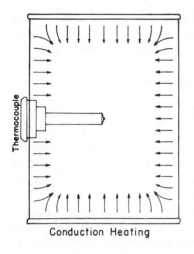
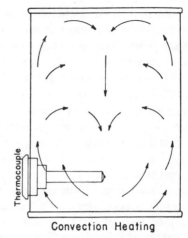

Conduction Heating   Convection Heating

Courtesy American Can Co.

FIG. 83. THERMOCOUPLE PLACEMENT WHEN HEATING IS PRIMARILY BY CONDUCTION OR CONVECTION

Courtesy American Can Co.

FIG. 84. CANS IN RETORT READY FOR HEAT PENETRATION TEST

250° F or a lethal temperature close to it. This is due to the "come-up" time required for the retort to reach processing temperature plus the time for heat penetration into the cans. We then add additional holding time and thus complete our sterilization requirement.

While a lethal effect at the cold point equivalent, for example, to 250° F for 2.5 min may be called for, this degree of lethality can be achieved by various equivalent time-temperature exposures. Further, since the temperature rise during heat penetration of the can also accomplishes a degree of microbial destruction this is commonly accounted for, and the required holding time decreased accordingly. The cans are now quickly cooled to prevent additional heat damage to the food. Because cooling is not instantaneous, some additional microbial destruction also occurs during the cooling period. Thus, to calculate effective retort process treatments, accurate heat penetration and cooling curves must be established. Total lethality of the process then represents a summation of the lethal effects of changing temperatures with time during the entire retort operation.

Since come-up time and penetration time will vary between different retorts, different size and shape of cans or bottles, and different compositions of foods, it is obvious that the required heat treatment must be determined for each specific case. A great deal of experience has been gained by the canning industry over the past 40 yr and mathematical formulas have been developed for calculating effective heat treatments if bacterial death curve data, heat penetration properties of the food, and certain characteristics of the retort are known. The formulas have been used to set up simple tables of heat treatments for different foods and can sizes and these can be found in appropriate canning references (Table 21). However, when a new product is developed such as a new baby food composition or perhaps

TABLE 21

PROCESS TIME FOR VEGETABLES IN 307 × 409 CANS AND NO. 303 GLASS JARS [1]

	Initial	307 × 409 Cans		No. 303 Jars	
Product	Temp, °F	Min at 240° F	Min at 250° F	Min at 240° F	Min at 250° F
Green beans, whole or cut	70	21	12	25	...
Lima beans, succulent	70	40	20	45	...
Beets, whole, cut, diced	70	35	23	35	...
Carrots, whole, cut	70	35	23	30	...
Corn, cream style	160	100	80	105	80
Corn, whole kernel in brine	100	55	30	50	30
Peas in brine	70	36	16	45	25
Peas and carrots	70	45	20	45	...
Potatoes, white, small whole	70	35	23	35	25
Pumpkin or squash	160	80	65	80	65

[1] From National Canners Assoc. (1966, 1971).

a special chow mein blend, then specific determinations of effective heat treatments along the described lines must be made.

PROTECTIVE EFFECTS OF FOOD CONSTITUENTS

There are several constituents of foods which protect microorganisms to various degrees against heat. Thus sugar in high concentration is protective to bacterial spores, and canned fruit in a sugar syrup generally requires a higher temperature or longer time for sterilization than the same fruit without sugar. Starch and protein in foods generally act somewhat like sugar. Fats and oils have a great protective effect upon microorganisms and their spores, and the mechanism of this protection involves interference with the penetration of wet heat. As has been noted, wet heat at a given temperature is more lethal than dry heat. Moisture is an effective conductor of heat and penetrates into microbial cells and spores. If microorganisms are trapped within fat globules then moisture can less readily penetrate into the cells and heating becomes more like dry heat. In the same can or food mass, organisms in the liquid phase may be quickly killed while most of an effective heat treatment is required for inactivation of the oil phase flora. This makes sterilization of meat products and fish packed in oil very difficult, and severe heat treatments required often adversely affect other food constituents. There is more fat and more sugar in ice cream mix than there is in milk, and for the same reasons ice cream mix must be pasteurized at a higher temperature or for a longer time than milk to accomplish equivalent bacterial destruction.

It must also be appreciated that in addition to any direct protective effects of food constituents on microorganisms there are the indirect effects related to differences in heat conductivity rates through different food materials. Thus fat is a poorer conductor of heat than water. Further, and often more important, are the effects related to food consistency and its influence on whether conduction or convection heating will take place. If sufficient starch or other thickener is added to a food composition to convert it from a convection heated system to a conduction heated system, then in addition to any direct microbial protection there will be a slowing down of the heat penetration rate to the cold point within the container or food mass, and this too will protect microorganisms. Interesting patents have recently been issued related to this very point. Many foods are supplemented with starch to increase their viscosity. Common starches in solution thicken upon heating. This results in a slowing down of the rate of convection within cans during retorting and the need for longer retort times. Special starches have been developed which do not thicken on early heating but instead thicken on later heating or on cooling. Foods supplemented with these starches retain maximum convection rates in the retort permitting shortened retort times and less heat damage. Then upon cooling the starch imparts the desired thickening. In a typical application a product like chow mein can be heated with less softening of the vegetables from excessive heating yet possess the desired viscosity in the liquid phase.

INOCULATED PACK STUDIES

The many variables discussed above make the calculation of safe heat treatments from formulas alone difficult and somewhat risky, especially when applied to new products. In practice, therefore, formulas based upon thermal death curves, heat penetration rates, and properties of specific retorts are used to gain an approximation of the safe heat treatment, but results are checked by what are termed inoculated pack studies.

In inoculated pack studies we inoculate a substantial population of a heat resistant food spoilage organism such as PA 3679 into cans of food and then process the cans in a retort. If formulas call for 60 min of heat, we may heat representative cans for 50, 55, 60, 65, and 70 min. The cans are then incubated at a temperature that would be favorable for growth of any surviving spores (Fig. 85). The cans are periodically examined for evidence of growth and spoilage, such as bulging from gas production. Samples of

Courtesy American Can Co.

FIG. 85. CANS BEING EXAMINED FOR BULGING AS EVIDENCE OF SPOILAGE

nonbulging cans also are examined bacteriologically. The shortest heat treatment which produces cans with no evidence of bacterial survival is then taken as the effective heat treatment to be used for subsequent commercial packs.

DIFFERENT TEMPERATURE-TIME COMBINATIONS

While temperature and time are required to destroy microorganisms, different temperature-time combinations that are equally effective in microbial destruction can be far different with regard to their damaging effect upon foods. This is of the greatest practical importance in modern heat processing and is the basis for several of the more advanced heat preservation methods.

If the time-temperature combinations required for destruction of *Cl. botulinum* in low-acid media are taken from thermal death curves the following will be found to be equally effective:

0.78 min at 260° F	10 min at 240° F
1.45 min at 255° F	36 min at 230° F
2.78 min at 250° F	150 min at 220° F
5.27 min at 245° F	330 min at 212° F

This illustrates the simple relationship that the higher the temperature the less time will be required for microbial destruction. This principle holds true for all types of microorganisms and spores. On the other hand foods are not equally resistant to these combinations and the more important factor in damaging foods with respect to color, flavor, texture and nutritional value is long time rather than high temperature. If we were to inoculate milk with *Cl. botulinum* and then heat samples for 330 min at 212° F, 10 min at 240° F, and less than 1 min at 260° F, which would produce equal microbial destruction, heat damage to the milk would be enormously different. The sample heated for 330 min would be thoroughly cooked in flavor and brown in color. The ten-minute sample would be almost as bad. The one-minute sample while still somewhat overheated would not be far different from unheated milk. This difference in sensitivity to time and temperature between microorganisms and various foods is a general phenomenon. It applies to milk, meat, juices, and generally all other heat sensitive food materials.

The greater relative sensitivity of microorganisms than food constituents to high temperatures can be quantitatively defined in terms of different temperature coefficients for their destruction. Thus, while each increase of 18° F in temperature approximately doubles the rate of chemical reactions contributing to food deterioration, these same 18° F increases, above the maximum temperature for growth, produce approximately a ten-fold increase in the rate of microbial destruction. Since higher temperatures permit use of shorter times for microbial destruction, and shorter times favor food quality retention, we employ high temperature-short time heating treatments rather than low temperature-long time heating treatments for heat sensitive foods whenever possible.

In pasteurizing certain acid fruit juices, for example, the industry formerly used treatments of about 145°F for 30 min. Today they use flash pasteurization such as 190°F for 1 min, 212°F for 12 sec, or 250°F for 2 sec. While bacterial destruction is very nearly equivalent, the 250°F two-second treatment gives the best quality juice with respect to flavor and vitamin retention. Such short holding times, however, require special equipment which is more difficult to design and generally is more expensive than the 145°F 30-min type of processing equipment.

HEATING MAY PRECEDE OR FOLLOW PACKAGING

The foregoing principles very largely determine the design parameters for heat preservation equipment and commercial practices. The food processor will employ no less than that heat treatment which gives the necessary degree of microorganism destruction. This is further ensured by periodic inspections from the Food and Drug Administration or equivalent local authorities. However, the food processor also will want to use the mildest effective heat treatment to ensure highest food quality.

It is convenient to separate heat preservation practices into two broad categories; one involves heating of foods in their final containers, the other employs heat prior to packaging. The latter category includes methods that are inherently less damaging to food quality where the food can be readily subdivided (such as liquids) for rapid heat exchange. However, these methods then require packaging under aseptic or nearly aseptic conditions to prevent or at least minimize recontamination. On the other hand, heating within the package frequently is less costly and produces quite acceptable quality with the majority of foods, and most of our present canned food supply is heated within the package.

Heating Food in Containers

Still Retort.—One of the simplest applications of heating food in containers is sterilization of cans in a still retort, that is, the cans remain still while they are being heated. Illustrations of typical equipment appeared in previous figures. In this type of retort, temperatures above 250°F generally may not be used or foods cook against the can walls. This is especially true of solid type foods which do not circulate within the cans by convection, but it also can be a problem with liquid foods. Because 250°F is the upper temperature, and there is relatively little movement in the cans, the heating time to bring the cold point to sterilizing temperature is relatively long; for a small can of peas it is about 40 min.

Agitating Retorts.—This time can be markedly reduced by shaking the cans during heating, especially with liquid or semiliquid type foods. Not only is processing time shortened but food quality is improved. This is accomplished with various kinds of agitating retorts, one type of which is seen in Fig. 86. Part of the wall has been cut away to show the cans resting in reels which rotate and thereby shake the contents. Forced convection within cans also depends upon degree of can filling, since some free headspace within cans is necessary for optimum food turnover within the cans. In addition to faster heating, since the can contents are in motion there is less chance for food to cook onto the can walls. This permits the use of higher temperatures than the 250° F upper limit for a still retort, which further speeds heating times.

Agitation may be of more than one type; for example cans may be made to turn end over end or to spin in an axial fashion with their length. Depending upon the physical properties of the food, one or another method may be more effective. The reduction in processing times possible with agitating retorts compared to still retorts is seen in Table 22. These substantial reductions in time with associated quality advantages would not be realized in foods that heat primarily by conduction, and for such foods the simpler and generally less costly still retorts may be quite satisfactory.

Pressure Considerations.—Whether still or agitating retorts are used, the high temperatures required for sterilization or commercial sterilization commonly are obtained from steam under pressure. Steam pressures of

Courtesy of FMC Corp.

FIG. 86. CUT-AWAY VIEW OF A CONTINUOUS AGITATING RETORT

TABLE 22

HIGHER TEMPERATURES AND FORCED CONVECTION OF AGITATING RETORT
SHORTEN PROCESS TIMES [1]

Product	Can Size	Process-Agitated at 260°F		Conventional	
		Time Min	Temp °F	Time Min	Temp °F
Peas	307 × 409	4.90	260	35	240
Carrots	307 × 409	3.40	260	30	240
Beets—sliced	307 × 409	4.10	260	30	240
Asparagus spears	307 × 409	4.50	270	16	248
Asparagus—cuts and tips	307 × 409	4.00	270	15	248
Cabbage	307 × 409	2.75	270	40	240
Asparagus—spears					
brine packed	307 × 409	5.20	260	50	240
brine packed	603 × 700	10.00	260	80	240
vacuum packed	307 × 306	5.00	260	35	250
Mushroom soup	603 × 700	19.00	260	..	..
Evaporated milk	300 × 314	2.25	200	18	240

[1] From Clifcorn et al. (1950).

approximately 10, 15, and 20 psi (above atmospheric) are required for heating at 240°, 250°, and 260° F. Moist foods in cans have part of their moisture converted to steam at these temperatures and produce equivalent pressures within the cans. An exception to this is when foods are canned under vacuum. Then the final pressure within a can will be less than the pressure in the retort to an extent determined by the degree of vacuum used at time of can closure. Control of pressure differences inside and outside of cans and other containers during and following heat treatment are of obvious importance to prevent mechanical damage to containers. Several techniques are employed to prevent such damage.

If degrees of vacuum within cans are such that retort pressures cause can collapse, then a heavier gage of steel may be called for. More commonly, pressure problems are due to greater pressures within the container than on its outside. This occurs when steam pressure is too rapidly released in closing down a batch-type retort or when heated containers are too suddenly conveyed from a continuous pressure retort to atmospheric pressure. The problem is greater in the case of glass jars than with cans since excessive internal pressure can easily blow the lids from glass jars since these generally have a weaker seal than the lids of cans. Thus in the case of retorting glass jars, provisions are made for air pressure over a layer of water to balance internal and external pressures. Partial cooling of containers before releasing them from retorts is the common way to decrease internal container pressure. Many continuous retorts, such as the agitating type in Fig. 86, provide semipressurized cooling zones following the heating zone just prior to release of cans to atmospheric pressure.

From Pflug et al. (1963)

FIG. 87. VERTICAL-SLOT RACK TO HOLD FLEXIBLE POUCHES
DURING RETORTING

With the increasing use of flexible packaging materials there is considerable interest in sterilizing foods in plastic pouches. Here pressure problems can be still greater than with glass jars. In addition, a uniform heat treatment requires that the pouches be evenly exposed to the heating medium rather than be allowed to pile up in the retort from water currents. One means of better controlling pouches during retorting is to sandwich the pouches between rigid supports (Fig. 87).

Hydrostatic Cooker and Cooler.—Continuous retorts (usually of the agitating type) are pressure-tight and built with special valves and locks for admitting and removing cans from the sterilizing chamber. Without these, pressure conditions would not be held constant and sterilizing temperatures could not be closely controlled. Another type of continuous pressure retort which is open to the atmosphere at the inlet and outlet ends is the hydrostatic pressure cooker and cooler.

This type of heating equipment consists essentially of a "U" tube with an enlarged lower section. Steam is admitted to the enlarged section and hot water fills one of the legs of the "U" while cool water fills the other leg (Fig. 88). Cans are carried by a chain conveyor down the hot water leg, through the steam zone which may involve an undulating path to increase residence time, and up the cool water leg. These legs are sufficiently

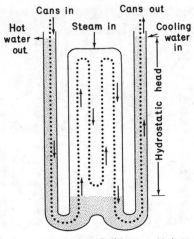

Courtesy Food Processing-Marketing

FIG. 88. HYDROSTATIC COOKER AND COOLER ILLUSTRATING
HOW STEAM PRESSURE IS BALANCED BY WATER HEADS

high to produce a hydrostatic head pressure to balance the steam pressure in the sterilizing zone. If a temperature of 260° F is used in the sterilizing zone then this would be equal to a pressure of about 20 psi (above atmospheric), which would be balanced by water heights of about 46 ft in the hot and cold legs.

As cans descend the hot water leg and enter the steam zone their internal pressure increases as food moisture begins to boil. But this is balanced by the increasing external hydrostatic pressure. Similarly, as high pressure cans pass through the water seal and ascend the cool water leg, their gradually reduced internal pressure is balanced by the decreasing hydrostatic head in this cool leg. In this way cans are not subjected to sudden changes in pressure. For this reason the system also is well suited to the retorting of foods and beverages in jars and bottles.

Direct Flame Sterilization.—Where sterilizing temperatures above 212° F are needed, steam under pressure generally is the heat exchange medium, and vessels capable of withstanding pressure add to the cost of equipment. A new method, recently introduced from Europe, employs direct flame to contact cans as the cans are rotated in the course of being conveyed past gas jets. Excellent rates of heating are claimed with high product quality and reduced processing costs, but commercial experience with this type of system is still somewhat limited.

In-Package Pasteurization.—In-package heating need not be to the point of sterilization or commercial sterilization. Tunnels of various designs are used to pasteurize food and beverages in cans, bottles, and jars

From Pflug and Esselen (1963)

FIG. 89. LOADING END OF CONTINUOUS STEAM HEATED PASTEURIZER

(Fig. 89). Hot water sprays or steam jets are directed at the containers and varying temperature zones progressing to cooling temperatures are commonly employed. Temperature changes must be gradual to prevent thermal shock to glass. Such systems are at atmospheric pressure. This is one of the methods of pasteurizing beer in containers.

Heating Food Prior to Packaging

As already stated, there are advantages to heating heat-sensitive foods prior to packaging. These are related to the ability to heat rapidly by exposing food in a subdivided state to a heat exchange surface or medium, rather than having to allow appreciable time for heat penetration into a relatively large volume of food in a container.

Batch Pasteurization.—One of the earliest and simplest methods of rendering liquid foods, such as milk, free of pathogens is to heat them in a vat with mild agitation. Raw milk commonly is pumped into a steam heated jacketed vat, brought to temperature, held for the prescribed time, and then pumped over a plate type cooler prior to bottling or paper cartoning. In the case of milk the product must be quickly brought to 145° F, held at this temperature for 30 min, and rapidly cooled. In addition to being freed of common pathogens this heat treatment also inactivates the milk enzyme lipase which otherwise would quickly cause the milk to become rancid. Batch pasteurization, also known as the holding method of pasteurization, is still widely practiced, especially in smaller dairies, but it has largely given way to high temperature-short time continuous pasteurization.

High Temperature-Short Time Pasteurization.—High temperature-short time (HTST) pasteurization of raw milk employs a temperature of at least 161° F for at least 15 sec. This is equivalent in bacterial destruction to the batch method.

In HTST pasteurization (Fig. 90) raw milk held in a cool storage tank is pumped through a plate type heat exchanger and brought to temperature. The key to the process now rests in ensuring that every particle of the milk remains at no lower than 161° F for no less than 15 sec. This is accomplished by pumping the heated milk through a holding tube of such length and diameter that it takes every milk particle at least 15 sec to pass through the tube. At the end of the tube is an accurate temperature sensing device and valve. Should any milk reach the end of the holding tube and be down in temperature even one degree, the valve known as a flow diversion valve checks this flow of milk and sends it back through the heat exchanger once again to be reheated. In this way no milk escapes the required heat treatment. Frequent checks of the equipment are made by

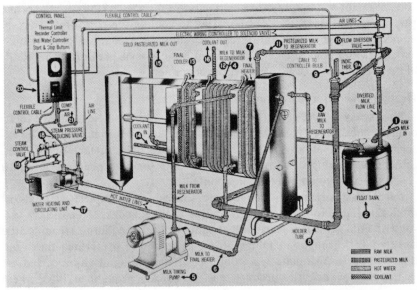

Courtesy of C. P. Div., St. Regis

FIG. 90. FLOW DIAGRAM OF A HIGH TEMPERATURE-SHORT TIME PASTEURIZATION
SYSTEM FOR MILK

authorized milk inspectors to help ensure its proper operation. After emerging from the holding tube the milk is cooled and may be cartoned or bottled. Cooling not only prevents further heat damage to the milk but also retards subsequent bacterial multiplication since the milk is not sterile.

Pasteurization by the HTST method is not limited to milk and is widely used in the food industry. However, times and temperatures vary in accordance with the effects of different foods upon microorganism survival, and the heat sensitivities of these foods.

Aseptic Canning.—It is possible to shorten sterilizing times down to seconds and even fractions of a second, and for many products this results in a marked improvement in quality. This can be done with canned foods by the methods of aseptic canning. Aseptic canning refers to a technique in which food is sterilized or commercially sterilized outside of the can and then aseptically placed in previously sterilized cans which are subsequently sealed. The point behind aseptic canning is that while food in a container will require many minutes or even hours, depending upon container size, to reach sterilizing temperature, food outside a container may be passed through an efficient heat exchanger and brought to sterilization temperature almost instantaneously. It then remains to provide sterile cans and lids and to fill the cans and seal them in an aseptic environment. Food temperatures employed may be as high as 300° F and sterilization takes place in 1 or 2 sec yielding food products of the highest quality.

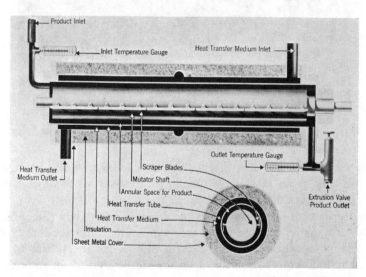

Courtesy of Girdler Corp.

FIG. 91. TUBULAR SCRAPED-SURFACE-TYPE HEAT EXCHANGER

Quick heating of liquid foods may be done in a plate-type heat exchanger (previous Fig. 39), or in a tubular scraped-surface-type heat exchanger (Fig. 91). This latter type consists essentially of a tube within a tube. Steam flows through the space between the tubes while food flows through the inner tube. The inner tube also is provided with a rotating shaft or mutator equipped with scraper blades to prevent food from burning onto the heat exchange surface. In contact with the hot surface the thin layer of food may be brought to sterilization temperature in a second or less. If it is desired to prolong residence time beyond this, then a holding tube is added as in the case of HTST pasteurization. Such rapid sterilization at extremely high temperatures, as 1 or 2 sec at 300° F, sometimes is referred to as ultra-high-temperature (UHT) sterilization. The sterile food must now be quickly cooled, since at these high temperatures product

Courtesy of James Dole Engineering Co.

FIG. 92. ASEPTIC CANNING LINE

quality can be impaired in seconds. Quick cooling can be accomplished with the same types of plate or tubular scraped-surface heat exchangers, used with refrigerants instead of steam.

The sterile cool food now enters the aseptic canning line (Fig. 92). This consists of a tunnel through which cans without their lids are conveyed and sterilized by superheated steam, a sterile filling zone also heated by steam where the food enters the cans, a heated sterile can lid dispenser, and a closing machine which seals cans under a steam heated sterile atmosphere. After cans are sealed they may be further cooled with sprays of

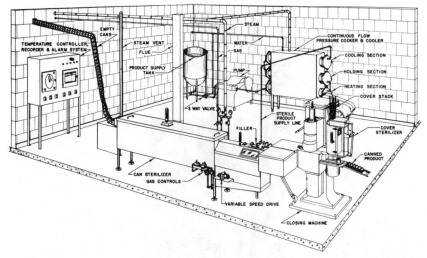

Courtesy of James Dole Engineering Co.

FIG. 93. PLANT LAYOUT COMBINING QUICK FOOD STERILIZATION EQUIP-
MENT AND ASEPTIC CANNING LINE

water. Not only must food temperature be accurately controlled before entering the aseptic canning line, but can and lid sterilization temperatures must also be controlled since tinplate begins to melt at about 450° F, and superheated steam can be higher than this in temperature. A complete plant layout, combining quick food sterilization equipment and the aseptic canning line is illustrated in Fig. 93.

Advances in Aseptic Canning.—The system pictured in Fig. 93 is suitable for liquid foods or foods of thin consistency, such as concentrated milk, soups, or possibly creamed corn. By changing the type of heat exchanger and the pumps and lines leading to the aseptic canning line, chunk type foods such as chow mein or chicken à la king can be aseptically canned. In this case intimate heat contact with chunk type foods to achieve rapid sterilization can be accomplished with direct steam injection type heat exchangers (Fig. 94). In using direct steam injection it is essential that the steam does not contain any impurities that may have come from the boiler. Today, there are direct steam injectors that generate steam from softened purified water to eliminate such impurities. Steam injection heating is not restricted to use with aseptic canning. Many foods are cooked, pasteurized, or otherwise quickly heated by this method.

Great quantities of food materials are used as intermediates in the production of further processed foods. This frequently requires packaging of such items as tomato paste or apricot puree in large containers such

Courtesy of The W. J. Fitzpatrick Co.

FIG. 94.   DIRECT STEAM INJECTION TYPE HEATER

as 55-gal. drums since smaller containers would involve unnecessary expense. The food manufacturer then may use the tomato paste in the production of ketchup or the apricot in bakery products. If such large volumes were to be sterilized for keeping properties in 55-gal. drums, then by the time the cold point reached sterilization temperature the product nearer the drum walls would be excessively scorched. Such items also can be quickly sterilized in efficient heat exchangers and aseptically drummed. In this case, large chambers have been developed in which the drums and lids are sterilized under superheated steam and product filled and sealed aseptically within the chamber. This technology has advanced to the point where sterile food can be aseptically filled into previously sterilized tank cars.

Aseptic packaging is not limited to metal containers. An aseptic bottling system for processing UHT sterilized cream has very recently been put on a commercial basis. However engineering problems related to glass breakage from thermal shock have not yet been completely eliminated.

Another form of aseptic packaging utilizes flexible packaging materials which are sterilized, formed, filled, and sealed in a continuous operation. In some cases the disinfectant property of hydrogen peroxide is combined with heat to make lower temperatures effective in sterilizing these less heat-resistant packaging materials. Coffee cream is put up in small single service paper packets this way. Chlorine and other chemicals can be expected to find wider use in such applications in the future.

Hot Pack or Hot Fill.—The terms hot pack or hot fill refer to the filling of previously pasteurized or sterilized foods, while still hot, into clean but not necessarily sterile containers, under clean but not necessarily aseptic conditions. Here we depend upon the heat of the food and some holding period before cooling the closed container to render the container commercially sterile.

Hot pack, as distinguished from aseptic canning, is most effective with acid foods since lower temperatures in the presence of acid are lethal; and further, below pH 4.5 *Clostridium botulinum* will not grow or produce toxin so this health hazard is not present. Hot pack with low-acid foods (above pH 4.5) is not feasible unless the product is recognized as being only pasteurized and will be stored under refrigeration; or, unless the hot pack treatment is combined with some additional means of preservation such as a very high sugar content. This is because the residual heat of the food in the absence of appreciable acid is not sufficient to guarantee destruction of spores that may be present on container surfaces or enter containers during filling and sealing. Even with acid foods, very definite food temperatures and holding times in the sealed containers before they are cooled for warehouse storage must be adhered to for hot pack processing to be effective. These temperatures and times depend upon the specific product's pH and other food characteristics.

In home canning, when fruit and sugar are boiled together to make jam, and the hot jam is poured into jars that have been previously boiled, the principle of hot pack is being employed. Home canning instructions further call for inverting the filled jars after a short time. This is to ensure that the hot acid product also contacts all surfaces of the jar lid for sterilization. But for home canning of meats and other low-acid foods directions always call for pressure cooking of closed containers as is done in conventional commercial retorting.

In commercial practice, most acid juices such as orange, grapefruit, grape, tomato, and various acid fruits as well as some acid vegetables such as sauerkraut, commonly are hot packed following prior pasteurization or sterilization. Typically, acid fruits and juices are first heated in the range

of about 170° to 210° F for about 30 to 60 sec, hot filled no lower than
170° F and often closer to 200° F, and held at this temperature for about
1 to 3 min including an inversion before cooling. In the case of tomato
juice, a common practice is HTST heating of the juice at 250° F for 0.7
min, cooling below the boiling point but not below 195° F for hot fill can
sterilization, and can holding for 3 min including an inversion before final
cooling. Precise times and temperatures depend upon the pH of the particular tomato juice batch, and can be confirmed by inoculated pack studies.

"Flash 18" Process.—Where conventional hot pack processing is
not feasible for low-acid foods, still another method of heating such
foods prior to packaging has found limited use. The "Flash 18" process,
also known as the Smith-Ball process after its originators, goes back to
about 1953. As previously indicated, low-acid foods require heating well
above 212° F for sterility. If filling of containers is attempted at such temperatures under atmospheric pressure, violent product boiling during can
filling and sealing occurs. The "Flash 18" process takes care of this boiling problem by placing the entire canning line, including operating personnel, within a room-like pressure chamber under a pressure of 18 to 20
psi (above atmospheric). Under this pressure water does not boil below a
temperature of approximately 255° to 260° F. Therefore, low-acid foods
can be presterilized by HTST techniques and pumped to the filling line
within the pressurized room without boiling over at the filler. Cans are
then sealed, held for an appropriate number of minutes and cooled. A filling temperature as high as 255° F for several minutes produces commercial
sterility in the previously nonsterile containers although the food in contact with the container wall is low in acid.

In this process operators can perform comfortably in the 18 to 20 psi
pressurized room. However, they must enter and leave the pressurized
room through a small antiroom that serves as an air lock. Here, on entering, pressure is gradually increased to accomodate them to the pressure
within the canning room. Also, they must undergo decompression back to
atmospheric pressure in the antiroom before returning to the normal environment.

Microwave Heating

Microwave energy produces heat in materials that absorb it. Microwave
energy and energies of closely related frequencies are finding ever increasing applications in the food industry. These include heat preservation.
Microwave energy heats foods in a unique fashion that largely eliminates
temperature gradients between the surface and center of food masses.
Foods do not heat from the outside to the inside as with conventional
heating since microwave penetration can generate heat throughout the

food mass simultaneously. In this case the concept of cold point, and the limitations of conventional heat penetration rates are not directly applicable. The use of microwaves can result in very rapid heating but requires special equipment, and often specific packaging materials since microwaves will not pass through tin cans or metal foils. Microwave heating also can produce major differences in food appearance and other properties compared with the more conventional methods of heating. More will be said about microwave heating in Chap. 11.

BIBLIOGRAPHY

ALSTRAND, D. V., and BENJAMIN, H. A. 1949. Thermal processing of canned foods in tin containers. V. Effect of retorting procedures on sterilization values in canned foods. Food Res. *14*, 253–260.

ANDERSON, E. E., ESSELEN, W. B., JR., and FELLERS, C. R. 1949. Effect of acid salt, sugar, and other food ingredients on thermal resistance of *Bacillus thermoacidurans*. Food Res. *14*, 499–510.

BALL, C. O. 1923. Thermal process time for canned foods. Natl. Res. Council Bull. 7.

BALL, C. O., and OLSON, F. C. W. 1957. Sterilization in Food Technology. McGraw-Hill Book Co, New York.

BIGELOW, W. D. 1921. The logarithmic nature of thermal death time curves. J. Infect. Diseases *29*, 528–532.

BOARD, R. W. 1953. Factors affecting the practical determination of thermal processes. Paper presented at 3rd Ann. Conv. Inst. Food Technologists, Australian Regional Sect., May.

BOYD, J. M., and BOCK, J. H. 1952. Vacuum in canned foods—vs. significance and the measurement. Natl. Canners Assoc. Inform. Letter *1371*, 41–44.

BRODY, A. L. 1971. Food canning in rigid and flexible packages. Critical Rev. Food Technol., July, 187–243.

CARLSON, V. R. 1969. Aseptic Processing. Cherry-Burrell Corp., Chicago.

CLIFCORN, L. E., PETERSON, G. T., BOYD, J. M., and O'NEIL, J. H. 1950. A new principle for agitating in processing canned foods. Bull. *20*. Continental Can Co., Chicago.

CURRAN, H. R. 1935. Influence of some environmental factors upon the thermal resistance of bacterial spores. J. Infect. Diseases *56*, 373–380.

DESROSIER, N. W. 1970. The Technology of Food Preservation, 3rd Edition. Avi Publishing Co., Westport, Conn.

ECKLUND, O. F. 1949. Apparatus for measurement of the rate of heat penetration in canned food. Food Technol. *3*, 231–233.

GILLESPY, P. G. 1951. Estimation of sterilizing values of processes as applied to canned food. I. Packs heating by conduction. J. Sci. Food Agr. *2*, 108–125.

GOFF, H. R. 1970. An outline of recent developments in aseptic processing. *In* Symp. Innovation in Food Engineering, Univ. of Calif. March 1970.

GOLDBLITH, S. A., JOSLYN, M. A., and NICKERSON, J. T. R. 1961 Introduction to Thermal Processing of Foods. Avi Publishing Co., Westport, Conn.

HALL, C. W., and TROUT, G. M. 1968. Milk Pasteurization. Avi Publishing Co., Westport, Conn.

KIRATSOUS, A. S., FRANCIS, F. J., and ZAHRADNIK, J. W. 1962. Temperature profiles of thickening agents in high temperature-short time and retort processing. Food Technol. *16*, No. 7, 107–110.

LOPEZ, A. 1969. A Complete Course in Canning. Canning Trade, Baltimore.

MERRILL, D. G. 1948. Heating rates of foods in glass and other containers. Ind. Eng. Chem. *40*, 2263–2269.

NATIONAL CANNERS ASSOC. 1959. An information bulletin on retort operation. Natl. Canners Assoc. Bull. *32-L*.

NATIONAL CANNERS ASSOC. 1966. Processes for low-acid canned foods in metal containers. Natl. Canners Assoc. Bull. *26-L*.

NATIONAL CANNERS ASSOC. 1968. Laboratory Manual for Food Canners and Processors, Vol. 1. Avi Publishing Co., Westport, Conn.

NATIONAL CANNERS ASSOC. 1971. Processes for low-acid canned foods in glass containers. Natl. Canners Assoc. Bull. *30-L*.

PEEPLES, M. L. 1962. Forced convection heat transfer characteristics of fluid milk products. A review. J. Dairy Sci. *45*, 293–302.

PFLUG, I. J., BOCK, J. H., and LONG, F. E. 1963. Sterilization of food in flexible packages. Food Technol. *17*, 1167–1172.

PFLUG, I. J., and ESSELEN, W. B. 1963. Food processing by heat sterilization *In* Food Processing Operations, Vol. 2. M. A. Joslyn, and J. L. Heid (Editors). Avi Publishing Co., Westport, Conn.

REED, J. M., BOHRER, C. W., and CAMERON, E. J. 1951. Spore destruction rate studies on organisms of significance in the processing of canned foods. Food Res. *16*, 383–408.

SCHULTZ, O. T., and OLSON, F. C. W. 1938. Thermal processing of canned foods in tin containers. I. Variation of heating rate with can size for products heating by convection. Food Res. *3*, 647–753.

SOGNEFEST, P., HAYS, G. L., WHEATON, E., and BENJAMIN, H. A. 1948. Effect of pH on thermal process requirements of canned food. Food Res. *13*, 400–416.

STUMBO, C. R. 1965. Thermobacteriology in Food Processing. Academic Press, New York.

CHAPTER 9

Cold Preservation and Processing

INTRODUCTION

Freezing and cold storage are among the oldest methods of food preservation, and in frigid climates foods naturally frozen were thawed and consumed by prehistoric man. In more recent times, such as the latter half of the nineteenth century, some fish, meat, and poultry were being frozen and commercially sold in the United States but the amounts were insignificant. These were frozen out of doors in winter months and shipped short distances in iced wagons. At the same time, ice-salt mixtures were being employed to a limited extent to obtain and hold somewhat lower temperatures than could be maintained with pure ice. It was not until 1875 that a mechanical ammonia refrigeration system capable of supporting commercial exploitation of refrigerated warehousing and of the freezing process was invented. The use of mechanical refrigeration to freeze food immediately was hampered by the lack of refrigerated warehousing facilities—a prime requirement for any refrigerated or frozen food industry. Over the next quarter century refrigerated warehouses came into existence in increasing numbers but store and household refrigerators were virtually nonexistent, to say nothing of food freezers. As late as the 1920's food delivered to a market in a frozen state commonly thawed before it could be brought home, or else thawed in household ice boxes and generally was of marginal to poor quality.

In the 1920's Clarence Birdseye entered the field, and through his researches on quick freezing processes, equipment, frozen products, and frozen food packaging our modern frozen food industry was initiated. Birdseye also pioneered in promoting consumer units of frozen foods through the next 20 yr. Acceptance grew rapidly as household refrigerators and freezers became more common. Today freezing as a food preservation method is steadily increasing in importance in terms of volume of food processed and value of product, and in the United States it is expected that freezing of foods will grow in volume to eventually approximate and perhaps equal canning as the two major methods of food preservation.

Currently one excellent measure of the technological development of a society is the extent of its refrigerated and frozen food processing, transportation, storage, and merchandising facilities. Long before these technological achievements were made, tribes and nations of temperate and colder climates were more fortunate than peoples in warmer climates since they could store their harvests and turn their attentions to other things, while peoples in warmer climates had to gather much of their food daily if it was to be edible. This situation still exists in the world today. Less developed regions generally are outstanding in their lack of refrigeration facilities and this makes the task of improving their food situation that much more difficult.

Refrigeration today markedly influences the practices of agriculture and marketing and sets the economic climate of the food industry. Great Britain, for example, depends upon Australia for her beef and mutton; without refrigeration in transit this would be impossible. The same situation exists with respect to eastern U.S. cities depending upon California for much of their fruits and vegetables. Refrigeration and cold storage equalize food prices throughout the year. Without them prices would be at a low at the time of harvest and extremely high later on, if indeed the foods were available at all.

DISTINCTION BETWEEN REFRIGERATION AND FREEZING

When we talk about cold preservation and processing we must make a distinction between refrigeration and cool storage on the one hand, and freezing and frozen storage on the other.

By cool storage we generally mean storage at temperatures above freezing, and this covers a range of about 60° F down to 28° F. Commercial and household refrigerators are usually run at 40° to 45° F. Commercial refrigerators will sometimes be operated at a slightly lower temperature where a particular food is being favored. While pure water will freeze at 32° F, most foods will not begin to freeze until about 28° F or lower is reached.

Frozen storage as the name implies, refers to storage at temperatures where the food is maintained in frozen condition. Good frozen storage generally means 0° F. or below.

Refrigerated or cool storage generally will preserve perishable foods for days or weeks depending upon the food. Frozen storage will preserve perishable foods for months or even years. The remarkable preservation potential of sufficiently low temperatures are interestingly emphasized when occasionally frozen mastodons and other ancient creatures are uncovered by explorers, and found still to be intact.

Further distinctions between refrigeration and freezing temperatures are related to microorganism activity (Fig. 95). Most food spoilage microorganisms grow rapidly at temperatures above 50° F. Some food poisoning organisms grow slowly down to 38° F. Psychrophilic organisms will grow slowly within the range of 40° to 15° F, provided the food is not solidly frozen. These will not produce food poisoning or disease but even

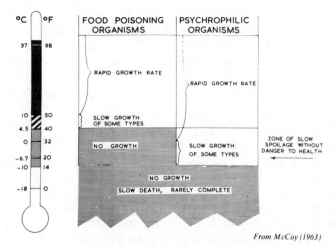

From McCoy (1963)

FIG. 95. SOME RELATIONSHIPS BETWEEN TEMPERATURE AND MICROBIAL GROWTH IN FOODS

below 25° will cause the food to deteriorate. Below 15° F there is no significant growth of microorganisms in food, instead there is a gradual decrease in the numbers of living organisms. But, as pointed out previously, destruction by cold of microorganisms is not complete; when the food is thawed there can be rapid microorganism multiplication and spoilage.

Because there are significant differences between refrigeration and freezing it is well to discuss these forms of cold preservation and processing separately.

REFRIGERATION AND COOL STORAGE

Gentle but of Short Duration

Refrigeration and cool storage in general is the gentlest method of food preservation. By and large it has relatively few adverse effects upon taste, texture, nutritive value, and overall changes in foods, provided simple rules are followed and storage periods are not excessive. One cannot say this of heat, dehydration, irradiation, and other methods of preservation which often immediately result in adverse changes in foods, however small.

While refrigeration and cool storage can be exceptionally gentle and will reduce the rate of food deterioration, with most foods it will not prevent it to anywhere the same degree as will heat, dehydration, irradiation, fermentation, or true freezing. This is apparent from Table 23 which indicates the generally useful storage life of plant and animal tissues at various temperatures. The cold temperature given is 32° F which is lower than most commercial or household refrigerators. Nevertheless, the life of such

TABLE 23

USEFUL STORAGE LIFE OF PLANT AND ANIMAL TISSUES
AT VARIOUS TEMPERATURES[1]

Food	Generalized Avg Useful Storage Life (Days) at: 32°F	72°F	100°F
Animal flesh	6–10	1	less than 1
Fish	2–7	1	less than 1
Poultry	5–18	1	less than 1
Dry meats and fish	1000 and more	350 and more	100 and more
Fruits	2–180	1–20	1–7
Dry fruits	1000 and more	350 and more	100 and more
Leafy vegetables	3–20	1–7	1–3
Root crops	90–300	7–50	2–20
Dry seeds	1000 and more	350 and more	100 and more

[1]From Desrosier (1961).

perishables as animal flesh, fish, poultry, and many fruits and vegetables, even at 32° F, is generally less than two weeks. At the more common refrigerator temperature of 42° F, storage life is often less than one week. On the other hand, these products held at 72° F or above may spoil in one day or less.

Must Provide Quick and Uninterrupted Cold

Ideally, refrigeration of perishables starts at time of harvest or slaughter and is maintained throughout transportation, warehousing, merchandising, and storage prior to ultimate use. This is not dictated from the standpoint of microbial spoilage alone. Many examples could be cited where a few hours delay between harvest or slaughter and refrigeration is sufficient to permit marked deterioration to occur.

This is particularly true with certain metabolically active fruits and vegetables. These not only will generate heat from respiration but will convert metabolites from one form to another. The loss of sweetness from sweet corn is an example of the latter (Table 24). At 32° F sweet corn can metabolize its own sugar to the extent that 8% is lost in 1 day and 22% is

TABLE 24

LOSS OF SWEETNESS IN SWEET CORN DURING STORAGE[1]

Hr Storage	Storage Temperature 32°F	68°F
	% Loss in Total Sugars	
24	8.1	25.6
48	14.5	45.7
72	18.0	55.5
96	22.0	62.1

[1]From Huelsen (1954).

lost in 4 days. However, the losses in sugar at 68°F can be of the order of 25% in one day and can far exceed this on a hot summer afternoon. To minimize such losses, cooling today is brought to the harvest field. Figure 96 shows one type of portable cooler. As they are picked, fruits or

Courtesy of Florida Div., FMC Corp.

FIG. 96. PORTABLE HYDRO-COOLER

vegetables pass through this hydro-cooler where they are sprayed with jets of cold water. The water also may contain a germicide to inactivate surface microorganisms. The cooled produce is then loaded into refrigerated trucks or railroad cars enroute to refrigerated warehouses.

Quick cooling does not simply mean immediate placement of bulk foods into a refrigerated railroad car or warehouse in all cases. Cooling is the taking of heat out of a body. If the body is large, the time to remove sufficient heat can be so long as to permit considerable food spoilage before effective preservation temperatures are reached. The hydro-cooler of Fig. 96 accomplishes rapid cooling aided by subdivision of the produce as it is fed through the machine. Similarly, subdivision of bulk produce favors cold air circulation in refrigerated storage rooms. Current use of cold nitrogen gas from evaporating liquid nitrogen in refrigerated trucks, rail cars, and ship holds also aids in providing intimate cold contact and quick cooling of produce. This has the further advantage of displacing air from the refrigerated area, which can be beneficial for certain products. Bulk liquids are best cooled rapidly by passing them through an efficient heat exchanger before putting them into refrigerated storage. Animal carcasses at time of slaughter are at a temperature of about 100°F, which must be lowered to about 35°F in less than 24 hr if quality is to be maintained.

Requirements of Refrigerated Storage

Principal among these are controlled low temperature, air circulation, humidity control, and modification of gas atmospheres.

Controlled Low Temperature.—Properly designed refrigerators, refrigerated storage rooms, and warehouses will provide sufficient refrigeration capacity and insulation to maintain the cold room within about ±2° F of the selected refrigeration temperature. In order to design a refrigerated space capable of maintaining this temperature, in addition to insulation requirements it is necessary to know in advance all factors that may generate heat within this space or influence ease of removal of heat from the space. These factors include such items as: the number of heat generating electric lights and electric motors that may be operating in the space, the number of people that may be working in the refrigerated space since they too generate heat, how often doors to the area will be open to permit entrance of warm air, and the kinds and amounts of food products that will be stored in the refrigerated area.

This latter item is of importance for two major reasons: first, the quantity of heat that must be removed from any amount of food to lower it from one temperature to another is determined by the specific heat of the particular food; and second, during and after cooling, such foods as fruits and vegetables respire and produce heat at varying rates. Both the specific heats and respiration rates of all important foods are known or can be closely estimated. These values, in addition to the items mentioned above, are necessary to calculate the "refrigeration load," which is the quantity of heat that must be removed from the product and the storage area in order to go from an initial temperature to the selected final temperature and then maintain this temperature for a specified time.

The differences between products with respect to heats evolved during respiration are seen for representative fruits and vegatables in Table 25. The amount of heat produced varies with each product, and like all metabolic activities decreases with storage temperature. Products with particularly high respiration rates, such as green beans, broccoli, sweet corn, green peas, spinach, and strawberries are particularly difficult to store. Such products if closely packed in a bin can rot in the center even when the surrounding air is cool. The relationships between specific heats of foods and calculation of refrigeration load will be discussed shortly in the section on freezing and frozen storage.

Air Circulation and Humidity.—Proper air circulation will help move heat away from the vicinity of food surfaces toward refrigerator cooling coils and plates. But the air that is circulated within a cold storage room must not be too moist or too dry. Air of high humidity can condense moisture on the surface of cold foods. If this is excessive, molds will grow on

TABLE 25

HEAT FROM THE RESPIRATION OF FRUITS AND VEGETABLES [1]

Commodity	Btu [2] per Ton per 24 Hr		
	32°F	40°F	60°F
Apples			
Jonathan or Winesap	300 to 800	590 to 840	2,270 to 3,470
Beans, green	5,500 to 6,160	9,160 to 11,390	32,090 to 44,130
Broccoli	7,450	11,000 to 17,600	33,870 to 50,000
Cabbage	1,200	1,670	4,080
Carrots, topped	2,130	3,470	8,080
Celery	1,620	2,420	8,220
Corn, sweet	6,560	9,390	38,410
Onions	600 to 1,100	1,760 to 1,980[3]	. . . . .
Oranges	420 to 1,030	1,300 to 1,560	3,650 to 5,170
Peaches	850 to 1,370	1,440 to 2,030	7,260 to 9,310
Pears, Bartlett	660 to 880	. . . . .	8,800 to 13,200
Peas, green	8,160	13,220	39,250
Potatoes	440 to 880	1,100 to 1,760	2,200 to 3,520
Spinach	4,240 to 4,860	7,850 to 11,210	36,920 to 38,000
Strawberries	2,730 to 3,800	3,660 to 6,750	15,460 to 20,280
Sweet potatoes	1,190 to 2,440	1,710 to 3,350	4,280 to 6,300
Tomatoes mature green	580	1,070	6,230
ripe	1,020	1,250	5,640

[1] From U.S. Dept. Agr. Ag. Handbook 66.
[2] Heat values obtained by multiplying respiration rate in mg of CO_2 per kilo per hour by 220.
[3] At 50°F.

these surfaces at common refrigeration temperatures. On the other hand if the air is too dry it will cause excessive drying out of foods. All foods are somewhat different with respect to supporting mold growth and tendency to dry out, and so for each an optimum balance must be reached. The optimum relative humidity to be maintained in cool storage rooms for most foods is well known. Typical data for many items along with their best temperatures for storage and their approximate storage lives are given in Table 26, which also includes data necessary for calculation of refrigeration loads. Most foods store best at refrigeration temperatures when the relative humidity of the air is between about 80 and 95%. This is generally related to the moisture content of foods and the ease with which they dry out. Thus celery and several other crisp vegetables will require a relative humidity of 90 to 95%, while nuts may do well at only 70%. On the other hand, dry and granular products such as powdered milk and eggs which have extended storage lives at refrigeration temperatures are favored by very dry atmospheres, and relative humidities above about 50% can cause excessive lumping and caking if packaging is not moisture tight.

When refrigerated storage is to be for prolonged periods various techniques are used to maintain quality. Foods that tend to lose moisture can be protected by several packaging methods. This is important since other-

TABLE 26

STORAGE REQUIREMENTS AND PROPERTIES OF PERISHABLE FOODS[5]

Commodity	Storage Temp.°F	Relative Humidity, %	Approximate Storage Life	Water Content, %	Average Freezing Point,°F	Specific Heat above Freezing[3]	Specific Heat below Freezing[3]	Latent Heat (Calculated)[4] Btu	Heat of Respiration Btu/Ton/24 Hr
Alfalfa meal[1]	30–40	70–75	…[1]	…[1]	…	…	…	…	1,500–12,380(70)
Apples	30–32	85–90	1–2 wk	84.1	28.2	0.87	0.45	121	
Apricots	31–32	85–90	1–2 wk	85.4	29.6	0.88	0.46	122	
Artichokes (globe)	31–32	90–95	2–5 mo	83.7	29.6	0.87	0.45	120	
Jerusalem	31–32	90–95		79.5	27.5	0.83	0.44	114	
Asparagus	32	90–95	3–4 wk	93.0	30.4	0.94	0.48	134	
Avocados	45–55	85–90	4 wk	65.4	30.0	0.72	0.40	94	
Bananas	…[1]	85–95	…[1]	74.8	29.6	0.80	0.42	108	
Beans (green or snap)	45	85–90	8–10 days	88.9	30.2	0.91	0.47	128	6,160–52,950(70)
lima	32–40	85–90	10–15 days	66.5	30.8	0.73	0.40	94	2,330–29,220(70)
Beer, barreled[1]	35–40	…	3–6 wk	90.2	28.0	0.92	…	…	
Beets bunch	32	90–95	10–11 days	…	…	…	…	…	
topped	32	90–95	1–3 mo	87.6	29.2	0.90	0.46	126	2,650–7,240
Blackberries	31–32	85–90	7 days	84.8	29.4	0.88	0.46	122	
Blueberries	31–32	85–90	3–6 wk	82.3	28.6	0.86	0.45	118	
Bread	0		Several wk	32–37		0.70	0.34	46–53	7,450–100,000
Broccoli, sprouting	32	90–95	7–10 days	89.9	30.3	0.92	0.47	130	
Brussels sprouts	32	90–95	3–4 wk	84.9	30.2	0.88	0.46	122	1,200–6,120(70)
Cabbage, late	32	90–95	3–4 mo	92.4	30.5	0.94	0.47	132	
Candy	0–34	40–65		…	…	…	…	…	
Carrots bunch	32	90–95	10–14 days	…	…	…	…	…	
prepackaged	32	80–90	3–4 wk	88.2	28.8	0.90	0.46	126	2,130–8,080
topped	32	90–95	4–5 mo	91.7	30.2	0.93	0.47	132	
Cauliflower	32	85–90	2–3 wk	88.3	30.2	0.91	0.46	126	
Celeriac	32	90–95	3–4 mo	93.7	30.9	0.95	0.48	135	1,620–14,150(70)
Celery	31–32	90–95	2–4 mo	83.0	27.7	0.87	0.45	120	1,249–13,200
Cherries	31–32	85–90	10–14 days	…	…	…	…	…	
Coffee (green)	35–37	80–85	2–4 mo	10–15	…	…	…	…	
Corn, sweet	31–32	85–90	4–8 days	73.9	30.8	0.79	0.42	106	6,560–61,950(80)

	Temp (°F)	Humidity (%)	Storage life	Water (%)	Freezing pt (°F)	Sp. heat above	Sp. heat below	Latent heat	
Cranberries	36–40	85–90	1–3 mo	87.4	30.0	0.90	0.46	124	
Cucumbers	45–50	90–95	10–14 days	96.1	30.5	0.97	0.49	137	720–1,800(50)
Currants	32	80–85	10–14 days	84.7	30.2	0.88	0.45	120	1,690–10,460
Dairy products									
butter	32–36	80–85	2 mo	15.5–16.5		0.33		23	
butter	−10 – −20	80–85	1 yr	15.5–16.5			0.25	23	
cheese	35	65–70	[1]	37–38	28.0	0.50	0.31	54	
cream (sweetened)	−15		Several mo						
ice cream	−15		Several mo		22–29	0.80	0.45	96	
skim milk									
dried	40	[1]	Several mo	3.5		0.23		5	
sweetened	35		Several mo						
unsweetened	−15		Short time	20.0	−4.2	0.36	0.26	29	
Dates	[1]	[1]							
Dewberries	31–32	85–90	7–10 days		29.2				
Dried fruits	32	50–60	9–12 mo			0.30–0.32		17–21	
Eggplant	45–50	85–90	10 days	92.7	30.4	0.94	0.48	132	
Eggs									
dried spray albumen	35	Low as possible	6 mo	Up to 6.0		0.25		9	
dried, whole	35	Low as possible	6 mo–1 yr	5.0		0.25	0.21	9	
dried, yolk	35	Low as possible	6 mo–1 yr	3.0		0.22	0.21	4	
fermented albumen	Rm temp	Low as possible	1 yr, plus	3–15		0.22–0.32		4–21	
frozen	−10–0		1 yr, plus	73		0.74	0.42	104	
shell	29–31[2]	85–90	8–9 mo	67.0	28.0	0.74	0.40	96	
shell, farm cooler	40–55	75		67.0	28.0	0.74	0.40	96	
Endive (escarole)	32	90–95	2–3 wk	93.3	31.1	0.94	0.48	132	
Figs									
dried	32–40	50–60	9–12 mo	24.0		0.39	0.27	34	
fresh	28–32	85–90	5–7 days	78.0	27.1	0.82	0.43	112	
Fish									
brine salted	40–50		10–12 mo			0.76	0.41	100	
fresh	33–40	90–95	5–20 days	62–85	28.0	0.80	0.40	89–122	
frozen	−10–0	90–95	8–10 mo	62–85		0.80	0.40	115	
mild cured	28–35	75–90	4–8 mo			0.76	0.41	100	
smoked	40–50	50–60	6–8 mo			0.70	0.39	92	
Frozen-pack fruits	−10–0		6–12 mo						
Frozen-pack vegetables	−10–0		6–12 mo						
Furs and fabrics[1]									
Garlic dry	32	70–75	6–8 mo	74.2	28.0	0.79	0.42	106	
Gooseberries	31–32	80–85	3–4 wk	88.9	30.0	0.90	0.46	126	

TABLE 26 (continued)

Commodity	Storage Temp, °F	Relative Humidity, %	Approximate Storage Life	Water Content, %	Average Freezing Point, °F	Specific Heat above Freezing[3]	Specific Heat below Freezing[3]	Latent Heat (Calculated)[4] Btu	Heat of Respiration Btu/Ton/24 Hr
Grapefruit	32–50	85–90	4–8 wk	88.8	28.6	0.91	0.46	126	950–6,840(90)
Grapes									
American type	31–32	85–90	3–8 wk	81.9	29.4	0.86	0.44	116	
European type	30–31	85–90	3–6 mo	81.6	27.1	0.86	0.44	116	
Honey	[1]	[1]	1 yr	18.0	...	0.35	0.26	26	
Hops	29–32	50–60	Several mo	...	...	...	...	...	
Horseradish	32	90–95	10–12 mo	73.4	26.4	0.78	0.42	104	
Kale	32	90–95	3–4 wk	86.6	30.7	0.89	0.46	124	
Kohlrabi	32	90–95	2–4 wk	90.1	30.0	0.92	0.47	128	
Lard (without antioxidant)	45	90–95	4–8 mo	0	...	...	...	...	
Lard (without antioxidant)	0	90–95	12–14 mo	0	...	...	...	...	
Leeks, green	32	90–95	1–3 mo	88.2	30.4	0.90	0.46	126	900–5,490(80)
Lettuce	32,55–58	85–90	1–4 mo	89.3	29.0	0.92	0.46	127	11,320–45,980
Limes	32	90–95	3–4 wk	94.8	31.2	0.96	0.48	136	
Logan blackberries	48–50	85–90	6–8 wk	86.0	28.2	0.89	0.46	122	
Malt syrup	31–32	85–90	7 days	82.9	29.5	0.86	0.45	118	
Mangoes	[1]	[1]	...	81.4	29.4	0.85	0.44	117	
Maple syrup	50	85–90	2–3 wk	36.0	...	0.49	0.31	52	
Meat									
bacon, frozen	−10–0	90–95	4–6 mo	13–29	...	...	...	...	
cured (farm style)	60–65	85	4–6 mo	...	...	0.30–0.43	0.24–0.29	18–41	
cured (packer style)	34–40	85	2–6 wk	...	...	...	...	...	
beef, fresh	32–34	88–92	1–6 wk	62–77	28–29	0.70–0.84	0.38–0.43	89–110	
frozen	−10–0	90–95	9–12 mo	...	...	...	...	...	
fat backs	38–40	85–90	0–3 mo	...	...	...	...	...	
hams and shoulders, fresh	32–34	85–90	7–12 days	47–54	28–29	0.58–0.63	0.34–0.36	67–77	
cured	60–65	50–60	0–3 yr	40–45	...	0.52–0.56	0.32–0.33	57–64	
frozen	−10–0	90–95	6–8 mo	...	...	...	...	...	

lamb, fresh	32–34	85–90	5–12 days	60–70	28–29	0.68–0.76	0.38–0.51	86–100	
frozen	−10–0	90–95	8–10 mo						
livers, frozen	−10–0	90–95	3–4 mo	70.0					
pork, fresh	32–34	85–90	3–7 days	35–42	28–29	0.48–0.54	0.30–0.32	50–60	
frozen	−10–0	90–95	4–6 mo						
sausage casings	40–45	85–90							
smoked sausage	40–45	85–90							
veal	32–34	90–95	5–10 days	70–80	28–29	0.76–0.84	0.42–0.51	100–114	
Melons									
cantaloupe and Persian	45–50	85–90	1–2 wk	92.7	29.9	0.94	0.48	132	1,230–8,500
Casaba	45–50	85–90	4–6 wk	92.7	29.9	0.94	0.48	132	
Honey Dew and Honey Ball	45–50	85–90	2–4 wk	92.6	29.8	0.94	0.48	132	
watermelons	36–40	85–90	2–3 wk	92.1	30.6	0.97	0.48	132	
Milk, powdered	32–40	Moistureproof containers	Several wk						
Mushrooms[1]	32–35	85–90	3–5 days	91.1	30.0	0.93	0.47	130	6,160–58,000(70)
Mushroom spawn									
grain spawn	32–40	75–80	2 wk						
manure spawn	34	75–80	8 mo						
Nursery stock	32–35	85–90	3–6 mo						
Nuts	32–50[1]	65–75	8–12 mo	3–6		0.22–0.25	0.21–0.22	4–8	
Oil (vegetable salad)	35		1 yr	0					
Okra	50	85–95	7–10 days	89.8	28.6	0.92	0.46	128	
Oleomargarine	35	60–70	1 yr	15.5		0.32	0.25	22	
Olives, fresh	45–50	85–90	4–6 wk	75.2	28.5	0.80	0.42	108	
Onions and onion sets	32	70–75	6–8 mo	87.5	30.1	0.90	0.46	124	
Oranges	32–34	85–90	8–12 wk	87.2	30.6	0.90	0.46	124	1,100–4,180(70)
Papayas	45	85–90	2–3 wk	90.8	30.1	0.82	0.47	130	1,030–9,420(90)
Parsnips	32	90–95	2–6 mo	78.6	29.8	0.84	0.46	112	
Peaches	31–32	85–90	2–4 wk	86.9	29.6	0.90	0.46	124	1,370–22,460(80)
Pears	29–31	85–90		82.7	27.7	0.86	0.45	118	880–13,200
Peas, green	32	85–90	1–2 wk	74.3	30.1	0.79	0.42	106	8,360–82,920(80)
Peppers, chili (dry)	32–40	65–75	6–9 mo	12.0	30.9	0.30	0.24	17	
Peppers, sweet	45–50	85–90	8–10 days	92.4	30.5	0.94	0.47	132	
Persimmons	30	85–90	2 mo	78.2	27.5	0.84	0.43	112	2,720–8,470
Pineapples									
mature green	50–60	85–90	3–4 wk		29.1				
ripe	40–45	85–90	2–4 wk	85.3	29.7	0.88	0.45	122	
Plums, including fresh prunes	31–32	80–85	2–4 wk[1]	85.7	28.7	0.88	0.45	123	

TABLE 26 (continued)

Commodity	Storage Temp, °F	Relative Humidity, %	Approximate Storage Life	Water Content, %	Average Freezing Point, °F	Specific Heat above Freezing[3]	Specific Heat below Freezing[3]	Latent Heat (Calculated)[4] Btu	Heat of Respiration Btu/Ton/24 Hr
Pomegranates	34–35	85–90	2–4 mo		26.5				
Popcorn, unpopped	32–40	85	...[1]	13.5		0.31	0.24	19	
Potatoes									880–3,530(70) (Irish Potatoes)
early crop	50–55	85–90	...[1]	77.8	30.0	0.82		111	
late crop	38–50[1]	85–90	...[1]		29.8		0.43		
Poultry									
fresh	32	...	1 wk	74.0	27.0	0.79		106	
frozen, eviscerated	–10–0	...	9–10 mo				0.37		
frozen, New York dressed		...	6–9 mo						
Pumpkins	50–55	70–75	2–6 mo	90.5	29.9	0.92	0.47	130	
Quinces	31–32	90–95	2–3 mo	85.3	28.1	0.88	0.45	122	
Rabbits									
fresh	32–34	90–95	1–5 days						
frozen	–10–0	90–95	0–6 mo						
Radishes, spring, bunched or prepackaged	32	90–95	10 days	93.6	30.1	0.95	0.48	134	
winter	32	90–95	2–4 mo	93.6		0.95	0.48	134	
Raspberries									
black	31–32	85–90	7 days	80.6	29.4	0.84	0.44	122	5,500–22,300
frozen (red or black)	–10–0	...	1 yr				0.45		
red	31–32	85–90	7 days	84.1	30.3	0.87	0.48	121	5,500–22,300
Rhubarb	32	90–95	2–3 wk	94.9	29.9	0.96	0.47	134	
Rutabagas	32	90–95	2–4 mo	89.1	29.7	0.91	0.44	127	
Salsify	32	90–95	2–4 mo	79.1	29.6	0.83	0.48	113	
Spinach	32	90–95	10–14 days	92.7	31.3	0.94		132	4,860–38,000
Squash									
acorn	45–50	75–85	4–5 wk		30.0				
summer	32–40	85–95	10–14 days	95.0	30.4	0.96		135	
winter	50–55	70–75	4–6 mo	88.6	29.8	0.91		127	
Strawberries									
fresh	31–32	85–90	7–10 days	89.9	30.2	0.92		129	3,800–46,400(80)
frozen	–10–0	...	1 yr	72.0			0.42	103	

Sugar, granulated	50–100	Below 60	1–3 yr	0.5	...	0.20	0.20	72	2,440–6,300
Sweet potatoes	55–60	90–95	4–6 mo	68.5	29.2	0.75	0.40	97	
Tangerines	31–38	90–95	3–4 wk	87.3	29.5	0.90	0.46	125	
Tomatoes									
mature green	55–70[1]	85–90[1]	2–5 wk	94.7	30.4	0.95	0.48	134	580–6,230
ripe	32	85–90[1]	7 days	94.1	30.4	0.95	0.48	134	1,020–5,640
Turnips, roots	32	90–95	4–5 mo	90.9	29.8	0.93	0.47	130	1,940–5,280
Vegetable seed	32–50	50–65	[1]	...	...	...	...	...	
Yeast, compressed baker's	31–32	...	...	70.9	...	0.77	0.41	102	

[1] See text of Chap. 23 in the ASRE Data Book, 1959, or Agr. Handbook 66. If not available for local examination, copies may be obtained from ASHRAE, New York, and from Supt. of Documents, Government Printing Office, Washington, D.C.

[2] Eggs with weak albumin freeze just below 30.

[3] Calculated by Siebel's formula, see pp. 23-01 of the ASRE Data Book, 1959. For values above freezing point $S = 0.008a + 0.20$. For values below freezing point $S = 0.003a + 0.20$. (Work on the Calorimetric determination of specific heats is now in progress at the University of Texas but values thus obtained are available for only a few products and therefore are not included in this tabulation.)

[4] Values for latent heat (latent heat of fusion) in Btu per pound, calculated by multiplying the % of water content by the latent heat of fusion of water, 143.4 Btu.

[5] Taken from ASRE Data Book, 1959, as modified by McCoy (1963).

wise there would be a continual migration of moisture from the food to the storage atmosphere and onto refrigerated coils and plates since moisture vapor tends to condense on cold surfaces.

Large cuts of meat are often covered by plastic sacks or they may be sprayed with various moisture-resistant coatings. Cheeses which are ripened for many months in cold warehouses are frequently protected with a wax dip. This not only minimizes moisture loss but affords protection against contamination and growth of surface molds. Eggs in the shell tend to lose moisture as well as carbon dioxide. This is retarded by dipping the eggs in a thin harmless oil, such as mineral oil, to seal the minute pores of the egg shell.

Beef that is tenderized by ageing in cool rooms often presents a problem (Fig. 97). Conventionally such ageing may be done at about 35° F for a

Courtesy of American Meat Institute

FIG. 97.   TENDERIZING BEEF BY AGEING IN COOL ROOM

period of several weeks. If the relative humidity of the storage room is much below 90% the beef dries out. If it is above 90% the beef will mold. Precise relative humidity is difficult to control. To retard mold growth and the development of surface bacterial slime, ultraviolet light is sometimes employed. In a particular accelerated ageing process known as the "Tenderay" process, beef is aged in 2 or 3 days by combining high humidity with a temperature of about 65° F. This also accelerates surface microbial growth which is kept in check by ultraviolet light. In applications such as this the dosage of ultraviolet irradiation must be controlled, since excessive exposure to ultraviolet light can cause surface fat to become rancid.

Modification of Gas Atmospheres.—Controlled atmosphere storage was mentioned briefly in Chap. 1. Apples and other fruits in cold storage respire, ripen, and then overripen. Respiration depends upon availability of oxygen and gives off carbon dioxide. Three ways to slow down respiration and the physiological changes that accompany it are reduced temperatures, depletion of oxygen, and increases in the level of carbon dioxide. The optimum temperatures, relative humidities, and gas compositions of the atmosphere differ somewhat for different fruits and for varieties of the same fruit. In the case of McIntosh apples, conditions include a temperature of 37° F, 85 to 90% RH, depletion of the normal 21% oxygen of air to 3%, increase of the normal 0.03% carbon dioxide of air to 3% and then after about 1 month to 5%, and makeup of the balance of the atmosphere with nitrogen or another inert gas. In practice the cold storage warehouse is made gas-tight, brought to temperature, filled with fruit, and sealed. Commercial gas generators then replace air with the chosen gas atmosphere and may also introduce water vapor to maintain the desired relative humidity. The warehouse is usually sealed for months until it is to be emptied. If a man must enter the warehouse to make repairs, an oxygen mask is required. Under these conditions apples retain quality in storage for better than six months.

Controlled atmosphere storage is not limited to the above application and there are various ramifications. In a sense controlled atmosphere storage is practiced whenever food is packaged in a container under vacuum, nitrogen, carbon dioxide or any other departure from the composition of air. With regard to refrigerated shipping and warehouse applications other examples of controlled or modified atmosphere storage include use of diphenyl vapors to inhibit mold growth on citrus fruits, and use of ethylene gas to speed ripening and color development of citrus fruits and bananas. The fact that liquid nitrogen cooling displaces air with nitrogen gas has already been mentioned, and considerable research is currently underway to determine the full potential of this kind of modified atmosphere storage. Since animal as well as plant tissues consume and give off gases it would be expected that gas equilibria would affect many food properties. This certainly is so with respect to the pigment changes of red meat, the growth and metabolic patterns of surface ripening as well as spoilage microorganisms, and the staling rate of cold storage eggs. In the latter case, besides oil dipping to minimize water and carbon dioxide losses, eggs have been stored in warehouses enriched with carbon dioxide to minimize loss of this gas which is associated with egg pH and freshness.

Food Variability in Refrigerated Storage

The specific changes that can occur in foods during cool storage are legion and influenced by such diverse factors as growing conditions and varieties of plants, feeding practices in the case of animals, conditions of harvest and slaughter, sanitation and damage to tissues, temperature of cool storage, mixture of foods in storage, and other variables.

Thus, Florida grapefruit stores well at 32° F while Texas Marsh grapefruit stores better at 52° F. McIntosh apples store well at 36° to 40° F but the Delicious apple does better at 32° F.

Pigs fed on substances high in unsaturated fats such as peanuts and soybeans produce softer pork and lard than the same animals fed on cereal grains. Flesh of the latter keeps better in cold storage.

Animals permitted to rest before slaughter build up glycogen (animal starch) reserves in their muscles. Following slaughter this is converted to lactic acid which is a mild preservative and enhances the keeping quality of meat in cold storage. Animals that are exercised or excited before slaughter use up their glycogen reserves, less is available for conversion to lactic acid, and keeping quality is impaired.

As has been pointed out earlier, too low temperatures of refrigeration can cause cold damage to fruits and vegetables even when these are not physically damaged by freezing (previous Table 16). This is not surprising since living plants would be expected to have optimum temperature requirements just as animals do. Many of the defects shown in Table 16 are of microbial origin, reflecting a weakened physiological state and a decrease in resistance to this kind of deterioration. In the case of bananas and tomatoes on the other hand, storage temperatures below about 55° F slow down the activities of natural ripening enzymes and result in poor ripened colors. Nevertheless, for the majority of perishable foods no cooling at all generally would be far worse than refrigeration temperatures that are somewhat too low.

Refrigerated storage permits exchange of flavors between many types of foods if they are stored near one another. For example, butter and milk will absorb odors from fish and from fruit as will eggs absorb odors from onions. Where possible different foods, especially odorous ones, should be stored separately but this is not always economically feasible. In many instances odor exchange can be entirely prevented by effective packaging.

The previously mentioned losses of sugar in the case of sweet corn (Table 24), even at refrigeration temperatures, are due to synthesis of starch from the sugar. But other changes in refrigerated storage represent

TABLE 27

LOSSES IN VITAMIN C IN SELECTED VEGETABLES ON COLD STORAGE[1]

Produce	Storage Conditions Days	Temp, °F	Losses, %
Asparagus	1	35	5
	7	32	50
Broccoli	1	46	20
	4	46	35
Green beans	1	46	10
	4	46	20
Spinach	2	32	5
	3	34	5

[1] From Desrosier (1970).

true nutrient losses, as in the case of vitamin destruction (Table 27). Thus, asparagus lost 50% of its vitamin C in 7 days at 32°F, broccoli lost 20% in just 1 day and 35% in 4 days at 46°F. In the case of the asparagus this loss occurred although 32°F is the optimum temperature for refrigerated storage of this vegetable. Other vitamin losses are common in many foods held for relatively short periods under refrigeration.

Still other common changes in foods during refrigerated storage involve loss of firmness and crispness in fruits and vegetables, changes in the colors of red meats, oxidation of fats, softening of the tissues and drippage from fish, staling of bread and cake, lumping and caking of granular foods, losses of flavor, and a host of microbial deteriorations often unique to a specific food and caused by the dominance of a particular spoilage organism. Some foods should not be refrigerated at all. Bread is an example. The rate of staling of bread is greater at refrigeration temperatures than it is at room temperature, however, staling can be arrested by freezing. These and other differences between foods at refrigerated temperatures are behind the storage requirements indicated in Table 26.

Benefits Other Than Preservation

In the food industry cooling generally is used for its preservation value. There are many situations, however, where cooling provides other advantages and improves the processing properties of foods. Cooling is employed to control the rates of certain chemical and enzymatic reactions as well as the rates of growth and metabolism of desirable food microorganisms. This is the case in the cool ripening of cheeses, cool ageing of beef, and cool ageing of wines. Cooling also improves the ease of peeling and depitting peaches for canning. Cooling citrus fruits reduces changes in flavor during extraction and straining of juice. Cooling improves the ease and efficiency of meat cutting and bread slicing. Cooling precipitates waxes from edible oils. Water for soft drinks is cooled before carbonating to increase the solubility of carbon dioxide. More will be said about these applications of cooling in later chapters.

Economic Considerations

Where cooling is used for preservation in the multiproduct warehouse, the supermarket, and the household refrigerator, unfortunately it is not always economical or practical to separate foods and provide each with their optimum temperature and humidity requirements. A compromise often is made and the refrigerated area is held somewhere within the 35° to 45° F range with no special provisions made to control humidity. Even under these conditions refrigeration provides major improvements with respect to safety, appearance, flavor, and nutritional value of our food supply. It further reduces losses from insects, parasites, and rodents.

FREEZING AND FROZEN STORAGE

As a preservation method, freezing takes over where refrigeration and cool storage leave off. Coupled with preservation, freezing has been a major factor in bringing convenience foods to the housewife, restaurant, and institutional feeding establishments. Because freezing properly done preserves foods without major changes in size, shape, texture, color, and flavor, freezing permits much of the work in preparing a food item or an entire meal to be done prior to the freezing step. This transfers operations that formerly had to be done by the housewife or chef to the food processor. Such diverse items as chicken pot pie, breaded fish sticks, ethnic entrées, whipped topping, chiffon and fruit pies, and complete dinners are today commonly prepared and arranged by assembly-line techniques in specialized industrial kitchens and then quickly frozen. The virtually unlimited items, many frozen in their final serving dishes by the hundreds of millions, represent a major revolution in the food industry and reflect gross changes in eating habits. These changes in the United States stem from such current social phenomena as the following: (1) More meals are eaten outside the home than ever before. This includes meals in restaurants, colleges, school lunch programs, hotels, airplanes, hospitals, etc. (2) There is an increasing shortage of skilled chefs and restaurant help in all of the above areas. (3) From crowded schools to high speed airlines there is increasing need for fast food preparation and service. (4) Labor costs are steadily rising, further forcing maximum use of convenience foods in food handling establishments.

At the present time no form of food preservation is as well suited to provide maximum convenience as is freezing. Thus while dehydrated foods offer convenience, they require reconstitution on an individual component basis to satisfy varying water needs, and then also require heating. Not so with frozen foods. Many items can be completely prepared and assembled together for a single thawing-heating operation. This ultimate in frozen foods rests on well-developed scientific principles.

Characteristics of Food Systems Being Frozen

Water when frozen can burst iron pipes and so it should not be surprising that unless properly controlled, freezing can disrupt food texture, break emulsions, denature proteins, and cause other changes of both physical and chemical nature. Many of these changes are related to food composition which in turn is influenced by agricultural practices long before the freezing process.

Food Composition.—It is a basic property of aqueous solutions that increasing their concentrations of dissolved solids will lower their freezing points. Thus the more salt, sugar, minerals, or proteins in a solution the lower its freezing point and the longer it will take to freeze when put into a freezing chamber. If water and juice are placed in a freezer the water will freeze first. Further, unless the temperature is considerably below the freezing point of pure water the juice will never freeze completely but rather will become icy and slushy. What really is happening here is that the water component of the juice freezes first and leaves the dissolved solids in a more concentrated solution which requires a still lower temperature to freeze it.

Since different foods have quite different compositions with respect to their levels of water and the kinds and amounts of solids dissolved in the water, it is to be expected that these will have different freezing points (Table 26), and under a given freezing condition will require different times to reach a solidly frozen state. This alone provides much of the explanation of why varieties of the same fruit or vegetable will behave differently on freezing. Varieties have somewhat different compositions. Even the same variety grown in a field under different irrigation and fertilization practices will have certain variations in composition, including differences in mineral content absorbed from the fertilizers. For this reason, frozen food producers who want to have strict control over the freezing processes will define varieties to be grown and may even supply seed and fertilizer to help guarantee controlled composition and other properties of raw materials.

Progressive Freezing.—A given unit of food, whether it is a bottle of milk, a cut of beef, or a can of sliced apples in sugar syrup will not freeze uniformly; that is, it will not suddenly change from liquid to solid. In the case of the bottle of milk placed in a freezer, for example, the liquid nearest the bottle wall will freeze first, and the first ice crystals will be pure water. As water continues to be frozen out, the milk will become more concentrated in minerals, proteins, lactose and fat. This concentrate which gradually freezes also becomes more concentrated as freezing proceeds. Finally a central core of highly concentrated unfrozen liquid remains, and if the temperature is sufficiently low this central core also will ultimately freeze solid.

Much the same occurs with solid foods as can be seen from the freezing curve for thin sections of beef (Fig. 98). This also reveals other properties of food systems during progressive freezing.

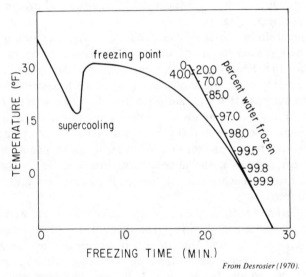

From Desrosier (1970).

FIG. 98.   FREEZING CURVE FOR THIN SECTIONS OF BEEF

We speak of the freezing point of pure water being 32° F, but actually water doesn't begin to freeze at 32° F. Instead, it generally becomes supercooled to a temperature several degrees below 32° F before some stimulus such as crystal nucleation or agitation initiates the freezing process. When this stimulation occurs there is an abrupt rise from the supercooled temperature to 32° F due to the evolution of the latent heat of crystallization. Even if the water is in an environment far below 32° F, so long as free water is freezing and giving up latent heat of crystallization or fusion the temperature of a pure water-ice mixture will not drop below 32° F. Only after all of the water has been converted to ice will the system drop below the equilibrium temperature of 32° F, and then rapidly approach the temperature of the freezing environment.

Much of this also is true for food systems containing water, but since foods contain dissolved solids, progressive freezing is somewhat more complex. In Fig. 98, the freezing curve for a thin section of beef was obtained by placing the beef in a freezing chamber well below 0° F and recording changing temperature of the beef with time as it underwent freezing. At the same time the percentage of water that was converted to ice was determined as a function of temperature or time. As the beef is chilled it first drops from its initial temperature to a supercooled temperature somewhat below its freezing point. Nucleation or agitation initiates formation of the first ice crystal and latent heat of fusion causes the temperature to rise to the freezing point, which is somewhat below 32° F because of the dissolved solids in the water phase.

Now if this were the freezing of pure water, the curve would not drop below the freezing point as long as liquid water remained. In the case of beef and other foods, however, the temperature continues to drop as more and more water is frozen out. This is largely because as more water is frozen out the concentration of solutes in the remaining water progressively increases and exerts a greater and greater freezing point depression on the remaining solution.

It also should be noted from Fig. 98 that while at about 25° F some 70% of the water is frozen, and the beef would appear solidly frozen, at 15° F about 3% of the water still remains unfrozen and even at 0° F not all of the water is completely frozen. These small quantities of unfrozen water are highly significant, particularly since within them are dissolved food solutes which are concentrated and are therefore more prone to reaction with one another and with other food constituents.

Since the compositions of foods differ, just as they have different initial freezing points they have characteristic freezing curves differing somewhat in shape. But generally one can identify the zone of supercooling, the inflection up to the freezing point, and the subsequent drop in temperature if there is a sufficient temperature differential between the freezing food and the freezer environment. This differential provides the driving force for continued heat transfer out of the food.

Concentration Effects.—For most foods to maintain quality in frozen storage the food must be solidly or very nearly solidly frozen. An unfrozen core or a partially frozen zone will deteriorate with respect to texture, color, flavor, and other properties. In addition to the possible growth of psychrophilic microorganisms, and to the greater action of enzymes when free water remains, a major reason for deterioration in partially frozen food is due to the high concentration of solutes in the remaining water. Thus when milk is slowly frozen, as can occur on the doorstep in winter, the concentration of minerals and salts can denature proteins and break fat emulsions which show up as curdling and butter granules. Flavor changes also occur.

Damage from the concentration effect can be of various kinds:

(1) If solutes precipitate or crystallize out of solution, as do excessive levels of lactose in freezing ice cream, then they can impart a gritty, sandy texture to the food.

(2) If solutes do not precipitate but remain in concentrated solution then they can denature proteins because of a "salting out" effect.

(3) Some solutes are acidic and upon concentration can cause the pH to drop below the isoelectric point (point of minimum solubility) of proteins and coagulate protein in this way.

(4) Colloidal suspensions are delicately poised with respect to their concentration of anions and cations. Some of these ions are essential to maintain colloids in suspension. Concentration or precipitation of these ions can disturb this balance.

(5) Gases in solution also are concentrated when water freezes out. This can cause supersaturation of the gases and ultimate forcing of them out of solution. Frozen beer or soda pop suffers such a defect.

(6) Further, the concentration effect can cause a dehydration of adjacent tissues at the microenvironmental level. Thus when ice crystals form in extracellular liquid, and solutes are concentrated in the vicinity of the ice crystals, water will diffuse from within the cells through the membranes into the region of high solute concentration to restore osmotic equilibrium. This shift of moisture is rarely completely reversed on thawing, and can result in loss of tissue turgor.

Ice Crystal Damage.—Solid foods from living tissues such as meats, fish, fruits, and vegetables are of cellular structure with delicate cell walls and cell membranes. Within and between the cells is water. When water freezes rapidly it forms minute ice crystals, when it freezes slowly it forms large ice crystals and clusters of crystals. Large ice crystals forming within or between cells can cause physical rupture and separation of cells which would be far less severe from more minute crystals. Figure 99 is a picture of cross sections of three asparagus spears; A was frozen fastest, B was frozen next fastest, and C was frozen slowest. Sample C had the largest ice crystals and the disruption of texture is extreme. Large ice crystal damage is detrimental not only to cellular foods, it also can disrupt frozen emulsions such as butter, frozen foams like ice cream, and frozen gels such as puddings and pie fillings. In the case of butter, ice crystals that grow within individual water droplets dispersed in the continuous fat phase can penetrate through the fat and merge. When such butter is later thawed water pockets and water drippage result. In the case of ice cream, large ice crystals can puncture frozen foam bubbles. Such a condition leads

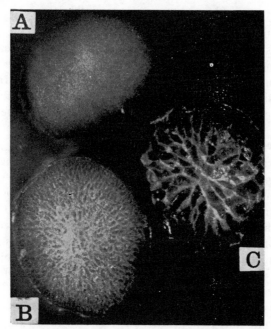

From Tressler and Evers (1957)

FIG. 99. CROSS SECTIONS OF ASPARAGUS SPEARS FROZEN AT DIFFERENT RATES: A—IMMERSION FREEZING (FASTEST); B— CONTACT FREEZING (INTERMEDIATE); C—STILL AIR FREEZING (SLOWEST)

to loss of volume on storage and during partial melting. Gels behave somewhat like butter, often exhibiting syneresis or water separation.

Rate of Freezing

There sometimes is disagreement between frozen food investigators whether the concentration effect or physical damage from large ice crystals is the more detrimental during freezing and frozen storage. Undoubtedly this depends upon the particular food system under consideration. However, in either case fast freezing is necessary for high quality.

Fast freezing produces minute ice crystals. Rapid or instantaneous freezing, however, also minimizes concentration effects by decreasing the time concentrated solutes will be in contact with food tissues, colloids, and individual constitutents during the transition from the unfrozen to the fully frozen state.

For these reasons particularly, all modern methods of freezing and all freezing devices are designed for very rapid freezing where high food quality can justify the cost. Regarding actual freezing rates, generally the faster the freezing rate the better is the product quality. However, from a practical standpoint, freezing rates equivalent to about one-half inch per hour are satisfactory for most products and are easy to realize in commercial equipment. This would mean that a flat package of food two inches thick and frozen from both major surfaces should be frozen (to 0° F or below) at its center in about two hours. Plate freezers easily do this, and liquid nitrogen freezers may cut down the time to a few minutes.

Choice of Final Temperature

A consideration of all factors including textural changes, enzymatic and nonenzymatic chemical reactions, microbiological changes, and costs, leads to the general conclusion that foods should be frozen to an internal temperature of 0° F or lower and kept at 0° F or lower throughout their entire history of frozen transport and frozen storage. Economic considerations generally preclude temperatures below about −20° F during transport and storage, although many foods commonly are frozen to temperatures somewhat below −20° F in an effort to achieve the advantages of rapid freezing.

The choice of 0° F or below as the maximum recommended temperature for freezing and storage is based on substantial data, and a compromise between quality and cost. Microbiologically, 0° F storage would not be strictly required since pathogens do not grow below about 38° F and normal food spoilage organisms do not grow below about 15° F. On the other hand, transportation and frozen storage facilities are expected to vary somewhat below and above any chosen temperature setting. Since some spoilage organisms can grow in the vicinity of 20° F, a choice of 0° F provides a reasonable measure of safety against these and a still greater margin of safety against pathogens; and indeed frozen foods have enjoyed an excellent public health record over the years.

For control of enzymatic reactions 0° F is not exceptionally low since some enzymes retain activity even at −100° F, although reaction rates are extremely slow. Enzyme reaction rates are faster in supercooled water than in frozen water at the same temperature. In most foods there remains considerable unfrozen water at 15° F, and long term storage at 15° F results in severe enzymatic deterioration of food quality, especially of an oxidative nature. Storage at 0° F sufficiently retards the actions of many food enzymes, but exceptions exist in the case of fruits and vegetables. In these cases the enzymes are inactivated prior to freezing by heat blanching or chemical treatment.

As for nonenzymatic chemical reactions, these are not entirely stopped at 0° F but proceed very slowly. In the freezing zone, the generalized statement that reaction rates are approximately halved for every 18° F drop in temperature does not hold well, since many reactions proceed in solution, and in this zone solution concentration is changing rapidly with the freezing of water. Suffice it to say that the lower the temperature the slower the reaction rates, and the less unfrozen water present to serve as solvent for chemical reactants.

The overall effects of low temperature on long term storage of various foods are indicated in Table 28. Considering vegetables, fruits,

TABLE 28

APPROXIMATE NUMBER OF MONTHS OF HIGH QUALITY
STORAGE LIFE[1]

Product	Storage Temperature		
	0°F	10°F	20°F
Orange juice (heated)	27	10	4
Peaches	12	<2	6 days
Strawberries	12	2.4	10 days
Cauliflower	12	2.4	10 days
Green beans	11–12	3	1
Green peas	11–12	3	1
Spinach	6–7	<3	$3/_4$
Raw chicken (adequately packaged)	27	15½	<8
Fried chicken	<3	<30 days	<18 days
Turkey pies or dinners	>30	9½	2½
Beef (raw)	13–14	5	<2
Pork (raw)	10	<4	<1.5
Lean fish (raw)	3	<2¼	<1.5
Fat fish (raw)	2	1½	0.8

[1]From U.S. Dept. Agr. (1960); Van Arsdel (1961).

and nonfatty meats properly packaged and frozen, quality storage life of many at 0° F is of the order of 12 months or longer. Most fish are less stable. At higher temperatures of 15° to 20° F quality may be retained for periods of only days or a few weeks, depending upon product.

Initial quality and subsequent storage life would be still better for many foods if they were frozen and stored well below 0° F. It is relatively easy to freeze foods to −20° F and even lower by several methods, and the costs would not be excessive. What is more difficult and would be very expensive, however, is maintaining the food at −20° F or below through refrigerated transportation and warehouse or supermarket cabinet storage. Many refrigerated trucks on the road today are not capable of holding a temperature of even 0° F, and supermarket display cases often are above 0° F near the top, although they may be colder below.

The Association of Food and Drug Officials of the United States recognizing this situation has proposed a frozen food code known as the AFDOUS code. This is designed to assure that all frozen food be stored and merchandised at a temperature not over 0° F. To accomplish this the AFDOUS code would require disposal of all trucks, rail cars, etc., and display cabinets that do not meet the 0° F standard. It also calls for disposal of frozen food above 0° F. Several states have adopted the AFDOUS code or modifications of it but compliance is not yet nation-wide. Taking a conservative position from the standpoint of public health, the Food and Drug Administration is strongly in support of the AFDOUS code.

Damage from Intermittent Thawing

The kinds of damage that can occur to foods during slow freezing also occur during slow thawing; and nothing is more detrimental to the quality of frozen foods than repeated freezing and thawing during storage. Nor need repeated thawings be complete. Complete thawing in storage is rare and generally occurs only when there is complete breakdown of the cold storage equipment. This is easily recognized and quickly corrected. However, there is not a commercial frozen food distribution or storage system that doesn't have a measurable temperature cycle. Such cycles are part of current temperature control systems, and it is not uncommon for a frozen storage chamber to go from its maximum to its minimum temperature and back again on roughly a two hour cycle. This could mean 360 cycles a month and over 4,000 cycles a year.

As little as a 5° F fluctuation in freezer storage temperature above and below the zero mark can be damaging to many foods. Above 10° F, thawing intensifies the concentration effect. Upon refreezing, water melted from small ice crystals tends to bathe unmelted crystals causing them to grow in size. Whatever the temperature fluctuation in the storage area, because heat transfer has a finite rate there will be a lag effect in the food itself, and the food generally will experience less of a temperature range than the room or cabinet. Nevertheless, room or cabinet temperature variations of greater than a few degrees from the zero mark over a period of weeks or months will noticeably damage quality of most frozen foods, and such freezer storage facilities are in need of correction.

Frozen foods being thawed for ultimate use also are subject to quality loss, especially if thawing is slow. Once again concentration effects can occur. The most concentrated solutions that freeze last are the first to thaw. These commonly are eutectic mixtures.

A eutectic mixture is a solution of such composition that it freezes (or thaws) as such rather than becoming more concentrated due to further separation of pure ice. In other words, the eutectic mixture freezes (and thaws) as a mixture, and the frozen eutectic will have a constant proportion of ice crystals intermingled with solute crystals. The temperature at which a eutectic mixture is formed is called the eutectic temperature or eutectic point. A dilute solution of NaCl in water under freezing conditions will first freeze out pure water and become more concentrated in NaCl. At $-6°$ F remaining water and salt would consist of a mixture of 23% NaCl and 77% water. This would freeze into eutectic ice of the same composition. Where ice from pure water has a melting point of 32° F, eutectic ice could be removed from the system and would have a melting point of $-6°$ F, and therefore such ice would be a better refrigerant than pure water ice and has been used as such commercially.

Food materials are complex mixtures and pass through several eutectic compositions in the course of becoming solidly frozen. The opposite occurs on thawing, the last eutectics to freeze being the first to thaw. If thawing is slow there is more time for food constituents to be in contact with concentrated eutectic mixtures and damaging concentration effects are intensified.

Another reason why quick final thawing is superior to slow thawing is seen in Table 29. Large volumes of frozen food, such as a 30-lb can of

TABLE 29

EFFECT OF THAWING ON THE MICROBIOLOGY OF FROZEN
WHOLE EGG MEATS[1]

Method	Hours Required	% Increase in Microbial Count During Thawing
In air at 80°F	23	1,000
In air at 70°F	36	750
In air at 45°F	63	225
In running water 60°F	15	250
In running water 70°F	12	300
Agitated water 60°F	9	40
Dielectric heat	15 min	Negligible

[1]From Weiser *et al.* (1971).

frozen whole egg, can take anywhere from 20 to 60 hr of thawing time in air depending upon the air temperature. Cool running water and other techniques can markedly reduce this time. Since bacteria survive the freezing process, when times are long and temperatures of the product rise there is considerable opportunity for bacterial multiplication.

Refrigeration Requirements

We speak of the product refrigeration load as that quantity of heat which must be removed in order to reduce the temperature of the product from its initial temperature to the temperature consistent with good frozen food storage.

If the food is cooled from above its freezing point to a storage temperature below its freezing point, then quantitatively this refrigeration load is made up of three parts: These are the number of Btu/lb of food that must be removed to cool the food from its initial temperature to its freezing point, plus the number of Btu/lb which must be removed to cause a change of state at the freezing point, plus the number of Btu/lb that must be removed to lower the temperature of the frozen product to the specified storage temperature.

Definitions and Heat Constants.—A Btu or British Thermal Unit is the quantity of heat which will raise or lower the temperature of one pound of water 1°F through the range of 32°F to 212°F at normal atmospheric pressure.

The specific heat of a substance is the ratio of the heat required to raise or lower the temperature of unit mass of the substance 1°F compared to the heat required to raise or lower the temperature of unit mass of water 1°F. Since the specific heat of water is taken as the standard and is 1, it follows that the specific heat of any substance is the amount of heat in Btu required to raise or lower the temperature of one pound of the substance 1°F.

There are two types of heat, namely sensible heat and latent heat. Sensible heat may be defined as the heat we readily perceive by the sense of touch and which produces a temperature rise or fall as heat is added or removed from a substance. Latent heat is the quantity of heat required to change the state or condition under which a substance exists, without changing its temperature. Thus a definite quantity of heat must be removed from water at 32°F to change it to ice at 32°F. The same amount of heat must be added to ice at 32°F to change it to water at 32°F. This is known as the latent heat of fusion or crystallization. Similarly in going from water at 212°F to steam at 212°F we must supply the latent heat of evaporation. In freezing we are interested in the latent heat of fusion, and this in the case of water is 144 Btu/lb. It is quantitatively different from 144 Btu/lb for substances other than water.

With regard to specific heat, the specific heat of a material is different in the liquid state and in the frozen state. That is, a different number of Btu/lb is required to raise or lower the temperature of a material 1°F depending upon whether we are above or below its freezing point.

The specific and latent heats of foods are known, and are used to determine refrigeration requirements for cooling, freezing, and storage. Typical values for a few foods are given in Table 30, and more extensive

TABLE 30

SPECIFIC AND LATENT HEATS OF FOODS[1]

Food Product	Specific Heat Btu/Lb Freezing Before	After	Latent Heat of Fusion, Btu/Lb
Asparagus	0.94	0.48	134.
Bacon	0.50	0.30	29
Blackberries	0.88	0.46	122
Beef			
lean	0.77	0.40	100
fat	0.60	0.35	79
dried	0.34	0.26	22
Cabbage	0.94	0.47	132
Carrots	0.90	0.46	126
Eggs	0.76	0.40	100
Fish	0.76	0.41	101
Green peas	0.79	0.42	106
Lamb	0.67	0.30	83
Milk	0.93	0.49	124
Oysters, shelled	0.90	0.46	125
Poultry, fresh	0.79	0.37	106
Pork, fresh	0.68	0.38	86
String beans	0.91	0.47	128
Veal	0.71	0.39	91
Water	1.00	0.48	144

[1] Data from ASHRAE Handbook of Fundamentals, 1967.

lists can be found in handbooks of the ASRE and ASHRAE (Table 26) and handbooks of the U.S. Dept. of Agr.

Calculation of Refrigeration Load.—Table 30 not only provides data for calculation of refrigeration requirements but also gives clues to the freezing behavior of different foods.

Water at the bottom of this table has a specific heat before freezing of 1.00, a latent heat of fusion of 144, and a specific heat after freezing of 0.48. Therefore, if we wanted to freeze a pound of water from 60°F to 0°F, we would have to remove 1 Btu/degree F from 60°F down to 32°F, plus 144 Btu to go from water to ice at 32°F, plus 0.48 Btu/degree F from 32°F down to 0°F. This would be equal to 28 + 144 + 15 or 187 Btu.

Using the same method, the following general equations will permit us to calculate the Btu to be removed to cool and freeze any quantity of food material from any starting temperature to any frozen storage temperature, provided we know the freezing point of the food material:

$$H_1 = (S_L)(W)(T_i - T_f) \qquad H_3 = (S_S)(W)(T_f - T_s)$$

$$H_2 = (H_F)(W) \qquad H_{fs} = H_1 + H_2 + H_3$$

Thus, H_1 would be the number of Btu to cool the food from its initial temperature to its freezing point and would be equal to S_L (the specific heat of the food above its freezing point) times W (its weight in pounds) times $T_i - T_f$ (the difference between the initial temperature and the freezing point in degrees F).

H_2 would be the number of Btu required to change the food from the "liquid" state to the frozen state at its freezing point, and would be equal to H_F (the latent heat of fusion of the food) times W (its weight).

H_3 would be the number of Btu required to lower the frozen food from its freezing point to the desired storage temperature, and would be equal to S_S (the specific heat of the food below its freezing point) times W (the weight of the food) times $T_f - T_s$ (the difference between the freezing point and the desired storage temperature).

H_{fs}, the total Btu requirement would be equal to $H_1 + H_2 + H_3$.

Table 30 also indicates some important differences between foods. Foods which are high in water, such as asparagus, cabbage, and milk, have heat constants very close to those of water, and foods low in water have lower heat constants. This says that foods low in water require less Btu per unit weight to be removed to cool and freeze them than foods higher in water. This is further brought out in the case of beef, comparing the constants for lean beef, fatty beef, and dried beef. Specific heats before and after freezing, as well as latent heats of fusion, go down as the food contains less water.

To use the specific heat data, the freezing point of the particular food must be known. This is usually given in handbooks, along with moisture contents of foods and the specific and latent heat constants (Table 26). The satisfactory use of such data depends upon the purpose for which calculations are being made and the degree of accuracy that is needed.

Specific and latent heat values given in handbooks strictly apply only at the moisture content of the food for which they were established. Thus, the published value for latent heat of fusion of sweet corn of 75% moisture is 106 Btu/lb. But sweet corn can vary by more than 10% in water content. As pointed out by Tressler and Evers (1957) if the sweet corn comes down to 64% moisture, than the latent heat of fusion would be found on careful calorimetric measurement to be not 106 Btu/lb but 91.7 Btu/lb.

For research purposes it sometimes is necessary to know refrigeration requirements with a high degree of accuracy, then heat constants based on calorimetric measurements at specific moisture contents are required. But generally in commercial practice, refrigeration requirements may be estimated quite well from average handbook values. Further, for practical purposes, where the actual freezing point of a food is not known, the value of 28° F is assumed to be the freezing point of most foods.

Where handbook values are not available, as would be the case for a new product of a proprietary nature, or a natural product of altered moisture content, three simple formulas are commonly used to estimate heat constants.

For specific heat of a food before freezing:

Specific heat = 0.008 (% water) + 0.20

For specific heat after freezing:

Specific heat = 0.003 (% water) + 0.20

For latent heat of fusion in Btu/lb :

$$\text{Latent heat} = \frac{144 \, (\% \text{ water in food})}{100}$$

When the product refrigeration load is calculated in Btu by the methods described, it often is expressed in terms of the standard refrigeration unit, namely tons of refrigeration. A ton of refrigeration is the number of Btu required to convert 1 ton of water at 32° F to 1 ton of ice at 32° F in 24 hr. Since the latent heat of fusion for water is 144 Btu/lb, a ton of refrigeration is 144 times 2,000 lb, or 288,000 Btu/24 hr.

Therefore the required refrigeration load in Btu divided by 288,000 equals the tons of refrigeration required to bring the food batch to its storage temperature. The refrigeration engineer than adds to this the additional refrigeration requirements to cool down the cold storage room or cabinet, and to maintain it at proper storage temperature against heat pickup through poor insulation, food respiration, opening of doors, electric motors, etc.

Factors Determining Freezing Rate

Quite apart from the absolute refrigeration requirements to freeze foods there are the factors that affect freezing rates and thereby help determine quality.

The rate of cooling and freezing food may be expressed generally as a function of two variables, namely the driving force divided by the sum of resistances to heat transfer. The driving force is simply the temperature difference between the product and the cooling medium. The resistances depend upon such factors as air velocity, thickness of product, geometry of the system, and composition of the product. Geometry of the system could include such factors as degree of contact of the refrigerant with the food to be cooled, extent of agitation, in a continuous cooling and freezing system whether the refrigerant is circulated counter or cocurrent to the direction of movement of the food, and so on. Composition of the product, on the other hand, not only involves the chemical composition and the thermal conductivities of various constituents, but also the physical arrangement of constituents; for example, the way the fat is distributed within a cut of meat and the direction of orientation of muscle fibers in relation to a refrigerating surface.

Food Composition.—Like metals and other materials, food constituents have different thermal conductivity properties which change with temperature. The greater the conductivity the greater the cooling and freezing rate, other things being equal. In the cooling and freezing temperature range, heat conductivities of water change little until there is a phase change of the water to ice. Then the thermal conductivity of ice is far greater than that of water, and the thermal conductivity of a food increases rapidly as it passes from the unfrozen to the frozen state.

Fat has a much lower thermal conductivity than water, and air has a thermal conductivity far less than that of water or fat.

We therefore can draw some inferences with respect to composition of a food product and freezing rate under controlled freezing conditions:

(1) Rates of cooling and freezing will be influenced by composition, with high levels of fat or entrapped air tending to have a negative influence.

(2) Rates of cooling and freezing are not constant during the processes since water is going to ice and thermal conductivities are changing.

(3) We may expect influences on freezing rate from differences in physical structure of foods. Thus if we had two food systems both containing 50% fat and 50% moisture, but one was an oil-in-water emulsion and the other was a water-in-oil emulsion, the two foods would be expected to have different thermal conductivity properties. Here the oil-in-water emulsion, with water being the continuous phase, should have greater thermal conductivity values at different temperatures than the corresponding water-in-oil emulsion of the same chemical composition. Other things being equal, the oil-in-water emulsion should freeze at a faster rate than the water-in-oil emulsion.

(4) Similarly, structural systems like cuts of meat should conduct heat at different rates depending upon whether the meat is in contact with a refrigerated surface in a direction parallel or perpendicular to the layers of fat, and to the direction of orientation of the muscle fibers. We can make educated guesses as to how heat transfer will be affected by these variations, but unfortunately there is very little published work on food systems along these lines.

Noncompositional Influences.—As for the other variables that affect freezing rate, such as air velocity, product thickness, agitation, and degree of contact between food and cooling medium, these effects are well known, follow the simpler rules of heat transfer, and largely determine the design of freezer systems. It is easy to cite the directional effects of such variables upon freezing rate, and these will apply in virtually any system design. However, a quantitative measure of the effects of these variables generally must be established experimentally for each different food and system geometry to have validity.

Each of the following will apply in any system design: (1) the greater the temperature differential between the food and the refrigerant the greater the freezing rate; (2) the thinner the food piece or food package the greater the freezing rate; (3) the greater the velocity of refrigerated air or circulating refrigerant the greater the freezing rate; (4) the more intimate the contact between the food and the cooling medium the greater the freezing rate; and (5) the greater the refrigerating effect or heat capacity of the refrigerant the greater the freezing rate.

In this latter case, if the refrigerant is a liquid which expands to a gas -then the refrigerating effect is determined largely by its particular latent heat of vaporization. If the refrigerant does not undergo phase change, such as a salt-brine, then its refrigerating effect is determined by its heat capacity, or specific heat. More will be said about refrigeration effect under liquid nitrogen freezing.

The order of magnitude of some of these major variables on freezing rate can be substantial. Thus, lowering air temperature in a tunnel-type freezer from 0° F to −20° F can commonly shorten freezing time of small cakes from 40 min to about 20 min. Spraying with liquid nitrogen at −320° F would cut freezing time to under 2 min. Lowering of freezer temperatures to very low levels, however, does not give a straight-line freezing rate response, and the increased rate from lower temperatures tends to drop off, especially at freezer temperatures below about −50° F.

In still air at 0° F, small items such as individual fruits or small fish fillets may freeze in about three hours. Increasing the air velocity at this temperature to 250 ft/min will decrease freezing time of these items to about 1 hr, while an air velocity of 1,000 ft/min will further decrease freezing time to about 40 min. Whether in cold air or in any other flowing refrigerant, increased velocity speeds freezing by carrying heat away from the surface of food and rapidly replacing warmed refrigerant with cold refrigerant to maintain maximum temperature differential between the food and the refrigerant. But here too it will be found that freezing rate does not increase linearly with air velocity.

The effect of food or package thickness on freezing rate is such that when common food packages are doubled from about 2 to 4 in. in thickness, freezing time increases about 2.5 fold. But the slope of the thickness curve is such that as we continue to increase product thickness the rate of increase in freezing time goes up faster than the rate of change in thickness. Thus 30-lb cans of liquid eggs or fruit may require 48 to 72 hr to become thoroughly frozen throughout. Commercial 55-gal. drums of fruit juices may require more than a week unless the juice was first slush frozen by being passed through a heat exchanger prior to being filled into the large drums.

Methods of Food Freezing

There are three basic freezing methods in commercial use, these are freezing in air, freezing by indirect contact with the refrigerant, and freezing by direct immersion in a refrigerating medium. These three basic methods can be further subdivided in various ways, one division is indicated in Table 31.

TABLE 31

COMMERCIAL FREEZING METHODS

Air Freezing	Indirect Contact Freezing	Immersion Freezing
Still-air "sharp" freezer	Single plate	Heat exchange fluid
Blast freezer	Double plate	Compressed gas
Fluidized-bed freezer	Pressure plate	Refrigerant spray
	Slush freezer	

Thus cold air may be used with various degrees of velocity progressing from still-air "sharp" freezing to the high velocity blast freezer tunnel. The velocity of the air also may be used to subdivide and move particles of materials to be frozen, as in the case of fluidized-bed freezing.

Indirect contact freezing includes those methods in which the food or the food package is in contact with a surface which in turn is cooled by a refrigerant, but the food or food package does not contact the refrigerant directly. In the case of solid foods or foods in containers this most commonly involves providing a flat surface or nearly flat surface in contact with refrigerated plates, which may contact 1 or 2 surfaces of the food or package. In the case of liquid foods and purées, the food is pumped through a cold wall heat exchanger and frozen to the slush condition.

Immersion freezing implies direct contact of the food or package with the refrigerant either by submerging the food in the cold liquid or spraying the cold liquid onto the food or package surface.

With the exception of still-air "sharp" freezing, all of the methods may be engineered for batch, semicontinuous, or continuous operation. Also with the exception of still-air "sharp" freezing, all of the other methods generally are referred to as fast freezing methods.

Air Freezing.—The oldest and least expensive air freezing method from an equipment standpoint is still-air "sharp" freezing. Here the food is simply placed in an insulated cold room at a temperature usually maintained in the range of $-10°$ F to $-20°$ F (previous Fig. 41). The method introduced in 1861 became termed "sharp" freezing since anything below zero was then considered very low temperatures. While there is some air movement by natural convection, and in some cases gentle air movement is promoted by placing circulating fans in the room, the method is essentially a still air freezing method to be clearly distinguished from air blast freezing, which employs air velocities that may exceed hurricane speeds. Depending upon size of food items or packages and degree of separation between units, freezing time can be several hours to several days. Sharp freezers remain today a very important freezing method. Sharp freezing conditions also are essentially the freezing conditions that exist in home freezers, except temperatures commonly are closer to $0°$ F than to $-10°$ F or $-20°$ F. Commercially, sharp freezers often double as frozen storage rooms where space permits.

In contrast to sharp freezers, air blast freezers typically are operated at temperatures of $-20°$ to $-50°$ F and forced air velocities of 2,000 to 3,000 ft/min. Under such conditions, 30-lb cans of eggs or fruit that take 72 hr to freeze through in a sharp freezer may be frozen in about 12 to 18 hr. Blast freezers are of many designs; from rooms where food is frozen as a batch, to tunnels through which carts or a belt may be moved continuously. The tunnel blast freezer in Fig. 100 combines an overhead conveyor belt with a lower level track for moving food carts. Particulate unpackaged foods, such as loose vegetables, are automatically fed onto the moving belt whose speed is adjustable according to the required freezing time. Frozen product is dropped from the belt into a collection hopper at the opposite end of the tunnel. Independently, loose foods or packaged cartons loaded on the carts can be moved through the tunnel at a selected rate.

Other designs make use of vertical movement of food on trays. The trays of particulate products such as peas or beans are automatically moved upward through a cold air blast. Freezing time of such particulates in thin layers may be of the order of 15 min. Today along with foods frozen as a single block in a package, vegetables and other particulate items, such as shrimp, are individually frozen so that they can be poured from a bag for greater convenience. These go by the term IQF, which refers to individually quick frozen. Since there is some tendency for such particulates to stick together during freezing, product mechanically dislodged from trays may be passed through a breaker device to disaggregate large clusters before being conveyed under cold air to packaging.

In air blast type systems, manufacturers have developed numerous

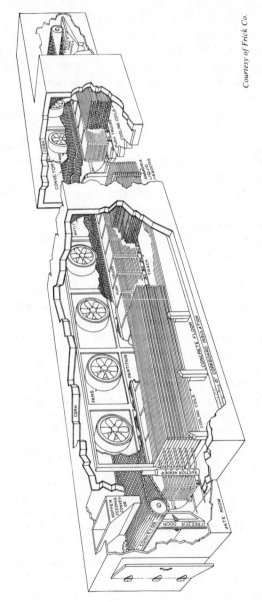

Courtesy of Frick Co.

FIG. 100.   FRICK TUNNEL FREEZER WITH CONVEYOR BELT AND FOOD CARTS

patterns of cold air flow to pass over, under, or through the product. Frequently the principle of countercurrent air flow is employed to bring the coldest air into contact with the already frozen product as it is about to leave the tunnel or column. In this way freezing is progressive and there is no tendency for product to rise in temperature and partially thaw through the freezing process, as would be possible in a cocurrent system, where coldest air enters with unfrozen product and tends to rise in temperature through the tunnel as product gives up heat and freezes.

Modern blast freezers also provide means to overcome major drawbacks inherent in high velocity air freezers. Whenever unwrapped food is placed in a cold zone there is a tendency of the food to lose moisture, whether during freezing or after the food is frozen. In a freezer this can have two consequences; frosting over of refrigerated coils or plates with need for frequent defrosting to maintain heat exchanger efficiency, and drying out of food at its surface resulting in the common defect known as freezer burn. This situation is markedly accelerated in blast freezers where the air is moving at high velocity. When food is frozen and water vapor molecules are removed from the frozen surface by the dryer cold air we have the condition of sublimation, or a crude form of freeze drying, and this is essentially what freezer burn is.

To minimize freezer burn which produces unsightly food surface appearance, nutrient loss, and other defects in unpackaged foods, two techniques are employed. One is the practice of prechilling food with air of high relative humidity at about 25° F. In this case the food partially frozen in the humid air undergoes minimum moisture loss. Then the prechilled surface-frozen food is moved into a second colder zone where it is quickly finish-frozen. The rapid finish-freezing in colder air provides minimum time for the already cold product to lose more moisture, which also decreases the defrosting requirement on freezer coils. The other technique is to wet the unpackaged food pieces in the prechilling zone so as to freeze a thin ice glaze around each food piece or particle. The glazed particles are then moved to the colder zone for quick finish-freezing. The glaze will sublime slightly, but will protect the underlying food from the defects of freezer burn. These techniques are employed in continuous blast freezers of various designs by providing a series of humidity and temperature controlled zones (Fig. 101). To minimize condensation and freezing of moisture on freezer coils, it is common to maintain freezer coils in these zones only very slightly lower in temperature than the circulating air. The problems of freezer burn and frosted coils, of course, are markedly less when packaged foods are frozen.

In various air-type freezers, cold air is blown up through a wire mesh belt that supports and conveys the product. This imparts to particulate foods a slight vibratory motion of the particles which accelerates

Courtesy of Frick Co.

FIG. 101. CONTINUOUS BLAST FREEZER WITH HUMIDITY AND TEMPERATURE
CONTROLLED ZONES FOR GLAZING AND FREEZING

freezing rate. When the air velocity is increased to the point where it just exceeds the velocity of free fall of the particles we get the condition of fluidization and fluidized-bed freezing. The dancing-boiling motion given to peas being fluidized-bed frozen is seen in Fig. 102. This not only gives subdivision of product and intimate contact of each particle with the cold air, but keeps clusters from freezing together and so is particularly well suited to production of frozen items in the IQF form. Freezing times commonly are in the order of minutes.

Several types of fluidized-bed freezers are in commercial use. The workings of one continuous type are shown in Fig. 103. Particulate foods are fed by a shaker onto a porous trough at the right. The food may be prechilled and even moistened if it is desired to produce a frozen glaze around each particle. The high velocity refrigerated air fluidizes the product, freezes it, and moves it in continuous flow from right to left for collection and packaging. This unit has another interesting feature that can be seen from the diagram at the left in Fig. 103. This is the method of continuous and automatic defrost. Air is blown via the fan through the cooling coils and up through the porous food trough. The cold air, now

Courtesy of Frigoscandia AB, Sweden

FIG. 102. "BOILING" MOTION OF PEAS DURING FLUIDIZED-BED
FREEZING

moistened from the food, is recirculated to conserve refrigeration. It tends to condense its moisture onto the cooling coils. But a spray of propylene glycol antifreeze is maintained over the cooling coils to melt ice as it would be formed. In this way the cooling coils are maintained at maximum operating efficiency. The glycol solution is bled off to an evaporator where the accumulated water is easily removed.

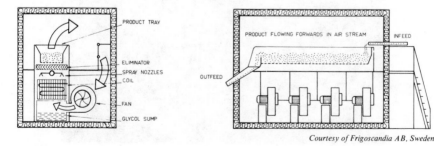

Courtesy of Frigoscandia AB, Sweden

FIG. 103. DIAGRAM OF CONTINUOUS FLUIDIZED-BED FREEZER AND METHOD FOR
DEFROSTING

Indirect Contact Freezing.—While it is of course possible to place solid food directly onto the surface of a block of ice or a block of Dry Ice this is rarely done commercially. Rather, the food is placed on plates, trays, belts, or other cold walls which are chilled by circulating refrigerant, and so the food is in direct contact with the cold wall but in indirect contact with the refrigerant. One should not confuse certain forms of indirect contact freezing with direct immersion freezing. The distinguishing feature always is whether the food or its intimate package is in direct contact with the refrigerant. If a slice of meat or a film-wrapped slice of meat is itself immersed into a brine bath or sprayed with brine this is direct immersion freezing. If the same meat is placed in a metal pail and the pail immersed in the brine then the food and its wrapper would be undergoing indirect contact freezing, and such systems have seen limited use.

The more important indirect contact freezers are typified by the Birdseye Multiplate Freezer of Fig. 104. This consists of a number of metal shelves or plates through which refrigerant is circulated. The food, usually as flat packages, is placed between shelves and there is provision

Courtesy of General Foods Corp.

FIG. 104.   BIRDSEYE MULTIPLATE FREEZER

after loading for applying pressure to squeeze the shelves into more intimate contact with the top and bottom of the packages for faster freezing. All is enclosed within an insulated cabinet. Depending upon refrigerant temperature, package size, degree of contact, and the type of food, freezing time is of the order of 1 to 2 hr for 1.5- to 2.0-in. thick commercial packages. This unit is a batch freezer.

Quite similar are various automatic plate freezers. These have provisions for automatically loading shelves from the packaging line. As a shelf is loaded it is moved into pressure contact with the preceding shelf and into an insulated zone where freezing proceeds. At the rear of the freezing zone frozen packages are discharged one shelf at a time, and the empty shelves return to the loading position once again. The Amerio and the Knowles automatic package freezers operate in this fashion. The CP continuous vertical-plate freezer is somewhat more elaborate in design (Fig. 105). Here, after double plate contact, the frozen packages will be automatically unloaded and conveyed to cartoning.

Courtesy of CP Division, St. Regis

FIG. 105.   FOOD PACKAGES BEING AUTOMATICALLY LOADED INTO TOP OF A CP CONTINUOUS VERTICAL-PLATE FREEZER

In all of these indirect contact plate or shelf freezing machines, efficiency is dependent upon the extent of contact between the plates and the food. For this reason packages should be well filled or slightly overfilled to make good pressure contact with the plates, and solid compact products such as meat or fish fillets freeze more rapidly than shrimp or vegetables where the individual pieces are separated from one another by small air spaces.

Indirect contact freezers for liquid foods and purées are quite different. They generally take the form of the tubular scraped surface type heat exchangers previously described (previous Fig. 22, 91), with refrigerant rather than steam on the side of the wall opposite the food. As was the case when this equipment (Fig. 91) was used for heating, the liquid food is pumped through the inside tube with its rotating shaft or mutator. This occupies most of the inner tube space and so the food is forced to pass through the remaining annulus as a thin layer in contact with the cold wall. Scraper blades attached to and rotating with the mutator continually scrape the cold wall as food tends to freeze onto it. This speeds the freezing rate three ways: (1) it keeps the cold wall free of a frozen insulating food layer buildup, which would minimize the temperature differential between the unfrozen food and the effective cold wall; (2) it shaves ice crystals from the cold wall as freezing progresses and these ice crystals seed the unfrozen portion of the food, promoting further freezing within the mass; and (3) the scraper blades (and mutator) keep the mass in motion, continually bringing new portions of food into contact with the cold wall.

Freezing is virtually instantaneous, occurring in a matter of seconds. In this type of unit freezing is never carried to completion, or else the frozen product would set up in the tube and choke off continuous flow. Instead the product is frozen to the slush condition, packaged, and then hard frozen in an air blast or immersion-type freezer.

Immersion Freezing.—As we have said, in immersion freezing we may immerse the loose food or packages containing the food directly into the refrigerating medium. Or we may spray the refrigerant onto the food or package. It should be appreciated that in a strict sense air freezing is a kind of immersion freezing. However, immersion freezing generally is meant to apply to refrigerants other than cold air. The advantages of direct immersion freezing include the following:

(1) There is intimate contact between the food or package and the refrigerant, and therefore resistance to heat transfer is minimized. This is particularly important with irregularly shaped food pieces that we wish to freeze very rapidly, such as loose shrimp, mushrooms, and the like.

(2) Loose food pieces can be frozen individually by immersion freezing, as they can by air freezing, but immersion freezing has the advantage of minimizing their contact with air during freezing, which can be desirable for foods sensitive to oxidation.

(3) For some foods, the speed of immersion freezing with cryogenic

liquids produces quality unattainable by any other currently known freezing method.

Direct immersion freezing immediately places limitations on the refrigerants that may be used, especially if they are to come into contact with unpackaged foods. These include the requirements of nontoxicity, purity, cleanliness, freedom from foreign tastes and odors, absence of foreign colors or bleaching agents, etc. Similarly when the food is packaged, nontoxicity and noncorrosiveness to the packaging material are important. The refrigerants for immersion freezing are of two broad classes; namely the low freezing point liquids which are chilled by indirect contact with another refrigerant, and the cryogenic liquids, such as compressed liquified nitrogen, which owe their cooling effect to their own evaporation.

The low freezing point liquids that have been used for contact with nonpackaged foods have commonly included solutions of sugars, sodium chloride, and glycerol. These must be used at sufficient concentration to remain liquid at 0°F or lower to be effective. In the case of sodium chloride brine, for example, this requires a concentration of about 21%. One can go as low in temperature as −6°F with a 23% brine, but this is the eutectic point, and at lower temperatures a salt and water mixture freezes out of solution, so the lowest practical brine freezing temperature is −6°F. Brine cannot be used with unpackaged foods that should not become salty, and today brine for direct immersion freezing is largely restricted to freezing of fish at sea. Sugar solutions have been used to freeze fruits, but the difficulty here is that to reach a freezing point of −5.9°F one must go to 62% sucrose, which becomes very viscous at the low temperature. Still lower freezing temperatures are not practicable because −5.9°F is the eutectic point in this case, and lower temperatures freeze out a mixture of sugar-water crystals. Glycerol-water mixtures have been used to freeze fruit, but like sugar cannot be used for foods that should not become sweet. One can get down to −52°F with a 67% glycerol solution in water. Another low freezing point liquid related to glycerol is propylene glycol. A 60% propylene glycol-40% water mixture will not freeze until −60°F is reached. Propylene glycol is nontoxic but has an acrid taste. For this reason its use in immersion freezing is generally limited to packaged foods.

Commercial equipment for immersion freezing with low freezing point liquids is typified by the continuous round shell direct immersion freezer which is well suited to the freezing of food in cans (Fig. 106). The shell has a large diameter closed tubular reel that rotates within it. The cans are positioned at the periphery of this rotating reel, and refrigerant is circulated in the annulus between the outer shell and the inner reel. Since

Courtesy of FMC Corp.

FIG. 106.   CONTINUOUS ROUND SHELL DIRECT IMMERSION FREEZER

the inner reel is closed at its ends, refrigerant flows only through the space
occupied by the cans, reducing the volume of refrigerant needed. In a
typical operation about 300 to 400 6-oz cans will be fed into the unit and
will emerge frozen per minute. Residence time or freezing time can be
in the order of 30 min. Rotation of the cans as they pass through this unit
imparts motion to fluid foods in the cans as they freeze; this contributes
to a faster, more uniform, small ice crystal type of freezing. Another type
of immersion freezer for cans was the Finnegan tubular freezer. Cans
were introduced into the top of a battery of vertical tubes that were only
slightly greater in diameter than the cans. The tubes were rifled so as to
give the cans a spiral motion and keep their contents in gentle motion
during freezing. Refrigerant was pumped through the tubes in a direction
countercurrent to the continuous forward motion of the cans. With
refrigerant at $-30°$ F, gallon cans of orange juice froze in about 45 min.
The Finnegan freezer was an excellent piece of equipment for freezing
juice in relatively large cans. However, since large units of single strength
juice are seldom frozen today, this freezer is no longer manufactured or
used.

   Immersion Freezing with Cryogenic Liquids.—Freezing with cryogenic
liquids is rapidly gaining the prestige position in freezing that freeze dry-

ing is enjoying in the field of dehydration. When we speak of cryogenic liquids we mean liquefied gases of extremely low boiling point, such as liquid nitrogen at $-320°$ F, and liquid carbon dioxide at $-110°$ F. Today liquid nitrogen is by far the most important cryogenic liquid in immersion freezing of foods.

The major advantages to liquid nitrogen freezing are the following:

(1) The boiling point of liquid nitrogen at atmospheric pressure is $-320°$ F. This means that the immersion liquid undergoing slow boiling is at $-320°$ F which provides a great driving force for heat transfer.

(2) Liquid nitrogen like other immersion fluids intimately contacts all portions of irregularly shaped foods, thus minimizing resistance to heat transfer.

(3) Since the cold temperature results from evaporation of the liquid nitrogen there is no need for a primary refrigerant to cool this medium.

(4) Liquid nitrogen is nontoxic and inert to food constituents. Moreover, by displacing air from the food it can minimize oxidative changes during freezing and through packaged storage.

(5) Because of the speed of liquid nitrogen freezing, with certain products in the form of large food pieces it can give a quality unattainable by any other commercial freezing method. While many products do not require such fast freezing for good quality, some products such as tomato slices cannot be frozen by any other method without excessive tissue damage. Nevertheless, even with liquid nitrogen, satisfactory freezing of tomato slices further depends upon the use of very meaty Italian-type tomatoes which are relatively resistant to cellular disruption. Other potential new products also are attainable. Orange segments have been liquid nitrogen frozen and then in their brittle state fragmented into individual juice cells with the juice cell walls largely unruptured. Such juice cells have had interest as possible flavoring components for addition to such foods as ice cream and the like.

The major disadvantage of liquid nitrogen freezing generally cited has to do with costs, but depending upon product this objection may be invalid.

Some additional properties of liquid nitrogen have to do with its heat capacity or refrigerating effect. In being vaporized from a liquid at $-320°$ F to a gas at $-320°$ F each pound of liquid nitrogen absorbs 86 Btu, the latent heat of vaporization. Then each pound of gas at $-320°$ F absorbs another 80 Btu in rising in temperature to $0°$ F; this is simply the specific heat of the gaseous nitrogen times the temperature rise from $-320°$ F to $0°$ F. Thus, the total heat uptake of the liquid at $-320°$ F going to zero is 166 Btu/lb.

This is very important in the design of spraying type liquid nitrogen freezers. To get the maximum freezing effect from spraying we want the nitrogen to impinge upon the food surface as liquid droplets rather than as a cold gas. As liquid droplets we gain the cooling effect of the latent heat of vaporization plus the sensible heat of gas temperature rise, or 166 Btu/lb of liquid. If the spray permits the liquid to vaporize before contacting the food then we take only 80 Btu/lb of gas from the food in going from a gas temperature of $-320°$ F to $0°$ F.

The principles of manufacture and handling of liquid nitrogen should be understood. Essentially, liquid nitrogen is manufactured by compressing air and simultaneously removing the heat of compression. The cooled compressed air is then allowed to expand through specially designed valves. This expansion causes the air to further chill itself to the point of liquefaction, producing a mixture principally of liquid nitrogen and liquid oxygen. Since liquid oxygen has a higher boiling point than liquid nitrogen, namely $-297°$ F, the oxygen and nitrogen can be separated by distillation. Liquid nitrogen with its lower boiling point of $-320°$ F comes off first and goes to a gas. The gaseous nitrogen can be recompressed as above. In recent years technological advances in the production of liquid gases have stemmed from the needs of the space program where liquid oxygen is an important fuel.

At $-320°$ F and at atmospheric pressure liquid nitrogen boils gently. It does not produce an excessive pressure of nitrogen gas above the liquid if placed in a vessel and maintained at $-320°$ F, and this is the key to liquid nitrogen storage and handling. Liquid nitrogen is transported and stored at $-320°$ F by housing it in large insulated tanks of the thermos bottle or Dewar flask type. So long as insulation maintains this low temperature, pressure developed in the tank is comparatively small and not dangerous. In contrast, compressed nitrogen gas at room temperature is under great pressure and requires storage in the familiar high pressure steel gas cylinders.

Manufacturers of liquid nitrogen deliver it in tank truck quantities to insulated storage tanks at food plants. Filling is done simply by hose connection from the tank truck, often making use of the slight pressure of nitrogen gas above the liquid in the tank truck to force the liquid nitrogen through the hose into the storage vessel. The same procedure is used to deliver liquid nitrogen from the storage vessel to the liquid nitrogen food freezer or to a refrigerated truck for transporting frozen food (Fig. 107).

The food freezing equipment itself is undergoing rapid development and change but much of the equipment is essentially of tunnel construction with a continuous mesh belt (Fig. 108). The earlier practice of submerging the food under liquid nitrogen has largely given way to more efficient use

Courtesy D. C. Brown, Air Products and Chemicals, Inc.

FIG. 107. TRANSFERRING LIQUID NITROGEN FROM STORAGE TANK TO REFRIGERATED TRUCK

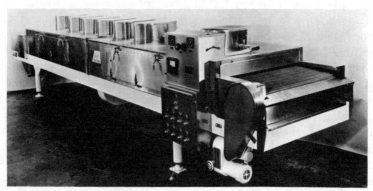

Courtesy of Air Reduction Co., Inc.

FIG. 108. LIQUID NITROGEN SPRAY FREEZING UNIT

of liquid nitrogen sprays. Design features are aimed at depositing the spray as a liquid onto the food surface, minimizing sensible heat loss through insulation, and in very large installations provisions may be engineered to recover and recompress the vaporized nitrogen for reuse. When liquid nitrogen contacts the relatively warm food it boils violently. In most installations it is not recompressed, but the spent nitrogen gas which still may be in the range of about 0°F to 40°F is vented to contact and prechill incoming food, or to cool a refrigerated storage room.

While liquid nitrogen is capable of freezing food down to −320°F, as was indicated earlier this is virtually never done, and in addition to unnecessary cost could even be damaging to some foods. The food is seldom frozen to a temperature below −50°F, and quality results largely from the speed at which this temperature is reached. In the case of many fruit, vegetable, meat, and fish items this may require of the order of 1 to 3 min.

Much shrimp is liquid nitrogen frozen in the IQF form. Typically the shrimp enter the freezing tunnel at one end and a liquid nitrogen spray is directed at the conveyor belt at the opposite end of the tunnel. The spray vaporizes and cold nitrogen gas is directed through the tunnel to meet the incoming shrimp in a countercurrent fashion. The incoming shrimp thus are first chilled by the cold gas to about 30°F before they reach the spray. Then they are passed under the liquid spray and are frozen to a surface temperature of about −300°F. The shrimp are then moved through an equilibration zone where the cold surface and warmer core equilibrate to a uniform temperature of about −50°F. The shrimp are then passed through a controlled water spray, where the stored refrigeration of the shrimp freezes a thin ice glaze protective against subsequent dehydration in storage. The shrimp then emerge from the glaze spray at about −20°F for packaging and storage at about −10°F.

Generally liquid nitrogen freezing will produce less dehydration loss during freezing and less drip loss during thawing than other freezing methods. This can amount to as much as 5% of the weight of some foods. If the food is worth $1.00/lb the savings in weight loss would amount to $0.05/lb of product. This sort of thing must be taken into account when comparing the true costs of liquid nitrogen freezing or any other kind of freezing. In some cases liquid nitrogen freezing, generally found to be more expensive than other methods, may actually be found to be less costly under such analysis. This type of subtlety, frequently product specific, is to be found in all types of food processing and adds to the difficulty of developing true cost comparisons. In any event, even while liquid nitrogen freezing is in the process of revealing its attributes, the constant evolution of processing methods continues.

Cryogenic freezing with carbon dioxide has taken two forms. In one, powdered Dry Ice which sublimes at $-110°F$ is mechanically mixed with the food to be frozen. In the other, liquid carbon dioxide under high pressure is sprayed onto the food surface. As pressure is released in the course of spraying, the liquid carbon dioxide becomes Dry Ice snow at $-110°F$. There are applications where frozen food quality with this refrigerant are essentially equal to that of liquid nitrogen freezing. In such cases, since a given weight of Dry Ice will absorb over twice as many Btu of heat in vaporizing as does liquid nitrogen, the use of carbon dioxide may well have economic advantages over liquid nitrogen freezing.

"Freon" Freezing.—The newest entry into the competition between fast freezing methods is direct contact of the food with a special "Freon" refrigerant approved by the FDA for this application. Freon is the trademark for a family of fluorocarbons manufactured by DuPont and commonly used as refrigerants, solvents, and propellants for aerosols. The highly purified food grade Freon has a boiling point at atmospheric pressure of $-22°F$. Although not nearly as cold as liquid nitrogen or Dry Ice, evaporating Freon does have a substantial heat of vaporization which is taken advantage of in the DuPont system. Equipment consists essentially of a conveyor belt that transports food under sprays of liquid Freon within the freezing chamber. Because Freon is substantially higher in cost than an equivalent weight of liquid nitrogen or carbon dioxide the economic feasibility of the system depends upon a highly efficient recovery of the Freon which vaporizes on contact with the food. This is achieved by capturing the Freon vapors which are then recondensed by a conventional refrigeration unit in the system and recycled continuously. Several Freon freezers have recently gone into commercial operation and claims have been made for exceptional frozen product quality at costs lower than can be achieved with either liquid nitrogen or carbon dioxide.

Packaging Considerations

The packaging of frozen foods imposes certain special requirements. Because of the tendency of water vapor to sublime from frozen food surfaces to colder surfaces in freezers and storage rooms, packaging materials for frozen foods should have a high degree of water vapor impermeability. Most foods expand on freezing, some to the extent of 10% of their volume. Therefore packages in which food is frozen should be strong, have a degree of flexibility, or should not be completely filled. As with all foods that may be stored for months or years, packages should be protective against light and air. Because frozen foods generally will be thawed at time of use in their containers, packages should be liquid tight to prevent leaking on thawing. Many packages and packaging materials such as cans, metal foils, waxed papers, plastic coated cardboards, and plastic films are all satisfactory for frozen foods. Glass generally is not satisfactory for frozen foods due to breakage from expansion and from thermal shocks. Packaging will be considered in more detail in a later chapter.

BIBLIOGRAPHY

AMERICAN SOCIETY OF REFRIGERATING ENGINEERS, 1956–1957, 1959, and AMERICAN SOCIETY OF HEATING, REFRIGERATING AND VENTILATING ENGINEERS, 1969, 1970, 1971. Refrigerating Data Books. ASHRAE, New York.

ANON. 1960. Liquid nitrogen process. ASHRAE J. 2, No. 5, 23.

ANON. 1961. Truck refrigeration with liquid nitrogen offers low investment cost. Refrig., Serv. Contr. 29, No. 6, 24.

ANON. 1967. ASHRAE Handbook of Fundamentals. ASHRAE, New York.

BRODY, A. L., and BEDROSIAN, K. 1961. Effect of room temperature vs. refrigerated storage on quality of canned fruit and vegetable products. Food Technol. 15, 367–370.

BROWN, D. C. 1967. The application of cryogenic fluids to the freezing of foods. Advan. Cryog. Eng. 12. Plenum Press, New York.

DAUGHTERS, M. R., and GLENN, D. S. 1946. The role of water in freezing foods. Refrig. Eng. 52, 137–140.

DESROSIER, N. W. 1961. Attack on Starvation. Avi Publishing Co., Westport, Conn.

DESROSIER, N. W. 1970. The Technology of Food Preservation, 3rd Edition. Avi Publishing Co., Westport, Conn.

FENNEMA, O., and POWRIE, W. D. 1964. Fundamentals of low temperature food preservation. In Advances in Food Research, Vol. 13. Academic Press, New York.

FISHER, D. V. 1960. Cooling rates of apples packed in different bushel containers and stacked at different spacings in cold storage. ASHRAEJ. 2, No. 7, 53–56.

GORDON, J., PAYNE, I. R., STEPHENSON, K. Q., and CONE, J. F. 1965. The effect of freezing treatments on the quality of certain frozen foods. Penn. State Univ. Bull. 727.

GORTNER, W. A., ERDMAN, F. S., and MASTERMAN, N. K. 1948. Principles of Food Freezing. John Wiley & Sons, New York.

HAWTHORN, J., and ROLFE, E. J. (Editors) 1968. Low Temperature Biology of Foodstuffs. Pergamon Press, Oxford, England.

HAYES, K. M., KANE, J. J., MACLINN, W. A., and COLLINS, S. C. 1961. Liquefied gases —new techniques in food preservation. ASHRAE J. 3, No. 9, 78–83.

HENNEY, C. F., and McCOY, D. C. 1954. Mechanical refrigeration for railroad refrigerator cars. Refrig. Eng. 62, No. 10, 41–48.

HUELSEN, W. A. 1954. Sweet Corn. Interscience Publishers, New York.

LAWLER, F. K., and TRAUBERMAN, L. 1969. What to know about Freon freezing. Food Eng. 41, No. 4, 67–72.

MATCHES, J. R., and LISTON, J. 1968. Low temperature growth of Salmonella. J. Food Sci. 33, No. 6, 641–645.

McCOY, D. C. 1963. Refrigeration in food processing. In Food Processing Operations, Vol. 1. M. A. Joslyn, and J. L. Heid (Editors). Avi Publishing Co., Westport, Conn.

MILLER, A. T., EL-BISI, H. M., SAWYER, F. M. 1964. Microbiological and public health aspects of prepared frozen foods—A review. Univ. Mass. Bull. 548.

PENCE, J. W. et al. 1955. Studies on the preservation of bread by freezing. Food Technol. 9, 495–499.

RAMSBOTTOM, J. M., and ROSCHEN, H. L. 1949. Edible life of meats in household refrigerators. Refrig. Eng. 57, No. 4, 327–350.

SHUMAN, A. C. 1956. Measurement of crystallization in foods. Proc. First Intern. Symp. Food Physics 1, 85–97.

SLAVIN, J. W. 1958. Methods of freezing used in the fisheries—A review. Fishing Gaz. Ann. Rev. 75, 176–186.

SMITH, A. U. (Editor) 1970. Current Trends in Cryobiology. Plenum Press, New York.

SMOCK, R. M., and VAN DOREN, A. 1939. Studies with modified atmosphere storage of apples. Refrig. Eng. 38, No. 3, 163–166.

TRESSLER, D. K., and EVERS, C. F. 1957. The Freezing Preservation of Foods, Vol. 1 and 2. Avi Publishing Co., Westport, Conn.

TRESSLER, D. K., VAN ARSDEL, W. B., and COPLEY, M. J. (Editors) 1968. The Freezing Preservation of Foods, 4th Edition, Vols. 1, 2, 3, and 4. Avi Publishing Co., Westport, Conn.

U.S. DEPT. AGR. 1960. Conference on Freezer Food Quality. U.S. Dept. Agr., Agr. Res. Serv. 74–21.

VAN ARSDEL, W. B. 1961. Alignment chart speeds computation of quality changes in frozen foods. Food Process. 22, No. 12, 40.

VAN ARSDEL, W. B., COPLEY, M. J., and OLSON, R. L. (Editors) 1969. Quality and Stability of Frozen Foods. Wiley-Interscience, New York.

WEIL, B. H., and STERNE, F. 1948. Literature search on preservation of foods by freezing. Georgia School Technol., Atlanta.

WEISER, H. H., MOUNTNEY, G. J., and GOULD, W. A. 1971. Practical Food Microbiology and Technology, 2nd Edition. Avi Publishing Co., Westport, Conn.

WRIGHT, R. C., ROSE, D. H., and WHITEMAN, T. M. 1954. The commercial storage of fruits, vegetables, and florist and nursery stock. U.S. Dept. Agr. Handbook 66.

CHAPTER 10

Food Dehydration and Concentration

INTRODUCTION

Water is removed from foods under natural field conditions, by a variety of controlled dehydration processes, and as a consequence of such common operations as cooking and baking. In each case some degree of drying and concentrating of food constituents occurs. However, in modern food processing, such terms as food dehydration and food concentration have acquired rather special meanings which need some clarification.

Drying has been a means of preserving foods from earliest times. Its application in simplest form undoubtedly was learned from observing nature. Grains in the field dry on the stalk by exposure to the sun. Often a sufficient degree of dryness is achieved, for example about 14% final moisture in the case of grains, to require no further drying by man to accomplish effective preservation. This also is true of many plant seeds and spices, and is approached by certain fruits such as dates and figs which develop high sugar contents as they tend to dry out on the tree. Man must have observed these naturally sun dried products before learning to dry fish and thin slices of meat by hanging them in the air and sun. Where drying of these animal products took a long time bacterial spoilage during the slow operation occurred, and so the use of smoke and salt as further preservative agents in combination with drying gradually evolved.

Sun drying is still in use in many parts of the world including the United States (Fig. 109). Sun drying is used to prepare raisins and prunes; to dry apricots, dates, figs, and the like; and of course to dry grains prior to harvest. But while sun drying in some parts of the world and for certain products is the most economical kind of drying, it has several obvious disadvantages. Thus, sun drying is dependent upon the elements which are beyond strict control; it is slow and not suitable for many high quality products; it generally will not lower moisture contents below about 15%, which is too high for storage stability of numerous food products; it requires considerable acreage; and the food being exposed is subject to contamination and losses from dust, insects, rodents, and the like.

It was to be expected, therefore, that food drying would be brought indoors where the drying operation could be better controlled. Efforts at artificial drying with heated air date back to the close of the eighteenth century. It is artificial drying under controlled conditions that the term food dehydration refers to today. But in modern food processing food dehydration has a still more specific meaning in contrast to a number of processes that remove water from foods.

238

Courtesy of U. S. Dept. Agr.

FIG. 109.   GRAPES ON TRAYS DRYING IN THE SUN

When we fry potatoes, toast cereals, broil steak, or bake bread we remove water. However, the frying, toasting, broiling, and baking operations do much more than simply remove water. They bring about several other changes such as cooking, browning, and tenderizing. These foods are changed substantially in addition to being decreased in water content, and we desire these changes quite beyond any preservation value. Such processes are characterized by the changes they make in foods beyond water removal.

Then there are the processes we refer to as evaporation or concentration. These are designed to remove only part of the water of foods; perhaps ⅓ to ⅔ of the water as in the preparation of syrups, evaporated milk, tomato paste, and condensed soups. These processes also do not come under the currently accepted meaning of the term food dehydration.

By food dehydration we generally mean virtually complete water removal from foods under controlled conditions which cause minimum or ideally no other changes in the food properties. Such foods, depending upon the item, commonly are dried to final moistures within the range of about 1 to 5%. Examples are dried milk and eggs, potato flakes, instant coffee, and orange juice crystals. Such products will have storage stability at room temperature of a year or longer. A major criterion of quality of dehydrated foods is that when they are reconstituted by the addition of water they be very close to, or virtually indistinguishable from, the original food material used in their preparation. In food dehydration, the technological challenge is especially difficult since very low moisture levels for maximum product stability are not easily obtained with minimum change to food materials. Further, such optimization frequently can be approached only at the expense of increased drying costs. With sensitive foods, product quality and processing costs also usually are correlated in the case of concentration processes.

FOOD DEHYDRATION

Why Foods Are Dried

Preservation is the principal reason but not the only reason we dehydrate foods. In addition to preservation we dehydrate foods to decrease weight and bulk (Fig. 110). Since orange juice contains approximately 12% solids, if we remove all of the water we are left with ⅛ the weight, that is, 8 oz of

FIG. 110.   WEIGHT AND VOLUME RELATIONSHIPS IN DEHYDRATED JUICES

liquid orange juice yield approximately 1 oz of dried solids. To reconstitute, 7 oz of water are added at the time of food consumption. In the case of juices, the bulk or volume of the powders also is less than the original juices, although rarely are the powders decreased in volume to the same extent that they are reduced in weight. These reductions in weight and bulk can result in economies in shipping and in cost of containers, but this is not always the case with dehydrated foods.

Some drying processes are chosen to retain the size and shape of the original food. Freeze drying of large food pieces is such a process. In Fig. 111 the freeze-dried steak on the left has essentially the same volume as

Courtesy of Food Processing-Marketing

Fig. 111.   Freeze-Dried Steaks

the original steak. Savings may be made in shipping costs from reduced weight, but not in size of containers in this instance. Further, sometimes shipping costs are not based on weight but are based on volume. In such a case the freeze-dried steaks would not be cheaper to package or ship than their original counterparts.

A third reason for dehydration is the production of convenience items. Good examples of this would be instant coffee and instant mashed potatoes. In both cases all brewing or cooking steps are completed before the products are dried. The consumer simply adds water and stirs or mixes. Regardless of the reasons for water removal, food dehydration processes are based on sound scientific principles.

Heat and Mass Transfer

Whatever method of drying we employ, food dehydration involves two occurrences: (1) we must get heat into the product; and (2) we must get moisture out of the product.

These two occurrences are not always favored by the same operating conditions. For example, food may be pressed between two heated plates. This would give close contact and improve heat transfer into the food through top and bottom, but the same close contact of the plates would interfere with the escape of free moisture. It might be better to use one bottom hot plate to get heat in, and a free surface on top of the food to let moisture out. These two occurrences involve heat transfer in and mass transfer out; by mass transfer we mean water transfer. In food dehydration we generally are interested in a maximum drying rate and so every effort is made to speed heat and mass transfer rates. The following considerations are important in this regard.

Surface Area.—Generally we subdivide food to be dehydrated into small pieces or thin layers to speed heat and mass transfer. Subdivision speeds drying for two reasons. First, larger surface area provides more surface in contact with the heating medium and more surface from which the moisture can escape. Second, smaller particles or thinner layers reduce the distance heat must travel to the center of the food, and reduce the distance through which moisture in the center of the food must travel to reach the surface and escape. Nearly all types of food driers make use of a condition of large surface area of the food to be dried.

Temperature.—The greater the temperature difference between the heating medium and the food the greater will be the rate of heat transfer into the food, which provides the driving force for moisture removal. When the heating medium is air, temperature plays a second important role. As water is driven from the food in the form of water vapor it must be carried away, or else the moisture will create a saturated atmosphere at the food's surface which will slow down the rate of subsequent water removal. The hotter the air the more moisture it will hold before becoming saturated. Thus, high temperature air in the vicinity of the dehydrating food will take up the moisture being driven from the food to a greater extent than will cooler air. Obviously, a greater volume of air also can take up more moisture than a lesser volume of air.

Air Velocity.—Not only will heated air take up more moisture than cool air, but air in motion will be still more effective. Air in motion, that is high velocity air, in addition to taking up moisture will sweep it away from the drying food's surface, preventing the moisture from creating a saturated atmosphere which would slow down subsequent moisture removal. This is why clothes dry more rapidly on a windy day.

Dryness of Air.—When air is the drying medium or food is dried in air, the drier the air the more rapid is the rate of drying. Dry air is capable of absorbing and holding moisture. Moist air is closer to saturation and so can absorb and hold less additional moisture than if it were dry.

But the dryness of the air also determines how low a moisture content the food product can be dried to. Dehydrated foods are hygroscopic. Each food has its own equilibrium relative humidity. This is the humidity at a given temperature where the food will neither lose moisture to the atmosphere nor pick up moisture from the atmosphere. Below this atmospheric humidity level food can be further dried. Above this humidity it cannot, rather it picks up moisture from the atmosphere. For any product we can determine this equilibrium relative humidity at different temperatures by exposing the dried product to different humidity atmospheres in bell jars. We then weigh the product after several hours of exposure. The humidity at which the product neither loses nor gains moisture is the

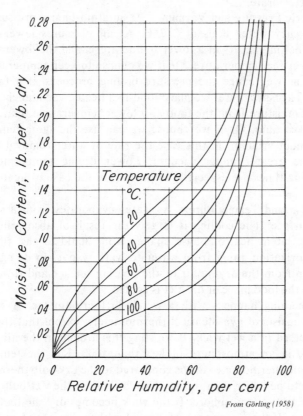

From Görling (1958)

FIG. 112. WATER SORPTION ISOTHERMS OF POTATO

equilibrium relative humidity. If we then plot the data we get water sorption isotherms such as seen in Fig. 112. Such data can tell us, for example, that at 212° F and 40% RH, potato comes into equilibrium at 4% moisture; if we wish to dry it down to 2% moisture (Fig. 112) with 212° F air, then this air must be at about 15% RH. Similar water sorption isotherms have been established for a wide variety of food products and can be found in appropriate references. But for a new product, a mixture of ingredients such as a dehydrated soup, or a new variety of fruit or vegetable, it usually is necessary to experimentally determine the isotherms for the specific product. With this information we can select the temperature and humidity of the drying air to be most effective. Equilibrium relative humidity data also are important when we consider storage of the dried product. If the food is packaged in a container that is not moisture tight, and is stored in an atmosphere above the dried food's equilibrium relative humidity, then the food will gradually pick up moisture and may cake or otherwise deteriorate.

Atmospheric Pressure and Vacuum.—At an atmospheric pressure of 760 mm of mercury water boils at 212° F. At all pressures lower than atmospheric, boiling occurs at a lower temperature, and the lower the pressure the lower the temperature. Or if we choose to keep temperature constant, then as we reduce the pressure boiling proceeds at a faster and faster rate. This says that if we place food in a heated vacuum chamber we can remove moisture from the food at a lower temperature than if we did not employ vacuum. Or if we choose we can use the same temperature with or without vacuum, in this case the rate of water removal from the food will be greater under vacuum. Lower drying temperatures and shorter drying times are especially important in the case of heat-sensitive foods.

Evaporation and Temperature.—As water evaporates from a surface it cools the surface. The cooling is largely the result of absorption by the water of the latent heat of phase change from liquid to gas, that is the heat of vaporization going from water to water vapor. In doing this the heat is taken from the drying air or the heating surface and from the hot food, and so the food piece or droplet is cooled.

The same thing happens with a wet bulb thermometer. A sling psychrometer consists of two identical thermometers, except that the bulb of one is immersed in a wet wick. If we sling this around in the air to speed evaporation, in an atmosphere of less than 100% RH the temperature of the wet bulb thermometer drops compared to the dry bulb thermometer. It continues to be lower then the dry bulb as long as the wet bulb can give off moisture to the atmosphere. If the wick becomes dry the temperature ceases to drop. If the air is at a high humidity then the rate of evaporation and the amount of water vapor evaporated from the wet wick is less then that evaporated at lower humidity. The extent of the wet bulb temperature depression is a measure of relative humidity.

A particle or piece of solid food, or a droplet of liquid food, while it is being dehydrated acts as a wet bulb so long as it still contains free water. There are several important consequences of this:

(1) Regardless of the temperature of the drying air or heating surface, the temperature of the food will not be substantially higher than the temperature of a wet bulb so long as water is evaporating rapidly. Thus, in a spray drier the incoming air may be at 400° F and the exit air at perhaps 250° F, but the food particle while drying may be no higher than about 160° F.

(2) As the moisture content of the food particle decreases and evaporation slows down, the particle rises in temperature. When there is virtually no more free water, then the food particle in the above spray drying example rises in temperature to that of the 400° F incoming air, and the exit air also approaches 400° F if there are no other heat losses through the drier.

(3) Since foods are heat sensitive we generally must get them out of high temperature driers long before they reach such high temperatures (as the above 400° F); or if this can't be done then we design equipment so that foods receive this kind of heat for only an extremely short time.

(4) As a further consequence, unless preheated specifically for the purpose, virtually no quality dehydrated food emerges from a drier in a sterile condition. While a large proportion of the microbial load is killed during most drying operations, many bacterial spores are not. This becomes still more significant as the dehydration method is designed to be more gentle to protect highly delicate food types. In freeze drying, for example, comparatively few microorganisms are destroyed, and indeed freeze drying has been used for many years as a method of preserving the viability of bacterial cultures. The non-sterilizing aspects of food dehydration also apply to certain natural food enzymes which may survive drying conditions.

Time and Temperature.—Since all important methods of food dehydration employ heat, and food constituents are sensitive to heat, compromises must be made between maximum possible drying rate and maintenance of food quality. As was the case in the use of heat for pasteurization and sterilization, with few exceptions drying processes which employ high temperatures for short times do less damage to food than drying processes employing lower temperatures for longer times. Thus, vegetable pieces dried in a properly designed oven in four hours would retain greater quality than the same product sun dried over two days. Several drying processes will achieve dehydration in a matter of minutes or even less if the food is sufficiently subdivided.

One process, namely freeze drying which will be discussed further on, may appear to contradict the high temperature-short time principle since drying may take eight hours or more and still produce excellent quality. However, in this case the product is dried directly from the frozen state, and at such low temperatures that there is little deterioration.

Normal Drying Curve

When foods are dried they do not lose water at a constant rate all the way down to bone dryness. On the contrary, as drying progresses the rate of water removal under any set of fixed conditions drops off. This is seen in Fig. 113 for carrot dice. In practice while we may remove 90% of a product's water in four hours it may require another four hours to remove most of the remaining 10%, and this becomes asymptotic so that zero moisture is never reached under practical operating conditions. At the beginning of drying, and for some time thereafter, generally water continues to evaporate from the food piece at a rather constant rate as if it were drying from

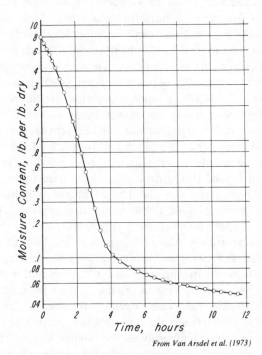

From Van Arsdel et al. (1973)

FIG. 113. CHANGES IN MOISTURE CONTENT OF CARROT DICE
DURING DEHYDRATION

a free surface. This is referred to as the constant rate period of drying, and in Fig. 113 it goes on for about four hours. This is followed by an inflection in the drying curve which leads into the falling rate period of drying.

These changes during dehydration can be largely explained in terms of heat and mass transfer phenomena. A cube of food in the course of dehydration will lose moisture from its surfaces and gradually develop a thick dried layer with remaining moisture largely confined to its center. From the center to the surface a moisture gradient will be established. As a result, the outside dried layer will form an insulation barrier against rapid heat transfer into the food piece, especially since the evaporating water leaves air voids behind it. In addition to less driving force from decreased heat transfer, the centrally remaining water also now has farther to travel to get out of the food piece than did surface moisture at the start of drying. In addition, as the food dries it approaches its normal equilibrium relative humidity. As it does, it begins to pick up molecules of water vapor from the drying atmosphere as fast as it loses them. When these rates are equal, drying ceases.

These are not the only food changes that contribute to the shape of the typical drying curve, although they are major factors. The precise shape of the normal drying curve varies with different food materials, for different types of driers, and in response to varying drying conditions such as temperature, humidity, air velocity, direction of the air, thickness of the food, and other factors. But the drying of most food materials generally shows periods of constant and falling rate, and the removal of water below about two per cent without damage to the product is exceedingly difficult.

Properties of Food Materials

The physical factors affecting heat and mass transfer such as temperature, humidity, air velocity, geometry to produce maximum surface area, and the like are usually relatively easy to optimize and control, and largely determine drier design. Far more subtle are some of the properties of food materials, and how they may change during dehydration and affect drying rates and final product quality. In the case of food freezing, it was pointed out that various food properties affect heat transfer. The picture is more complex with regard to dehydration since food raw material properties affect both heat and mass transfer, and both can have gross effects on characteristics of the dried products.

Constituent Orientation.—Few foods approach homogeneity at the molecular level. A piece of meat will have lean and fat interlaced or marbled together. We place a layer of fat or oil over a bottle of liquid to keep it from evaporating. We therefore can expect that a piece of meat being dried will give up water at different rates in the regions of fat and lean, especially if the water must escape through a fat layer. This suggests that where fat occurs in layers, we can achieve faster drying if we orient the meat's position relative to the source of heat so that moisture escapes in a line parallel to the layers of fat rather than having it pass through them. The same principle can apply to layers of muscle fibers. The rate of drying will differ depending upon whether orientation with respect to the heat source, such as a heated plate, encourages moisture to escape parallel with or transverse to the stratification of muscle fibers. Parallel escape generally gives faster drying.

Constituent orientation also applies in food emulsions. If in the food piece or droplet, water is emulsified in oil so that the oil is the continuous phase and coats the moisture droplets, then dehydration should be slower than if the emulsion is reversed and water is the continuous phase. Sometimes we can control this in a manufactured food to be dried, but more often we must take what nature gives us.

Solute Concentration.—Solutes in solution elevate the boiling point of water systems. This also occurs in food dehydration processes. Other things being equal we can expect foods high in sugar or other low molecular weight solutes to dry slower than foods low in these solubles. What is more, the concentration of solutes becomes greater in the remaining water as drying progresses. This is another factor that slows down drying, and contributes to the falling rate period in the drying curves of many foods.

Binding of Water.—Water escapes freely from a surface when its vapor pressure is greater than the vapor pressure of the atmosphere above it. But as a product dries and its free water is progressively removed the vapor pressure of a unit area of the product decreases. This is because there is less remaining water per unit volume and per unit area, and also because some of the product's water is held or bound by chemical and physical forces to solid constituents of the food.

Free water is easiest to remove and evaporates first. Additional water may be loosely held by forces of adsorption to food solids. More difficult water to remove is that which enters into colloidal gels such as when starch, pectin, or other gums are present. Still more difficult is the removal of chemically bound water in the form of hydrates such as glucose monohydrate or hydrates of inorganic salts. These phenomena also contribute to the flattening of normal drying curves with time.

Cellular Structure.—Solid foods of natural tissue have a cellular structure. Moisture exists between and within the cells. When the tissue is alive the cell walls and membranes hold moisture within the cells. Such cells have turgor, rather than exhibiting leakage or bleeding.

When the animal or plant is killed the cells become more permeable to moisture. When the tissue is blanched or cooked the cells may become still more permeable to moisture; and generally cooked vegetables, meat, or fish will dry more easily than their fresh counterparts, provided cooking doesn't cause excessive toughening or shrinking.

Shrinkage, Case Hardening, Thermoplasticity.—Even when the cells are killed they still retain varying degrees of elasticity; they will stretch or shrink under stress. If the stress is excessive then their elastic limit is exceeded and they will not return to their original shape on removal of the stress. One of the most obvious changes during dehydration of cellular as well as noncellular foods is shrinkage.

If we had a perfectly elastic material under turgor and removed moisture evenly throughout the mass then the material would shrink in an even linear fashion with removal of moisture. This uniform shrinkage is rarely seen in food materials being dehydrated since the food pieces generally do not have perfect elasticity, and water is not removed evenly throughout the food piece as it is dried. Different food materials exhibit different shrinkage patterns in the course of dehydration. Typical changes of vegetable dice during dehydration are indicated in Fig. 114. The original

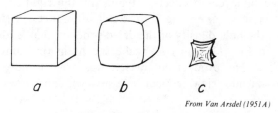

From Van Arsdel (1951A)

FIG. 114. CHANGES IN SHAPE OF VEGETABLE DICE DURING
DRYING

piece before drying is represented by (a). The effect of surface shrinkage is seen in (b), where the edges and corners gradually pull in giving the cube a more rounded appearance in the early stages of drying. Continued dehydration gradually removes water from deeper and deeper layers and finally from the center. This causes continued shrinkage toward the center and the concave cube appearance as in (c).

An extreme case of this is seen in the cross section of a completely dehydrated carrot cube (Fig. 115). In this case drying and shrinking must have occurred slowly and uniformly from the surface inward, since in cross section the pieces appear to have a uniformly dense interior. Often with quick high-temperature drying of food pieces the surface becomes dry and rigid long before the center has dried out. Then when the center dries and

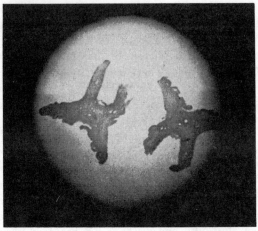

From Reeve (1942)

FIG. 115. CROSS SECTION OF COMPLETELY DEHYDRATED CARROT
DICE

shrinks, it pulls away from the rigid surface layers causing internal splits, voids, and honeycomb effects. Meanwhile the rigid surface does not become as concave as in Fig. 115. Such differences in shrinkage patterns can affect the bulk density of the dried product, that is, the weight per unit volume. In Fig. 116 the two beakers contain the same weight of dried potato dice. The product on the left was dried rapidly under conditions which produced a rigid less concave surface, and more internal shrinkage

From Van Arsdel (1951A)

FIG. 116. RELATIVE BULK OF RAPIDLY AND SLOWLY DRIED POTATO DICE

and air voids. The product on the right, dried slowly, is more concave and dense; it has about twice the bulk density (or half the specific volume) of the product on the left.

Both kinds of dried product have advantages and disadvantages. For example, the less dense product will absorb water and reconstitute quicker, is more attractive and more closely resembles the original material, and may be psychologically more acceptable to consumers who frequently interpret greater volume as more substance even though weight is the same. On the other hand this less dense product is more expensive to package, ship, and store, and because of its air voids may be more easily oxidized or otherwise have shortened storage stability. The less dense product often is favored when it is to be sold directly to the consumer who values appearance and quick reconstitution of the product. The more dense product frequently is preferred by the food manufacturer who purchases dehydrated ingredients for further processing and has reconstitution kettles and mixers; he may be less concerned with reconstitution rate than with container, shipping, and storage cost savings.

A special condition related to shrinkage and sealing of the surface of a food piece is known as case hardening. This may occur when there is a very high surface temperature and unbalanced drying of the piece so that a dry skin forms quickly, before most of the internal moisture has had opportunity to migrate to the surface. The rather impermeable skin then traps much of the remaining water within the particle, and drying rate drops off severely.

Case hardening is more common with some foods than others; it is particularly common with foods that contain dissolved sugars and other solutes in high concentration. This can be explained from the various ways water may escape from a product during dehydration. Some of the water moves through cell walls and membranes of cellular foods by molecular diffusion. If the membranes are highly selective against solutes then the water will leave dissolved substances behind. Water also may be heated to water vapor within the food piece and escape as water vapor molecules free of solute. But food pieces and food purées being dried also contain voids, cracks, and pores of various diameters down to minute capillary size. Water in foods rises in these pores and capillaries, many of which lead to the food surface. Capillary water carries sugars, salts, and other materials in solution to the surface of food pieces during dehydration. Then at the surface the water is evaporated and the solutes are deposited. This is what causes a sticky, sugary exudate on the surface of some fruits in the early stages of drying. This can seal off the surface pores and cracks, which also are shrinking during drying. The combined effects of shrinking and pore clogging from solutes contributes to case hardening. Where case hardening is a problem it generally can be minimized by lower surface temperatures to promote a more gradual drying throughout the food piece.

Many foods are also thermoplastic materials, that is, they soften on heating. A cellular food, such as plant and animal tissue, has structure and some rigidity even at drying temperatures. A fruit or vegetable juice, on the other hand, lacks structure and is high in sugars and other materials that soften and melt at the elevated temperatures of drying. Thus, if orange juice or a sugar syrup are dried on a pan or on a heated belt, even after all of the water has been removed the solids will be in a thermoplastic tacky condition, giving the impression that they still contain moisture. They also will stick to the pan or belt and be difficult to remove. However, on cooling, the thermoplastic solids harden into a crystalline or amorphous glass form. In this more brittle condition they generally are more easily removed from the pan or belt. Most belt type driers are equipped with a cooling zone just prior to a scraper knife to facilitate removal of this type of material from the drier.

Food Porosity.—Many drying techniques or pretreatments given to food before drying are aimed at making the structure more porous so as to facilitate mass transfer and thereby speed drying rate. But in some instances even though potential mass transfer rates are speeded by puffing or otherwise opening the structure, drying rate is not speeded. Porous sponge-like structures are excellent insulating bodies and generally will slow down the rate of heat transfer into the food. The net result then depends on whether the effect of porosity is greater on speeding mass transfer or slowing heat transfer rates in the particular food material and drying system.

From Feustel et al. (1964)

FIG. 117. POTATO PUFFS MADE UNDER CONDITIONS OF RAPID DRYING AND INTERNAL STEAM ESCAPE

Porosity may be developed by creating steam pressure within the product and a case hardened surface through rapid drying. The escaping steam tends to puff such a product as in the case of the potato puffs of Fig. 117. Porosity also can be developed by whipping or foaming a food liquid or purée prior to drying. A stable foam that resists collapse during drying is then desired. Porosity can be developed in a vacuum drier by rapid escape of water vapor into the high vacuum, and by still other means.

Quite apart from its effect on drying rate, any process that retains or creates a highly porous structure does many of the other things discussed in relation to internal voids. The porous product has the advantages of quick solubility or reconstitution and greater volume appearance, but the disadvantages of increased bulk and generally shorter storage stability because of increased surface exposure to air, light, etc.

Chemical and Other Changes.—A great range of chemical changes can take place during food dehydration along with the physical changes described above, and these contribute to final quality of both the dried items and their reconstituted counterparts in terms of food color, flavor, texture, viscosity, reconstitution rate, nutritional value, and storage stability. These changes frequently are product specific, but a few major types occur with virtually all foods undergoing dehydration, and the extent of these changes depends upon the composition of the food and the severity of the drying method.

Browning reactions may be from any of the usual causes, including enzymatic oxidations of polyphenols and other susceptible compounds if the oxidizing enzymes are not inactivated. Drying temperatures, because of the water evaporation cooling effect, often are not sufficient to destroy these enzymes during drying and so it is common to pasteurize or blanch foods with heat or chemicals prior to drying. Caramelization of sugars and scorching of other materials if heat is excessive is another common type of browning. Highly important in food dehydration is nonenzymatic or Maillard browning from reaction of aldehyde and amino groups of sugars and proteins. Maillard-type browning, like other chemical reactions, is favored by high temperature and by high concentration of reactive groups in the presence of some water. In the course of dehydration reactive groups are concentrated. Maillard browning generally proceeds most rapidly during drying when the moisture content is decreased to the range of about 20 to 15%. As moisture content drops further, the rate of Maillard browning slows down, so that in dried products below about two per cent moisture further color change from this kind of browning is minimally perceptible even on long range storage. In designing a drying system or heating schedule we therefore try to dehydrate rapidly through the 20 to 15% moisture range so as to minimize time for Maillard browning at this optimum condition.

Another common consequence of dehydration is some loss in the ease of rehydration. Some of this is physical from shrinkage and distortion of cells and capillaries, but much also is chemical or physicochemical at the colloidal level. Heat, and the salt concentration effects from water removal can partially denature proteins which cannot then fully reabsorb and bind water. Starches and gums also may be altered and become less hydrophilic. Sugars and salts escape from damaged cells into the water used to reconstitute dehydrated foods, resulting in loss of turgor. These and other chemical changes make reabsorption of water by the dried products somewhat less than equal to the original water content and contribute to altered texture.

Still another common chemical change associated with dehydration is some loss of volatile flavor constituents. This invariably occurs to at least a slight degree. Complete prevention of this loss has as yet proven virtually impossible, and so methods of trapping and condensing the evolved vapors from the drier and adding them back to the dried product are sometimes employed. Additional techniques involve add-back of essences and flavor preparations derived from other sources, as well as methods of minimizing flavor loss by incorporating gums and other materials into certain liquid foods prior to drying. Some of these materials have flavor fixative properties, others work by coating dried particles and providing a physical barrier against volatile loss.

Optimization of Variables

The above principles are taken into account in the design of food dehydration equipment. Efforts are made to balance dehydration conditions to produce maximum drying rate with minimum product damage at the most economical drying cost. Food dehydration is truly an area where the food scientist and chemical engineer must work together to achieve optimum results.

There are mathematical relationships between each of the major controllable drying variables and heat and mass transfer. But there are also the peculiarities of food materials such that optimum drying conditions are seldom the same for two different products.

Engineering calculations usually based on model systems can go a long way toward selecting favorable drying conditions, but seldom are sufficient in themselves to predict accurately drying behavior. This is because food materials are highly variable in initial composition, in amounts of free and bound water, in shrinkage and solute migration patterns, and most important, in changing properties throughout the drying operation. This is especially so in the falling rate period of the drying curve, where quality and economics are most affected.

For these reasons, in selecting and optimizing a drying process, the experimental approach with the food to be dried must always supplement engineering calculations based on less variable model systems.

Drying Methods and Equipment

There are several basic drying methods and a far greater number of modifications of the basic methods. The method of choice very much depends upon the type of food to be dried, the quality level that must be achieved, and the cost that can be justified. Starch sells for about ten cents/lb while orange juice crystals sell for over a dollar/lb; we can afford to use a more delicate and generally more expensive drying method to dehydrate orange juice, and orange juice needs the milder drying method since it is far more sensitive than starch.

Some of the more common drying methods include drum drying, spray drying, vacuum shelf drying, vacuum belt drying, atmospheric belt drying, freeze drying, fluidized-bed drying, rotary drying, cabinet drying, kiln drying, tunnel drying, and others. Some of these methods are particularly suited to liquid foods and cannot handle solid food pieces, others are suitable for solid foods or mixtures containing food pieces.

One useful division of drier types separates them into air convection driers, drum or roller driers, and vacuum driers. Using this breakdown, Table 32 indicates the applicability of the more common drier types to

TABLE 32

COMMON DRIER TYPES USED FOR LIQUID AND SOLID FOODS

Drier Type	Usual Food Type
Air Convection Driers	
kiln	pieces
cabinet, tray, or pan	pieces, purées, liquids
tunnel	pieces
continuous conveyor belt	purées, liquids
belt trough	pieces
air lift	small pieces, granules
fluidized bed	small pieces, granules
spray	liquids, purées
Drum or Roller Driers	
atmospheric	purées, liquids
vacuum	purées, liquids
Vacuum Driers	
vacuum shelf	pieces, purées, liquids
vacuum belt	purées, liquids
freeze driers	pieces, liquids

liquid and solid type foods. In air convection driers, heated air is put into intimate contact with the food material and supplies a major source of the heat for evaporation. If liquid, the food may be sprayed, or poured into pans or on belts. Pieces may be supported in any number of ways. Although heated moving air is common to this group of driers, additional heat also may be supplied by heated tray or belt supports. Drum or roller driers are limited to use with purées, mashes, and liquid foods that can be applied as thin films. Vacuum driers may employ any degree of vacuum to lower the boiling point of water. Freeze driers are special kinds of vacuum driers generally operated at a pressure below 5 mm of mercury so as to sublime water vapor directly from ice without going through the liquid phase. But such a division is not rigid since many driers are combinations. Thus we can place a drum drier in a vacuum chamber or blow high velocity heated air over the drum to speed drying, and both practices are done commercially.

Air Convection Driers.—All air convection driers have some sort of insulated enclosure, a means of circulating air through the enclosure, and a means of heating this air. They also will have various means of product support, special devices for dried product collection, some will have air driers to lower drying air humidity, and will be equipped with various kinds of instrumentation and controls.

Movement of air generally will be controlled by fans, blowers, and baffles. Air volume and velocity will affect drying rate, but its static pressure also is important since products being dried become very light and can be blown off trays or belts. Air flow patterns are complex when they encounter surfaces and their velocities and pressures in contact with food are seldom comparable with measurements made on the main air stream, but such measurements usually can be correlated with drying behavior. Nevertheless, if two driers are said to have an air velocity of 1,000 ft/min, this measurement is usually made in a convenient place in the drier. If the driers are of different geometries, the surface of the food in the two driers probably encounter different velocities.

The air may be heated by direct or indirect methods. In direct heating the air is in direct contact with flame or combustion gases. In indirect heating the air is in contact with a hot surface, such as being blown across pipes or fins heated by steam, flame, or electricity. The important point is that indirect heating leaves the air uncontaminated. On the other hand in direct heating the fuel is seldom completely oxidized to carbon dioxide and water. Incomplete combustion leaves gases and traces of soot and this is picked up by the air and can be transferred to the food product. Direct heating of air also contributes small amounts of moisture to the air since moisture is a product of combustion, but this is usually insignificant except with very hygroscopic foods. These disadvantages are balanced by the generally lower cost of direct heating of air compared to indirect heating, and both methods are widely used in food dehydration.

Kiln Drier.—One of the simplest kinds of air convection drier is the kiln drier. Kiln driers of early design were generally two story constructions (Fig. 118). A furnace or burner on the lower floor generated heat, and warm air would rise through a slotted floor to the upper story. Food such as apple slices would be spread out on the slotted floor and turned over periodically. This kind of drier generally will not reduce moisture to below about ten per cent. It is still in use for apple slices.

Courtesy J. O'Connell Co., Sebastopol, Calif.

FIG. 118.   APPLE RINGS BEING DRIED IN A KILN DRIER

Cabinet, Tray, and Pan Driers.—A step more advanced is the cabinet drier in which food may be loaded on trays or pans in comparatively thin layers up to a few inches. A typical construction for this type of drier is seen in Fig. 119. Fresh air enters the cabinet (b), is drawn by the fan through the heater coils (c), and is then blown across the food trays to exhaust (h). In this case the air is being heated by the indirect method. Screens filter out any dust that may be in the air. The air passes across and between the trays in this design. Other designs have perforated trays and the air may be directed up through these. In Fig. 119 the air is exhausted to the atmosphere after one pass rather than being recirculated within the system. In recirculating designs, the moisture laden air, after evaporating water from the food, would have to be dried before being recirculated,

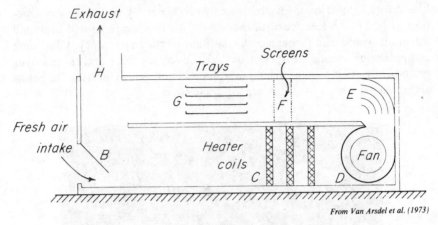

From Van Arsdel et al. (1973)

FIG. 119.   ONE TYPE OF CABINET OR TRAY DRIER

or else it would soon become saturated and further drying of the food would
stop. In such a case the air could be dried by passing it through a desiccant
such as a bed of silica gel, or condensing moisture out by passing the moist
air over cold plates or coils. Note also that if we are not going to dry
the exhaust air for recirculation, then the exhaust vent (Fig. 119) should
not be close to the fresh air intake area, otherwise the moist exhaust air
will be drawn back through the drier and drying efficiency will be lost.

Cabinet tray and pan driers such as this are usually for small scale
operations. They are comparatively inexpensive and easy to set in terms of
drying conditions. They may run up to 25 trays high, and will operate with
air temperatures of the order of 200° F dry bulb, and air velocities of
about 500 to 1,000 ft/min across the trays. They commonly are used to dry
fruit and vegetable pieces, and depending upon the food and the desired
final moisture, drying time may be of the order of 10 or even 20 hr.

Tunnel and Continuous Belt Driers.—For larger operations we elongate
the cabinet, place the trays on carts and we have a tunnel drier (Fig. 120).

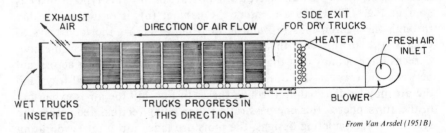

From Van Arsdel (1951B)

FIG. 120.   TYPICAL COUNTERFLOW TUNNEL DRIER CONSTRUCTION

If drying time to the desired moisture is 10 hr then each wheeled cart of trays will take 10 hr to pass through the tunnel. When a dry cart emerges it makes room to load another wet cart into the opposite end of the tunnel. Such an operation then becomes semicontinuous.

A main construction feature by which tunnel driers differ has to do with the direction of air flow relative to tray movement. In the construction shown in Fig. 120 the wet food carts move from left to right. The drying air moves across the trays from right to left. This is the counterflow or counter-current principle. Its significance is that the air, when it is hottest and driest, contacts the nearly dry product, whereas the initial drying of entering carts gets cooler, moister air that has cooled and picked up moisture going through the tunnel. This means that initial product temperature and moisture gradients will not be as great, and the product is less likely to undergo case hardening or other surface shrinkage leaving wet centers. Further, lower final moistures can be reached since the driest product encounters the driest air. In contrast, there also are cocurrent flow tunnels with the incoming trays and incoming hottest driest air traveling in the same direction. In this case rapid initial drying and slow final drying can cause case hardening and internal splits and porosity as centers finally dry, which sometimes is desirable in special products.

Just as carts of trays can be moved through a heated tunnel, so a continuous belt may be driven through a tunnel or oven enclosure. Then we have a continuous belt or conveyor drier, and a great number of designs are possible. Some of the more common features can be uniform automatic feeding of product to the belt in a controlled thin layer, zoned heat and air flow control in different sections, tumbling over of product onto a second strand of belt, automatic collection of dried product, and of course continuous operation. We generally refer to the drying capacity of such driers in terms of weight of product dried from one moisture level to another per square foot of belt surface per hour. This also can be expressed in terms of pounds of water removed per square foot of belt surface per hour under defined operating conditions.

Belt Trough Drier.—A special kind of air convection belt drier is the belt trough drier (Fig. 121). Here the belt forms a trough. The belt is usually of metal mesh and heated air is blown up through the mesh. The belt moves continuously keeping the food pieces in the trough in constant motion to continuously expose new surface. This speeds drying, and with air of about 275° F vegetable pieces may be dried to the 7 to 5% moisture range in about 1 hr.

But not all products may be dried this way since certain sizes and shapes do not readily tumble. Fragile apple wedges may break. Onion slices tend to separate and become entangled. Fruit pieces that exude sugar on

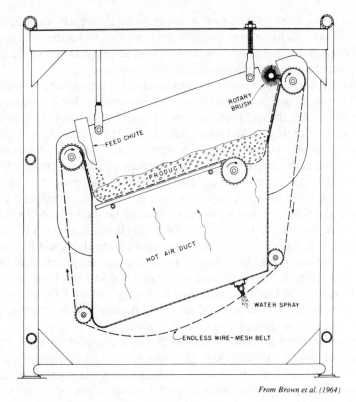

From Brown et al. (1964)

FIG. 121.   BELT TROUGH DRIER CONSTRUCTION

drying tend to stick together and clump with the tumbling motion. These are but a few additional factors that must be considered in selecting a drier for a particular food.

Air Lift Drier.—Going a step beyond tumbling to expose surface area of food particles we have several types of pneumatic conveyor driers. These generally are used to finish-dry materials that have been partially dried by other methods, usually to about 25% moisture, or at least sufficiently low so that the material becomes granular rather than having a tendency to clump and mat. One type of air lift drier is seen in Fig. 122. This might be used to finish-dry semimoist granules coming from a drum drier. Such granules at about 25% moisture can be brought to about 6% moisture more efficiently in a heated air stream than on the drum. This is because the more difficult moisture to remove in this falling rate period of dehydration is more easily evaporated from suspended particles in intimate contact with the heating medium. The suspended particles when

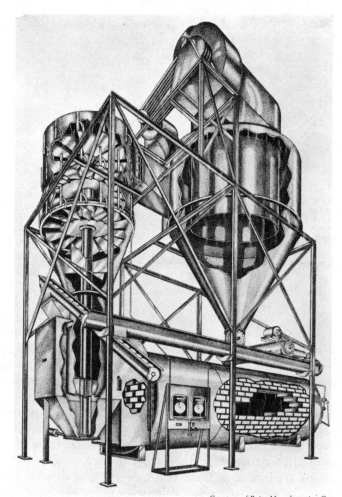

Courtesy of Reitz Manufacturing Co.

FIG. 122. ONE TYPE OF AIR LIFT DRIER

dry are separated from the air and collected in a cyclone type separator which will be described under spray driers.

Fluidized-Bed Drier.—Another type of pneumatic conveyor drier is the fluidized bed drier. This is similar in principle and construction to the fluidized-bed freezer described in the preceding chapter. In fluidized-bed drying (Fig. 123) heated air is blown up through the food particles with just enough force to suspend the particles in a gentle boiling motion. Semidry particles such as potato granules enter at the left and gradually migrate to the right where they are discharged dry. Heated air is introduced

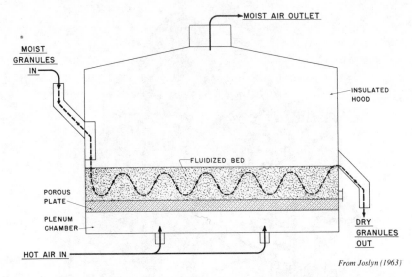

MOIST AIR OUTLET

MOIST
GRANULES
IN

INSULATED
HOOD

FLUIDIZED BED

POROUS
PLATE

PLENUM
CHAMBER

DRY
GRANULES
OUT

HOT AIR IN

From Joslyn (1963)

FIG. 123. CONSTRUCTION FEATURES OF A FLUIDIZED-BED DRIER

through a porous plate that supports the bed of granules. The moist air is exhausted at the top. The process is continuous and the length of time particles remain in the drier can be regulated by the depth of the bed and other means. This type of drying can be used to dehydrate grains, peas, and other particulates.

Spray Driers.—By far the most important kind of air convection drier is the spray drier. Spray driers turn out a greater tonnage of dehydrated food products than all other kinds of driers combined, and there are various types of spray driers designed for specific food products.

Spray driers are limited to foods that can be atomized, such as liquids and low viscosity pastes or purées. Atomization into minute droplets results in drying in a matter of seconds with common inlet air temperatures of about 400° F. Since evaporative cooling of particles seldom permits them to reach above about 180° F, and properly designed systems quickly remove the dried particles from heated zones, this method of dehydration can produce exceptionally high quality with many highly heat sensitive materials, including milk, eggs, and coffee.

In typical spray drying we introduce the liquid food as a fine spray or mist into a tower or chamber along with heated air. As the small droplets make intimate contact with the heated air they flash off their moisture, become small particles, and drop to the bottom of the tower from where they are removed. The heated air which has now become moist is withdrawn from the tower by a blower or fan. The process is continuous in that liquid food continues to be pumped into the chamber and atomized, along with dry heated air to replace the moist air that is withdrawn, and the dried product is removed from the chamber as it descends.

The principal components of the spray drying system will differ in construction depending upon the product to be dried. In the case of milk the system will include tanks for holding the liquid, a high pressure pump for introducing the liquid into the tower, spray nozzles or a similar device for atomizing the food, a heated air source with blower, a secondary collection vessel for accumulating product drawn from the tower, and means for exhausting the moistened air (Fig. 124).

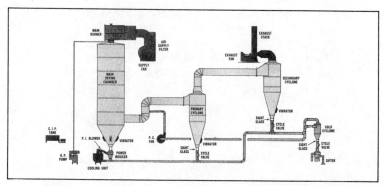

Courtesy of The DeLaval Separator Co.

Fig. 124.   Diagram of Spray Drying System Suitable for Milk

As for the drying tower or chamber, its main purpose is to provide intimate mixing of heated air with finely dispersed droplets. As in the various spray drier types of Fig. 125, the heated air and the atomized droplets may enter the tower together at the top or bottom or may enter separately, the particles may be made to descend straight down or take a spiral path, and the chamber may be vertical or horizontal.

As in tunnel driers, if there is cocurrent introduction of droplets and air then we get quick initial drying and slower final drying; countercurrent streams may be favored for highly hygroscopic materials. Further, if we introduce the liquid product at the top of the tower it descends through and out of the tower in one pass. But if we introduce the product at the bottom of the tower, it first ascends and then descends and its time in the drier can thus be made longer. This also is true if the droplets are given a spiral motion in the tower. We may want this longer residence time to bring the particles down to a lower moisture content. Or we may wish to have particles grow in size in the drier. In this case the longer residence time gives

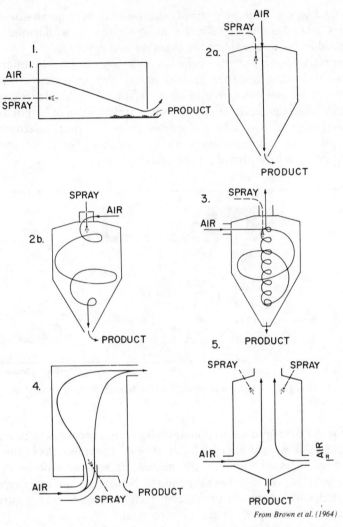

FIG. 125. SOME TYPES OF SPRAY DRIERS

greater opportunity for dry particles to collide with less-dry particles and form clusters. This is one way to carry out the instantizing process of agglomeration, which yields clusters that have many voids, sink in water, and are therefore easier to dissolve than certain spray dried particles which are small in size, float on water, and are difficult to wet.

As important to dried product characteristics as the geometry and air pattern in the chamber is the nature of the atomization. Atomizers are of two main types; pressure spray nozzles, and centrifugal spinning disks or baskets. Spinning disks and baskets, from which deposited food throws out droplets, are favored where passage through a fine-hole pressure nozzle can damage the food, as might be the case in denaturing proteins of egg white. Viscous liquids and purees with fine pulp also may not be able to pass through a fine pressure nozzle, but can be easily spun from a high-speed, rotating disk.

We not only want small droplets for quick drying, but need uniform droplet size for even drying. Actually, the size and trajectory of the largest droplets determine drying time, and as a consequence the size of the drying chamber. No atomizers have yet been developed which produce all droplets of the same size, but the object of their design is to make droplet size as uniform as possible for several reasons. If not uniform, the small droplets dry first and then overdry before the larger droplets have become dry. The droplet size determines the final dried particle size; if dried particle size varies substantially then settling and stratification of fines may occur in the final package. Particle size affects solubility rate. Large particles may sink and fines generally float on water, making for uneven wetting and reconstitution of nonuniform products. Further, very small droplets in an atomized distribution dry as minute fines. These are hard to recover as product from the drier since they tend to be lost with the exit air even as the collection system is made highly efficient. Entrainment loss with the exit air is largely made up of these minute fines.

During atomization the angle of departure from a spray nozzle or the trajectory from a spinning disk also must be considered. As droplets descend the drying chamber they go from a liquid to a sticky condition and then to dryness. If they encounter the drier wall when dry they do not stick. But if their trajectory causes them to hit the drier wall before they are dry they stick and build up as a cake, become heat damaged, and are difficult to remove. Trajectory generally is designed to prevent or minimize wall contact in the early stages of drying.

The appearance, size, shape, density, and solubility of the final spray dried particle can be variously affected by nozzle pressure, shear, liquid viscosity, surface tension, nature of the solids, etc. Generally, spray dried particles have a spherical shape (Fig. 126). which is the form assumed by free floating liquid bodies. Sometimes if drying is extremely rapid, the droplets are dehydrated as they emerge from the atomizer before they have had time to form a spherical shape. Then the dried particles may be irregular or dumb-bell shaped. When drying is appropriately controlled, water vapor escaping from droplets can be made to leave voids and hollows in the dried particles, which give lighter density, but also more surface for possible oxidative deterioration.

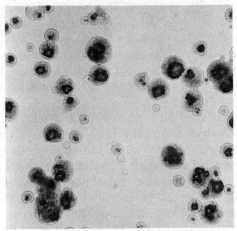

From Coulter and Jenness (1945)

FIG. 126. PHOTOMICROGRAPH OF SPRAY DRIED WHOLE MILK
PARTICLES × 220

Powder collectors may simply be zones in the conical base of the drying chamber from which product can be periodically removed. More commonly collectors will consist of secondary smaller conical structures known as cyclone separators (see Fig. 124). In this case the exit air from the drying chamber carries the dried particles into the cyclone separator, where the air acquires a whirling motion, throwing dried particles against the conical wall. The particles settle for easy removal while the nearly particle-free air exits at the top. Since the exit air is never entirely free of fine particles, another kind of collector may be employed above the cyclone. This is a bag collector or filter just preceeding air exhaust to the atmosphere. Product fines remaining in the bag collector for long periods exposed to heated exiting air generally become heat damaged, and represent lower quality product.

There is additional variation in design and operation of spray driers for special product requirements. One method foams the liquid food, such as milk or coffee, before spraying it into the drier. The result is faster drying rate from the expanded foamed-droplet surface area, and lighter density dried product. This is known as foam-spray drying.

It was stated that when particles are dry they do not stick to the drier wall. This is not true in the case of thermoplastic substances such as juices high in sugar. Even when dry, these melt, stick, and build up on the wall. One kind of spray drier has a double wall and circulates cold water or cool air so as to chill the lower portion of the inner wall where dried juice particles would accumulate. Thus prevented from melting and fusing, these juices too may be spray dried and collected in particulate form.

Another type of spray drier has been developed especially to handle thermoplastic materials and other highly heat-sensitive foods. This is known as the BIRS spray drier. The BIRS drier (Fig. 127) uses counter-current cool dry air of about 86° F and 3% RH. To give the droplets sprayed in at the top of the tower sufficient time to dry at this relatively low temperature the drying tower is built exceptionally tall. It may be 220 ft high and 50 ft in diameter. As droplets descend they dry in about 90 sec. Products like orange, lemon, and tomato juices, otherwise difficult to spray

From Sivetz and Foote (1963)

Fig. 127. BIRS Countercurrent Spray Drier

dry because of thermoplasticity, can be quality dried this way. Because there is not rapid escape of steam from particles in this cool process, such particles are less puffed and more dense than many conventionally spray dried products. Low temperature also favors flavor retention.

Drum or Roller Driers.—In drum or roller drying, liquid foods, purées, pastes, and mashes are applied in a thin layer onto the surface of a revolving heated drum. The drum generally is heated from within by steam.

One may have a single drum or a pair of drums (Fig. 128). The food may be applied between the nip where two drums come together, and then the clearance between the drums determines the thickness of the applied food layer. Or the food can be applied to other areas of the drum. Food is applied continuously and the thin layer loses moisture. At a point on the drum or drums a scraper blade is positioned to peel the thin dried layer of food from the drums. The speed of the drums is so regulated that the

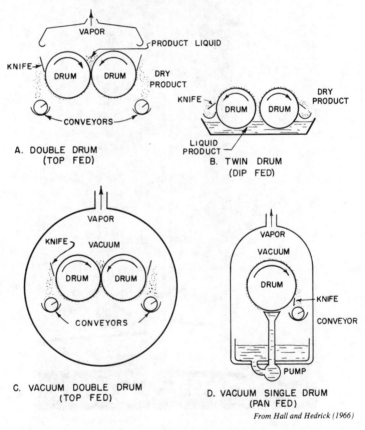

From Hall and Hedrick (1966)

FIG. 128.   TYPES OF DRUM DRIERS

layer of food will be dry when it reaches the scraper blade, which also is referred to as a doctor blade. The layer of food is dried in one revolution of the drum, and is scraped from the drum before that position of the drum returns to the point where more wet food is applied. Using steam under pressure in the drum, the temperature of the drum surface may be well above 212° F, and often is maintained at about 300° F. With a food film commonly less than 1/16 in. thick, drying can be completed in one minute or less depending upon the food material. Other features of drum driers include hoods above drums to withdraw moisture vapor, and conveyors in troughs to receive and move dried product.

Typical products dried on drums include milk, potato mash, heat-tolerant purées such as tomato paste, and animal feeds. But drum drying has some inherent limitations which restrict the kinds of foods to which it is applicable. To effectuate rapid drying, drum surface temperature must be high, generally above 250°F. This gives products a more cooked flavor and color than when they are dried at a lower temperature. Drying temperature can of course be lowered by constructing the drums within a vacuum chamber (Fig. 128), but this increases equipment and operating costs over atmospheric drum or spray drying.

A second limitation is the difficulty of providing zoned temperature control needed to vary the drying temperature profile. This is particularly important with thermoplastic food materials. While dried milk and dried potato are easily scraped from the hot drum in friable sheet form, this is not the case with many dried fruits, juices, and other products which tend to be sticky and semimolten when hot. Such products tend to crimp, roll up, and otherwise accumulate and stick to the doctor blade in a taffy-like mass.

This condition can be substantially improved by a cold zone to make the tacky material brittle just prior to the doctor blade. But zone-controlled chilling is not as easy to accomplish on a drum of limited diameter, and therefore limited arc, as it would be in perhaps 20 ft of length of a horizontal drying belt 150 ft long. One means of chilling is by impinging a stream of cool air onto a segment of the product on the drum prior to the doctor blade. A system for doing this and providing additional zoned temperature control around the drum is seen in Fig. 129.

For relatively heat-resistant food products drum drying is one of the least expensive dehydration methods. Drum dried foods generally will have a somewhat more "cooked" character than the same materials spray dried; thus drum dried milk is not up to beverage quality but is satisfactory as an ingredient in less delicately flavored manufactured foods. More delicate vacuum drum drying or zone-controlled drum drying increases dehydration costs.

Courtesy of Jones Div., Beloit Corp.

FIG. 129.   DOUBLE DRUM DRIER WITH ZONED TEMPERATURE CONTROL

Vacuum Driers.—Vacuum dehydration methods are capable of producing the highest quality dried products, but costs of vacuum drying generally also are higher than other methods which do not employ vacuum. In vacuum drying, the temperature of the food and the rate of water removal are controlled by regulating the degree of vacuum and the intensity of heat input. Heat transfer to the food is largely by conduction and radiation. Vacuum drying methods usually can be controlled with a higher degree of accuracy than methods depending upon air convection heating.

All vacuum drying systems have four essential elements. These include a vacuum chamber of heavy construction to withstand outside air pressures that may exceed internal pressure by as much as 2,000 lb per sq ft; means to supply heat; a device for producing and maintaining the vacuum; and components to collect water vapor as it is evaporated from the food. Typical arrangements of these elements are seen in Fig. 130.

The vacuum chamber generally will contain shelves or other supports to hold the food, and these shelves may be heated electrically or by circulating a heated fluid through them. The heated shelves are called platens. The platens convey heat to the food in contact with them by conduction, but where several platens are one above another they also radiate heat to the food on the platen below. In addition, special radiant heat sources such as infrared elements can be focused onto the food to supplement the heat conducted from platen contact.

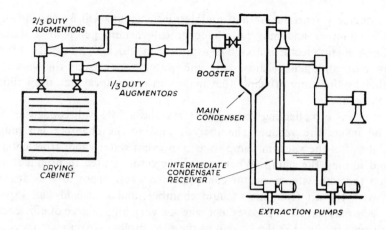

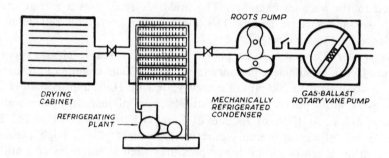

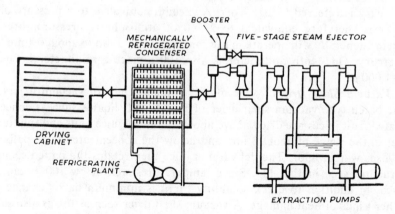

FIG. 130. ELEMENTS OF VACUUM DEHYDRATION SYSTEMS

The device for producing and maintaining vacuum will be outside the vacuum chamber and may be a mechanical vacuum pump or a steam ejector. A steam ejector is a kind of aspirator in which high velocity steam jetting past an opening draws air and water vapor from the vacuum chamber by the same principle that makes an insect spray gun draw fluid from the can.

The means of collecting water vapor may be a cold wall condenser. It may be inside the vacuum chamber or outside the chamber but must come ahead of the vacuum pump so as to prevent water vapor from entering and fouling the pump. When a steam ejector is used to produce the vacuum the same steam ejector can condense water vapor as it is drawn along with the air from the vacuum chamber, and so a cold wall vapor condenser may not be needed except where a very high degree of efficiency is required. In Fig. 130 the system at the top employs steam ejectors connected to the vacuum chamber. The middle system uses a refrigerated condenser and vacuum pumps. The lower system employs a refrigerated condenser and steam ejectors.

Degree of Vacuum.—Atmospheric pressure at sea level is approximately 15 psi, or sufficient pressure to support a 30 in. column of mercury. This is equivalent to 760 mm of mercury, or 1 in. Hg is approximately 25 mm. At 1 atmosphere, or 30 in., or 760 mm of mercury, pure water boils at 212° F. At 10 in. or 250 mm of mercury pure water boils at 162° F. At 2 in. or 50 mm of mercury pure water boils at 101° F. High vacuum dehydration operates at still lower pressures such as fractions of a millimeter of mercury. In Europe, a pressure equivalent to a millimeter of mercury is referred to as a Torr. A vacuum equivalent to a pressure of 2 Torr is therefore equivalent to 2/760 of atmospheric pressure. Freeze drying generally will operate in the range of 2 mm down to about 0.1 mm of mercury. One-tenth millimeter is also 100 μ since a millimeter is equal to 1,000 μ.

Vacuum Shelf Driers.—One of the simplest kinds of vacuum driers is the batch type vacuum shelf drier of Fig. 131. If liquids such as concentrated fruit juices are dried above about 5 mm the juice boils and splatters, but in the range of about 3 mm and below the concentrated juice puffs as it loses water vapor. The dehydrated juice then retains the puffed spongy structure seen in Fig. 131. Since temperatures well below 100° F can be used, in addition to quick solubility there is minimum flavor change or other kinds of heat damage. A vacuum shelf drier such as this is also suitable for the dehydration of food pieces. In this case the rigidity of the solid food prevents major puffing, although there also is a tendency to minimize shrinkage.

Continuous Vacuum Belt Drier.—Vacuum driers can be engineered

From Ponting et al. (1964)

FIG. 131. BATCH TYPE VACUUM SHELF DRIER

for continuous operation. A diagram of a continuous vacuum belt drier is
shown in Fig. 132. This drier is used commercially to dehydrate high
quality citrus juice crystals, instant tea, and other delicate liquid foods.

The drier consists of a horizontal tank-like chamber connected to a
vacuum producing, moisture condensing system. The chamber is about 55
ft long and 12 ft in diameter. Within the chamber are mounted two revolving hollow drums. Around the drums is connected a stainless steel
belt which moves in a counter-clockwise direction. The drum on the right
is heated with steam confined within it. This drum heats the belt passing
over it by conduction. As the belt moves it is further heated by infrared

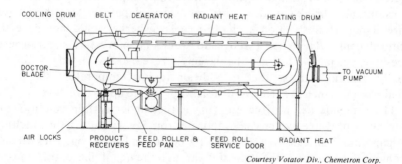

Courtesy Votator Div., Chemetron Corp.

FIG. 132. CONTINUOUS VACUUM BELT DRIER

radiant elements. The drum to the left is cooled with cold water circulated within it and cools the belt passing over it. The liquid food in the form of a concentrate is pumped into a feed pan under the lower belt strand. An applicator roller dipping into the liquid continuously applies a thin coating of the food onto the lower surface of the moving belt. As the belt moves over the heating drum and past the radiant heaters the food rapidly dries in the vacuum which is equivalent to about 2 mm Hg. When the food reaches the cooling drum it is down to about two per cent moisture. At the bottom of the cooling drum is a doctor blade which scrapes the cooled, embrittled product into a collection vessel. The belt scraped free of product receives additional liquid food as it passes the applicator roller and the process repeats in continuous fashion.

Products dried with this equipment have a slightly puffed structure. If desired, a greater degree of puffing can be achieved as has been done in the case of milk. This can be accomplished by pumping nitrogen gas under pressure into the milk prior to drying. Some of the gas goes into solution in the milk. Upon entering the vacuum chamber this gas violently comes out of solution and further puffs the milk as it is being dried.

Freeze Drying.—In recent years, freeze drying has been developed to a highly advanced state. Much of the development work has been aimed at optimizing the process and equipment to reduce drying costs, which still may be of the order of 2 to 5 times greater per pound of water removed than other common drying methods. Freeze drying can be used to dehydrate sensitive high value liquid foods such as coffee and juices, but it is especially suited to dry solid foods of high value such as strawberries, whole shrimp, chicken dice, mushroom slices, and sometimes food pieces as large as steaks and chops. These types of foods, in addition to having delicate flavors and colors, have textural and appearance attributes which cannot be well preserved by any current drying method except freeze drying. A whole strawberry, for example, is soft, fragile, and almost all water. Any conventional drying method that employs heat would cause considerable shrinkage, distortion, and loss of natural strawberry texture. Upon reconstitution such a dried strawberry would not have the natural color, flavor, or turgor and would be more like a strawberry preserve or jam. This can be largely prevented by drying from the solidly frozen state, so that in addition to low temperature the frozen food has no chance to shrink or distort while giving up its moisture.

The principle behind freeze drying is that under certain conditions of low vapor pressure, water can evaporate from ice without the ice melting. When a material can exist as a solid, a liquid, and a gas, but goes directly from a solid to a gas without passing through the liquid phase, the material is said to sublime. Dry Ice sublimes at atmospheric pressure and room temperature. Frozen water will sublime if the temperature is 32° F or below and the frozen water is placed in a vacuum chamber at a pressure of 4.7 mm or less. Under such conditions the water will remain frozen and water molecules will leave the ice block at a faster rate than water molecules from the surrounding atmosphere reenter the frozen block.

Figure 133 is a diagrammatic illustration of a food piece being freeze-dried. Within the vacuum chamber heat is applied to the frozen food to

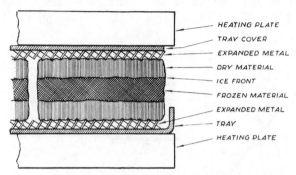

HEATING PLATE
TRAY COVER
EXPANDED METAL
DRY MATERIAL
ICE FRONT
FROZEN MATERIAL
EXPANDED METAL
TRAY
HEATING PLATE

Courtesy of Columbine Press, Gr. Brit., and A/S Atlas, Denmark

FIG. 133. ILLUSTRATION OF FOOD PIECE BEING FREEZE-DRIED

speed sublimation, and if the vacuum is maintained sufficiently high, usually within the range of about 0.1 to 2 mm Hg, and the heat is controlled so as to be just short of melting the ice, moisture vapor will sublime at a near maximum rate. Sublimation takes place from the surface of the ice, and so as it continues the ice front recedes towards the center of the food piece; that is, the food dries from the surface inward. Finally, the last of the ice sublimes and the food is below 5% moisture. Since the frozen food remains rigid during sublimation, escaping water molecules leave voids behind them, resulting in a porous sponge-like dried structure. Thus, freeze-dried foods reconstitute rapidly but also must be protected from ready absorption of atmospheric moisture and oxygen by proper packaging.

In this diagram a heating plate is positioned above and below the food to increase heat transfer rate, but an open space is left with expanded metal so as not to seal off escape of sublimed water molecules. Nevertheless, as drying progresses and the ice front recedes, drying rate drops off for several reasons. Thus, the porous dried layer ahead of the receding ice layer acts as an effective insulator against further heat transfer, the porous layer slows down the rate of escape of water molecules subliming from the ice surface, and other phenomena previously described exert their effects. But in well engineered freeze-drying systems, it generally will be found that interference by the growing porous dried layer against efficient heat transfer rather than against mass transfer is the most important factor limiting drying rate. Some of the more practical means of increasing overall drying rates have therefore made use of energy sources with penetrating power, such as infrared and microwave radiations, to pass through dried food layers into the receding ice core.

A typical freeze-drying curve for asparagus is seen in Fig. 134. This figure also has plotted temperatures of the heating plates and the food

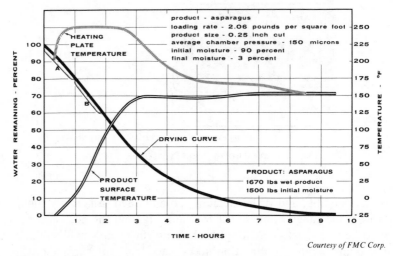

Courtesy of FMC Corp.

FIG. 134. DRYING CURVE AND SIGNIFICANT TEMPERATURE CHANGES DURING FREEZE DEHYDRATION OF ASPARAGUS

surface during the drying run. At the start of the drying operation no moisture has yet been removed, and the frozen product is somewhat below −25° F at its center and surface. The chamber is evacuated to a pressure of 150 μ and the heating platen is set at 250° F. As drying progresses and ice sublimes, the food surface temperature begins to rise from contact with the heated platen but the receding ice core remains frozen, cooled by the latent heat of sublimation. The platen temperature now must be regulated to establish a delicate balance. We want maximum heat to provide the driving force for rapid sublimation, but the heat must not be sufficiently great to melt the ice. If the ice were pure water its melting point would be 32° F, but since some of the ice is frozen with solute as a eutectic, the maximum ice temperature that can be tolerated is usually somewhat below 25° F, depending upon the particular food. As more and more ice sublimes, the dried shell surface temperature continues to rise approaching the 250° F platen. It then becomes necessary to decrease gradually the platen temperature to about 150° F to prevent scorching of the dried food surface. As the platen temperature is decreased, heat transfer to the remaining ice core also drops off, augmenting the insulating effect of the growing dried layer. The result is further decrease in drying rate. Ultimately all of the ice is sublimed, the entire dried mass reaches the 150° F temperature of the heating platen, and moisture is down to about 3%. This may require 9 hr or longer. The dried product can now be removed from the vacuum chamber. However, the dried porous product is under high vacuum, and so if the vacuum is broken by admitting air the product would instantaneously absorb this air into its pores resulting in impaired storage stability. It therefore is common practice to break the vacuum with inert nitrogen gas. The nitrogen impregnated product is then packaged, also under nitrogen.

Today, food companies wishing to install freeze-drying equipment on a major scale must consider the process from an overall systems approach. This will include material handling, the freezing operation, loading of drier trays, the drying operation, high vacuum and condenser require-

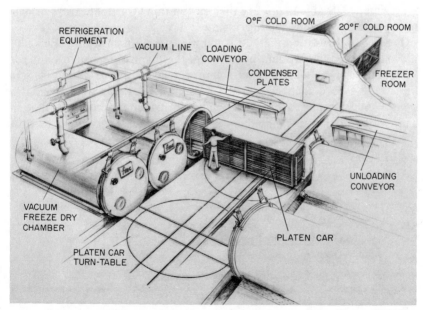

Courtesy of FMC Corp.

FIG. 135. FREEZE-DRYING PLANT

ments, unloading of trays, packaging requirements, and of course equipment, labor, and utility costs. Many equipment companies have designed total systems which can be custom engineered for a specific product and the needs of the manufacturer. It is common for such equipment companies, working with the food manufacturer, to design and install entire freeze-drying plants. Seldom are two such plants quite the same. One type of plant layout is seen in Fig. 135.

Atmospheric Drying of Foams.—Vacuum drying methods, and freeze drying in particular, can produce dehydrated foods of exceptional quality. Where liquids and purées are involved, however, it sometimes is possible to approach vacuum drying quality at atmospheric pressure with less expensive equipment and operating costs. This has been done in some instances by drying prefoamed liquid foods. As mentioned earlier, foaming is for the purpose of exposing enormous surface area for quick moisture escape. This in turn can permit rapid atmospheric drying at somewhat reduced temperatures. In this type of drying, naturally foaming foods such as egg white will be mechanically whipped to a foam density of about 0.3 gm per cc. Foods that do not whip as readily, such as concentrated citrus juices, fruit purées, and tomato paste are supplemented with low levels of an edible whipping agent belonging to such groups of materials as vegetable proteins, carbohydrate gums, or monoglyceride emulsifiers prior to being whipped. Stable foams are then cast in thin layers onto trays or belts and are dried by various heating schemes.

One such dehydration method is known as foam-mat drying (Fig. 136). In a particular type of foam-mat drying, the foam is deposited on a perforated tray or belt support as a uniform layer approximately 1/8 in. thick. Just before the perforated support enters the heated oven it is given a mild air blast from below. This forms small craters in the stiff foam which further expands foam surface and increases drying rate. At

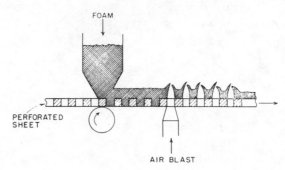

Courtesy of U. S. Dept. Agr., Western Regional Res. Lab.

FIG. 136. CRATERING TECHNIQUE OF FOAM-MAT DRYING

oven temperatures of about 180° F, foam layers of many foods can be dried to about 2–3% moisture in approximately 12 min.

Another system casts similar stable foams on a nonperforated stainless steel belt at a uniform thickness of approximately 1/64 in. The belt is heated from below by condensing steam and from above by high velocity heated air. Product temperature is kept below 180° F, and drying time is of the order of one minute or less. Exceptionally rapid drying rates are due largely to the extreme thinness of the foam layers and to the method of heating by condensing steam. When steam condenses under the belt it gives up both sensible heat and latent heat of condensation, which together provide a substantial driving force to evaporate food moisture. An illustration of the integrated equipment employed in this system is seen in Fig. 137.

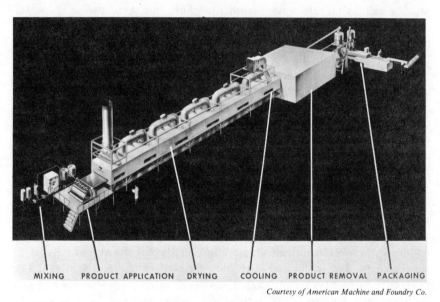

MIXING   PRODUCT APPLICATION   DRYING   COOLING   PRODUCT REMOVAL   PACKAGING

Courtesy of American Machine and Foundry Co.

FIG. 137.   MICROFLAKE FOOD DEHYDRATION SYSTEM

FOOD CONCENTRATION

Foods are concentrated for many of the same reasons that they are dehydrated. Concentration can be a form of preservation, but this is true only for some foods. Concentration reduces weight and volume and results in immediate economic advantages. Nearly all liquid foods to be dehydrated are concentrated before they are dried. This is because in the early stages of water removal moisture can be more economically removed in highly efficient evaporators than in dehydration equipment. Further, increased viscosity from concentration often is needed to prevent liquids from running off drying surfaces, or to facilitate foaming or puffing. Foods are also concentrated because the concentrated forms have become desirable components of diet in their own right. Thus, fruit juice plus sugar with concentration becomes jelly.

There are many examples of concentrated foods such as frozen orange juice concentrate and canned soups which are easily recognized because of the need to add back water before they are consumed. However, maple syrup and butter are somewhat less obvious concentrated foods. In the case of maple syrup the dilute maple tree sap is concentrated from about 2% solids to 66% solids by boiling off water in open pans or kettles. In making butter, constitutents of cream are concentrated from about 40% solids to 85% solids by breaking the fat emulsion and draining the buttermilk, which is largely water, from the churn. In these two cases water removal is accompanied by other changes that we wish to achieve. As in dehydration, however, most food concentration aims at minimal alteration of food constitutents.

The more common concentrated foods include such items as evaporated and sweetened condensed milks, fruit and vegetable juices and nectars, sugar syrups and flavored syrups, jams and jellies, tomato paste, many types of fruit purées used by bakers, candymakers, and other food manufacturers, and many more. Currently there is research going on in the concentration of beer and vinegar.

Aspects of Preservation

The levels of water in virtually all concentrated foods are in themselves more than enough to permit microbial growth. Yet while many concentrated foods such as nonacid fruit and vegetable purées may quickly undergo microbial spoilage unless additionally processed, such items as sugar syrups, and jellies and jams are relatively immune to spoilage. The difference, of course, is in what is dissolved in the remaining water and what osmotic concentration is reached. Sugar and salt in concentrated solution have high osmotic pressures. When these are sufficient to draw water from microbial cells, or prevent normal diffusion of water into these cells a preservative condition exists. Heavy syrups and similar products will keep indefinitely without refrigeration even if exposed to microbial contamination, provided they are not diluted above a critical concentration by moisture pickup.

The critical concentration of sugar in water to prevent microbial growth will vary depending upon the type of microorganism and the presence of other food constituents, but usually 70% sucrose in solution will stop growth of all microorganisms in foods. Less than this concentration may be effective, but for shorter periods of time, unless the foods contain acid or they are refrigerated. Salt becomes highly preservative when its concentration is increased, and levels of about 18 to 25% in solution generally will prevent all growth of microorganisms in foods. Except in the case of certain briny condiments, however, this level is rarely tolerated in foods. Removal of water by concentration also increases the level of food acids in solution. This is particularly significant in concentrated fruit juices.

In the sugar industry, juice squeezed from sugar cane contains approximately 15% sucrose and is highly perishable. Evaporators are an essential part of the equipment in sugar processing plants and are used to remove most of the water from cane or beet juice prior to subsequent crystallization steps in the production of dry granulated sugar. However, concentrated syrups with sugar levels of approximately 70% also are sold as important items of commerce. These syrups, with consistencies similar to honey, are pumped into tank cars and delivered to storage tanks of bakeries and confectionery manufacturers (Fig. 138). Preservation is quite satisfactory provided there is no moisture condensation from the air onto

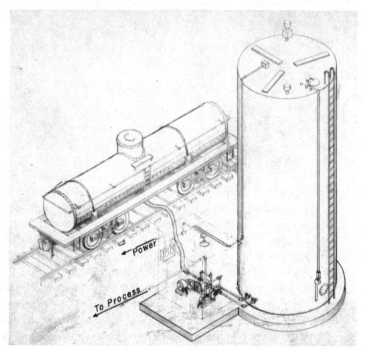

From Kelly (1964)

FIG. 138.   TYPICAL LIQUID SUGAR STORAGE INSTALLATION WITH 25,000 GAL. STORAGE TANK

interior tank surfaces. Sugar in this form, already in solution and easy to pump, is more convenient and economical than granulated sugar to use in many manufacturing operations.

Reduced Weight and Volume

While the preservation effects of food concentration are important, the principal reason for most food concentration today is to reduce food weight and bulk. Tomato pulp, which is ground tomato minus the skins and seeds, has a solids content of only 6%, and so a gallon can would contain only 1/2 lb of tomato solids (Table 33). Concentrated to 32% solids the same

TABLE 33

SPECIFIC GRAVITY AND SOLIDS RELATIONSHIP OF TOMATO PULP AND COMMERCIAL
TOMATO CONCENTRATES[1]

Total Solids, %	Specific Gravity at 68°F	Dry Tomato Solids per Gal. at 68°F, Lb
6.0 Tomato pulp	1.025	0.51
10.8 ⎫	1.045	0.94
12.0 ⎪ Tomato purée	1.050	1.05
14.2 ⎬	1.060	1.25
16.5 ⎭	1.070	1.47
25.0 ⎫	1.107	2.31
26.0 ⎪	1.112	2.41
28.0 ⎬ Tomato paste	1.120	2.61
30.0 ⎪	1.129	2.82
32.0 ⎭	1.138	3.03

[1] With permission; From "A Laboratory Manual for the Canning Industry." 1956. 2nd Edition   Natl. Canners Assoc., Washington, D. C.

gallon can would contain 3 lb of tomato solids, or six times the value of product. For a manufacturer needing tomato solids, such as a producer of soups, canned spaghetti, or frozen pizzas, the savings from concentration are enormous in cans, transportation costs, warehousing costs, and handling costs throughout his operations. This is especially so since much of the U. S. tomato crop is grown in the Sacramento Valley area of California and shipped to manufacturing plants in Chicago and Eastern areas of the country. For the same reasons, hundreds of millions of pounds of concentrated fruits and vegetables, milk products, and other commodities are used industrially, in restaurant operations, and in the home. Large quantities of concentrated buttermilk, whey, blood, and other food by-products also are ultimately used in animal feeds by poultry and livestock growers.

Methods of Concentration

Solar Concentration.—As in food dehydration, one of the simplest methods of evaporating water is with solar energy. This was done to derive salt from sea water since earliest times, and is still practiced today in the United States. Over a million tons of salt are produced by solar evaporation each year in the San Francisco bay area (Fig. 139). The sun and wind evaporate water from sea brine in man-made lagoons. This method is extremely slow in terms of evaporation rate, and is suitable only for salt.

Courtesy of Leslie Salt Co.

FIG. 139. SALT CONCENTRATION OF OCEAN WATER BY SOLAR EVAPORATION

Open Kettles.—Some foods can be satisfactorily concentrated in open kettles that are heated by steam. This is the case for some jellies and jams and for certain types of soups. However, high temperatures and long concentration times damage most foods. In addition, thickening and burn-on of product to the kettle wall gradually lowers the efficiency of heat transfer and slows the concentration process. Kettles and pans are still widely used in the manufacture of maple syrup, but here high heat is desirable to produce color from caramelized sugar and to develop typical flavor.

Flash Evaporators.—By subdividing the food material and bringing it into direct contact with the heating medium we can markedly speed con-

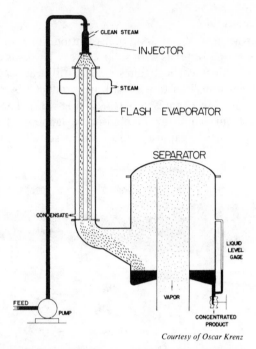

FIG. 140.   COMPONENTS OF FLASH EVAPORATOR

centration. This is done in flash evaporators of the kind seen in Fig. 140. Clean steam superheated at about 300° F is injected into the food which is pumped into an evaporation tube where boiling occurs. The boiling mixture then enters a separator vessel in which the concentrated food is drawn off at the bottom and the steam plus water vapor from the food is evacuated through a separate outlet. Because temperatures are high, foods that lose volatile flavor constituents will yield these to the exiting steam and water vapor. These can be separated from the vapor by essence recovery equipment on the basis of different boiling points between the essences and water.

Thin-Film Evaporators.—In thin-film evaporators, one type of which is seen in Fig. 141, food to be concentrated is pumped into a vertical cylinder which has a rotating element that spreads the food into a thin layer on the cylinder wall. The cylinder wall of double jacket construction usually is heated by steam. Water is quickly flashed from the thin food layer and the concentrated food is simultaneously wiped from the cylinder wall. The concentrated food and water vapor are continuously discharged to an external separator, from which product is removed at the bottom and water vapor passes to a condenser. Product temperature may reach

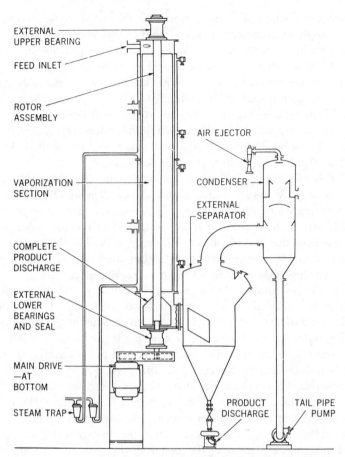

EXTERNAL
UPPER BEARING

FEED INLET

ROTOR
ASSEMBLY

AIR EJECTOR

VAPORIZATION
SECTION

CONDENSER

EXTERNAL
SEPARATOR

COMPLETE
PRODUCT
DISCHARGE

EXTERNAL
LOWER
BEARINGS
AND SEAL

MAIN DRIVE
—AT
BOTTOM

STEAM TRAP

PRODUCT
DISCHARGE

TAIL PIPE
PUMP

Courtesy of Buflovak Equipment Div., Blaw-Knox Co.

FIG. 141. AGITATED THIN-FILM EVAPORATOR

185°F or higher, but since residence time of the concentrating food in the heated cylinder may be less than a minute heat damage is minimal.

Vacuum Evaporators.—Heat sensitive foods are most commonly concentrated in low temperature vacuum evaporators. The thin-film type evaporators frequently are operated under vacuum by connecting a vacuum pump or steam ejector to the condenser.

It is common to construct several vacuumized vessels in series so that the food product moves from one vacuum chamber to the next and thereby becomes progressively more concentrated in stages. With such an arrangement the successive stages are maintained at progressively higher degrees of vacuum, and the hot water vapor arising from the first stage is used to heat the second stage, the vapor from the second stage heats the third stage, etc. In this way maximum use of heat energy is made. Such a system is called a multiple effect vacuum evaporator and is illustrated in previous Fig. 43. Multiple effect vacuum evaporators become sizable and expensive. Systems employed in the grape juice industry continuously concentrate juice from an initial solids content of 15% to a final solids concentration of 72% at rates as high as 4,500 gal. of single strength juice per hour. The system illustrated in Fig. 43 is capable of concentrating tomato juice from an initial solids level of 6% to a final solids concentration of 30% at a rate of 14,000 gal. of single strength juice per hour.

Even with efficient vacuum evaporator systems where water may boil at 80° F or slightly lower, some volatile flavor compounds are lost with the evaporating water vapor. These volatile essences can be recovered, or "stripped," from the water vapor and returned to the cool concentrated food as has been mentioned earlier. However, it is possible to concentrate foods at still lower temperatures and further minimize heat damage and volatile flavor loss. One method is known as freeze concentration.

Freeze Concentration.—As discussed previously, when a solid or liquid food is frozen all of its components do not freeze at once. First to freeze is some of the water which forms ice crystals in the mixture. The remaining unfrozen food solution is now higher in solids concentration. This concentration effect continues as more and more water is frozen out of the mixture. Ultimately the entire mixture freezes.

It is possible, before the entire mixture freezes, to separate the initially formed ice crystals. One way of doing this is to centrifuge the partially frozen slush through a fine mesh screen. The concentrated unfrozen food solution passes through the screen while the frozen water crystals are retained and can be discarded. By repeating this process several times on the concentrated unfrozen food solution its final concentration can be increased several fold. By such a process (Fig. 142), up to 80% of the water has been removed from beer. Since alcohol has a lower freezing point than water the beer concentrate retains the alcohol. Freeze concentration has been known for many years, and has been applied commercially to orange juice. However, high processing costs, due largely to losses of juice occluded to the ice crystals, have limited the number of installations to date.

Reverse Osmosis.—Low temperature concentration processes employing perm-selective membranes are currently being actively studied. Osmosis is the process involving the movement of water through a perm-selective membrane from a region of high concentration to a region of lower concentration. The region of lower concentration generally contains solutes in solution and has associated with it an osmotic pressure. It is possible to

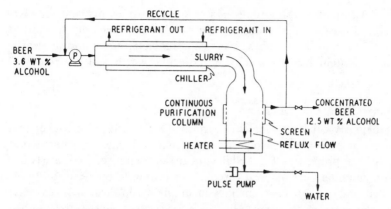

Flow diagram of Phillips fractional crystalliza-tion or freeze-drying process for concentration of beer. Single strength beer is blended with a recycle stream of concentrate and cooled in a conventional crystal forming and growing unit, producing a thick crystal slurry much like soft sherbet. From the crystal forming unit the slurry enters the crystal purification column where the non-frozen concentrate is removed through a wall filter (flow through filter is con-trollable) leaving a crystal bed. (In one of Phillips' commercial adaptation of this process the crystal bed is moved through the column hydraulically.)

A heater melts the forward surface of the crys-tal bed and yields a liquid-water product. Water exits from the melt end at a tempera-ture just above 32 F and can be reused. Some of this water is forced back through the crystal bed and as it undergoes refreezing and sub-sequent remelting performs the same rectify-ing action as does reflux in a fractional distilla-tion column. About 99 per cent of the water entering the column in crystal (ice) form is eventually removed.

Beers tested by this process ranged from con-ventional types to malt liquor. In each case up to 80 per cent of the water was removed with less than 0.1 per cent of beer components.

Courtesy Food Processing-Marketing

Fig. 142. Flow Diagram of Freeze Concentration Process for Beer

reverse the normal flow of water through the membrane by applying pres-sure on the solute side of the membrane in excess of the osmotic pressure. This is reverse osmosis.

Applied to food concentration, reverse osmosis processes involve pump-ing liquid foods under pressure against a perm-selective membrane in a suitable support. Equipment may be similar to pressure filters in design. If the membrane is of suitable perm-selectivity then water will pass through it but food solutes of low molecular weight, as well as larger constituents, will be retained and concentrated. The future success of food concentra-tion by reverse osmosis will be largely dependent upon membrane prop-erties such as water permeability rate, solute rejection rate, and length of useful membrane life. Different membranes will be required for different foods. Synthetic membranes are today being fabricated with considerable control over their physical and chemical properties. Some of these mem-branes, by allowing passage of low molecular weight solutes with the water, in addition to concentrating solids also affect a change in product composition by altering the ratios of solid components retained. Known as ultrafiltration, this technique is now used commercially to modify the composition of cheese whey, increasing its lactalbumin and decreasing its lactose content after the still lower molecular weight salts are removed.

Changes From Concentration

Obviously concentration that exposes food to 212°F or higher temperatures for prolonged periods can cause major changes in organoleptic and nutritional properties. Cooked flavors and darkening of color are two of the more common heat induced results. In addition to the desirability of controlled amounts of these changes in maple syrup, heat induced reactions also characterize certain candies such as caramel, and in caramel production sugar-milk mixtures are intentionally concentrated at high temperature. With most other foods, however, the lower the concentration temperature the better, since we most often want the reconstituted concentrated food to resemble as closely as possible the natural single-strength product. Even at the lowest temperatures, however, concentration can cause other changes that are undesirable. Two such changes involve sugars and proteins.

All sugars have an upper limit of concentration in water beyond which they are not soluble. Thus at room temperature sucrose is soluble to the extent of about 2 parts sugar in 1 part water. If we evaporate water beyond this concentration level the sugar crystallizes out. This can result in gritty, sugary jellies or jams which are undesirable. It also results in a condition known as "sandiness" in certain milk products when lactose crystallizes due to overconcentration. Since the amount of sugar that can be in solution decreases with decreasing temperature, a concentrated product may be smooth in texture at room temperature but become gritty or sandy when put into a refrigerator. This condition occurs in the manufacture of ice cream due to lactose crystallization during freezing if the concentration of lactose from concentrated milk ingredients is excessive.

As for effects on proteins, it has been pointed out that proteins can be easily denatured and precipitated from solution. One cause of denaturation can be high concentration of salts and minerals in solution with the protein. As we concentrate protein-containing foods such as milk, the concentration of all dissolved solids increases. The concentration of milk salts and minerals can become sufficiently high to partially denature the milk protein and cause it to slowly gel. The gelling may not show up immediately but only after weeks or months of storage, as frequently occurs in cans of evaporated and certain other condensed milks. The gelation of concentrated milk and other proteinaceous foods is an extremely complex phenomenon and is affected by many variables in addition to degree of concentration.

Microbial destruction, another type of change that may occur during concentration, will be largely dependent upon temperature. Concentration at a temperature of 212° F or slightly above will kill many microorganisms but cannot be depended upon to destroy bacterial spores. When the food contains acid, such as fruit juices, the kill will be greater, but again sterility is unlikely. On the other hand, when concentration is done under vacuum many bacterial types not only survive the low temperatures but multiply in the concentrating equipment. It therefore is necessary to stop frequently and sanitize low temperature evaporators, and where sterile concentrated foods are required, to resort to an additional preservation treatment.

INTERMEDIATE MOISTURE FOODS

The term "water activity" was briefly described in Chap. 7. In recent years adjustment and control of water activity to preserve semimoist foods has attracted increasing attention. Intermediate moisture foods or semimoist foods, in one form or another, have been important items of diet for a very long time. Generally they contain moderate levels of moisture, of the order of 20 to 50% by weight, which is less than is normally present in natural fruits, vegetables, or meats and more moisture than is left in conventionally dehydrated products. But in addition, intermediate moisture foods have dissolved in this moisture concentrations of solutes sufficient to decrease water activity below that required to support microbial growth. As a consequence intermediate moisture foods do not require refrigeration to prevent microbial deterioration. In the past there have been various kinds of intermediate moisture foods: natural intermediate moisture products such as honey; manufactured confectionery products high in sugar, plus jellies, jams, and bakery items such as fruit cakes; and partially dried products including figs, dates, jerky, pemmican, pepperoni, and the like. Sweetened condensed milk with a sugar level of about 63% based on the water content also could be considered an intermediate moisture food. In all of these products preservation is partially from high osmotic pressure associated with the high concentration of solutes; in some, additional preservative effect is contributed by salt, acid, and other specific solutes.

Current interest in this area, however, represents a new look at what possibly can be done in the creation of new products based on intermediate moisture phenomena. This is due in very large part to the success and excellent record of stability of manufactured moist dog foods within the past decade, and encouragement in the form of research contracts for the investigation of the feasibility of adapting this technology to the production of various intermediate moisture items for military and space flight personnel. This latter interest has been motivated by the potentials intermediate moisture technology offers for producing ration items with such positive attributes as: elimination of refrigeration requirement; high caloric density; moist texture without the need for water reconstitution; and relief from the problem of package breakage and subsequent food spoilage associated with air drops and other conditions of rough handling. In this latter case, even if packages are damaged, intermediate moisture foods are not readily subject to spoilage because of their low water activity. Packaging requirements for intermediate moisture foods are simplified because of this; they seldom will require more than enclosure within inexpensive protective wrappers.

Several of these properties offer obvious marketing advantages for consumer foods.

Principles Underlying Technology

Essential to any discussion of intermediate moisture foods is an understanding of the term "water activity" and its relationship to food properties and stability. Water activity (a_w) may be defined in a number of ways. Qualitatively, a_w is a measure of unbound, free water in a system available to support biological and chemical reactions. Water activity, not absolute water content, is what bacteria, enzymes, and chemical reactants encounter and are affected by at the microenvironmental level in food materials. Two foods with the same water content can have very different a_w values depending upon the degree to which the water is free or otherwise bound to food constituents.

Figure 142A is a representative water sorption isotherm for a given food at a given temperature. It shows the final moisture content the food will have when it reaches moisture equilibrium with atmospheres of differ-

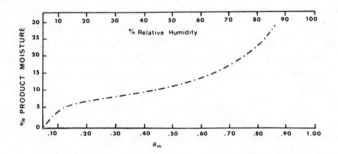

FIG. 142A. MOISTURE SORPTION ISOTHERM

ent relative humidities. Thus, this food, at the temperature for which this sorption isotherm was established, will ultimately attain a moisture content of 20% at 75% RH. If this food were previously dehydrated to below 20% moisture and placed in an atmosphere of 75% RH, it would absorb moisture until it reached 20%. Conversely, if this food were moistened to greater than 20% water and then placed at 75% RH it would lose moisture until it reached the equilibrium value of 20%. Under such conditions some foods may reach moisture equilibrium in the very short time of a few hours, others may require days or even weeks. When a food is in moisture equilibrium with its environment then the a_w of the food will be quantitatively equal to the RH divided by 100.

Water activity can be defined in still other terms in accordance with Raoult's law. Thus, a_w of a solution is quantitatively equal to the vapor pressure of the solution divided by the vapor pressure of pure water. This also is equal to the mole fraction of pure water in the solution, which is equivalent to the number of moles of water in the solution divided by the total number of moles present. Thus, a 1 molal solution of sucrose would contain 1 mole of sucrose and 55.5 moles of water (1,000 gm/18 gm), and under ideal solution behavior conditions would have an a_w value of 55.5/56.5 or 0.9823. Such a solution would be quite dilute and if it constituted the water phase of a food would not of itself generally inhibit microbial growth.

Determining Water Activity

The foregoing relationships provide the means for measuring a food's a_w at various moisture contents and temperatures. One method involves placing aliquots of the food in jars maintained at a fixed temperature and at different relative humidities with standard sulfuric acid or salt solutions. The aliquots are periodically weighed until they reach moisture equilibrium as indicated by no further gain or loss in weight. Equilibrium moisture content of each aliquot is next plotted at its corresponding RH. This plot yields a moisture sorption isotherm for the specific food (at the temperature chosen) of the kind indicated in Fig. 142A. From the resulting moisture sorption isotherm curve the RH divided by 100 corresponding to each moisture content is equal to the food's a_w at that moisture level. In practice, the a_w of an experimental food formulation can be readily determined instrumentally. In this case, a sample of the food is placed in a vessel of limited headspace at a chosen temperature. The vessel is provided with a sensitive hygrometer sensor not in contact with the food but connected to a potentiometric recorder. As the food exchanges moisture with the headspace a curve of RH is traced. The food's a_w then corresponds to the RH/100 at equilibrium.

As was stated earlier, a_w is a measure of free or available water, to be distinguished from unavailable or bound water. These states of water also bear a relationship to the characteristic sigmoid shapes of water sorption isotherm curves of various foods. Thus, according to theory, most of the water corresponding to the portion of the curve below its first inflection point (below 5% moisture in Fig. 142A) is believed to be tightly-bound water—often referred to as an adsorbed monomolecular layer of water. Moisture corresponding to the region above this point and up to the curve's second inflection point (about 20% moisture in Fig. 142A) is thought to exist largely as multimolecular layers of water less tightly held to food constituent surfaces. Beyond this second inflection point moisture generally is considered to be largely free water condensed in capillaries and interstices within the food. In this latter portion of the sorption isotherm curve small changes in moisture content result in great changes in a food's a_w.

Of the greatest importance with respect to intermediate moisture foods is the effect of a_w on microorganism growth. The a_w values for growth of most food-associated bacteria, yeasts, and molds have received considerable study. The minimum a_w below which most important food bacteria will not grow is of the order of 0.90 or greater, depending upon the specific bacterium. Some halophilic bacteria may grow down to an a_w of 0.75, and certain osmophilic yeasts even lower, but these seldom are important causes of food spoilage. Molds are more resistant to dryness than most bacteria and frequently will grow well on foods having an a_w of about 0.80, however slow growth may appear after several months at room temperature on some foods even at an a_w as low as 0.70. At a_w values below 0.65 mold growth is completely inhibited, but such low a_w generally is not applicable in the fabrication of intermediate moisture foods. This level would correspond to total moisture content well below 20% in many foods; such foods would lose chewiness and approach a truly dehydrated product. For most items, a_w values between 0.70 and 0.85 are required for semimoist texture. These levels are sufficiently low to inhibit common food spoilage bacteria. Where they are not sufficiently low for long term inhibition of mold growth, an antimycotic such as potassium sorbate is included in the food formulation to augment the preservative effect.

While a_w values for microbial inhibition commonly are cited in the literature to 2 or 3 decimal places, this should not convey the impression that an a_w given as a minimum for growth of a particular microorganism is an absolute value. It can be influenced somewhat by such factors as the food's pH, temperature, nutritional status in terms of microbial requirements, and the nature of specific solutes in the water phase. Although these influences frequently are small, it is prudent to confirm the efficacy of a target a_w to prevent microbial spoilage of a new intermediate moisture formulation by running appropriate bacterial plate counts. Bacteriological tests also are necessary from a public health standpoint.

When attempting to fabricate an intermediate moisture food, one selects an appropriate target a_w then considers formula ingredients to provide solute concentrations to yield the desired a_w. The total solute concentration corresponding to any a_w can be easily calculated from equations based on Raoult's law provided the food's water phase behaves as an ideal solution.

As solutions become more concentrated and more complex, however, they fail to behave in ideal fashion; then calculations relating solute concentrations and a_w become only approximations. For an a_w of 0.995, for example, theory calls for a total solute concentration of 0.281 molal. Sucrose and glycerol, which do not dissociate in solution, closely approach this ideal. Sodium chloride and calcium chloride, which dissociate to yield 2 and 3 ions, respectively, also approach ideal behavior in such dilute solutions when we account for the sum of the concentrations of their ions. However, in concentrated solutions, solutes become more effective in lowering a_w than would be predicted on the basis of ideal behavior. This is not due to suppression of ion dissociation, which in itself would be expected to contribute an opposite effect, but rather is thought to result from increased total hydration of large numbers of solute molecules which decrease the probability of occurrence of unattached water molecules. This also is so with nondissociating solutes such as sucrose and glycerol, favored ingredients in the formulation of intermediate moisture foods. Such phenomena make it necessary to augment mathematical calculation of a_w by experimental measurement when attempting to establish intermediate moisture food compositions.

Much of what has been said thus far with regard to a_w has had to do with microbial inhibition. It also should be clear, however, that a_w affects many other properties of foods, including chemical reactivity and equilibria, enzymatic activity, flavor, texture, color, and stability of nutrients. More will be said about some of these effects shortly.

Products and Technology

The ingredient composition of a typical hamburger-like, semimoist dog food will contain about 20% moisture, contributed largely from chopped meat by-products. The water-soluble solids dissolved in this moisture, particularly sucrose added in high concentration and some salt, will then produce a water phase with an a_w of about 0.78. This value is sufficient to control bacteria, but for long-term room temperature stability against mold growth, potassium sorbate is added. Propylene glycol in the formula provides some additional antimycotic activity, contributes slightly to lowering a_w, and serves the additional function of contributing to the moist chewy texture through its plasticizing humectant properties. The remaining ingredients satisfy the nutritional and organoleptic qualities of a meat-like dog food.

As for manufacturing processes, these vary, but generally involve applying pasteurization-cooking temperatures to a homogeneous mixture of all heat-resistant ingredients; subsequent incorporation of the more heat-sensitive colors, flavors and nutrient supplements; extrusion to form ground chopped meat-like texture; and, if desired, passage through a patty-maker to form hamburger-like patties. Pasteurization-cooking and extrusion can be combined in a cooker-extruder. Simple packaging in protective films is sufficient, and the product retains adequate stability even if packets are opened and subsequently reclosed. The processing heat treatment serves to cook the meat, hasten the establishment of moisture equilibrium throughout the product, and decrease initial microbial load. It does not inactivate bacterial spores but the low a_w prevents their germination.

With regard to new intermediate moisture foods for humans, progress recently has been reported by researchers of the General Foods Corp. working under contracts from the U.S. Army Natick Laboratories. Contracts involved demonstrating feasibility of producing such items as intermediate moisture diced chicken, ground beef, diced carrots, beef stew, barbecued pork, and apple pie filling. To be acceptable, rather specific natural textures were required for these products. This required departing from the practice of grinding and mixing ingredients as is common in dog food preparation. Two approaches were studied. One involved infusing low a_w solutions into previously dehydrated foods, most of which were freeze dried to take advantage of their retained texture and sponge-like absorptive structure. The second approach infused solutes into naturally moist foods by cooking them in low a_w solutions. Infusing solutions were formulated to compensate for the diluting effect of the foods' natural water contents upon desired final a_w.

To decrease a_w without imparting excessive sweetness to certain products, glycerol was used in preference to the sucrose found acceptable in intermediate moisture dog foods.

Final a_w values for the experimental intermediate moisture foods ranged from 0.71 to 0.81. Yeast, mold, and bacterial plate counts revealed no significant microbial growth in any of the products during 4 months of storage at 100.4°F, but sensory evaluation rated flavor and texture of these products considerably below conventionally canned or freshly prepared comparable products. Further product improvement work has extended this technology to the preparation of such additional intermediate moisture items as chicken à la king, ham in cream sauce, Hungarian goulash, etc. Several of these items involve a number of distinct food components that must be individually distinguishable in the final preparation if the item is to be considered of high quality.

It is a property of a_w that when food components differing in a_w are put into the same system or package, components of higher a_w give up moisture to components of lower a_w until the mixture reaches a single equilibrium a_w. A practical consequence of this is that each component of a mixture can be prepared separately under specific optimum conditions of formulation and infusion. When these components are subsequently blended and reach the equilibrium a_w of the mixture, they will retain different total water contents in keeping with their individual water sorption isotherms, and different textures influenced by these water contents. This principle is employed in producing complex mixtures.

Problems Remaining

Product development based on intermediate moisture technology must include some further considerations. Levels of a_w that prevent microbial growth but retain semimoist food texture generally are not sufficiently low to inhibit the activities of food enzymes. Numerous examples of enzymatic hydrolyses and oxidations of food substrates at low a_w have been demonstrated. Therefore low a_w is not used to control enzymatic changes in intermediate moisture foods. Instead, enzymes are inactivated by cooking, pasteurizing, or blanching before, during, or following solute infusion. Or, enzyme effects may be controlled by the use of sulfur dioxide, ascorbic acid-citric acid, and other treatments well known to the food technologist. Nonenzymatic reactions, including Maillard browning, also proceed at a_w values consistent with semimoist texture if precautions common to the manufacture of other food products are not employed.

Sugar and glycerol are two important ingredients for decreasing a_w. The tastes of both, however, are objectionable in many food products. Tasteless ingredients that could replace sugar and glycerol are currently being sought. Protein derivatives and dextrins with appreciable water-binding capacity hold promise here.

With regard to microbial inhibition, low a_w is effective and safe only if there is true equilibrium throughout the aqueous phase and at water-solid interfaces. Problems can occur with certain kinds of food structures and emulsions that may interfere with solute diffusion. Thus, an oil-in-water system is easier to infuse with aqueous solutes than a water-in-oil system in which fat is the continuous phase. This latter type of system can be readily processed, however, if solutes are added to the water phase prior to forming the emulsion.

Finally, the acceptability ratings of many experimental products must be improved and more learned about nutrient stability at intermediate moisture levels if intermediate moisture foods for human consumption are to make major gains. However, the potentials for such items as nonrefrigerated, shelf-stable sandwich spreads, salad mixes, an unlimited range of fillings for snack foods, and perhaps still more sophisticated products justify continued research.

BIBLIOGRAPHY

ACKER, L. 1969. Water activity and enzyme activity. Food Technol. 23, 1257–1258, 1261, 1264, 1269–1270.

ANON. 1963. New concepts spark evaporation. Food Eng. 35, No. 2, 68–70.

ANON. 1969. More flavorful fruit and vegetable powders. Food Process. 30, No. 1, 30–31.

BOMBEN, J. L., GUADAGNI, D. G., and HARRIS, J. G. 1969. Aroma concentration for dehydrated foods. Food Technol. 23, 83–86.

BONE, D. P. 1969. Water activity—its chemistry and applications. Food Prod. Develop. 3, No. 5, 81, 84–85, 88, 90, 92, 94.

BROWN, A. H., VAN ARSDEL, W. B., and LOWE, E. 1964. Drying methods and driers. In Food Dehydration, Vol. 2. W. B. Van Arsdel, and M. J. Copley (Editors). Avi Publishing Co., Westport, Conn.

CECIL, S. R., and WOODROOF, J. G. 1962. Long-term storage of military rations. Georgia Agr. Expt. Sta. Tech. Bull. N.S. 25.

COTSON, S., and SMITH, D. B. (Editors) 1963. Freeze-Drying of Foodstuffs. Columbine Press, Manchester and London.

COULTER, S. T., and JENNESS, R. 1945. Packing dry whole milk in inert gas. Minnesota Agr. Expt. Sta. Tech. Bull. 167.

DEDERT, W. G., and MOORE, J. G. 1963. New trends in evaporation. Ind. Eng. Chem. 55, June, 57–62.

FEINBERG, B. 1964. Concentration by evaporation. In Food Processing Operations, Vol. 3. M. A. Joslyn, and J. L. Heid (Editors). Avi Publishing Co., Westport, Conn.

FUESTEL, I. C., HENDEL, C. E. and JUILLY, M. E. 1964. Potatoes. In Food Dehydration, Vol 2. W. B. Van Arsdel, and M. J. Copley (Editors). Avi Publishing Co., Westport, Conn.

FISHER, F. R. (Editor) 1962. Freeze-drying of foods. Conf. sponsored jointly by QM Food Container Inst. and Nat. Acad. Sci.—Nat. Res. Council, Apr. 12–14, 1961, Chicago.

GÖRLING, P. 1958. Physical phenomena during the drying of foodstuffs. In Fundamental Aspects of the Dehydration of Foodstuffs. Soc. Chem. Ind. 1958, 42–53.

HALL, C. W., and HEDRICK, T. I. 1971. Drying of Milk and Milk Products, 2nd Edition. Avi Publishing Co., Westport, Conn.

HOLLIS, F., KAPLOW, M., HALIK, J., and NORDSTROM, H. 1969. Parameters for moisture content for stabilization of food products (Phase II). 70-12-FL. U.S. Army Natick Lab. Tech. Rept. 70-12-FL.

HOLLIS, F., KAPLOW, M., KLOSE, R., and HALIK, J. 1968. Parameters for moisture content for stabilization of food products. U.S. Army Natick Lab. Tech. Rept. 69-26-FL.

JOSLYN, M. A. 1961. Concentration by freezing. In Fruit and Vegetable Juice Processing Technology. D. K. Tressler, and M. A. Joslyn (Editors). Avi Publishing Co., Westport, Conn.

JOSLYN, M. A. 1963. Food processing by drying and dehydration. In Food Processing

Operations, Vol. 2. M. A. Joslyn, and J. L. Heid (Editors). Avi Publishing Co., Westport, Conn.

KELLY, N. 1964. Sugar. *In* Food Processing Operations, Vol. 3. M. A. Joslyn, and J. L. Heid (Editors). Avi Publishing Co., Westport, Conn.

LAPPLE, W. C., and CLARK, W. E. 1955. Drying methods and equipment. Chem. Eng. *62*, No. 10, 191–210.

LABUZA, T. P. 1968. Sorption phenomena in foods. Food Technol. *22*, 263–265, 268, 270, 272.

MILLEVILLE, H. P. 1962. High-quality concentrates. Food Process. *23*, No. 10. 59–62.

MOORE, J. G., and HESSLER, W. E. 1963. Evaporation of heat sensitive materials. Chem. Eng. Progr. *59*, Feb., 87–92.

NAIR, J. H. 1962. Freeze-dry systems changing. Food Eng. *34*, No. 6, 41–43.

NATIONAL CANNERS ASSOC. 1956. A Laboratory Manual for the Canning Industry, 2nd Edition. Natl. Canners Assoc., Washington, D.C.

NOWLIN, R. L., and HENWOOD, C. I., JR., 1955. Flash evaporation now applied to grape juice concentrate. Wines Vines *36*, No. 1, 25.

OSBORNE, R. J., POTTER, N. N., FIORE, J. V., and KELY, T. K. 1966. Method of drying foamed materials, e.g., foods. U.S. Pat. 3,266,559. Aug. 16.

PERRY, R. H., CHILTON, C. H., and KIRKPATRICK, S. D. (Editors) 1963. Chemical Engineers Handbook, 4th Edition. McGraw-Hill Book Co., New York.

PONTING, J. D., STANLEY, W. L., and COPLEY, M. J. 1964. Fruit and vegetable juices. *In* Food Dehydration, Vol. 2. W. B. Van Arsdel, and M. J. Copley (Editors). Avi Publishing Co., Westport, Conn.

POTTER, N. N. 1970. Intermediate moisture foods: principles and technology. Food Prod. Develop. *4*, No. 7, 38, 41, 44–45, 48.

POTTER, N. N., OSBORNE, R. J., KELLY, T. K., and MOSHY, R. J. 1964. The AMF Microflake food dehydration process. Res. Develop. Assoc. U.S. Army Natick Lab. Activities Rept. *16*, 194–200. Natick, Mass.

REEVE, R. M. 1942. Facts of vegetable dehydration revealed by microscope. Food Ind. *14*, No. 12, 51–54.

ROCKLAND, L. B. 1969. Water activity and storage stability. Food Technol. *23*, 1241–1246, 1248, 1251.

SCOTT, W. J. 1957. Water relations of food spoilage microorganisms. *In* Advances in Food Research, Vol. 7. Academic Press, New York.

SELTZER, E., and SETTELMEYER, J. T. 1949. Spray drying of foods. *In* Advances in Food Research, Vol. 6. Academic Press, New York.

SIVETZ, M., and FOOTE, H. E. 1963. Coffee Processing Technology, Vol. 1. Avi Publishing Co., Westport, Conn.

TRESSLER, D. K., and JOSLYN, M. A. (Editors) 1971. Fruit and Vegetable Juice Processing Technology, 2nd Edition. Avi Publishing Co., Westport, Conn.

VAN ARSDEL, W. B. 1951A. Principles of the drying process, with special reference to vegetable dehydration. U.S. Dept. Agr. Bur. Circ. *AIC-300*.

VAN ARSDEL, W. B. 1951B. Tunnel-and-truck dehydrators, as used in vegetable dehydration. U.S. Dept. Agr., Bur. Agr. Ind. Chem. *AIC-308*.

VAN ARSDEL, W. B., COPLEY, M. J. and MORGAN, A. I., JR. (Editors) 1973. Food Dehydration, 2nd Edition, Vols. 1 and 2. Avi Publishing Co., Westport, Conn.

WALKER, L. H. 1961. Volatile flavor recovery. *In* Fruit and Vegetable Juice Processing Technology. D. K. Tressler, and M. A. Joslyn (Editors). Avi Publishing Co., Westport, Conn.

CHAPTER 11

Food Irradiation and Microwave Heating

INTRODUCTION

Food irradiation and microwave heating are entirely different processes with distinct and separate objectives. Nevertheless, it is appropriate to consider them in a single chapter since they do share some common features. Both food irradiation and microwave heating employ radiant energies that produce their effects upon being absorbed within the food. Both require special equipment to generate and focus this energy, as well as to prevent potentially harmful effects to humans. Irradiation and microwave heating represent relatively new technologies as applied to foods. Although having received intensive investigation in recent years, both must be considered to be not yet fully researched nor exploited in terms of their full potentials. Food irradiation is seen primarily as a preservation method, but also has potential as a more general unit operation to produce specific changes in food materials. Microwave energy, on the other hand, has been employed especially to produce rapid and unique heating effects, one application of which can be food preservation.

FOOD IRRADIATION

The several preservation methods described in previous chapters all have origins dating back to primitive times. Not so with food irradiation. The discoveries of artifically produced radiations such as X-rays and radioactivity of natural materials were made as recently as 1895–1896. Food irradiation studies are still more current, having not begun in earnest until shortly after World War II. The impetus to this research resulted largely from intensive investigations of nuclear energy, which led to developments in the economic production of radioactive isotopes and to evolution of high energy accelerators. In the relatively short period since World War II, food irradiation has been investigated with an intensity equalled by no previous food preservation or processing method. Much of this work has had to do with safety and wholesomeness of irradiated products. In 1963, the U.S. Food and Drug Administration approved irradiation-sterilized bacon as the first in a growing list of proposed products. This very approval, which limited types of energy sources and doses that could be employed, is currently being reassessed.

Kinds of Energy

There are several forms of radiant energy emitted from different sources. These belong to the electromagnetic spectrum of radiations and differ in wavelength, frequency, penetrating power, and various effects they have upon biological systems. Some of these forms of radiant energy and their bactericidal effects are indicated in Table 34.

TABLE 34

BACTERICIDAL EFFECTS OF DIFFERENT WAVELENGTHS OF RADIANT ENERGY[1]

Classification	Wavelength Angstroms	Germicidal Effects
Invisible Long		
radio	very long	none
infrared heat	8,000 and longer	temperature may be raised
Visible		
red, orange, yellow, green, blue, violet	4,000 to 8,000	little or none
Invisible Short		
ultraviolet total range	136 to 4,000	
	3,200 to 4,000	photographic and fluorescent range
	2,800 to 3,200	human skin tanning, anti-rachitic-vitamin D
	2,000 to 2,800	maximum germicidal power
	1,500 to 2,000	Shuman region
	1,000	ozone forming, germicidal in proper concentration
X-rays	1,000 to 1,500	
Alpha, beta, and gamma rays	less than 1,000	germicidal
Cosmic rays	Very short	probably germicidal

[1]From Weiser et al. (1971).

A light bulb emits visible energy. This energy is radiated from the bulb filament and travels in all directions, however, it can be focused and aimed at a target as in aiming a flashlight beam. Similarly heat is a form of energy. An infrared heat lamp contains a glowing element which radiates infrared energy. This energy can be directed at a person's back or onto a steak. The back or steak absorbs the infrared energy and becomes warm or indeed cooked if the quantity of the absorbed energy is sufficiently high.

There also are sources that radiate forms of energy which produce neither light nor heat, and can not readily be detected by the human eye or sense of touch. Thus, one does not ordinarily see or feel radio waves, ultraviolet light, or cosmic rays, but they are present nevertheless.

Energy radiations are emitted from the breakdown of atomic structure. Materials that undergo such changes are said to have radioactivity. Some elements such as uranium are naturally radioactive, others can be made radioactive by high energy bombardment of their atoms, as in the case of Co^{60}. Another form of energy is associated with the flow of electrons such as can be emitted from a cathode tube. These electrons or cathode rays can be given various degrees of acceleration and increased energy by passage through special electronic devices.

Some of the kinds of energy indicated above are used to a limited degree in food preservation. Thus, ultraviolet light, especially within the wavelength range of 2,000 to 2,800 angstroms, is employed to inactivate microorganisms on the surface of foods. The severe limitation here is the low degree of penetration of ultraviolet light into foods, restricting its usefulness to surface treatment or to food liquids that can be exposed in thin layers. Treatment of equipment surfaces, water, and air used in food plants are additional current applications of ultraviolet light. X-rays have greater penetrating power than ultraviolet light and have received consideration as a means of preserving foods. However, X-rays cannot easily be focused, leading to low efficiency of use with current equipment. Thus X-ray food applications to date have been experimental rather than commercial.

When the term food irradiation is currently used it generally is understood to mean processing with a limited number of kinds of radiant energy that together are referred to as ionizing radiations. These are chosen for penetrating power and inability to produce significant radioactivity in treated foods. They also do not produce significant heat in foods and so the additional term "cold sterilization" has been applied to this kind of food preservation.

Ionizing Radiations and Sources

The principal ionizing radiations used in food irradiation include gamma rays from radioactive elements, and electron beams produced in machines such as a Van de Graaff generator or a linear accelerator.

Radioactive Fuels.—Natural radioactive elements and artificially induced radioactive isotopes which can be produced in nuclear reactors emit a variety of radiations and energy particles during radioactive decay. Among these are alpha particles which are really helium atoms minus two outer electrons, beta particles or rays which are high energy electrons also referred to as cathode rays, gamma rays or photons which are a type of X-ray, and neutrons. These radiations have different penetrating powers. Thus, alpha particles will not even penetrate a sheet of paper, beta particles or electrons are more penetrating but can be stopped by a sheet of aluminum, and gamma rays are highly penetrating and will go through a block of lead if it is not too thick. Neutrons have great penetrating power and are of such high energy that they can alter atomic structure and thus make elements that they happen to strike radioactive. Such elements in turn emit their own high energy radiations.

In food irradiation we wish to use emissions that have good penetrating power so that they will not only inactivate surface microorganisms and enzymes but will produce these effects deep within the food. On the other hand, we do not wish to use such high energy emissions as neutrons which additionally would break down atomic structures in the food and make the food radioactive. For food irradiation we therefore principally employ gamma rays and beta particles.

Gamma and beta rays used in food irradiation may be derived from spent uranium fuel elements after their use in a nuclear reactor. These fuel elements which eventually develop fission fragments and other impurities, making them unsuitable for further use in the nuclear reactor, still possess intense radioactivity. Such spent fuel elements can be placed in an appropriately shielded and enclosed region, and the food brought into the path of their radiation. In early experimental food irradiation facilities (Fig. 143) such spent fuel elements (indicated by arrows) were placed

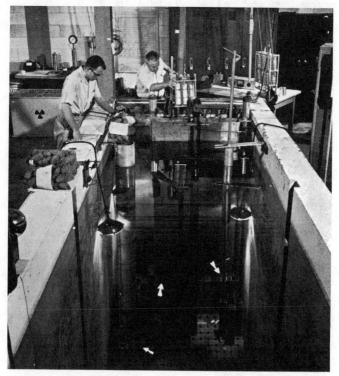

Courtesy of Phillips Petroleum Co.

FIG. 143. EARLY RADIATION FACILITY USING SPENT FUEL ELEMENTS

in shielded pits under about 16 ft of water. Containers of food were lowered into vertical cylinders immersed in the water and surrounded by the
fuel elements at the bottom of the pit. The containers were then held there
for sufficient time to absorb an appropriate radiation dose. Current facilities are less cumbersome and make considerable use of artificially induced radioactive elements such as Co^{60} for the radiating fuel. Where
Co^{60} is used, it is employed primarily as a gamma ray source, since beta
particles may be more efficiently produced by electronic machines.

Electron Accelerators.—Beta particles or electrons can be produced in a
Van de Graaff electrostatic generator (Fig. 144). In such a device an end-

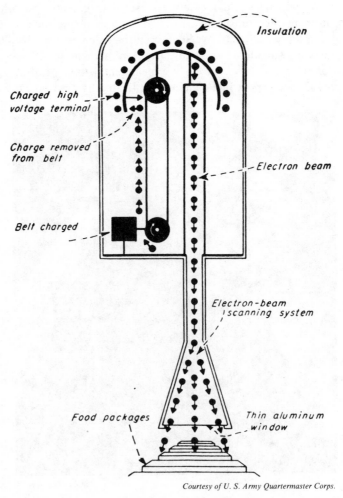

Courtesy of U. S. Army Quartermaster Corps.

FIG. 144. DIAGRAM OF A VAN DE GRAAFF ELECTRON ACCELERATOR

less belt of nonconducting material transports an electric charge from an electron source such as a heated cathode filament to a dome which acquires a high voltage. From the dome an electron beam can be made to accelerate through a cylindrical vacuum tube and out through a thin aluminum window. Food to be irradiated can then be passed under this window to receive an appropriate radiation dose. In related machines, electron streams can be given various degrees of beam power by increasing voltages, and through other means. One type of linear electron accelerator capable of producing electron energies of 50 Mev is seen in Fig. 145. One Mev is a million electron volts.

Courtesy of High Voltage Engineering Corp.

FIG. 145.   LINEAR ACCELERATOR, 50 MEV ELECTRONS

Units of Radiation

Various terms have been used to quantitatively express radiation intensity and radiation dosage:

(1) A roentgen of radiation is equivalent to the quantity of radiation received in one hour from a one gram source of radium at a distance of one yard. This is also the quantity of radiation that will produce 2.08 ×

10^9 ion pairs per cubic centimeter of dry air, or one electrostatic unit of charge of either sign per cubic centimeter of air under standard conditions of temperature and pressure.

(2) The energy required to produce ion pairs in air can also be expressed in terms of electron volts. In this case approximately 32.5 electron volts are required to produce one ion pair in air. An electron volt is also the energy equivalent of 1.6×10^{-12} erg. An erg is the energy equivalent of 10^{-7} joules. One joule per second is equivalent to one watt of power.

(3) The term roentgen equivalent physical (rep) refers to a quantity of ionizing radiation absorbed by materials. The absorption of 1 rep by food or soft tissues is equivalent to the absorption of 93 ergs of energy per cubic centimeter of material. The rep in earlier literature was given a somewhat lower energy equivalent of 84 ergs which has led to some confusion. The rep has now largely been replaced by the unit of radiation known as the rad.

(4) The rad also is a measure of energy absorbed. It has a quantitative equivalent of 100 ergs of energy absorbed per gram of material receiving ionizing radiation.

In irradiation processes what is important is the dose or quantity of radiation that a substrate receives, that is, the number of units of radiation energy absorbed. Different materials absorb radiation energy to different degrees. This is so even when such materials are exposed to the same radiation source for the same length of time. Under such conditions two different food materials would be exposed to the same amount of emitted radiation energy, but one will have absorbed more of this energy and so will have received a greater number of rads than the other.

A rad of radiation dosage represents the same amount of absorbed energy whether it comes from gamma rays, beta particles, or a mixture of the two. We may express the magnitude of a radioactive isotope power source in terms of curies, which is a measure of disintegrations per second. We may express the strength of gamma radiations in terms of roentgens. The intensity or energy level of beta particles emitted from a linear electron accelerator is generally defined in terms of electron volts. However, the length of time food is exposed to such sources, and the absorption properties of the food (and its container) will determine the number of rads received by the food, which is the effective dosage that produces changes in the food's microflora, enzymes, and other constituents.

Mechanisms of Action of Radiations

Ionizing radiations penetrate food materials to varying degrees depending upon the nature of the food and the characteristics of the radiations.

Gamma rays have greater penetrating power than beta particles. The efficacy of radiations in producing radiation effects, however, also is dependent upon their abilities to alter molecules and their ionization potential, that is, their abilities to knock electrons out of atoms of the materials through which they pass. Beta particles generally have greater ability to produce ionizations in matter through which they pass than gamma rays. Electron beams of higher energy levels will have greater depths of penetration and produce more altered molecules and total ionization along their traveled paths than lower energy electron beams.

Just as neutrons possessed of extremely high energy can alter atomic nuclei so as to make them radioactive, there are energy levels beyond which gamma rays and electron beams may induce radioactivity in foods. These energy levels are far in excess of what is needed to alter molecules, produce ionization, and inactivate microorganisms in foods. They also are far in excess of the energy levels of such isotope sources as Co^{60} and Cs^{137}, or 10 Mev electron beams, that have been permitted by the U.S. Food and Drug Administration for irradiation processing of approved foods.

When ionizing radiations of approved energy levels pass through foods there are collisions between the ionizing radiations and food particles at the molecular and atomic levels. Ion pair production results when the energy from these collisions is sufficient to dislodge an electron from an atomic orbit. Molecular changes occur when collisions provide sufficient energy to break chemical bonds between atoms; an important consequence of this is the formation of free radicals.

Free radicals are parts of molecules, groups of atoms, or single atoms, that possess an unpaired electron. Stable molecules almost always possess an even number of electrons, and an unpaired electron configuration is an extremely unstable form. Free radicals, therefore, have a great tendency to react with one another and with other molecules to pair their odd electrons and attain stability.

The formation of ion pairs, free radicals, reaction of free radicals with other molecules, recombination of free radicals, and related physical and chemical phenomena provide the mechanisms by which microorganisms, enzymes, and food constituents are altered during irradiation.

Direct Effects.—In the case of living cells and tissues, destructive effects and mutations from radiation were originally thought to be due primarily to direct contacts of high energy rays and particles with vital centers of cells, much as a bullet hits a specific target. The same theory of action was extended to explain changes in nonliving materials and foods. Thus, for example, a change in the color or texture of a food would be due to direct collision of a gamma ray or high energy beta particle with a specific pigment or protein molecule. Such direct hits unquestionably do occur, but their frequency of occurrence at a given radiation dose probably is not sufficient to explain the major portion of radiation effects in a given substrate.

Indirect Effects.—Direct hits need not occur for radiation effects in living or nonliving substrates. Just as radiations colliding with a cell or specific food molecule would produce ion pairs and free radicals, much the same occurs when high energy radiations pass through water. In this case water molecules are altered to yield highly reactive hydrogen and hydroxyl radicals. These radicals can react with each other, with dissolved oxygen in the water, and with the widest range of other organic and inorganic molecules and ions that may be dissolved or suspended in the water. Thus two hydroxyl radicals upon combining form hydrogen peroxide,

$$\cdot OH + \cdot OH \rightarrow H_2O_2.$$

Two hydrogen radicals produce hydrogen gas,

$$\cdot H + \cdot H \rightarrow H_2.$$

A hydrogen radical plus dissolved oxygen yield a peroxide radical,

$$\cdot H + O_2 \rightarrow \cdot HO_2.$$

Two peroxide radicals produce hydrogen peroxide,

$$\cdot HO_2 + \cdot HO_2 \rightarrow H_2O_2 + O_2.$$

Hydrogen peroxide is a strong oxidizing agent and a biological poison. Hydroxyl and hydrogen radicals are strong oxidizing and reducing agents, respectively. They also can enter into reaction with organic materials and grossly alter molecular structure. Since living cells and food materials are mostly water, the activity imparted to this solvent by radiation constitutes a most important factor contributing to lethality or sublethal changes in living cells, and alteration of food constituents.

A substrate receiving ionizing radiation probably will experience to some extent the direct effects cited above; it will certainly be affected by the indirect effects.

In food irradiation preservation it is an ultimate goal to inactivate undesirable microorganisms and enzymes but produce minimum changes in other food constituents. Microorganisms and enzymes can be inactivated by direct hits from radiations as well as from indirect effects. Other food constituents, largely in aqueous solution, undoubtedly are greatly affected by indirect effects from free radicals produced during radiolysis of water. It therefore has been attempted to minimize changes in foods during irradiation by limiting indirect effects.

Attempts to Limit Indirect Effects.—Efforts here have been largely directed at minimizing free radical formation from water, and minimizing reaction of free radicals with food constituents. Three approaches that have had varying degrees of success, depending upon the food material, illustrate this reasoning:

(1) Irradiation from the frozen state.—Free radicals are produced even in frozen water, though possibly to a lesser extent. However, the frozen state hinders free radical diffusion and migration to food constituents beyond the site of free radical production. This would be expected to limit undesirable reactions.

(2) Irradiation in a vacuum or under inert atmosphere.—As indicated above, a hydrogen radical reacting with oxygen will produce a highly oxidative peroxide radical. Peroxide radicals produce hydrogen peroxide. By removing oxygen from the system such reactions are minimized and food constituents may be somewhat protected. However, removal of oxygen and minimization of these reactions also has a protective effect upon food microorganisms, somewhat limiting the benefits that can be obtained. There also is the problem of getting oxygen out of food systems.

(3) Addition of free radical scavengers.—Ascorbic acid is an example of a compound that has a great affinity for free radicals. Addition of ascorbic acid and certain other materials to food systems results in consumption of free radicals through reaction with these, and a sparing of other sensitive pigments, flavor compounds, and food constituents. But a problem exists in incorporating such scavengers throughout non-liquid foods.

Each of these approaches, and several others, not only protect food constituents but offer some protection to microorganisms and undesirable food enzymes, generally necessitating an increased radiation dosage for food preservation.

Gross Effects of Ionizing Radiations

It is beyond the scope of this chapter to consider the many changes that occur within living systems and biological materials exposed to radiation. Suffice it to say that ionizing radiations can alter the structures of organic and biochemical compounds essential to normal life when these radiations are received in high dosage. Thus they may stunt, alter, or kill plants, animals, and microorganisms. In foods, excessive dosage will adversely affect proteins, carbohydrates, fats, vitamins, pigments, flavors, enzymes, etc. Excessive dosage also can change the protective properties of certain packaging materials such as plastic films and plastic or enamel interior can coatings. In this latter case, however, such dosages generally are in excess of sterilizing or pasteurizing requirements compatible with acceptable food quality. Where they are not, rigid containers such as tin or aluminum cans, more resistant to irradiation, are used for foods treated in their final package.

Excessive dosage has meaning only in terms of specific substrates. As in the case of heat, different food materials vary greatly in sensitivity to ionizing radiations. Bacon, for example, can withstand a radiation dosage of 5.6 Mrad (an Mrad or megarad is one million rads) and retain highly satisfactory organoleptic qualities. Such bacon is microbiologically sterile. Certain proteins, on the other hand, become highly disorganized at far

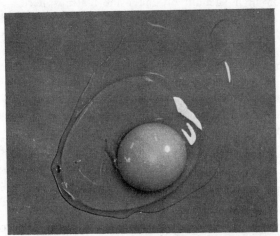

Control

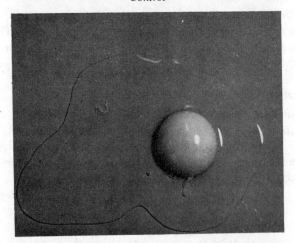

Courtesy of McArdle and Desrosier

FIG. 146.   RADIATION EFFECTS OF 600,000 RADS ON FRESH EGG

lower doses, showing varying degrees of molecular uncoiling, unfolding, coagulation, molecular cleavage, and splitting out of amino acids, odorous compounds, and ammonia. Egg white is a particularly sensitive mixture of proteins. In Fig. 146 are seen two originally similar fresh whole eggs. The control egg was not irradiated. The bottom egg was irradiated and a thin, watery condition of the egg white resulted. This undesirable change occurred with a radiation dose of 600,000 rads or 0.6 Mrad.

It is important to note that while 0.6 Mrad damaged the egg white, this dosage is less than sufficient to ensure sterility of the egg if it contained spores of certain bacteria. Therefore a higher dosage to ensure sterility would be impractical since it would make the fresh egg quite unacceptable for most food uses. Many foods cannot be irradiation sterilized for similar reasons. Some of these, however, are given improved keeping quality by irradiation pasteurization at lower doses.

Some of the more important overall effects and uses of different irradiation doses are indicated in Fig. 147. Approximately 500 rads will kill humans. About 10,000 rads will inhibit sprouting of potatoes and slightly more will destroy insects. Several hundred thousand rads will kill yeasts and molds, and this level will pasteurize many of our foods. Complete destruction of bacterial spores, producing food sterility, requires several million rads.

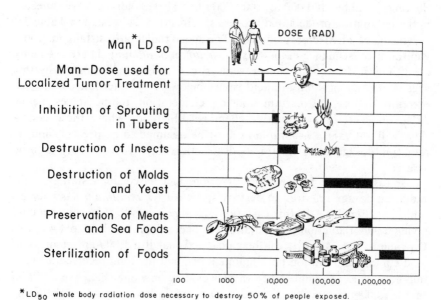

Man*LD$_{50}$

Man—Dose used for
Localized Tumor Treatment

Inhibition of Sprouting
in Tubers

Destruction of Insects

Destruction of Molds
and Yeast

Preservation of Meats
and Sea Foods

Sterilization of Foods

DOSE (RAD)

100   1000   10,000   100,000   1,000,000

*LD$_{50}$ whole body radiation dose necessary to destroy 50% of people exposed.

From Goldblith (1963)

FIG. 147. APPROXIMATE DOSAGES OF IONIZING RADIATION FOR SPECIFIC EFFECTS

Dose Determining Factors

Where the purpose of irradiation is food preservation, choice of dosage must take in several factors. The more important of these include safety and wholesomeness of the treated food, resistance of the food to organoleptic quality damage, resistance of microorganisms, resistance of food enzymes, and cost. Safety and wholesomeness involve considerations beyond freedom from dangerous radioactivity and absence of pathogens, and will be discussed later on.

Resistance of Food.—No simple generalizations can be given here. Foods vary widely in chemical composition, physical structure, and degree of change that is accepted before quality is considered sacrificed. Chemical and physical structure of natural foods of course vary even at the species and variety levels. These differences in foods set their own upper limits of radiation dose with respect to quality acceptability. Much of the acceptability data on specific foods has been obtained in studies conducted with volunteer troops of the U.S. Army. By way of example, pork loin, chicken, bacon, and shrimp have withstood sterilizing doses of 4.8 Mrad well. In some instances off-flavors detected in newly irradiated items largely disappear on storage. Some vegetables also have tolerated 4.8 Mrad. Various fruits have withstood sterilizing doses of 2.4 Mrad. More sensitive meats, fish, and fruits have been found quite acceptable at pasteurizing doses in the range of about 100,000 to 1,000,000 rads. These tolerances are reflected in the irradiation product and process specifications suggested in Table 35.

Resistance of Microorganisms.—The most radiation-resistant microorganism of consequence in foods is *Clostridium botulinum*. There are many conditions in foods that can prevent growth and toxin formation by this organism. Among them are acid values below pH 4.5, aerobic conditions, extreme dryness of certain foods, refrigeration temperatures below 38°F, and certain preservative chemicals. In foods where these conditions will not exist *Cl. botulinum* must be assumed to be present, and irradiation dosage sufficient for its destruction employed, if safety is to be assured.

As was the case for heat preservation, and based upon similar logic, radiation dosage required to destroy spores of *Cl. botulinum* has been established (Fig. 148). In this case the D_M value refers to the radiation dose giving a 90% reduction in population. In beef substrate (above pH 4.5) this D_M value is 0.4 Mrad. It can be calculated that if a 1,000-gm quantity of food contained a million botulinum spores, and the food received a radiation dose of 12 D_M values, then there would be only one chance in a billion that a 1,000-gm can of such food would contain live spores (in calculating one should not overlook the fact that a rad is an amount of energy per *gram* of material). A 12 D_M dosage (12 × 0.4 Mrad) is 4.8 Mrad. Such a dosage provides a wide margin of safety.

TABLE 35

SUMMARY OF FOOD IRRADIATION PRODUCT AND PROCESS SPECIFICATIONS[1]

Product	Process	Dose, Rads	Dosimeter	Package Requirements	Storage Temperature	Estimated Useful Storage Life
Potatoes	Sprout inhibition	7,500	ferrous sulfate	stored in open containers or in porous containers	41°F, 85% RH	2 yr or more
					68°F	10 mo or less
Flour	Insect destruction	50,000	ferrous sulfate	sealed paper or cloth bags, and overwrapped to prevent reinfestation	room temp	2 yr or more
					40°F	5 yr or more
Berries	Pasteurization (mold destruction)	150,000	cobalt glass	sealed in oxygen, CO_2 permeable film	34°F	21 days or more
Sliced meat and fish	Pasteurization (bacteria, yeast, mold, parasites, insects)	1,000,000	ceric sulfate	sealed in gas proof container	32°F	60 days or more
Animal, fish, and vegetable tissue	Heat inactivation of enzymes (165°F). Radiation sterilization	4,500,000	ceric sulfate	vacuum sealed in durable container (tin can) with odor scavenger	room temp	2 yr or more
					32°F	5 yr
Fruits	Heat inactivation of enzymes (165°F). Radiation sterilization	2,400,000	ceric sulfate	vacuum sealed in durable container (tin can) with odor scavenger	room temp	2 yr or more
					32°F	5 yr

[1] From Desrosier and Rosenstock (1960).

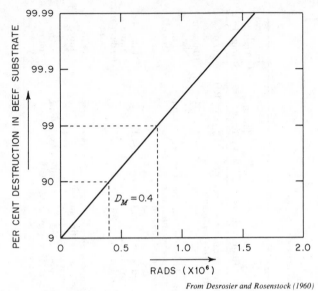

From Desrosier and Rosenstock (1960)

FIG. 148.   THE D_M VALUE FOR *Clostridium botulinum*

For foods with pH values below 4.5, *Cl. botulinum* is not a problem but other spoilage organisms must be inactivated. The most resistant of these has been found to have a D_M value of about 0.2 Mrad. For sterilization with a substantial margin of safety 12 D_M values (equivalent to 2.4 Mrad) also may be employed here.

Resistance of Enzymes.—Most food enzymes are more resistant to ionizing radiations than even spores of *Cl. botulinum*. Enzyme destruction curves comparable to bacterial destruction curves have been established (Fig. 149). It has been found that D_E values (radiation doses producing 90% reduction in enzyme activity) are of the order of 5 Mrad. Four D_E values would produce nearly total enzyme destruction, but such a dosage of 20 Mrad would be highly destructive to food constituents and might also impair safety of foods. For these reasons irradiation alone is not suitable where substantial enzyme destruction is required for storage stability.

This problem has been resolved by the use of various combination processes. Enzymes are readily inactivated by heat (blanching) and by certain chemicals. Temperatures of about 160° F for a few minutes are fairly effective. The combination of microorganism-destructive radiation doses plus such heat treatments are extremely effective. This is the basis of the heat-irradiation process specifications indicated at the bottom of Table 35.

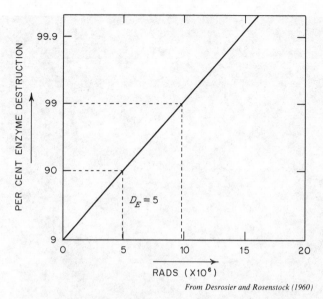

From Desrosier and Rosenstock (1960)

FIG. 149. THE D_E VALUE FOR ENZYMES

Cost Considerations.—Cost is another dose determining factor. Higher doses are obtained by using stronger radiation sources or by exposing foods to less intense radiations for longer periods of time. Either practice increases processing costs. In the case of some foods, irradiation pasteurization may be economically feasible while irradiation sterilization would not be. More broadly speaking, cost can determine whether irradiation processing should be used at all. It must be appreciated that generally there will be more than one practical method to preserve a given food. At the present time preservation by irradiation is more costly than preservation by heat, refrigeration, or freezing. Where these methods are applicable there would be little incentive to use irradiation.

On the other hand, there are applications where irradiation is uniquely suitable. Low dose irradiation pasteurization has extended the normal storage life of refrigerated marine products, fruits, and vegetables from a few days up to periods of several weeks. This can profoundly influence marketing practices. The military faces different problems, often having to operate under field conditions where refrigeration is not available. Heat preserved foods and dehydrated foods are used in such cases, but many products are markedly altered by such processing. Because irradiation can produce cold sterilization it can yield some preserved foods with little if any of the changes generally caused by high temperatures. Thus, radiation-sterilized bacon will retain essentially all of its preradiation attributes

Courtesy of U. S. Army Quartermaster Corp.

FIG. 150. RADIATION STERILIZED SHRIMP STORED ONE YEAR AT ROOM TEMPERATURE (4.8 MEGARADS)

even after a year or more of room temperature storage. The remarkable potentials of irradiation stabilization are further indicated by the irradiated shrimp and chicken of Fig. 150 and 151, which were stored for a year at room temperature before being prepared as illustrated. Notwithstanding such quality changes as may have occurred from irradiation, no currently known processing method is capable of this degree of room temperature preservation, regardless of cost.

Controlling the Radiation Process

There are many similarities between radiation preservation and the principles discussed in the chapter on heat preservation and processing. Like heat, radiations capable of cold sterilization are subject to the following considerations:

(1) Radiations can destroy microorganisms and inactivate many food enzymes but they also can damage food constituents and so radiation dose must be carefully controlled.

(2) If food is to be sterilized, then the radiation dose must be sufficient to destroy the most radiation-resistant pathogenic and spoilage-causing organisms that may be present. Dosage to inactivate *Cl. botulinum* spores with a substantial margin of safety satisfy this requirement.

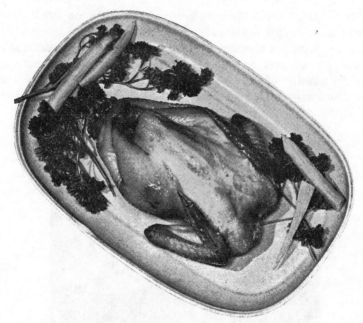

Courtesy of U. S. Army Quartermaster Corp.

FIG. 151. RADIATION STABILIZED CHICKEN STORED ONE YEAR AT
ROOM TEMPERATURE (4.8 MEGARADS)

(3) As with heat, it is not just the intensity of the radiation source that is important but the amount of radiation that the food absorbs, and so we have the element of time. The longer the food is in the radiation path the more that it will absorb.

(4) As with heat, we must provide radiation energy in such a manner that it reaches every particle of food within the mass or container. In the case of heat, we had the advantages of conduction and natural convection to help distribute heat throughout the container. In the case of cold sterilization by irradiation, with the exception of limited diffusion of free radicals (indirect effect), these do not occur and we must ensure an adequate killing dose by uniformly irradiating throughout the entire food mass. This brings in the problems of dosimetry and means of measuring irradiation dose.

Radiation Dosimeters.—In the case of heat it will be recalled that a temperature sensing thermocouple was placed at the cold point of cans and after sterilizing temperature was reached, additional processing time was employed. The measurement of radiation is made with various kinds of dosimeters which undergo change in proportion to energy received.

One of the most useful kinds of dosimeters is based on the property of specially prepared cobalt glass strips to change color on irradiation; the degree of color change being a measure of total radiation absorbed. If the cobalt glass strips are then positioned on a frame which is sealed in a can together with the food, and the can is irradiated, we have a means of detecting the quantity of radiation absorbed throughout various positions of the can. Such a dosimeter is seen in Fig. 152. If any portion of the can and

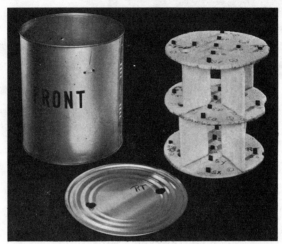

Courtesy of U. S. Army Quartermaster Corp.

Fig. 152.   Dosimeter Using Cobalt Glass Strips

the food within it fail to absorb the required number of rads then the cobalt glass strips in that portion of the can also will not have absorbed the radiation and the corresponding color change will not have occurred. If all of the strips have changed color equivalent to a sterilizing number of rads then it may be assumed all of the food also has absorbed this number of rads. Excessive irradiation can be as objectionable as under-irradiation and this too will be revealed by the degree of color change. It is necessary, of course, only to include a small number of dosimeters among many cans receiving the same radiation treatment to monitor the operation.

Safety and Wholesomeness of Irradiated Foods

The complex question of safety and wholesomeness of irradiated foods has been investigated in the United States by the Office of the Surgeon General of the Department of the Army, the Atomic Energy Commission, the National Bureau of Standards, the Food and Drug Administration, and others. Intensive studies also have been conducted by similar groups in other countries.

In addition to safety from a microbiological standpoint, since irradiation can alter chemical molecules, and in sufficient dose induce radioactivity, these studies have been concerned with such aspects as: (a) effects of irradiation treatments on the nutrient value of foods; (b) possible production of toxic substances from irradiation; (c) possible production of carcinogenic substances in irradiated foods; and (d) possible production of harmful radioactivity in irradiation treated foods.

After some 20 yr of the most intensive investigation that any food preservation method had ever received, the following was the general consensus up to 1968:

(1) Irradiated foods, on the whole, were as nutritious as their heat processed counterparts. Irradiation did destroy various amounts of various nutrients, but the losses generally were of the same degree as from heat processing.

(2) Significant levels of toxic or carcinogenic substances were not produced in foods when they were irradiated with FDA-approved dosages from approved radiation sources. Substantial margins of safety had been built into the upper levels of doses approved.

(3) At approved doses, sterilized or pasteurized foods were safe from a microbiological standpoint.

(4) Irradiation with FDA-approved dosages from approved sources did not contribute harmful levels of radioactivity to foods. Substantial margins of safety had been built into approved processes. It had been pointed out that all foods, water, and the air we breathe contain low levels of radioactivity, as does the human body. These levels, contributed to by radiations from the sun, are part of our natural environment. Sometimes they are increased by poorly controlled or ill-used man-made atomic power. But the natural low levels of food radioactivity were not raised to anywhere near harmful levels with approved radiation treatments.

Because of the complexity of the safety and wholesomeness aspects, in the United States a high degree of control over this kind of processing has always been exercised. The law requires that a petition must be filed with and approved by the Food and Drug Administration before any new food may be irradiation processed and widely distributed. This also applies to the use of irradiation sources not previously "cleared." Prior to 1968 some of the more significant approvals had included sterilization of bacon with dose levels up to 5.6 Mrad; insect deinfestation of wheat and wheat products with levels up to 50,000 rads; sprout inhibition of potatoes with levels up to 10,000 rads (see Fig. 153); and sterilization of selected packaging materials with (X-ray) dose levels up to 1 Mrad. Additional petitions had been filed, among them an Army petition for clearance of irradiation sterilized smoked ham.

In 1968 the FDA informed the Army that it could not grant approval of

Courtesy of Brownell

FIG. 153. TREATED AND CONTROL POTATOES STORED ONE
YEAR AT 41°F

their irradiated ham petition on the basis of certain toxicological observations made by FDA scientists on the Army data. Shortly thereafter, the FDA revoked its earlier approval of irradiation sterilized bacon on the grounds that it needed to have further proof of safety. More definitive animal feeding tests presently are being considered. Until additional data are available the question of wholesomeness of irradiated foods remains unresolved.

Radiation as a Unit Operation

The abilities of ionizing radiations to alter molecules and promote chemical reactions have found wide application in a number of fields. This can also be true in food processing for purposes other than preservation.

Closely related to preservation are the needs for ridding foods and feeds of contaminating pathogenic organisms such as *Salmonella* and anthrax bacteria.

Beyond microorganism destruction ionizing radiations can hydrolyze and further modify proteins, starches, and cellulose. As a result irradiation is capable of improving nutritive values of certain plant materials, tenderizing vegetables and meats, lowering roasting requirements of coffee beans, and improving the water absorbing properties of several dehydrated foods. Irradiation of selected materials and mixtures also can yield new flavors.

Ionizing radiations can promote polymerization reactions. This has been used to alter the properties of plastics. Some of the improved features such as increased tensile strength, and moisture and swelling resistance, are directly applicable to the packaging of foods.

As a unit operation and processing tool for the food industry, irradiation studies have only begun. It is to be expected that many new applications will be found in the years ahead.

The Future for Food Irradiation

Food irradiation will not replace all other preservation methods. Sterilizing doses of irradiation can deteriorate various properties of many foods, spanning a wide range of organoleptic changes. In some of these cases lower doses of irradiation, to prolong storage life under refrigeration, are proving technically and economically feasible. Irradiation pasteurization of harvested fruits and vegetables and freshly caught seafoods are in this class.

How important food irradiation will eventually become is difficult to assess at this time. Much will depend upon future policies of the FDA and similar agencies abroad relative to safety and approval of specific foods so processed. Currently irradiation to deinfest grains and prevent sprouting of potatoes and other vegetables is practiced in several countries.

It is agreed that improved keeping qualities and microbiological safety from irradiation could play a substantial role in international food exports and imports of the future. To this end, meetings under world Food and Agriculture Organization sponsorship have been held to consider the problems of drafting uniform guidelines and legislation pertaining to international traffic in irradiated foods of established safety.

The potentials for irradiation in less developed regions would be of the greatest significance if means of financing processing facilities could be found. Such regions may be almost entirely lacking in refrigeration facilities, and losses from insects and spoilage often account for more than half of total production. Here it must be recognized however, that as with heat, irradiation has no residual preservative effect upon treated food. That is, once a storage bin of irradiated grain or a container of irradiated food is opened it is subject to recontamination and spoilage like any other food.

While the future of food irradiation is yet to be determined, equipment manufacturers continue to devise and improve irradiation facilities.

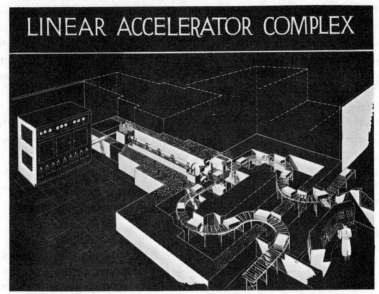

Courtesy of U. S. Army Quartermaster Corp.

FIG. 154.   LINEAR ACCELERATOR COMPLEX

Figure 154 is a diagram of a linear accelerator complex designed to irradiate food continuously as it is automatically conveyed past the high energy electron source. The thick walls of the labyrinth enclosing the electron accelerator are to protect operating personnel from stray radiations. Figure 155 illustrates a mobile gamma irradiator designed to be driven to the place of harvest or to a conventional food processing plant. Other con-

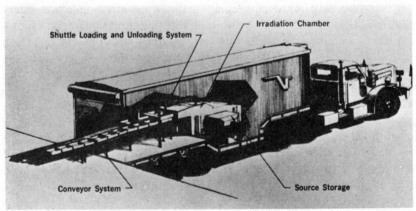

Courtesy of U. S. Atomic Energy Commission

FIG. 155.   MOBILE GAMMA IRRADIATOR

cepts have included irradiators mounted on rail cars and aboard ship to treat grain at the site of storage elevators and to preserve fish at sea.

MICROWAVE HEATING

Unlike ionizing radiations, microwave energy in food applications is used for its heating properties. Microwave energy is similar to the energy that carries radio and television programs and to the energy involved in the direction of signals by radar. Radar emits electronic radiations in the form of microwaves which travel to a target and are then absorbed, transmitted, or reflected. When they are reflected, the microwaves return to a receiver and indicate the range and bearing of the object struck. Some materials absorb rather than reflect microwaves. When this occurs the microwaves impart their energy to the absorbing medium in the form of heat. The industrial potential of microwave heating began to be appreciated during World War II, following intensive investigation of radar.

Properties of Microwaves

Microwaves are electromagnetic waves of radiant energy, differing from such other electromagnetic radiations as light waves and radio waves primarily in wavelength and frequency. In Table 34, microwaves would fall between radio waves and infrared radiations with wavelengths in the range of about 250 million to 7.5 billion angstroms which is equivalent to about 1 to 30 in. The wavelengths of radio waves and infrared radiations, in comparison are measured in miles and thousandths of an inch, respectively (254,000,000 angstrom units equals 1 in.). Wavelengths of electromagnetic energy are inversely related to frequency, which is the rapidity with which the waveform occurs. Microwave wavelengths of about 1 to 30 in. correspond to frequencies of about 20,000 to 400 megahertz. A megahertz (MHz) is a million cycles per sec. Common alternating electric current has a frequency of only 60Hz (cycles per sec). Because microwave frequencies are close to the frequencies of radio waves and overlap the radar range they can interfere with communication processes, and so the use of specific microwave frequencies come under the regulations of the Federal Communications Commission. For food applications the approved and most commonly used microwave frequencies are 2,450 MHz and 915 MHz.

Microwaves, like light, travel in straight lines. They are reflected by metals; pass through air and many, but not all types of glass, paper, and plastic materials; and are absorbed by several food constituents including water. When they are reflected they do not impart heat to the reflecting surface. To the extent that they are absorbed they heat the absorbing material. In heating the material they lose electromagnetic energy. The terms "loss factor" and "loss tangent" are used to indicate the microwave energy "lost" in passing through, or being entirely absorbed by various materials under defined conditions. Materials that are highly absorbent of microwaves are said to be highly "lossy." Highly lossy materials are rapidly heated by microwaves. Loss tangents for various substances are given in Table 36. Since foods differ in composition, including physical distribution of components within a given food, foods vary in their heating patterns from microwave radiation.

TABLE 36

LOSS TANGENTS FOR VARIOUS SUBSTANCES $(\times 10^4)$[1]

Material	900 MHz	2,450 MHz
Water 59°F	700	1,700
Water 131°F	300	700
Water 203°F	200	450
0.1 Molal NaCl solution	6,700	3,400
Steak	7,000	4,000
Suet	1,100	700
Polyethylene	2	2
Teflon	2	2
Paper	660	660
Paraffin wax	2	2

[1] From Food Engineering (1964).

The loss factor also is a measure of the degree of penetration of microwaves into materials. Since microwaves lose energy in the form of heat as they penetrate materials, the greater the loss factor, and the more heat that is produced, the shorter is the distance they can penetrate before all of their energy is consumed. In Table 36 it is seen that 900 MHz microwaves exhibit different energy losses than 2,450 MHz microwaves in certain materials while the reverse is true in other materials. Where depth of penetration is desired in a given material one can choose the microwave frequency with the lower loss factor. Thus it can be shown that under similar conditions by the time half of their incident energy is lost, 900 MHz microwaves will penetrate water to a depth of three inches while 2,450 MHz microwaves will penetrate to only a depth of ½ in.

Mechanism of Microwave Heating

Common alternating electric current reverses its direction 60 times a second. Microwaves do the same, but at frequencies corresponding to 915 or 2,450 MHz. Food and certain other materials contain molecules that act as dipoles, that is, they exhibit positive and negative charges at opposite ends of the molecule. Such molecules also are said to be polar. Water molecules are polar with the negative charge centered near the oxygen atom and the positive charge nearer the hydrogen atoms.

When microwaves pass into foods, water molecules and other polar molecules tend to align themselves with the electric field. But the electric field reverses 915 or 2,450 million times per second. The molecules attempting to oscillate at such frequencies generate intermolecular friction which quickly causes the food to heat. Quite the same phenomenon occurs in dielectric heating, which is like microwave heating but employs radiations in the frequency range of about 1 to 150 MHz. While microwaves thus generate heat within the food, as was stated, components with different loss factors will not immediately heat up equally. However, as heat is generated it also will be conducted between food components, tending to equalize temperature. In liquid foods this will also be helped by convection. However, these secondary effects must not be confused with the prime mechanism of intermolecular friction which occurs within the food at the sites of billions of molecules simultaneously.

Differences from Conventional Heating

In conventional heating, such as with direct flame, heated air, infrared elements, direct contact with a hot plate, etc., the heat source causes food molecules to react from the surface inward, so that successive layers of molecules heat in turn. This produces a temperature gradient which can burn the outside of a piece of food long before the temperature within has risen appreciably. This is why steak can be crusted on the outside while still rare on the inside.

In contrast, microwaves penetrate food pieces up to a few inches of thickness uniformly, setting all water molecules and other polar molecules in motion at the same time. Heat is not passed by conduction from the surface inward, but instead it is generated quickly and quite uniformly throughout the mass. The result is an internal boiling away of moisture. The steam also heats adjacent food solids by conduction. Incidentally, so long as there is free water being converted to steam, the temperature of the food piece does not rise much above the boiling point of water, except as the steam within the food may be under some pressure as it attempts to escape. As a result there is virtually no surface browning or crusting from excessive surface heat. This is a limitation of microwaves in such operations as bread baking, meat cooking, and the like, where crusting or browned surfaces are desired. In such cases, if microwave heating is employed, it must be preceded or followed by a conventional kind of heating to produce such surfaces. On the other hand, nonthermal-gradient microwave heating lends itself to numerous special applications, as indicated in the list of food applications at the end of this chapter.

Microwave Generators and Equipment

The most commonly used type of microwave generator is an electronic device called a magnetron. The components of a magnetron are seen in Fig. 156. A magnetron is a kind of electron tube within a magnetic field

FIG. 156. COMPONENTS OF A CAVITY MAGNETRON

1. Air-cooled anode showing multi-cavity arrangement 2. Permanent magnet 3. Cathode assembly 4. Antenna radiating element 5. Mounting blocks

which propagates high frequency radiant energy. The power output of different size magnetrons is rated in kilowatts. A larger magnetron, or several smaller ones working together, will heat a given quantity of food to a given temperature in a shorter time. It also is well to recognize that since microwave energy heats only objects into which it is absorbed there is a relationship between food load and heating time to a given temperature. Thus, two pounds of water will take essentially twice the time to bring to a boil as will one pound of water.

A simple microwave oven consists of a metal cabinet into which is inserted a magnetron (Fig. 157). The cabinet frequently is equipped with a metal "fan" which distributes the microwaves throughout the cabinet as they are reflected and bounce off of the metal fan blades. The microwaves also are reflected and bounce between the metal cabinet walls. Food placed in such an oven (generally raised above the oven floor by a screen or rack through which microwaves can pass) is thus contacted by microwaves from all directions. This speeds heating time and facilitates steam escape. If the

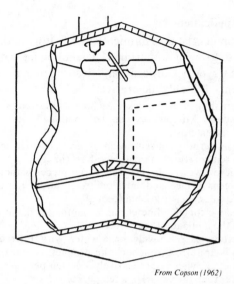

From Copson (1962)

FIG. 157. SIMPLE MICROWAVE OVEN CONSTRUCTION WITH
MAGNETRON AT TOP

food is wrapped, the wrapper should be perforated, or otherwise allow for steam escape to prevent it from bursting. Microwave radiations are not dangerous when confined within properly designed equipment. Since microwaves can cause damage to the eyes and other tissues that may absorb them, safety engineering of microwave ovens and related equipment has evolved to a high degree. All microwave ovens have interlocks or equivalent devices which cut off the power supply when the oven door is opened.

More complex microwave tunnel ovens frequently are equipped with an endless moving belt of low loss material on which food is conveyed past magnetrons in continuous fashion. Such ovens generally are open at the inlet and outlet ends to receive and discharge the product. In such a case the microwaves are prevented from escaping through the open ends by providing trapping materials which absorb stray microwaves, by providing metal reflectors to turn would-be stray microwaves back into the oven chamber, and by other means.

It is also possible to heat liquid materials continously with microwaves. In this case the liquid may be pumped through a coil of low loss glass or like material placed within the microwave heating zone. Or the magnetron(s) may be positioned surrounding a low loss tube through which the liquid is pumped.

Microwave Food Applications

The current and potential uses of microwave heating in the food industry are many and are of growing importance. The following industrial applications listing by the Cryodry Corporation, a leading manufacturer of microwave heating systems, is highly illustrative:

(1) **Baking.**—Internal heating quickly achieves desired final temperature throughout the product. Microwaves can be combined with external heating by air or infrared to obtain crust.

(2) **Concentrating.**—Permits concentration of heat-sensitive solutions and slurries at relatively low temperatures in relatively short times.

(3) **Cooking.**—Microwaves cook relatively large pieces without high temperature gradients between surface and interior. Well suited for continuous cooking of meals for large volume institutional feeding.

(4) **Curing.**—Effective for glue-line curing of laminates (as in packaging) without direct heating of the laminates themselves.

(5) **Drying.**—Microwaves selectively heat water with little direct heating of most solids. Drying is uniform throughout the product; preexisting moisture gradients are evened out. Drying is at relatively low temperatures; no part of the product need be hotter than the vaporizing temperature.

(6) **Enzyme Inactivation (Blanching).**—Rapid uniform heating to the inactivating temperature can control and terminate enzymatic reactions. Microwaves are especially adaptable to blanching of fruits and vegetables without leaching losses associated with hot water or steam. Also does not overcook the outside before core enzymes are inactivated.

(7) **Finish Drying.**—When most of the water has been removed by conventional heating methods, microwaves remove the last few percentages of moisture from the interior of the product quickly, and without overheating the already dried material.

(8) **Freeze Drying.**—The ability of microwave energy to selectively heat ice crystals in matter makes it attractive for accelerating the final stages of freeze drying.

(9) **Heating.**—Almost any heat transfer problem can benefit from the use of microwaves because of their ability to heat in depth without high temperature gradients.

(10) **Pasteurizing.**—Microwaves heat a product rapidly and uniformly without the overheating associated with external, high temperature heating methods.

(11) **Precooking.**—Microwaves are well suited for precooking "heat and serve" items because there need be no overcooking of the surface and cooking losses can be negligible. When the consumer reheats the food by conventional methods the desired texture and appearance of conventionally cooked items can be imparted.

(12) **Puffing and Foaming.**—Rapid internal heating by microwaves causes puffing or foaming when the rate of heat transfer is made greater than the rate of vapor transfer out of the product interior. May be applied to the puffing of snack foods and other materials.

(13) **Solvent Removal.**—Many solvents other than water are efficiently vaporized by microwaves, permitting solvent removal at relatively low temperatures.

(14) **Sterilizing.**—Where adequate temperatures may be reached (acid foods), quick, uniform come-up time may permit high temperature-short time sterilization. Selective heating of moisture-containing microorganisms makes possible the

sterilizing of such materials as glass and plastic films, which are not themselves heated appreciably by microwaves. This application must be considered cautiously since escaping steam temperatures generally are not sufficient to kill bacterial spores.

(15) **Tempering.**—Because the microwave heating effect is roughly proportional to moisture content, microwaves can equalize the moisture in a product which came from a process in a nonuniform condition.

(16) **Thawing.**—Controlled, rapid thawing of bulk items is possible due to substantial penetration of microwaves into frozen materials.

It must be recognized that several of the above applications may be achieved by still other heating methods or combination processes. The choice of method must then depend upon relative product quality and cost.

BIBLIOGRAPHY

ANON. 1964. Commercial radiation processes. Food Process. *25*, No. 12, 67–71, 76, 78.
BROWNELL, L. W. *et al.* 1957. Storage properties of gamma irradiated potatoes. Food Technol. *11*, 306–312.
COPSON, D. A. 1962. Microwave Heating, In Freeze Drying, Electronic Ovens, and Other Applications. Avi Publishing Co., Westport, Conn.
CRYODRY CORPORATION. 1965. Cryodry Industrial Brochure. San Ramon, Calif.
DAVIS, C. O., SMITH, O., and OLANDER, J. 1965. Microwave processing of potato chips. Potato Chipper *25*, No. 2, 38; No. 3, 72; No. 4, 78.
DESROSIER, N. W. 1970. The Technology of Food Preservation, 3rd Edition. Avi Publishing Co., Westport, Conn.
DESROSIER, N. W., and ROSENSTOCK, H. M. 1960. Radiation Technology in Food, Agriculture, and Biology. Avi Publishing Co., Westport, Conn.
GLASS, R. A., and SMITH, H. D. 1959. Radioactivities produced in foods by high energy electrons: Summary technical report of the Stanford Research Inst. with the Dept. of the Army, Contract *DA 19-129-QM-4100*, No. *10, S-572*.
GOLDBLITH, S. A. 1963. Radiation processing of foods and drugs. *In* Food Processing Operations, Vol. 1. M. A. Joslyn, and J. L. Heid (Editors). Avi Publishing Co., Westport, Conn.
GOLDBLITH, S. A. 1964. World wide status of the treatment of foods by ionizing energy. Proc. Intern. Conf. on Radiation Preservation of Foods, MIT, Boston, Mass. Sept. 28–30.
GOLDBLITH, S. A. 1966. The wholesomeness of irradiated foods: past history, present status, international aspects, and future outlook. Food Technol. *20*, 191–196.
GOLDBLITH, S. A. 1970. Sane perspectives regarding radiation effects. Food Technol. *24*, 250, 252, 254, 256.
JEPPSON, M. R. 1964. Consider microwaves. Food Eng. *36*, No. 11, 49–52.
MACHURECK, E. 1964. Radiation preservation of marine products: U.S.A.E.C. programme. Food Irradiation *4*, A2–A7.
MAURER, R. L., TREMBLAY, M. R., and CHADWICK, E. A. 1971. Microwave processing of pasta. Food Technol. *25*, 1244–1246, 1249.
McARDLE, F. J., and DESROSIER, N. W. 1955. Influence of ionizing radiations upon some protein components of selected foods. Food Technol. *9*, 527–532.
RAICA, N. *et al.* 1963. Wholesomeness of irradiated food. Proc. Intern. Conf. Radiation Research, U.S. Army Natick Laboratories, Natick, Mass., Jan. 14–16, 168–184.
READ, M. S. 1959. The effects of ionizing radiations on the nutritive value of foods. Proc. Intern. Conf. Preservation of Foods by Ionizing Radiations. Mass. Inst. of Technol., July 27–30. 138–152.
ROCKWELL, W. C., LOWE, E., HUXSOLL, C.C., and MORGAN, A. I., JR. 1967. Apparatus for experimental microwave processing. Food Technol. *21*, 1257–1258.

SCHULTZ, H. W., and LEE, J. S. 1966. Food preservation by irradiation, present status. Food Technol. 20, 136–141.

SHEA, K. G. 1963–1964. AEC Program on low-dose irradiation processing of food. Isotopes Radiation Tech. 1, 181–188.

URROWS, G. M. 1964. Food Preservation by Irradiation. U.S. Atomic Energy Comm., Div. Tech. Inform., Washington, D.C.

U.S. ARMY QUARTERMASTER RESEARCH and ENGINEERING COMMAND. 1961. Preservation of Food by Low-Dose Ionizing Energy. QM Research and Engineering Command, Natick, Mass.

U.S. ATOMIC ENERGY COMMISSION. 1963. Radiation pasteurization of foods. Summaries of accomplishment. TID-7684, Isotopes—Industrial Technology (TID 4500, 28th Edition). Washington, D.C.

U.S. ATOMIC ENERGY COMMISSION. 1964. Summaries of accomplishment. CONF-641002, Isotopes—Industrial Technology (TID-4500, 37th Edition). Washington, D.C.

WEISER, H. H., MOUNTNEY, G. L., and GOULD, W. A. 1971. Practical Food Microbiology and Technology, 2nd Edition. Avi Publishing Co., Westport, Conn.

YOUNG, F. R. et al. 1964. Report of The Working Party on Irradiation of Food. Her Majesty's Stationery Office, London.

CHAPTER 12

Food Fermentations

INTRODUCTION

Natural fermentations occur when environmental conditions permit interaction between microorganisms and susceptible organic substrates. Such interactions are fundamental to the decomposition of natural materials, and to the ultimate return of chemical elements to the soil and air without which life could not be sustained.

Natural fermentations have played a vital role in man's development from earliest times to the present. Some of these fermentations made changes in food materials that were quickly recognized to be desirable. Thus, for example, fruit and fruit juices left to the elements acquired an alcoholic flavor. Milk on standing became mildly acidic. These changes in foods tasted good and so early civilizations encouraged the conditions that permitted them to occur. Sometimes the desired results were obtained repeatedly, but this was not always so. Early man also discovered that certain alcoholic fruit juices and sour milks would keep well and so he converted part of his food supply into these forms as a means of preservation. This was several thousand years before any basic knowledge of fermentation processes had been gained. By trial and error it was gradually learned to use natural fermentation to advantage. Not only was a degree of preservation of many otherwise perishable foods accomplished, but at the same time man became accustomed to the texture and taste attributes of these fermented items.

Today we understand the principles of food preservation and have methods that are superior to fermentation as means of preserving many foods. Thus in technically advanced societies the major importance of fermented foods has come to be the variety they add to our diets. However, in many less developed areas of the world, fermentation, along with natural drying, are the major food preservation methods, and as such are vital to survival of more than half of the world's current population.

The various preservation methods discussed thus far, based on the applications of heat, cold, removal of water, radiations, and other principles, all had the common objective of decreasing the numbers of living organisms in foods, or at least holding them in check against further multiplication. Fermentation processes, whether for preservation purposes or not, in contrast, encourage the multiplication of microorganisms and their metabolic activities in foods. But the organisms that are en-

329

TABLE 37

SOME INDUSTRIAL FERMENTATIONS IN FOOD INDUSTRIES[1]

Lactic acid bacteria
  Vegetables and fruits
    cucumbers → dill pickles, sour pickles, salt stock
    olives → green olives, ripe olives
    cabbage → sauerkraut
    turnips → sauerrüben
    lettuce → lettuce kraut
    mixed vegetables, turnips, radish, cabbage → Paw Tsay
    mixed vegetables in Chinese cabbage → Kimchi
    vegetables and milk → Tarhana
    vegetables and rice → Sajur asin
    dough and milk → Kishk
    coffee cherries → coffee beans
    vanilla beans → vanilla
    taro → poi
  Meats → sausages such as salami, Thuringer, summer, pork roll, Lebanon bologna,
      cervelat
  Dairy products
    sour cream
    sour milk drinks—acidophilus, yoghurt, cultured buttermilk, Bulgarian, skyr,
             gioddu, leban, dadhi, taette, mazun
    butter—sour cream butter, cultured butter, ghee
    cheese—unripened → cottage, pot, schmierkase, cream
             whey → mysost, primost, ricotta, schottengsied.
             ripened → Cheddar, American, Edam, Gouda, Cheshire,
                provolone
Lactic acid bacteria with other microorganisms
  Dairy products
    with other bacteria
      propionic acid bacteria—Emmenthaler, Swiss, Samso, Gruyére cheeses
      surface ripening bacteria—Limburger, brick, Trappist, Münster, Port de Salut
    with yeasts—kefir, kumiss or kumys
    with molds—Roquefort, Camembert, Brie, hand, Gorgonzola, Stilton, Blue
  Vegetable products
    with yeasts—Nukamiso pickles
    with mold—tempeh, soya sauce
Acetic acid bacteria—wine, cider, malt, honey, or any alcoholic and sugary or starchy
    products may be converted to vinegar
Yeasts
  malt → beer, ale, porter, stout, bock, Pilsner
  fruit → wine, vermouth
  wines → brandy
  molasses → rum
  grain mash → whiskey
  rice → saké, sonti
  agave → pulque
  bread doughs → bread
Yeasts with lactic acid bacteria
  cereal products → sour dough bread, sour dough pancakes, rye bread
  ginger plant → ginger beer
  beans → vermicelli
Yeasts with acetic acid bacteria
  cacao beans
  citron
Mold and other organisms
  soybeans—miso, chiang, su fu, tamari sauce, soy sauce
  fish and rice-lao, chao.

[1] From Pederson (1963).

couraged are from a select group and their metabolic activities and end products are highly desirable. The extent of this desirability is emphasized by the partial list of fermented foods from various parts of the world in Table 37.

FERMENTATION

Definitions

The term "fermentation" has come to have somewhat different meanings as its underlying causes have become better understood. The derivation of the word fermentation signifies a gentle bubbling or boiling condition. The term was first applied to the production of wine more than a thousand years ago. The bubbling action was due to carbon dioxide gas liberated during the conversion of sugar, although this reaction was yet to be defined. When it was, following the studies of Gay-Lussac, fermentation came to mean the breakdown of sugar into alcohol and carbon dioxide. Pasteur later demonstrated the relationship of yeast to this reaction, and the word fermentation became associated with microorganisms, and still later with enzymes. The early research on fermentation dealt mostly with carbohydrates and reactions that liberated carbon dioxide gas. It was soon recognized, however, that microorganisms or enzymes acting on sugars did not always evolve gas. Further, many of the microorganisms and enzymes studied also had the ability to break down noncarbohydrate materials such as proteins and fats, which yielded carbon dioxide, other gases, and a wide range of additional materials.

Currently the term fermentation is used in various ways which require clarification. When chemical change is discussed at the molecular level, in the context of comparative physiology and biochemistry, the term fermentation is correctly employed to describe the breakdown of carbohydrate materials under *anaerobic* conditions.

In a somewhat broader and less precise sense of usage, where primary interest is in describing the end products rather than the mechanisms of biochemical reactions, the term fermentation refers to breakdown of carbohydrate and carbohydrate-like materials under either *anaerobic* or *aerobic* conditions. Thus conversion of lactose to lactic acid by *Streptococcus lactis* bacteria is favored by anaerobic conditions and is true fermentation. Conversion of ethyl alcohol to acetic acid by *Acetobacter aceti* bacteria is favored by aerobic conditions and is more correctly termed an oxidation than a fermentation. Common usage frequently overlooks this distinction and considers both types of reactions to be fermentations. In this and subsequent chapters the common usage of the term fermentation, which refers to both the anaerobic and aerobic breakdown of carbohydrates will be followed.

But the word fermentation also is used in a still broader and less precise manner. We say "fermented foods" to describe a special class of food products. These foods are characterized by various kinds of carbohydrate breakdown; but seldom is carbohydrate the only constituent acted upon. In fermented foods we are virtually always dealing with a complex mixture of carbohydrates, proteins, fats, etc., undergoing modification simultaneously, or in some sequence, under the action of a variety of microorganism and enzyme types present. This creates the need for additional terms to distinguish between major types of change. Those reactions involving carbohydrates and carbohydrate-like materials (true fermentations) are referred to as "fermentative." Changes in proteinaceous materials are designated "proteolytic" or "putrefactive." Breakdowns of fatty substances are described as "lipolytic." When complex foods are "fermented" under natural conditions they invariably undergo different degrees of each of these types of change. Whether fermentative, proteolytic, or lipolytic end products dominate will depend upon the nature of the food, the types of microorganisms present, and environmental conditions affecting their growth and metabolic patterns. In specific food fermentations we of course endeavor to control the types of microorganisms and environmental conditions to produce desired product characteristics.

Additional Benefits from Fermentation

In addition to the roles of fermentation in preservation and providing variety to man's diet there are further important consequences of fermentation. Several of the end products of food fermentation, particularly acids and alcohols, are inhibitory to the common pathogenic microorganisms that may find their way into foods. The inability of *Clostridium botulinum* to grow and produce toxin at pH values below 4.5 has already been cited.

When microorganisms ferment food constituents they derive energy in the process. To the extent that food constituents are oxidized, their remaining energy potential for humans is decreased. Compounds that are completely oxidized by fermentation to such end products as carbon dioxide and water retain no further energy value for man. Most controlled food fermentations, however, yield such major end products as alcohols, organic acids, aldehydes, and ketones. These compounds are only slightly more oxidized than their parent substrates, and so still retain much of the energy potential of the starting materials. Fermentation processes are attended by slight temperature increases. The energy dissipated as heat represents a fraction of the total energy potential of the original food material no longer recoverable for nutritional purposes. Nevertheless, the important food fermentations associated with a wide variety of preserved foods are economical in terms of energy consumption, still leaving much of the original caloric value of the natural material for man.

Fermented foods often are actually *more* nutritious than their unfermented counterparts. This can come about in at least three different ways. Microorganisms not only are catabolic, breaking down more complex compounds, but they also are metabolic and synthesize several complex vitamins and other growth factors. In fact the industrial production of such materials as riboflavin, vitamin B_{12}, and the precursor of vitamin C is largely by special fermentation processes.

The second important way in which fermented foods can be enhanced nutritionally has to do with the liberation of nutrients locked into plant structures and cells by indigestible materials. This is especially true in the case of certain grains and seeds. The milling processes do much to release nutrients from such items by physically rupturing cellulosic and hemicellulosic structures surrounding the endosperm, which is rich in digestible carbohydrates and proteins. Crude milling, however, practiced in many less developed regions, often is inadequate to release the full nutritional value of such plant products; even after cooking, some of the entrapped nutrients may remain unavailable to the digestive processes of man. Fermentation, especially by certain molds, breaks down indigestible protective coatings and cell walls both chemically and physically. Molds are rich in cellulose-splitting enzymes, but in addition mold growth penetrates food structures by way of its hair-like mycelia. This alters texture and makes the structures more permeable to the water of cooking or steeping as well as to man's digestive juices. Similar phenomena result from the enzymatic actions of yeasts and bacteria.

A third mechanism by which fermentation can enhance nutritional value, especially of plant materials, involves enzymatic splitting of cellulose, hemicellulose, and related polymers not digestible by man into simpler sugars and sugar derivatives. This goes on naturally in the rumen of the cow through the enzymatic action of protozoa and bacteria. It also occurs in the process of preparing silage for animal feeding. German scientists did much the same thing during the time of World War I when they used inorganic acids to hydrolyze the cellulose of wood as a means of producing sugar. Cellulosic materials in fermented foods similarly can be nutritionally improved for man by the action of microbial enzymes.

Of course such changes are accompanied by gross changes in texture and appearance of the starting food materials, just as all fermented foods are markedly altered from their unfermented counterparts. Such changes are not looked upon as quality defects. Quite the contrary, particularly in areas of the world where most of man's nutrients are derived from plant sources, food materials markedly altered by fermentation commonly are more frequent and relished items of diet than are the natural plant components.

Types of Microbial Changes in Foods

The normal microbial flora associated with foods can produce a very wide range of breakdown products. Depending upon the major food substrates attacked these microorganisms are designated proteolytic, lipolytic, and fermentative. Because of their generally broad complement of enzymes, few types of microorganisms are exclusively proteolytic, lipolytic, or fermentative. Rather, most types exhibit varying degrees of each property, depending upon environmental conditions and other factors. Nevertheless, many organisms are characteristically dominant in one or another of these three basic kinds of change produced in food.

Generally speaking, proteolytic organisms which break down proteins and other nitrogenous compounds give rise to putrid and rotten odors and flavors which are considered undesirable in man's food supply beyond certain rather low levels. Similarly, lipolytic organisms which attack fats, phospholipids, and related materials give rise to rancid and fishy odors and flavors not desired in most foods beyond minor levels. On the other hand, fermentative organisms convert carbohydrates and carbohydrate derivatives largely to alcohols, acids, and carbon dioxide. These end products are not generally offensive to man's tastes and add zest to many of his foods.

Most important from the standpoint of food preservation, the alcohol and acid produced by fermentative organisms in sufficient concentration are inhibitory to many proteolytic and lipolytic organisms that are capable of food spoilage if not controlled. Herein lies the principle of preservation by fermentation; encourage the growth and metabolism of alcohol and acid forming microorganisms and suppress or control the growth of proteolytic and lipolytic types. Once the fermentative organisms are heavily established they limit growth of the other types, not only by virtue of their production of alcohol and acid, but also because they compete for and consume certain constituents of the food that otherwise would be utilized by the proteolytic and lipolytic organisms.

These statements, correct in principle, underlie production practices of many fermented foods. However, fermentation technology is complex, due to the large number of microorganism types and enzymes on the one hand, and the diversity of food systems on the other. We are almost never dealing with a model system in which one or two organism types work on one or two food constituents. In practice we seldom want only alcohol or acid production to the total exclusion of protein and fat breakdown. The clean, tart taste of fresh cottage cheese is largely due to the conversion by fermentation of lactose into lactic acid. On the other hand, the more complex flavors of Cheddar and Limburger cheese are due to different degrees of protein and fat breakdown in addition to lactic acid fermentation. We desire these balanced flavors in certain foods, and so control through fermentation processes the balance of microorganism types that may grow in the foods.

Some of the more common and significant types of microbial activity in foods are indicated in Table 38. The complex intermediate steps leading to the final results are omitted.

TABLE 38

SOME MICROBIAL ACTIVITIES IN FOODS

Substrate, Organism	Reaction Products
Sugar + *Saccharomyces* Yeast	= alcohol + CO_2 (wine)
Alcohol + O_2 + *Acetobacter* Bacteria	= acetic acid + H_2O (vinegar)
Sugar + *Streptococcus lactis*	= lactic acid (curd)
Acid + O_2 + Molds	= loss of acidity
Protein + *Proteus* Bacteria	= amines + NH_3 (putrid)
Fat + *Alcaligenes* Bacteria	= fatty acids (rancid)
Food + *Clostridium botulinum*	= toxins

Sugar fermented by yeasts, such as *Saccharomyces cerevisiae* and *Saccharomyces ellipsoideus* yields ethyl alcohol and carbon dioxide in accordance with the following overall reaction:

$$C_6H_{12}O_6 + \text{yeast} = 2\,C_2H_5OH + 2\,CO_2$$

This is the basis of wine and beer production and the leavening of bread.

Alcohol from yeast fermented cider, in the presence of oxygen, will be further fermented by bacteria such as *Acetobacter aceti* to acetic acid as in the reaction:

$$C_2H_5OH + O_2 + \textit{Acetobacter aceti} = CH_3COOH + H_2O$$

This is the mechanism of vinegar production.

The sugar of milk, fermented by *Streptococcus lactis* bacteria, gives lactic acid which curdles the milk to yield cottage cheese, or curd from which other cheeses can be made.

Acids produced from fermentation, in the presence of oxygen can be further broken down by molds. When this happens the preservative action of the acid against other microorganisms is lost.

Proteins broken down by proteolytic bacteria such as *Proteus vulgaris* and other organisms yield a wide range of nitrogen-containing compounds which give putrid and decayed odors to food.

Lipids broken down by lipolytic bacteria such as *Alcaligenes lipolyticus* and other organisms yield fatty acids. These and their subsequent breakdown products contribute to rancid and fishy odors.

Low acid foods supporting growth of *Clostridium botulinum* may contain toxins produced by this bacterium. This food poisoning organism will not grow in fermented foods high in acid.

It should be appreciated that the types of activities indicated in Table 38 can lead to many interesting and highly significant sequences of reactions. These sequences are either prevented or encouraged, as indicated below, depending upon the type of fermented food being produced.

Controlling Fermentations in Various Foods

Among the many factors that influence microorganism growth and metabolism, the most common means of controlling the course of food fermentations include level of acid, level of alcohol, use of starters, temperature, level of oxygen, and salt. These factors also determine the organism types that may grow in the fermented food on later storage.

Acid.—The inhibitory effects of acid are exerted whether the acid is added directly to the food, is a natural constituent of the food, or is produced in the food by fermentation. If it is not a natural constituent of the food (as in oranges or lemons), then the acid must be added or formed by fermentation quickly, before spoilage or otherwise harmful types of microorganisms have a chance to increase substantially in numbers and produce their effects.

Food containing acid may be in a state of preservation, but if oxygen is available and surface molds grow and further ferment the acid its preservative power is lost. In this way we may gradually develop proteolytic and lipolytic activity on the surface of such food. This can occur during the ripening of Cheddar cheese and constitutes a defect. Acid level also can be effectively decreased by neutralization. Certain yeasts will tolerate moderately high acid conditions and produce alkaline end products, such as ammonia, from the breakdown of protein. These neutralize previously formed acid and permit subsequent growth of proteolytic and lipolytic bacterial types. This is desirable and is encouraged in the surface-ripening of Limburger cheese.

These types of changes also occur when raw milk is allowed to ferment naturally (Fig. 158). Raw milk generally will be contaminated with a wide variety of types of microorganisms. After a short period during which freshly drawn raw milk fails to support microbial growth (period of germicidal action), *Streptococcus lactis* dominates the fermentation and produces lactic acid. Eventually, this organism is inhibited from further growth by its own acidity. Bacteria of the genus *Lactobacillus,* also com-

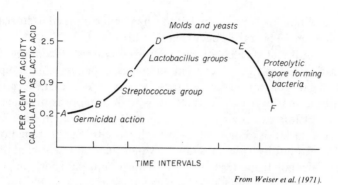

TIME INTERVALS

From Weiser et al. (1971).

FIG. 158. SEQUENCE OF CHANGES IN RAW MILK IN RELATION
TO ACID CONCENTRATION

mon to milk, are still more acid tolerant than *Streptococcus lactis*. The lactobacilli now take over the fermentation and produce still more acid until the new level becomes inhibitory to their further growth. In the high acid environment these lactobacilli gradually die off, and acid tolerant yeasts and molds become established. The molds oxidize acid and the yeasts produce alkaline end products from proteolysis, both of which gradually decrease the acid level to the point where proteolytic and lipolytic spoilage bacteria find the medium satisfactory. These organisms now grow, and especially from further proteolytic activity, decrease the milk acidity to the point where it can become more alkaline than the original raw milk. During the period of *Streptococcus* and *Lactobacillus* growth, the milk clots and the curd becomes firm, with little evidence of gas accumulation or development of off-odors. Mold and yeast growth followed by proteolytic and lipolytic bacterial growth digest this curd, produce a gassy condition, and develop off-odors characteristic of putrefaction.

In breadmaking we ferment the sugars of dough with yeast. This produces alcohol, carbon dioxide, and minor fermentation products. In typical white bread, the fermentation is not intended for preservation purposes and provides little protection of this kind. Here we are interested in the leavening power of the carbon dioxide gas and the flavors from fermentation. However, there are many varieties of sour breads where the yeast fermentation is accompanied by lactic acid fermentations from organisms of the *Lactobacillus* group. In addition to imparting characteristic flavor, the acid inhibits growth of sporeforming bacteria of the genus *Bacillus* in the dough and later in the bread. The spores of this genus if present in the dough survive the temperatures of baking. They then may produce a gummy condition known as ropy bread when nonacid bread is stored under damp conditions. This rarely occurs in sour breads.

Alcohol.—Like acid, alcohol can be a preservative, depending upon its concentration. The alcohol content of wines depends in part upon the original sugar content of the grapes, the type of yeast, fermentation temperature, and level of oxygen. Just as with organisms producing acid, yeasts cannot tolerate their own alcohol and other fermentation products beyond certain levels. For many yeasts this occurs in the range of about 12 to 15% alcohol by volume. Natural wines generally will contain about 9 to 13% alcohol from fermentation. This is not sufficient in itself for complete preservation, and so such wines must receive in addition a mild pasteurization treatment. Fortified wines are natural wines to which additional alcohol is added to bring the final alcohol concentration up to about 20% by volume. Such wines may not require further pasteurization.

Use of Starters.—When a particular type of microorganism is present in large numbers and is multiplying it usually dominates its environment and keeps down the growth of other microorganism types. In early times, a winemaker or cheesemaker used this principle, without quite knowing why, when he poured part of a former batch of wine into grape juice, or cheese milk into fresh milk for the next batch. Such practices continue today in many areas of the world. Figure 159 illustrates one kind of primitive cheesemaking currently practiced in Nepal in the Himalayas. Milk from the yak ox ferments under natural conditions until sufficient acid is

Courtesy of FAO

FIG. 159. A METHOD OF CHEESEMAKING STILL PRACTICED IN NEPAL IN THE HIMALAYAS

produced to coagulate curd. The curd is squeezed through the fingers into noodle-like forms which then are dried in the sun. The fermented milk from one day's operation is used as a starter to initiate fermentation of the next day's production.

In contrast, in technologically advanced countries we help ensure a controlled condition of fermentation by using starters of pure cultures obtained from commercial laboratories. These cultures can be had in dehydrated and in concentrated frozen form (Fig. 160). Such cultures

Courtesy of Dairy Technics

FIG. 160. CONCENTRATED FROZEN LACTIC CULTURE

have been developed from selected strains of lactic acid organisms outstanding for their quick and dependable acid production under cheese-making conditions. This often means resistance of strains to such additional factors as traces of antibiotics and pesticide residues that may find their way into the cheese milk from farm operations, as well as resistance to bacterial viruses, all of which could otherwise interfere with starter activity. Similarly, special cultures are available for the production of wine, beer, vinegar, pickles, sausage, bread, and other fermented foods. In using starters, frequently we heat-treat the juice, milk, or other material to inactivate detrimental types of contaminating organisms prior to starter addition.

Temperature.—Various microorganism types may dominate a mixed fermentation depending upon the fermentation temperature. The sauerkraut fermentation is particularly sensitive to temperature. The effects temperature can have in this fermentation upon final acid concentration, and time to reach various acidities are indicated in Table 39.

TABLE 39

EFFECT OF FERMENTATION TEMPERATURE ON BACTERIAL GROWTH AND
ACID PRODUCTION IN SAUERKRAUT WITH 2.25 PERCENT SALT ADDED[1]

Temperature, °F	Days	Total Acid, %	Total Bacterial Count, × 100,000/Ml
45	1	0.04	40
	10	0.48	2,640
	20	0.70	2,105
64	1	0.16	2,150
	10	1.23	2,330
	20	1.71	560
89	1	0.71	6,400
	10	2.02	725
	20	...	...
98	1	0.72	15,600
	10	1.76	48
	20	...	...

[1] From Pederson and Albury (1954).

In sauerkraut production three major types of organisms convert the sugar of cabbage juice to acetic acid, lactic acid, and other products of fermentation. These include such bacteria as *Leuconostoc mesenteroides, Lactobacillus cucumeris,* and *Lactobacillus pentoaceticus. Leuconostoc mesenteroides* produces acetic acid, some lactic acid, alcohol, and carbon dioxide. The alcohol and acids also combine to form esters which contribute to final flavor. *Lactobacillus cucumeris* produces additional lactic acid where *Leuconostoc mesenteroides* leaves off. *Lactobacillus pentoaceticus* produces still more lactic acid after *Lactobacillus cucumeris* ceases to be active. The desirable sequence of these fermentations is indicated in Fig. 161.

Leuconostoc mesenteroides requires cool temperatures of the order of 70°F for optimum growth and fermentation in sauerkraut manufacture. The lactobacilli tolerate higher temperatures.

If temperatures much above 70°F are employed in the initial stages of the fermentation the lactobacilli easily outgrow *Leuconostoc mesenteroides* and then their high levels of acid production further prevent growth and fermentation of *Leuconostoc mesenteroides.* Under these conditions acetic acid, alcohol, and other desirable products of *Leuconostoc*

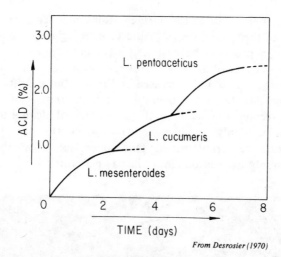

FIG. 161. SEQUENCE OF ACID FERMENTATIONS IN SAUERKRAUT MANUFACTURE

mesenteroides fermentation would not be formed. The sauerkraut fermentation therefore employs initial low temperatures, which then may be increased somewhat in the later stages of fermentation. This is but one example of how we provide optimum temperature for the type of organism desired.

Level of Oxygen.—The aerobic nature of molds has been amply discussed. The acetobacter important in vinegar making is an aerobe, it requires oxygen. The yeast which produces alcohol from sugar does it better in the absence of oxygen. *Clostridium botulinum* is a strict anaerobe. We provide or remove air or oxygen as required to encourage or inhibit particular microorganisms.

An organism may have different requirements with respect to oxygen for growth, that is cell multiplication, than it has for fermentation activity. Bakers' yeast (*Saccharomyces cerevisiae*) and wine yeast (*Saccharomyces ellipsoideus*) are good examples of this. Both grow better and produce greater cell masses under aerobic conditions; but they ferment sugars more rapidly under anaerobic conditions. Thus, in the commercial production of bakers' yeast, the yeast is grown under aerobic conditions by bubbling air through a yeast-inoculated molasses solution in large tanks. Fermentation is favored in the breadmaking operation (after sufficient yeast population is established) by the relatively anaerobic conditions of large dough masses.

In vinegar manufacture, the fermentations are separated principally on the basis of the relationships of the fermenting organisms to oxygen. In this two step process, the first step involving conversion of the sugar of apple juice to alcohol may be begun under aerobic conditions to stimulate yeast *growth* and increased cell mass. But conditions are soon made anaerobic to favor the actual yeast *fermentation* of the sugar to alcohol. The second step involving the conversion of alcohol to acetic acid is promoted by highly aerobic conditions since this transformation is really an oxidative fermentation. This conversion of alcohol to acetic acid is commonly carried out in a vinegar generator (Fig. 162). Vinegar

Courtesy of Food Processing-Marketing

FIG. 162.   COMMERCIAL VINEGAR GENERATORS

generators differ in design but generally consist of large tanks or vats packed with wood shavings to provide a large aerobic surface area. The alcoholic cider, after heavy inoculation with vinegar bacteria, is trickled through the wood shavings while air is blown up through the shavings. The vinegar is removed from the generator when its acetic acid concentration reaches four percent (or somewhat higher), since this is the minimum legal level for acetic acid in vinegar. Operation of a vinegar generator demands close control. Aerobic conditions can encourage mold development, and as has been pointed out molds can further break down acid. In addition, excessive aeration can itself oxidize acetic acid further to carbon dioxide and water.

Salt.—Microorganisms can be separated on the basis of salt tolerance. The lactic acid producing organisms used in fermenting olives, pickles, sauerkraut, certain meat sausages, and similar products generally are tolerant to moderate salt concentrations of the order of 10 to 18%. Many proteolytic and other spoilage organism types that can infect pickle and sauerkraut vats are not tolerant to salt above about 2.5%, and especially are not tolerant to the combination of salt and acid.

In these fermentations, added salt gives the lactic acid producing organisms an advantage in getting under way even if proteolytic types are present on the cucumbers or cabbage. Once underway, the acid produced by the lactic acid organisms plus the salt provides strong inhibition against proteolytic and other spoilage types. The salt added to vegetable fermentations also draws water and sugar out of the vegetables. The sugar entering the salt brine provides readily available carbohydrate for continued fermentation in the brine, which complements fermentation within the vegetable tissue from inward diffusion of lactic acid microorganisms.

Water drawn from the vegetables also tends to dilute the brine and so salt must be frequently added to maintain the brine's preservative salt level. In the production of sauerkraut, approximately 2.0 to 2.5% salt generally is added to the cabbage; the major preservative effect coming from the acidity formed. Olives are placed in salt brines of about 7 to 10%, and cucumbers commonly are fermented in brines maintained at about 15 to 18% salt.

Quite the same principle applies in the making of cheese. It is common practice to salt cheese curd to control proteolytic organisms during the long ripening periods, which may be in excess of a year for certain types of cheese. In this case various salt tolerant lactobacilli continue to produce acid and further modify the cheese curd during the ripening period.

Many sausage types owe their unique flavors to fermentations by strains of *Leuconostoc, Lactobacillus*, and *Pediococcus* bacteria. Generally fermentations by these organisms in meat products produce a less acid condition than is common in fermented vegetables. Such products as fermented sauerkraut and pickles have acidities in the range of about pH 2.5 to 3.5. Fermented meat sausages commonly have acidities in the range of pH 4.0 to 5.5. This degree of acidity, in itself, would be marginal as a preservative were it not augmented by the presence of salt and other curing chemicals in the sausages, plus the effects from smoking, cooking, and partial drying of certain of these products (Fig. 163).

Courtesy of Swift and Co. (Mr. Ed Hois)

FIG. 163. DRY SAUSAGE HANGING ROOM

Fermentation Technology

The above discussion is intended to do little more than highlight some of the more important principles underlying food fermentations. The fermented food industries, although highly developed, still rely on much know-how and art in their fermentation processes. For each class of fermented foods there are many recipes and procedural differences, especially between various manufacturers.

Actually in the case of most fermented foods the fermentation steps really constitute a unit process, preceded and followed by other food manufacturing unit operations. More will be said about the production of cheese, bread, beer, and other fermented foods in subsequent chapters dealing with specific food commodities.

A great deal is not known about the microbiology and fermentation patterns of some of the most important foods in the world. This includes the many types of fermented pastes and beers of tribal Africa and South America, and the numerous fermented soybean foods of Asia. Food preservation by fermentation often can be achieved with far less complex or costly equipment than most other preservation methods require. Fermented foods of a wide variety also are traditional and well accepted by the peoples of many developing regions.

BIBLIOGRAPHY

AMERICAN MEAT INSTITUTE. 1953. Sausage and Ready to Eat Meats. Univ. Chicago, Chicago.

AMERINE, M. A., BERG, H. W., and CRUESS, W. V. 1972. Technology of Wine Making, 3rd Edition. Avi Publishing Co., Westport, Conn.

BINSTED, R., DEVEY, J. D., and DAKIN, J. C. 1962. Pickle and Sauce Making. Food Trade Review, London.

CAMPBELL, C. H., ISKER, R. A., and MACLINN, W. A. 1954. Campbell's Book—A Manual on Canning, Preserving, and Pickling. Vance Publishing Corp. Chicago.

DESROSIER, N. W. 1970. The Technology of Food Preservation, 3rd Edition. Avi Publishing Co., Westport, Conn.

FELLERS, C. R. 1960. Effects of fermentations on food nutrients. In Nutritional Evaluation of Food Processing. R.S. Harris, and H. Von Loesecke (Editors). Reprinted in 1971 by Avi Publishing Co., Westport, Conn.

FRAZIER, W. C. 1967. Food Microbiology, 2nd Edition. McGraw-Hill Book Co., New York.

HAMMER, B. W., and BABEL, F. J. 1957. Dairy Bacteriology. John Wiley & Sons, New York.

HARGROVE, R. E. 1970. Fermentation products from skim milk. In Byproducts from Milk. B. H. Webb, and E. O. Whittier (Editors). Avi Publishing Co., Westport, Conn.

HARRIS, F. 1951. Pickling and Preserving. Abeland Press, New York.

KOSIKOWSKI, F. 1970. Cheese and Fermented Milk Foods. Published by the author, Ithaca, N.Y.

MARTH, E. H. 1970. Fermentation products from whey. In Byproducts from Milk. B. H. Webb, and E. O. Whittier (Editors). Avi Publishing Co., Westport, Conn.

MASELLI, J. A. 1958. Brew processes: the general history. Bakers Weekly 168, No. 6, 30–32.

PEDERSON, C. S. 1960. Sauerkraut. In Advances in Food Research, Vol. 10, Academic Press, New York.

PEDERSON, C. S. 1963. Processing by fermentation. In Food Processing Operations, Vol. 2. M. A. Joslyn, and J. L. Heid (Editors). Avi Publishing Co., Westport, Conn.

PEDERSON, C. S. 1971. Microbiology of Food Fermentations. Avi Publishing Co., Westport, Conn.

PEDERSON, C. S., and ALBURY, M. N. 1954. The influence of salt and temperature on the microflora of sauerkraut fermentation. Food Technol. 8, 1–5.

PEDERSON, C. S., and BEATTIE, H. G. 1943. Vinegar making. N.Y. Agr. Expt. Sta. Circ. 148.

PETERSON, M. S., and TRESSLER, D. K. (Editors) 1963. Food Technology the World Over, Vols. 1 and 2. Avi Publishing Co., Westport, Conn.

POMERANZ, Y., and SHELLENBERGER, J. A. 1971. Bread Science and Technology. Avi Publishing Co., Westport, Conn.

PYLER, E. J. 1952. Baking Science and Technology, Vols. 1 and 2. Siebel Publishing Co., Chicago.

UNDERKOFLER, L. A., and HICKEY, R. J. 1954. Industrial Fermentations, Vols. 1 and 2. Chemical Publishing Co., New York.

WALLERSTEIN LABORATORIES. 1955. Bottle beer quality—a 10 year research record. Wallerstein Laboratories, New York.

WEISER, H. H., MOUNTNEY, G. J., and GOULD, W. A. 1971. Practical Food Microbiology and Technology, 2nd Edition. Avi Publishing Co., Westport, Conn.

WHITE, J. 1954. Yeast Technology. John Wiley & Sons, New York.

CHAPTER 13

Milk and Milk Products

INTRODUCTION

The terms milk and milk products are used in the food industry to cover a very wide range of raw materials and manufactured items. No attempt is made in this chapter to deal with all of them. Rather, it is hoped to convey some understanding of the properties and processing of fluid milk and some of the more important products manufactured from it, such as specialty milks, ice cream, and cheese. Butter, along with the nondairy product margarine, is left for the later chapter on fats and oils.

Fluid milk is the parent substance. This milk may be processed to be consumed as fluid whole milk, the familiar beverage. Commonly in the United States it is pasteurized and homogenized, and its composition is very close to what it was when taken from the cow.

But milk also may be separated into its principal components such as cream and skim milk. These are sold and used as products in their own right. Or they may be further processed into butter, cheese, ice cream, and other well-known dairy products. Similarly, the parent milk may be modified by condensing, drying, flavoring, fortifying, demineralizing, and still other treatments of it. Further, the whole milk or its components may be used as such or combined in various proportions for incorporation into numerous manufactured food products, such as milk chocolate, bread, cakes, sausage meat products, confectionery items, soups, and many other food products not primarily of dairy origin.

FLUID MILK AND SOME OF ITS DERIVATIVES

Milk as a Lacteal Fluid

Milk is the normal secretion of the mammary glands of all mammals. Its purpose in nature is to nourish the young of the particular species of animal producing it. The nutritional needs of different species varies and so it is not surprising that the milk from different mammals differs in composition.

Table 40 gives typical analyses of milks produced by various animals and used for human food. While the cow is the principal source of milk for human consumption in the United States and many other parts of the world, in India most milk is obtained from the buffalo. In southern Europe the milk of goats and sheep predominates, as does the milk of the reindeer in Lapland.

TABLE 40

TYPICAL ANALYSES OF MILKS USED FOR HUMAN FOOD (PERCENT)[1]

	Total Solids	Fat	Crude Protein	Casein	Lactose	Ash
Cow	12.60	3.80	3.35	2.78	4.75	0.70
Goat	13.18	4.24	3.70	2.80	4.51	0.78
Sheep	17.00	5.30	6.30	4.60	4.60	0.80
Water buffalo	16.77	7.45	3.78	3.00	4.88	0.78
Zebu	13.45	4.97	3.18	2.38	4.59	0.74

[1] From Herrington (1963).

The principal constituents of milk including fat, protein (primarily casein), milk sugar or lactose, and the minerals of milk which collectively are referred to as ash, vary in amounts in the milks of different animal species. In addition, with the exception of lactose, each of these components from different mammals varies somewhat in chemical, physical, and biological properties. Thus the fatty acids of goat's milk fat have different melting points, susceptibility to oxidation, and flavor characteristics than those of cow's milk. Similarly, milk protein of various species may differ with respect to heat sensitivity, nutritional properties, and ability to produce allergic reactions in other species.

This high degree of variability between the milks of different animals becomes especially important in processing operations. Thus the conditions for condensing, drying, cheesemaking, etc., that are optimum for cow's milk may not be at all satsifactory when applied to a dairy situation in India. In the remainder of this chapter, unless otherwise indicated, discussion will apply to the milk from cows.

A typical composition of cow's milk is given in Table 41. But even the milk from cows will vary in composition depending upon many factors. These include the breed of cow, individuality of the animal, age of the animal, stage of lactation, season of the year, the cow's feed, time of milking, period of time between milkings, the physiological condition of the cow

TABLE 41

APPROXIMATE COMPOSITION OF COW'S MILK

Constituents	%
Water	87.1
Fat	3.9
Protein	3.3
Lactose (milk sugar)	5.0
Ash (minerals)	0.7
	100.0
Solids-not-fat	9.0
Total solids	12.9

TABLE 42

APPROXIMATE MILK EQUIVALENTS OF DAIRY PRODUCTS[1]

Product	Lb Milk Required to Make 1 Lb of Product
Butter	22.8
Cheese	10.0
Condensed milk—whole	2.3
Evaporated milk—whole	2.4
Powdered milk	7.6
Powdered cream	19.0
Ice cream—per gal.[2]	15.0
Ice cream—per gal.[3] (eliminating fat from butter and concentrated milk)	12.0
Cottage cheese	6.25 (skim milk)
Nonfat dry milk solids	11.0 (skim milk)

[1] From Dept. Agr. and Milk Industry Foundation (1960).
[2] The milk equivalent of ice cream per gallon is 15 lb.
[3] Plant reports indicate that 81.24 % of the butterfat in ice cream is from milk and cream. Thus the milk equivalent of the milk and cream in ice cream is about 12 lb.

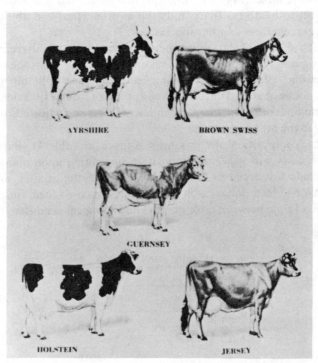

AYRSHIRE   BROWN SWISS

GUERNSEY

HOLSTEIN   JERSEY

From Lampert (1965)

FIG. 164.   VARIOUS BREEDS OF DAIRY COWS

including whether it is calm or excited, whether it is receiving drugs, and so on. All of these factors also affect the quality of the milk. Because of these sources of variation, seldom will literature values on the composition of milk agree exactly. Nevertheless, it is useful to remember the approximate composition of cow's milk since most commercial milk supplies contain the mixed milk from several farms and variations tend to average out. The approximate composition of milk in Table 41 is on such a mixed milk. We refer to all of the solids in milk as "total solids," in this case approximately 13%. The terms "solids-not-fat" or "milk solids-not-fat" (msnf) refer to total solids minus the fat, in this case 9%. Milk solids-not-fat also are referred to as "serum solids." The market price of milk purchased in bulk generally is based on its fat content and to a lesser extent on its solids-not-fat content. These solids of milk further determine the approximate yields of other dairy products that can be manufactured from the milk (Table 42).

The most important single factor governing the composition of cow's milk is the breed of the cow. The principal milk producing breeds (Fig. 164) are the Ayrshire, Brown Swiss, Guernsey, Holstein, and Jersey. Holsteins generally produce the most milk but Guernseys and Jerseys produce milk with the highest fat contents (around 5%).

Legal Standards

Milk is the most legally controlled of all food commodities. The minimum standard for fat is regulated by law in each state and values have ranged from 3.0 to 3.8%. Regulations in most states also cover total solids which have ranged from 11.2 to 12.25%. There also are federal standards of composition, and regulations against conditions that would constitute adulteration for milk and all important milk products that enter interstate commerce.

In addition, each state and many cities regulate veterinary inspections on farms, and sanitary requirements throughout the entire chain of milk handling and milk processing operations. This is essential to protect health since milk improperly handled can be a source of serious disease to all age groups. Milk has been referred to as man's most nearly perfect food from a nutritional standpoint. Its wholesomeness and acceptability further depend upon the strictest sanitary control, and the sanitary practices employed by the dairy industry have for many years been the guide to the entire food industry.

Milk is also highly regulated with respect to pricing structure and permissible marketing practices. An example of the former is that the same supply of milk often will be priced according to the end use to which it will be put. Thus a supplier generally must charge more for milk going into fluid whole milk channels than he can for milk to be used for manufactured products such as cheese or butter, even when the same milk source is used for both purposes. Control over marketing practices has included laws in some states against standardizing high and low fat milks by the addition of butterfat or skim milk although the final blend may be well above the legal minimum fat content.

Many dairy laws with respect to pricing and marketing originally were established to protect the interests of producers and processors in a given region. Often with time, however, such regulations tend to restrict rather than help a particular segment of the food industry. This has been particularly true in the dairy industry, especially as nondairy or partial-dairy substitute products such as margarine, certain coffee whiteners, and synthetic milks have grown in importance.

Milk Production Practices

Milk is produced from blood constituents in the udder of the cow. The milking operation stimulates release of blood hormones which in turn act on muscles in the udder causing let-down of milk into the four teat canals. Hand milking in the United States is largely a thing of the past. Milking machines working on a vacuum principle squeeze and suck milk from the teat canals into receiving vessels; or the milk is drawn under vacuum from the milking machine cups through pipes leading to a bulk holding tank in another room.

This tank is provided with refrigeration to quickly cool the milk down to the 40° to 50°F range to prevent bacterial multiplication. Milk secreted by a healthy udder is sterile but quickly becomes contaminated with microorganisms from the external body of the cow and from milk handling equipment. Milk should not be held in the cold tank on the farm more than two days before it is transported to a milk receiving station or milk processing plant. Often it is transported the same day it is produced.

From smaller farms the cooled milk may be shipped by truck in ten-gallon milk cans. However, larger farms utilize tank truck transportation. The milk is pumped into insulated stainless steel tanks which can hold up to 5,000 gal. The tank truck driver records the weight of milk collected and removes a small sample for later analysis of fat and total solids upon which to base price to the farmer.

The milk in ten-gallon cans or in tank trucks may go directly to a milk processing plant or, if there is not enough of it, the milk may be brought to a central receiving station where it is pooled. Here high fat milk may be blended with low fat milk before it is shipped to the processing plant. Such a blending of natural milks is considered legal even in states where standardization by the addition of butterfat or skim milk is not permitted.

Quality Control Tests

Upon receipt of the milk at the processing plant several inspections and tests may be run to control the quality of the incoming product. Some of these tests may have been done at an earlier receiving station. These tests commonly include determination of fat and total solids by chemical or physical analyses; estimation of sediment by forcing the milk through filter pads and noting the residue left on the pad; determination of bacterial counts, especially total count, coliform count, and yeast and mold count; determination of freezing point as an index to possible water pick-up; and evaluation of milk flavor. Under special circumstances tests for detection of antibiotic residues from treated cows, and for pesticide residues that may get into the milk from the cow's feed or from other farm use also may be made.

Bacterial counts play a major role in the sanitary quality of milk upon which grades are largely based. Generally fluid whole milk for consumer use, also referred to as market milk, has higher standards placed upon it than milk which will be used for manufacturing purposes. The Milk Ordinance and Code of the United States Public Health Service provides an excellent guide to the setting of microbiological and sanitary standards, and many cities and states have adopted or patterned their milk regulations after this code. Among various grades of milk and cream recognized by the U.S. Public Health Service Milk Ordinance and Code are Grade A Raw Milk for Pasteurization, which may not exceed a bacterial plate count or direct microscope clump count of 200,000 per ml; Grade A Pasteurized Milk, which may not exceed a total bacterial count of 30,000 per ml or a coliform count of 10 per ml; and Grade B Pasteurized Milk, which may not have been made from raw milk exceeding a bacterial count of 1,000,000 per ml prior to pasteurization or exceed a bacterial count of 50,000 per ml after pasteurization. These bacterial counts are among many other requirements that have gone into establishing the grades. Not all states or cities conform to these grade requirements. Some have more stringent regulations and do not permit the sale of market milk below Grade A.

As for flavor, much milk is received that is not of top quality. Milk may acquire off-flavors from many sources such as unusual feeds, absorption of odors from unclean barns, flavors or odors from excessive bacterial multiplication, rancid flavor from the action of the natural milk lipase enzyme breaking down fat, and a variety of oxidized flavors often caused by the milk coming into contact with traces of copper or iron in valves, pipes, or other milk handling equipment. As little as one part of copper in 10 million parts of milk can cause oxidized flavors that vary in degree and are described as metallic, cardboard, oily, fishy, and so on. For this reason iron and copper must be kept from coming into direct contact with product, or with cleaning water that can contaminate equipment surfaces contacting product, and the metal of choice in milk handling operations is stainless steel.

The type of off-flavor in milk is generally a good clue to its cause, as are defects uncovered by the other quality control tests. Defects are reported to farmers with suggested methods of correction. Acceptable milk is now ready for processing.

Milk Processing Operations

The first step in processing may be a further blending of different batches to a specified fat content. All the while the milk is held cold, preferably at about 40° F.

Clarification.—The milk generally is next passed through a centrifugal clarifier (Fig. 165). This machine removes sediment, body cells from the cow's udder, and some bacteria. Removal of these impurities in the clarifier is facilitated by distributing the milk in thin layers over conical disks which revolve at high speed. Since the milk is in thin layers, these impurities, which differ in density from the liquid milk, need travel only a very short distance under the influence of centrifugal force to be removed from the milk.

Clarification is by no means intended to rid the milk completely of bacteria and the clarifier was not designed for this purpose. A special machine known as a Bactofuge, operating under centrifugal force of a greater order of magnitude, has been designed for a high degree of bacterial removal. But even such machines fail to remove all bacteria from milk and could not be depended upon to remove all pathogens. The clarified milk is now ready for pasteurization if it is to be processed as market milk.

Pasteurization.—The aim of pasteurization in the case of milk is to rid the milk of any disease producing organisms it may contain and to reduce substantially the total bacterial count for improved keeping quality. Pasteurization also destroys lipase and other natural milk enzymes. Pasteurization temperatures and times for many years were selected to ensure destruction of *Mycobacterium tuberculosis,* the highly heat resistant nonsporeforming bacterium that can transmit tuberculosis to man. A treatment of 143° F for 30 min or its equivalent was employed. In more recent years it was discovered that the organism causing Q fever was slightly more resistant than the tuberculosis organism and required a treatment of 145° F for 30 min, or its equivalent, to ensure its destruction.

The two accepted methods for milk pasteurization today include the batch or holding method of heating every particle of milk to not less than 145° F and holding at this temperature for not less than 30 min, and the high temperature–short time (HTST) method of heating every particle of milk to not less than 161° F and holding for not less than 15 sec.

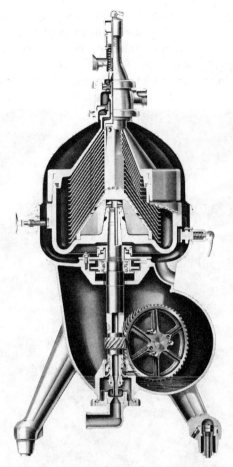

Courtesy of De Laval Separator Co.

FIG. 165. CENTRIFUGAL MILK CLARIFIER

As has been pointed out earlier, pasteurized milk is not sterile and so it must be quickly cooled following pasteurization to prevent multiplication of surviving bacteria. Pasteurization at these temperatures does not produce an objectionable cooked flavor in milk and has no important effect upon the nutritional value of milk. While slight vitamin destruction may occur, this is easily made up by other foods in a normal diet.

Batch pasteurization is carried out in heated vats provided with an agitator to ensure uniform heating, a cover to prevent contamination during the 30 min holding period, and a recording thermometer to trace a permanent record of the time-temperature treatment.

High temperature–short time pasteurization requires the more complex system described in Chap. 8, with its heating plates, holding tube, flow diversion valve, and time-temperature recording charts. Such a HTST system is seen in Fig. 166, which also includes such additional equipment as a vacuum chamber in the center and a homogenizer to the right.

Courtesy of C. P. Div., St. Regis

FIG. 166. TYPICAL MILK PROCESSING ROOM

All pasteurization equipment must be of approved design, and frequent visits from milk inspectors are a check on proper equipment operation.

Raw milk contains several enzymes. One such enzyme of considerable importance in public health work is alkaline phosphatase. This enzyme has heat destruction characteristics that closely approximate the time-temperature exposures of proper pasteurization. Therefore if alkaline phosphatase activity beyond a certain level is found in pasteurized milk it is evidence of inadequate processing. This enzyme has the ability to liberate phenol from phenol-phosphoric acid compounds. Free phenol gives a deep blue color with certain organic compounds. This is the basis for the phosphatase test. In one form of the phosphatase test, disodium phenyl phosphate is the source of phenol and 2,6,dichloroquinone-chlorimide is the indicator reagent. Milk is incubated with the disodium phenyl phosphate and then the indicator reagent is added. A blue color indicates improper pasteurization or recontamination with unpasteurized product.

Homogenization.—After pasteurization the milk may be homogenized, or homogenization may come just before the pasteurization step.

Milk and cream have countless fat globules that vary from about 1/10 to 20 μ in diameter (Fig. 167). These fat globules have a tendency to gather

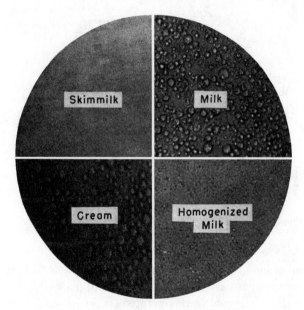

From Maryland Agricultural Experiment Station Bull. 454

FIG. 167.   THE MICROSCOPIC APPEARANCE OF FAT GLOBULES

into clumps and rise due to their lighter density than skim milk. Skim milk from which the cream has been removed has virtually no fat globules. The purpose of homogenization is to subdivide the fat globules and clumps in milk to such small size that they will no longer rise to the top of the milk as a distinct layer in the time before the milk is normally consumed. This is an advantage since it makes the milk in a bottle or container more uniform and prevents the first person using the bottle from getting more cream. In addition, subdivision and uniform dispersion of the fat gives homogenized milk a richer taste and a whiter color in the bottle, as well as greater whitening power when added to coffee, than the same milk not homogenized.

One type of homogenizer valve assembly is seen in Fig. 168. Large fat globules of milk entering at the bottom are sheared as they are pumped under pressure through a tortuous path. They emerge at the top about 1/10 of their original diameter.

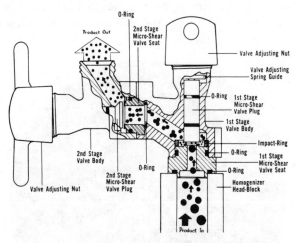

Courtesy of C. P. Div., St. Regis

FIG. 168. DIAGRAM OF TWO-STAGE HOMOGENIZER VALVE ASSEMBLY

Homogenization and cooling of the milk is followed by bottling or containerization in paper cartons and other types of packages. The containers of milk are then delivered in refrigerated trucks to supermarkets, restaurants, or homes.

Related Milk Products

The above processing sequence is basic to the production of market milk. However, slight departures or additional steps in the sequence are employed to produce a number of closely related milk products.

Vitamin D Milk.—Milk drawn from the cow normally contains vitamin D, but the amount varies with the cow's diet, and with her exposure to sunlight. Since the diet of most children is deficient in vitamin D it has become common practice to add the vitamin to milk. Milk can be increased in vitamin D activity by irradiating the milk with ultraviolet light, which in effect converts the milk sterol, 7-dehydrocholesterol, into vitamin D_3. But the vitamin D level that can be produced this way is somewhat limited. More practical has been the adding of a vitamin D concentrate to the milk at a level to bring the potency up to at least 400 units of vitamin D per quart. Most of the milk consumed in the United States has this vitamin D addition. It is generally added before pasteurization.

Multi-Vitamin Mineral Milk.—Nutritionists and physicians generally oppose the indiscriminate fortifying of general purpose foods since normal variety in diet tends to supply all needed vitamins, and further, there is evidence that excesses of certain vitamins can be harmful. Nevertheless, a fortified milk has been approved to meet the demand in some areas.

Vitamins and minerals in this case usually are added to milk to give each quart the minimum daily requirement of vitamin A, vitamin D, thiamine, riboflavin, niacin, iron, and iodine. Vitamin C is not commonly added since it is quickly destroyed during milk processing and normal storage. Such fortified milk represents but a small fraction of current total milk production.

Low Sodium Milk.—People with high blood pressure or edema may be on a restricted sodium diet. Low sodium milk is available in a number of cities. It is prepared by passing the milk through an ion exchange resin that replaces sodium with potassium. Low sodium milk generally contains about 3 to 10 mg of sodium per 100 ml, whereas untreated milk will contain about 50 mg/100 ml.

Soft Curd Milk.—The casein of milk coagulates and forms curd when acted upon by enzymes and acid of the stomach. This curd may be harder or softer depending upon the amount of casein and calcium in the milk and

Courtesy of Evaporated Milk Association

FIG. 169. CURDS FROM DIFFERENT MILKS

other factors. Human breast milk forms a soft fluffy curd. Pasteurized cow's milk forms a harder more compact curd (Fig. 169). Soft curd milk may be easier to digest by infants and young children. Various treatments are known for producing soft curd milk. These include heat treatments comparable to those used in producing evaporated milk, removal of some calcium by ion exchange, treatment of the milk with enzymes, and other methods. Soft curd milks are commercially available.

Regarding digestibility of milk by infants, human milk is more easily digested than cow's milk. Cow's milk is substantially higher in protein and lower in sugar than human milk. To correct these differences, in preparing infant formulas it is common practice to dilute cow's milk with water and to add sugar, making it more like human milk.

Sterile Milk.—Milk may be sterilized rather than pasteurized by using more severe heat treatments. If the temperature is sufficiently high the time may be very short, preventing cooked flavor and color change. A typical heat treatment is of the order of 300° F for 2 to 3 sec. The milk is then aseptically packaged, usually in tin cans. Sterile milk has found its greatest use to date in places where refrigeration is not generally available such as parts of Europe, aboard ships, and by the Armed Forces abroad.

Evaporated Milk.—Evaporated milk is the most widely used form of concentrated milk. It is concentrated to approximately 2.25 times the solids of normal whole milk. In its processing, generally raw whole milk is clarified, concentrated, fortified with vitamin D (to give 400 units per quart when the evaporated milk is diluted with an equal volume of water), homogenized, filled into cans, sterilized in the cans in large continuous pressure retorts at temperatures of about 245° F for 15 min, and cooled. This heat treatment gives evaporated milk its characteristic caramelized cooked color and flavor.

Currently whole milk is being concentrated approximately 2:1 and 3:1 and sterilized outside the can by HTST techniques followed by aseptic canning. This gives sterile 2:1 evaporated milk and sterile 3:1 concentrate without cooked color and flavor. These products can be of excellent quality but equipment costs usually are somewhat higher.

As mentioned in the chapter on drying and concentration, when concentrated milks are heated the proteins have a tendency to gel and thicken on storage. Various stabilizing phosphates and other salts may be used in prescribed low levels to minimize this problem, but its complete elimination is rarely achieved.

Sweetened Condensed Milk.—Unlike evaporated milk, sweetened condensed milk is not sterile. But multiplication of bacteria present in this product is prevented by the preservative action of sugar. The product is made from pasteurized milk that is concentrated and then supplemented with sucrose. Concentration and sugar addition are adjusted to give a sugar concentration of about 63% in the water of the final product. Preservation of milk with sugar has largely given way to milk preservation by heat. However, the combination of sugar and milk solids is convenient in food manufacture, and large amounts of sweetened condensed milk are today used by the baking, ice cream, and confectionery industries. A further comparison of the different steps involved in the manufacture of evaporated milk and sweetened condensed milk is seen in Fig. 170.

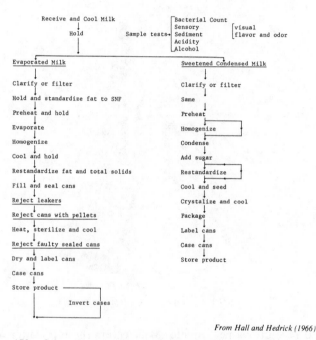

From Hall and Hedrick (1966)

FIG. 170. STEPS INVOLVED IN EVAPORATED MILK AND SWEETENED CONDENSED MILK PROCESSING

Dried Whole Milk.—Whole milk is dehydrated to about 97% solids principally by spray drying and vacuum drying. The drying operation is quite efficient but on storage the whole milk product soon acquires off-flavors, frequently of an oxidized character. How to completely prevent these off-flavors is still not known, and this is why dried whole milk of beverage quality is not yet as important a commercial product as is dried skim milk of beverage quality. However, large quantities of dried whole milk are used in the manufacture of other food products where storage flavor is not as apparent.

Separation of Milk

All of the above products result largely from processing whole milk that has not been separated into its components. But milk can be readily separated into its two principal fractions, cream and skim milk.

The separation is made in a centrifugal cream separator which looks quite like a milk clarifier but has separate discharge nozzles for cream and skim milk (Fig. 171). The cream separator bowl rotates at a speed of several

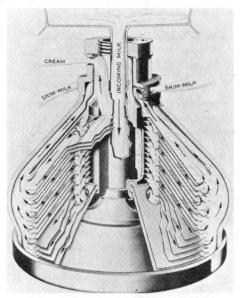

Courtesy of De Laval Separator Co.

FIG. 171.   BOWL OF CREAM SEPARATOR

thousand revolutions per minute. Milk enters the top center of the bowl. The skim milk having a heavier density than the whole milk or cream is driven by centrifugal force to the outside of the bowl, while the lighter cream moves toward the center of the bowl. The machine can be adjusted to separate cream over a wide range of fat contents for different uses.

Skim milk may be used directly as a beverage or it may be concentrated or dried for use in manufactured foods and animal feeds. Similarly cream may be used directly, or it may be frozen, concentrated, dried, or further separated to produce butter oil and serum solids. All of these forms are used in manufactured foods.

Milk Substitutes

The prices of milk, cream, and other dairy products are largely determined by their milk fat (butterfat) contents. Butterfat for many years has sold for about five times the price of common vegetable fats and oils. As will be discussed in the later chapter on fats and oils, current technology can modify many fats and oils of vegetable, marine, or animal origin to perform nearly interchangeably in numerous food applications. This of course is the basis for the margarine industry.

In more recent years various substitutes for dairy products other than butter have become commercially important. These have included vegetable fat frozen desserts (ice cream substitutes), vegetable fat coffee whiteners, and vegetable fat whipped toppings. Vegetable fat milk substitutes, sometimes referred to as filled milks, also have appeared. Among milk substitutes there is a legal distinction between terms used to differentiate products. When these milk substitutes are made by combining nondairy fats or oils with certain classes of milk solids the resulting products are referred to as filled milks. The term imitation milk, on the other hand, is used to describe products that resemble milk but contain neither milk fat nor other important dairy ingredients.

Today it is possible to manufacture fluid milk substitutes of truly excellent quality. Generally such products are made from skim milk or reconstituted skim milk powder plus coconut fat or some other vegetable fat. Commonly additional ingredients such as mono- and diglyceride emulsifiers, carotene (for color), vitamin D, and other substances are added. The products are pasteurized, homogenized, packaged, and marketed quite like market milk. These filled milks may not be called milk but go under such names as *Melloream* (*Mellorine* is the name of a vegetable fat ice cream), protein drink, and other trade names. These products are commonly sold in various countries of Europe but as yet are prohibited from interstate commerce in the United States. However, such milk substitutes are legal products *within* several of the states. Presently there is much debate on the desirability of establishing minimum standards of composition for such products, in view of the important role milk has in the diets of persons of all ages. It is likely that such products will become more important in the future.

Imitation milks and beverages made from soybean protein and vegetable oils represent a still further departure from natural milk. Such products are now being manufactured and sold in countries of Asia and other regions. Carefully formulated they can be of considerable importance nutritionally, since they generally can be produced at a lower cost than natural milk.

While filled and imitation milk products have been cited by some as a threat to the future of the dairy industry, their importance in this regard presently is difficult to assess. Many major food commodities are currently experiencing competition from substitute foods and this tendency may be expected to increase. Balancing this, however, is a growing appreciation of the special attributes of milk proteins, lactose, butterfat, and modified forms of these, and they are increasingly being used as functional and nutritional ingredients in other manufactured foods.

ICE CREAM AND RELATED PRODUCTS

Ice cream has been called "The Great American Dessert," and currently in the United States about 1 billion gallons of ice cream and related items are consumed annually.

Ice cream as we know it today is the result of an evolution of about five centuries that began in Europe. Its origin may have been in the practice of runners bringing snow from the tops of mountains to cool the beverages of royalty. It later was learned that beverages and fruit juices could be frozen by stirring in a vessel chilled on the outside with a mixture of salt and ice. Such products frozen to a slush consistency were much like our ices of today. Gradually small amounts of cream and milk were mixed into such items giving products similar to our current sherbets which are really ices containing low levels of dairy ingredients. As more milk and cream were introduced, the products more closely resembled our present day ice cream. Ice cream recognizable as such was known in England in the early 1700's, but was still a rare item when served in the United States to White House guests by Dolley Madison in 1809.

In the early 1900's, ice cream plants in the United States still were using ice and salt freezers of the type seen in Fig. 172. Today multicylinder con-

Courtesy of Ice Cream Trade Journal

FIG. 172.   ICE AND SALT FREEZER OF EARLY 1900'S

tinuous freezers can turn out over 1,000 gal. of uniformly frozen ice cream per hour.

Composition of Ice Cream

Dairy ingredients in many forms are used in the manufacture of ice cream and related products. These may include whole milk, skim milk, cream, frozen cream, butter, butter oil (which contains about 99% butterfat), condensed milk products, and dried milk products. The composition of ice cream will be made up of milk fat (butterfat) and milk solids-not-fat derived from the above ingredients, plus sugar, stabilizer, emulsifier, flavoring materials, water, and air.

The mixture of these constituents, before the air is incorporated and the mixture frozen, is known as the ice cream mix. The mix composition may be made richer or leaner in fat, msnf, and total solids depending upon market requirements; but in addition, a mix of chosen composition can be formulated from various combinations of the basic dairy ingredients to supply the fat and msnf. In typical commercial operations the supply and cost of dairy ingredients varies throughout the year, and so the ice cream plant manager frequently is recalculating his chosen mix formulas to keep overall ice cream compositions constant at the lowest possible cost.

Typical compositions of commercial ice creams and related products

TABLE 43

APPROXIMATE COMPOSITION OF COMMERCIAL ICE CREAM AND RELATED PRODUCTS[1]

Milk Fat %	MSNF %	Sugar %	Stabilizer and Emulsifier %	Approximate Total Solids %
		Economy Ice Cream		
10	10 to 11	13 to 15	0.30 to 0.50	35.0 to 37.0
12	9 to 10	13 to 15	0.25 to 0.50	
		Good Average Ice Cream		
12	11	15	0.30	
14	8 to 9	13 to 16	0.20 to 0.40	37.5 to 39.0
		Deluxe Ice Cream		
16	7 to 8	13 to 16	0.20 to 0.40	
18	6 to 7	13 to 16	0.25	40.0 to 41.0
20	5 to 6	14 to 17	0.25	
		Ice Milk		
3	14	14	0.45	31.4
		Good Average Ice Milk (Soft Serve)		
4	12.0	13.5	0.40	
5	11.5	13.0	0.40	29.0 to 30.0
6	11.5	13.0	0.35	
		Sherbet		
1 to 3	1 to 3	26 to 35	0.40 to 0.50	28.0 to 36.0
		Ice		
..	...	26 to 35	0.40 to 0.50	26.0 to 35.0

[1]From Arbuckle (1972).

are seen in Table 43. A good average ice cream would contain about 12% milk fat, 11% msnf, 15% sugar, 0.2% stabilizer, 0.2% emulsifier, and a trace of vanilla. This would give 38.4% total solids and the remainder would be water. To this might be added other ingredients such as nuts, fruit, chocolate, eggs, additional flavorings, etc. Such a formula changes quickly as we produce deluxe and French ice creams that may have 18% fat, economy ice creams that may have 10% fat, ice milk products that may have only 4% fat, fruit flavored sherbets that usually will contain less than 2% fat, and fruit ices that generally contain no fat.

Milk fat is the most expensive major ingredient of ice cream and so the higher the fat content generally the more expensive the product. There are state and federal regulations covering compositions of frozen desserts, and these are largely based upon milk fat and total milk solids contents. Thus, according to federal standards, plain ice cream may contain no less than 10% milk fat and 20% total milk solids, while fruit, nut, or chocolate ice cream may contain no less than 8% milk fat and 16% total milk solids. There are also allowances for other ingredients. Products with leaner compositions may not be called ice cream. Federal standards also specify minimum compositions of ice milk and other frozen desserts.

Air and Overrun.—These compositions are based on the ice cream exclusive of air, that is, percentages are based on weight of the ice cream. But ice cream is made to contain a great deal of air and is truly a whipped product. This air, uniformly whipped into the product as small air cells, is necessary to prevent the ice cream from being too dense, too hard, and too cold in the mouth.

The increase in volume caused by whipping air into the mix during the freezing process is known as overrun. The usual range of overrun in ice cream is from 70 to 100%. If ice cream has 100% overrun then it has a volume of air equal to the volume of mix that was frozen. In other words one gallon of mix makes two gallons of frozen ice cream of 100% overrun.

The overrun of any ice cream can be calculated from the formula:

$$\% \text{ overrun} = \frac{\text{vol of ice cream} - \text{vol of mix}}{\text{volume of mix}} \times 100$$

The maximum allowable overrun also is specified in federal and state standards by defining the minimum permissible weight per gallon of product.

Functions of Ingredients

Some of the more important functions of the major ingredients are as follows:

Milk Fat.—The fat gives the product a rich flavor and improves body and texture. The fat also is a concentrated source of calories and contributes heavily to the energy value of ice cream.

MSNF.—The milk solids-not-fat contribute to the flavor and also give body and a desirable texture to the product. Higher levels of msnf also permit higher overruns without textural breakdown.

Sugar.—The sugar not only adds sweetness to the product but lowers the freezing point of the mix so that it does not freeze solid in the freezer. The sugar may be sucrose from cane or beet sources or it may be dextrose from corn syrup.

Stabilizers.—Stabilizers are generally gums such as gelatin, gum guar, gum karaya, seaweed gums, pectin, or manufactured gums such as carboxymethyl cellulose types which are cellulose derivatives. The stabilizers form gels with the water in the formula and thereby improve body and texture. They also give a drier product which does not melt as rapidly or leak water. The stabilizers by binding water also help to prevent large ice crystals from forming during freezing, which would give the product a coarse texture.

Emulsifiers.—Egg yolk is a good natural emulsifier due to its content of lecithin. Commercial emulsifiers are numerous and generally contain monoglycerides and diglycerides. The emulsifiers help disperse the fat globules throughout the mix and prevent them from clumping together and churning out as butter granules during the freezing-mixing operation. Emulsifiers also improve whipping properties to reach desired overrun. Emulsifiers further help to make the ice cream dry and stiff.

Flavors.—The flavors give variety. Vanilla is still the most popular flavor followed by chocolate, strawberry, and a very large number of fruit, nut, and other additions.

Manufacturing Procedure

The first step in preparing the mix is to combine the liquid ingredients in a heated mixing vat and bring them to about 110° F. The sugar and dry ingredients are next added to the warm mix which helps dissolve them. Gross particulates such as nuts or fruits are not added at this time since they would be disintegrated during subsequent processing. Instead they are added during the freezing step.

Pasteurization.—The mix is now pasteurized by a batch or continuous heating process. Pasteurization temperatures are higher than for plain milk since the high fat and sugar contents tend to protect bacteria from heat destruction. Common temperatures for batch pasteurization are 160° F for 30 min, and for continuous HTST pasteurization 180° F for 25 sec. Except for the higher temperature, pasteurization equipment is much the same as used for milk.

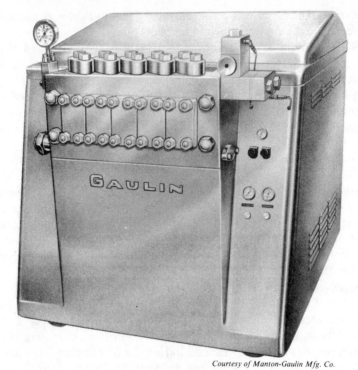

Courtesy of Manton-Gaulin Mfg. Co.

FIG. 173.   ICE CREAM HOMOGENIZER

Homogenization.—The pasteurized mix is next homogenized at the temperature it comes from the pasteurizer. A two-stage homogenizer may be used (Fig. 173) with the mix pumped at a pressure of 2,500 psi through the first stage valve and 600 psi through the second stage valve. Homogenization breaks up fat globules and fat globule clumps, and together with the added emulsifiers prevents churning of fat into butter granules during the freezing operation. Homogenization also improves the overall body and texture of ice cream. After homogenization the mix is cooled to 30°–40° F.

Ageing the Mix.—The next step is ageing. The mix is held anywhere from 3 to 24 hr at a temperature of 40° F or lower (Fig. 174). Ageing does the following: it provides time for the melted fat to solidify, the gelatin or other stabilizer swells and combines with water, the milk proteins also swell with water, and the viscosity of the mix is increased. These changes lead to quicker whipping to desired overrun in the freezer, smoother ice cream body and texture, and slower ice cream melt-down. Some manufacturers of stabilizers and emulsifiers claim that through the use of their products ageing time may be drastically reduced or even eliminated, but ageing is still employed in many ice cream plants.

Courtesy of Creamery Package Mfg. Co.

FIG. 174. STORAGE TANKS FOR AGEING ICE CREAM MIX

Freezing.—The mix is now ready to be frozen. The cold mix at about 30° to 40° F is pumped to a batch or continuous freezer. Continuous freezers with multiple freezing chambers such as seen in Fig. 175 are more common in large manufacturing operations.

Mix and air enter the freezing cylinders which are chilled by circulating refrigerant between double walls. The purposes of the freezing operation are mainly two; to freeze the mix to about 22° F, and to beat in and subdivide air cells.

Freezing must be quick to prevent the growth of large ice crystals that would coarsen texture, and air cells must be small and evenly distributed to give a stable frozen foam. These are accomplished within the freezing chamber, which is of the scraped surface type described in Chapter 9. The freezing chamber is provided with a special mixing element or dasher (see previous Fig. 38). The rotating dasher with its sharp scraper blades shaves the layers of frozen ice cream off the inner freezer wall as they are formed. This prevents buildup of an insulating layer which would otherwise decrease freezing efficiency of the still colder freezer wall. The ice cream scrapings mixed into the remaining mix in the freezing cylinder also serve to seed the mix with small ice crystals which speed freezing of the mass. The dasher's rods and bars also beat air into the freezing mass, much as in the whipping of cream or egg white.

Mix passing through the freezer cylinder is frozen and whipped in about 30 sec or less to a temperature of about 22° F. At this temperature not all of the water is frozen, and the ice cream is semisolid, in which condition it is easily pumped out of the cylinder as a continuous extrusion by the incoming unfrozen mix and the propelling action of the dasher.

The semisolid ice cream emerging from the freezer goes directly into packaging cartons or drums. The consistency of the ice cream entering the cartons is that of soft ice cream-like products sold at roadside stands.

Novelty Ice Cream.—Various kinds of nozzles and filling attachments are available to make novelty ice cream as the product is extruded from the freezer cylinder. Thus, for example, with the rig at the top of Fig. 176 three flavors can be pumped from three freezer cylinders through a three compartment square nozzle to give the common vanilla, chocolate, strawberry block.

Ice Cream Hardening.—The cartons of semisolid ice cream now go to a

Courtesy of Cherry-Burrell Corp.

FIG. 175. MULTIPLE CHAMBER CONTINUOUS ICE CREAM FREEZER

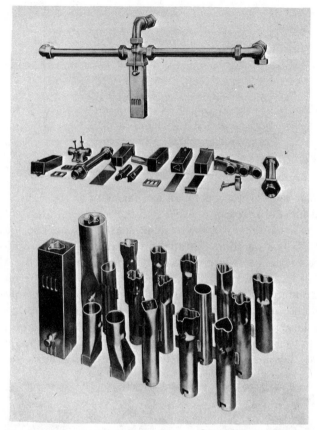

Courtesy of Cherry-Burrell Corp.

FIG. 176.   FILLING ATTACHMENTS FOR NOVELTY ICE CREAM PRODUCTS

hardening room where a temperature of about −30° F is maintained. Storage in the hardening room freezes most of the remaining water and makes the ice cream stiff. When stiff the product is ready for sale.

Ice Cream Physical Structure

The physical structure of ice cream should be understood since changes in physical structure are the cause of several common defects in this product.

We have said that ice cream is a foam containing air cells which constitute overrun, and that the overrun will give ice cream with approximately twice the volume of the original mix. The dairy foam illustrated in Fig. 177 is similar to the foam in ice cream. In the frozen ice cream foam the films of mix surround the air cells. The fat globules are dispersed within the films or layers of mix. Also within the films are the frozen ice crystals.

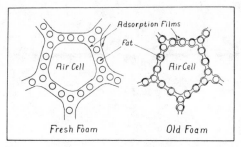

From Sommer (1951)

FIG. 177.   DIAGRAM OF THREE PHASE DAIRY FOAM SYSTEM

As ice cream ages in storage, foams can shrink as on the right. In addition, weakened films of mix can collapse and the ice cream loses volume. This can be excessive if the mix is low in solids, and represents a serious defect.

Figure 178 is a photomicrograph of the internal structure of ice cream with more detail. The white areas marked *b* are the air cells. All the rest are films of frozen mix surrounding the air cells. Within the films are ice crystals, solidified fat globules, and insoluble as well as dissolved sugars, salts, proteins, and other mix constituents. If the ice crystals marked *a* become too large, as occurs when fluctuating storage temperatures permit repeated partial thawings and refreezings, the ice cream becomes coarse and icy. If there is too much lactose from excessive milk solids and it

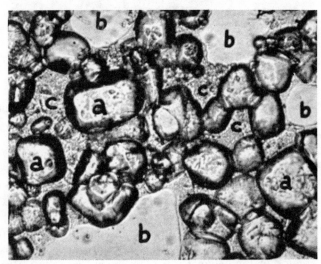

From Arbuckle (1940)

FIG. 178.   PHOTOMICROGRAPH OF THE INTERNAL STRUCTURE OF ICE CREAM

should crystallize out the ice cream becomes grainy or sandy. In addition to foam collapse and loss of overrun from formulas low in solids, excessive shrinkage can result from partial melting at too high a freezer storage temperature. There also is shrinkage due to mechanical compaction when ice cream is dipped from tubs to make cones. This is called dipping loss.

Other textural defects may include gummy, crumbly, curdy, watery, and so on due largely to poor mix formulations. Ice cream also may have flavor defects common to other dairy products such as cooked flavor, oxidized flavor, or even rancidity if made from off-flavor dairy ingredients. In addition it may have a host of unnatural flavors from poor quality flavoring ingredients.

Other Frozen Desserts

Some of these have already been mentioned (Table 43), and there are many more depending upon formula. All are manufactured with much the same equipment and in accordance with the same principles used in making ice cream. Several of these frozen desserts are simply varieties of ice cream. Thus we have plain ice cream, fruit ice cream, and nut ice cream with about 8 to 14% milk fat, deluxe ice creams with about 16 to 20% milk fat, French ice cream and frozen custard which contain liberal quantities of egg yolk, parfait and spumoni which are high in fat and generally also contain fruits and nuts, etc.

Lower fat products include "soft ice cream" and "soft ice milk" with milk fat contents from about 6% down to about 3%. These are the popular products served directly from the freezer at drive-ins and other retail establishments. In many marketing areas these products may not be called ice cream but instead are referred to as "soft serve" or by trade names.

Sherbets usually contain less than 2% milk fat and corresponding low levels of other milk solids. Sherbets, which are principally water, sugar, and tart fruit flavorings, have low overruns of the order of 30 to 40%. Ices are similar to sherbets but generally contain no dairy products and also have low overruns of about 25 to 30%.

Many of the above products and related items are loosely referred to by different names in different parts of the country. Federal standards for such products, however, are quite specific.

In addition, some ice cream and ice milk type products are being manufactured with vegetable fat in place of milk fat. Since vegetable fat is less expensive then milk fat obviously there is a cost advantage in manufacture. Such products are illegal in some states. Where they are legal, federal law requires that they be labeled imitation ice cream or imitation ice milk if they move in interstate commerce. This is to protect dairy interests and to eliminate any question of intended deception.

CHEESE

In addition to being delightful foods that contribute variety and interest to our diets, cheeses of various kinds always have been important sources of nutrients to man wherever milk producing animals could be raised. While today the gourmet may pay several dollars per pound for an imported cheese, at the other extreme, in less developed regions where milk rapidly spoils because of lack of refrigeration, cheese may be a staple of diet (Fig. 179) sometimes made under the most primitive conditions.

Courtesy of FAO

FIG. 179. NEPALESE CHEESEMAKER FOLLOWS HERDS OF YAK IN HIMALAYAS

Kinds of Cheese

We might define cheese as the product made from the curd of the milk of cows and other animals, the curd being obtained by the coagulation of the milk casein with an enzyme (usually rennin), an acid (usually lactic acid), and with or without further treatment of the curd by heat, pressure, salt, and ripening (usually with selected microorganisms). Even this broad approximate definition doesn't cover all cheeses, since some are made from milk whey solids that remain after removal of coagulated casein.

Cheesemaking is an old process and still retains aspects of an art even when practiced in the most modern plants. Part of this is due to the natural variation common to milk, and the imperfect controllability of microbial populations.

The basic cheese types evolved as products of different types of milk, regional environmental conditions, accidents, and gradual improvements by trial and error. There are over 800 names of cheeses but many of the names really describe similar products made in different localities or often in different sizes and shapes. Of these, however, there are basically only about 18 distinct types of natural cheeses, reflecting the different processes by which they are made. These include brick, Camembert, Cheddar, cottage, cream, Edam, Gouda, hand, Limburger, Neufchatel, Parmesan, Provolone, Romano, Roquefort, sapsago, Swiss, Trappist, and whey cheeses.

If we take Cheddar as an example of a distinct natural type, then we can see how some of the multiplicity of subtypes and different names come about. In Fig. 180 are types of cheese hoops in which Cheddars may be

Courtesy of Damrow Brothers Co.

FIG. 180. VARIOUS TYPES OF CHEESE HOOPS

pressed, giving rise to different sizes and shapes. The cheeses then get such names as Longhorns, Picnics, Daisies, Twins, and so on. But they all are of the Cheddar type.

Classification by Texture and Kind of Ripening.—A useful means of classifying the types and important varieties of cheeses is indicated in Table

TABLE 44

CLASSIFICATION OF CHEESES[1]

Unripened:
　Low Fat—cottage, pot, bakers'.
　High Fat—cream, Neufchatel (as made in United States).
　Ripened: Bel Paese, Brie, Camembert, cooked, hand, Neufchatel (as made in
　　France).
SEMISOFT:
　Ripened principally by bacteria: brick, Munster.
　Ripened by bacteria and surface microorganisms: Limburger, Port du Salut,
　　Trappist.
　Ripened principally by blue mold in interior: Roquefort, Gorgonzola, Blue,
　　Stilton, Wensleydale.
HARD:
　Ripened by bacteria, without eyes: Cheddar, Granular, Caciocavallo.
　Ripened by bacteria, with eyes: Swiss, Emmentaler, Gruyere.
VERY HARD (grating):
　Ripened by bacteria: Asiago old, Parmesan, Romano, sapsago, Spalen.
PROCESS CHEESES:
　Pasteurized, cold-pack, related products.
WHEY CHEESES:
　Mysost, Primost, Ricotta.

[1]From U. S. Dept. Agr. Handbook No. 54 (1953).

44. It is based largely on the textural properties of the cheeses and the primary kind of ripening. Thus we have hard cheeses, semihard cheeses, and soft cheeses depending upon their moisture content; and they may be ripened by bacteria or molds, or they may be unripened. The bacteria may produce gas, and so form eyes as in the case of Swiss cheese, or they may not produce gas as in the case of Cheddar and so no eyes are formed. Among the soft and semisoft cheeses, Limburger is ripened primarily by bacteria, and Camembert by a mold; cottage cheese is not ripened.

The classification is extended to include "Process" cheeses which are essentially melted or blended forms of the above cheeses, and whey cheeses which are made from the whey remaining after coagulation and removal of the casein. Whey cheeses are high in β-lactoglobulin and α-lactalbumin, the second and third principal proteins in amount in milk. These are not coagulated by rennin or by the acid in most cheese making processes and so they remain soluble in the whey. However, they can be easily coagulated from the whey as curds by heating.

All of the major types of cheese can fit into a classification such as the above. The approximate percentage compositions of several of these cheeses are seen in Table 45.

Cheddar Cheese, Curdmaking and Subsequent Operations

All cheese types begin with curdmaking, and then involve various manipulations of the curd or whey. Illustrative of the cheese making process is

TABLE 45

APPROXIMATE PERCENTAGE COMPOSITION OF SOME VARIETIES OF CHEESE[1]

Variety	Moisture	Fat	Protein	Ash (Salt-free)	Salt	Calcium	Phosphorus
Brick.........	41.3	31.0	22.1	1.2	1.8	—	—
Brie.........	51.3	26.1	19.6	1.5	1.5	—	—
Camembert.........	50.3	26.0	19.8	1.2	2.5	0.68	0.50
Cheddar.........	37.5	32.8	24.2	1.9	1.5	0.86	0.6
Cottage							
uncreamed	79.5	0.3	15.0	0.8	1.0	0.10	0.15
creamed.........	79.2	4.3	13.2	0.8	1.0	0.12	0.15
Cream.........	54.0	35.0	7.6	0.5	1.0	0.3	0.2
Edam	39.5	23.8	30.6	2.3	2.8	0.85	0.55
Gorgonzola	35.8	32.0	26.0	2.6	2.4	—	—
Limburger.........	45.5	28.0	22.0	2.0	2.1	0.5	0.4
Neufchatel	55.0	25.0	16.0	1.3	1.0	—	—
Parmesan.........	31.0	27.5	37.5	3.0	1.8	1.2	1.0
Roquefort.........	39.5	33.0	22.0	2.3	4.2	0.65	0.45
Swiss.........	39.0	28.0	27.0	2.0	1.2	0.9	0.75

[1] From Lampert (1965).

the preparation of Cheddar, the most popular cheese in America, Canada, and England.

Milk contains fat, proteins (principally casein, less β-lactoglobulin and still less α-lactalbumin), lactose, minerals, and water. When acid, or the enzyme rennin, or both are added to milk there is a coagulation of the casein which traps much of the fat, some of the lactose, and some of the water and minerals. This is the curd. The remaining liquid and its dissolved lactose, proteins, minerals, and other minor constituents is the whey. In making Cheddar cheese, curd is formed under controlled conditions of temperature, acidity, and rennin concentration. This gives curd of the desired moisture content and texture for subsequent processing.

Cheese curd can be made from raw or pasteurized milk. When it is made from raw milk the FDA requires that the finished cheese be ripened for sixty days or more as a safeguard against pathogens, since such storage under the acid conditions of the cheese destroys the common disease producing organisms that could be present in the milk. But most Cheddar cheese is made from pasteurized milk since pasteurization also destroys most spoilage types of organisms and undesirable milk enzymes and gives better control over subsequent fermentation of the curd.

Setting the Milk.—The pasteurized whole milk is added to the vat, brought to about 87° F, and a lactic acid producing starter culture of *Streptococcus lactis* is added at a level of about 1.0% based on the milk. At this point color may be added to the stirred milk if the Cheddar is to be of the orange colored type. After about 30 min a mildly acidic condition of about 0.2% acidity (calculated as lactic acid) will exist and the rennin in the form of a dilute solution is added as in Fig. 181. The commercial rennin

From Kosikowski (1970)

FIG. 181. ADDING RENNET EXTRACT TO MILK FOR CHEDDAR CHEESE; A CLASS AT CORNELL UNIVERSITY

preparation is known as rennet. While the name rennin refers to the pure enzyme, the commercial rennet, obtained from the fourth stomach of the calf, contains rennin and small amounts of other materials. The mild acidity improves the coagulating property of the rennin.

Stirring is now stopped and the milk is allowed to set. In about 30 more minutes a uniform custard-like curd forms throughout the vat. Acid continues to be formed, as it will throughout the curd making operation. The combination of rennin and acid forms a curd with a desirable elastic texture which when subsequently heated or pressed will shrink and squeeze out much of the trapped whey.

Cutting the Curd.—The next step after setting is cutting the curd. This is done with curd knives that are made up of wires strung across a frame. One knife has the wires going vertically and the other horizontally. By drawing the knives through the length of the vat (Fig. 182) and then back

From Lampert (1965)

FIG. 182. CUTTING THE CURD FOR CHEDDAR CHEESE

and forth with the width of the vat, the curd is cut into small cubes. In the case of Cheddar these cubes may be from $\frac{1}{4}$ to $\frac{1}{2}$ in. on a side. The smaller the cube the more surface area, and so the quicker and more complete is the removal of whey from the cubes, which can lead to a drier cheese. The curd for different types of cheese, therefore, is cut into different size cubes.

Cooking.—After the cutting step, which may take only 5 to 10 min, the cubes are gently agitated and the jacketed vat is heated with steam to raise the temperature of the curds and whey. The temperature is brought to about 100° F over a 30 min period and held at 100° F for about 45 min longer. This is known as cooking.

Cooking at 100° F further helps to squeeze the whey from the curd cubes. Heat increases the rate of acid production and makes the curd cubes shrink. Both help expel the whey and toughen the curd cubes which now take on a more rounded cottage cheese-like form. During cooking the curds continue to be gently agitated. We are now ready to drain the whey.

Draining Whey and Matting Curd.—Agitation of the curds is stopped and they are permitted to settle. The whey is drained from the cheese vat and the curds are trenched along the sides of the vat, as seen in Fig. 183,

Courtesy of Manufactured Milk Products Journal

FIG. 183.   DRAINING WHEY AND TRENCHING CURD FOR CHEDDAR
CHEESE

to further facilitate whey drainage. After all of the whey has been drained, the curds are allowed to mat for about 15 min. During matting the individual curd pieces fuse together to form a continuous rubbery slab.

The process of matting and subsequent handling of matted curd is known as cheddaring and is unique to the production of the Cheddar type of cheese. Cheddaring involves cutting the matted curd into blocks, turning the blocks at 15 min intervals, and then piling the blocks on one another 2 or 3 deep. The purpose of cheddaring is to allow acid formation to continue, and to squeeze whey from the curd. The weight of the blocks on one another actually is a mild form of pressure. During the cheddaring the vat is maintained warm. The cheddaring operation of stacking and turning the blocks goes on for about 2 hr or until the whey coming from the blocks reaches between 0.5 to 0.6% acid.

Milling and Salting.—The curd blocks or slabs are now ready for the milling and salting operation. The rubbery slabs of cheddared curd are passed through a mill which cuts the blocks into pieces about ⅝ in. square and about 2 in. long (Fig. 184).

Courtesy of Dairymens League Coop.

FIG. 184. MILLING OF CHEDDAR CURD BLOCKS

The milled pieces are next spread out over the floor of the vat and sprinkled with salt. The amount of salt is about 2.5 lb/100 lb of curd. The salt and curd are stirred to uniformly distribute the salt. The purposes of the salt are three-fold. The salt further draws whey out of the curd by osmosis. The salt acts as a preservative, holding down proteolytic and other types of spoilage organisms that might otherwise grow in later stages of the cheesemaking operation. The salt also adds flavor to the final cheese.

Pressing.—The milled and salted curd pieces are now placed in hoops fitted with cheesecloth and the hoops are placed in a hydraulic press. Pressing at about 20 psi pressure is continued overnight. Pressing has several effects. It determines the final moisture that the finished cheese will have. The more moisture or whey retained in the cheese from the press, the more acidity that can be fermented from it. This is turn affects the final texture of the cheese and what microorganisms can grow during the subsequent ripening period. And of course pressing determines the final shape of the cheese.

Curing or Ripening.—After overnight pressing the cheese is removed from the hoop and placed in a cool drying room at about 60° F and 60% relative humidity for 3 or 4 days. This causes mild surface drying and forms a slight rind. To prevent mold from growing on the surface of the cheese, the cheese block or wheel is now dipped in hot paraffin. The wax coating in addition to preventing surface molding also prevents the cheese from excessive drying out during the long ripening or ageing period. The waxed cheese is now boxed and placed in the curing room for ripening. The curing or ripening room generally will be at about 36° F and 85% RH.

Ripening is continued for at least 60 days whether the cheese milk was raw or pasteurized. For peak flavor ripening may be continued for 12 months or longer. During this period bacteria in the cheese and enzymes in the rennet preparation modify the cheese texture, flavor, and color by continuing to ferment residual lactose and other organic compounds into acids and aroma compounds, by partial hydrolysis of the milk fat and further breakdown of fatty acids, and by mild proteolysis of the protein. In the case of Cheddar these changes are comparatively mild because of

Courtesy of Alfa-Laval AB, Stockholm-Tumba, Sweden

FIG. 185. A MECHANIZED CHEESEMAKING OPERATION IN EUROPE

the types of organisms present, which are primarily of the lactic acid type, and due to the relatively low moisture content. The flavor is correspondingly mild when compared, for example, to Roquefort or Limburger cheese.

Advanced Processes.—Obviously there is much hand labor in conventional Cheddar making and so considerable research has been directed to the development of mechanized and continuous cheesemaking processes. Several mechanized schemes have been devised over the past dozen or so years; among them the Ched-O-Matic and the Curd-A-Matic processes in the United States, and various other processes in Europe and Australia (Fig. 185). Most of these processes retain the classical steps of conventional Cheddar production and replace hand operations with mechanical equivalents.

More recently, an important departure from conventional cheesemaking has involved cold milk renneting. In conventional cheesemaking, rennet is added to warm milk and the system is permitted to set and form the curd. If rennet is added to cold milk the casein is altered but the milk remains a liquid. If such milk is subsequently heated to 90° F instantaneous gelling occurs. It is thus possible to work with a liquid system which is more easily pumped, metered, etc., and then generate coagulated curd continuously by passing the liquid through a heat exchanger. Such practices lend themselves to improved processing methods and may be expected to influence cheesemaking processes of the future.

Cottage Cheese

Cottage cheese is an example of a low fat, soft cheese, generally coagulated with lactic acid rather than rennin. The curd is left in particulate form, that is it is not pressed. Further, it is not aged or ripened under long storage.

Starting with pasteurized skim milk rather than whole milk, the curd forming operations have many similarities to the early stages of Cheddar making (Fig. 186). The steps are as follows:

(1) Pasteurized skim milk is warmed in a vat to 72° F.
(2) A lactic starter (at about 1% level) is added to produce acid. In addition to *S. lactis,* the starter usually contains *Leuconostoc citrovorum,* a flavor producing bacterium.
(3) The vat is set and fermented for about 14 hr (long set method).
(4) The coagulated milk is cut into $\frac{1}{4}$ in. cubes as in the upper left of Fig. 186.
(5) The curd cubes are cooked for about 90 min with stirring, gradually increasing the temperature to 120° F.
(6) After cooking the whey is drained and the curd is washed with cold water to remove excess whey and limit acidity.
(7) The curd is trenched to drain all water.
(8) The curd may now be mildly salted, as a mild preservative measure and for flavor.

From Kosikowski (1970)

FIG. 186.   BASIC STEPS IN COTTAGE CHEESEMAKING

(9) The curd also may be blended with sweet or soured cream to give 4% fat. The product is then called creamed cottage cheese.

Cottage cheese is packaged as loose curd particles and undergoes no further processing. It is highly perishable and must be kept refrigerated.

The principal variations in cottage cheesemaking have to do with the length of fermentation time in the vat. The 14-hr holding time at 72° F is known as the "long set" method. By using a larger amount of lactic starter (about 6%) and a higher temperature of 90°F the proper degree of acidity for coagulation and curd cutting can be reduced to 5 hr and this is known as the "short set" method. Another variation employs low levels of rennet plus the starter for milk coagulation.

Swiss Cheese

Like Cheddar, this is a hard-type cheese. But it is characterized by the formation of large holes or eyes and a sweet nutty flavor. This is obtained through the activities of an organism known as *Propionibacterium shermanii*. This organism follows the lactic acid organisms and further ferments their lactic acid (now in the form of lactate) to propionic acid and carbon dioxide. The propionic acid contributes to the nutty flavor and the carbon dioxide gas collects in pockets within the ripening curd and forms the eyes.

Swiss cheese, also known as Emmental cheese, generally is made from raw milk. To the milk in large kettles is added a multiple organism starter. Present are lactic acid organisms including *Lactobacillus bulgaricus*, and a heat tolerant streptococcus, namely *Streptococcus thermophilus*, which produces lactic acid through the rather high cooking temperatures of about 128°F which the curd undergoes during processing. The starter may contain the eye forming *Propionibacterium* or this may come in with the raw milk. Follwing an initial period of lactic acid fermentation, rennet is added to the kettle to coagulate the milk. The curd is cut with a harp-like wire knife into rice-size particles. The curds and whey are now heated and cooked at about 128°F for about an hour.

Unlike Cheddar making, at this point the stirred heated curd is allowed to settle, a cloth with a fitted steel strip edge is slid under the curd, and the entire curd mass is hoisted from the kettle to drain (Fig. 187).

The entire curd from a kettle is placed in a single large hoop in which it is pressed for one day to form a beginning rind. The cheese wheel which may weigh somewhat more than 200 lb is now removed from the hoop and placed in a large brine tank at about 50°F (Fig. 188). It floats in this brine for about three days and its top is periodically salted. The salt removes still more water from the cheese surfaces than could be removed by pressing and thus produces the heavy protective rind.

The cheese is next removed from the brine to a warm ripening room which is maintained at about 70°F and 85% RH. The cheese remains here for about five weeks during which time the eyes are formed by the fermentation of the *Propionibacterium* at the relatively warm temperature. As the eyes are formed the cheese becomes somewhat rounded (Fig. 189). The opening of the eyes also changes the sound of the cheese when it is thumped with the finger. After about 5 weeks, the cheese is moved to a

Courtesy of Valio Finnish Coop. Dairies Assoc., Helsinki, Finland

FIG. 187.   DRAINING SWISS CHEESE CURD PRIOR TO PLACING
IT IN THE HOOP

Courtesy of Swiss Cheese Union Inc., Berne, Switzerland

FIG. 188.   SALTING WHEELS OF SWISS CHEESE

Courtesy of Swiss Cheese Union Inc., Berne, Switzerland

FIG. 189. SWISS CHEESE IN CURING ROOM

colder curing room at about 45° F. Here it remains from 4 to 12 months to develop the full sweet nutty flavor.

In judging the quality of Swiss cheese much emphasis is given to the size, shape, and gloss of the eyes (Fig. 190). This is not for appearance alone. Proper eye formation is an index of several other quality factors. For example, if the acidity is not properly controlled to produce a chewy elastic texture then the curd would not be able to stretch and form the eye

Courtesy of Swiss Cheese Union Inc., Berne, Switzerland

FIG. 190. TYPICAL EYE FORMATION IN QUALITY SWISS CHEESE

under the pressure of the generated carbon dioxide. Thus, excessive acid gives a brittle curd which forms cracks rather than eyes. So the eyes also are an index of texture. Similarly, the same organism that forms the eyes produces the propionic acid necessary for the sweet nutty flavor. Good eye formation indicates active fermentation by this organism and well-developed flavor.

Blue-Veined Cheeses

The family of blue-veined cheeses is typified by a semisoft texture and blue mold growing throughout the curd. There are four well-known varieties of blue-veined cheeses. Three are made from cow's milk and they are Blue cheese, made in Denmark, the United States, and other countries; Stilton, made in England; and Gorgonzola, made in Italy. The fourth and perhaps the most famous blue-veined cheese is Roquefort, which is made from sheep's milk and is a product of France.

All of the blue-veined cheeses acquire the characteristic blue marbling by having their curd inoculated with the blue-green mold *Penicillium roqueforti* prior to being hooped and pressed. Mold growth is encouraged during the ripening period which can be from 3 to 10 months at cool, moist, cave-like conditions of 40° F and 90% RH.

Molds are aerobic and so generally grow on the surface of cheeses and other foods. To permit the mold to grow throughout the cheese mass it is common practice to pierce the pressed cheese when it is placed in the curing room. This allows air to penetrate the cheese and support mold growth throughout the mass. The blue-green color is from spores of the mold, and in Fig. 191 can be seen the darkened lines where mold growth is heavy

Courtesy of Danish Dairy Assoc., Aarhus, Denmark

FIG. 191. DANISH BLUE CHEESE SHOWING HEAVY MOLD GROWTH ALONG AIR CHANNELS

along the pierced air channels. *Penicillium roqueforti* not only produces the mottled blue color but is an active splitter of milk fat. This gives rise to fatty acids and ketones which contribute to the sharp, peppery flavor of blue-veined cheeses.

Camembert

Another mold ripened cheese is Camembert, which like Roquefort originated in France. However, this cheese is characterized by a soft cream-colored curd and a white felt-like mold growth which covers its entire surface (Fig. 192). The mold is *Penicillium camemberti*, and it is inoculated

Courtesy of The Borden Co.

FIG. 192. CAMEMBERT CHEESE SHOWING WHITE SURFACE MOLD
DURING CURING

onto the pressed cheese curd after removal from the hoop by spraying a mist of mold spores onto the cheese surfaces. Ripening, as in the case of Roquefort, is under damp conditions of about 45° F and 95% RH. But ripening time is only about three weeks. *Penicillium camemberti* is highly proteolytic and it breaks down the curd protein, from the surface inward, to the texture of soft butter. If proteolysis goes too far, because of prolonged storage in the supermarket or the home, the cheese develops a strong ammoniacal odor.

semisoft cheese which, like Camembert, is ripened from
\ with a characteristic proteolytic decomposition. How-
... ripening agent is a surface bacterium called *Bacterium*

Process Cheese and Related Products

All of the cheeses described thus far are referred to as natural cheeses.
That is, they are produced through a series of natural curd making and
ripening operations (cottage cheese is unripened). Process cheese is the
name given to cheese made by mixing or grinding different lots of natural
cheeses together and then melting them into a uniform mass.

This is done in part because different lots of natural cheese vary in such
characteristics as moisture, acidity, texture, flavor, and age. A highly
acidic cheese, for example, can be blended with a bland cheese to yield a
totally acceptable product. However, process cheeses have become so
popular in their own right that they have necessitated plants for the production of natural cheese solely intended for conversion to process cheese.

In making process cheese, the mixed lots are melted together by heating
to about 160° F. This also pasteurizes the cheese. Emulsifiers such as
sodium citrate and disodium phosphate are added to prevent fat separation, and to add smoothness to the texture. The hot melted cheese is then
poured into cartons (Fig. 193) and allowed to cool and solidify. The best
known process cheese is the popular American cheese made from blended
and melted Cheddar.

Process cheese may be used to prepare process cheese foods and spreads
by mixing in additional dairy ingredients, fruits, vegetables, meats, etc.
The designations "Process Cheese Food" and "Process Cheese Spread"
may be used only when the final products meet minimal federal standards
with respect to solids, fat, and proportion of cheese to noncheese substances. Thus, Process Cheese Food must contain no less than 51% cheese,
no less than 23% fat, and no more than 44% moisture.

There are several other related dairy foods that enjoy popularity. Junket
dessert is sweet milk plus flavor that is coagulated with rennet to a custard-
like consistency. Cultured buttermilk is pasteurized skim milk (or partially
skimmed milk) mildly coagulated with lactic acid culture (containing
Leuconostoc bacteria for flavor) and consumed as a beverage. At one time
sour buttermilk was the liquid drained from the butter churn and allowed
to ferment naturally, but today's cultured buttermilk is the result of a well
controlled process. Sour cream is fresh pasteurized cream mildly coagulated with lactic acid culture plus *Leuconostoc* flavor bacteria. It is higher
in fat and heavier in consistency than cultured buttermilk. Yoghurt is
pasteurized whole milk coagulated to a custard-like consistency with a

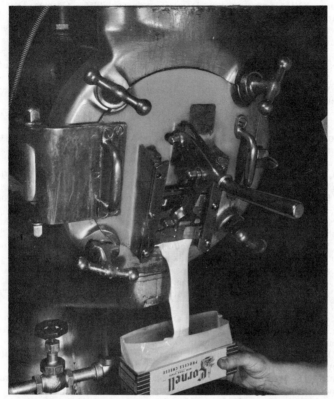

From Kosikowski (1970)

FIG. 193. HAND FILLING HOT MELTED PROCESS CHEESE INTO
CARTONS

mixed lactic acid culture containing *Lactobacillus bulgaricus* and *Streptococcus thermophilus*. It may be flavored or unflavored. The refreshing
qualities of yoghurt are rather new to the United States, but in parts of
Europe and in many areas of Africa and Asia naturally fermented yoghurt
is a staple of diet.

BIBLIOGRAPHY

AGR. MARKETING SERV., U.S. DEPT. AGR. 1959. Federal and State Standards for the
Composition of Milk Products. USDA Agr. Handbook *51*.
AMERICAN PUBLIC HEALTH ASSOCIATION. 1967. Standard Methods for the Examina-
tion of Dairy Products. 12th Edition. New York.
ANON. 1965. Milk Facts. Milk Industry Foundation, Washington, D.C.
ARBUCKLE, W. S. 1940. A microscopical and statistical analysis of texture and structure
of ice cream as affected by composition, physical properties, and processing methods.
Missouri Agr. Expt. Sta. Res. Bull. *320*.
ARBUCKLE, W. S. 1972. Ice Cream, 2nd Edition. Avi Publishing Co., Westport, Conn.

ASSOCIATION XVII INTERNATIONAL DAIRY CONGRESS. 1966. German Dairying. The Association, Munich.
FARRALL, A. W. 1963. Engineering for Dairy and Food Products. John Wiley & Sons, New York.
FOSTER, E. M. *et al.* 1957. Dairy Microbiology. Prentice-Hall, Englewood Cliffs, N.J.
FRANDSEN, J. H. (Editor) 1958. Dairy Handbook and Dictionary. Published by the author, Amherst, Mass.
HALL, C. W., and HEDRICK, T. I. 1971. Drying of Milk and Milk Products, 2nd Edition. Avi Publishing Co., Westport, Conn.
HALL, C. W., and TROUT, G. M. 1968. Milk Pasteurization. Avi Publishing Co., Westport, Conn.
HENDERSON, J. L. 1971. The Fluid-Milk Industry. Avi Publishing Co., Westport, Conn.
HERRINGTON, B. L. 1963. Dairy products. *In* Food Processing Operations, Vol. 1. M. A. Joslyn, and J. L. Heid (Editors). Avi Publishing Co., Westport, Conn.
JACOBSON, R. E., and BARTLETT, R. W. 1963. The ice cream and frozen dessert industry—changes and challenges. Illinois Agr. Expt. Sta. Bull. *694*, Urbana.
JUDKINS, H. F., and KEENER, H. A. 1960. Milk Production and Processing. John Wiley & Sons, New York.
KOSIKOWSKI, F. 1970. Cheese and Fermented Milk Foods. Published by the author, Ithaca, N.Y.
LAMPERT, L.M. 1965. Modern Dairy Products. Chemical Publishing Co., New York.
MILK INDUSTRY FOUNDATION. 1960. Milk Facts *29*, Washington, D.C.
NICKERSON, R. A. 1960. Chemical composition of milk. J. Dairy Sci. *43*, 598–606.
OLSON, T. M. 1950. Elements of Dairying. Macmillan Co., New York.
POTTER, N. N. 1967. *Salmonella* contamination. Am. Dairy Rev. *29*, No. 9, 70, 75–76, 124–127.
SANDERS, G. P. 1953. Cheese Varieties and Descriptions. U.S. Dept. Agr. Handbook *54*.
SMALL, E., and FENTON, E. F. 1964. A summary of laws and regulations affecting the cheese industry. U.S. Dept. Agr. Handbook *265*.
SOMMER, H. H. 1951. The Theory and Practice of Ice Cream Making, 6th Edition. Published by the author, Madison, Wisc.
U.S. DEPT. HEALTH, EDUCATION AND WELFARE. 1965. Grade "A" Pasteurized Milk Ordinance. Public Health Service Pub. *229*, Washington, D.C.
VAN SLYKE, L. L., and PRICE, W. V. 1952. Cheese. Orange Judd Co., New York.
WEBB, H. W., and JOHNSON, A. H. (Editors) 1965. Fundamentals of Dairy Chemistry. Avi Publishing Co., Westport, Conn.
WEBB, B. H., and WHITTIER, E. O. (Editors) 1970. Byproducts from Milk. Avi Publishing Co., Westport, Conn.
WORLD HEALTH ORGANIZATION. 1962. Milk Hygiene. Monograph Ser. *48*. FAO-WHO, Geneva, Switzerland.

CHAPTER 14

Meat, Poultry, and Eggs

INTRODUCTION

The consumption of large quantities of animal products generally is well correlated with the affluence of a society. This is related to the efficiencies of nutrient production in nature. Before animals, birds, and fish can provide food for man in terms of flesh, eggs, or milk they must satisfy their own physiological requirements for energy and synthesis. These requirements are met largely through the consumption of plant materials, which if consumed directly by man, could support a substantially greater population than can the animal products derived from them. This is true with respect to total available calories, protein, and all other nutrients needed to sustain life.

Nevertheless, the human appetite always has had a strong preference for animal foods, and man has been more than willing to expend the greater effort generally required to satisfy this appetite where natural conditions have permitted. Today, in agriculturally advanced societies, it is possible to convert grain into flesh at rates of about 2.1 lb per pound of chicken, 4 lb per pound of pork, and 10 lb per pound of beef. These conversion ratios are largely responsible for the relative prices of food from these sources.

In addition to preferences based on palatability, foods from animal products (including fish, which will be discussed in the next chapter) represent concentrated sources of most of the nutrients required by man. This is to be expected since the tissues and body fluids of man are very much like their counterparts in other animals with respect to the elements and compounds they contain. While it is probably true that man could supply all of his nutritional needs from plant sources, this would require the consumption of a sizable number of plant types and an uncommon sophistication with respect to choices if no animal products supplemented such a diet. This would be especially so with respect to meeting the requirements for all essential amino acids, vitamins, and minerals.

MEAT AND MEAT PRODUCTS

Meat and meat products generally are understood to include the skeletal tissues or flesh of cattle, hogs, sheep, and other animals. Also included are the glands and organs of these animals such as tongue, liver, heart, kidneys, brain and so on. In a broader sense meat also includes the flesh of poultry and fish, but these are generally considered separate from the red meats of four legged animals.

In the United States, our principal sources of meat are cattle which yield beef; calves which yield veal; hogs which yield hams, pork, and bacon; sheep which yield mutton; and young sheep which yield lamb.

But meat products also include the many by-products from animal slaughter such as animal gut used for sausage casings; the fat of the meat which is rendered into tallow and lard; hides and wool; animal scrap, bone, and blood used in poultry and other feeds; and such products as gelatin, chemicals, enzymes, and hormones used by the food, pharmaceutical, and other industries. For this reason the major meat processing companies are seldom in a single business.

In addition to farm animals yielding meat, which is one of our most important sources of high quality protein, vitamins, minerals, and other nutrients, the management of meat-yielding animals also contributes to soil fertility, and is a means of converting large quantities of plant roughage materials unsuited for human consumption into highly acceptable human food.

The size of the meat industry within the enormous food industry is in itself great, being third in the United States after the steel and automobile industries. In one year Americans consume over 35 billion pounds of various meat products, beef and pork being the favorites. This is worth about $27 billion and represents about 30¢ of every dollar spent on food. Further, the Food and Agriculture Organization of the United Nations forecasts that world demand for meat by 1980 will be 40% greater than in 1970.

Government Surveillance

Essential to the meat industry are two kinds of government surveillance, these are Grading and Meat Inspection.

Grading.—The need for grading is very clear. Like all of nature's products meat is very heterogenous. Animal carcasses are of all sizes, from many breeds, of varying ages, and have been fed on many different kinds of feeds. These factors result in cuts of meat varying in yield, tenderness, flavor, cook-out losses, and general overall quality. A uniform system of federal grading is essential to ensure that the wholesale buyer and ultimately the retail customer gets what he pays for.

Grading is based on such factors as contour of the meat, amount of fat, degree of marbling of the fat, texture and firmness of the lean, and color. Generally the best cuts of beef have more fat and the fat is well marbled throughout the lean. This results in greater tenderness and better flavor, as in the case of the Prime cut (Fig. 194) which is the highest grade for beef. Subsequent grades in the case of beef, in order of decreasing

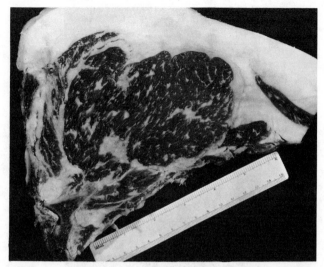

Courtesy of Prof. J. R. Stouffer, Cornell University

FIG. 194.   U. S. DEPARTMENT OF AGRICULTURE PRIME GRADE
BEEF

quality, are Choice, Good, Standard, Commercial, Utility, and Cutter-Canner. The grades, however, have very little relationship to the nutritional value of the cuts.

Consumers will readily agree on the overall palatability scores of meat cooked from different grades. The Prime grade will cost the most and get the highest score. Generally Prime cuts are sold to the better hotels, restaurants and clubs. Most beef found in retail stores for home use is of the Choice and Good grades. Standard, Commercial, and lower grades are used chiefly in processed meat products and inexpensive hamburgers. Grading usually is done at the place of slaughter.

An interesting experimental technique that may influence future grading and the purchase price paid for animals involves the use of ultrasonic energy to reveal the gross structure of meat prior to animal slaughter. Meat, fat, and bone reflect ultrasonic energy differently. By radiating such energy over the body of a live animal and recording the reflected energy pattern it is possible to develop an X-ray-like cross sectional view of portions of the animal carcass. In this way purchases of live meat-yielding animals can be made more efficient in terms of intended end use than is now possible. Figure 195 shows the kind of information that can be obtained on the live animal by this method and how it correlates with the structure of meat cuts obtained from the same animal after slaughter.

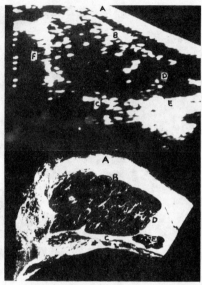

Courtesy of Prof. J. R. Stouffer, Cornell University

FIG. 195. REFLECTED ULTRASONIC ENERGY PATTERN FROM
LIVE STEER AND CORRESPONDING BEEF CUT FROM SAME ANIMAL

Meat Inspection for Wholesomeness.—This is done by federal meat inspectors on all meat going into interstate commerce, in accordance with The Federal Meat Inspection Act of 1906. Its purpose is to safeguard health by ensuring a clean, wholesome, disease-free meat supply that is without adulteration. Unlike grading practices by USDA Agricultural Marketing Service representatives which are largely optional, this kind of meat inspection is mandatory.

If animals are diseased the meat can carry a wide variety of organisms pathogenic to man. These may include species capable of causing tuberculosis, brucellosis, anthrax, trichinosis, salmonellosis, etc. There are some 70 such diseases that animals can transmit to man. For this reason, inspections are made by trained veterinarians or persons under their supervision at places of animal slaughter and at meat processing facilities.

Until very recently mandatory inspection of meat for wholesomeness applied at the federal level only to meat entering interstate commerce. The different states and many cities had their own laws to cover safety of meats that remained within the states. This led to abuses in some cases. To further ensure consumer health, a federal law enacted in 1967 now requires that all of the states adopt and enforce meat inspection practices at least comparable in thoroughness to the federal meat inspection laws.

Slaughtering and Related Practices

There has been a law in the United States since 1958 that all animals coming under federal inspection must be rendered insensible to pain before being hoisted by their hind legs and stuck in the neck for bleeding. An exception exists in slaughtering according to religious ritual.

One common humane method of rendering the animal insensible is by striking it on the head with an air or gunpowder-driven blunt or penetrating device. This has largely replaced stunning with a sledge hammer. Another method employs an electric shock, and a third method uses a tunnel filled with carbon dioxide through which the animal passes.

After stunning, hoisting, and bleeding, a modern slaughterhouse is an efficient continuous disassembly line. Virtually every component of the animal body is utilized, including the hide, viscera, blood, and carcass. The skinned, washed, and deviscerated carcass is then moved by mono-rail into a chill room where the deepest part of the meat reaches 35° F in about 36 hr. This prevents rapid bacterial spoilage.

Resting of Animals.—There is another practice to help delay bacterial spoilage. Animals store glycogen in their muscles as a source of reserve energy. After the animal is killed this glycogen is converted under the anaerobic conditions in the muscles into lactic acid. This gives the muscles increased acidity which acts as a mild preservative. But if animals are excited or exercised before slaughter then the glycogen is largely consumed and there is very little left to be converted to lactic acid in the postmortem tissues. Such meat can spoil more quickly. This is one reason for the common practice of resting animals before slaughter. Additional research has shown that antemortem stress also can affect other carcass characteristics such as the defects of dark-cutting beef, and pale, soft, watery pork.

Structure and Composition of Meat

The gross structure of cuts of meat can be seen in Fig. 194 and 195. The dark areas are principal muscles and the white areas are fat; however, microscopic observation is required to see the fine structure of the muscles.

Figure 196 is a diagram of a longitudinal section of lean muscle showing that the muscle is composed of bundles of hair-like muscle fibers. These protein muscle fibers are held together by proteinaceous connective tissue which merges to form a tendon which in turn connects the muscle to a bone. The muscle fibers themselves are formed from cells that merge and give the hair-like structures. The protein of the muscle fiber is called myosin. The connective tissue contains two proteins called collagen and elastin. Collagen on heating in the presence of moisture dissolves and

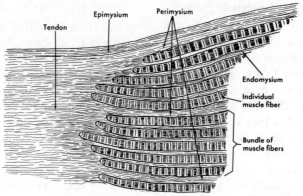

From Griswold (1962)

FIG. 196. DIAGRAM OF A LONGITUDINAL SECTION OF LEAN MUSCLE

yields gelatin. Elastin is tougher and is a constituent of the ligaments. A cooked chicken leg nicely reveals the bundles of muscle fibers, the connective tissue between the bundles of muscle fibers, and the gelatinous substance in the connective tissue which is dissolved collagen.

When an animal is well fed, fat penetrates between the muscle fiber bundles and this is fat marbling. There are relationships between muscle

TABLE 46

GENERAL COMPOSITION OF FOODS OF ANIMAL ORIGIN[1]

Food	—% Composition—Edible Portion—				
	Carbo-hydrate	Protein	Fat	Ash	Water
Meat					
beef, medium fat.............................	...	17.5	22.0	0.9	60.0
veal, medium fat.............................	...	18.8	14.0	1.0	66.0
pork, medium fat............................	...	11.9	45.0	0.6	42.0
lamb, medium fat............................	...	15.7	27.7	0.8	56.0
horse, medium fat..........................	1.0	20.0	4.0	1.0	74.0
Poultry					
chicken....................................	...	20.2	12.6	1.0	66.0
duck.......................................	...	16.2	30.0	1.0	52.8
turkey.....................................	...	20.1	20.2	1.0	58.3
Fish					
non-fatty fillet	...	16.4	0.5	1.3	81.8
fatty fish fillet..............................	...	20.0	10.0	1.4	68.6
crustaceans................................	2.6	14.6	1.7	1.8	79.3
dried fish..................................	...	60.0	21.0	15.0	4.0
Milk					
cow, whole.................................	5.0	3.5	3.5	0.7	87.3
goat, whole................................	4.5	3.8	4.5	0.8	86.4
Cheese					
hard, whole milk...........................	2.0	25.0	31.0	5.0	37.0
soft, partly whole milk	5.0	15.0	7.0	3.0	70.0

[1] From Food Composition Tables, F.A.O., United Nations, Rome.

structure and meat tenderness. Thinner muscle fibers are more tender than thicker muscle fibers, and thinner muscle fibers are more common in young animals. Marbled fat within the muscles makes for more tenderness. On cooking, muscle fibers will contract and may become tougher, but cooking also melts the fat and dissolves the collagen into soluble gelatin, so the overall effect is increased tenderness.

The compositions of meat cuts will vary with the relative amounts of fat and lean, but a typical cut of beef may contain 60% water, 22% fat, 18% protein, and 1.0% ash. Compositions of the meats of other food animals, poultry, fish, and some milk products are given in Table 46 for comparison.

Ageing of Meat

When an animal is killed, within a few hours rigor mortis sets in with a contraction of muscle fibers and an increasing toughness of the meat (Fig. 197). This is thought to be due to the formation of lactic acid which

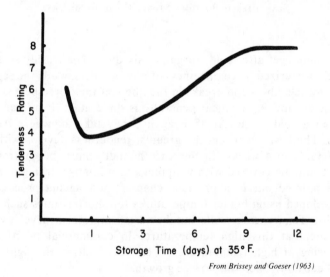

From Brissey and Goeser (1963)

FIG. 197. EFFECT OF AGEING ON TENDERNESS OF BEEF

accumulates in the muscles of newly killed animals. If the meat is held cool, rigor mortis subsides in about two days, the muscles become soft again, and there is a progressive tenderization of the meat over the next several weeks. The tenderization is believed to be due principally to natural proteolytic enzymes in the meat, which slowly break down the connective tissue between the muscle fibers as well as the muscle fibers themselves.

Figure 198 compares photomicrographs of raw beef freshly slaughtered

Courtesy of Dr. Pauline Paul

FIG. 198. PHOTOMICROGRAPHS OF RAW BEEF: TOP—FRESHLY
SLAUGHTERED; BOTTOM—STORED COLD FOR SIX DAYS

and the same beef after cold storage of six days. The freshly slaughtered beef is characterized by compactness of muscle fibers, while the separation between muscle fibers and breaks in the fibers of the stored beef is evident.

Ageing or ripening of meat generally is done at 35° F by hanging the carcass in a cold room. At 35° F ageing may take anywhere from 1 to 4 weeks. The best flavor and the greatest tenderness develop with ageing at 35° F for 2 to 4 weeks. In this case humidity must be controlled and the meat may be covered with wrappings to minimize drying and weight loss. As pointed out in a previous chapter, new ageing processes have been developed using higher temperatures for shorter times such as 68° F for 48 hr. Tenderness results but bacterial slime also develops quickly on the meat at this high temperature. In commercial practice where quick ageing at high temperatures is employed ultraviolet light may be used to keep down bacterial surface growth.

Not all beef is deliberately aged for increased tenderness and flavor before being shipped by meat packing companies due to the cost involved. Further, some beef that is used for sausage manufacture may not be aged or even cooled following slaughter. This so-called "hot beef" that has not yet passed through complete rigor mortis has superior water holding characteristics over cold stored beef, a desirable property in the making of sausage meat emulsions. This superior water holding capacity of hot beef also can be retained for later use if the beef is rapidly frozen before rigor has had time to subside.

Artificial Tenderizing

Cold room storage results in natural ageing or ripening of the meat with tenderizing from the meat's natural enzymes. There are several artificial means of tenderizing meat to various degrees.

Meat may be tenderized by mechanical means such as pounding, cutting, or separating and breaking meat fibers with ultrasonic vibrations.

Meat may be tenderized somewhat by the use of low levels of salt. Salt solubilizes meat proteins. Salt draws water to itself; therefore, if salt is placed within the meat as in ground hamburger it holds water within the mass. If it is placed on the surface of the meat (as in the case of cheese) it draws moisture out of the mass to the surface. Phosphate salts may be even more effective than common table salt in this respect, and either may be blended into ground meat or diffused into the flesh of fish to help retain juices and minimize bleeding or drip losses.

A third artificial tenderizing method involves the addition of enzymes to the meat, such as bromelin from pineapple, ficin from figs, trypsin from pancreas, or papain from papaya. The native practice in tropical countries of wrapping meat in papaya leaves before cooking results in this kind of tenderization. Enzymes may be applied to meat surfaces but penetration is slow, and so injection into the meat or into the bloodstream of the living animal before slaughter is more effective for large cuts. If this is done then any additional cold room ageing time requirement is markedly reduced. Tenderizing enzymes will function before cooking and during the cooking operation until the meat temperature reaches about 180° F, then they become heat inactivated.

Curing of Meat

While ageing or ripening by cold room storage, or tenderizing by the methods mentioned, have as their prime objective increased tenderness, the curing of meat is a different process and has additional objectives. Curing refers to modifications of the meat that affect preservation, flavor, color, and tenderness due to added curing ingredients. Proper ageing still leaves the meat recognizable as a fresh cut, but curing is designed to grossly alter the nature of the meat and produce distinct products such as smoked and salted bacon, ham, corned beef, and highly flavored sausages including bologna and frankfurters.

Originally, curing treatments were practiced as a means of preserving meat before the days of refrigeration, and curing goes back to about 1500 BC. In less developed areas without modern preservation facilities, the prime objective of curing still is preservation. But where more effective preservation methods are available the prime purpose of curing is to produce unique flavored meat products, and a special purpose is to preserve the red color of meat. Thus, cured corned beef when cooked remains red while beef that is not cured turns brown on cooking. Similarly, cured ham retains its red color through cooking but uncured pork becomes brown.

The principal ingredients used for curing or pickling meat are: (1) common salt—which is a mild preservative and adds flavor; (2) sodium nitrate and sodium nitrite—which are red color fixatives; (3) sugar—which helps stabilize color and also adds flavor; and (4) spices—mainly for flavor.

These ingredients are available in numerous commercial mixtures and may be applied to meat in dry form by rubbing on surfaces or mixing into ground meats. In the case of hams or corned beef they may be applied as a wet cure or pickle, by soaking in vats. When the meat cut is large and penetration of the cure is slow, the cure may be pumped into the meat via an artery as is common with large hams, or the cure may be injected with multiple needles into slabs of bacon bellies as in Fig. 199.

Courtesy of Swift and Co. (Mr. Ed Hois)

FIG. 199. AUTOMATIC MULTIPLE NEEDLE INJECTION OF CURE INTO BACON

Meat Pigments and Color Changes

One of the principal objectives of curing is to stabilize the red color of meat and this requires some understanding of the pigments of meat and their color changes. This is most important because the consumer attaches great significance to red meat color in her purchases. The color changes that can occur in meat are complex in their chemistry and it is intended here only to indicate a few principles (Fig. 200).

The chief muscle pigment is a protein called myoglobin and it has a

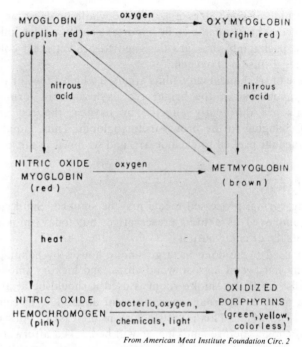

From American Meat Institute Foundation Circ. 2

FIG. 200. COLOR CHANGES OBSERVED DURING THE CURING AND HANDLING OF MEATS

purplish color. When it is exposed to oxygen it becomes oxymyoglobin which has a bright red color. Thus when fresh meat is first cut it is purple in color but its surface quickly becomes bright red upon exposure to air. Large cuts may be bright red on the surface but more purplish in the interior due to less oxygen within. The desirable bright red of oxymyoglobin on exposure to air is not entirely stable and on prolonged exposure and excessive oxidation it can shift to metmyoglobin which has a brownish color.

When fresh meat is cooked these protein pigments are denatured and also produce a brown color. Steak cooked to a rare condition has less of the oxymyoglobin denatured and is more pink. Well-done meat is more denatured and is more brown. But meats cured with nitrates are red and remain red through cooking. The nitrates plus myoglobin produce nitric oxide myoglobin in cured meats which is red. Nitric oxide myoglobin on cooking is converted to nitric oxide hemochromogen which is pink or red as in cooked ham and bacon.

These pigment shifts, some of which are reversible, are affected by oxygen, acidity of the meat, and exposure to light; and the combination determines which pigments will dominate. Within the normal pigment shifts, the color of meat does not indicate wholesomeness or nutritional value; however, the red color is an important positive sales influence. For this reason, packaging films are designed to protect meat color, largely by controlling diffusion of oxygen.

In the case of fresh meat cuts, films are used which allow air to penetrate and keep myoglobin in the bright red oxymyoglobin form. However, cured meats are differently affected by oxygen; the red nitric oxide myoglobin changing to the brown metmyoglobin. Thus, cured meats are generally vacuum packed to exclude air, and wrapped in air impermeable films.

Smoking of Meats

Following curing, processed meats may be smoked. Smoking also was originally employed as a mild preservative, but today smoking is used mostly for its flavor contribution.

Smoking used to be done in large smoke houses by hanging the meat over burning hardwood logs or wood chips, and hickory smoke was preferred for flavor. If the smoke room is used it should be at about 135° F to give the meat an internal temperature of about 125° F; smoking may take from 18 to 24 hr. This is satisfactory in the case of pork products if the meat is cooked before smoking or will be cooked afterward. If, however, the meat is to be a ready-to-eat product without additional heat, then smoking must bring pork products to an internal temperature of 137° F or higher to ensure destruction of the trichinosis parasite, and this is included in the federal meat inspection laws. In Fig. 201 hams are being removed from a typical cabinet-type smokehouse.

Today there are several ways to generate smoke remotely and then circulate it into a smoke room or smoke tunnel (Fig. 202). In addition smoke can be generated in a special device without fire by high speed frictional contact with the wood. The smoke also can be given an electric charge and electrostatically deposited onto the meat surface. There also are synthetic solutions of the chemicals from smoke, but their use is legally restricted to only limited products.

Sausages and Table-Ready-Meats

Cured meats especially, and uncured meats to a lesser extent find their way into enormous quantities of sausage products. There are over 200 kinds of sausage products sold in the United States, the most popular of which are frankfurters. Most have their origins in countries outside the United States and are sold in the larger American cities where the population is of many origins.

Classifications of sausage types are confusing, but generally break down into whether the ground meat is fresh or cured, and whether the sausage

Courtesy of Swift and Co. (Mr. Ed Hois)

FIG. 201. HAMS BEING REMOVED FROM A CABINET-TYPE SMOKE-HOUSE

Courtesy of Swift and Co. (Mr. Ed. Hois)

FIG. 202. MECHANICAL SAWDUST BURNER AND SMOKEHOUSE CONTROLLERS

is cooked or uncooked, smoked or unsmoked, and dried or not in manufacture. Examples would be frankfurters—which generally are mildly cured, cooked, and smoked; fresh pork sausage—which is not cooked, smoked, or cured in manufacture; and Italian salami—which is cured and dried.

Many sausages are prepared within a casing. Natural casings are made from cleaned animal intestines, the different sizes being used for different types of sausages. But natural casings are expensive and nonuniform and so today artificial casings are more important. These casings are extruded tubes of Saran, Cellophane, polyethylene, or other film plastics. The casings hold the ground meat together and prevent excessive moisture and fat losses during the cooking and smoking operations. Large sausages such as bologna may have the casing removed after cooking and smoking, and then be sliced and packaged. Such products are known as table-ready-meats.

Frankfurter Manufacture.—The most important sausage product in the United States is frankfurters, and except for size its production method is the same as for bologna.

Generally franks are made from finely ground cured beef which is referred to as a frankfurter meat emulsion. The emulsion is pumped into

Courtesy of Swift and Co. (Mr. Ed Hois)

FIG. 203. FRANKFURTER EMULSION IN CONTINUOUS LENGTH OF CASING BEING LINKED AND LOADED FOR SUBSEQUENT PROCESSING

great lengths of artificial casing which is automatically twisted every six inches to form the links (Fig. 203). Following this procedure, the links are cooked by passing through hot water or steam and then hung for smoking, or smoking may precede the final cook.

Skinless franks are very popular, but they go through the same process-

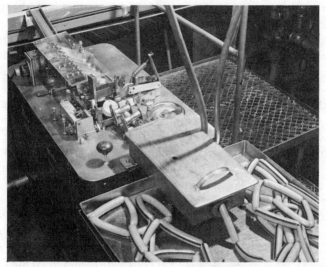

Courtesy of Swift and Co. (Mr. Ed Hois)

FIG. 204. EQUIPMENT FOR PEELING CASINGS IN MANUFACTURE
OF SKINLESS FRANKFURTERS

Courtesy of Ideal Tool and Manufacturing Co.

FIG. 205. CONTINUOUS FRANKFURTER PROCESSING EQUIPMENT

ing within casings. Then as a last step after smoking, the casing is mechanically peeled from the now congealed form, which had its shape set within the casing during cooking. Where skinless franks are to be peeled by machine (Fig. 204), the casing often is made with a black stripe so that any casings missed by the machine can be seen and peeled later by hand.

Even these mechanical operations which today dominate the frankfurter industry are somewhat cumbersome, and so new continuous frankfurter processes have appeared on the scene. One such process is the Tender-frank Process of Swift and Company. No casings are used and all operations of forming, cooking, and smoking are done as frankfurters are conveyed through the apparatus of Fig. 205. In continuous fashion the meat emulsion is injected into frank-shaped molds. The meat emulsion is coagulated in the molds with electronically generated heat. The franks are then conveyed through the tunnel in which they are smoked and then cooled, and from which they emerge for packaging at a rate of about 1000 lb per hr. This process has not yet seen wide commercial use.

Freezing of Meat

Meat may be frozen and held in frozen storage for months in the case of pork and fatty meats, and for years in the case of beef. The shorter time for pork and fatty meats is limited by gradual development of oxidized fat flavors. As with other frozen foods, quality demands that the meat be quick frozen and then not thaw and refreeze so as to rupture tissues and result in excessive bleeding and drip when the product is finally thawed and cooked. Few cured meats or sausages are commercially frozen since salt in their formulations markedly increases the rate of fat oxidation and development of rancid flavors. Further, frozen storage tends to alter the flavor of the seasoning spices used in many sausage products.

Fresh meat cuts properly wrapped store well in frozen condition but are not popular in supermarkets because the housewife likes to see and feel frost-free meats and associates quality with unfrozen bright red cuts. Satisfied, she then takes the meat home and often as not stores it in her own freezer. Restaurant operators use a great deal more frozen meat which the customer doesn't see, and the military buys great quantities, some of which is imported from Australia and New Zealand. Meat cutting in supermarkets is labor consuming, and as the cost of labor continues to increase it is to be expected that there will be a shift to more centralized meat cutting at packing plants. Then frozen meat cuts marketed at the retail level could become far more important. A new system for packaging meat cuts for freezing utilizes a special clear ionomer plastic film which is made to fit skin-tight over the meat by passing the film-enclosed meat through a vacuum chamber before heat sealing the film package. The tight conformity of the film to the meat prevents air pockets where frost could form during freezing and display. Such frozen meat cuts are reported to retain excellent color and are more attractive than when frost is evident under the wrapper. The overall quality and nutritive value of properly packaged and frozen meat are usually excellent.

A special use of freezing temperatures has to do with the destruction of the trichinosis parasite in pork products. As was stated earlier, smoking or cooking to an internal temperature of 137°F ensures destruction of the larvae of this organism. Frozen storage of pork products in accordance with the standards of temperature and time indicated in Table 47 also

TABLE 47

U. S. DEPARTMENT OF AGRICULTURE STANDARDS FOR PORK FREEZING[1]

Temperature, °F	Time for 6-In. Diam, Days	Time for 6- to 27-In. Diam, Days
+ 5	20	30
− 10	10	20
− 20	6	12

[1]From Mohler in Federal Register 5, No. 26, 615 (1940).

destroys this organism and is another recommended treatment by the U.S. Dept. of Agr. to render pork products safe. Concern over treatments for the safety of pork products is due in part to the fact that normal meat inspection practices are unable to detect the presence of trichina organisms with certainty.

Cooking of Meat

Cooking can make meat more or less tender than the original raw cut. When meat is cooked there are three tenderizing influences: fat melts and contributes to tenderness; connective collagen dissolves in the hot liquids and becomes soft gelatin; and muscle fibers separate and the tissue becomes more tender. There also are two toughening influences: overheating can cause the muscle fibers to contract and the meat to shrink and become tougher; and moisture evaporates and the dried out tissue becomes tougher.

Generally lower cooking temperatures for a longer period of time produce more tender results than higher temperatures for short periods of time to any given degree of doneness. Depending upon the cooking method this can become quite complicated, especially with the newer methods of microwave, dielectric, and infrared heating, and much research remains to be done.

As for the nutritional value of cooked meat it generally remains very high. Normal cooking procedures do little to change the high value of the meat proteins, and minerals are heat resistant. Some minerals are lost in meat drippings, but on the other hand cooking dissolves some calcium from bone and so enriches the meat in this mineral. The B vitamins are heat sensitive and so cooking to well-doneness will cause about a ten per cent greater destruction of these vitamins than cooking to the rare condition. Even to the well-done stage most meats retain about 70% of the B vitamins present in the uncooked meat.

POULTRY

In the United States, poultry types include principally chickens, turkeys, ducks, and geese, and the amounts consumed are in this order. Poultry is raised for meat and for eggs. We will first consider poultry for meat and confine discussion to chicken since much of the same technology applies to the other types of birds.

Production Considerations

Years ago most chicken meat came from egg-laying flocks, but today to satisfy the great demand for meat, special genetic strains of meat broilers are produced with optimum characteristics of rapid growth, disease resistance, and good meat qualities such as tenderness and flavor. Chicken breeds include types with white feathers and types with brown and black feathers. The white feathered types are favored for meat broilers because of the absence of dark pinfeathers and their lighter skin color which consumers prefer.

Broiler farms are often quite large and raise several million birds per year. Baby chicks are highly susceptible to many diseases and so raisers of broilers must practice a rigid husbandry with respect to bird housing, temperature and humidity control, extreme sanitation, and rigid feeding practices.

A remarkable achievement of breeders, poultry nutritionists, and feed manufacturers is that with today's advanced technology it is common to raise a 4 lb broiler in just 8 weeks with a feed conversion of 2.1 lb of feed per pound of bird. In other words a 4-lb broiler is raised from a chick on just about 8.4 lb of feed. This is one reason why chicken may be purchased for ½ or ⅓ the price of beef, which has a far less efficient feed conversion ratio.

The market classification of poultry is generally based on the bird's age and live weight. Going from smaller and younger to larger and older birds the following designations are given to chickens; broiler or fryer, roaster, capon, stag, stewing chicken, and old rooster. The tenderness of the flesh generally decreases in the same order. Broilers or fryers are

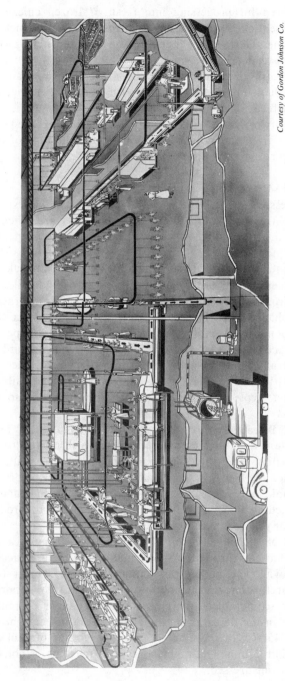

FIG. 206. JOHNSON SYSTEM OF POULTRY PROCESSING

generally preferred for processing into fresh or frozen chicken where tenderness is essential. Processors of canned chicken or chicken soup are able to use the older and tougher birds because the sterilization heat of canning usually tenderizes the meat.

Within these marketing classes there also are U.S. grade standards for quality of individual birds based on feathering, shape, fleshing, fat, and freedom from defects. There are three quality grades, namely A Quality or No. 1, B Quality or No. 2, and C Quality or No. 3. Birds are purchased by the processor from the grower depending upon the type of products he will manufacture and competitive price.

Processing Plant Operations

Plants for dressing poultry will vary in size up to the largest that can process 10,000 birds per hour. These modern plants are efficient continuous line facilities in which the birds are moved from operation to operation via monorail, as in Fig. 206. Live birds are shackled, electrically stunned, bled, scalded to facilitate feather removal, plucked of feathers, eviscerated, government inspected, washed and chilled, dried, packaged, and frozen if production calls for freezing. The operations can be partially mechanized and highly efficient in large plants since the birds purchased are remarkably uniform with respect to size, shape, weight, and other characteristics. To ensure high quality uniform birds, large processors generally contract with the growers far in advance and set up rigid specifications on the kind of bird they want. Small details on each of the processing steps in dressing the birds are important to produce optimum results.

Slaughter and Bleeding.—Birds generally are not fed for 12 hr before slaughter to ensure that their crops are empty, which makes for cleaner operations. Bleeding time depends upon efficiency of the cut, type of bird, and whether the bird was electrically stunned or not before cutting. Bleeding may take anywhere from 1 to 3 min depending upon these factors. But bleeding must be quite complete in order to produce the desirable white or yellow skin color in the final dressed bird.

Scalding.—After bleeding the birds are conveyed through a scalding tank. Scalding loosens the feathers and makes for easier plucking and pinfeather removal. The higher the temperature the shorter the time required, but careful time and temperature control is very important because at higher temperatures there is a greater danger of removal of portions of skin in the defeathering machines. Scalding may be done at 140° F in about 45 sec, or more safely with less chance of skin removal at 125° F in about 2 min. Optimum conditions must be established for the kind of bird being dressed.

Defeathering.—Defeathering is commonly done mechanically by a

Courtesy of Gordon Johnson Co.

FIG. 207. AUTOMATIC RUBBER-FINGERED FEATHER PICKER

Courtesy of Wilson and Co.

FIG. 208. EVISCERATION AND PREPARATION FOR GOVERNMENT INSPECTION

device that has a multiplicity of rotating rubber fingers (Fig. 207). This removes all but a few remaining pinfeathers which are then removed by hand.

Eviscerating.—This is generally done in a separate cool room (Fig. 208). Evisceration includes inspection of the viscera by a veterinarian or someone under his supervision. The lungs and other organs that are difficult to dislodge may be removed by suction tubes. Birds passing inspection are thoroughly washed.

Chilling.—The washed birds are now rapidly chilled from about 90° F to 35° F to prevent bacterial spoilage and to preserve quality. Chilling is done with ice slush, and the birds absorb a small amount of moisture from the slush which makes them more succulent after packaging. But the maximum allowable water pickup is fixed by law. After chilling, birds are drained of excess moisture and are sized and graded for quality.

Packaging.—The graded poultry may now be packaged as fresh poultry in boxes surrounded by crushed ice. If so, birds must be kept below 40° F and moved to retail channels rapidly since shelf-life may be only a few days. Shelf-life will depend upon the bacterial load (Fig. 209). Should this be about 10,000 organisms per square centimeter of surface, which is not uncommon, odor and slime will develop even at 40° F in about 6 days.

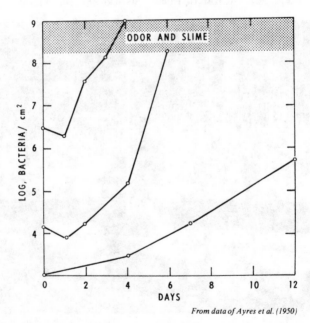

From data of Ayres et al. (1950)

Fig. 209. Effect of Initial Bacterial Load on Shelf-Life
of Chicken Meat at 40°F

To prolong storage life much poultry is individually wrapped in low moisture and low oxygen transmission films or bags and is frozen. When this is done the bags are made to fit snugly, and the birds are vacuum packed in the bags to remove all air since the fat of chicken is highly susceptible to oxidation. This type of wrapping is further described in the chapter on packaging.

Government Inspection.—The U.S. Poultry Products Inspection Act of 1957 states that all poultry sold in interstate commerce must be inspected for wholesomeness and therefore must be processed in plants having government inspection service. Poultry is inspected live prior to slaughter, during evisceration, and during or after packaging. This inspection to protect the public health is mandatory. Inspection for quality grading by USDA Agricultural Marketing Service representatives is optional to the plant owner as in the case of meat. In Fig. 210 are seen the two types of marks that may appear on poultry and represent these different forms of inspection.

Courtesy of U. S. Dept. Agr.

FIG. 210. THE U. S. DEPT. AGR. GRADE SHIELD OF QUALITY, AND INSPECTION MARK OF WHOLESOMENESS

Tenderness and Flavor

As in the case of red meats, tenderness of poultry flesh is favored by young birds, by less connective tissue as in the case of breast meat compared with thigh meat, by more fat within the tissue, and by growing birds in confined quarters without exercise as compared with exercised birds grown on open range.

In addition, as in the case of meat and fish, poultry enters into a state of rigor mortis soon after being killed. Rigor mortis is associated with a conversion of glycogen to lactic acid which has a mild preservative effect on the flesh. It is also associated with a contraction of the muscles and a stiffening of the tissues. Rigor mortis naturally subsides in poultry with a relaxation of the muscles after about ten hours or less. If poultry is cooked or frozen while the meat is in a state of rigor mortis the meat will be excessively tough, and this is avoided in good processing schedules.

The flavor of chicken meat that has not undergone spoilage is mild and pleasing. It can be intensified by the use of the chemical monosodium glutamate and this compound often is added to poultry and poultry products to enhance flavor. Chicken meat flavor also is affected by the feed received during growing. Excessive amounts of fish meal in the feed can give poultry a fishy flavor.

Contributing to tenderness and flavor, while at the same time providing added convenience during cooking, has been the development of the self-basting bird intended for roasting. This is presently more common with turkey but can also be applied to chicken. To prepare self-basting birds the manufacturer injects basting liquid at several points under the skin of the bird before packaging and freezing. The basting liquid generally contains vegetable oils, water, salt, emulsifiers, and artificial flavor and color. During roasting the basting liquid moistens the skin and flesh and contributes succulence.

Nutritive Value

The composition of the edible parts of chicken depends upon the cut and the method of cooking. Roasted white meat without the skin will contain about 64% water, 32% protein, and 3.5% fat. Roasted dark meat without the skin contains about 65% water, 28% protein, and 6% fat. The skin is higher in fat. Chicken flesh contains more protein and less fat than red meat. The protein is of excellent quality and contains all of the essential amino acids needed by man. The fat is more unsaturated than the fat of red meat and this is considered beneficial by nutritionists. Like other animal tissue, poultry flesh is a good source of B vitamins and minerals. Because of its high protein to fat ratio it is a favored food for weight watchers, older people who must restrict their intake of fat, and patients with vascular sclerotic tendencies. But poultry is also an all around excellent food from babyhood to old age.

EGGS

As with broilers for meat, special strains of chickens are bred for large scale egg production. Today, on the average, a quality hen lays about 220 eggs per year, and in the United States about 70 billion eggs are produced each year. About 90% of these are consumed as such in the form of shell eggs. The remainder is mostly frozen and dried. Most of these are used in the bakery, confectionery, and noodle industries, although there are also many minor chemical and pharmaceutical uses, especially for the egg white or albumen.

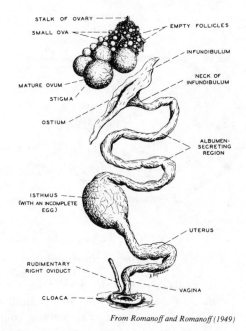

STALK OF OVARY

SMALL OVA

EMPTY FOLLICLES

INFUNDIBULUM

NECK OF INFUNDIBULUM

MATURE OVUM

STIGMA

OSTIUM

ALBUMEN-SECRETING REGION

ISTHMUS (WITH AN INCOMPLETE EGG)

UTERUS

RUDIMENTARY RIGHT OVIDUCT

CLOACA

VAGINA

From Romanoff and Romanoff (1949)

FIG. 211.   REPRODUCTIVE ORGANS OF THE HEN

Egg Formation and Structure

Eggs are produced not for man but for reproduction (Fig. 211). Yolks containing the female germ cell are formed in the chicken's ovaries. These yolks drop into the mouth of the oviduct and then slowly pass down the oviduct. As they do, they are covered with layers of egg white from albumen secreting cells, then with membranous tissue from other protein secreting cells, and finally with calcium and other minerals from mineral secreting cells near the bottom of the oviduct. This results in the egg shell.

This goes on whether the hen is fertilized or not. In fertilization, the sperm travels up the oviduct to the yolks and, if fertilization is to take place, must reach them before the albumen and shell are deposited.

This sequence of events helps to explain several defects possible in shell eggs for human food: fertilized egg yolks produce embryos; ruptures in the ovary or oviduct can produce blood spots and sometimes meat specks; diseases of the ovary or oviduct can produce infected eggs with bacteria or parasites inside a sound shell; however, the contents of eggs from a healthy bird in unbroken shells generally are sterile when freshly laid.

The structure of the egg follows from the sequence of events in the

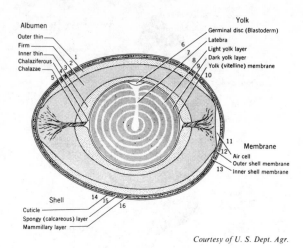

Albumen
Outer thin
Firm
Inner thin
Chalaziferous
Chalazae
1
2
3
4
5

Yolk
Germinal disc (Blastoderm)
Latebra
Light yolk layer
Dark yolk layer
Yolk (vitelline) membrane
6
7
8
9
10

11
12
Membrane
Air cell
Outer shell membrane
13
Inner shell membrane

Shell
14
15
16
Cuticle
Spongy (calcareous) layer
Mammillary layer

Courtesy of U. S. Dept. Agr.

FIG. 212.   STRUCTURE OF THE HEN'S EGG

oviduct (Fig. 212). The central yolk is surrounded by a membrane called the vitelline membrane. Immediately beyond this is another membranous layer known as the chalaziferous layer. The yolk is connected to thick or firm albumen by two extensions of the chalaziferous layer called chalazas. The yolk further is surrounded by layers of thin and thick albumen, and outside of these by another layer of thin albumen. This is surrounded by the shell which has two inside shell membranes and an outer protective layer known as cuticle or "bloom."

The shell is porous which allows for gases to pass in and out of the egg for the developing embryo in the case of a fertilized egg. On ageing, as air enters through the shell, the air cell at the blunt end between the shell membrane and the shell enlarges; a large air cell is an indication of storage and less fresh quality. When eggs are washed the cuticle or bloom on the outside is removed exposing the open pores of the egg shell. Under these conditions bacteria can more easily enter the egg contents through the shell pores.

Composition

Eggs contain about 2 parts white to 1 part yolk by weight. The whole mixed egg contains about 65% water, 12% protein, and 11% fat. But the compositions of the white and the yolk differ considerably. Virtually all of the fat is in the yolk, and when eggs are separated into white and yolk we want to keep it this way since small amounts of fat adversely affect the whipping property of egg white. The 12% solids of egg white is virtually all protein (Table 48). The yolk is rich in fat soluble vitamins A, D, E, and K and in phospholipids including the emulsifier lecithin.

TABLE 48

CHEMICAL COMPOSITION OF THE HEN'S EGG[1]

Fraction	%	% of Constituents			
		Water	Protein	Fat	Ash
Whole egg	100	65.5	11.8	11.0	11.7
White	58	88.0	11.0	0.2	0.8
Yolk	31	48.0	17.5	32.5	2.0
		calcium carbonate	magnesium carbonate	calcium phosphate	organic matter
Shell	11	94.0	1.0	1.0	4.0

[1]From U.S. Dept. Agr. Agricultural Handbook 75.

Nutritionally, eggs are a good source of fat, protein, vitamins, and minerals, especially iron.

Quality Factors

Eggs may range in size from Peewee to Jumbo classifications but quality grades are independent of size.

The most common method of grading eggs is by candling, in which the egg is held up to a light source. Candling will reveal many defects such as a cracked shell, a fertilized yolk, a blood spot, an enlarged air cell, firmness of white which becomes thinner on ageing, and position of yolk which tends to drift off center when the egg becomes stale. The extent of staleness also can be seen in broken out eggs (previous Fig. 66). Fresh eggs have a high yolk rather than a flat yolk and a larger amount of thick white relative to runny thin white. This causes a stale egg to spread out over a larger area than a fresh egg. Egg quality grades are based largely on these measures of freshness, since fresher eggs taste better, are nutritionally superior, are easier to separate into whites and yolks for manufacturing purposes, and perform better in whipping and baking applications.

The shell color of eggs depends upon the breed of chicken, but the yolk color depends largely upon the chicken's feed. Feeds high in carotenoids produce darker yolks, which are favored in some markets and in food manufacture to give a golden color to baked goods and products like noodles and mayonnaise.

Egg Storage

Because there is an abundance of eggs produced in the spring of the year eggs must be stored. Fresh eggs to be frozen or dried also may be stored before such processing. Storage is best at a temperature slightly above the freezing point of the egg. A temperature of 30° F in warehouses is ideal; to minimize moisture loss from eggs the relative humidity may be as high as 90%. In proper cold storage Grade A quality can be maintained for as long as six months. Immediately after laying, and during storage, eggs lose carbon dioxide through the porous shell, making the eggs more alkaline. The loss of carbon dioxide also is associated with the staling process, and some lengthening of storage stability can be achieved by storing the eggs under carbon dioxide to minimize carbon dioxide loss.

More common, however, is the practice of dipping eggs to be stored in a light mineral oil. This closes the pores of the egg shell and retards both carbon dioxide and moisture loss. Another method of prolonging storage life is known as thermostabilization. The eggs are dipped in hot water or hot oil for a brief period to coagulate a thin layer of albumen around the inside of the shell and thus further seal it. The heat also kills some of the surface bacteria.

Bacterial Infection

As stated earlier, the contents of freshly laid eggs generally are sterile. However, the shell surface will contain many bacteria, especially when the shell becomes soiled with chicken droppings. Even if the shell is not cracked it can be permeable to invasion of bacteria through the natural shell pores. When eggs are washed the shell cuticle is easily removed. If washing is not complete and the eggs are not dried then bacteria are especially likely to pass via the water through the shell. If the eggs are washed with warm water, increased temperature can make gases within the shell expand and escape through the pores. Then when the egg cools, a reduced pressure can result within the shell. This tends to draw bacteria and moisture from a wet shell into the egg through the pores. When there are sufficient bacteria the egg may rot. Cracked shells are obviously worse.

A particular group of bacteria belonging to the genus *Salmonella* is pathogenic to man and is found in chicken droppings. It is extremely difficult to keep *Salmonella* organisms out of egg products and *Salmonella* infected eggs have caused numerous outbreaks of disease in man.

Pasteurization.—Because of the prevalence of *Salmonella* infections, U.S. food laws and the laws of several other countries now require that all commercial eggs broken out of the shell for manufacturing use be pasteurized. This is a new law in the United States, having been extended to egg white in 1966. Pasteurization of whole egg and egg yolk had been practiced for many years but this was not the case with egg white. Egg white especially is very sensitive to heat being easily coagulated very near efficient pasteurization temperatures, and for this reason an effective pasteurization treatment with minimal damage to the egg white was slow in being developed. The current pasterurization conditions for egg white or whole egg in the United States involve heating to the range of 140°

to 143° F and holding for periods of 3.5 to 4.0 min. Egg white also may be pasteurized at lower temperatures of 125° to 127° F combined with hydrogen peroxide. In one method the liquid whites are heated to this temperature and held for 1.5 min. Hydrogen peroxide at a level of 0.075 to 0.10% is metered into the egg white which is held at 125° to 127° F for 2 min. more. The hydrogen peroxide is then broken down to water and oxygen by the addition of the enzyme catalase. Pasteurization processes may vary, but the eggs must be *Salmonella*-free and meet other bacteriological standards.

Freezing Eggs

Large quantities of eggs for food manufacturing use are preserved by freezing. This is not done in the shell but rather with the liquid contents of the egg which may be frozen as the whole egg or separated into yolk and white or various mixtures of yolk and white for special food uses.

Freezing plants generally are combined with egg breaking facilities. The egg breaking section of the plant receives eggs, may wash and dry them, and then breaks the egg contents from the shell (Fig. 213).

Operators do this by striking the shell against a knife edge and letting the contents drop into a whole egg cup. If separation of whites and yolks is desired, then the contents are dropped over a small teaspoon-like yolk cup suspended over two larger cups. The yolk settles in the small yolk cup and the white overflows into the egg white cup below. A ring is brought

Courtesy of Tranin Egg Co.

FIG. 213. HAND-OPERATED BREAKING ROOM FORMERLY USED BY TRANIN EGG CO.

down over the small yolk cup to sever any white that adheres. The yolk is then flipped into the larger yolk cup below. After three eggs have been broken into the cups below the cups are sniffed for evidence of bacterial spoilage. Good eggs are transferred to collection pails.

In modern plants this hand breaking operation has been almost entirely replaced by automatic egg breaking machines (Fig. 213A). Where one operator can break and separate 60 to 90 doz eggs per hour by hand, an operator-inspector can break and separate 600 doz eggs per hour with these automatic machines. The operator-inspector also performs the very important function of rejecting spoiled eggs, one of which can ruin hundreds of pounds of good product. The common bacteria that are found in bad eggs generally fluoresce under ultraviolet light. This property has been used to help identify eggs to be rejected.

FIG. 213A. A BATTERY OF NINE SEYMOUR EGG BREAKING MACHINES.

The whole or separated eggs are now mixed for uniformity, screened to remove chalaza, membranes, or bits of shell, pasteurized, and placed in 10- or 30-lb cans or other suitable containers for freezing. Freezing generally is done in a sharp freezer room with circulating air at $-20°$ F. Freezing may take from about 48 to 72 hr.

Egg white and whole egg may be frozen as such, but egg yolk may not be frozen without additives since by itself it becomes gummy and thick, a condition known as gelation. Gelation of egg yolk on freezing is prevented by the addition of sugar or salt at a level of 10%, or addition of glycerin at a level of 5%. Sugar yolk is the product that goes to bakers, confectioners, and other users that can tolerate sugar in their end products, while mayonnaise manufacturers may use salt yolk. These ingredients may be dissolved in the yolk during mixing and prior to screening.

Dried Eggs

The whites, yolks, or whole eggs after pasteurization may be dried by any of several methods including spray drying, tray drying, foam drying, or freeze drying. Egg white contains traces of glucose. Whichever dehydration method is used, on drying or during subsequent storage at temperatures much above freezing the glucose combines with egg proteins and the Maillard browning reaction occurs. This discolors the dried egg white. It has been found possible to prevent this browning reaction by removing glucose through fermentation by yeasts or with commercial enzymes. This is known as desugaring and is a step practiced prior to the drying of all egg white.

BIBLIOGRAPHY

AMERICAN MEAT INSTITUTE FOUNDATION. 1960. The Science of Meat and Meat Products. W. H. Freeman & Co., San Francisco, Calif.

ANON. 1960. Food Composition Tables. FAO, Rome.

ANON. 1965. Manual of Meat Inspection Procedures. U.S. Dept. Agr.

ANON. 1967. Regulations governing the grading and inspection of egg products. U.S. Dept. Agr., Agr. Marketing Serv. Effective Jan. 1, 1967.

AYRES, J. C., OGILVY, W. S., and STEWART, G. F. 1950. Postmortem changes in stored meats. I. Microorganisms associated with development of slime on eviscerated cut-up poultry, Food Technol. 4, 199–205.

BERGQUIST, D. H. 1973. Eggs. In Food Dehydration, 2nd Edition, Vol. 2. W. B. Van Arsdel, M. J. Copley and A. I. Morgan, Jr. (Editors). Avi Publishing Co., Westport, Conn.

BRANDLY, P. J., MIGAKI, G., and TAYLOR, K. E. 1966. Meat Hygiene, 3rd Edition. Lea and Febiger, Philadelphia.

BRATZLER, L. J. 1968. The preparation for freezing and freezing of meats. In The Freezing Preservation of Foods, 4th Edition, Vol. 3. D. K. Tressler, W. B. Van Arsdel, and M. J. Copley (Editors). Avi Publishing Co., Westport, Conn.

BRISSEY, G. E., and GOESER, P. A. 1963. Aging, curing and smoking of meats. In Food Processing Operations, Vol. 1. M. A. Joslyn, and J. L. Heid (Editors). Avi Publishing Co., Westport, Conn.

BROOKS, J., and TAYLOR, D. J. 1955. Eggs and egg products. Gr. Brit. Dept. Sci. Ind. Res., Food Invest. Spec. Rept. 60. Her Majesty's Stationery Office, London.

CLINGER, C., YOUNG, A., PRUDENT, I., and WINTER, A. R. 1951. The influence of pasteurization, freezing, and storage on the functional properties of egg white. Food Technol. 5, 166–170.

FORSYTHE, R., and MIYAHARA, T. 1959. The use of modern egg solids in baking. Baker's Dig. 33, No. 2, 57–86.

GOESER, P. A., and URBAIN, W. M. 1963. Cattle, hogs and sheep. In Food Processing Operations, Vol. 2. M. A. Joslyn, and J. L. Heid (Editors). Avi Publishing Co., Westport, Conn.

GRISWOLD, R. M. 1962. The Experimental Study of Foods. Houghton Mifflin Co., Boston, Mass.

JENSEN, L. B. 1954. Microbiology of Meats, 3rd Edition. Garrard Press, Champaign, Ill.

KAHLENBERG, O. J., and GORMAN, J. M. 1968. The preparation for freezing and freezing of eggs. *In* The Freezing Preservation of Foods, 4th Edition, Vol. 3. D. K. Tressler, W. B. Van Arsdel, and M. J. Copley (Editors). Avi Publishing Co., Westport, Conn.

KARMAS, E. 1970. Fresh Meat Processing 1970. Food Process. Rev. *12*. Noyes Data Corp., Park Ridge, N.J.

KARMAS, E. 1970. Meat Product Manufacture 1970. Food Process. Rev. *14*. Noyes Data Corp., Park Ridge, N.J.

KARMAS, E. 1972. Sausage Processing 1972. Food Process. Rev. *24*. Noyes Data Corp., Park Ridge, N.J.

KLOSE, A. A. 1968. Poultry: processing and freezing. *In* The Freezing Preservation of Foods, 4th Edition, Vol. 3. D. K. Tressler, W. B. Van Arsdel, and M. J. Copley (Editors). Avi Publishing Co., Westport, Conn.

KLOSE, A. A., and OLCOTT, H. S. 1964. Meat, poultry, and sea foods. *In* Food Dehydration, Vol. 2. W. B. Van Arsdel, and M. J. Copley (Editors). Avi Publishing Co., Westport, Conn.

LEVIE, A. 1970. The Meat Handbook, 3rd Edition. Avi Publishing Co., Westport, Conn.

MILLARES, R., and FELLERS, C. R. 1949. Vitamin and amino acid content of processed chicken meat products. Food Res. *14*, 131–143.

MOHLER, F. L. 1940. U.S. Dept. Agr. standards for pork freezing. Federal Register *5*, No. 26, 615.

MOUNTNEY, G. J. 1966. Poultry Products Technology. Avi Publishing Co., Westport, Conn.

NIVEN, C. F., JR. 1951. Influence of microbes upon the color of meats. Am. Meat Inst. Found. Circ. *2*.

NORTH, M. O. 1972. Commercial Chicken Production Manual. Avi Publishing Co., Westport, Conn.

ROMANOFF, A. L., and ROMANOFF, A. J. 1949. The Avian Egg. John Wiley & Sons, New York.

SCHWEIGERT, B. S. 1953. Meat in human nutrition. Am. Meat Inst. Found. Circ. *8*.

SELTZER, E. 1961. Importance of selection and processing method for successful freeze-drying of chicken. Food Technol. *15*, No. 7, 18, 20, 22.

STEWART, G. F., HANSON, H. L., and LOWE, B. 1945. Effects of aging, freezing rate, and storage period on palatability of broilers. Food Res. *10*, 16–27.

STRANDINE, E. J. 1963. Poultry production and processing. *In* Food Processing Operations, Vol. 2. M. A. Joslyn, and J. L. Heid (Editors). Avi Publishing Co., Westport, Conn.

STRANDINE, E. J., KOONZ, C. H., and RAMSBOTTOM, J. M. 1949. A study of variations in muscles of beef and chicken. J. Animal Sci. *8*, 483–494.

STRINGER, W. C., BILSKIE, M. E., and NAUMANN, H. D. 1969. Microbial profiles of fresh beef. Food Technol. *23*, 97–102.

U.S. DEPT. AGR. 1964. Egg Grading Manual. USDA Agr. Handbook *75*.

U.S. DEPT. AGR. 1966. The destruction of Salmonellae. Rept. Western Experiment Station Collaborators Conference. USDA Agr. Res. Serv. *ARS 74–34*, Albany, Calif.

U.S. DEPT. AGR., CONSUMER MARKETING SERV., POULTRY DIV. 1966. Regulations governing the grading and inspection of poultry and edible products thereof and U.S. classes, standards, and grades with respect thereto. Aug. 1.

VAN ARSDEL, W. B., COPLEY, M. J., and MORGAN, A. I., JR. (Editors) 1973. Food Dehydration, 2nd Edition, Vol. 1 and 2. Avi Publishing Co., Westport, Conn.

WALKER, H. W., and AYRES, J. C. 1956. Incidence and kinds of microorganisms associated with commercially dressed poultry. Appl. Microbiol. *4*, 345–349.

WATTS, B. M. 1962. Meat Products *In* Symposium on Foods: Lipids and Their Oxidation. H. W. Schultz, E. A. Day, and R. O. Sinnhuber (Editors). Avi Publishing Co., Westport, Conn.

WEISS, G. H. 1971. Poultry Processing 1971. Food Process. Rev. *20*. Noyes Data Corp., Park Ridge, N.J.

WILCOX, G. 1971. Eggs, Cheese and Yogurt Processing 1971. Food Process. Rev. *17*. Noyes Data Corp., Park Ridge, N.J.

WINTER, A. R., and FUNK, E. M. 1951. Poultry Science and Practice. J. B. Lippincott Co., Philadelphia.

ZABIK, M. E., and FIGA, J. E. 1968. Comparison of frozen, foam-spray-dried, freeze-dried, and spray-dried eggs. Food Technol. *22*, 1169–1175.

CHAPTER 15

Seafoods

INTRODUCTION

Our principal seafoods are made up of salt water fish, some fresh water lake fish, and salt water shellfish and crustaceans such as shrimp, lobster, and crab. These natural foods also are converted into great quantities of manufactured or processed seafoods, most of which are frozen or canned. Examples are the popular precooked, breaded, and frozen fish sticks, fillets, and shrimp, as well as canned tuna, salmon, and sardines. In addition, smaller quantities of fish are salted, smoked, pickled, or dried. Currently Americans consume about 11 lb of fish per capita per year, which is below 8% of their meat consumption, but in several other parts of the world the picture is reversed. The U.S. consumption of ocean products far exceeds the domestic catch, and it has been estimated that if this trend continues about 70% of the seafoods consumed in the United States by 1980 will be from imports.

There are about 50 major species of fish, shellfish, and crustaceans available to Americans throughout the year varying with the season. For the last 15 yr or so the two most important kinds on an economic basis have been shrimp and tuna with shrimp currently in the lead. The trend is toward still greater consumption of shrimp, shellfish, and fish processed by freezing and canning, while consumption of fresh fish and fish cured by smoking, salting, and pickling is decreasing.

Americans consume only certain parts of most fish, principally the muscles. Remaining parts plus enormous quantities of menhaden, a fish not used for human food, go into animal and poultry feeds and pet foods. This represents about 50% of the weight of the fish catch, some of which man gets back indirectly in the forms of flesh and eggs.

FISH PROCUREMENT

The procurement of fish for food represents a unique phenomenon in modern food gathering and has great significance upon quality of fish. In our modern agriculture we have considerable control over plants and animals. We harvest and slaughter at times and in places largely of our own choosing. Hogs and cattle are fattened under our control and then brought to the place of slaughter according to schedule so that subsequent processing and refrigeration may follow immediately under optimized conditions. Not so with most fish. While we do "farm" some oysters,

424

lobsters, and some trout in hatcheries, most fish are pursued and hunted and may be caught hundreds of miles from adequate processing facilities. These fish may lie in the fishing vessel for a week or two poorly iced, which generally is insufficient refrigeration, before being returned to port. Such "fresh fish" is not fresh at all, its quality is quite poor and becomes much worse before it reaches the consumer. This is aggravated by the fact that fish tissue is generally more perishable than most animal tissue under any circumstances, for reasons which will be indicated farther on.

Years ago the waters of the Americas and other coastal nations were only lightly fished by small boats. Fish were plentiful and boats returned to port in a day or so. Under such conditions iced fish could be of high quality. In more recent years with the North Sea and the North Atlantic waters rapidly becoming fished out, due to sonar and other electronic devices for locating fish, and large trawler operations, vessels must travel farther out, e.g., into the Arctic waters to find fish. Under such conditions since fish would have to remain in the ship's hold for three weeks or more, the need to prevent spoilage by processing on board has become essential.

Figure 214 is a sketch of a typical ocean-going fishing trawler that can stay at sea for about 80 days. Ships such as this may have automatic equipment for eviscerating and cleaning fish and for converting livers to fish oil. They also have filleting machines, quick freezing facilities, and fish meal processing plants to convert less edible portions of the fish to by-products. This is the current trend in the fishing industry of major fishing countries and will improve fish quality in the years ahead. Unfortunately, the United States has only a few vessels so equipped. As yet, most of the fishing boats are small, and the major current problems of the food scientist in the area of seafoods are related to maintaining fresh fish quality.

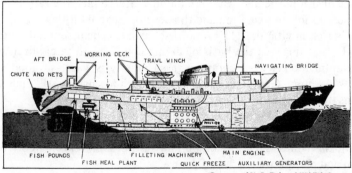

Courtesy of U. S. Fish and Wildlife Service

FIG. 214. OCEAN GOING FISHING TRAWLER WITH FACILITIES FOR PROCESSING AT SEA

MARINE FISH

One useful division of salt water fish separates them into two groups that are found in different depths of water, and correlated with this are great differences in the fish's fat content. Thus there is the group which is found in the middle and surface water layers of the sea. This group is called pelagic fish and includes such important types as herring, mackerel, salmon, tuna, sardines, and anchovies. This group includes many of the fatty fish which in some instances have muscle containing 20% fat. The other group is found at or near the bottom of the sea ordinarily on the continental shelves. This group is called demersal fish and includes cod, haddock, whiting, flat fish such as flounder and halibut, ocean perch, shrimp, oysters, clams, and crab. Demersal fish usually have less than 5% fat and often less than 1% fat in the muscle. This big difference between pelagic and demersal fish should be appreciated by dieters.

Composition and Nutrition

The composition and nutritional properties of the edible muscle of fish of a given species are quite variable depending upon season of the year, degree of maturity, and other factors. The herring, for example, may vary in muscle fat from about 8 to 20% with changes in the season and available food supply. The compositions of most fish will fall in the ranges of about 18 to 35% total solids, 14 to 20% protein, 0.2 to 20% fat, and 1.0 to 1.8% ash (previous Table 46).

Nutritionally, fish proteins are of a very high degree of digestibility and are at least as good as red meat with respect to content of essential amino acids. Consequently, the most important function of fish in all major fish-eating countries of the world is to provide high quality protein.

The fats of fish also are readily digestible and rich in unsaturated fatty acids, and so nutritionists and physicians frequently emphasize the importance of fish in the diet. But like all unsaturated fats, the fats of fish are highly susceptible to oxidation and the development of off-flavors.

Fish is rich in vitamins. The fat of fish is an excellent source of vitamins A and D, and this was the basis of giving cod liver oil to children before multivitamin tablets were common. Fish muscle is a fair to good source of the B vitamins. Generally shellfish and crustaceans are still richer in B vitamins than finny fish.

Sea fish are a good source of important minerals and an excellent source of iodine in particular. Fish are lower in iron than most meats. Canned fish with the bones, such as salmon and sardines, are excellent sources of calcium and phosphorus.

Spoilage Factors

It was stated that fish tissue generally is more perishable than animal tissue, and this is true even under conditions of refrigerated handling. Beyond this generalization it is really quite difficult to make broad statements in terms of storage life of freshly caught fish because of the many variables that are encountered. Differences in tissue compositions of species, influence of season of the year on these compositions, differences between fresh and salt water fish and the effects of salt on the normal microflora of these fish, and varying procurement and holding practices on board fishing vessels are among these variables. Further, there presently are no rigid criteria which adequately separate such terms as truly "fresh," "good," or "acceptable." Certainly fish quality begins to change as soon as it is taken from the water, and "fresh" fish that is quite acceptable commercially is not fully the equivalent of the product when caught.

Data in Table 49 reflect commerical acceptability. Freshly caught fish at a moderate temperature of 60°F remains good for only one day or less.

TABLE 49

STABILITY OF SOME FISH PRODUCTS

| Product | Approximate Number of Days Remaining in Good Condition | |
	At 32°F [1]	At 60°F
Fresh cod	14	1
Fresh salmon	12	1
Fresh halibut	14	1
Finnan haddie	28	2
Kippers	28	2
Salt herring	1 yr	3 to 4 mo
Dried salt cod	1 yr	4 to 6 mo

[1] Assuming fish are immediately iced and never allowed to warm up.

On ice at 32°F finny fish may remain good for periods up to about 14 days, but this is not true of all species. In contrast, beef may be aged at 35°F for several weeks to improve its texture and flavor. Even with mild salting and smoking, as in the case of finnan haddie and kippers, the fish may remain good at 32°F for only a few weeks. Heavy salting and drying will of course preserve fish for long periods, but in the United States these forms of fish are not favored and frozen and canned products are preferred. There are several important reasons why fresh fish spoil rapidly, and these are microbiological, physiological, and chemical in origin.

Microbiological.—While the flesh of healthy live fish is bacteriologically sterile, there are large numbers of many types of bacteria in the surface slime and digestive tracts of living fish. When the fish is killed these bacteria rapidly attack all constitutents of the tissues. Furthermore, since these bacteria live on the cold blooded fish at rather low ocean temperatures they are well adapted to cold and continue to grow even under common refrigeration conditions.

Physiological.—Fish struggle when caught and use up virtually all of the glycogen in their muscles. When killed there is little glycogen left to be converted to lactic acid, and so preservative action from muscle lactic acid to slow bacterial growth is limited. This is in contrast to animal meat where animals are rested before slaughter to build up glycogen reserves.

Chemical.—Associated with the fat of fish are phospholipids rich in trimethylamine. Trimethylamine split from phospholipids by bacteria and natural fish enzymes has a strong fishy odor. In fact this is what gives fish much of its characteristic fishy odor. It is interesting to note that fish as taken from the water have little or no odor. Yet virtually all fish products that we encounter have a fishy odor and this is evidence of some deterioration. The fishy odor from liberated trimethylamine is then further augmented by odorous products of fat degradation. The fats of fish are highly unsaturated and become easily oxidized. This results in additional oxidized and rancid off-odors and -flavors.

Preservation Methods

With such a great tendency of fish toward spoilage we would expect a number of methods of preservation to have received consideration, and this is so. The earliest methods were curing with smoke and salt and subsequent drying. This is effective, but except for limited specialty items most Americans do not like highly salted or smoked fish as a major item in their diet.

Chemical preservatives can prolong storage life of fish, and chemicals such as mild acids, sodium benzoate, and the fumigant gas ethylene oxide have been used, but these are not permitted as preservatives for fish in most countries. In the United States, the antibiotic aureomycin had been allowed in low levels, and when used the practice had been to incorporate aureomycin into the ice used for packing fish on shipboard and in transit. The melting ice then held down bacterial growth. But this application is now prohibited in line with the government's continuing program to limit use of physiologically active chemicals in foods.

In recent years irradiation with Cobalt 60 to pasteurization doses has received much interest as an effective means of prolonging storage life of fresh refrigerated fish by additional periods of about 2 to 3 weeks. Experimental irradiation facilities have been operated at the port of Gloucester, Massachusetts and other locations to determine commercial feasibility and to establish data to support petition to the FDA for this irradiation application. But by far the current methods of greatest importance in preserving quality fish products still are freezing and canning.

Shipboard Operations

Freezing can give excellent or poor quality results depending upon how quickly the freezing is done after the fish is caught and upon freezing and storage temperatures. Ideally, fish should be gutted and frozen within two hours of being caught, and they should be frozen down to –20° F or below and held at this temperature. Unfortunately this is difficult to accomplish at sea, and even supermarket frozen food cabinets generally are not held below the 0° F to 5° F range.

When fish are not processed and hard-frozen on board ship, and they generally are not except on the newer floating factory-type vessels, they commonly are stored with layers of ice at 32° F or in refrigerated chilled sea water at about 30° F. When the catch is held this way for a week or longer it is no longer truly fresh on arrival at port. In Fig. 215 halibut is

Courtesy of U. S. Fish and Wildlife Service

FIG. 215. UNLOADING HALIBUT FROM THE COLD HOLD OF A FISHING
VESSEL

seen being unloaded from the cold hold of a fishing vessel. Not all fish held on ice or in chilled sea water is gutted on board ship, frequently this is done when the fish reaches port. Tuna often are chilled in ship brine wells down to 10° F ungutted. This partially freezes the fish. The tuna are then thawed and gutted several weeks later in processing plants.

Processing Plant Operations

Some fish processing plants are located at dockside. When they are not the fish are packed with ice in wooden boxes and sent to the processing plant where the fish are washed, gutted if not previously done, and then scaled, skinned, or filleted. There are machines for gutting, skinning, and

Courtesy of Pacific Fisherman

FIG. 216.   FISH FILLETING LINE

filleting but much of this work is still done by hand since machines need to be set for a given size of fish and size varies considerably (Fig. 216).

Freezing.—Fillets may be wrapped a few to a package for retail trade or packaged in sizable boxes and then frozen. The small packages may be frozen in contact freezers of the type used to freeze retail portions of vegetables. The large boxes are frozen in room and tunnel blast freezers, preferably to a temperature of −20° F or below.

Cleaned whole fish also are frozen in the round (Fig. 217). This often is done with the larger fish, which after freezing are sawed perpendicular to their length into fish steaks of which salmon and halibut are the most popular. When individual fish are frozen they are usually glazed. The dippings and freezings may be repeated several times to build up a thick glaze to protect the frozen fish within from surface oxidation and from freezer burn during frozen storage. Glazing also is practiced with frozen shrimp. When steaks are cut from large frozen fish the newly cut surfaces are sometimes glazed to improve their keeping quality. All glazed frozen fish still require protective packaging in wrapping materials that are air- and moisture-tight.

Today much fish goes into the preparation of prebreaded, precooked, and frozen fish sticks and individual fish portions. Generally the fish fillets that were block frozen in large boxes are used for this and they are cut to fish stick or portion size on band saws from the frozen blocks. The frozen por-

Courtesy of Pacific Fisherman

FIG. 217.   FROZEN FISH BEING STACKED IN COLD STORAGE ROOM

tions are then battered and breaded and automatically conveyed to deep fat fryers (Fig. 218). The fried pieces are then cooled, packaged, and re-frozen.

The storage life of quality frozen fish further depends upon its fat content. High quality, low-fat fish stored in the frozen state at –5° F to – 10° F may retain its quality for as long as two years.

Canning Fish.—While high-fat fish do not store as well as low-fat fish in the frozen state, the oily fish are most suitable for canning. Important

Courtesy of J. W. Greer

FIG. 218.   FISH PORTIONS BEING BREADED PRIOR TO FRYING

Courtesy of Starkist Foods, Inc.

FIG. 219.   RAW TUNA BEING MOVED INTO PRECOOKER

Courtesy of Starkist Foods, Inc.

FIG. 220.   LIGHT AND DARK MEAT BEING SEPARATED FROM
PRECOOKED TUNA

examples are salmon, tuna, sardines, and herring. In the case of salmon, tuna, and sardines, additional fish or vegetable oil commonly is added to the fish prior to can closure.

Very briefly the canned tuna operation involves the following steps:

(1) Thaw the partially frozen tuna received from the fishing vessel.

(2) Eviscerate, clean, and sort tuna for size.

(3) Precook whole tuna in steam ovens (Fig. 219) to soften flesh for easy separation.

(4) Let cool overnight, and then separate the light and the dark colored meat (Fig. 220). The white meat gets the premium price, and the separation is still largely a hand operation which may involve 100 workers in a large plant.

(5) The tuna meat is now compacted by machine into a cylindrical shape and portions are cut off and automatically filled into cans.

(6) Salt and vegetable oil are added to the cans.

(7) The cans are vacuum sealed and sterilized in a retort. The color of the flesh may darken somewhat due to browning reactions on heating.

The canned product has a shelf-life of several years.

THE MERCURY PROBLEM

Mercury occurs at varying levels in the soil, in rocks, in bodies of fresh water, and in the sea. It may occur in both water-soluble and relatively insoluble forms. In bodies of water near certain types of industrial manufacturing operations mercury levels may be unnaturally high due to industrial pollution. But even without such pollution remote inland lakes and the oceans always have contained substantial quantities of mercury, and it has been estimated that natural processes, such as the weathering of rocks and erosion, carry mercury to the ocean in an amount equal to 2.5×10^6 kg/year. For the mercury concentrations of sea water, figures ranging from 0.03 to 2.0 parts per billion have been published, depending upon area, depth, and other factors. The mean mercury content of sea water has been reported at 0.15 ppb.

Plants, animals, and fish also accumulate different levels of mercury in their tissues. In the case of fish this depends not only upon the level of mercury in the water, but also on the type of fish, its natural food chain, and the age of the fish. Older and larger fish of a given species tend to be higher in mercury content, believed due to the longer time they have had to concentrate it in their tissues from their food supply. Because mercury in sufficient concentration is toxic, the regulatory agencies of various countries have set upper limits of mercury permitted in foods. In the case of fish, the U.S. Food and Drug Administration's recommended maximum level for mercury has been 0.5 ppm. In some other countries this level is higher.

Such levels are established on the basis of toxicological data plus an appropriate safety factor. At the present time, however, no one knows the absolute threshold level that is toxic in man.

In 1970 a Canadian scientist discovered high concentrations of mercury in certain species of freshwater fish. As a result Canadian and U.S. authorities banned commercial and sport fishing in several lakes and rivers. Later in the year an American scientist discovered levels of mercury in excess of 0.5 ppm in some commercial cans of tuna and in frozen swordfish steaks. Promptly a million cans of tuna and most frozen swordfish were taken off the American market. Subsequent intensive testing revealed that only a small fraction of commercial tuna contained mercury in excess of 0.5 ppm. However, it was found that 95% of 853 samples of swordfish contained greater than 0.5 ppm, with levels in excess of 1.0 ppm not uncommon. Many other species of salt water fish have been tested including cod, salmon, halibut, haddock, hake, herring, mackerel, perch, sardine, shrimp, and others, without finding high levels of mercury.

In mid-1971 the FDA warned consumers to stop eating swordfish and the swordfish industry in the United States essentially ceased to exist. Tuna stocks that contained greater than 0.5 ppm of mercury have been removed from commercial outlets, and currently tuna is inspected for mercury as it is packed.

The above events have focused attention on the mercury contents of other foods, as well as the need for more information on the toxicology of mercury and its compounds. Research also has been initiated on possible means of rendering mercury less harmful to humans.

SHELLFISH

The term shellfish as generally used refers to the true shellfish, such as oysters and clams, as well as the crustaceans. The high degree of perishability of the finny fish is shared by the shellfish, except that most shellfish are even more perishable. Lobsters and crabs, for example, are best kept alive up to the point of their cooking or freezing, otherwise they deteriorate in quality in a matter of a day or less.

Shrimp

The most important seafood in the United States from an economic standpoint is shrimp. These are caught in large trawling nets mostly near U.S. coastal waters of the South Atlantic, Pacific, and the Gulf of Mexico. Many are frozen in the raw state and in the breaded and precooked condition. Many are canned and freeze-dried.

After capture heads are removed, the sooner the better the quality. This often is done on the shrimp boats. The landed iced shrimp are then unloaded at the processing plant (Fig. 221) where they are washed and

Courtesy of U. S. Bureau of Commercial Fisheries

FIG. 221. UNLOADING SHRIMP AT GULF COAST PROCESSING PLANT

sorted according to size. They then may be inspected, packed, and frozen in the shell without deveining. On the other hand, shrimp for breading and precooking prior to freezing are automatically peeled of shell and mechanically deveined by splitting and washing out the vein-like intestine.

Shrimp should be consumed or processed within five days of being caught even though they are iced. In addition to continued bacterial activity the iced shrimp will darken in color and may become black due to natural enzymatic action. This common darkening is seen in Fig. 222 where the shrimp on the right were held on ice for five days before being frozen. The light colored shrimp on the left were frozen immediately after catching. Shrimp quality is especially favored by very rapid freezing, such as is achieved with liquid nitrogen. Texture, color, and flavor are superior and drip loss is minimized when cryogenic freezing is used. However, these advantages are largely lost when shrimp are frozen by slower methods at sea and held on ice prior to arrival at the processing plant. To avoid this some processors are supplying liquid nitrogen to the shrimp boats. The pH of shrimp tissue is a fairly good index of shrimp quality. Freshly caught shrimp has a flesh pH of about 7.2, which increases even in ice storage. Quality remains generally good up to a pH of about 7.7. Above a pH of 7.9 the shrimp become progressively spoiled.

Oysters and Clams

These shellfish remain essentially fixed in their environments and are harvested by raking the bottom or digging from the mud close to shore.

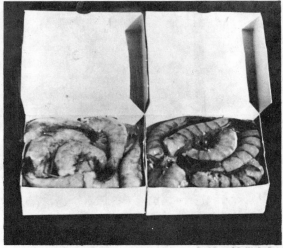

Courtesy of C. W. DuBois

FIG. 222. SHRIMP DARKEN IF HELD BEFORE FREEZING: LEFT—
FROZEN IMMEDIATELY AFTER CATCHING; RIGHT—ICED FIVE
DAYS BEFORE FREEZING

The U.S. oyster industry is concentrated in the Chesapeake Bay area and
Long Island Sound, with lesser amounts of oysters coming from coastal
waters of the South Atlantic and the North Pacific States. The clam industry is more widely scattered along the entire seacoast.

Live oysters and clams are removed from the shell by hand (Fig. 223),
washed, sorted for size, and then further processed. Processing may simply
involve packing in cans or jars and shipping in ice to market. Oysters and
clams also are canned and sterilized in retorts, and to a lesser extent are
frozen. The frozen products may later be used in the manufacture of stews
and chowders.

When the shore from which clams or oysters are taken is near a city
the water can be polluted from sewage waste. This is particularly serious
because oysters and clams frequently are eaten raw with no heat treatment
to inactivate pathogenic organisms that these shellfish may carry. Outbreaks of infectious hepatitis have been traced to uncooked clams and
oysters. For these reasons commercial plants handling oysters and clams
operate under regulations of the U.S. Public Health Service and usually
also under state regulations.

FISH MEAL AND FISH FLOUR

For many years the parts of fish not used for human food, as well as
whole fish of less favored species, have been ground up, dehydrated, and

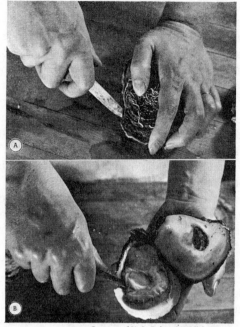

Courtesy of U. S. Fish and Wildlife Service

FIG. 223.   SHUCKING AN OYSTER

converted to fish meal for animal and poultry feed. Such fish meal generally had a fishy odor and a high bacterial content and was not considered for human food.

In recent years ways have been found to extract oils and fatty substances from ground fish tissue to an extent that no fishy odor or flavor remains. This extracted tissue can be heated, stripped of solvent, and then dehydrated and milled to a bland, highly nutritious powder rich in high quality protein and minerals. When produced under proper bacteriological and sanitary control from selected species of fish the product is known as fish protein concentrate or fish flour, and is approved by the U.S. FDA and regulatory agencies of other countries as a human food. However, as yet this industry is of limited commercial importance.

Initial approval of fish protein concentrate for human consumption took many years to acquire because the product, to be produced economically, had to be made from the entire fish including the entrails. While this disturbed some people from an esthetic point of view the product was quite wholesome, being sterile or nearly so. More recently an economic process has been developed by Astra of Sweden for producing a similar product from eviscerated fish. This product has been termed eviscerated fish protein. Both types of product offer great promise as an inexpensive high protein food supplement, especially in exploding population areas. The esthetic issue also is placed in proper perspective when one recognizes that sardines, oysters, clams, and certain other forms of fish are commonly eaten in the whole, ungutted condition.

Shortages of food and especially high quality protein in several areas of the world can be alleviated by food from the sea. However, this often does not mean the feeding of fish as such. In many areas of the world people may never have seen or eaten a fish and would be reluctant to accept fish in the natural form if it were made available. Further, the highly perishable nature of fresh fish, the refrigeration requirements of frozen fish, and the bulky properties of canned fish seriously limit these forms as feasible sources of nutrients in regions where transportation and refrigeration facilities are virtually lacking.

Recognizing such problems the Food and Agriculture Organization of the United Nations has listed the qualities that a food being added to the local diet in a developing area should possess. These include:

(1) Keeping qualities such that it is possible to store the item for long periods at tropical temperatures and under adverse conditions without loss of quality; (2) acceptance and easy incorporation into local diets; (3) cost should be as low as possible; (4) nutritive value should be as high as is possible; and (5) manufacture should be easily carried out on both a large and small scale.

Fish flour when properly manufactured and packaged can retain its bland taste and nutritive properties almost indefinitely. The bland powder can be readily incorporated into a wide variety of basic local foods as an enrichment without adverse affects upon acceptability of these items. Fish flour can contain 85 to 92% of high quality protein. It has been estimated that for a cost of approximately one-half cent per day per person fish flour could balance the diets of people around the world. It is expected that fish flour will find increasingly important applications in helping to alleviate world protein shortages.

BIBLIOGRAPHY

ANON. 1967. Fish protein concentrate, how made, where used. Food Eng. *39*, No. 5, 72–75.
BORGSTROM, G. (Editor) 1961–1965. Fish as Food, Vols. 1, 2, 3, and 4. Academic Press, New York, London.
BRODY, J. 1965. Fishery By-Products Technology. Avi Publishing Co., Westport, Conn.
BROWN, D. C. 1965. The use of liquid nitrogen in the shrimp industry. 18th Ann. Session, Gulf and Caribbean Fisheries Inst., Nov. 15, Miami Beach.
BURGESS, G. H. O., CUTTING, C. L., LOVERN, J. A., and WATERMAN, J. J. (Editors) 1965. Fish Handling and Processing. Her Majesty's Stationery Office, Edinburgh.
CONNELL, J. J. 1962. Fish muscle proteins. *In* Recent Advances in Food Science. J. Hawthorn, and J. M. Leitch (Editors). Butterworths, London.
CRAWFORD, L., and FINCH, R. 1968. Quality changes in albacore tuna during storage on ice and in refrigerated sea water. Food Technol. *22*, 1289–1292.

CUTTING, C. L. 1955. Fish Saving, A History of Fish Processing from Ancient to Modern Times. Leonard Hill Publisher, London.

DASSOW, J. A., and McNEELY, R. L. 1963. Commercial fishery methods. *In* Food Processing Operations, Vol. 1. M. A. Joslyn, and J. L. Heid (Editors). Avi Publishing Co., Westport, Conn.

DUMONT, W. H., and SUNDSTROM, G. T. 1961. Commercial fishing gear of the United States. U.S. Fish Wildlife Serv. Circ. *109.*

DYER, D. J., and DINGLE, J. R. 1961. Fish proteins, with special reference to freezing. *In* Fish as Food, Vol. 1. G. Borgstrom (Editor). Academic Press, New York, London.

FRIBERG, L. T., and VOSTAL, J. J. 1972. Mercury in the Environment. Chemical Rubber Co., Cleveland.

GILLIES, M. 1971. Seafood Processing 1971. Food Process. Rev. *22.* Noyes Data Corp., Park Ridge, N.J.

HEEN, E., and KRENZER, R. (Editors) 1962. Fish in Nutrition. Fishing News (Books), London.

JACQUOT, R. 1961. Organic constituents of fish and other aquatic animal foods. *In* Fish as Food, Vol. 1. G. Borgstrom (Editor). Academic Press, New York, London.

JARVIS, N. D. 1943. Principles and methods in canning of fishery products. U.S. Fish Wildlife Serv. Res. Rept. *7.*

JONES, N. R. 1962. Browning reaction in dried fish products. *In* Recent Advances in Food Science. J. Hawthorn, and J. M. Leitch (Editors). Butterworths, London.

LAWLER, F. K. 1970. Pure fish protein. Food Eng. *42,* No. 8, 61–65.

OLLEY, J., PIRIE, R., and WATSON, H. 1962. Lipase and phospholipase activity in fish skeletal muscle and its relationship to protein denaturation. J. Sci. Food Agr. *13,* 501–516.

PYKE, M. 1964. Food Science and Technology. John Murray, London.

SLAVIN, J. W. 1958. Methods of freezing used in the fisheries, a review. Fishing Gaz. Ann. Rev. *75,* 176.

STANSBY, M. E. 1963. Processing of seafoods. *In* Food Processing Operations, Vol. 1. M. A. Joslyn, and J. L. Heid (Editors). Avi Publishing Co., Westport, Conn.

STANSBY, M. E. (Editor). 1967. Fish Oils, Their Chemistry, Technology, Stability, Nutritional Properties, and Uses. Avi Publishing Co., Westport, Conn.

TRESSLER, D. K., and LEMON, J. M. (Editors) 1950. Marine Products of Commerce, 2nd Edition. Reinhold Publishing Co., New York.

TRESSLER, D. K., VAN ARSDEL, W. B., and COPLEY, M. J. 1968. The Freezing Preservation of Foods, 4th Edition, Vols. 2 and 3. Avi Publishing Co., Westport, Conn.

U.S. DEPT. INTERIOR. 1964. Fish Protein Concentrate. Booklets *1–5.* Washington, D.C.

U.S. FISH and WILDLIFE SERVICE. 1965. Guide for buying fresh fish and shellfish. U.S. Fish Wildlife Serv. Circ. *214.*

CHAPTER 16

Fats, Oils, and Their Products

INTRODUCTION

Several properties of fats and oils have been referred to in previous chapters; such as their being made up of esters of glycerol and fatty acids, their susceptibility to oxidation and rancidity, their shortening, lubricating, and whipping properties, their high caloric value, and so on. The terms fat and oil only indicate whether the material is liquid or solid at ordinary room temperature. Fats that are liquid at room temperature are called oils.

PROPERTIES DETERMINED BY COMPOSITION

The structural formula of a typical triglyceride molecule of a fat is seen in Fig. 224. In this case three different fatty acids are esterified or connected to glycerol. There are numerous different fatty acids and which ones are esterified to glycerol largely determine the properties of the fats, including whether they are solid or liquid at room temperature. It is well to review some of the more important properties these different fatty acids contribute to fats before considering the processing and utilization of fats and oils.

Short chain fatty acids give softer fats of lower melting points than do long chain fatty acids.

Fatty acids can have points of unsaturation within their molecules due to the absence of hydrogen atoms at these points. These are the points of double bonds in the fatty acid formulas. In the triglyceride molecule of Fig. 224 all three fatty acids are of the same length, that is they each contain 18 carbon atoms. But the degree of unsaturation of each is different. The top fatty acid, namely stearic acid, has no unsaturation. The next one down, oleic acid, has one double bond and is missing only two hydrogen atoms. The third fatty acid is linoleic acid, it has two double bonds and is missing four hydrogen atoms, it is still more unsaturated.

The greater the degree of unsaturation in the fatty acids of the fat molecules the softer will be the fat, and the lower will be its melting point. When there is a considerable degree of unsaturation the fat will be liquid at room temperature and will be called an oil.

By chemical means, we can add hydrogen to an oil, saturate its fatty acids, and thereby convert it to a solid. This is the process of hydrogenation which commonly converts a vegetable oil to a solid shortening. If we partially hydrogenate we get an intermediate degree of solidification.

440

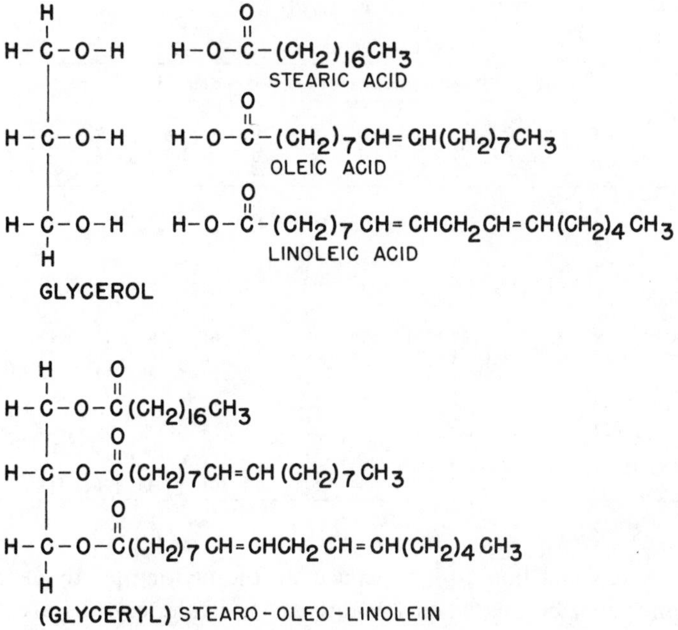

H   O
| ||
H-C-O-H   H-O-C-(CH$_2$)$_{16}$CH$_3$
| STEARIC ACID
| O
| ||
H-C-O-H   H-O-C-(CH$_2$)$_7$CH=CH(CH$_2$)$_7$CH$_3$
| OLEIC ACID
| O
| ||
H-C-O-H   H-O-C-(CH$_2$)$_7$CH=CHCH$_2$CH=CH(CH$_2$)$_4$CH$_3$
| LINOLEIC ACID
H
GLYCEROL

H   O
| ||
H-C-O-C(CH$_2$)$_{16}$CH$_3$
| O
| ||
H-C-O-C(CH$_2$)$_7$CH=CH(CH$_2$)$_7$CH$_3$
| O
| ||
H-C-O-C(CH$_2$)$_7$CH=CHCH$_2$CH=CH(CH$_2$)$_4$CH$_3$
|
H
(GLYCERYL) STEARO-OLEO-LINOLEIN

From Weiss (1963)

FIG. 224. STRUCTURAL FORMULA OF A TYPICAL TRIGLYCERIDE MOLECULE AND ITS COMPONENTS

Unsaturated fatty acids are highly sensitive to oxygen attack at the points of unsaturation. Therefore, hydrogenation which saturates the fat also makes the fat more resistant to oxidation and more stable against oxidized flavor development.

Most natural fats do not contain only one kind of triglyceride molcule. A given fat will generally contain a mixture of triglyceride molecules which will differ in the lengths and in the degrees of unsaturation of their fatty acids (Tables 50 and 51). Because of this some molecules in the fat will be softer and some harder. The overall fat may be in liquid form at room temperature but actually contain some solid fat molecules suspended in the liquid oil. Should the liquid fat be cooled, more of the fat molecules will solidify and they may form fat crystals which separate from the liquid oil portion. This is one property that is used in separating fats into liquid and solid fractions. The liquid fraction will then have a lower melting point and the solid fraction a higher melting point than the original mixture, and both fractions will be suitable for different food uses.

Figure 225 is a photomicrograph of a vegetable shortening with solidified fat crystals suspended in the liquid oil portion. The proportions

TABLE 50

VEGETABLE FATS AND OILS [1]

Typical Percentage Composition and Iodine Value

Fatty Acid	Carbon Atoms	Cocoa Butter	Coconut	Corn	Cotton-seed	Olive	Palm	Palm Kernel	Peanut	Rape-seed	Saf-flower	Sesame	Soy-bean	Sun-flower
Caprylic	8	..	6	...	...	..	..	3	...	...	...	...	...	...
Capric	10	..	6	...	...	..	..	4	...	...	...	...	...	...
Lauric	12	..	44	...	...	..	..	51	...	...	...	...	...	...
Myristic	14	..	18	...	1	..	1	17	...	...	...	...	...	...
Palmitic	16	24	11	13	24	13	48	8	6	4	8	10	12	8
Palmitoleic	16	..	..	...	1	1	..	..	...	..	..	..	..	..
Stearic	18	35	6	4	3	2	4	2	5	2	3	5	2	5
Oleic	18	39	7	29	18	75	38	13	61	19	13	40	24	21
Linoleic	18	2	2	54	53	9	9	2	22	14	75	43	54	66
Linolenic	18	..	..	...	...	..	..	..	...	8	1	2	8	...
Arachidic	20	..	..	...	...	..	..	..	2	...	...	...	...	...
Gadoleic	20	..	..	...	...	..	..	..	...	13	...	...	...	...
Behenic	22	..	..	...	...	..	..	..	3	...	...	...	...	...
Erucic	22	..	..	...	...	..	..	..	...	40	...	...	...	...
Lignoceric	24	..	..	...	...	..	..	..	1	...	...	...	...	...
Iodine value		37	9	127	109	84	51	16	101	104	146	114	134	134

[1] From Weiss (1963).

of fat crystals and liquid oil depend upon the melting points of the crystals, which will be low when the fatty acids in the crystals are of short length or are highly unsaturated. When this shortening is chilled, more crystals form and the shortening stiffens. When the shortening is heated the crystals melt and the shortening becomes a liquid oil.

The fat and oil chemist and processor have as their raw material a very versatile group of substances. With respect to texture they may choose natural fats with different properties (Table 52). Thus the fat from cocoa

TABLE 51

ANIMAL FATS AND OILS [1]

Fatty Acid	Carbon Atoms	Typical Percentage Composition and Iodine Value		
		Butter	Lard	Tallow
Butyric	4	3	..	..
Caproic	6	3	..	..
Caprylic	8	2	..	..
Capric	10	3	..	..
Lauric	12	3	..	..
Myristic	14	10	1	3
Myristoleic	14	1	..	..
Palmitic	16	26	25	28
Palmitoleic	16	1	2	3
Stearic	18	15	13	23
Oleic	18	29	47	40
Linoleic	18	2	12	2
Linolenic	18	2	..	..
Iodine value	..	35	63	41

[1] From Weiss (1963).

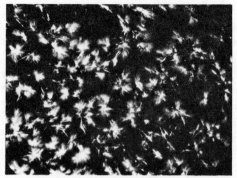

Courtesy of V. C. Mehlenbacher, Garrard Press

FIG. 225. PHOTOMICROGRAPH OF A SHORTENING SHOWING
SOLIDIFIED FAT CRYSTALS SUSPENDED IN LIQUID OIL

TABLE 52

PHYSICAL CHARACTERISTICS OF FOOD FATS—RAW MATERIALS[1]

Fat	Solid Fat Index at °F					Melting Point, °F (Capillary)
	50	70	80	92	100	
Butter	32	12	9	3	0	97
Cocoa butter	62	48	8	0	0	85
Coconut oil	55	27	0	0	0	79
Lard	25	20	12	4	2	110
Palm oil	34	12	9	6	4	103
Palm kernel oil	49	33	13	0	0	84
Tallow	39	30	28	23	18	118

[1] From Weiss (1963).

TABLE 53

PHYSICAL CHARACTERISTICS OF TYPICAL FAT PRODUCTS[1]

Product	Solid Fat Index at °F					Melting Point, °F (Capillary)	Consistency (Bloom) @75°F
	50	70	80	92	100		
Shortenings							
cake and icing	28	23	22	18	15	124	40
cake mix	40	31	29	21	15	118	75
coating fat, winter	65	55	45	19	1	103	Hard & brittle
coating fat, summer	67	58	51	31	18	118	Hard & brittle
frying	44	28	22	11	5	109	70
pie crust	33	28	22	10	8	118	70
yeast dough	26	20	12	6	3	115	50
Margarines							
table (premium)	24	12	8	2	0	98	15
table (regular)	28	16	12	3	0	100	25
cake	29	19	17	11	7	115	40
pastry, roll-in	25	21	20	18	15	122	80
puff paste	28	25	24	22	19	124	110

[1] From Weiss (1963).

known as cocoa butter is solid at temperatures below 86° F. On the other hand the fat pressed from peanuts is an oil, it is liquid at room temperature.

But the fat and oil chemist and processor also can modify fats and oils of a given kind very readily by hydrogenation to make them stiffer, by temperature controlled crystallization followed by separation into stiff and liquid portions, and by still other means. The processor can then further blend various natural, hydrogenated, or crystallized fats into an endless number of mixtures and thereby further tailor special fats for the widest range of uses (Table 53).

SOURCES OF FATS AND OILS

Fats and oils may be of vegetable, animal, and marine origin. Examples of vegetable fats include such solid fats as cocoa butter, and such liquid oils as corn oil, soybean oil, cottonseed oil, peanut oil, olive oil, and many more. Animal fats include lard from hogs, tallow from beef, and butter-fat from milk. Fish oils include cod liver oil, oil from menhaden, and usually whale oil, although the whale is really a mammal.

Some of these fats and oils are chosen for food uses because of special flavor attributes. This is so in the case of lard which contributes a meaty flavor, olive oil which has a distinctive flavor on salads, and butterfat which has a buttery aroma and flavor. But for the very large uses of fats such as shortenings, margarines, and frying fats, today we rely on chemical and physical methods such as hydrogenation and crystallization to make many of the natural fats interchangeable with respect to texture and physical properties. Where permitted by law we also may add flavors to duplicate or even improve upon a specific natural fat.

In the past, there has been great prejudice in certain countries for or against one or another type of fat. Part of this undoubtedly developed from availability, and to retain competitive advantage. In France, margarine developed around 1870 was made from melted down animal fat. Animal fat margarine is still important in Europe, and there are several European countries, as well as Canada, where margarine is made from hydrogenated and deodorized fish oil. But in the United States most margarine is made from vegetable oils, and a fish oil margarine (if known to the consumer) would probably not be readily accepted. But the product could be made to spread and taste quite satisfactorily.

There has been fierce competition between industries on the matter of fats. The butter industry versus the margarine industry is an example. Lard shortening versus vegetable shortening is another example. But economics and availability of different fats have become the deciding factors. Butterfat at about 70 cents per pound, many vegetable oils at about 18 cents per pound, and lard and tallow at about 10 cents per pound clearly dictate what fats will be used when the fats can be made interchangeable for a specific application by modern technology.

Because the fats do vary widely in price, and often can be made interchangeable or nearly so, it is important that deception be prevented and the customer indeed gets what he chooses to purchase. Thus there are federal standards of identity for foods, labeling requirements for nonstandardized foods, and analytical tests to distinguish between certain fats to prevent adulteration. Butter cannot be called butter if it contains any fat other than butterfat. This is also true of olive oil. Imitation cocoa and chocolate products must be appropriately labeled when they contain vegetable fats other than cocoa butter.

But margarine, shortenings, frying fats, and many other products will be made of various fats, and of blends, very largely dependent upon availability and price which may change daily. There is no question of deception when the food standards are met or ingredients are declared on package labels of nonstandardized foods. Rather, the interchangeable use of fats is a matter of good technology and sound economics.

FUNCTIONAL PROPERTIES OF FATS

Apart from flavor differences, when fats are used as shortenings, tenderizers, lubricants, frying media, whipping agents, and for other purposes there are special requirements in each of these capacities.

In the case of butter or table margarine, a plastic condition is required such that the butter or margarine will not become too hard in the refrigerator to spread, or too soft on a summer day so that it will run.

In the case of salad oils we want the oil to be clear and to pour. It should not contain high melting point molecules that will solidify and crystallize when the salad oil is placed under refrigeration.

The same is true of the oils used in the preparation of mayonnaise. The oils should not form crystals when the mayonnaise is refrigerated since these fat crystals could disrupt the state of emulsion and cause the mayonnaise to separate into fat and liquid phases.

Chocolate products should not melt at room temperature. We want the chocolate to be brittle and to snap when bitten into. Yet the chocolate should melt quickly in the mouth. Cocoa butter melts sharply above an 86° to 96° F range and possesses these desirable properties. Chocolate substitutes contain fats other than cocoa butter that may have been tailored to closely match these properties of cocoa butter. In the case of chocolate-type coatings for certain confections and crackers, however, it may not be the objective to match chocolate, but rather to produce a coating with a higher melting point to prevent melting in the hand.

Where the fat is to be whipped and hold air, as in the case of butter-cream type icings, partially solidified shortenings generally produce a firmer whip than liquid oils. Also where shortening is to be used in baked goods a partially solidified fat generally functions better than most liquid oils, since the oils tend to separate and collect in pockets in the baked item.

Optimum fats for some of these and other applications cannot always be obtained from nature. More generally they must be fabricated from a variety of fats and oils that have undergone various degrees of modification and blending. This is particularly true today where fats and oils are used in manufactured foods increasingly produced with automatic equipment. Thus, the requirements of a shortening used in the high speed continuous bread making process are different from those of a shortening for bread made by the batch method.

PRODUCTION AND PROCESSING METHODS

There are but a few basic production methods to obtain fats and oils from animal, marine, and vegetable sources. These include rendering, pressure expelling, and solvent extraction. These are followed by various refining and modifying procedures.

Rendering

Lard is obtained from hogs and tallow from beef by the process of rendering. Rendering consists of heating meat scraps so as to cause the fat to melt. The melted fat then rises and water and remaining tissue settle below. The melted fat is then separated by skimming or centrifugation. We can have dry heat rendering which cooks the tissue under vacuum to remove moisture, wet rendering which utilizes water and steam, or low temperature rendering which uses just enough heat to melt the fat. Low temperature rendering can produce a fat of lighter color, but where more meaty flavor is desired higher temperature rendering is used. Rendering also is used to obtain oil from whale blubber or fish tissue. In its simplest form rendering can be carried out in a heated kettle; but large capacity modern rendering plants are highly engineered and some employ continuous rendering methods.

Pressing or Expelling

Various types of mechanical presses and expellers are used to squeeze oil from oilseeds. Seeds are usually first cooked slightly to partially break down the cell structure and to melt the fat for easier release of oil. The seeds also may be ground or cracked for the same purpose. The heat from cooking or grinding the seeds should not be excessive or it may darken the color of the oil. Where such seeds as corn are used for oil

Courtesy of Corn Industries Research Foundation, Inc.

FIG. 226.   ANDERSON EXPELLERS USED IN SEED OIL EXTRACTION

only the germ is pressed. The expellers in Fig. 226 are continuous screw-type presses commonly used in the production of corn oil. The expelled oil is usually further clarified of seed residues by next being pumped through multiple cloths in a filter press (Fig. 227).

Courtesy of Corn Industries Research Foundation, Inc.

FIG. 227.   FILTER PRESSES FOR CLARIFYING CORN OIL

Solvent Extraction

It is very common in large scale operations to remove the oil from cracked seeds at low temperatures with a nontoxic fat solvent such as hexane. The solvent is percolated through the seeds, and after the oil is extracted, the solvent is distilled from the oil and recovered for reuse.

Courtesy of Procter and Gamble

FIG. 228. STAGES IN PRODUCTION OF SOYBEAN OIL: (UPPER LEFT) SOYBEANS; (UPPER RIGHT) FLAKED BEANS FOR SOLVENT EXTRACTION; (LOWER LEFT) SOYBEAN OIL; (LOWER RIGHT) RESIDUAL GROUND MEAL

Solvent extraction frequently will get more oil out of seeds than is possible by pressing. Combined processes employ pressing to remove most of the oil followed by solvent extraction to recover final traces. The oil-free residual seed meal then will be ground for animal feed. The stages in solvent extraction of soybeans are indicated in Fig. 228.

Degumming

Vegetable oils from the press or from solvent extraction always contain fat-like substances such as phosopholipids or fat-protein complexes which are gummy. When wetted with water these materials become insoluble in the oil and settle out. This is one way to obtain the phospholipid lecithin.

Refining

While water will settle much of the gummy material, use of alkali solution will settle additional minor impurities from the oil. This will include free fatty acids which combine with alkali to form soaps. These soaps can be removed by filtration or centrifugation. This treatment with alkali is known as refining.

Bleaching

Even after degumming and refining, the oil from seeds will contain various plant pigments such as chlorophyll and carotene. These can be removed by passing heated oil over charcoal or various adsorbent clays and earths. Animal fats generally can be bleached by heat alone.

Deodorization

Natural fats and oils from seeds, meat, and fish contain various odorous compounds. Some of these are desirable as in the case of olive oil, cocoa butter, lard, fresh butterfat, and chicken fat, and these odors are not deliberately removed. But many other oils such as fish oils and several seed oils have disagreeable odors. These odors are removed by heat and vacuum. The heat is often supplied by injecting steam into the fat in low pressure evaporators.

Hydrogenation

Hydrogenation to saturate fatty acid double bonds is carried out by whipping deaerated hot oil with hydrogen gas plus a nickel catalyst in a closed vessel, known as a converter. When the desired degree of hardening of the fat is reached the unreacted hydrogen gas is removed from the vessel by vacuum and the nickel catalyst is removed by filtration (Fig. 229).

Winterizing

As has been said, fats and oils are made up principally of various triglycerides in a mixture. The triglycerides containing more saturated fatty acids, and fatty acids of longer chain lengths, tend to crystallize out and settle from the mixture when an oil is chilled. Where we do not want crystallization and settling in a refrigerated product such as a salad oil,

Courtesy of Procter and Gamble

FIG. 229.   COMMERCIAL SCALE HYDROGENATION OF FATS

we crystallize by cooling and remove the crystals before the final product is bottled. The precooling treatment to remove fat crystals is known as winterizing. It may be done by simply setting barrels of oil in a cold room at a selected temperature that is lower than the salad oil will later experience in the refrigerator, or by continuous processing through precisely controlled heat exchangers.

Plasticizing and Tempering

The consistency and functional properties of more solid fats also are largely influenced by their state of crystallization. A given fat or oil can therefore be modified by chilling and by agitation, both of which influence crystallization rate and crystal form. If a heated fat is allowed to slowly cool to a solidification temperature it will have a different crystalline structure than if it is rapidly chilled to the same temperature; rapid chilling with agitation causes further differences. Controlled chilling with or without agitation to influence a fat's consistency and functional properties is referred to as plasticizing. It generally is done by pumping the melted fat or oil through a tubular scraped surface type heat exchanger for supercooling, and then through a second chilled cylinder provided with a high speed shaft containing rows of pins that alternate with pins on the cylinder wall to provide intensive agitation. For some applications the crystallized fat also will be given a controlled degree of aeration by introducing measured amounts of air or nitrogen prior to chilling. A freshly plasticized fat then will undergo further changes in consistency and functional properties upon standing. After a period of about 2 to 4 days at a temperature of about 80°F these changes essentially cease. Holding a newly plasticized fat at a controlled temperature until its properties become stabilized is known as tempering. The chemical or physical basis for tempering is poorly understood, but such improvements in tempered shortenings as increased ability to emulsify water or air, as in a cake batter or creamed icing, are easily demonstrated.

Monoglyceride and Diglyceride Preparation

Glycerol esters containing one or two fatty acid residues can be prepared from triglycerides plus about one-fifth their weight of additional glycerol. If the mixture is heated to about 400°F in the presence of a sodium hydroxide catalyst some of the fatty acid molecules migrate from the triglycerides. These react with free hydroxyl groups of the added glycerol. Since there is an excess of glycerol relative to total available fatty acid molecules, some of the hydroxyl groups of the glycerol must remain unesterified. The reaction is carried out under an inert gas or under vacuum to prevent oxidation.

Monoglycerides and diglycerides are both hydrophilic because of their free hydroxyl groups and hydrophobic due to their fatty acid residues. They are thus partially soluble in water and partially soluble in fat, which makes them excellent emulsifying agents. Monoglycerides and diglycerides are commonly added to shortenings and many other food products for their emulsifying properties.

PRODUCTS MADE FROM FATS AND OILS

The food manufacturer may now use the many forms of fats and oils as ingredients in the widest variety of food products, or further process the fats and oils into manufactured oleaginous products, a few of which are described below.

Butter

The raw material for butter making is milk fat usually in the form of cream. The cream is separated from the milk to contain about 30 to 35% fat. The cream is pasteurized at a somewhat higher temperature than for pasteurizing milk since the high fat content has a slight protective effect on bacteria. Sometimes the cream is slightly acidic due to lactic acid from fermentation of the cream when it is separated on the farms and goes through several days of handling. When this is so the cream is neutralized with a food grade alkali prior to pasteurization.

Depending upon the color of the cream a vegetable coloring material such as extract of annatto seed or carotene may be added to deepen the yellow color. A measured amount of a lactic acid, diacetyl-producing bacterial culture also may be added to the cream to enhance the butter flavor. The cream is now ready for churning.

Churning whether done as a batch operation or in a continuous process is a mechanical agitation designed to reverse the natural emulsion in cream.

Cream will have its fat globules suspended in water such that the water is the continuous phase and the fat globules are the dispersed or discontinuous phase. The fat globules each are surrounded by a kind of phospholipid membrane, which contains lecithin, that helps to keep the globules emulsified or suspended in the water phase. The mechanical agitation of churning breaks this membrane-like surface of the fat globules and causes globules to collide with one another. As a result the globules clump together and form small butter granules, these grow in size and separate from the water phase of the cream. The resulting water phase or serum is known as buttermilk.

In the churn, with the breaking of the emulsion, the butter granules mat together into a large mass of solid fat since the churn is operated at about 50° F. At this point the agitation or tumbling action of the churn is stopped and most of the buttermilk is drained from the churn. The state of the emulsion is now reversed. The mass of butterfat is the major component and it traps about 15% of buttermilk within it. The butterfat is now the continuous phase, and the remaining buttermilk which is largely water with dissolved lactose, casein, and other milk solids is suspended as droplets within the mass of fat. This condition results after about 40 min of batch churning.

The butter mass in a batch-type churn now appears as in Fig. 230. The mass next is washed with pure water by turning a hose into the churn to remove surface adhering buttermilk. At this point the wash water is drained and salt is added to the churn. A small amount of pure water also may be added to contribute the maximum amount of water permitted by law in the final butter. The churn again is closed and given further tumbling action to work the butter. The purpose of working is to uniformly disperse the salt and to subdivide the water droplets into smaller and smaller size. Subdivision of water droplets by proper working in the churn prevents these droplets from running together and causing leaky butter.

The salt which is added at a level of about 2.5% of the final butter contributes flavor. But the salt also acts as a preservative. All of the salt goes into solution in the water droplets, and since the amount of water is only about 15%, the salt concentration in the water is actually about 7 times the 2.5% salt added. At this concentration the salt is a strong

Courtesy of J. A. Gosselin Co., Ltd.

FIG. 230. BUTTER MASS IN BATCH TYPE CHURN

Courtesy of Anderson Bros. Mfg. Co.

FIG. 231. CONTINUOUS BUTTERMAKING CHURN

preservative within the water droplets and largely prevents the growth of spoilage bacteria in these droplets.

The butter may now be packaged in tubs or large cartons or it may be packaged in smaller units with a machine known as a butter printer. In this case the butter is loaded into the hopper of the machine from where it is mechanically extruded in the shape desired, cut to size, and wrapped.

Butter also may be made by any of several high speed continuous processes but the basic principles cited for the batch churning operation apply to all. Typically, cream is pumped into cylindrical chilled churns that look somewhat like an ice cream freezer (Fig. 231). High speed mixing within the cylinder forms the butter granules in a matter of seconds. The butter granules may be mechanically forced through perforated plates while the buttermilk simultaneously is drained from the cylinder. A salt solution is injected into an extension of the cylinder where the butter is further worked as it is extruded. The continuously extruded butter goes directly to automatic packaging equipment.

There is a legal standard for butter stating that the fat must be entirely from butterfat and that the finished product must contain not less than 80% of butterfat by weight. Color and salt are optional.

Margarine

This term applies to certain types of shortenings as well as table spreads. The consumption of table spreads in the United States has remained rather constant over the last 30 yr, but where butter has declined in popularity margarine has increased. Much of this is due to the difference in price of the two products.

In the United States, margarine is made largely from vegetable oils that have been hydrogenated or crystallized for the proper spreading texture. The vegetable oils may also be blended with lesser quantities of animal fats. The choice and blending of oils depend upon seasonal availability and price. Like butter, legal table margarine must contain no less than 80% of fat. Since the oils are naturally almost 100% fat, water is added (usually in the form of milk or cream) to produce the desired water in oil emulsion which is physically quite the same as in butter. To the oil and water phases are added emulsifiers, salt, butter flavor, color, and permissible chemical preservatives such as sodium benzoate. Vitamins A and D also may be added.

In manufacture two mixtures usually are made; one of the oil and all other fat soluble ingredients, and the other of water and all water soluble ingredients. These two mixtures are then emulsified in a vat with vigorous agitation, which distributes the water phase as small droplets throughout the continuous oil phase. The emulsion which would quickly separate if not stiffened by chilling is now quickly cooled. In modern continuous systems (Fig. 232) this is done by pumping the emulsion through a series of heat exchangers which may have special agitators to further subdivide the water droplets throughout the fat as it stiffens. The emulsion is next

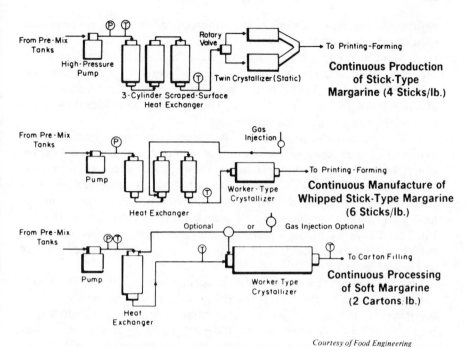

Courtesy of Food Engineering

FIG. 232. DIAGRAMS OF MARGARINE CHILLING AND CRYSTALLIZING SYSTEMS

passed through a chilled crystallizer to further solidify and plasticize the fat. Proper temperature control to develop optimum sized fat crystals is most important for producing the desired semiplastic consistency. The semisolid margarine is continuously extruded and packaged as in continuous butter making.

While butter may contain only butterfat, margarine is not so restricted as to kind of fat and some vegetable fat margarines are actually made to contain some butter in the amount of about 5 to 10% to enhance flavor.

Both butter and margarine are highly concentrated and dense foods. For easier spreadability and to cut down on calorie consumption there are whipped butters and whipped margarines sold today. These products are made by whipping air or nitrogen gas into butter or margarine to increase their volume by about 50%.

Shortenings and Frying Oils

Margarine is one type of bakery shortening. It is usually chosen when flavor is a consideration. Its flavor results largely from milk ingredients in its composition. Other bakery shortenings do not contain milk ingredients and are essentially flavorless. Some bakery shortenings will be made entirely of vegetable oils, such as cottonseed, peanut, and soybean oils. Others, particularly those favored for flaky pie crusts will be made of lard. Many will contain blends of vegetable and animal fats. Emulsified shortenings in addition will contain monoglycerides, diglycerides, and related compounds. These permit cakes to be made with higher levels of water and sugar, and therefore to be more moist and tender than would be possible with unemulsified shortenings.

Shortenings may be prepared to all degrees of stiffness including pourability. Pourable shortenings are easily pumped and metered but are generally not equal to the plastic shortenings in bakery performance. One important function of a shortening is to hold air, whether beaten in a cake batter or creamed with other icing ingredients. This ability to hold air generally is enhanced by a plastic consistency of the shortening. Further, following baking, plastic shortenings remain dispersed within baked goods where liquid shortenings have a greater tendency to leak and collect in pockets.

Plastic shortenings not only differ in degree of hardness, but two shortenings with the same initial hardness can have different softening properties as they are subjected to the same conditions of elevated temperature. This results from the different melting points of various triglycerides in their separate mixtures. Such shortenings are said to have different plastic ranges. That is, they will remain semisolid over a wider or narrower temperature range. In Tables 52 and 53 the term "Solid Fat Index" appears. Solid Fat Index is a measure of the solidity of fats at various temperatures; it is related to the percentage of the fat that exists in crystalline form as distinct from melted oil at these temperatures. Solid Fat Index curves therefore correlate well with plastic ranges of fats and shortenings.

A shortening that remains plastic over a wide range of temperature (long plastic range) is suited to most bakery operations. On the other hand, for frying doughnuts a long plastic range offers no advantages. On the contrary, shortenings with short plastic ranges and low melting points are preferred for frying operations. These properties minimize greasiness from unmelted fat in the mouth when fried items are eaten.

Frying fats have additional requirements that are different from bakery shortenings. While shortenings in baked goods seldom are exposed to temperatures much above the boiling point of water during baking, frying fats and oils are generally heated to temperatures of about 325° to 375° F in the frying kettle. Monoglycerides and diglycerides decompose at such temperatures and produce smoke and therefore are not added to frying fats. Frying fats exposed to these high temperatures also must be given considerable stability against darkening, pyrolytic decomposition leading to gum formation, and oxidation. This generally calls for hydrogenation. Fats at high temperatures also have a tendency to foam in the frying kettle. This may be minimized by the incorporation of such materials as methyl silicones into the frying fats.

In fat and oil technology we frequently encounter requirements that appear somewhat contradictory. Thus, for example, we want frying fats with maximum stability, but also with low melting points to minimize greasiness in the mouth. Hydrogenation can contribute to the former but may aggravate the latter. On the other hand, fats with saturated shorter chain fatty acids can have both stability and relatively low melting points without hydrogenation. While there is often more than one approach to solve such problems, the solution frequently must involve compromise influenced by the specific food application.

Mayonnaise and Salad Dressings

Standards of Identity for mayonnaise in the United States require that this emulsified semisolid food be made from vegetable oil, acetic or citric acid, and egg yolk. It may further contain salt, natural sweeteners, spices, and various flavoring ingredients from natural sources. The oil level may not be less than 65% by weight of the mayonnaise. The acid is a microbial preservative and must be present to the extent of 2.5% by weight. The egg yolk provides emulsifying properties and the yolk further gives the mayonnaise a pale yellow color which may not be imitated or intensified by ingredients other than yolk.

Commercial mayonnaise generally will contain 77 to 82% of a winterized salad oil, 5.3 to 5.8% liquid egg yolk, 2.8 to 4.5% of a 10% acetic acid vinegar, small amounts of salt, sugar, and spices, and additional water to make 100%. In mayonnaise the oil phase is present in greater quantity than the water phase. Generally the phase in greater quantity becomes the external or continuous phase when emulsions are made. In the case of mayonnaise, however, we seek to reverse this and produce an oil in water emulsion to give the characteristic viscosity, mouth feel, and taste. Such an "unnatural" emulsion is difficult to prepare and tends to be relatively unstable. If the oil used in its preparation is not properly winterized then fat crystallization in a refrigerator will break the emulsion. Even when the oil is winterized the mayonnaise emulsion quickly breaks upon freezing.

Mayonnaise is prepared commercially by both batch and continuous methods and there are many variations with respect to order and rates of ingredient additions to the mixers. Two-stage mixing is commonly employed with high speed turbine blades in the first stage followed by yet more severe shearing of the oil into fine droplets in the second stage.

The second stage mixer may possess close clearance whirling teeth as in a colloid mill. Mayonnaise may be whipped with small quantities of inert gas such as nitrogen or carbon dioxide to produce a finished product specific gravity of 0.88 to 0.92. The gas commonly is pumped along with the emulsion into the second stage mixer of enclosed design where the high shear mixing under pressure subdivides the gas into minute bubbles, which further contribute to "body" or firmness and texture. Mayonnaise with the same ingredient composition can be highly variable with respect to such properties as firmness, smoothness, sheen, spooning characteristics, and taste, and these properties are greatly influenced by the conditions of mixing. Mayonnaise is preserved against microbial spoilage by its acid content but it is very sensitive to oxidative deterioration of flavor and should be refrigerated after jars are opened.

Salad dressings may be of the spoonable or pourable type. Spoonable salad dressings may be very similar to mayonnaise but generally contain less oil (35 to 50%) and contain starch paste as a thickener. The egg yolk, vinegar, and seasonings perform the same functions as in mayonnaise, and principles with respect to mixing and emulsion stability are similar except that special care must be given to starch cooking to develop desired degree of thickening. For example, if the starch-water suspension is cooked together with the vinegar acid hydrolysis tends to thin the starch paste. It therefore is preferred to add vinegar to the previously cooked starch paste, which is then blended with the oil, egg yolk, and other ingredients prior to final mixing-emulsification.

Pourable salad dressings, of which French dressing is an example, contain oil, vinegar, spices, and other ingredients. Pourable dressings may be of the emulsified type or of the kind that readily separate into an oil and aqueous layer and are commonly shaken before use. Emulsifiers vary and include numerous gums as well as egg yolk. In the United States, French dressing composition is covered by a Standard of Identity which includes a minimum oil level of 35%, although higher levels of oil are common. Other pourable salad dressings can be quite variable in composition and flavoring ingredients. The separating types are well mixed but need not be emulsified prior to bottling.

QUALITY CONTROL TESTS

Generally fats and oils are tested for the following purposes: to gain information related to performance in specific food applications; to measure degree of deterioration (such as oxidation or rancidity) as well as stability of the fat against such change; to check fat properties against purchase specifications; and to identify fats and oils against possible misrepresentation or adulteration. The important physical and chemical properties of fats and oils have been measured in various ways which have created a number of terms commonly associated with the properties of fats.

Chemical Tests

The degree of unsaturation of the fatty acids in a fat or oil can be quantitatively expressed by the Iodine Value of the fat. Iodine Value refers to the number of grams of iodine absorbed by 100 gm of fat. Since the iodine reacts at the sites of unsaturation much as would hydrogen in hydrogenation, the higher the Iodine Value the greater the degree of unsaturation that existed in the fat.

The degree of oxidation that has taken place in a fat or oil can be expressed in terms of Peroxide Value. When the double bonds of unsaturated fats become oxidized peroxides are among the oxidation products formed. Under standard conditions these peroxides can liberate iodine from potassium iodide added to the system. The amount of iodine liberated is then a measure of peroxide content, which correlates with degree of oxidation already experienced by the fat and probable tendency of the fat to subsequent oxidative rancidity. Oxidative rancidity results from the liberation of odorous products of unsaturated fatty acid breakdown. These commonly include such compounds as aldehydes, ketones, and shorter chain fatty acids. This is the type of fat deterioration that can often be prevented or minimized by the addition of chemical antioxidants, such as butylated hydroxyanisole (BHA) and butylated hydroxytoluene (BHT) commonly seen on ingredient labels of fat-containing foods.

Fats also are degraded by the process of hydrolysis, which in the presence of moisture splits triglycerides into their basic components of glycerol and free fatty acids. The free fatty acids, especially if they are of short chain length, are odorous in themselves and contribute to rancid flavors and odors in fats and oils. This type of deterioration, referred to as hydrolytic rancidity, is to be distinguished from oxidative rancidity mentioned above. Hydrolytic rancidity does not require oxygen to occur, but is favored by the presence of moisture, high temperatures, and natural lipolytic enzymes. The term Acid Value refers to a measure of free fatty acids present in a fat. Acid Value is defined as the number of milligrams of potassium hydroxide necessary to neutralize one gram of the fat or oil.

The average molecular weight of the fatty acids in a fat, which influences firmness of the fat as well as flavor and odor properties (low molecular weight fatty acids are more odorous), is another useful measure made on fats and oils. Average molecular weight of the fatty acids in a fat is indicated by Saponification Value. Saponification Value is the number of milligrams of potassium hydroxide required to saponify (convert to soap) one gram of fat. Since one gram of fat must contain more fatty acids if they are of short chain length or less fatty acids if they are of long chain length, and the fatty acids react with the alkali to give the soap, it follows that Saponification Value increases and decreases inversely with average molecular weight.

The above are but a few of the chemical tests that have been applied to fats and oils. Much that they can tell us can be learned today more quickly by instrumental analytical methods such as gas chromatography and infrared absorption analysis, and many of the classical chemical tests are rapidly being replaced by these newer methods.

Physical Tests

These generally are related to consistency of the fat under different temperature conditions. Most fats and oils do not melt or solidify sharply at a given temperature. Rather, because fats and oils are mixtures of triglyceride molecules each with their own melting point, fats melt or solidify gradually over a temperature range.

There are various tests to indicate the beginning of melting of a fat or oil previously chilled to a specified temperature. In one type, the temperature at which the chilled cloudy fat within a capillary tube loses its cloudiness from melting of its solidified crystals is taken as the melting point. In another the temperature at which chilled fat in a capillary tube softens just enough to slide within the tube is considered the melting point. A related type of test measures the temperature for a melted fat to go to the crystalline state by observing the point at which cloudiness of the fat is complete. This test can then be extended to determine the temperature at which the cloudy fat congeals.

The Solid Fat Index, mentioned earlier, is a measure of solidity of fats and is related to the percentage of the fat that is crystalline at specific temperatures. Crystallinity is measured by changes in volume that occur when fat crystals melt. The experimental method is referred to as dilatometry.

As with the chemical tests, more sophisticated instrumental methods can be used to gain information on the state of crystallinity in a fat. One of these is X-ray diffraction and is based on the ability of crystals to deflect an X-ray beam according to the spacing between molecules within the crystal.

Additional Tests

The consistency of semisolid fats can easily be measured by their resistance to penetration of a needle, ring, or cone. The response of fats and oils to frying temperatures can be indicated by such measurements as smoke point, flash point, and fire point, which correspond to rising temperatures at which these occurrences begin.

Many of the above chemical and physical tests are highly useful in identification and quality control of fats and oils as food ingredients (Table 54). Frequently, however, they may not correlate closely with optimum performance of a given fat in a specific application. For this reason actual performance tests with the fat may be indispensable. Performance tests are essentially scaled down versions of the actual application in which the fat will be used. Sometimes they impose still more severe conditions than will be encountered in the corresponding commercial operation to add conservatism to the evaluation.

TABLE 54

REFINED CORN OIL ANALYTICAL DATA [1]

Property	Value
Acidity (free fatty acid as oleic)	0.020 to 0.050
Acid value	0.04 to 0.10
Color (Lovibond)	20 to 25 yellow
	2.5 to 5 red
Cold test	Clear
Saponification value	189 to 191
Iodine value	125 to 128
Hehner value	93 to 96
Titer	64° to 68°F
Melting point	4° to 12°F
Smoke point	430° to 500°F
Solidifying point	−4° to 14°F
Flash point	575° to 640°F
Fire point	590° to 700°F
Specific gravity	0.918 to 0.925
Pounds per gallon	7.672 at 70°F

[1] Anon. (1957).

Effective performance tests on fats and oils (or any other ingredients) will differ between plants manufacturing the same type products when there are differences in recipe, manufacturing procedures, or even stability requirements under varying distribution and marketing condition. Thus, performance tests on shortening for cakes prepared in a small retail bakery would be different from the tests to be performed in a large wholesale bakery employing automated high speed operations, and exposing its finished products to the variables associated with national distribution.

BIBLIOGRAPHY

AMERICAN OIL CHEMISTS' SOCIETY. 1967. Official Methods of Analysis. Am. Oil Chemists' Soc., Chicago.

ANON. 1957. Corn Oil. Corn Ind. Res. Found., Washington, D.C.

BEDNARCYK, N. E. 1969. Edible Oils and Fats 1969. Food Process. Rev. 5. Noyes Data Corp. Park Ridge, N.J.

BRINK, M. F., and KRITCHEVSKY, D. (Editors) 1968. Dairy Lipids and Lipid Metabolism. Avi Publishing Co., Westport, Conn.

BRAVERMAN, J. B. S. 1963. Introduction to The Biochemistry of Foods. Elsevier Publishing Co., Amsterdam, London, New York.

COX, H. E., and PEARSON, D. 1962. The Chemical Analysis of Foods. Chemical Publishing Co., New York.

DANIELSON, C. V., and KNAPE, S. D. 1958. Salad dressing, mayonnaise and related products, 1957. U.S. Dept. Com.

DEUEL, H. J., JR. 1955. The Lipids, Vol. 1. Interscience Publishers, New York.

ECKEY, E. W. 1954. Vegetable Fats and Oils. Reinhold Publishing Corp. New York.

HOFFMANN, G. 1962. Vegetable oils. In Symposium on Foods: Lipids and Their Oxidation. H. W. Schultz, E. A. Day, and R. O. Sinnhuber (Editors). Avi Publishing Co., Westport, Conn.

MATZ, S. A. 1970. Cereal Technology. Avi Publishing Co., Westport, Conn.

MEHLENBACHER, V. C. 1960. The Analysis of Fats and Oils. Garrard Press, Champaign, Ill.

MEYER, R. I. 1959. Production of oils from cereal grains. In The Chemistry and Technology of Cereals as Food and Feed. S. A. Matz (Editor). Avi Publishing Co., Westport, Conn. (Out of print.)

MOHR, W., and VON DRACHENFELS, H. J. 1956. Consistency of butter and margarine. Fette Seifen Anstrichmittel 58, 609–613.

MOHR, W., and VON DRACHENFELS, H. J. 1956. Observations on frozen sections of butter as a method for the study of the disposition of crystals and distribution of water in butter. Milchwissenchaft 11, 228–234.

MULDER, H. 1953. The consistency of butter. In Foodstuffs: Their Plasticity, Fluidity, and Consistency. G. W. Scott Blair (Editor). Interscience Publishers, New York.

OLCOTT, H. S. 1962. Marine products. In Symposium on Foods: Lipids and Their Oxidation. H. W. Schultz, E. A. Day, and R. O. Sinnhuber (Editors). Avi Publishing Co., Westport, Conn.

PALTON, S. 1962. Dairy products. In Symposium on Foods: Lipids and Their Oxidation. H. W. Schultz, E. A. Day, and R. O. Sinnhuber (Editors). Avi Publishing Co., Westport, Conn.

SCHULTZ, H. W., DAY, E. A., and SINNHUBER, R. O. (Editors) 1962. Symposium on Foods: Lipids and Their Oxidation. Avi Publishing Co., Westport, Conn.

SCHWEITZER, M. K. 1951. Continuous Processing of Fats. Leonard Hill Publisher, London.

STANSBY, M. E. (Editor) 1967. Fish Oils, their Chemistry, Technology, Stability, Nutritional Properties, and Uses. Avi Publishing Co., Westport, Conn.

SWERN, D. (Editor) 1964. Bailey's Industrial Oil and Fat Products, 3rd Edition. Interscience Publishers Div., John Wiley & Sons, New York.

WATTS, B. M. 1962. Meat products. In Symposium on Foods: Lipids and Their Oxidation. H. W. Schultz, E. A. Day, and R. O. Sinnhuber (Editors). Avi Publishing Co., Westport, Conn.

WEISS, T. J. 1963. Fats and oils. In Food Processing Operations, Vol. 2. M. A. Joslyn, and J. L. Heid (Editors). Avi Publishing Co., Westport, Conn.

WEISS, T. J. 1970. Food Oils and their Uses. Avi Publishing Co., Westport, Conn.

WILLIAMS, K. A. 1950. Oils, Fats and Fatty Foods, 3rd Edition. Blakiston Co., Philadelphia.

WOERFEL, J. B. 1960. Shortenings. In Bakery Technology and Engineering. S. A. Matz (Editor). Avi Publishing Co., Westport, Conn.

CHAPTER 17

Cereal Grains and Their Processing

INTRODUCTION

The cereal grains provide the world's most important source of calories. These grains are consumed as such or in slightly modified form as major items of diet; they are further processed into flour, starch, oil, bran, sugar syrups, and numerous additional ingredients used in the manufacture of other foods; and they are fed to livestock and thereby converted into meat, milk, and eggs.

On a worldwide basis, rice is the most important cereal crop, supplying the major food of more than half of the world's population. This rice is grown largely in Asia where about 93% of the world's crop is produced. Actually the world acreage in wheat is about twice that of rice, but the yield of rice per acre is slightly more than double that of wheat accounting for the greater quantity of rice produced.

The principal cereal grains grown in the United States are corn, wheat, oats, sorghum, barley, rye, rice, and buckwheat. In the United States corn is by far the largest cereal crop, in recent years averaging about 4 billion bushels, but most of it is used for feeding livestock. Wheat at about 1.3 billion bushels per year is the largest U.S. cereal crop used for human food.

GENERAL COMPOSITIONS AND STRUCTURES

The major constituents of the principal cereal grains are seen in Table 55. These grains contain about 10 to 14% moisture, 58 to 72% carbohydrate, 8

TABLE 55

TYPICAL PERCENTAGE COMPOSITIONS OF CEREAL GRAINS

Grain	Moisture	Carbohydrate	Protein	Fat	Indigestible Fiber	Calories (Per 100 Gm)
Corn	11	72	10	4	2	352
Wheat	11	69	13	2	3	340
Oats	13	58	10	5	10	317
Sorghum	11	70	12	4	2	348
Barley	14	63	12	2	6	320
Rye	11	71	12	2	2	321
Rice	11	65	8	2	9	310
Buckwheat	10	64	11	2	11	318

to 13% protein, 2 to 5% fat, and anywhere from 2 to 11% indigestible fiber. They also contain about 300 to 350 Cal per 100 gm quantity. While these are typical values, compositions will vary slightly depending upon varieties of the particular grain, geographical and weather conditions, and other factors.

The moisture contents of 10 to 14% represent properly ripened and dried grains. When the grains from the field are substantially higher than this they must be dried to this moisture range otherwise they may mold and rot in storage before they are further processed. It is to be noted that the cereal grains contain about two-thirds carbohydrate, and this is in the form

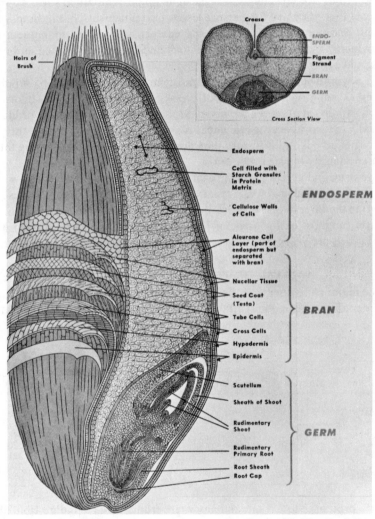

Courtesy of The Wheat Flour Institute

FIG. 233. STRUCTURE OF A WHEAT KERNEL

of digestible starches and sugars. The operations of milling generally will remove indigestible fiber and fat from these grains when they are to be consumed for human food.

With respect to comparative structure there are a few important features that the cereal grains have in common and these form the basis for subsequent milling and other processing operations. All of the cereal grains are plant seeds and as such contain a large centrally located starchy endosperm which also is rich in protein, protective outer layers such as hull and bran, and an embryo or germ usually located near the bottom of the seed. These portions are seen in the diagrams for wheat and corn in Fig. 233 and 234.

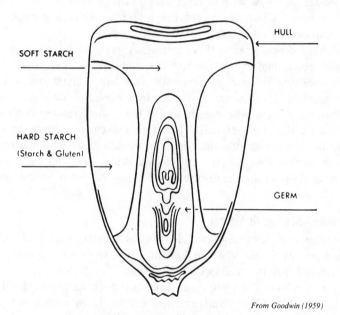

From Goodwin (1959)

FIG. 234.   DIAGRAM OF A CORN KERNEL

For most food uses we remove the hulls which are largely indigestible by man, the bran which is dark colored, and the germ which is high in oil, is enzymatically active, and under certain conditions would be likely to produce a rancid condition in the grain. Thus we are primarily interested in the starchy, proteinaceous endosperm. Since the bran is rich in B vitamins and minerals it is common practice to add these back to processed grains from which bran has been removed and this is known as enrichment.

Besides indigestibility of hulls, bran color, and possible rancidity from the germs, further reason for removing these components in many cases is to improve the functional properties of the endosperm in manufactured food use. For example, white bread made from wheat flour would have less acceptable color, flavor, and volume if the bran and germ were not removed before the flour was ground. However, there also are applications where we do not remove hulls, bran, or germ, but utilize the unmilled whole grain. Grain for animal feed is an example. Sprouted barley used for its malting effect in the brewing industry is another example. Let us now look at some of the principal cereal grains individually with respect to their processing and utilization.

WHEAT

The reader may now wish to refer back to the section on "Bread Producing Operations" Chap. 2, where the interrelationships between wheat, milling, and bread making were briefly described.

As with all cereal grains, there are many varieties of wheat grown for high yield, resistance to weather, insects, and disease, and grown for optimum composition for special food uses. In Chap. 2 hard and soft wheats were mentioned. Hard wheat is higher in protein, yields a stronger flour which forms a more elastic dough, and is better for bread making where a strong elastic dough is essential for high leavened volume. In contrast soft wheat is lower in protein, yields a weaker flour which forms weak doughs or batters, and is better for cake making. In either case, wherever wheat is used for human consumption the majority of it is first converted to flour.

Conventional Milling of Wheat

The miller receives the wheat, cleans it of foreign seeds and soil, soaks or conditions the wheat to about 17% moisture to give it optimum milling properties and then proceeds with the milling.

Milling involves a progressive series of disintegrations followed by sievings (Fig. 235). The disintegrations are made by rollers set progressively closer and closer together. The first rollers break open the bran and free the germ from the endosperm. The second and third rollers further pulverize the rather brittle endosperm and flatten out the more semiplastic germ. The flakes of bran and flattened germ are removed by the sieves under these first few sets of rollers. The pulverized endosperm is run through successive rollers set still closer together to grind it into finer and finer flour, which also is sifted under each set of rollers to remove last traces of bran.

From such an operation several flour fractions having finer and finer endosperm particles are collected. What is more, these finer fractions will contain progressively lower and lower amounts of ground up contaminating germ or bran, some of which always gets through the earlier sieves. As a

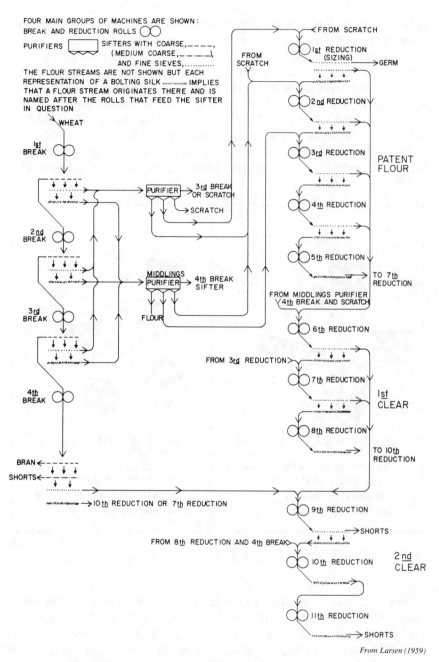

FIG. 235. FLOW DIAGRAM OF TYPICAL WHEAT MILLING SYSTEM

From Larsen (1959)

result, as the flour is progressively milled it becomes whiter in color, better in bread-making quality, but lower in vitamin and mineral content.

The resulting flour, no matter how fine it is ground by this milling procedure, will have a starch and protein composition which is a consequence of the variety and kind of wheat that was ground. If the wheat was a hard wheat then the protein to starch ratio in the flour will be greater than if the wheat was a soft wheat. Thus the kind of flour that can be milled by such a procedure is largely dependent upon the kind of wheat available.

Figure 236 is a diagram of two finely milled flours. The endosperm contains both protein (the dark matter) and starch granules (the white matter

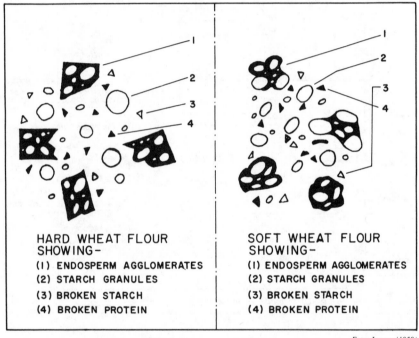

HARD WHEAT FLOUR
SHOWING–
(1) ENDOSPERM AGGLOMERATES
(2) STARCH GRANULES
(3) BROKEN STARCH
(4) BROKEN PROTEIN

SOFT WHEAT FLOUR
SHOWING–
(1) ENDOSPERM AGGLOMERATES
(2) STARCH GRANULES
(3) BROKEN STARCH
(4) BROKEN PROTEIN

From Larsen (1959)

FIG. 236.   PARTICLE TYPES PRESENT IN HARD AND SOFT WHEAT FLOUR

in this diagram). In addition to the large mixed endosperm agglomerates, there are smaller fragmented starch and protein particles. The fragmented starch and protein particles are too close in size to be further separated from one another by the sieves of the conventional milling operation. If they could be, then this would make it possible to separate any flour into fractions differing in protein and starch contents. Such a separation could yield both a hard and a soft flour from the same wheat. Further, a naturally hard wheat could be made to yield a soft flour plus a protein fraction just as a naturally soft wheat could be made to yield a hard flour plus a starch fraction.

Turbomilling and Air Classification

It is now possible to make this separation of flour into higher protein or higher starch fractions and the method is known as turbomilling. In turbomilling, flour from conventional milling is further reduced in particle size in special high speed turbo grinders which cause the endosperm agglomerates to abrade against each other in a high speed air vortex.

While the resulting protein and starch particles are too close in size to be separated by sieves, they do differ sufficiently in particle size, shape, and density to be separable in a stream of turbulent air. In this case the slightly finer protein particles rise and the starch particles settle in the stream of air. The flour and air mixture is blown into a specially designed air classifier, which then may impose centrifugal force on the suspended particles, and two fractions of flour differing in protein and starch concentrations are recovered.

Turbomilling, a development of the late 1950's, probably is the greatest milling advance of the past century since we now have the power to separate flour into fractions and then blend the fractions in any desired ratio. Thus we can custom blend flours for bread making, cake making, cookie making, and many other specific applications.

Uses of Wheat Flour

The uses of wheat flour in the baking industry include the making of breads, sweet doughs, cakes, biscuits, doughnuts, crackers, and the like. Some of the unit operations and kinds of equipment used in producing and shaping bread dough were indicated in Chap. 2 (Fig. 15 through 18). Further principles of baking will be discussed in the latter half of the present chapter.

Wheat flour is also used in making breakfast cereals, gravies, soups, confections, and other articles. But a principal use of wheat flour second only to baked goods is the preparation of alimentary pastes, such as macaroni, spaghetti, and other forms of noodles. Alimentary pastes like bakery doughs contain mostly flour and water. They also may contain eggs, salt, and other minor ingredients. But they differ from bakery doughs in that the alimentary pastes are not leavened.

The unleavened dough is formed by mixing the ingredients in the ratio of about 100 parts of hard wheat flour to 30 parts of water. The dough then may be extruded in a thin sheet (Fig. 237) which is cut into flat noodles

Courtesy of Braibanti and Co.

FIG. 237.   EXTRUDED NOODLE DOUGH BEING FED TO CUTTER

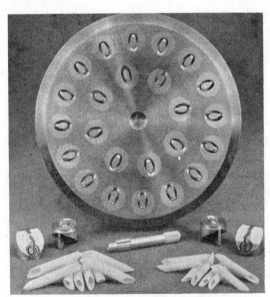

Courtesy of Glenn G. Hoskins Co.

FIG. 238.   DIE FOR EXTRUDING MACARONI

and dried in an oven to about 12% moisture. Or the unleavened dough may be extruded in dozens of other shapes depending upon the choice of dies. Figure 238 indicates the way macaroni with a hole in the middle is extruded. It also is oven dried to about 12% moisture.

RICE

As previously indicated, rice is the world's most important human food crop. Where wheat for the most part is ground into flour, most of the world's rice is consumed as the intact grain, minus hull, bran, and germ. Therefore the milling process must be designed not to disintegrate the endosperm core of the seed.

Rice Milling

This is done with a series of machines which first feed whole grains of rice between abrasive discs or moving rubber belts. These machines are known as shellers or hullers. They do not crush the grains but instead rub the outer layer of hull from the underlying kernels. The hulls are now separated from the kernels by jets of air and the kernels which are known as brown rice move to another abrasive device called a rice milling machine. Here remaining inner layers of bran and germ are dislodged by the rubbing action of a ribbed rotor. The endosperms with bran and germ removed can now be further polished to a white high glossy finish.

As in the case of wheat, the higher the degree of milling or polishing the lower are the remaining vitamin and mineral contents. This is particularly serious in the case of rice because entire populations depend upon rice as their principal staple of diet.

Rice Enrichment

There are two major ways to enrich rice and they differ from the simple admixture of vitamins and minerals in powder form as may be done in the case of flour.

One method is to coat the polished rice with the enrichment mixture and then to further coat the grains with a waterproof edible film material. Upon hardening the film material prevents the enrichment ingredients from dissolving away when the marketed rice is washed, as is common practice.

The second important method involves parboiling or steeping the whole rice grains in hot water before removal of hulls, bran, and germ in milling. Parboiling may be for about ten hours at 160° F, although several other time-temperature combinations can be used. This causes the B vitamins and minerals from the hulls, bran, and germ to leach into the endosperm. The rice is then dried, milled, and polished as before. Parboiled rice processed for enrichment also has been referred to as converted rice.

The principal nutrients with which we want to enrich rice are thiamine, niacin, and iron, and these are particularly effective in reducing incidence of beriberi where polished rice is a major item of diet. Legislation requires all rice sold in Puerto Rico to be enriched. In the United States, the state of South Carolina, which consumes considerable rice, also has made it mandatory that rice sold within the state be enriched. This is not required in other states, although most of the rice sold in the United States is enriched. To be called enriched rice in the United States, the product must meet the standards indicated in Table 56.

TABLE 56

FEDERAL STANDARDS [1] FOR RICE ENRICHMENT

	Minimum Mg/Lb	Maximum Mg/Lb
Thiamine	2.0	4.0
Riboflavin [2]	1.2	2.4
Niacin	16	32
Iron	13	26
Calcium [3]	500	1,000
Vitamin D [3]	250	1,000

[1]Anon. (1957, 1958).
[2]Held in abeyance.
[3]Optional ingredients.

Improved Varieties

Plant breeders are continuously at work improving the yields and properties of cereal grains. This includes considerations of soil types, weather conditions, response to fertilizer application, resistance to disease and insect attack, nutritional quality, storage stability, milling properties, cooking and processing characteristics, and other factors. In the case of rice the continual world shortage may be somewhat relieved by a high yielding strain designated IR-8, developed at the International Rice Research Institute in the Philippines. IR-8 has proven especially high yielding in the tropics since seed became available in 1966. Acceptability of the cooked rice by consumers in most parts of tropical Asia also appears adequate. Other high yield varieties with still better milling and cooking characteristics continue to be sought by government sponsored breeding programs in several countries. While this is going on it is of interest to note that rice as a diet staple may give way when wheat becomes available in the form of bread and pasta. This tendency is now being seen in Japan and in parts of Indonesia.

Rice Products

Rice can be made quick-cooking or almost instant in terms of preparation time. This is done by precooking the rice to gelatinize the starch, and then drying the rice under conditions which will give the rice an expanded internal structure for quick absorption of water during subsequent preparation. Many patents exist.

Rice may be ground into flour and as such is used by people who are allergic to wheat flour. Rice is a source of starch. It is the grain that is used in preparing the Japanese fermented alcoholic beverage sake. Rice hulls, bran, and germ also are used as animal feed.

CORN

Corn is the largest U. S. cereal grain crop but as we have said, most of it is fed to farm animals. For this use it is commonly dried on the cob.

Corn is consumed as human food in various forms. In its harvested wet form it is consumed as a vegetable. The kernels of a special variety may be dried and consumed as pop corn. Pop corn pops because on heating, moisture in the center of the kernels turns to steam and this escapes with force sufficient to explode the kernels. Pop corn might therefore be considered the original puffed cereal.

But the majority of corn consumed as human food has undergone milling and is consumed as a specific or modified fraction of the original cereal grain. Like the other cereal grains, corn is milled to remove hulls and germ. Both are fed to livestock. In addition the germ is the important source of corn oil. Corn is milled in two basic ways known as dry milling and wet milling.

Dry Milling

Corn kernels are first conditioned to about 21% moisture and then passed between special rotating cones which loosen the hulls and germ from the endosperm. The entire mixture is next dried to about 15% moisture to facilitate subsequent roller milling and sieving. The hulls may now be removed by jets of air. From here on the milling is not much different than in the case of wheat. The endosperm and loosened germs are passed through rollers which flatten the germs and crush the more brittle endosperm. Sieving now easily separates the flattened germs from the endosperm particles. The endosperm may be recovered in the form of coarse grits or corn meal, or it may be passed through finer rollers and reduced to corn flour.

Wet Milling

Wet milling is different. Its objective is to use water as a means of softening the corn kernels, floating off the lighter oil bearing germs, removing the hulls, and then separating the endosperm starch and protein as distinct fractions from the water suspension.

After cleaning the corn kernels the first step in wet milling is steeping the kernels in large tanks of warm water which generally contain acid and sulfur dioxide as a mild preservative. In Fig. 239 softened kernels may be

Courtesy of Corn Industries Research Foundation, Inc.

FIG. 239. SOFTENED CORN KERNELS DROPPING FROM STEEPING TANK ONTO CONVEYOR FOR SUBSEQUENT GRINDING

seen being dropped from the overhead steeping tanks onto a conveyor trough.

The softened kernels are next run through an attrition mill which breaks up the kernels. The pasty mass from this mill is then pumped to water-filled settling troughs. Here the lighter density rubbery germs float to the top and are skimmed off to be pressed for oil. The slurry now contains the hulls and the protein and starch fractions of the endosperm. The water slurry is passed through screens which next remove the hulls.

The remaining water slurry containing the starch and protein fractions is now passed through high speed centrifuges, such as seen in Fig. 240, which separate the heavier starch from the lighter protein. The starch fraction is finally dried to yield the familiar corn starch. The protein fraction is also dried to yield corn gluten which is rich in the corn protein known as zein. Corn gluten is commonly used in animal feeds. Separated zein has industrial uses including some as a food ingredient. The corn starch

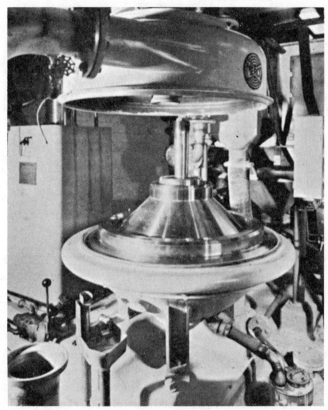

Courtesy of Corn Industries Research Foundation, Inc.

FIG. 240. OPEN VIEW OF CENTRIFUGE FOR SEPARATING GLUTEN FROM STARCH

can be used as such in manufactured foods or be further converted into corn syrup by the hydrolytic action of acid or starch splitting enzymes. The relationships between these various products from the wet milling of corn are seen in Fig. 241.

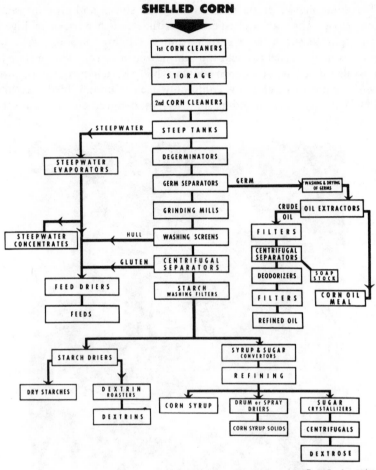

From Goodwin (1959)

FIG. 241. FLOW DIAGRAM OF THE WET-MILLING PROCESS

BARLEY, OATS, RYE

Each of these is used for animal feed. Barley and rye also provide sources of fermentable carbohydrate in the production of fermented beverages and distilled liquors. The flour of rye after removal of bran and germ is used in mixture with wheat flour in the production of rye bread. Rye flour cannot be used alone for this purpose since its protein would not form films sufficiently strong to support an expanded bread structure. Most oats for human consumption are marketed as rolled oat breakfast cereals.

Barley is also used to produce barley malt. In this case the whole barley seed is steeped in water to allow the live germ to sprout. The sprouted barley having initiated growth now becomes much increased in enzymatic activity, especially starch-digesting amylase activity. The sprouted barley is next dried under mild heat so as not to inactivate its enzymes. The sprouted dried barley, now known as malt, is used in the brewing industry to help digest starchy material into sugars for rapid yeast fermentation. The malt also has a distinctive flavor which contributes to the flavor of brewed beverages such as beer. Malt further adds flavor to breakfast cereals and malted-milk concentrates. Malt syrups also find use in various bakery operations where amylase activity is desired.

BREAKFAST CEREALS

The cereal grains find an important use in the manufacture of breakfast cereals. Most breakfast cereals are made from the endosperm of wheat, corn, rice, and oats. The endosperm may simply be broken or pressed, with or without toasting, to yield such uncooked cereals as farina and oatmeal.

From Matz (1959)

FIG. 242.   A SET OF CEREAL FLAKING ROLLS

But far more popular in the United States are the ready-to-eat cereals. For these the endosperm may be broken or ground into a mash, and then converted into flakes by squeezing the broken grits or mash between rollers. The mash also can be extruded into numerous shapes. Or the endosperm may be kept intact as kernels to be puffed, as in the case of puffed rice. But in all cases the flaked, formed, or puffed cereal must be oven cooked and dried to develop toasted flavor and to obtain the crisp, brittle textures desired. This crispness requires that many of the ready-to-eat breakfast cereals be dried to about 3 to 5% moisture.

In Fig. 242 is a set of flaking rolls that may be used for producing corn flakes. The course pieces of corn endosperm or grits are cooked and then partially dried to a firm plastic consistency. The grits are then passed through these rolls which squeeze them into individual flakes. The flakes are oven toasted and dried to about 3% moisture.

Wheat or rice endosperms to be puffed are first cooked and then partially dried as individual kernels. These are next placed in a puffing gun which heats the kernels under pressure converting moisture within the kernels into steam. Suddenly the gun is opened and the steam under pressure within the kernels expands explosively and puffs the kernels (Fig. 243). In

Courtesy of Quaker Oats Co.

FIG. 243.   DOUGH PIECES EXPLODING FROM EXPERIMENTAL PUFFING GUN

some cases mashes of cereal doughs are extruded into moist pellet forms. The pellets may be puffed in the same manner. The puffed cereals are toasted, often sugar coated, and dried.

SOME PRINCIPLES OF BAKING

Wheat flours find their principal applications in the production of bakery products. Bakery products for the most part differ from other wheat products such as alimentary pastes or noodles and unpuffed breakfast cereals in that bakery products are leavened, that is they are raised to yield baked goods of low density.

The term baking really defines the operation of heating dough products in an oven, but since there are many steps that must take place before the oven if baking is to be successful, the term baking has come to mean all of the science and technology that must precede the oven as well as the oven heating step itself. We will consider baking in this broader sense.

While there are a great many bakery products which grade one into another in terms of their formulas, methods of preparation, and product characteristics, it is possible to divide bakery products according to the way in which they are leavened. This will not give a perfect division but nonetheless a useful one. Such a division might be made as follows:

(1) Yeast raised goods—includes breads and sweet doughs leavened by carbon dioxide from yeast fermentation.
(2) Chemically leavened goods—includes layer cakes, doughnuts, and biscuits raised by carbon dioxide from baking powders and chemical agents.
(3) Air leavened goods—includes angel cakes and sponge cakes made without baking powder.
(4) Partially leavened goods—includes pie crusts, certain crackers, and other items where no intentional leavening agents are used yet a slight leavening occurs from expanding steam and other gases during the oven baking operation.

This kind of division refers to the intended source of the leavening gas, however the intended source is not the only source of leavening as will be seen shortly.

Leavening gas can produce leavening only if it is trapped in a system that will hold the gas and expand along with the gas. Therefore, much of cereal science related to baking technology is really the engineering of food structures through the formation of correct doughs and batters to trap leavening gases, and then the coagulation or fixing of these structures by the application of heat. This brings in the need to understand further some of the properties of flour and certain other baking ingredients.

Major Baking Ingredients and Their Functions

Gluten and Starch of Wheat Flour.—The principal functional protein of wheat flour is gluten. Gluten has the important property that when it is moistened and worked by mechanical action it forms an elastic dough. This dough may be stretched in two directions and form sheets or films, or it may be stretched in all directions under the pressure of expanding gas and form bubbles as does bubble gum. However, unlike bubble gum, the films weaken and then break down under excessive mechanical action such as overmixing of the dough. Additionally, upon exposure to sufficient heat the gluten coagulates and forms a semirigid structure. If the gluten has been expanded by gas prior to being heated then this fairly rigid structure will be of a cellular character such as the inside of a loaf of bread.

The gluten of wheat flour has starch associated with it. Wheat starch does not form films as does gluten, but, when heated, the moistened starch forms a paste and stiffens, or more correctly gelatinizes.

Thus these major constituents of wheat flour together are capable of forming a batter or dough depending upon the amount of water employed; and both the gluten and starch contribute to the semirigid structures resulting when such batters or doughs are heated.

The character of the dough or batter will depend considerably upon the type of flour used. As indicated earlier, strong flours containing more gluten, and gluten of a quality that will stretch farther before tearing, are the kind chosen for making bread because bread dough must be able to expand to a great degree and yield baked products of especially light density. Weaker flours generally contain less gluten and their films tear more readily; further, such films are less tough, and when baked yield structures that are less chewy and more tender. This is the kind of flour selected for making cakes and related products where more tender and friable structures are desired. Figure 244 shows unbaked and baked doughs that were

Courtesy of The Wheat Flour Institute

FIG. 244. UNBAKED AND BAKED GLUTEN DOUGHS FROM SAME WEIGHT OF (LEFT TO RIGHT) CAKE FLOUR, ALL-PURPOSE FLOUR, AND BREAD FLOUR

made from gluten separated from the same weight of cake flour, bread flour, and an intermediate flour known as all-purpose flour.

Leavening Agents.—As implied earlier, the effective leavening agents do not include only yeast and baking powders. Water in doughs or batters turns to steam in the oven and the expanding steam contributes to leavening. Air in a dough or a batter similarly expands when heated in the oven and contributes to leavening. It, therefore, should be appreciated that in yeast leavened or chemically leavened goods, although carbon dioxide from fermentation or from baking powder is a major leavening gas it is supplemented with expanding steam and expanding air from oven heat. A closer look at leaveners also will show that not only are the amounts of gas they produce important, but equally important are the rates of gas production and the time of gas production.

Yeast.—Yeast used in baking may be in the moist pressed cake form or in the dehydrated granular form. In either case the yeast consists of billions of living cells of *Saccharomyces cerevisiae*. In the bread making process and related sweet dough processes, yeast ferments simple sugars and produces carbon dioxide and alcohol. This fermentation is gradual, beginning slowly and increasing in rate with time. The increase in rate with time is due to two conditions in a dough: (1) yeast cells are multiplying and their enzymes are becoming more active while the dough is prepared and held, and (2) sugar for fermentation is gradually being liberated from starch in the dough by the action of natural flour enzymes.

This gradual production of carbon dioxide is desirable in contrast to an immediate burst of gas because the film-forming property of gluten also is developed gradually as the dough is being hydrated and mechanically kneaded. If the gas were to evolve before the film-forming property became developed then the gas would escape entrapment and there would be no leavening. Further, in the operations involved in converting the large dough mass into individual loaf-size pieces there is considerable rough handling which tends to knock gas out of the rising dough pieces. Gradual and continued production of carbon dioxide up to the point of oven baking replenishes the lost gas and maximizes leavening.

The distribution of gas bubbles in the elastic dough prior to baking, the delicate structure of the leavened dough, and the origin of the cellular structure of the baked loaf can be seen in Fig. 245. The amounts of leavening gases and their rates of production must be balanced against the rate of development of the film-forming structure and its strength to hold the gas prior to and during baking.

In the baking operation itself heat kills the yeast, inactivates its enzymes, and fermentation to produce more carbon dioxide ceases. However, the bubbles already formed enlarge under the influence of heat due to expan-

Courtesy of The Wheat Flour Institute

FIG. 245.   GAS BUBBLES IN EXPANDING DOUGH PRIOR TO BAKING

sion of carbon dioxide, expansion of entrapped air, and conversion of water into steam. As the temperature of the loaf rises starch gelatinizes, gluten coagulates, and a semirigid, less fragile structure results.

Baking Powders.—Baking powders used in making cakes and related goods contain particles of sodium bicarbonate as a source of carbon dioxide, and particles of an edible acid to generate the carbon dioxide when water and heat are supplied. The simplified overall reaction in the case of a baking powder containing monocalcium phosphate as the baking acid can be visualized as follows:

$$3CaH_4(PO_4)_2 + 8NaHCO_3 \rightarrow Ca_3(PO_4)_2 + 4Na_2HPO_4 + 8CO_2 + 8H_2O$$

Monocalcium   Tricalcium   Disodium
phosphate   phosphate   phosphate

Such a reaction can take place too rapidly and so its speed and time of occurrence must be controlled. It is in the differences in times and rates of reactions that various baking powders differ, and baking powders are formulated to produce controlled release of gas for specific bakery product applications.

For example, in making cakes all ingredients may be mixed together (Fig. 246) and then deposited as a fluid batter into pans from a large bakery hopper. The fluid batter with its weak cake flour has very little gluten development or other means to hold evolved carbon dioxide. Thus, if there

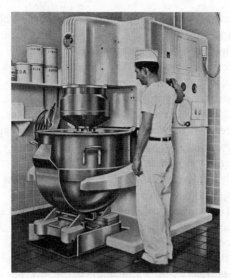

Courtesy of American Machine and Foundry Co.

FIG. 246. BATCH MIXING OF CAKE BATTER

is a major carbon dioxide evolution during mixing or holding of batters, the gas will largely escape from the batter and leavening power will be lost. However, when the batter is placed in the oven starch gelatinizes, gluten coagulates, and egg proteins if present coagulate. If gas is produced while this is taking place in the oven then the gas will be trapped and expand the solidifying mass giving the desired volume increase and cellular structure.

On the other hand, one can have too much gas evolution in the oven due to an excessive amount of baking powder. This tends to overexpand the gas cells which become weakened and collapse. The result is a coarse grain structure with lowered volume. It also is possible to produce gas in the oven too slowly. When this happens the gluten, starch, and eggs set the structure and the crust is formed before all of the gas is released. The late gas can then rupture the crumb structure and produce cracks in the surface crust.

We regulate the times and rates of gas evolution from baking powders by the selection of different baking acids which react faster or slower with the sodium bicarbonate. These acids also may be used in different particle sizes, or they may be coated with various materials to control their rates of solution and thereby further control their rates of reaction with sodium bicarbonate.

Baking powders are of two principal kinds: fast or slow acting. Some are double-acting powders. These will contain both a fast and a slow reacting acid in combination with sodium bicarbonate. Double-acting baking powders are compounded to give a quick burst of carbon dioxide in the batter stage to lighten the batter and make mixing easier, especially for the housewife who may mix by hand, and then to liberate additional carbon dioxide in the oven when the structure is being set.

Eggs.—In addition to their nutrient, flavor, and color contributions, eggs can function as a principal structure builder in cakes. Like gluten, egg white is a mixture of proteins. It forms films and entraps air when it is whipped, and on heating it coagulates to produce rigidity. The proteins of egg yolk have similar properties. This is particularly important when eggs are combined with relatively low levels of a weak flour, as is the case in the preparation of angel cakes and sponge cakes.

In these cakes the eggs are whipped and gently folded together with the other ingredients. The entrapped air in the egg foam is the primary leavening system since generally no baking powder is used. In the oven, the gluten, starch, and egg stiffen and the subdivided air bubbles expand from heat. Steam generated from water enters the air bubbles and further serves to expand them. This is one reason why the whipping quality and foam stability of eggs is so important to the baker.

Shortening.—Unlike flour and eggs which are structure builders and are tougheners, shortening is a tenderizer. But in many recipes, additionally, the beating of shortening is called for to entrap air prior to the incorporation of other ingredients to finish the batter. When the batter is baked in the oven the shortening melts and releases the air bubbles which contribute to the leavening action of baking powder and expanding steam. The melted shortening then deposits around the cell walls of the coagulating structure to contribute a tenderizing effect and lubricate the texture.

The grain of cakes being fine or coarse in cellular structure and the cake volume will be affected by the number and size of air bubbles and water droplets trapped in the beaten shortening. These in turn are determined by the plasticity of the shortening and the use of emulsifiers. The state of emulsion also will be affected by the other ingredients present and the sequence in which they are incorporated into the batter. The photomicrographs in Fig. 247 are of two layer cake batters with the shortening stained by a fat soluble dye. The spheres are mostly air bubbles within fat globules. Such differences between batters may be produced, for example, by creaming the shortening and sugar together prior to mixing in the remaining ingredients in contrast to beating all of the ingredients together in a single step. Such modifications in mixing procedure can easily give differences in grain structure and cake volume from the same ingredient formulation.

Sugar.—Sugar like shortening is a tenderizer in baked goods. It also has other attributes as do all of the ingredients used in baking. Besides

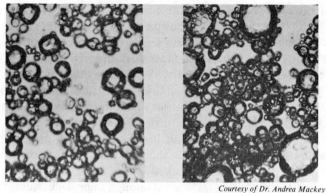

Courtesy of Dr. Andrea Mackey

FIG. 247. PHOTOMICROGRAPHS OF LAYER CAKE BATTERS SHOWING
AIR BUBBLES WITHIN FAT GLOBULES

sweetness, sugar in the form of sucrose provides additional fermentable substrate in yeast raised goods. Bakers' yeast cannot ferment sucrose directly, but hydrolyzes it first by means of the enzyme invertase into glucose and fructose. The yeast then immediately ferments the glucose, and after the glucose is consumed it proceeds to ferment the fructose. Sugar also has moisture retaining properties in baked goods. In this respect the hydrolytic products of sucrose, namely glucose and fructose which together are referred to as invert sugar, usually are superior to sucrose. This is one reason why invert sugar syrups are frequently used in addition to sucrose in various baked goods made without yeast. Corn syrups from the hydrolysis of starch, which contain glucose, maltose, and dextrins also have this moisture retaining property. Sucrose, fructose, glucose, maltose, and dextrins further contribute to the different kinds of browning that baked goods develop in the oven.

The Baking Step

Baking is a heating process in which many reactions occur at different rates. Some of these reactions include the following: (1) evolution and expansion of gases; (2) coagulation of gluten and eggs, and gelatinization of starch; (3) partial dehydration from evaporation of water; (4) development of flavors; (5) changes of color due to Maillard browning reactions between milk, gluten, and egg proteins with reducing sugars, as well as other chemical color changes; (6) crust formation from surface dehydration; and (7) crust darkening from Maillard browning reactions and caramelization of sugars.

The rates of these different reactions and the order in which they occur depend to a large extent upon the rate of heat transfer through the batter or dough. If the crust forms before the center of the mass is baked, because of too high top heat compared to bottom heat, or too hot an oven, then the center of the baked item may remain soggy, or late escaping gas may crack the crust. Quite apart from the temperature distribution in the oven, the rate of heat transfer also is affected by the nature of the baking pan.

Shiny pans reflect heat and slow down heat transfer into the pan contents. Dull and dark colored pans absorb heat more rapidly and speed heat transfer. The shape of pans also is obviously important, and a shallow pan with the batter or dough in a thin layer will develop different thermal gradients and give different results than a smaller deeper pan containing the same weight of material to be baked.

Were all of the preceding factors not enough to provide causes for variations in baked goods, there also is the effect of altitude. Unless otherwise indicated, most bakery formulas were developed for use at altitudes approaching sea level. At elevations of about 3,000 ft and higher, excessive expansion of leavening gases under reduced atmospheric pressure causes stretching and weakening of the cellular structure being formed in the oven. The result can be collapsed items of coarse and irregular grain. Corrective measures at high altitudes therefore call for cake formulas with less baking powder, the use of more tougheners such as more flour or stronger flour, or decreased levels of tenderizers such as shortening and sugars. Because of their tougher doughs bread formulas are less sensitive to altitude than cake formulas.

The varieties of breads, cakes, and other bakery items can run into the thousands as ingredients, formulas, and preparation methods are changed. Today the principles of cereal chemistry and baking technology are well understood and the many possible variables can be kept under fairly rigid control in large modern bakeries. This permits automated high speed operations with uniform producton rates of tens of thousands of units per hour. In smaller bakeries and in the home, however, baking remains more of an art than a science.

BIBLIOGRAPHY

AMERICAN ASSOCIATION OF CEREAL CHEMISTS. 1962. Cereal Laboratory Methods. 7th Edition. Am. Assoc. Cereal Chemists, Minneapolis.
AMERICAN ASSOCIATION OF CEREAL CHEMISTS. 1966. Continuous bread-making. Cereal Sci. Today (Special Issue) Sept.
ANON. 1957. Rice. Federal Register 22, 6887–6888.
ANON. 1958. Rice. Federal Register 23, 1170–1171.
CARSON, G. 1957. Corn Flake Crusade. Rinehart and Co., New York.
DANIELS, R. 1970. Modern Breakfast Cereal Processes 1970. Food Process. Rev. 13. Noyes Data Corp., Park Ridge, N.J.
DANIELS, R. 1970. Rice and Bulgur Quick-Cooking Processes 1970. Food Process. Rev. 16. Noyes Data Corp., Park Ridge, N.J.

GOODWIN, J. T.   1959.   Wet-milling. *In* The Chemistry and Technology of Cereals as Food and Feed. S. A. Matz (Editor). Avi Publishing Co., Westport, Conn. (Out of print.)

GUTTERSON, M.   1969.   Baked Goods Production Practices 1969. Food Process. Rev. *9*. Noyes Data Corp., Park Ridge, N.J.

HARRELL, C. G.   1964.   Cereal grain production and processing. *In* Food Processing Operations, Vol. 3. M. A. Joslyn, and J. L. Heid (Editors). Avi Publishing Co., Westport, Conn.

HUMMEL, C.   1966.   Macaroni Products—Manufacture, Processing and Packing, 2nd Edition. Food Trade Review, London.

INGLETT, G. E. (Editor)   1970.   Corn: Culture, Processing, Products. Avi Publishing Co., Westport, Conn.

JONES, C. R.   1960.   New developments in milling process. Milling *135*, No. 19, 494–495, 498–499; No. 20, 524–526; No. 21, 558–559, 562.

JONES, C. R., HOLTON, P., and STEVENS, D. J.   1960.   The separation of flour into fractions of different protein content by means of air classification. J. Biochem. Microbiol. Technol. Eng. *1*, 77–98.

KELLY, K. M.   1961.   Cake batter mixing—continuous-batch. Proc. Am. Soc. Bakery Engrs. *1961*, 260–264.

KENT-JONES, D. W., and AMOS, A. J.   1967.   Modern Cereal Chemistry, 6th Edition. Food Trade Review, London.

LACHMANN, A.   1970.   Starches and Corn Syrups 1970. *In* Food Process. Rev. Noyes Data Corp., Park Ridge, N.J.

LARSEN, R. A.   1959.   Milling. *In* The Chemistry and Technology of Cereals as Food and Feed, S. A. Matz (Editor). Avi Publishing Co., Westport, Conn. (Out of print.)

MATZ, S. A.   1968.   Cookie and Cracker Technology. Avi Publishing Co., Westport, Conn.

MATZ, S. A.   1969.   Cereal Science. Avi Publishing Co., Westport, Conn.

MATZ, S. A.   1970.   Cereal Technology. Avi Publishing Co., Westport, Conn.

MATZ, S. A.   1972.   Bakery Technology and Engineering, 2nd Edition. Avi Publishing Co., Westport, Conn.

POMERANZ, Y., and SHELLENBERGER, J. A.   1971.   Bread Science and Technology. Avi Publishing Co., Westport, Conn.

POTTER, N. N., KELLY, T. K., and ZANG, J. A.   1966.   Apparatus for Rapid Mixing. U.S. Pat. 3,280,764. Oct. 25.

PYLER, E. J.   1952.   Baking Science and Technology, Vols. 1 and 2. Siebel Publishing Co., Chicago.

SULTAN, W. J.   1969.   Practical Baking, 2nd Edition. Avi Publishing Co., Westport, Conn.

WITT, P. R., JR.   1959.   Malting. *In* The Chemistry and Technology of Cereals as Food and Feed. S. A. Matz (Editor). Avi Publishing Co., Westport, Conn. (Out of print.)

CHAPTER 18

Vegetables, Fruits and Juices

INTRODUCTION

Vegetables and fruits have many similarities with respect to their compositions, methods of cultivation and harvesting, storage properties, and processing. In fact many vegetables may be considered fruits in the true botanical sense. Botanically, fruits are those portions of the plant which house seeds. Therefore such items as tomatoes, cucumbers, eggplant, peppers, okra, sweet corn, and others would be classified as fruits on this basis. However, the important distinction between fruits and vegetables has come to be made on a usage basis. Those plant items that are generally eaten with the main course of a meal are considered to be vegetables. Those that commonly are eaten as dessert are considered fruits. This is the distinction made by the food processor, certain marketing laws, and the consuming public, and this distinction will be followed in this discussion.

GENERAL PROPERTIES OF VEGETABLES AND FRUITS

The vegetables are derived from various parts of plants, and it is sometimes useful to associate different vegetables with the parts of the plant they represent since this provides clues to some of the characteristics we may expect in these items. Thus, onions are the bulb portion of the plant. Bulbs are really underground buds having fleshy leaves, and this characteristic is readily apparent in the structure of the onion. Broccoli and cauliflower are true flowers. Tomatoes and peppers are the seed-bearing fruit. Peas and shelled beans are the seeds. We expect seeds to be high in starch and protein and relatively low in moisture and this is the case for these vegetables. Green beans are the seeds and their pods. Celery is the stalk of the plant. Since stalks are supporting and conducting structures they would be expected to possess mechanical strength and tubular elements. Asparagus is a kind of stalk with leaves. Potatoes are fleshy stems or tubers. The eyes of potatoes are buds, as would be expected to be found on stems, and from which new plants may arise. Carrots are roots. A classification based on such morphological features is seen in Table 57.

Fruits, the dessert items, are the mature ovaries of plants with their seeds. The edible portion of most fruits is the fleshy part of the pericarp or vessel surrounding the seeds. Fruits in general are acidic and sugary. They commonly are grouped into several major divisions, depending principally upon botanical structure, chemical composition, and climatic require-

488

TABLE 57

CLASSIFICATION OF VEGETABLES[1]

	Examples
Earth vegetables	
roots	sweet potatoes, carrots
modified stems	
corms	taro
tubers	potatoes
modified buds	
bulbs	onions, garlic
Herbage vegetables	
leaves	cabbage, spinach, lettuce
petioles (leaf stalk)	celery, rhubarb
flower buds	cauliflower, artichokes
sprouts, shoots (young stems)	asparagus, bamboo shoots
Fruit vegetables	
legumes	peas, green beans
cereals	sweet corn
vine fruits	squash, cucumber
berry fruits	tomato, egg plant
tree fruits	avocado, breadfruit

[1]From Feinberg (1973).

ments. Thus, berries are fruits which are generally small and quite fragile, although cranberries are rather tough. Grapes are also physically fragile and grow in clusters. Melons, on the other hand, are large and have a tough outer rind. Drupes contain single pits and include such items as apricots, cherries, peaches, and plums. Pomes contain many pits, and are represented by apples, quince, and pears. Citrus fruits are chacteristically high in citric acid, as are oranges, grapefruit, and lemons. Tropical and subtropical fruits include bananas, dates, figs, pineapples, papayas, mangos, and others which require warm climates, but exclude the separate group of citrus fruits.

GROSS COMPOSITION

The compositions of representative vegetables and fruits in comparison with a few of the cereal grains are seen in Table 58. Compositions of vegetables and fruits not only vary for a given kind in accordance with botanical variety, cultivation practices, and weather, but change with the degree of maturity prior to harvest, and the condition of ripeness, which is progressive after harvest and is further influenced by storage conditions. Nevertheless, some generalizations can be made.

Most fresh vegetables and fruits are high in water, low in protein, and low in fat. In these cases water contents will generally be greater than 70% and frequently greater than 85%. Commonly protein contents will not be greater than 3.5% or fat contents greater than 0.5%. Exceptions exist in the case of dates and raisins which are substantially lower in moisture

TABLE 58

TYPICAL PERCENTAGE COMPOSITION OF FOODS OF PLANT ORIGIN [1]

	Percentage Composition—Edible Portion				
Food	Carbo-hydrate	Protein	Fat	Ash	Water
Cereals					
wheat flour, white	73.9	10.5	1.9	1.7	12
rice, milled, white...............	78.9	6.7	0.7	0.7	13
maize (corn) whole grain	72.9	9.5	4.3	1.3	12
Earth vegetables					
potatoes, white	18.9	2.0	0.1	1.0	78
sweet potatoes..................	27.3	1.3	0.4	1.0	70
Vegetables					
carrots........................	9.1	1.1	0.2	1.0	88.6
radishes.......................	4.2	1.1	0.1	0.9	93.7
asparagus	4.1	2.1	0.2	0.7	92.9
beans, snap, green	7.6	2.4	0.2	0.7	89.1
peas, fresh	17.0	6.7	0.4	0.9	75.0
lettuce	2.8	1.3	0.2	0.9	94.8
Fruits					
banana........................	24.0	1.3	0.4	0.8	73.5
orange	11.3	0.9	0.2	0.5	87.1
apple.........................	15.0	0.3	0.4	0.3	84.0
strawberries	8.3	0.8	0.5	0.5	89.9
melon.........................	6.0	0.6	0.2	0.4	92.8

[1] From Food Composition Tables, F.A.O., United Nations, Rome.

but cannot be considered fresh in the above sense; legumes such as peas and certain beans which are higher in protein; a few vegetables such as sweet corn which are slightly higher in fat; and avocados which are substantially higher in fat. On the other hand, vegetables and fruits are important sources of both digestible and indigestible carbohydrates. The digestible carbohydrates are present largely in the forms of sugars and starches while the indigestible cellulosic materials provide roughage important to normal digestion. Fruits and vegetables also are important sources of minerals and certain vitamins, especially vitamins A and C. The precursors of vitamin A, including β-carotene and certain other carotenoids are to be found particularly in the yellow-orange fruits and vegetables, and in the green leafy vegetables. Citrus fruits are excellent sources of vitamin C, but green leafy vegetables and tomatoes are also good sources. Potatoes further provide an important source of vitamin C to the diets of many countries. This is not so much due to the level of vitamin C in potatoes, which is not especially high, but rather to the large quantities of potatoes consumed.

STRUCTURAL FEATURES

The structural unit of the edible portion of most fruits and vegetables is the parenchyma cell (Fig. 248). While parenchyma cells of different fruits

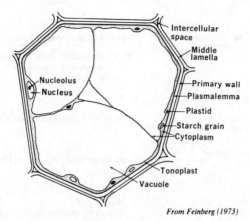

Intercellular space

Middle lamella

Nucleolus

Nucleus

Primary wall

Plasmalemma

Plastid

Starch grain

Cytoplasm

Tonoplast

Vacuole

From Feinberg (1973)

FIG. 248.   DIAGRAM OF A PARENCHYMA CELL

and vegetables differ somewhat in gross size and appearance, all have essentially the same fundamental structure. Parenchyma cells of plants differ from animal cells in that the actively metabolizing protoplast portion of plant cells represents only a small fraction, of the order of five per cent, of the total cell volume. This protoplast is rather film-like, and is pressed against the cell wall by the large water-filled central vacuole. The protoplast has inner and outer semipermeable membrane layers between which is confined the cytoplasm and its nucleus. The cytoplasm contains various inclusions, among them starch granules and plastids such as the chloroplasts and other pigment-containing chromoplasts. The cell wall, cellulosic in nature, contributes rigidity to the parenchyma cell and confines the outer protoplasmic membrane. It also is the structure against which other parenchyma cells are cemented to form extensive three-dimensional tissue masses. The layer between cell walls of adjacent parenchyma cells is referred to as middle lamella, and is composed largely of pectic and polysaccharide cement-like materials. Air spaces also exist, especially at the angles formed where several cells come together.

The relationships between these structures and their chemical compositions are further indicated in Table 59. The parenchyma cells will vary in size from plant to plant but are quite large when compared to bacterial or yeast cells. The larger parenchyma cells may have volumes many thousand times greater than a typical bacterial cell.

There are additional types of cells other than parenchyma cells that make up the familiar structures of fruits and vegetables. These include various types of conducting cells which are tube-like and distribute water and salts throughout the plant. Such cells produce fibrous structures toughened by the presence of cellulose and the wood-like substance lignin.

TABLE 59

COMPONENTS OF THE CELL—STRUCTURAL AND CHEMICAL [1]

Vacuole	H_2O, inorganic salts, organic acids, oil droplets, sugars, water-soluble pigments, amino acids, vitamins
Protoplast membrane	
tonoplast (inner) plasmalemma (outer)	protein, lipoprotein, phospholipids, phytic acid
nucleus	nucleoprotein, nucleic acids, enzymes (protein)
cytoplasm	
active	
chloroplasts	chlorophyll
mesoplasm (ground substance)	enzymes, intermediary metabolites, nucleic acid
mitochondria	enzymes (protein), Fe, Cu, Mo vitamin co-enzyme
microsomes	nucleoproteins, enzymes (proteins), nucleic acid
inert	
starch grains	reserve carbohydrate (starch), phosphorus
aleurone	reserve protein
chromoplast	pigments (carotenoids)
oil droplets	triglycerides of fatty acids
crystals	calcium oxalate, etc.
Cell Wall	
primary wall	cellulose, hemicellulose, pectic substances and noncellulose polysaccharide
middle lamella	pectic substances and noncellulose polysaccharides, Mg, Ca
plasmodesmata	cytoplasmic strands interconnecting cytoplasm of cells through pores in the cell wall
surface materials (cutin or cuticle)	esters of long chain fatty acids and long chain alcohols

[1]From Feinberg (1973).

Cellulose, lignin, and pectic substances also occur in specialized supporting cells which increase in importance as plants become older. An important structural feature of all plants, and of fruits and vegetables is protective tissue. This can take many forms but usually is made up of specialized parenchyma cells that are pressed compactly together to form a skin, peel, or rind. Surface cells of these protective structures on leaves, stems, or fruit secrete waxy cutin and form a water impermeable cuticle. These surface tissues, especially on leaves and young stems will also contain numerous valve-like cellular structures, the stomata, through which moisture and gases can pass.

Turgor and Texture

The range of textures that are encountered in fresh and cooked vegetables and fruits is indeed great, and to a large extent can be explained in terms of changes in specific cellular components. Since plant tissues gen-

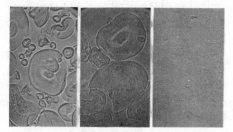

Courtesy of Univ. of Illinois Agr. Expt. Sta.

FIG. 249.   PROGRESSIVE GELATINIZATION OF STARCH GRANULES

On the other hand, starch swelling together with osmotic pressure can be so great as to cause plant cells to burst. When this happens the viscous colloidal starch suspension oozes from the cells and imparts pastiness to the system. The same occurs when cells containing much starch are ruptured by processing conditions. This is particularly important in the case of potato products. The desirable texture of mashed potatoes and other potato products is a mealiness rather than a stickiness or pastiness. Therefore, in the production of dehydrated potato granules and flakes much of the technology of mixing and drying is aimed at minimizing both cell rupture and release of free starch. The same is true in cooking and mashing of fresh potatoes, which if excessive can produce undesirable pastiness.

Sources of Color and Color Changes

In addition to a great range of textures, much of the interest that fruits and vegetables add to our diets is due to their delightful and variable colors. The pigments and color precursors of fruits and vegetables occur for the most part in the cellular plastid inclusions such as the chloroplasts and other chromoplasts, and to a lesser extent dissolved in fat droplets or water within the cell protoplast and vacuole. These pigments are classified into four major groups which include the chlorophylls, carotenoids, anthocyanins, and anthoxanthins. Pigments belonging to the latter two groups also are referred to as flavonoids, and include the tannins.

The Chlorophylls.—The chlorophylls are largely contained within the chloroplasts and have a primary role in the photosynthetic production of carbohydrates from carbon dioxide and water. The bright green color of leaves and other parts of plants is due largely to the oil-soluble chlorophylls, which in nature are bound to protein molecules in highly organized complexes.

When the plant cells are killed by ageing, processing, or cooking, the protein of these complexes is denatured and the chlorophyll may be released. Such chlorophyll is highly unstable and rapidly changes in color to olive green or brown. This color change is believed to be due to the conversion of chlorophyll to the compound pheophytin.

Conversion to pheophytin is favored by acid pH but does not occur readily under alkaline conditions. For this reason peas, beans, spinach, and other green vegetables which tend to lose their bright green colors on heating can be largely protected against such color changes by the addition of sodium bicarbonate or other alkali to the cooking or canning water. However, this practice is not looked upon favorably nor used commercially because alkaline pH also has a softening effect on cellulose and vegetable texture, and further is destructive at cooking temperatures to vitamin C and thiamine.

The Carotenoids.—Pigments belonging to this group are fat-soluble and range in color from yellow through orange to red. They often occur along with the chlorophylls in the chloroplasts, but also are present in other chromoplasts and may occur free in fat droplets. Important carotenoids include the orange carotenes of carrot, corn, apricot, peach, citrus fruits, and squash; the red lycopene of tomato, watermelon, and apricot; the yellow-orange xanthophylls of corn, peach, paprika, and squash; and the yellow-orange crocetin of the spice saffron. These and other carotenoids seldom occur singly within plant cells.

A major importance of some of the carotenoids is their relationship to vitamin A. A molecule of orange β-carotene is converted into two molecules of colorless vitamin A in the animal body. Such other carotenoids as α-carotene, γ-carotene, and cryptoxanthin also are precursors of vitamin A, but because of minor differences in chemical structure one molecule of each of these yields only one molecule of vitamin A.

In food processing the carotenoids are fairly resistant to heat, changes in pH, and water leaching since they are fat-soluble. However, they are very sensitive to oxidation, which results in both color loss and destruction of vitamin A activity.

The Flavonoids.—Pigments and color precursors belonging to this class are water-soluble and commonly are present in the juices of fruits and vegetables. The flavonoids include the purple, blue, and red anthocyanins of grapes, berries, beets, eggplant, and cherry; the yellow anthoxanthins of light colored fruits and vegetables such as apple, onion, potato, and cauliflower; and the colorless catechins and leucoanthocyanins which are food tannins and are found in apples, grapes, tea, and other plant tissues. These colorless tannin compounds are easily converted to brown pigments upon reaction with metal ions.

Properties of the anthocyanins include a shifting of colors with pH. Thus many of the anthocyanins which are violet or blue in alkaline media become red upon addition of acid. Cooking of beets with vinegar tends to shift the color from a purplish red to a brighter red, while alkaline water can influence the color of red fruits and vegetables toward violet and gray-blue. The anthocyanins also tend toward the violet and blue hues upon reaction with metal ions, which is one reason for lacquering the inside of metal cans when the true color of anthocyanin-containing fruits and vegetables is to be preserved. The water-soluble property of anthocyanins also results in easy leaching of these pigments from cut fruits and vegetables during processing and cooking.

The yellow anthoxanthins also are pH sensitive tending toward a deeper yellow in alkaline media. Thus potatoes or apples become somewhat yellow when cooked in water with a pH of 8 or higher, which is common in many areas. Acidification of the water to pH 6 or lower favors a whiter color.

The colorless tannin compounds upon reaction with metal ions form a range of dark colored complexes which may be red, brown, green, gray, or black. The various shades of these colored complexes depend upon the particular tannin, the specific metal ion, pH, concentration of the complex, and other factors not yet fully understood.

Water-soluble tannins appear in the juices squeezed from grapes, apples, and other fruits as well as the brews from extraction of tea and coffee. The color and clarity of tea are influenced by the hardness and pH of the brewing water. Alkaline waters that contain calcium and magnesium favor the formation of dark brown tannin complexes which precipitate when the tea is cooled. If acid in the form of lemon juice is added to such tea its color lightens and the precipitate tends to dissolve. Iron from equipment or from pitted tin cans has caused a number of unexpected colors to develop in products containing tannins, such as coffee, cocoa, and foods flavored with these.

The tannins also are important because they possess astringency which influences flavor and contributes body to such beverages as coffee, tea, wine, apple cider, and beer. Excessive astringency causes a puckery sensation in the mouth, which is the condition produced when tea becomes high in tannins from overbrewing.

ACTIVITIES OF LIVING SYSTEMS

Repeated reference has been made to the live state of fruits and vegetables after harvest. Continued respiration gives off carbon dioxide, moisture, and heat which influence storage, packaging, and refrigeration requirements. Continued transpiration adds to moisture evolved and further influences packaging requirements (Chap. 9, 21).

Further activities of fruits and vegetables, before and after harvest, include changes in carbohydrates, pectins, organic acids, and the effects these have on various quality attributes of the products.

As for changes in carbohydrates, few generalizations can be given with respect to starches and sugars. In some plant products sugars quickly decrease and starch increases in amount soon after harvest. This is the case for ripe sweet corn which can suffer flavor and texture quality losses in a very few hours after harvest. Unripe fruit, in contrast, frequently is high in starch and low in sugars. Continued ripening after harvest generally results in a decrease in starch and an increase in sugars as in the case of apples and pears. However, this does not necessarily mean that the starch is the source of the newly formed sugars. Further, the courses of change in starch and sugars are markedly influenced by post-harvest storage temperatures. Thus potatoes stored below about 50° F continue to build up high levels of sugars, while the same potatoes stored above 50° F do not. This is taken advantage of in the storage of potatoes for dehydration. Here we want potatoes that are low in reducing sugars so as to minimize Maillard browning reactions during drying and subsequent storage of the dried product. Such potatoes are stored above 50° F prior to being further processed.

After harvest the changes in pectins of fruits and vegetables are more predictable. Generally there is a decrease in water-insoluble pectic substance and a corresponding increase in water-soluble pectin. This contributes to the gradual softening of fruits and vegetables during storage and ripening. Further breakdown of water-soluble pectin by pectin methyl esterase also occurs.

The organic acids of fruits generally decrease during storage and ripening. This occurs in apples and pears and is especially important in the case of oranges. Oranges have a long ripening period on the tree and time of picking is largely determined by degree of acidity and sugar content which have major effects upon juice quality.

It is to be recognized that as acids disappear on ripening they influence more than just tartness of fruits. Since many of the plant pigments are sensitive to acid, fruit color would be expected to change. Additionally, the viscosity of pectin gel is affected by acid and sugar contents, both of which change with ripening. Further consequences of the live state of vegetables and fruits are indicated in the following sections on harvesting and processing.

HARVESTING AND PROCESSING OF VEGETABLES

Vegetable Varieties

The food scientist and vegetable processor must appreciate the substantial differences that varieties of a given vegetable will possess. In addition to variety and genetic strain differences with respect to weather, insect, and disease resistance, varieties of a given vegetable will differ in size, shape, time of maturity, and resistance to physical damage. These latter factors are of the greatest importance in the design and use of mechanical harvesting devices.

A variety difference with respect to resistance to tomato cracking is seen in Fig. 250. Varietal differences then further extend into warehouse

Courtesy of Campbell Soup Co.

FIG. 250. RADIAL AND CONCENTRIC CRACKING VARIETIES COMPARED WITH RESISTANT TOMATO TYPE

storage stability, and suitability for such processing methods as canning, freezing, pickling, or drying. A variety of peas that is suitable for canning may be quite unsatisfactory for freezing, and varieties of potatoes that are preferred for freezing may be less satisfactory for drying or potato chip manufacture. This should be expected since different varieties of a given vegetable will vary somewhat in chemical composition, cellular structure, and biological activity of their enzyme systems. Because of the importance of varietal differences, large food companies commonly provide special seed of their choice to farmers whose crops they contract to buy a year in advance. They also frequently manage their own vegetable farms to further guarantee a sufficient supply of high quality uniform raw materials.

Harvesting and Pre-Processing Considerations

When vegetables are maturing in the field they are changing from day to day. There is a time when the vegetable will be at peak quality from the standpoint of color, texture, and flavor. This peak quality is quick in passing and may last only a day. Harvesting and processing of several vegetables, including tomatoes, corn, and peas are rigidly scheduled to capture this peak quality.

After the vegetable is harvested it may quickly pass beyond the peak quality condition. This is independent of microbial spoilage. In a study on sweet corn (previous Table 24), in just 24 hr at room temperature 26% of the total sugars were lost with a comparable loss of sweetness in the corn. Even when stored just above freezing at 32° F, 8% of the sugar was lost in

24 hr and 22% in 4 days. Some of this sugar was probably converted to starch. Some was burned up in the process of respiration. In similar fashion, peas and lima beans can lose over 50% of their sugar in just one day at room temperature; losses are slower under refrigeration but there is still a great change in vegetable sweetness and freshness of flavor within 2 or 3 days. Not all losses of sugar are due to their consumption during respiration or their conversion to starch. Asparagus can convert some of its sugar into fibrous tissue after harvest and this contributes to a more woody texture.

Along with the loss of sugar, the evolution of heat can be a serious problem when large stockpiles of vegetables are transported or held prior to processing. At room temperature, some vegetables will liberate heat at a rate of 120,000 Btu/ton/day. This is enough for each ton of vegetables to melt 800 lb of ice per day. Since the heat further deteriorates the vegetables and speeds microorganism growth, the harvested vegetables must be cooled if not processed immediately.

But cooling only slows down the rate of deterioration, it does not prevent it, and vegetables differ in their resistance to cold storage. As pointed out in Chap. 7 each vegetable has its optimum cold storage temperature which may be between about 32°F to 50°F. Colder storage than 45°F in the case of cucumbers, for example, will result in pitting, soft spots, and decay. What actually happens is that at too low a temperature the normal metabolism of the living vegetable is altered and various abnormalities occur along with decreased resistance to invasion by microorganisms that are present and can grow at the low storage temperature.

The continual loss of water by harvested vegetables due to transpiration, respiration, and physical drying of cut surfaces results in wilting of leafy vegetables, loss of plumpness of fleshy vegetables, and loss of weight of both. And moisture loss cannot be completely and effectively prevented by hermetic packaging. This was tried with plastic bags for fresh vegetables in supermarkets, but the bags became moisture fogged, and deterioration of certain vegetables was accelerated because of buildup of CO_2 and decrease of oxygen in the package. It therefore is common to perforate such bags to prevent these defects as well as to minimize high humidity in the package which would encourage microbial growth.

Shippers of fresh vegetables and vegetable processors, whether they can, freeze, dehydrate, or manufacture soups or ketchup, appreciate the instability and perishability of vegetables and so do everything they can to minimize delays in processing of the fresh product. In many processing plants it is common practice to process vegetables immediately as they are received from the fields. To ensure a steady supply of top quality produce during the harvesting period the large food processor will employ trained field men; they will advise on growing practices and on spacing of plantings so that vegetables will mature and can be harvested in rhythm with the processing plant capabilities. This minimizes pileup and need for storage.

Post-Harvest Practices

Cooling of harvested vegetables in the field is common practice (previous Fig. 96). Liquid nitrogen-cooled trucks may next provide transportation of fresh produce to the processing plant or directly to market. Upon arrival of vegetables at the processing plant the usual operations of cleaning, grading, peeling, cutting, and the like are performed using a moderate amount of equipment, but a good deal of hand labor also still remains.

Washing.—The washing equipment, like all equipment subsequently used, will depend upon the size, shape, and fragility of the particular kind of vegetable. A flotation cleaner for peas and other small vegetables is shown in Fig. 251. The principle of its operation is that sound peas will

Courtesy of Key Equipment Co.

FIG. 251. FLOTATION CLEANER FOR SHELLED PEAS

sink while broken peas, weed seeds, and certain other kinds of contamination will float provided a liquid of the proper density is employed. In this case, a mineral oil-water emulsion is used and its density can be further controlled by frothing the mixture with air. The sound peas which sink are moved on to further processing and the floating debris is pumped to waste.

Another type of washer is the rotary washer in which vegetables are tumbled while they are sprayed with jets of water. This type of washer should not be used to clean fragile vegetables. Washing is used not only to remove field soil and surface microorganisms, but also to remove fungicides, insecticides, and other pesticides, since there are laws specifying maximum levels of these materials that may be retained on the vegetable; and in most cases the allowable residual level is virtually zero. Modern instruments can detect many pesticide residues at levels as low as a few parts per billion. Wash water containing detergents and other sanitizers may completely remove these residues.

Fragile vegetables such as asparagus are valued for their wholeness and cannot be washed in agitating equipment that would break them up. Asparagus may be washed by gentle spraying on a belt.

Skin Removal.—Some vegetables require skin removal. This can be done in various ways. Skins can be softened from the underlying tissue by submerging vegetables in hot alkali solution. Lye may be used at a concentration of about 1% and at about 200° F. The vegetables with loosened skins are then conveyed under high velocity jets of water which wash away the skins and any residual lye (previous Fig. 34).

Other vegetables with a thick skin such as beets and sweet potatoes are peeled with steam under pressure as they pass through cylindrical vessels. This softens the skin and the underlying tissue. When the pressure is suddenly released, steam under the skin expands and causes the skins to puff and crack. The skins are then washed away with jets of water.

Still other vegetables such as onions and peppers are best skinned by exposing them to direct flame or to hot gases in rotary tube flame peelers of the type seen in Fig. 252. Here too, heat causes steam to develop under skins and puff them so that they can be washed away with water.

Courtesy of Gentry Co.

FIG. 252. ROTARY TUBE FLAME PEELERS FOR ONIONS AND PEPPERS

Cutting and Trimming.—Many vegetables require various kinds of cutting, stemming, pitting, or coring. Asparagus spears are cut to precise length. The clippings from the base of the stalk are more fibrous and tougher than the prized stalk. The clippings go into soups and other heated products where heat tenderizes them. Brussels sprouts are trimmed largely by hand by pressing the base against a rapidly rotating knife. Green beans are cut by machine into several different shapes along the length of the vegetable or transverse to the length. Olives are pitted by aligning them in small cups and then mechanically pushing plungers through the olives (Fig. 253). Pimientos may then be mechanically stuffed into the holes.

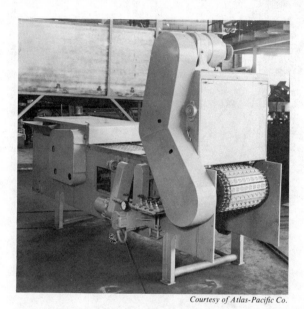

Courtesy of Atlas-Pacific Co.

FIG. 253.   OLIVE ORIENTOR AND PITTER

Blanching.—Most vegetables that ao not receive a severe heat treatment (as would be obtained in normal canning) must be heated to inactivate natural enzymes before they are processed or held in storage for any length of time. This special heat treatment to inactivate enzymes is known as blanching. Blanching is not indiscriminate heating. Too little is ineffective, and too much damages the vegetables by excessive cooking, especially where the fresh character of the vegetable is subsequently to be preserved by freezing. Blanching is essential where vegetables are to be frozen because while freezing slows down enzyme action it does not destroy or completely stop it. If blanching did not precede freezing then the product, which is often held in the frozen state for many months, would slowly develop many off-flavors and off-colors, and other kinds of enzymatic spoilage might result.

Two of the more heat resistant enzymes important in vegetables are catalase and peroxidase. If these are destroyed then the other significant enzymes in vegetables also will have been inactivated. The heat treatments to destroy catalase and peroxidase in different vegetables are known (Fig. 254), and sensitive chemical tests have been developed to detect the amounts of these enzymes that might survive a blanching treatment.

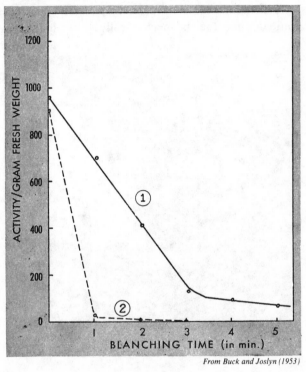

From Buck and Joslyn (1953)

FIG. 254. WATER-BLANCH TIME OF BROCCOLI AT 212°F RE-QUIRED TO INACTIVATE (1) PEROXIDASE, AND (2) CATALASE

Because various types of vegetables differ in size, shape, heat conductivity, and the natural levels of their enzymes, blanching treatments had to be established on an experimental basis. As with sterilization of food in cans, the larger the food item the longer it takes for heat to reach the center. Peas are more rapidly blanched than corn on the cob. Small vegetables may be adequately blanched in boiling water in a minute or two, large vegetables may require several minutes (Table 60). Blanching with steam under pressure at higher temperatures requires shorter times but processors must work out their own conditions depending upon specific product and method of heating.

In Fig. 255 ears of sweet corn are seen emerging from a steam blancher.

TABLE 60

BLANCHING TIME FOR VEGETABLES FOR FREEZING [1]

Vegetable	Blanching Time in Water at 212°F
Asparagus	Min
small ($^5/_{16}$ in. diam or less at butt)	2
medium ($^6/_{16}$ to $^9/_{16}$ in. diam at butt)	3
large ($^{10}/_{16}$ in. diam and larger at butt)	4
Beans, green and wax	
small (less than $18^1/_2/64$ in. diam or Sieve No. 2 and smaller)	$1-1^1/_2$
medium ($18^1/_2/64$ to $24/64$ in. diam or No. 3 and 4)	2–3
large ($24/64$ in. diam and larger or No. 5 and larger)	3–4
Beets	
small, whole ($1^1/_4$ in. diam or less)	3–5
diced ($1^3/_4$ to $2^1/_4$ in. diam)	3
cook in boiling water 2 min, peel, dice and blanch or cook through, then dice.	
Broccoli	
cut into pieces not more than 1 in. thick.	2–3
Cabbage (summer)	
chop coarsely.	$1-1^1/_2$
Cauliflower	
break into flowerettes or curds not over 2 in. in length by $1^1/_2$ diam.	3
Corn, (cut or whole kernel)	
blanch on cob, cool, then cut.	2–3
Corn-on-cob	
small (less than $1^5/_8$ in. diam at butt)	7
medium ($1^5/_8$ to 2 in. diam at butt)	9
large (over 2 in. diam at butt)	11
Peas	$1-1^1/_2$
Spinach	$1^1/_2$
Swiss Chard	2

[1] Atkinson and Strachan (1951).

Courtesy of Western Canner and Packer

FIG. 255.   STEAM BLANCHING CORN ON THE COB

Since much of the enzyme activity is within the corn cob a compromise is made to destroy perhaps only 90% of the enzyme activity, since heat to destroy 100% could overly soften the corn kernels and do more damage to quality of the product to be frozen than would the slight residual enzyme. Blanching with microwave energy, in order to rapidly heat the center of large items before the surfaces are overcooked, is receiving considerable interest in applications such as this.

Canning.—Great quantities of vegetable products are canned. A typical flow sheet for a vegetable canning operation (which also largely applies to fruits) is seen in Fig. 256. The unit operations performed in sequence in-

Courtesy of American Can Co.

FIG. 256. TYPICAL VEGETABLE CANNING OPERATIONS

clude harvesting, receiving, washing, grading, heat blanching, peeling and coring, can filling, exhausting to remove air, sealing, retorting, cooling, labeling, and packing. The vegetable may be canned whole, diced, puréed, as juice, and so on.

HARVESTING AND PROCESSING OF FRUITS

Fruit Varieties

As with vegetables, the diversity of kinds of fruit is further enlarged by the numerous varieties of a given fruit. Thus there are about 1,000 varieties of apples and about 3,000 varieties of pears, but of these only a few are commercially important. Some fruit is marketed fresh but more of it is processed into a wide range of different products, and it is here that specific varieties of a given fruit become especially significant. For example, apples are utilized in the following ways: consumed fresh, applesauce, canned apple slices, apple juice and cider, jellies, frozen slices, and dried slices. Apple varieties will differ in such properties as: resistance to weather, insects, disease, time of maturity and yield, storage stability, color of flesh, firmness when cooked, amount of juice, level of acidity, and level of solids. For optimum results apple varieties must be matched to particular end uses, and processing plants frequently are equipped to manufacture the products for which the local apple varieties are best suited. This is also true of other fruits. Knowledge of varietal differences for the various fruits is highly specific, and for this reason when a fruit processing use is contemplated it is best to consult with local State Agricultural Experiment Stations or equivalent agencies.

Fruit Quality

Fruit quality goes back to tree stock, growing practices, and weather conditions. Closer to the shipper and processor, however, are the degrees of maturity and ripeness when picked and the method of picking or harvesting. There is a distinction between maturity and ripeness of a fruit. Maturity is the condition when the fruit is ready to eat or if picked will become ready to eat on further ripening. Ripeness is that optimum condition when color, flavor, and texture have developed to their peak. Some fruits are picked when they are mature but are not yet ripe. This is especially true of very soft fruits like cherries and peaches, which when fully ripe are so soft as to be damaged by the act of picking itself. Further, since many fruits continue to ripen off the tree, unless they were to be processed quickly some would become over-ripe before they could be utilized if picked at peak ripeness.

When to Pick.—The proper time to pick fruit depends upon several factors. These include the variety, location, weather, ease of removal from the tree which changes with time, and the purpose to which the fruit will be put. Oranges, for example, change with respect to both sugar and acid as they ripen on the tree. Sugars increase and acid decreases. The ratio of sugar to acid determines the taste and acceptability of the fruit and the juice. In Florida, there are laws that prohibit picking until a certain sugar-acid ratio has been reached. This is to uphold quality since citrus fruits once picked cease to ripen further. In the case of many fruits to be canned, on the other hand, fruits are picked before they are fully ripe in terms of eating texture since canning will further soften the fruit.

Quality Measurements.—Many quality measurements can be made before a fruit crop is picked to determine if proper maturity or degree of ripeness has developed. Color may be measured with instruments of the kind discussed in Chap. 6, or by comparing color of fruit on the tree with standard picture charts.

Texture may be measured by compression, as with the simple type of plunger seen in Fig. 257, which is pressed into the fruit and gives a read-

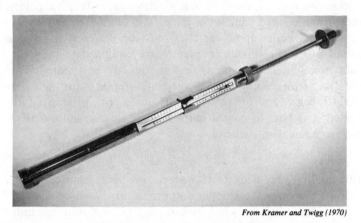

From Kramer and Twigg (1970)

FIG. 257.   FRUIT PRESSURE TESTER

ing as the spring contracts. Where individual units of a harvest may vary, as in the case of cranberries, an interesting separator is used after picking which is based on texture. Firm cranberries bounce; soft, overripe, or rotten ones don't bounce as high. So the cranberries are given a chance to bounce over a wooden barrier (Fig. 258), if they make it they are accepted, those that don't bounce over the barrier are automatically separated and used for less demanding purposes.

As fruits mature on the tree their concentration of juice solids, which are mostly sugar, changes. The concentration of soluble solids in the juice can be estimated with a refractometer or a hydrometer. The former measures

Photo by R. W. Abbott, Courtesy of National Cranberry Assoc.

FIG. 258. SEPARATOR FOR ELIMINATING SOFT CRANBERRIES

the ability of solutions to bend or refract a light beam, which is proportional to the solution's concentration; a hydrometer is a weighted spindle with a graduated neck which floats in the juice at a height related to its density.

The acid content of fruit, as we have said, changes with maturity and affects flavor. Acid concentration can be measured by a simple chemical titration on the fruit juice. But for many fruits the tartness and flavor are really affected by the ratio of sugar to acid. Percentage of soluble solids, which are largely sugars, is generally expressed in degrees Brix, which relates specific gravity of a solution to an equivalent concentration of pure

TABLE 61

SEASONAL CHANGES IN BRIX, ACID, AND RATIOS OF GRAPEFRUIT JUICE [1]

| | Texas[2] | | | Florida[3] | | |
	% Acid	Brix	Ratio	% Acid	Brix	Ratio
November	1.35	10.80	8.00	1.47	10.05	6.84
December	1.45	11.10	7.65	1.44	10.25	7.12
January	1.41	11.35	8.05	1.38	10.25	7.43
February	1.31	11.30	8.62	1.34	10.30	7.69
March	1.18	11.20	9.48	1.29	10.30	7.95
April	1.07	11.00	10.28	1.22	10.15	8.32
May	0.95	10.75	11.32	1.11	9.80	8.84
Average	1.245	11.07	9.05	1.32	10.15	7.79

[1] From Burdick (1961).
[2] Data covers five normal seasons in Texas.
[3] Data obtained from Harding and Fisher (1945).

sucrose. Therefore, in describing the taste or tartness of several fruits and fruit juices, the terms "sugar to acid ratio" or "Brix to acid ratio" are commonly used. The higher the Brix the greater the sugar concentration in the juice; the higher the Brix to acid ratio the sweeter and less tart is the juice. The seasonal changes in degrees Brix, acid content, and Brix to acid ratio for grapefruit juice are seen in Table 61. The relationships of these quantities to quality standards of grapefruit juice are seen in Table 62.

TABLE 62

SUMMARY OF STANDARDS FOR GRAPEFRUIT JUCIES[1,4]

	% Acid		Degrees Brix		Ratio	
	Min.	Max.	Min.	Max.	Min.	Max.
Fancy or Grade "A"						
grapefruit..................	0.90	2.00	9.5	None	7:1	14:1
grapefruit "sweet"..........	1.00	2.00	12.5	[3]	9:1[3]	14:1
blended with orange........	0.80	1.70	10.0	None	8:1	17:1
blended "sweet"............	0.80	1.70	12.5	[2]	10:1[2]	17:1
Standard or Grade "C"						
grapefruit..................	0.75	None	9.0	None	6.5:1	None
grapefruit "sweet"..........	0.85	None	12.5	[3]	9:1	None
blended with orange........	0.65	1.80	9.5	None	7.5:1	None
blended "sweet"............	0.65	1.80	12.5	[2]	10:1[2]	None

[1] These standards as established by the U. S. Dept. Agr. are subject to frequent revision. Data given are those in effect August 1952.
[2] When the Brix is above 16, the ratio may be less than 10:1.
[3] When the Brix is above 16, the ratio may be less than 9:1.
[4] From Burdick (1961).

Harvesting and Processing

The above and other measurements, plus experience, tell when fruit is ready for harvesting and subsequent processing. A large amount of the harvesting of most fruit crops is still done by hand. This labor may represent almost half of the cost of growing the fruit. Therefore, mechanical harvesting is currently one of the most active fields of research for the agricultural engineer, but also requires geneticists to breed fruit of nearly equal size, that matures uniformly, and that is resistant to mechanical damage. And mechanical damage can be subtle. For example, cherries that are not to be processed immediately frequently are picked with their stems attached to avoid the small break in the flesh that would allow microbial invasion. This is why fresh cherries with stems are seen in the supermarket.

Harvested fruit is washed to remove soil, microorganisms, and pesticide residues. It is further sorted for size and quality much as are vegetables. Fresh fruit that is not marketed as such may be processed in many ways, one of the more important being freezing.

Freezing.—Large amounts of high quality fruit are frozen for home, restaurant, and manufacturing use by the baking and other food industries. Freezing is generally superior to canning when we want to preserve the firmness of fruits. As was the case with vegetables, fruit to be frozen must be stabilized against enzymatic changes during frozen storage and on thawing.

The principal enzymatic changes that are objectionable in the case of frozen fruits are oxidations which cause darkening of color and alterations of flavor. A color change of particular importance is enzymatic browning of the lighter colored fruits such as apples, peaches, and bananas. This is believed due to oxidations of pigment precursors, often referred to as catechol-tannin substrates, by enzymes of the group known as phenol oxidases and polyphenol oxidases. Depending upon the intended end use for the frozen fruit, various methods are employed to inactivate these enzymes or otherwise prevent oxidation.

Heat Blanching.—Generally heat blanching is not used on fruits because of turgor loss from heat damage and the associated sogginess and juice drainage after thawing. Instead, chemicals are commonly used without heat to inactivate the oxidative enzymes or to act as antioxidants, and they are combined with other treatments as indicated below. An exception exists in the case of fruit slices to be frozen for later use in pies. Since the frozen fruit ultimately will receive heating during the baking operation, heat blanching before freezing is still sometimes practiced. In this case it may be combined with the use of calcium salts in the blanching water, or added after blanching, to firm the fruit by forming calcium pectates. It also is not uncommon to add pectin, carboxymethyl cellulose, alginates, and other colloidal thickeners to such fruit prior to freezing.

Ascorbic Acid Dip.—Ascorbic acid or vitamin C minimizes fruit oxidation primarily by acting as an antioxidant and itself becoming oxidized in preference to the catechol-tannin compounds. Ascorbic acid frequently is used by being dissolved in a sugar syrup. Levels of 0.05% to 0.2% ascorbic acid in an apple-syrup or a peach-syrup mixture usually are effective provided there is time for penetration prior to the freezing step. Peaches so treated may not darken in frozen storage at 0° F in two years (Fig. 259). It has been found that increased acidity also helps retard oxidative color changes and so ascorbic acid plus citric acid may be used together. Citric acid further reacts with (chelates) metal ions and thus removes these catalysts of oxidation from the system.

Sulfur Dioxide Dip.—Sulfur dioxide may function in several ways. Sulfur dioxide is an enzyme poison against common oxidizing enzymes. It also has antioxidant properties, that is, it is an oxygen acceptor (as is ascorbic acid). Further, SO_2 minimizes nonenzymatic Maillard type browning by

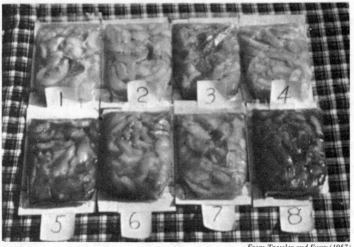

From Tressler and Evers (1957)

FIG. 259.   DARKENING OF SLICED PEACHES RETARDED BY ASCORBIC ACID

reacting with aldehyde groups of sugars so that they are no longer free to combine with amino acids. Sulfur dioxide also interferes with microbial growth.

When used to prevent oxidation of frozen fruit two factors must be considered. Sulfur dioxide must be given time to penetrate the fruit tissue, and SO_2 must not be used in excess because it has a characteristic unpleasant taste and odor and state and federal laws limit the SO_2 content of fruit. Commonly a 0.25% solution of SO_2, or its SO_2 equivalent in the form of solutions of sodium sulfite, sodium bisulfite, or sodium metabisulfite are used. Fruit slices are dipped in the solution for about one minute and then removed so as not to absorb too much SO_2. Then the slices are allowed to stand for about two hours for penetration of the SO_2 throughout the tissue before freezing, since penetration will not readily occur after freezing.

Sugar Syrup.—Sugar syrup addition, one of the oldest methods of minimizing oxidation, was used long before the causative reactions were understood and remains today a common practice for this purpose. Sugar syrup minimizes oxidation by coating the fruit and thereby preventing contact with atmospheric oxygen. Sugar syrup also offers some protection against loss of volatile fruit esters, and it contributes sweet taste to otherwise tart fruit. Today it is common to dissolve ascorbic acid and citric acid in the sugar syrup for added effect, or to include sugar syrup after an SO_2 treatment.

Vacuum Treatment.—When employed, vacuum treatments generally are used in combination with one of the chemical dips or with sugar syrup. The fruit submerged in the dip or in the syrup is placed in a closed vessel and vacuum is applied to draw air from the fruit tissue. Then when the vacuum is broken the chemical dip or syrup enters the voids from which air was removed, effecting better penetration of the solution.

Concentration and Drying.—The high moisture contents of many fruits necessitate their being puréed and concentrated to 2 or 3 times their natural solids contents for more economical handling and shipping where this physical form can be used. Or the fruits may be dried for various purposes to different moisture levels (Chap. 10). Where the fruit is only partially dried, as in the case of dried apricots, pears, prunes, figs, and raisins, these products are still largely prepared by sun drying in open wooden trays. When fruits are dried under such temperature conditions that do not inactivate their oxidative enzymes, SO_2 is commonly employed to minimize browning much as in the case of fruit freezing. The SO_2 also keeps down microbial growth during the slow, low temperature drying process. Sulfur dioxide finds further use in fruit juice production to minimize oxidative changes where relatively low heat treatments are employed so as not to damage delicate juice flavor.

FRUIT JUICES

In Chap. 2, the steps in the manufacture of frozen orange juice concentrate (previous Fig. 19 to 22) were traced. Several of these steps also are common to the manufacture of other juices, but equipment varies depending upon properties of the different fruits. In the production of most juice types the major steps involve: extraction of the juice, clarification of the juice, juice deaeration, pasteurization, concentration (if solids are to be increased), essence add-back, canning or bottling, and freezing if the juice is to be marketed in this form.

Extraction

In the case of orange and grapefruit, where the peel contains bitter oils, the juice extractor is especially designed to cause the peel oil to run down the outside of the fruit and not enter the juice stream (Fig. 260 and previous Fig. 20). But bitter peel oil is not a problem in the case of apples. Here the whole apple is pressed after grinding. One type of high pressure apple press is seen in Fig. 261.

Clarification

The juice pressed from most fruits contains small quantities of suspended pulp, which is often removed. This may be done with fine filters, but since these have a tendency to clog, it is common to use high speed centri-

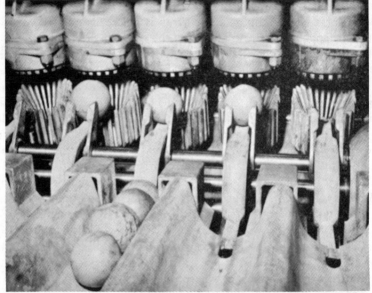

Courtesy Florida Div., FMC Corp.

FIG. 260.   FMC IN-LINE JUICE EXTRACTOR

From Aitken (1961)

FIG. 261.   PRESSING APPLE PULP

fuges which separate the juice from the pulp according to their differences in density.

Many persons prefer crystal clear apple juice. To clarify the juice it is necessary to treat the juice beyond simple filtration or centrifugation since very minute particles of pulp and colloidal materials may not be removed with filters or centrifuges. This fine pulp is suspended in the juice by the natural pectic substances of the fruit. Commercial enzyme preparations which digest pectic substances may be added. This results in a settling out of the fine pulp, which makes filtering or centrifuging more effective. Orange juice on the other hand is more acceptable if it retains a slight cloud of suspended pulp and so this is not removed.

Deaeration

Orange juice contains entrapped air and is deaerated by being sprayed into a vacuum deaerator (Fig. 262), which minimizes subsequent destruction of vitamin C and other changes due to oxygen.

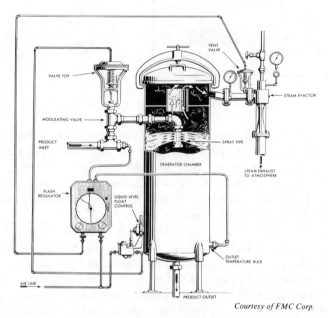

Courtesy of FMC Corp.

FIG. 262. REX MICRO-FILM DEAERATOR

Additional Steps

The juices are generally pasteurized to decrease microbial growth and to inactivate natural enzymes. All natural juices are low in solids and so it is common to concentrate many of them whether they are to be frozen or not. When this is done, low temperature vacuum evaporation generally is employed to retain maximum flavor. Nevertheless, along with water removal there is always the evaporation of some of the juices' volatile essences (Chap. 10). Therefore the evaporated water and essence coming from the vacuum evaporator is not discarded but is passed through an

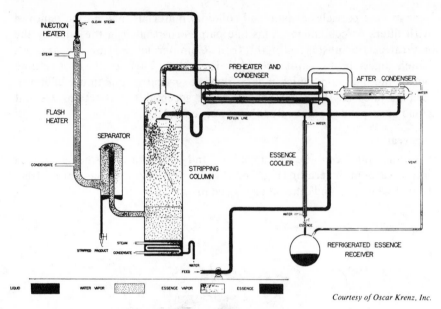

Courtesy of Oscar Krenz, Inc.

FIG. 263. DIAGRAM OF ESSENCE RECOVERY SYSTEM

essence recovery unit. Such units which distil the essence from the water and recondense it are designed specifically for the kind of juice being processed (Fig. 263). The essence is then added back to the concentrated juice to enhance flavor. The juice may now be chilled, canned, and frozen. Or, if not to be frozen, the juice may be given a final heat treatment to ensure low bacterial count and then be canned or bottled.

There are many kinds of juices and juice blends now offered for sale. Several of them are rich sources of vitamin C. In the case of apple juice, which is naturally low in vitamin C, fortification of the juice with vitamin C may be practiced. In England and other parts of Europe fruit drinks are popular which use the juice of citrus fruits plus much of the peel and pulp. These are ground together to yield beverages known as squashes.

Whenever fruit is processed or juice produced there always remain the fruit wastes including peels, pits, and other nonjuice solids. Some of this finds its way into certain confectionery and lower grade jelly products, pectin manufacture, recovery of chemicals, and limited use in animal feeds.

BIBLIOGRAPHY

AITKEN, H. C. 1961. Apple juice. *In* Fruit and Vegetable Juice Processing Technology. D. K. Tressler and M. A. Joslyn (Editors). Avi Publishing Co., Westport, Conn.

AMERINE, M. A., BERG, H. W., and CRUESS, W. V. 1972. Technology of Wine Making, 3rd Edition. Avi Publishing Co., Westport, Conn.

ANON. 1960. Food Composition Tables. Food Agr. Organ. United Nations, Rome, Italy.

ATKINSON, F. E., and STRACHAN, C. C. 1951. Freezing of fruits and vegetables. Can. Dept. Agr. Exptl. Farms Serv., Dominion Exptl. Sta. Progr. Rept. *1937–1948*, 63–64.

BROWN, R. 1960. The plant cell and its inclusions. *In* Plant Physiology, Vol. 1A. F. C. Steward (Editor). Academic Press, New York.

BUCK, P. A., and JOSLYN, M. A. 1953. Broccoli processing. Accumulation of alcohol in underscalded frozen broccoli. J. Agr. Food Chem. *1*, 309–312.

BURDICK, E. M. 1961. Grapefruit juice. *In* Fruit and Vegetable Juice Processing Technology. D. K. Tressler and M. A. Joslyn (Editors). Avi Publishing Co., Westport, Conn.

CRUESS, W. V. 1958. Commercial Fruit and Vegetable Products, 3rd Edition. McGraw-Hill Book Co., New York.

EDMOND, J. B. 1971. Sweet Potatoes: Production, Processing, Marketing. Avi Publishing Co., Westport, Conn.

ESAU, K. 1953. Plant Anatomy. John Wiley & Sons, New York.

FEINBERG, B. 1973. Vegetables. *In* Food Dehydration, 2nd Edition, Vol. 2. W. B. Van Arsdel, M. J. Copley, and A. I. Morgan, Jr. (Editors). Avi Publishing Co., Westport, Conn.

GARREN, R., JR., and LAGERSTEDT, H. B. 1964. Raw products: small fruits. *In* Food Processing Operations, Vol. 3. M. A. Joslyn, and J. L. Heid (Editors). Avi Publishing Co., Westport, Conn.

GOOSE, P., and BINSTED, R. 1964. Tomato Paste. Food Trade Press, London.

GUTTERSON, M. 1970. Fruit Juice Technology 1970. Food Process. Rev. *15*. Noyes Data Corp., Park Ridge, N.J.

GUTTERSON, M. 1971. Fruit Processing 1971. Food Process. Rev. *21*. Noyes Data Corp., Park Ridge, N.J.

GUTTERSON, M. 1971. Vegetable Processing 1971. Food Process. Rev. *19*. Noyes Data Corp., Park Ridge, N.J.

HARDING, P. L., and FISHER, D. F. 1945. Seasonal changes in Florida grapefruit. U.S. Dept. Agr. Tech. Bull. *886*.

HUELSEN, W. A. 1954. Sweet Corn. Interscience Publishers, New York.

JACOBS, M. (Editor) 1951. The Chemistry and Technology of Food and Food Products, 2nd Edition, Vol. 2. Interscience Publishers, New York.

JUDGE, E. E. 1971. The Almanac of the Canning, Freezing, Preserving Industries. E. E. Judge, Westminster, Md.

KRAMER, A., and TWIGG, B. E. 1970. Quality Control for the Food Industry, 3rd Edition, Vol. 1. Avi Publishing Co., Westport, Conn.

MAKOWER, R. U. 1960. Chemical inactivation of enzymes in vegetables before dehydration. Food Technol. *14*, 160–164.

MORRIS, H. J. 1958. Rapid peroxidase test for better control of blanching. *ARS 74-10*, U.S. Dept. Agr., Albany, Calif.

REEVE, R. M. 1963. Estimation of extracellular starch of dehydrated potatoes. J. Food Sci. *28*, 198–206.

SMITH, O. 1968. Potatoes: Production, Storing, Processing. Avi Publishing Co., Westport, Conn.

SOULE, M. J., JR., and LAWRENCE, F. P. 1958. Testing oranges for processing. Florida Agr. Ext. Serv. Circ. *184*.

TALBURT, W. F., and SMITH, O. 1967. Potato Processing, 2nd Edition. Avi Publishing Co., Westport, Conn.

TRESSLER, D. K., and EVERS, C. F. 1957. The Freezing Preservation of Foods. Avi Publishing Co., Westport, Conn.

TRESSLER, D. K., and JOSLYN, M. A. (Editors). 1971. Fruit and Vegetable Juice Processing Technology, 2nd Edition. Avi Publishing Co., Westport, Conn.

TRESSLER, D. K., VAN ARSDEL, W. B., and COPLEY, M. J. (Editors) 1968. The Freezing Preservation of Foods, 4th Edition, Vols. 2, 3. Avi Publishing Co., Westport, Conn.

WOODROOF, J. G. 1963. Receiving and preparing fruits and vegetables for processing. *In* Food Processing Operations, Vol. 1. M. A. Joslyn, and J. L. Heid (Editors). Avi Publishing Co., Westport, Conn.

CHAPTER 19

Beverages

INTRODUCTION

There are several kinds of beverages which are not consumed for their food value, but rather for their thirst quenching properties or for their stimulating effects. In this chapter we will consider three major groups, namely the carbonated nonalcoholic beverages or soft drinks of which "soda pop" is characteristic, the carbonated or noncarbonated mildly alcoholic beverages beer and wine, and the nonalcoholic, noncarbonated stimulating beverages coffee and tea.

Each of these beverages must be considered important foods in the broad sense since all are made from food ingredients, all are subject to the Pure Food Law, all are consumed in truly enormous quantities, and in some countries and areas they may actually be more safely consumed than the local water supply. Further, beer, wine, and carbonated soft drinks (with the exception of dietetic formulations) furnish calories, and coffee as well as tea, although noncaloric, frequently are consumed with cream or sugar and thus are vehicles of caloric intake. The technologies of each of these beverages and their ingredients are comprehensive studies in themselves and so all that is intended here is to briefly indicate the more important aspects of their production.

CARBONATED NONALCOHOLIC BEVERAGES

These beverages of which "soda pop" is the prime example are generally sweetened, flavored, acidified, colored, artificially carbonated, and sometimes chemically preserved. Their origin goes back to Greek and Roman times when naturally occurring mineral waters were prized for "medicinal" and refreshing qualities. But it was not until about 1767, when the British scientist Joseph Priestley found that he could artificially carbonate water, that the carbonated beverage industry got its start. An early method of obtaining the carbon dioxide was by acidification of sodium bicarbonate or sodium carbonate, and from the use of these sodium salts came the name "soda" which remains today although most carbon dioxide is no longer generated in this fashion. Gradually fruit juices and extracts were added to carbonated water for improved flavor. Today, the U.S. carbonated soft drink industry manufactures beverages worth over three billion dollars per year at wholesale. In this country alone there are over 3,000 soft drink bottling plants and over forty billion bottles and cans of soda are consumed annually.

Ingredients and Manufacture

The major ingredients of carbonated soft drink beverages are sugar, flavorings, colors, acids, water, and carbon dioxide. Typical compositions with respect to sugar, carbon dioxide, and acidity are given in Table 63, although the products of different manufacturers may vary somewhat from these values.

TABLE 63

COMPOSITION OF CARBONATED BEVERAGES

Flavor	Sugar °Brix	Carbonation Gas Volume	Acid %	pH
Cola flavors	10.5	3.4	0.09	2.6
Root beer	9.9	3.3	0.04	4.0
Ginger ales	9.5	3.8	0.10	—
Cream (vanilla)	11.2	2.6	0.02	—
Lemon and lime	12.6	2.4	0.10	3.0
Orange	13.4	2.3	0.19	3.4
Cherry	12.0	2.4	0.09	3.7
Raspberry	12.3	3.0	0.13	3.0
Grape	13.2	2.2	0.10	3.0

Sugar.—This is mostly sucrose, purchased as a pure colorless syrup from the manufacturer or made into a syrup at the beverage plant from high purity crystalline sugar. The sugar syrup is later supplemented with the flavoring, coloring, and acid ingredients and may be stabilized with a preservative. The finished beverage will contain about 8 to 14% of sugar. The sugar not only contributes sweetness and calories to the drink but also adds body and mouth feel. For this reason when dietetic beverages are made with a nonnutritive sweetener such as saccharin to replace all or much of the sugar, a bodying agent such as carboxymethyl cellulose or a pectin is required. Until recently dietetic beverages were formulated using 0.25% sodium cyclamate plus 0.01% saccharin to replace all of the sugar. In 1969 cyclamates were banned from the U.S. food supply. Presently saccharin, at a level of approximately $\frac{1}{7}$ of a gram per 12-oz bottle, is the nonnutritive sweetener used in dietetic carbonated soft drinks, which account for less than 10% of total soft drink sales.

Flavorings.—These come in the forms of synthetic flavor compounds, natural flavor extracts, and fruit juice concentrates. These flavors must be stable under the acidic conditions of the beverage and on exposure to light for a year or more, since the bottled drinks may be held this long or longer. The flavors do not have to be stable to heat much over 100°F since the beverage is not commonly heat sterilized or pasteurized.

An artificial fruit flavor containing synthetic flavor compounds and natural flavor extracts (Table 64) may have over two dozen different flavor constituents. Cola flavors may be equally or more complex, and

TABLE 64

RASPBERRY FLAVOR FORMULATION[1]

Ingredient	Parts
Ethyl methylphenylglycidate	400
Benzylidene isopropylidene acetone	100
Methoxyacetoxyacetophenone	60
Benzyl acetate	50
Phenethyl alcohol	50
Essence of Portugal	50
Isobutyl acetate	40
Vanillin	30
Methylionone	25
beta-Ionone	25
Coumarin substitute	10
Iris concrete essence	15
Ethyl acetate	10
Ethyl caproate	10
Isoamyl caproate	10
Hexanyl acetate	10
Hexenyl acetate	10
Methyl salicylate	10
Ethyl benzoate	10
Methyl butanol	10
Bornyl salicylate	10
Essence of clove	10
Essence of geranium	10
Hexyl alcohol	5
Hexenol	5
Anisaldehyde	5
Benzaldehyde	5
Acetylmethylcarbinol	3
Biacetyl	2

[1] From Benezet (1951).

their compositions are guarded secrets, sometimes formulated to contain ingredients that will add to the difficulty of chemical analysis and duplication by competitors. Cola flavors generally contain a source of caffeine which is a mild stimulant. When fruit derivatives which contain flavor oils are used it is necessary to employ an emulsifying agent to keep the oils from separating out in the beverage. Water soluble gums at low levels are the principal emulsifiers employed for this purpose.

Colors.—Most important coloring agents for soft drinks are the synthetic colors, particularly the certified coal tar colors. These have been approved by the Food and Drug Administration and all certified batches of such colors must meet stringent chemical purity standards in their manufacture. Caramel from burned sugar, a nonsynthetic color, also is commonly used. These coloring materials are much preferred over the natural fruit colors because of their greater coloring power and color stability. Even when natural fruit extracts or juices are used their colors are generally supplemented with the synthetic colors.

Acid.—Carbon dioxide in solution contributes to acidity, but this is supplemented with additional acid in most carbonated drinks. The main reason for acidification is to enhance the beverage flavors. The principal acids used are phosphoric, citric, tartaric, and malic acids. Of these all but phosphoric are important natural acids of fruits and so they are used mainly to enhance fruit flavored drinks, with citric being the most widely employed. Phosphoric is the acid of choice in the case of colas, root beer, and other nonfruit drinks.

In addition to flavor enhancement, the acid contributes preservative action in the nonheat-treated beverage. However, unless a very high degree of sanitation is employed in soft drink manufacture, the pH imparted by the acid, even in combination with acidic fruit juices, is not sufficient to ensure long term microbial stability. For this reason an additional preservative may be necessary, and this is usually sodium benzoate at a level of about 0.03 to 0.05% in the final beverage. In the acid drink sodium benzoate is converted to benzoic acid which is its more effective preservative form.

Water.—Water is the major ingredient in carbonated soft drinks and may be present to the extent of 92%. It is essential that the water be as nearly chemically pure as is commercially feasible since traces of impurities react with various constituents of the drink. In this respect municipal drinking water, although satisfactory from a bacteriological standpoint, generally is not satisfactory from a chemical purity consideration, and the standard for beverage water seen in Table 65 would not be met by most municipal water supplies.

TABLE 65

LABORATORY STANDARDS FOR WATER TO BE USED IN
PREPARING FRUIT JUICE BEVERAGES[1]

	Maximum
Alkalinity	50 ppm
Total solids	500 ppm
Iron	0.1 ppm
Manganese	0.1 ppm
Turbidity	5 ppm
Color	Colorless
Residual chlorine	None
Odor	None
Taste	No off taste
Organic matter	No objectionable content

[1] From Phillips (1971).

Thus, alkalinity must be low to prevent neutralization of the acid used in the beverage, which would alter flavor and decrease the preservative property of the beverage. Iron and manganese must be low to prevent reaction with coloring agents and flavor components. Residual chlorine must be virtually nonexistent since it adversely affects the flavor of the drink. Turbidity and color must be low for an attractive appearance of the drink. Organic matter as well as inorganic solids must be low since colloidal particles provide nuclei for carbon dioxide accumulation and release from solution, which results in beverages boiling and gushing at time of filling or opening of bottles.

To achieve these high water standards, bottling plants will generally further condition water with such additional treatments as chemical precipitation of minerals, deionization, activated charcoal to remove odors, flavors, and residual chlorine, final paper filtration to remove traces that may pass the carbon filter, and deaeration to remove oxygen. While the water supply in a bottling plant can be adequately controlled by these methods, the big problem occurs when the syrups and flavor bases are shipped to various locations to be used in soda fountains and vending machines. In these locations the waters will vary and frequently not meet the tight specifications of the bottling plant. Then the quality of the drink suffers and varies from location to location even though the syrup formula is constant.

Carbon Dioxide.—The sparkle and zest of this class of beverages are the result of their content of carbon dioxide gas. Carbon dioxide can be obtained from carbonates, limestone, the burning of organic fuels, and industrial fermentation processes. The soft drink bottler today buys his carbon dioxide in high pressure cylinders from manufacturers who produce the gas to comply with food purity regulations. In the cylinders, the gas under pressure exists as a liquid. The amount of CO_2 used in the beverage will depend upon the particular flavor and brand of the beverage. The CO_2 enhances flavor, contributes acidic preservative action, produces the tingling effect on the tongue, and gives the sparkling effervescent appearance to the beverage.

Carbon dioxide is dissolved in the beverage usually in the range of about 1.5 to 4 volumes of gas (under standard conditions of temperature and pressure) to each volume of liquid. This is done with a carbonator of which there are several designs. In all, however, carbonation is speeded by providing a large surface area between the liquid and the CO_2 gas, cooling the liquid since the solubility of CO_2 in water is greater the lower the temperature, and applying pressure to force more CO_2 into solution. In the type of carbonator illustrated in Fig. 264, the CO_2 is brought into contact with a large surface of water that flows over refrigerated plates within a pressurized vessel. In practice the entire flavored drink may be carbonated, or only the water may be carbonated for subsequent mixture with the flavored syrup.

Plant Layout.—A common installation for a soft drink mixing, carbonating, and bottling operation is indicated in Fig. 265. Flavored syrup con-

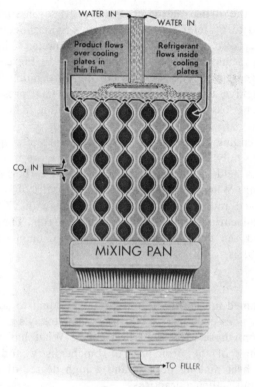

FIG. 264. COMBINATION COOLER-CARBONATOR

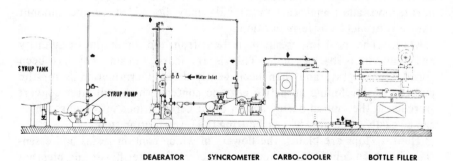

FIG. 265. SOFT DRINK MIXING, CARBONATING, AND BOTTLING INSTALLATION

taining all of the drink ingredients except the remaining water and CO_2 is pumped to a metering device called a Syncrometer. Treated and deaerated water also is pumped to the Syncrometer. This device then meters the syrup and water in fixed proportion to the carbonator. The carbonated beverage then goes to the bottling or canning line where it is admitted to highly sanitized containers under a CO_2 pressurized atmosphere to prevent loss of CO_2 and beverage boiling. The containers are then capped; they are not subsequently heat treated.

In modern vending machines that dispense drinks into open paper cups the procedure is only slightly different. Here the syrup from the beverage manufacturer is held in one tank and pressurized carbon dioxide is held in a second tank. When a drink is called for a squirt of syrup is pumped into the cup and municipal water is combined with CO_2 as it passes through a small carbonator on the way to the cup. Thus the water is carbonated and the drink is mixed in the cup, upon demand, on an individual cup basis.

BEER

Beer is consumed in quantities approximately equal to soft drinks. The brewing of beer goes back over 6,000 years, but today's practices are not far different from those used in earliest times. What has been gained is an understanding of the principles of biochemistry and microbiology underlying the beer making process and a high degree of sanitation and efficiency in manufacturing practices.

Raw Materials and Manufacture

The principal raw materials of beer manufacture are the cereal grains, particularly malted barley, rice, and corn which supply carbohydrates for fermentation by *Saccharomyces* yeast into ethyl alcohol and carbon dioxide. In addition, hops from the flower of a plant are used to intensify flavor, and additional carbon dioxide may be added to the amount naturally produced by fermentation.

Malt.—The most important ingredient from the standpoint of quantity and function is barley malt. This is the barley grain that has been germinated slightly and then been gently dried. Germination is for the purpose of developing an active enzyme content which will later convert starches in the malted barley and in other cereal grains into sugars which can be easily fermented by yeast during the fermentation step.

Hops.—Hops are plants, the flowers of which contain resins and essential oils which contribute to beer a characteristic bitter flavor and pleasant aroma. Hops also contain tannins which add to beer color. Materials extracted from hops during brewing also have mild preservative properties and add foam-holding capacity to the beer. All of these functions, however, are secondary to the role of hops in flavor and aroma.

Cereal Adjuncts.—These are cereal grains in addition to malted barley, such as corn, rice, and other cereals which are added to provide additional carbohydrates, principally starch, for conversion to sugar for subsequent fermentation.

Mashing.—The first step in beermaking is to combine the malted barley and cereal adjuncts with water and mildly cook the mixture, known as mash, to extract readily soluble materials and to gelatinize the starches, thus making them more susceptible to extraction and enzymatic breakdown into dextrins and sugars. The mild cooking also releases proteins from the grains which undergo enzymatic breakdown into compounds of lower molecular weight.

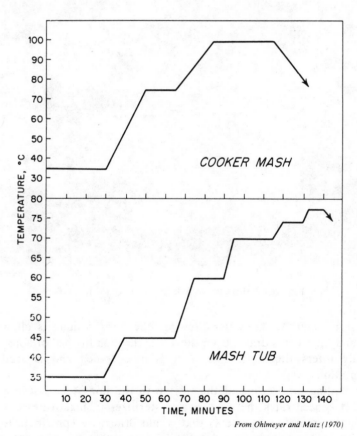

From Ohlmeyer and Matz (1970)

FIG. 266. TEMPERATURE-TIME SCHEDULE FOR TWO STAGES OF MASHING

These changes are brought about in specially designed tanks and the overall operation is known as mashing. Mashing may begin at about 100° F and gradually have the temperature of the mash raised to about 170° F. This heating is done in steps with rest periods of about 30 min between gradual temperature rises provided for specific amylases and proteinases to function before they are heat inactivated (Fig. 266). The mash tank is further designed so that upon completion of mashing, the liquid fraction, now high in yeast fermentable sugars, can be separated from the spent grains. The liquid fraction is known as wort.

Brewing.—The wort is next pumped to the brew kettle. The hops are added to the wort (Fig. 267) and the mixture is brewed by boiling in the

Courtesy of Falstaff Brewing Corp.

FIG. 267. HOPS BEING ADDED TO THE BREW KETTLE

kettle for about 2.5 hr. After brewing, the hops residue is allowed to settle and the wort is drawn from the kettle through the bed of hops which partially filters the wort. The wort is now cooled and is ready for fermentation.

The boiling or brewing of the wort with the hops serves several purposes. It concentrates the wort, nearly sterilizes it, inactivates enzymes, precipitates remaining proteins that would otherwise contribute to beer turbidity, caramelizes sugars slightly, and extracts the flavor, preservative, and tannin-like substances from the hops.

Fermentation.—The cooled wort is now inoculated with *Saccharomyces* yeast and fermentation of the sugar formed from starch during mashing proceeds. Fermentation in tanks, under near sterile conditions with respect to contaminating microorganisms, is carried out at temperatures within a range of about 38° to 57° F depending upon the strain of yeast and the brewery. The fermentation is complete in about nine days. It produces an alcohol content in the wort of about 4.6% by volume, which would be 9.2 proof. Fermentation also lowers the pH of the wort to about 4.0, and produces dissolved carbon dioxide in the wort to the extent of about 0.3% by weight.

Storage.—The beer is now quickly chilled to 32° F, passed through filters to remove most of the yeast and other suspended materials, and pumped into pressure storage tanks generally located in the cellar of the brewery (Fig. 268). The young or "green" beer is stored or "lagered" in

Courtesy of Falstaff Brewing Corp.

FIG. 268. PRESSURE STORAGE TANKS BEHIND CELLAR WALLS

these tanks for from several weeks to several months. During this period of storage at 32° F there is further settling of finely suspended proteins, yeast cells, and other remaining materials, and a development of esters and other flavor compounds, all of which contribute to improved body and a more mellow flavor.

While in storage additional carbon dioxide generally is added to the beer to increase the level developed and absorbed during fermentation, and to purge the beer of any oxygen that may be present and would adversely affect storage life. This may be done by periodically pumping the beer through a carbonator or bubbling carbon dioxide into the storage tank.

Another property of beer is known as chill haze. This is a condition caused by remaining traces of degraded proteins and tannins which form a colloidal haze when beer is cooled to low temperatures. To prevent this from occurring in the finished product various chill-proofing treatments may be given to the beer during the storage period. These generally include the addition of earths or clays to adsorb the colloidal materials, or use of proteolytic enzymes to further solubilize the protein fraction.

Finishing Steps.—After storage the beer is given a last fine filtration to yield a sparkling clear beverage. It may be further carbonated to insure a level of approximately 0.5% of CO_2 by weight in the product. The beer is now filled into casks, bottles, or cans under pressure of carbon dioxide to prevent gushing and foaming and to preclude air. The filling operation is known as racking. An analysis of the product at this stage reveals the complexity of its composition (Table 66).

Such beer in its closed container is not sterile, and although it has some degree of preservation from its hops and from mild acidity, micro-organisms present will grow on storage. Therefore beer in bottles and cans is pasteurized at about 140° F for several minutes within the container. This does not sterilize the beer but prolongs shelf-life substantially. Nevertheless, bottled or canned beer is not a truly stable product and in sufficient time the pasteurized beer in cans or bottles may develop sourness and off-flavors from slow microorganism growth. This is delayed by storing the canned or bottled beer under refrigeration. Frequently beer in casks, the well known draft beer, is not pasteurized since it is consumed rapidly in taverns before it has a chance to spoil. Because it is not pasteurized it has a flavor considered by many to be superior to canned or bottled beer.

Cold Pasteurization.—For many years attempts were made to capture the unheated flavor of casked draft beer in bottles and cans for home use. Recently, success was achieved by using a cold pasteurization technique. This employs newly developed micro-porous membrane filters which

TABLE 66

ANALYSIS OF A TYPICAL BEER[10]

Specific gravity[1]	1.0121
Beer Balling, %[1]	3.093
Saccharometer, %[1]	3.10
Alcohol by weight, %[1]	3.63
Alcohol by volume, %[1]	4.60
Real extract, %[1]	4.73
Extract of original wort (2A + E), %	11.99
Original balling, %[1]	11.80
Reducing sugars, %[1]	1.160
Degree wort sugar, %[1]	71.30
Degree attenuation, %[1] (real degree of fermentation)	60.00
pH[1]	4.35
Color,° L[1]	2.94
Air, cc[2]	1.20
Nitrogen, cc[2]	1.01
Oxygen, cc[2]	0.19
Oxygen/air, %[2]	15.80
CO_2 % by wt[1]	0.460
Acidity, %[1]	0.135
Erythro-dextrins (iodine reaction)[1]	0
Amylo-dextrins (iodine reaction)[1]	0
Dextrins, %[1]	2.73
Iron, ppm[1]	0.175
Indicator-Time test, sec[3]	290.0
Surface tension, dynes[4]	46.00
Surface activity[4]	0.367
$CaSO_4$, ppm[5]	256.00
NaCl, ppm[5]	153.00
Foam sigma	109.00
Foam density	20.40
Tannins, ppm[6]	55.40
Viscosity, cp[4]	1.057
SO_2, ppm[7]	13.20
Ash, %[1]	0.148
Diacetyl, ppm[1]	0.210
Copper, ppm[8]	0.245
Fractional carbohydrates, %[9]	
Glucose	0.001
Fructose	Trace
Sucrose	Trace
Maltose	0.10
Maltotriose	0.20
Maltotetraose	0.45
Higher saccharides	3.04
Total saccharides	3.83
Fractional proteins, %[4]	
Total protein	0.299
High molecular	0.0710
Medium molecular	0.100
Low molecular	0.0951
Non-protein N	0.0290
High/total	23.30
Medium/total	33.20
Low/total	31.60
Non-protein/total	9.6
Calories[4]	168.30

[1] Anon. 1964.
[2] Roberts *et al.* (1947).
[3] Gray and Stone (1939).
[4] Any standard method.
[5] Stone *et al.* (1951).
[6] Stone and Gray (1948).
[7] Monier-Williams (1940).
[8] Stone (1942).
[9] McFarlane *et al.* (1954).
[10] Ohlmeyer (1970).

can hold back the majority of bacteria and larger yeasts. Using filtration of this kind rather than heat, microbial numbers are effectively decreased and the flavor of draft beer is largely preserved. This is the method that has given rise to recent advertisements of draft beer in cans. In Fig. 269

Courtesy of Millipore Corporation

FIG. 269. FILTRATION ASSEMBLY HOUSING MICRO-POROUS
MEMBRANE DISCS AHEAD OF CANNER

is seen a filtration assembly housing two sets of micro-porous membrane discs connected in series. From here the beer is aseptically filled into commercially sterile cans or bottles seen to the right. Cold pasteurization with micro-porous filters also is finding application in the processing of other heat sensitive liquids such as pulp-free fruit juices and wines.

WINE

Like beer making, the fermentation of grapes to make wine goes back to at least 4000 B.C. In recent years annual world production of wine has been estimated at over 8 billion gallons, of which more than $\frac{1}{3}$ continues to be produced in France and Italy. U.S. production is very considerably smaller (about 250 million gallons), but has been growing at the rate of about 10% per year. In the United States, the principal wine producing regions are California and the Finger Lakes area of New York. Wine can be made from many fruits and berries but the grape is by far the most popular and most often used raw material.

Wine Varieties

The varieties and names given to wines are legion and reflect countries and regions of origin, variety of grape used in their manufacture, and certain properties of the wines such as degree of sweetness, color, alcohol content, and effervescence. In the United States, the Wine Advisory Board has grouped wines into five classes that are designated appetizer wines, red table wines, white table wines, sweet dessert wines, and sparkling wines. While these classes are somewhat descriptive, greater insight can be had from a consideration of some of the general characteristics of grape wines and how they are brought about.

Color.—Grape varieties range in skin color from deep purple through red to pale green. Red wines result when the crushed grape skins, pulp, and seeds of purple or red varieties are allowed to remain with the juice during the fermentation period. Alcohol produced contributes to pigment extraction. The longer the skins, pulp, and seeds are allowed to stay with the fermenting juice the deeper the color becomes. Pink or rosé wines can be produced by removing the nonjuice components or "pumace" from the mixture or "must" early through the fermentation period. White wines can be made from pigmented grapes but require removal of skins, pulp, and seeds prior to juice fermentation. White wines more commonly are made from white varieties of crushed grapes with removal of nonjuice solids prior to fermentation. Pink wines further can be prepared by blending white wines with small amounts of red wines. Final wine color also is determined by pigment stability during storage, which is dependent to a considerable degree upon grape variety.

Sweetness and Alcohol Content.—Sweetness and alcohol content are interrelated because fermentation uses up grape sugar. As more alcohol is produced sweetness decreases and when virtually all of the sugar is fermented the wine is without sweetness and is said to be "dry." Dry wines contain all of the alcohol that the specific grape is capable of yielding under the conditions of fermentation. This generally is between 12 to 14% of alcohol by volume.

The relationship between disappearance of sweetness and increase in alcohol content cannot be used to characterize wines, however, because both alcohol content and sweetness of finished wines can be further and independently adjusted. Thus a completely fermented dry wine of 14% alcohol can be made sweet after yeast removal by the addition of some unfermented juice. Similarly a sweet wine does not necessarily mean that alcohol content is low since additional alcohol can be added to a sweet wine in the form of distilled spirits. The wines in the United States designated table wines and sparkling wines generally will contain 10 to 14% alcohol by volume, appetizer and sweet dessert wines will contain over 14 but under 21% alcohol. Any of these classes may be red or white, and possess varying degrees of sweetness.

The terms "natural" and "fortified" also have been used in relation to alcohol content. Based on sugar content of the grapes, characteristics of the yeast culture, and fermentation practices employed, natural fermentation generally yields an alcohol concentration of less than 16% by volume. This alcohol concentration by itself is not sufficient to preserve "natural" wines and so a means of pasteurization must be employed. The term "light" wine also is used to describe a wine having an alcohol content from about 8 to 14%, here the term "light" has nothing to do with color. Fortified wines are those that have received additional distilled spirits to bring their alcohol content up to the range of 17 to 21% by volume. They are less perishable and may be stable without pasteurization.

Effervescence.—Wines will be either "still" or "sparkling" depending upon retention of carbon dioxide from natural fermentation, or sparkling wines may be artificially carbonated. The former are known as natural sparkling wines and the latter generally must be designated by some descriptive term, such as "carbonated wine."

During normal vat fermentation not enough carbon dioxide is retained by the wine to give it effervescence when bottled. Natural sparkling wines are made by adding about 2% sugar and a special alcohol-tolerant strain of wine yeast to previously fermented wine and giving it a second fermentation under conditions that prevent carbon dioxide loss. This second fermentation may be in the final bottle or in closed tanks from which the wine will be subsequently filtered and bottled. The preparation of bottle-fermented wines such as champagne involves an interesting technique for removing sedimented yeast, tartrates, and other fine particles that settle in the sealed bottle and would otherwise cloud the finished product. After secondary fermentation that may be complete in a month, the tightly stoppered bottles may be further rested for periods up to several years. Removal of sediment then involves placing bottles neck down in racks and periodic twirlings to move sediment down the neck toward the special stopper. Next the sediment-containing wine near the stopper is frozen by placing the necks of the inverted bottles in a refrigerant. The bottle is now set right-side-up, the stopper loosened, and carbon dioxide pressure below the frozen plug forces the plug containing the sediment out of the bottle. A small amount of wine or champagne is added to make up volume and the bottle is reclosed with its permanent cork.

Fermentation and Other Operations

As grapes mature the wine yeast *Saccharomyces ellipsoideus* naturally accumulates on the skins. When the crushed grapes or filtered juice is placed at a temperature of about 80°F the juice proceeds to ferment yielding essentially equal molar quantities of ethyl alcohol and CO_2 and traces of flavor compounds.

In commercial operation special strains of *S. ellipsoideus* may be used to supplement the natural inoculum and better control fermentation. Wine yeast is relatively resistant to sulfur dioxide and so this agent commonly is added to the grapes or must to help control undesirable microorganisms. Sulfur dioxide also is effective in inhibiting browning enzymes of the grapes and providing reducing conditions by reacting with oxygen. The sulfur dioxide treated must may next be fermented directly or pressed to remove pumace from the juice. Fermentation causes a rise in temperature and so cooling is required to prevent yeast inactivation. Fermentation under conditions of limited exposure to air may be to the point of complete exhaustion of the sugar, when it stops naturally, or fermentation may be interrupted prior to this point. At around 80°F this fermentation may last for some 4 to 10 days depending upon wine type.

After the fermentation has been completed naturally or stopped by addition of distilled spirits the next step is the first "racking," which involves allowing the wine to stand until most of the yeast cells and fine suspended materials settle out. The wine is then drawn off without disturbing the sediment or "lees." If lees are not quickly removed yeast will autolyze and contribute off-flavors to the wine. After the first racking the wine is further aged in casks or tanks that prevent entrance of air for periods of several months to years, during which last traces of sugar ferment and flavor further develops. During ageing additional rackings may be performed, and these will be followed by final filtration and stabilization treatments to produce brilliantly clear wines.

In addition to removal of last traces of colloidal materials that impair clarity, by fine filtration, stabilization also requires removal of the salts of tartaric acid. These tartrates, present in grape juice, tend to crystallize in the wine casks and if not completely removed from the wine before bottling slowly reappear as glass-like crystals in the final bottles on storage. Stabilization with respect to tartrates may involve chilling to promote crystallization prior to filtration, as in the case of winterizing oils, or removal of these salts by ion exchange treatments.

If the wine is not above 17% alcohol it now may be heat pasteurized, or cold pasteurized through microporous membrane filters, and bottled. Sparkling wines, whether secondary fermentation is carried out in bottles or in bulk, are not heat pasteurized although they generally contain not more than 14% alcohol. In this case depletion of nutrients from the previous double fermentation, a high concentration of carbon dioxide in solution, extreme cleanliness, and sometimes sulfur dioxide addition at time of final bottle closure all help to make microbial growth unlikely.

Naming of Wines

Originally wines were named for the region where the grapes were grown and the wine was produced. Such famous names as sherry originated in Jarez, Spain; port came from Oporto, Portugal; champagne from the district of Champagne near Paris; Chablis and Burgundy from districts to the south of Champagne; sauterne from Bordeaux in western France; Rhine wines from districts along the German Rhine; Marsala from Sicily; Chianti from the Italian district of Tuscany; etc. Grape varieties, soil, and climate contributed to the different characteristics of these wines. Today wines with similar characteristics are produced in many parts of the world, and to maintain identity as to type they frequently retain original names or derivatives thereof. In many countries, by international agreement and wine laws, when this is done and the original name is used it must be accompanied by the actual place of manufacture, e.g., New York State Port, California Champagne, Australian Sherry. The Treasury Department issues regulations governing the labeling and taxing of wines in the United States.

Among the most popular distinct wine types in the United States are the appetizer wines sherry and vermouth (vermouth is aromatically flavored with herbs or spice), the red table wines claret, Burgundy and Chianti, the white table wines Rhine wine and sauterne, the sweet dessert wines port, white port, muscatel, and Tokay, and the sparkling wines champagne and sparkling Burgundy. The price of wines includes federal taxation based on alcohol content and whether sparkling wines are carbonated artifically or by natural fermentation.

COFFEE

While there are considerable differences in their growing and processing, coffee and tea do share several common characteristics. Both contain virtually no food value in themselves and are consumed entirely for their refreshing and stimulating beverage properties. Both contain caffeine and this provides the physiologically stimulating effect. Both are grown in regions of tropical or near tropical climate and are important exports of these regions. Both are processed to develop flavor in the harvested bean or leaf and then are extracted or brewed to obtain this flavor in the beverage.

The United States consumes about half of the world's production of coffee as its favorite beverage which amounts to somewhat over 150 billion cups per year. Tea is far second to coffee in the United States, but in England, China, Japan, the Soviet Union, and certain other countries the picture is reversed.

Production Practices

Coffee trees are started in nurseries as seedlings which are later transferred to the plantation soil. After about five years the trees bear ripe fruit. The fruit and blossoms that appear on the branches of the trees are seen in Fig. 270. The fruit as it ripens turns red and is referred to

Courtesy of Pan American Coffee Bureau

Fig. 270.   Ripe Fruit and Blossoms of Coffee Tree

as cherries. When ripe the cherries are hand picked. The coffee tree yields about 2,000 to 4,000 cherries per year. Each cherry contains only two coffee beans and some 3,000 beans yield only about one pound of finished ground coffee.

Cross Section of Coffee Cherry

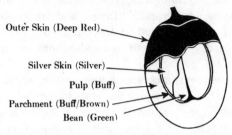

Outer Skin (Deep Red)

Silver Skin (Silver)

Pulp (Buff)

Parchment (Buff/Brown)

Bean (Green)

Courtesy of The Squier Corporation

FIG. 271.   STRUCTURE OF THE COFFEE CHERRY

The structure of the coffee cherry is seen in Fig. 271. The two coffee beans are covered by a thin parchment-like hull which is further surrounded by pulp. Both the pulp and hull are removed before the coffee beans are roasted for use.

The ripe coffee cherries are first passed through pulping machines which break and separate the pulp from the rest of the bean. Separation of the pulp leaves a mucilaginous coating on the beans which must be removed. This is done by various methods including natural microorganism fermentation of the beans heaped in large piles, use of commercial pectin digesting enzymes, or various washing treatments. After mucilage removal the beans which still contain an outer parchment look like the group on the right of Fig. 272.

The coffee beans are now partially dried either by being spread out in the sun or by machine driers. The object is to decrease coffee bean moisture from about 53% down to about 12%. Drying must be uniform throughout, and when sun drying is used the bean must be turned frequently. Drying by this method may take five days but is dependent upon the weather. During drying color and flavor attributes are modified within the beans, and overdrying or wide fluctuations in temperature give variable coffee bean quality. The advantages of machine drying with its time-temperature controllability are numerous. After drying to about 12% moisture the beans are ready to be hulled of the remaining thin layer of parchment and this is done with machines that apply friction to the hull and then remove it in a current of air.

Hulling is followed by sorting of the beans for color and defects. Just as both sun and machine drying are employed, the coffee production industry in its state of transition to modernization reveals other extremes. Hand sorting of beans moving along a belt is still practiced (Fig. 273). In contrast (Fig. 274), the coffee beans may be sorted electronically which

From Sivetz and Foote (1963)

FIG. 272. PULPED COFFEE BEFORE AND AFTER MUCILAGE
REMOVAL

is proving less costly and giving better quality control. In this case, the beans are picked up individually by vacuum and sorted by an electric eye.

The sorted beans are now graded for size, color, and by cup test to determine their potential brewing quality. Up to this point the beans are

Courtesy of Pan American Coffee Bureau

FIG. 273. HAND SORTING FROM MOVING BELT

Courtesy of Elexso Corp.

FIG. 274.   ELECTRONIC SORTING

still green. That is they have not yet been roasted. For cup testing (Fig. 275) small samples are roasted, ground, and brewed. But the graded coffee beans are shipped for the most part as green beans for further processing by the coffee manufacturer.

Courtesy of Pan American Coffee Bureau

FIG. 275.   CUP TESTING FOR BREWING QUALITY

Coffee Processing

Different manufacturers will favor various coffee blends and buy their beans from countries producing the required coffee types. The manufacturer will then custom blend for special market outlets.

Roasting.—After blending the important step is roasting, this is where the flavor of coffee as we recognize it is developed (Fig. 276). Equipment

Courtesy of National Coffee Association, U.S.A.

FIG. 276.   BATTERY OF COFFEE ROASTERS

is of either batch or continuous design and newer types of continuous roasters are highly automated with respect to temperature and humidity control, recirculation of roaster gases, and residence time of beans in the roaster. Some are even fed with green bean blends that are formulated and combined by computerized punch cards.

Much research has been carried out on the roasting step since various blends require different heat treatments to develop optimum flavor. Further, a given blend roasted to various degrees will yield coffees of different color and taste qualities favored by different markets. Current roasting practices will employ heating gas temperatures of about 500° F and roasting time will be about 5 min. The bean temperature will rise to about 400° F. All of the free moisture will be removed from the bean during roasting, and in addition the beans will lose about 5% more of their green bean weight as volatile chemical substances. One of the newer roasting processes employs heated nitrogen under pressure; among advantages claimed is improved flavor due in part to removal of oxygen.

TABLE 67

PARTICLE SIZE VERSUS NUMBER OF PARTICLES PER UNIT WEIGHT[1]

Particle Size Description	Size, Mm	No. Particles Per Gm	Increase Particles/Gm	Ratio of Increase	Total Area, Sq Cm/Gm
Whole bean	6.0	6	...	...	8
Cracked bean	3.0	48	42	1	16
Instant R & G for					
percolation	1.5	384	336	8	32
Regular	1.0	1,296	912	22	48
Drip	0.75	3,072	1,776	42	64
Fine	0.38	24,572	21,500	512	128

[1] From Sivetz and Foote (1963).

Grinding.—Following roasting the beans are cooled and ground. This is not as simple a step as might appear. The size to which the coffee is ground depends upon its intended end use (Table 67). This may be for home use in a vacuum, drip, or percolator brewer, or it may be for restaurant use in a larger urn, or for vending machine use where extremely fast brewing may be required, or for use in the manufacture of instant coffee. In each case, average particle size and particle size distribution affect the brewing time, the degree of turbidity in the cup, and other properties of the brewed beverage. Since the aroma and flavor properties of ground coffee are highly unstable to oxygen and to loss of volatiles, coffee that will undergo prolonged storage generally is packed in hermetic cans or jars under vacuum or under inert gas. Coffee for restaurants which is consumed more rapidly may be packed in sealed bags. Storage stability in each case also is affected by grind size.

Coffee Brewing.—The brewing of coffee to the correct strength and flavor depends upon several variables. These include ratio of coffee to water, particle size of the ground coffee, temperature of the water, mixing action in the brewer, and time. All will affect the amount of coffee solubles that are extracted from the ground bean. There is an optimum degree of extraction for best flavor, and extraction beyond this point removes bitter constituents from the bean and ruins the brew.

Optimum extraction can be measured by determining the soluble solids in the brew. This is done by measuring the brew density with a sensitive floating hydrometer. Such a hydrometer has been calibrated by the Coffee Brewing Institute and a chart has been developed relating extracted soluble solids to coffee strength (Fig. 277). Such measurements are very useful in developing brewing equipment of which there are scores of designs, and in quality control measurements on brewed coffee.

Machine Vending.—Machine vending of coffee has become a sizable business in itself, and since brewed coffee loses flavor and aroma even more rapidly than ground coffee some of the more advanced vending machines have been developed to brew coffee on an individual cup basis

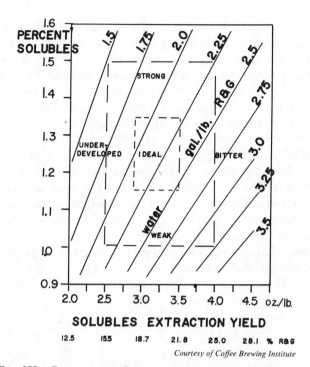

FIG. 277.   RELATIONSHIPS BETWEEN SOLUBLE SOLIDS AND COFFEE
STRENGTH AT DIFFERENT WATER TO COFFEE BREWING RATIOS

Courtesy of Rudd-Melikian, Inc.

FIG. 278.   TAPE OF INDIVIDUAL UNITS OF GROUND COFFEE FOR
VENDING MACHINE

upon demand. One such type of machine uses finely ground coffee in individual cup amounts packaged as pods in a water permeable paper tape (Fig. 278). These tapes are then rolled up and placed in the vending machine. On demand the tape is indexed past a one cup brewing chamber and a squirt of hot water is pumped through the pod of ground coffee for extraction of the soluble solids. Brewing is accomplished in about six seconds. The brew runs into a dispensed paper cup and the extracted coffee grounds remain in the tape for easy disposal.

Instant Coffee.—The biggest development in coffee technology of this century has been the development and gradual improvement of instant coffee. Instant coffee is made by dehydrating the brew, and manufacture of this product is carried out in plants that incorporate the most advanced extraction, dehydration, and essence recovery equipment to be found anywhere in the food industry.

Extraction.—Extraction of roasted ground beans is accomplished in an extraction battery that may consist of as many as 6 to 8 percolators connected to be operated as a single unit (Fig. 279). Percolators are run

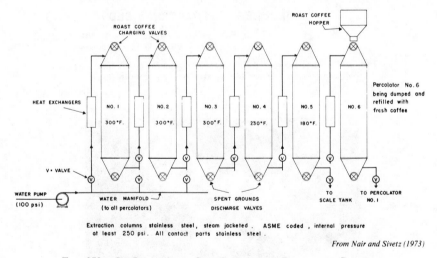

From Nair and Sivetz (1973)

FIG. 279. SIX PERCOLATOR COUNTERCURRENT EXTRACTION BATTERY

at different temperatures and extract is pumped from one to another at various stages of the brewing operation. Conditions are set to obtain maximum extraction without heat damage or overextraction of bitter constituents. Extraction also is designed to filter the brew through the coffee grounds and thereby remove fats and waxes which otherwise would adversely affect subsequent drying and storage stability. Efficient extraction using a temperature profile decreasing from about 300° to 160° F removes most of the readily soluble solids and hydrolyzes less soluble coffee bean carbohydrates (see Table 68) resulting in a total ex-

TABLE 68

CHEMICAL COMPOSITIONS SOLUBLE AND INSOLUBLE PORTIONS OF ROAST COFFEE (APPROXIMATE, DRY BASIS)[1]

	Solubles %	Insolubles %
Carbohydrates (53%)		
Reducing sugars	1–2	...
Caramelized sugars	10–17	7–0
Hemi-cellulose (hydrolyzable)	1	14
Fiber (not hydrolyzable)	...	22
Oils	...	15
Proteins ($N \times 6.25$); amino acids are soluble	1–2	11
Ash (oxide)	3	1
Acids, nonvolatile		
Chlorogenic	4.5	...
Caffeic	0.5	...
Quinic	0.5	...
Oxalic, Malic, Citric, Tartaric	1.0	...
Volatile acids	0.35	...
Trigonelline	1.0	...
Caffeine (Arabicas 1.0, Robustas 2.0%)	1.2	...
Phenolics (estimated)	2.0	...
Volatiles		
Carbon dioxide	Trace	2.0
Essence of aroma and flavor	0.04	...
Total	27 to 35	73 to 65

[1]From Sivetz (1963).

traction of about 40% of the weight of the roasted and ground bean. Without the high temperature (300° F) hydrolysis only about 20% of the bean weight would be extracted, which is about what is obtained in home and restaurant brewing.

The extract from the percolators must now be rapidly cooled and when possible dehydrated immediately, since coffee aroma and flavor can deteriorate somewhat in as little as six hours even when cooled to 40° F.

Dehydration.—The principal method of dehydrating the extract is by spray drying, and the spray drier designs are optimized especially for coffee. As with the spray drying of other products (Chap. 10) the size, shape, density, moisture content, solubility, and flavor properties of the dried particles depend upon such factors as the droplet size sprayed into the drier, the time required for the particle to descend, the temperature exposure, the trajectory of the droplet to prevent sticking to the drier wall, etc. A flow diagram of a typical instant coffee plant including spray drier is seen in Fig. 280.

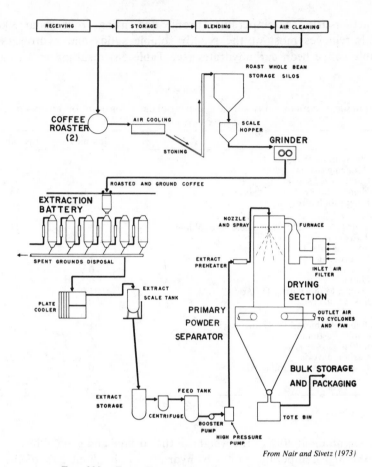

FIG. 280.   FLOW DIAGRAM OF INSTANT COFFEE PLANT

Aromatization.—Even the best instant coffee from the drier lacks the full flavor and aroma of freshly brewed coffee. An enormous amount of work has been done to remedy this and treatments of various kinds to improve flavor and aroma are referred to as aromatization. This generally involves adding back flavor and aroma constituents recovered during processing to the dry state. These flavor and aroma constituents have been trapped and recovered during roasting, grinding, and extracting, and have been obtained from oils pressed from the coffee bean. Hundreds of patents have been granted in this area alone. One interesting technique involves extraction of roasted and ground coffee with a coffee oil solvent such as liquid carbon dioxide. The cold CO_2 does not damage flavor and aroma compounds in the coffee oil, and further is easily separated from the extracted oil for recompression and reuse. The extracted oil is then sprayed onto the instant coffee. Such an aromatization scheme currently being used commercially is seen in Fig. 281. After CO_2 removal of the oil,

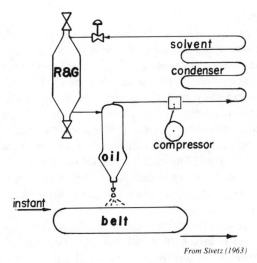

From Sivetz (1963)

FIG. 281. CLOSED CYCLE AROMATIZATION OF INSTANT COFFEE

the roasted and ground coffee is still highly suitable for extraction of water soluble solids in the regular extraction battery operation.

At present, considerable coffee extract is being dehydrated by freeze drying in an attempt to retain maximum flavor and aroma, and commercial products of high quality are available. Such products may or may not be further aromatized after freeze drying.

TEA

While coffee is derived from the beans (seeds) of the tree, tea comes from the young leaves of the tea bush. The tea bush is an evergreen and it is ready to yield tea leaves after about three years of growth. It then may yield for 25 to 50 yr depending upon growing conditions. The leaves are hand plucked from new shoots and about 6,000 leaves are needed to make one pound of manufactured tea. Depending upon climate, soil, and cultivation practices there are about 1,500 slightly different kinds of tea leaves which then can be further modified in processing. These contribute to differences in the final brew and provide opportunity for custom blending to satisfy regional preferences. Tea leaves contain three important kinds of constituents that affect brew·quality and these are caffeine which gives tea its stimulating effect; tannins and related compounds which contribute color and strength, often associated with the terms body and astringency; and essential oils which provide flavor and aroma.

Leaf Processing

There are three major classes of teas known as green, black, and Oolong teas, and the three types can be made from the same tea leaves depending upon how the leaf is processed. The differences result largely from enzymatic oxidations of the tannin compounds in the leaf. If the enzymes are allowed to act they turn the green leaf black much the same as a freshly cut apple blackens. If the enzymes in the leaf are inactivated by heat, as in blanching, then the leaf remains green. If a partial oxidation is allowed to occur by delayed heating then an intermediate tea of the Oolong type is obtained. The enzymatic oxidation of tea leaves is referred to as fermentation. Fermented leaves give black tea. Partially fermented leaves give Oolong tea. Along with the color differences there also are subtle flavor variations.

Black Tea.—The processing of tea to the dried leaf stage involves relatively few steps. In the case of black tea these include: (1) withering the plucked leaves to soften them and partially dry them; (2) passing the withered leaves under rollers to rupture cell walls and release the enzymes and juices; (3) fermenting the rolled leaves by exposing them to the air at about 80°F for about 2 to 5 hr (this relatively short time would be insufficient to bring about the desired color and flavor changes were the enzymes and juices not freed from the cells in the above rolling step); and (4) drying the fermented leaves in ovens at about 200° F, which inactivates the enzymes and decreases leaf moisture to about 4%. This drying step in the case of tea is known as firing.

Green and Oolong Tea.—In the case of green tea the steps involve: (1) steaming the plucked leaves to inactivate enzymes; (2) rolling the leaves as above since rupture of the cell walls also has the beneficial effect of making the leaves easier to extract during subsequent brewing; and (3) drying or firing the leaves. Oolong tea receives less steaming and a partial fermentation step before being fired.

Further Sub-Types.—Within each of the above broad classes of tea there are several sub-types and styles depending upon what country, region, and estate the tea came from; the season when the leaves were plucked; the size and shape of leaves which may be straight, curled, or twisted; and other characteristics, all of which affect cup quality. The percentages of the dry weight of leaves extractable as caffeine, tannin, and total soluble solids on brewing some of these teas are indicated in

TABLE 69

PERCENTAGES OF DRY WEIGHT OF LEAVES EXTRACTABLE AS CAFFEINE, TANNIN, AND
TOTAL SOLUBLE SOLIDS ON FIVE MINUTE INFUSION OF VARIOUS TEAS[1]

Infusion of	Caffeine %	Tannin %	Soluble solids %
Java black teas............................	2.7–4.4	6–20	16–26
Japan green teas	2.0–3.3	4–12	16–26
China black teas	2.0–3.7	5–10	16–22
Formosa Oolong teas	3.1–3.7	12–23	23–25
India black teas..........................	2.0–3.0	6–10	22–25

[1]From Deuss (1924).

Table 69. Regardless of type the dried tea leaves are now packed into chests and exported. The importer cup tests various lots for body, flavor, color, and clarity of the brew, and then custom blends for different markets. In the United States about 60% of the tea goes into tea bags, about 30% is sold as loose tea, and about 10% is used for the manufacture of instant tea.

Instant Tea

The manufacture of instant tea is in several ways like that of instant coffee, however, the state of technology is not nearly as advanced as in the case of coffee. Instant tea processing begins with extraction of the selected tea leaf blend; which is almost always of the fermented black tea types chosen for reddish color, relative freedom from haze, and strong flavor when brewed.

About ten parts of water are combined with one part of tea leaves by weight in the extractors and extraction is carried out at temperatures between about 140° to 212°F for 10 min. The final extract will contain about 4% solids, which represents approximately 85% of the soluble solids in the leaves. Departures from the above times and temperatures are common with different manufacturers.

This rather dilute extract is concentrated for more efficient dehydration, but just before concentration aromatics are distilled from the extract with specially designed flavor recovery equipment. The dearomatized extract is then concentrated in low temperature evaporators to between 25 to 55% solids for subsequent drying.

Instant tea has grown in popularity particularly for its convenient use in the preparation of iced tea. This, however, brings in a complication. Tea leaves and tea extract contain both caffeine and tannins. These are in solution in hot water, but in cold water some of the caffeine and tannins form a complex which gives a slight haze or turbidity to the brew known as "cloud" or "cream." Since iced tea is generally consumed in glasses rather than cups this turbidity is readily seen and detracts from the desirable quality attribute of clarity. This haze-forming property can be removed from the concentrate prior to drying. One method involves cooling the tea concentrate to about 50° F in order to encourage caffeine-tannin complex formation. The complex which gives a fine precipitate can then be removed by filtration or centrifugation. This is similar in principle to the chillproofing of beer and the winterizing of oils, although the hazes in each case differ in composition.

The concentrate with haze removed is now supplemented with tea essence distilled earlier and is ready for dehydration. It also is the practice of some manufacturers to supplement the tea concentrate with dextrins to provide a 50% tea solids and 50% carbohydrate solids mixture prior to drying. This tends to protect the delicate tea aroma during drying and yields a dried product with quicker solubility in cold water. In such a case bulk density of the product is controlled so that a teaspoonful gives about the same level of tea solids as does an instant tea dried without dextrins. A flow sheet of the overall instant tea manufacturing process is seen in Fig. 282.

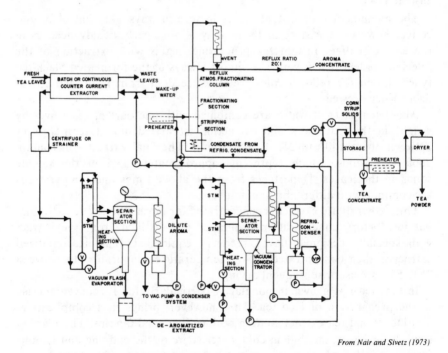

From Nair and Sivetz (1973)

Fig. 282. Flow Sheet of Instant Tea Process

Instant tea is dried primarily in spray driers and low temperature vacuum belt driers. Tea flavor and aroma is even more sensitive than that of coffee, and so the spray driers are operated under milder heat conditions than for coffee, which cuts down on their capacity. Freeze-dried tea also is being investigated.

BIBLIOGRAPHY

AMERINE, M. A., BERG, H. W., and CRUESS, W. V. 1972. Technology of Wine Making, 3rd Edition. Avi Publishing Co., Westport, Conn.

AMERINE, M. A., and SINGLETON, V. L. 1965. Wine—An Introduction for Americans. Univ. California Press, Los Angeles.

ANON. 1953. Technical Aspects of Cans and the Canning of Carbonated Beverages. American Can Co., New York.

ANON. 1964. Methods of Analysis, 8th Edition. American Society of Brewing Chemists, Milwaukee.

BALD, C., rewritten by C. J. HARRISON, 1953. Indian Tea, a Text Book on the Culture and Manufacture of Tea. Thacker, Sprink and Co., Calcutta, India.

BENEZET, L. 1951. The principal synthetic aromas in the food industry. La Perfumerie Moderne 43, No. 22, 61–78. (French)

COMPRESSED GAS ASSOCIATION. 1958. Carbon dioxide. Compressed Gas Assoc. Bull. G-6.

DE CLERCK, J. 1957. A Textbook of Brewing. English Edition. Chapman and Hall, London.

DEUSS, J. J. B. 1924. The chemical analysis of tea in relation to its quality. L'Agronomie Coloniale No. 80, 41–47. (French)

GRAY, P. P. and STONE, I. 1939. Oxidation in beers. I. A simplified method for measurement. Wallerstein Labs. Commun. 2, 5–16, 1940.

GUTCHO, M. 1969. Alcoholic Malt Beverages 1969. Food Process. Rev. 7. Noyes Data Corp., Park Ridge, N.J.

HARLER, C. R. 1933. The Culture and Marketing of Tea. Oxford University Press, New York.

HARRIS, G., BARTON-WRIGHT, E. C., and CURTIS, N. S. 1951. Carbohydrate composition of wort and some aspects of the biochemistry of fermentation. J. Inst. Brewing 57, 264–280.

JACOBS, M. B. 1959. Manufacture and Analysis of Carbonated Beverages. Chemical Publishing Co., New York.

JOSLYN, M. A. 1964. Gassing and deaeration in food processing. In Food Processing Operations, Vol. 3. M. A. Joslyn, and J. L. Heid (Editors). Avi Publishing Co., Westport, Conn.

KORAB, H. E. 1950. Technical Problems of Bottled Carbonated Beverage Manufacture. Am. Bottlers Carbonated Beverages, Washington, D. C.

LEE, S. 1958. Chemical engineering aspects of soluble coffee. Tea Coffee Trade J. 115, No. 5, 23–65.

McFARLANE, W. D., HELD, H. R., and BLINOFF, G. 1954. A simplified method for determining the total fermentable sugars in wort. Am. Soc. Brewing Chemists Proc. 1954, 121–127.

MEDBURY, H. E. 1945. The Manufacture of Bottled Carbonated Beverages. Am. Bottlers Carbonated Beverages, Washington, D. C.

MEDBURY, H. E. 1948. Modern practices in carbonated beverage plants. Food Ind. 20, 1133–1140.

MILLER, E. J. 1958. Carbon dioxide in water, in wine, in beer and in other beverages. Brochure, privately published. Berkeley, Calif.

MILLER, W. T., and HALE, J. F. 1949. Carbonated beverages. In Encyclopedia of Chemical Technology. R. E. Kirk, and D. F. Othmer (Editors). Interscience Publishers, New York.

MONIER-WILLIAMS, G. W. 1940. Official and Tentative Methods of Analysis, 5th Edition. Assoc. Offic. Agr. Chemists, Washington, D. C.

NAIR, J. H., and SIVETZ, M. 1973. Coffee and tea. *In* Food Dehydration, Vol. 2. W. B. Van Arsdel, M. J. Copley, and A. I. Morgan, Jr. (Editors). Avi Publishing Co., Westport, Conn.

NOLING, A. W. 1971. Beverage Literature: A Bibliography. Scarecrow Press, Metuchen, N.J.

OHLMEYER, D. W., and MATZ, S. A. 1970. Brewing. *In* Cereal Technology. S. A. Matz (Editor). Avi Publishing Co., Westport, Conn.

PEDERSON, C. S. 1971. Microbiology of Food Fermentations. Avi Publishing Co., Westport, Conn.

PHILLIPS, G. F. 1971. Imitation Fruit Flavored Beverages and Fruit Juice Bases. *In* Fruit and Vegetable Juice Processing Technology, 2nd Edition. D. K. Tressler and M. A. Joslyn (Editors). Avi Publishing Co., Westport, Conn.

PINTAURO, N. 1969. Soluble Coffee Manufacturing Processes 1969. Food Process. Rev. *8*. Noyes Data Corp., Park Ridge, N.J.

PINTAURO, N. 1970. Soluble Tea Production Processes 1970. Food Process. Rev. *11*. Noyes Data Corp., Park Ridge, N.J.

ROBERTS, M., LAUFER, S., and STEWART, E. D. 1947. Determination of air dissolved in storage beer. Am. Soc. Brewing Chemists Proc. *1947*, 87–92. Determination of air and oxygen in storage and finished beer. *Ibid* 92–100.

SANDEGREN, E. 1947. On the importance of proteins in brewing. Brewers Dig. *22*, No. 8, 47–52.

SIVETZ, M. 1962. Soluble coffee in transition. Coffee Tea Ind. *85*, No. 5, 6–8, 37.

SIVETZ, M. 1963. Coffee Processing Technology, Vol. 2. Avi Publishing Co., Westport, Conn.

SIVETZ, M., and FOOTE, H. E. 1963. Coffee Processing Technology, Vol. 1. Avi Publishing Co., Westport, Conn.

STONE, I. 1942. Determination of traces of copper in wort, beer, and yeast. Ind. Eng. Chem. Anal. Ed. *14*, 479–481.

STONE, I., and GRAY, P. P. 1948. Silica and tannin in worts and beers. Am. Soc. Brewing Chemists Proc. *1948*, 76–94.

STONE, I., GRAY, P. P., and KENIGSBERG, M. 1951. Flame photometry—sodium, potassium, and calcium in brewing materials. Am. Soc. Brewing Chemists Proc. *1951*, 8–20.

THORNEŘ, M. E., and HERZBERG, R. J. 1970. Food Beverage Service Handbook. Avi Publishing Co., Westport, Conn.

TRESSLER, D. K., and JOSLYN, M. A. 1971. Fruit and Vegetable Juice Processing Technology, 2nd Edition. Avi Publishing Co., Westport, Conn.

UKERS, W. H., and PRESCOTT, S. C. 1951. Coffee and tea. *In* The Chemistry and Technology of Food and Food Products, 2nd Edition, Vol. 2. M. B. Jacobs (Editor). Interscience Publishers, New York, London.

VALAER, P. 1951. Alcoholic beverages. *In* The Chemistry and Technology of Food and Food Products, 2nd Edition, Vol. 2. M. B. Jacobs (Editor). Interscience Publishers, New York, London.

WAECHTER, C. J. 1971. Plastic bottles for soft drinks and beer. Food Prod. Develop. *5*, No. 6, 74–75, 77.

WALLERSTEIN LABORATORIES. 1955. Bottled beer quality—a 10 year research record. Wallerstein Laboratories, New York.

WITT, P. R. JR. 1970. Malting. *In* Cereal Technology. S. A. Matz (Editor). Avi Publishing Co., Westport, Conn.

CHAPTER 20

Confectionery and Chocolate Products

INTRODUCTION

The technology of candy making is based largely on the science and art of manipulating sugar, the principal ingredient in candy, particularly to achieve special textural effects. This is accomplished primarily by controlling the state of crystallization of the sugar and the sugar-moisture ratio. While the confectioner has many ingredients besides sugar to modify his confections, such as milk products, egg white, food acids, gums, starches, fats, emulsifiers, flavors, nuts, fruits, chocolate, and others, all of these are secondary to sugar in determining the attributes that characterize the major candy types, and some of these ingredients are chosen especially for their influence upon the chemical and physical properties of sugar.

STRUCTURAL RELATIONSHIPS AND CONFECTIONERY TYPES

Sugar (sucrose) in confections may be crystalline and if so the crystals may be large or small; or the sugar may be noncrystalline, that is amorphous or glass-like. Whether crystalline or not the sugary structure may be hard or soft, softness being favored by a higher level of moisture, by air whipped into the sugary mass, and by the modifying influences of other ingredients.

Table 70 gives a simplified division of some major candy types. Candies that have sugar in the crystalline form include rock candy in which the en-

TABLE 70

MAJOR CANDY TYPES

Textural Property	Example
Crystalline sugar	
large crystals	rock candy
small crystals	fondant, fudge
Noncrystalline sugar	
hard candies	sour balls, butterscotch
brittles	peanut brittle
chewy candies	caramel, taffy
gummy candies	marshmallow, jellies, gumdrops

tire confection is a large sugar crystal, and fudges and fondants which contain smaller sugar crystals. A fondant is a saturated sugar solution in which small sugar crystals are dispersed. Examples of fondants would be cream centers, crystallized creams, and thin mints. Candies that contain the sugar in various degrees of crystallization also are referred to as grained candies.

Candies that have sugar in noncrystalline form include sour balls, butterscotch, and brittles, all of which have the sugar in an amorphous glass-like state, and all of which are hard, containing two per cent of moisture or less. Noncrystalline candies also include chewy types such as caramel and taffy with about 8 to 15% moisture, and gummy candies such as marshmallows, gumdrops, and jellies with higher moistures of about 15 to 22%. Marshmallows are further softened by having air whipped into them. Candies in which the sugar is noncrystalline are referred to as being nongrained.

While these candy types illustrate major varieties there are of course intermediate types but their preparation also is intermediate, following the same principles that govern sugar crystallization and water removal in the major types. The wide use of garnishes such as fruits, nuts, flavors, colors, and chocolate add interest and variety to the different candy types but the condition of the sugar and the degree of moisture are still recognizable.

The candy maker controls the state of crystallinity and the percentage of moisture in the finished confection largely by his choice of functional ingredients, his use of heat in cooking and concentrating his sugar syrups, and the way in which he cools these syrups including whether or not they are agitated.

INGREDIENTS

The variety of ingredients available to the confectionery manufacturer is indeed great. Some of these are indicated in Table 71 along with their gross compositions. From these the high energy value of the concentrated foods represented by various confections also can be judged. Some of these and other ingredients will be considered briefly with respect to their functional roles in candy making.

Sucrose

The principal sweetener and crystal former in candy making is sucrose, the sugar from sugar cane or sugar beets. At room temperature about two parts of sucrose can be dissolved in one part of water giving a concentrated solution of approximately 67%. If the solution is now cooled without agitation it becomes supersaturated. Upon further cooling, especially with agitation, the sucrose crystallizes and comes out of solution. Crystallization can be speeded enormously if even a single minute sucrose crystal is added to the supersaturated solution.

Greater concentrations of sucrose can be put into solution by raising the temperature. The higher the sucrose concentration the higher will be the

TABLE 71

GROSS COMPOSITIONS OF FOOD INGREDIENTS USED IN CONFECTIONERY MANUFACTURE[1]

Ingredient	Fuel Value Cal/100 Gm	Protein %	Fat %	Carbo-hydrates %	Ash %
Almonds	640	18.6	54.1	19.6	3.0
Coconuts (dry)	579	3.6	39.1	53.2	0.8
Chocolate (bitter)	570	5.5	52.9	18.0	3.2
Chocolate (sweet)	516	2.0	29.8	60.0	1.4
Chocolate (sweet milk)	542	6.0	33.5	54.0	1.7
Cocoa (average)	329	9.0	18.8	31.0	5.2
Corn starch	365	9.1	3.7	73.9	1.3
Cream (heavy)	337	2.3	35.0	3.2	0.5
Dairy butter	733	0.6	81.0	0.4	2.5
Eggs (total edible)	158	12.8	11.5	0.7	1.0
Fruits (fresh)					
apples (edible portion)	64	0.3	0.4	14.9	0.29
lemons (edible portion)	44	0.9	0.6	8.7	0.54
peaches (edible portion)	51	0.5	0.1	12.0	0.47
pears (edible portion)	70	0.7	0.4	15.8	0.39
oranges (edible portion)	50	0.9	0.2	11.2	0.47
pineapples (edible portion)	58	0.4	0.2	13.7	0.42
Figs (dried)	300	4.0	1.2	68.4	2.4
Raisins (seedless and seeded)	298	2.3	0.5	71.2	2.0
Gelatin (plain, dry)	343	85.6	0.1	0.0	1.3
Milk					
whole	69	3.5	3.9	4.9	0.7
condensed	327	8.1	8.4	54.8	1.7
evaporated	139	7.0	7.9	9.9	1.5
skim	36	3.5	0.2	5.0	0.8
Milk (dried)					
whole	496	25.8	26.7	38.0	6.0
skim	359	35.6	1.0	52.0	7.9
Milk (malted)	418	14.6	8.5	70.7	3.6
Nuts					
filberts	670	12.7	60.9	17.7	2.7
peanuts (roasted, edible portion)	600	26.9	44.2	23.6	2.7
pecans	747	9.4	73.0	13.0	1.6
walnuts (edible portion)	702	15.0	64.4	15.6	1.7
Sugars					
cane or beet	398	..	..	99.5	...
corn (refined dextrose, anhydrous)	398	..	..	99.5	...
maple	360	..	..	90.0	0.9
brown	382	..	..	95.5	1.2
Syrups					
cane	268	..	..	67.0	1.5
corn (commercial)	322	..	..	80.6	...
maple	256	..	..	64.0	0.7
sorghum	268	..	..	67.0	2.5
Honey (strained or extracted)	319	0.3	0.0	79.5	0.2
Molasses (light)	260	..	..	65.0	3.0

[1] From Schoen (1951).

boiling point of such solutions. Boiling point and sucrose concentration are related precisely, and this in fact is an important way the candy maker controls the final degree of water in his confection. He boils sugar and water to a selected temperature. When this temperature is reached with a given sugar such as sucrose the corresponding concentration of sugar and water in his boiling concentrated syrup will be as indicated in Table 72.

TABLE 72

CONCENTRATION OF SUGAR-WATER SYRUPS AT
DIFFERENT BOILING POINTS

% Sugar	Boiling Point, °F
30	213
40	214.3
50	215
60	217.5
70	222
80	233
90	253
95	284
97	303
98.2	320
99.5	330
99.6	340

The more concentrated solutions on cooling become highly supersaturated and may solidify as an amorphous glass, a totally crystalline mass, a partially crystalline mass with the crystals suspended in a glass, or they may partially solidify as a viscous or semiplastic crystalline suspension in the remaining saturated solution. An amorphous glass might be made into a sour ball, a totally crystalline mass would be rock candy, a partially crystalline mass with small crystals suspended in a glass would be suitable for the manufacture of partially grained confections, and the crystalline suspension in the saturated sugar solution could become a fondant cream center or a thin mint of the kind that is usually chocolate coated.

Invert Sugar

Another property of sucrose is its ability to be hydrolyzed by acids or enzymes into its two monosaccharides, glucose and fructose, according to the following equation:

$$C_{12}H_{22}O_{11} + H_2O \longrightarrow C_6H_{12}O_6 + C_6H_{12}O_6$$

Sucrose + Water $\longrightarrow$ Dextrose + Levulose

(100 lb) (5.26 lb)   (52.63 lb) (52.63 lb)

The confectionery trade refers to glucose as dextrose and fructose as levulose. The hydrolyzed mixture of dextrose and levulose is called invert sugar. One major importance of invert sugar is that it can prevent or help control the degree of sucrose crystallization. It can do this for at least two reasons. First, both dextrose and levulose crystallize more slowly than sucrose, and so substitution of part of the sucrose with invert sugar leaves less sucrose for rapid crystallization during cooling of syrups when most of the crystals are formed and during subsequent storage when additional crystals precipitate and grow in size. Second, a mixture of sucrose and invert sugar has greater solubility in water than sucrose alone. Increased solubility is equivalent to less crystallization.

Invert sugar may be obtained commercially as such and substituted for part of the sucrose in the candy formula, or it may be formed directly from the sucrose during candy making by including a food acid such as cream of tartar in the formula. During boiling of the sugar syrup the acid hydrolyzes part of the sucrose and the effects upon crystallization and other candy properties then are related to the concentration of invert sugar produced.

Invert sugar not only limits the amount of sucrose crystallization but it encourages the formation of small crystals essential to smoothness rather than grittiness in fondant creams, soft mints, and fudges. Additional properties of invert sugar include hygroscopicity which helps prevent more chewy candies from drying out and becoming overly brittle, and effects upon sweetness. With regard to sweetness the components of invert sugar differ from sucrose. Dextrose is less sweet and levulose is more sweet than sucrose. In mixture invert sugar and sucrose is sweeter than sucrose alone.

Corn Syrups and Other Sugars

Corn syrups are viscous liquids containing dextrose, maltose, higher sugars, and dextrins. They are produced by the hydrolysis of corn starch using acid or acid-enzyme treatments. The extent of hydrolysis or conversion to lower molecular weight substances is influenced and controlled by the time, temperature, pH, and choice of enzymes involved in these treatments, and a wide variety of syrup compositions is commercially available.

Corn syrups also retard crystallization of sucrose, and do so with less tendency toward hygroscopicity than invert sugar. Corn syrups further add viscosity to confections largely due to their dextrin content, reduce friability of the sugar structures from temperature or mechanical shock, slow dissolving rate of candies in the mouth, and contribute chewiness to confections.

Other sugars or sugar sources used in candy making include molasses, honey, and maple sugar, but these generally are used for their particular flavor properties rather than for special functional attributes.

Some Additional Ingredients

Other ingredients also have effects in controlling sucrose crystallization, although this may be secondary to the main reason for their use. Thus, besides the thickening and chewiness properties of starch, the whipping and toughening properties of egg white and gelatin, the flavor and coloring properties of milk, and the flavor, tenderizing, and lubricating qualities of fats, all of these ingredients interfere with sucrose crystal formation. This is due to adsorption of these materials onto crystal surfaces as they are forming, which produces a barrier between attractive forces of the crystal lattice and sucrose molecules in solution and thus limits the crystals from growing in size.

Some of the softer candies such as marshmallows, gumdrops, and jellies owe their chewiness in part to pectins, gums, and gelatin. The chewiness of caramel is due largely to prevention of the grained condition by corn syrup and invert sugar plus the chewiness of dextrins. These and other soft candies also are characterized by a moderate level of moisture as indicated earlier. When candy moisture is of the order of 20% or less, slight drying out on storage will have marked effects upon subtle optimum textures. In addition to protective packaging, humectants are used to hold moisture within such confections. Common humectants, in addition to invert sugar, include glycerin (glycerol) and sorbitol. Sorbitol is the six hydroxy alcohol formed from the reduction of glucose. Colloidal materials such as the pectins and gums which are hydrophilic also have humectant properties in confections.

Thus, the candy maker can combine a wide range of functional ingredients into an almost unlimited number of formulations to affect confectionery properties. The possibilities are further enlarged by the order of ingredient addition. If crystal inhibitors are added together with sucrose to the cooking kettle a different result will be obtained than when some of these ingredients are subsequently mixed into a smooth fondant produced with seeding, cooling, and agitation to promote rapid minute crystal formation. The hardness-softness aspect of texture, largely controlled by the amount of water boiled off in the cooking kettle prior to cooling and solidifying the batch, also is obviously affected by choice of ingredients. The incorporation of flavors, nuts, and fruits into the sugary mass further modifies the confection in a more easily predictable manner.

CHOCOLATE AND RELATED MATERIALS

Chocolate not only is one of the principal ingredients used by the confectioner, but its widely enjoyed flavor properties make it a favorite material of bakers, ice cream producers, and other food manufacturers. In its many forms chocolate may be consumed as a beverage, a syrup, a flavoring, a coating, or a confection in itself. It therefore warrants brief consideration in its own right before proceeding further with some of the processing practices of the confectionery manufacturer.

The Cacao Bean

Chocolate and related products begin with cacao beans which grow in elongated melon shaped seed pods attached to the cacao tree (Fig. 283).

Courtesy of Cadbury Brothers Ltd.

FIG. 283. HARVESTING CACAO FRUIT (SEED PODS) IN WEST AFRICA

The pods each contain about 25 to 40 cacao beans which are arranged in rows with the length of the pod around a central placenta. The rows of beans are surrounded by mucus and a pulpy layer beneath the pod husk.

The beans, which may be white or pale purple and are slightly larger than a coffee bean, are removed from the pod and given an opportunity to ferment microbiologically and enzymatically. This may be done by heaping the beans and covering them with leaves. Fermentation removes adhering pulp and mucus, kills the germ of the bean, and modifies flavor and color of the bean. After fermentation, the beans which are now cinnamon to brown in color are sun dried or machine dried to about 7% moisture to give them good keeping quality. Fermentation and drying also alter the seed coat, changing it to a friable skin which can be easily removed in a subsequent operation. The beans are now ready to be exported for further processing.

Cacao Bean Processing

At the chocolate and cocoa manufacturing plant the beans are roasted to further develop flavor and color. They are then passed through winnowing machines which remove seed coats and separate the germ. The hulled and germed beans are called nibs. The nibs are now passed through various types of mills where they are torn apart and ground releasing fat from the cells. The heat of grinding melts the fat and the ground nibs acquire a liquid consistency. The liquid discharged from the mill is known as chocolate liquor. These and subsequent manufacturing operations are indicated in Fig. 284.

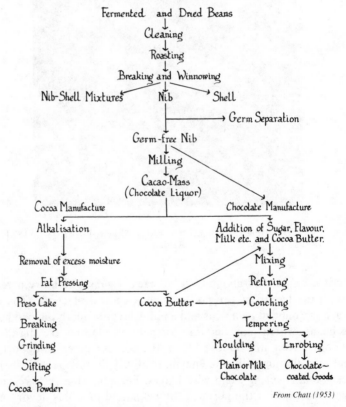

From Chatt (1953)

FIG. 284. FLOW SHEET OF COCOA AND CHOCOLATE MANUFACTURING PLANT OPERATIONS

Chocolate Liquor

Chocolate liquor contains approximately 55% fat, 17% carbohydrate most of which is digestible, 11% protein, 6% tannin compounds, 3% ash, 2.5% organic acids, 2% moisture, traces of caffeine, and about 1.5% of theobromine, the alkaloid related to caffeine which is responsible for the mildly stimulating properties of cocoa and chocolate.

This chocolate liquor upon cooling solidifies and is the familiar bitter chocolate used in baking and other applications. It also is the material which is further processed with sugar to yield sweet chocolate or with sugar and milk to produce milk chocolate. The chocolate liquor also may be partially defatted in a hydraulic press.

Cocoa Butter

The fat removed from chocolate liquor is known as cocoa butter. The brittle snap of chocolate at room temperature, and the quick melting properties in the mouth (releasing maximum flavor), are due to the rather narrow melting range of cocoa butter which is about 86° to 96° F. It is upon this temperature range for melting and solidification of cocoa butter components that tempering conditions for molten chocolate and subsequent storage temperatures for solidified chocolate are based. This is to prevent uncontrolled fat crystallization which gives chocolate an impaired texture and a gray surface appearance referred to as "fat bloom." This condition is not to be confused with "sugar bloom" which also occurs on chocolate surfaces from crystallization of sugar under poor temperature and humidity conditions.

Cocoa

After much of the cocoa butter is pressed from the chocolate liquor the remaining press cake is the raw material for the manufacture of cocoa or cocoa powder. The amounts of fat left in the press cake can be varied by the conditions of pressing, and on grinding of the press cake result in different cocoas which are classified according to their fat contents. The fat contents of cocoas are fixed by law. In the United States, for example, "breakfast cocoa" must contain a minimum of 22% cocoa fat, medium fat "cocoa" must contain between 10 and 22% fat, and products containing less than 10% fat must be labeled "low fat cocoas." It is also possible to further remove cocoa fat virtually completely by solvent extraction for special use cocoas. One such use is in the manufacture of chocolate flavored angel cakes where traces of fat would adversely affect the whipping properties of egg whites.

Some cocoa is treated with alkali to darken its color and modify its flavor. This is called "Dutch Process" cocoa since the process originated in Holland. Dutch Process cocoa may have a dark mahogany color and the flavor will generally be somewhat more bitter and astringent than the same material not treated. The "Dutching" treatment with alkali is usually applied to the nibs before they are made into chocolate liquor. One use for alkali treated cocoa is in the manufacture of dark colored devil's food cake.

Chocolate

There are many types of chocolate depending upon levels of chocolate liquor, added cocoa butter, sugar, milk, and other ingredients. In the United States "sweet chocolate" or "sweet chocolate coating" must contain at least 15%, "milk chocolate" at least 10%, and "bittersweet chocolate" at least 35% of chocolate liquor. The standards also are quite precise on other aspects of composition.

Courtesy of Baker Perkins Ltd.

FIG. 285.   FIVE-ROLL CHOCOLATE REFINER

The manufacture of chocolate begins with the combining of ingredients. A high quality sweet chocolate formulation might consist of 32% chocolate liquor, 16% additional cocoa butter, 50% sugar, and minor quantities of vanilla bean plus other materials. The mixture is next subjected to fine grinding referred to as "refining," by being passed through close clearance revolving rollers (Fig. 285). These reduce sugar crystals and other particulates to about 25 μ or less in size, and the mixture scraped from the rolls takes on the character of a flaky powder.

Chocolate is next "conched" or kneaded in special heated mixing tanks provided with pressure rollers that grind and aerate the now melted mass to develop increased smoothness, viscosity, and flavor (Fig. 286). Conching

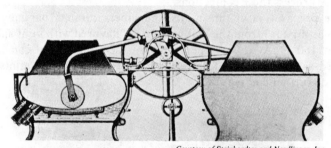

Courtesy of Steinhardter and Nordlinger, Inc.

FIG. 286.   CHOCOLATE CONCH MACHINE SHOWING ROLLER WITHIN CURVED TANK

may be at about 140° F and continue for periods from about 96 to 120 hr. Conching is not essential to chocolate manufacture but is rarely omitted in producing a really high quality product.

Following conching the liquid chocolate is tempered by being stirred in a heated and then cooled kettle to promote controlled crystallization of the cocoa fat. The object here is to melt all of the glycerides of the fat and then initiate uniform crystallization of the different glyceride fractions. This is in contrast to uncontrolled crystallization in which the higher melting point glycerides solidify within an oily mass. When the latter occurs, as mentioned earlier, uneven crystallization results in impaired chocolate texture and development of fat bloom on subsequent cool storage. Tempering conditions vary but may involve stirring at 130° F, cooling to about 90° F, and continued stirring for about one more hour. The thickened chocolate mass is now ready to be poured into molds for subsequent hardening or into tanks maintained at about 90° F for coating of confections.

Imitation Chocolate

There are also imitation chocolates in which some or all of the cocoa fat is replaced with other vegetable fats. These imitation chocolates are formulated for special applications such as the coating of ice cream bars, crackers, or candies, where selected vegetable fats can give the chocolate product improved coating properties or resistance to melting in the hand. In the latter case, a hydrogenated vegetable fat with a higher melting point than cocoa fat also will impart to the product a greater melt resistance during summer storage conditions.

CONFECTIONERY MANUFACTURING PRACTICES

The modern confectioner may employ batch or continuous processes for preparing and cooking his fondants, taffies, brittles, and hard candies. He uses a number of specialized machines to extrude, divide, enrobe, and otherwise process these confections.

In the preparation of thin mints, the supersaturated, partially crystallized sugar mixture from the boiling kettle is flavored with mint and cooled to about 160° F. At this temperature it is semiliquid and can be easily deposited as small dabs onto a moving belt (Fig. 287). The mints quickly solidify on further cooling.

From Barnett (1960)

FIG. 287. DEPOSITING THIN MINTS

Firmer chewy centers generally are extruded by being pressed through dies. The candy pieces are then cut off by the movement of a thin wire (Fig. 288). Like the thin mints they may travel on a moving belt to be covered or enrobed with molten chocolate.

Some candies are formed from a highly liquid mixture. They are given shape by molding before they harden. This may be done in a starch molding machine known as a Mogul (Fig. 289). In this case trays of powdered corn starch are continuously imprinted with concave impressions. The hot liquid candy is filled into the impressions as the trays are conveyed under a

Courtesy of Werner Machinery Co.

FIG. 288. EXTRUDING PLASTIC CENTERS

hopper. Quick cooling solidifies the candies which are then automatically dumped together with the starch from the trays over a screen which separates the candies from the starch. A brush further removes the starch from the candies and the starch is returned to the machine to be again imprinted. This is the way certain jellies, gum drops, marshmallows, and Easter egg centers are formed. Another type of forming utilizes metal, plastic, or rubber molds.

Other candies are aerated to give them softer texture. In the case of marshmallows and nougats this will involve formulations containing gelatin, egg white, or vegetable proteins that impart whipping properties,

Courtesy of Baker Perkins Ltd.

FIG. 289. STARCH MOLDING MACHINE

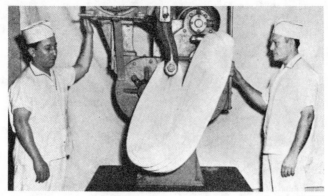

From Barnett (1960)

FIG. 290.   PULLING TAFFY

and aeration is achieved in batch or continuous mixers before the confections are molded. On the other hand, taffy is pulled (Fig. 290). With each fold of the taffy air is entrapped and with subsequent folds it is subdivided.

Various kinds of small and round candies are glazed by coating nuts and other centers with sugar. This is done by panning. The centers are added to revolving heated pans (Fig. 291) and a sugar syrup is sprayed into the pan. As the centers gently tumble they become uniformly coated with the syrup which dries as water is evaporated from the heated pan. The thickness of the glass-like sugar coating can be easily varied by continued syrup addition. This is the way candy coated chocolate centers that do not melt in

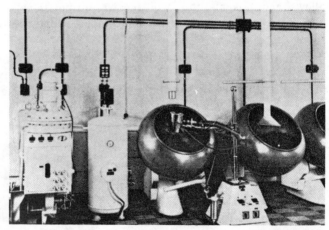

From Barnett (1960)

FIG. 291.   CANDY PANNING INSTALLATION

the hand are made. Candies also are coated with chocolate by this method except that the pans are chilled with cool air to solidify the chocolate coating. Chocolate panned items frequently are further polished or glazed. This is done by spraying a solution of gum arabic or zein into the pan after the chocolate coating is applied. Another polish is known as confectioners glaze, which is an edible shellac preparation. These glazes not only improve the glossy appearance of chocolate items but protect the chocolate from the effects of humidity and air in storage.

Larger candy pieces and those that are not round are coated with molten chocolate by the method known as enrobing. In this case the candy centers first are "bottomed" by passing on a screen over a layer of molten chocolate. They then pass through a tunnel in which they are showered by molten chocolate as seen in Fig. 292. Excess liquid chocolate is drained and

Courtesy of Werner Machinery Co.

FIG. 292. CENTERS ENTERING CHOCOLATE ENROBER

returned to the tunnel and the emerging pieces quickly cool solidifying the coating. It is in enrobing that special chocolate compositions with closely specified melting, covering, and solidifying properties are important. Uniform coating at high speeds requires close control of the temperatures of the incoming candy centers as well as the molten chocolate.

A special type of confection is of particular interest. This is the confection that has a liquid center and is typified by the chocolate covered cherries and fruits in a syrup. Since the center must be firm to be enrobed, the method of getting the liquid inside the chocolate shell is a good example of food processing ingenuity. First the fruit is covered with a sugar fondant in a form such as a starch mold and the fondant cools and solidifies. The firm fondant is now enrobed with chocolate in the usual way. However, the fondant is prepared with an invertase enzyme which slowly hydrolyzes sucrose to invert sugar. This inversion takes place during the normal storage of the candy. Invert sugar is more soluble than sucrose in the moisture of the fondant and so it melts under the chocolate layer and converts the firm center to a creamy liquid.

BIBLIOGRAPHY

ALIKONIS, J. J. 1953. Carbohydrates in confections. Am. Chem. Soc. Advan. Chem. *12,* 57–63.

ALIKONIS, J. J. 1955. Milk solids in confections. Chicago Dairy Tech. Soc. Symp., Dept. Food Technol., Univ. Illinois, Urbana.

ALIKONIS, J. J. 1964. Confectionery manufacture. *In* Food Processing Operations, Vol. 3. M. A. Joslyn, and J. L. Heid, (Editors). Avi Publishing Co., Westport, Conn.

BARNETT, C. D. 1960. Candy Making—As a Science and an Art. Magazines For Industry, New York. Formerly, Don Gussow Publications, New York.

BERGER, S. E., and CARR, D. R. 1966. Malic acid in place of citric acid in hard candy. Food Technol. *20,* 1477–1478.

CHATT, E. M. 1953. Cocoa, Cultivation, Processing, Analysis. Interscience Publishers, New York.

CICCONE, V. R. 1952. Cooking starch jellies continuously. Sixth Prod. Conf., Penn. Manuf. Confectioners Assoc., Lancaster, Pa.

FARRELL, K. E., and ALIKONIS, J. J. 1951. Improvement of chocolate type coating for use in Army rations. Food Technol. *5,* 288–290.

GUTTERSON, M. 1969. Confectionery Products Manufacturing Processes 1969. Food Process. Rev. *6.* Noyes Data Corp., Park Ridge, N.J.

HOYNAK, P. X., and BOLLENBACK, G. N. 1966. This is Liquid Sugar, 2nd Edition. Refined Syrups and Sugars, Yonkers, N.Y.

INTER-AMERICAN INSTITUTE OF AGRICULTURAL SCIENCES. 1949. Cacao Inform. Bull. *17.* Turrialba, Costa Rica.

KING, J. A. 1950. The art of candy making vs. science. Fourth Prod. Conf., Penn. Manuf. Confectioners Assoc., Lancaster, Pa.

KOOREMAN, J. A. 1952. Raw material processing techniques in gum candy. Confectioners J. *78,* No. 13, 44.

LANG, L. 1949. The role of sugar in candy making. Third Prod. Conf., Penn. Manuf. Confectioners Assoc., Lehigh Univ., Bethlehem, Pa.

MEEKER, E. W. 1950. Confectionery sweeteners. Food Technol. *4,* 361–365.

MINIFIE, B. W. 1970. Chocolate, Cocoa and Confectionery: Science and Technology. Avi Publishing Co., Westport, Conn.

PRATT, C. D. (Editor) 1970. Twenty Years of Confectionery and Chocolate Progress. Avi Publishing Co., Westport, Conn.

SCHOEN, M. 1951. Confectionery and cacao products. *In* The Chemistry and Technology of Food and Food Products, Vols. 2 and 3. M. B. Jacobs (Editor). Interscience Publishers, New York.

WOODROOF, J. G. 1966. Peanuts: Production, Processing, Products. Avi Publishing Co., Westport, Conn.

WOODROOF, J. G. 1967. Tree Nuts: Production, Processing, Products, Vols. 1 and 2. Avi Publishing Co., Westport, Conn.

WOODROOF, J. G. 1970. Coconuts: Production, Processing, Products. Avi Publishing Co., Westport, Conn.

CHAPTER 21

Food Packaging

INTRODUCTION

In earlier chapters, a number of food preservation methods were discussed. Packaging is still another preservation method, and indeed, faulty packaging will undo all that a food processor has attempted to accomplish by the most meticulous of manufacturing practices. But food packaging also performs many functions in addition to preservation, and few fields of activity essential to current distribution and merchandising of food materials are as dynamic and competitive as that of food packaging.

Food packaging employs a very wide variety of materials including rigid metals as in cans and drums; flexible metals as in aluminum and steel foils; glass as in jars and bottles; rigid and semirigid plastics as in canisters and squeeze bottles; flexible plastics of a wide variety of types as in pouches and meat wrappers; rigid cardboard, paper, and wood products as in boxes; flexible papers as in bags; and laminates or multilayers which may combine paper, plastic, and foil to achieve properties unattainable with any single component.

In addition to the many materials that are used, and their properties when in contact with different foods, food packaging also encompasses the equipment and machinery for producing or modifying certain packaging materials, for forming them into the final containers, for weighing and dispensing of food materials, for vacuumizing or gas flushing the containers, and for sealing the final packages. These packages in many instances then must withstand additional processing operations such as heat sterilization in pressure retorts, freezing and thawing in the case of frozen foods, and even final cooking or baking in the package in the case of numerous high-convenience items.

Packaging of foods has become so complex that an entire industry has developed to satisfy the need. Today, every sizable food company has a division of packaging, and several universities offer special curricula leading to a degree in package engineering. The food scientist and technologist certainly does not also have to become a packaging engineer to practice his profession, but he will find it impossible to prevent becoming involved in packaging problems. In many instances this will involve defining the kinds of protection essential to a food product, and specifying in quantitative terms what the package must do. There will be available considerable help in this from suppliers of packaging materials and equipment, but they in turn will depend upon the food scientist to make them aware of the peculiarities and subtleties of his particular food system. There are many hundreds of modified packaging materials and in the case of Cellophane alone there are over 100 types of Cellophane-containing films and laminates varying in such properties as moisture permeability, gas permeability, flexibility, stretch, burst strength, and so on. More often than not a new food product requires its own special package since maximum protection, economic considerations, and merchandising requirements change rapidly with variations in product composition, weight and form, and performance demands.

REQUIREMENTS AND FUNCTIONS OF CONTAINERS

The following are among the more important general requirements and functions of food containers: (1) nontoxic and compatible with the specific food; (2) sanitary protection; (3) moisture and fat protection; (4) gas and odor protection; (5) light protection; (6) resistance to impact; (7) transparency; (8) tamperproofness; (9) ease of opening; (10) pouring features; (11) reseal features; (12) ease of disposal; (13) size, shape, weight limitations; (14) appearance, printability; (15) low cost; and (16) special features.

We speak of primary and secondary containers. By primary container we mean one that comes in direct contact with the food such as a can or a jar. By secondary container we mean an outer box, case, or wrapper that may hold cans or jars but doesn't directly contact the food. Obviously primary containers must be nontoxic and compatible with the food, causing no color, flavor, or other foreign chemical reactions.

Sanitary protection means protection against introduction of microorganisms as well as dirt. It also implies resistance against the borings of insects and the sharp teeth of rodents.

Moisture protection is a two way affair. The food should not absorb moisture from the atmosphere, and moist foods should not lose moisture and dry out. There are exceptions such as permeable films to allow escape of moisture from respiring vegetables, as has been mentioned earlier. Fat protection is to keep fatty foods such as butter from staining through wrappings. A material that is moisture-proof is not necessarily impervious to fat since the latter may actually dissolve through the wrapping material as a solvent passes through a permselective membrane. Similarly a grease-proof material is not necessarily impervious to moisture.

Gas and odor protection also works two ways. Off-odors should be sealed out but desirable odors such as the aroma of coffee or the essence of vanilla should be sealed in. For storage stability of many foods we must seal oxygen out. Yet like moisture in the case of vegetables, there are some products which generate carbon dioxide which should escape from the package; this is the case in certain gas evolving doughs.

Resistance to impact is to prevent breakage of the package and subsequent product contamination; however, resistance to product damage from impact or other physical stress (such as protection of crackers from breaking) is also wanted.

Transparency and protection from light are conflictive. Transparency of the package is desirable because the customer likes to see what she is buying. This is no problem with foods that are not light sensitive. With those that are, and most foods are light sensitive at least to a small degree, choice of container must be based upon judgement, taking into account the probable normal shelf-life of the product and how much damage light will do in this length of time. Colored bottles for beer and other beverages and juices is a common compromise.

Tamperproofness is especially important in certain perishable foods. Consider the vile practice of a shopper opening a bottle of baby food, tasting it with the finger for acceptability, and then closing the jar and replacing it on the shelf. This has occurred enough times in the past to cause virtually a universal shift away from simple screw top covers for baby food jars. Today in place of these, lids with slightly concave domes that are drawn in when the jars are vacuum packed are the type used. Upon opening and breaking of the vacuum a click is heard as assurance to the customer that the air-tight seal has not been previously broken either by intent or from faulty closure during packaging. Other tamperproof devices for different products are cellulose bands which seal closure to container, and membranous films sealed across the mouth of a container beneath the removable lid. These also minimize chances of product leakage, gas transfer, and aroma loss.

Ease of opening is perhaps best exemplified by the modern pull tab beer and soda pop cans and the flip-off crown caps whose forerunners required a can or bottle opener. These technological developments had to balance minimum force for ease of opening against potential of bursting from internal pressure of carbon dioxide.

Pouring features apply to containers for many granular and particulate solids as well as liquids, from breakfast cereals to salt. The bridging and flowability properties of these materials determine the size and shape of pouring openings.

Resealability feature has long been provided in coffee cans, screw type bottle caps, and pressure lid jars, but only recently has it been successfully applied to loaves of bread to retard staling. Its effective application currently is in the form of plastic bags with a twist wire for repeated closings.

Ease of disposal is improved if the packages can be burned, crushed, or ground up. Metal containers are easily crushed and glass can be ground. Burning must not produce toxic or otherwise noxious fumes to pollute the air. Some rigid plastic materials are likely to be ruled out in the future because of difficulty of disposal.

Lighter weight is generally more economical for a given packaging material provided it gives adequate protection. Size and shape are generally merchandising decisions. Wherever possible, supermarket managers and housewives favor square over round containers to save space, but frequently square containers are more expensive to fabricate. Appearance and cost, after other criteria are met, also are merchandising decisions.

Special features may cover any novel function or property from aerosol dispensers to the compartmented aluminum dinner tray packages used to heat and serve the food. Some special feature containers will be described later on.

This partial list of container requirements and functions is sufficient to illustrate the variability that can be called for in a package, especially when one considers the thousands of different food items stocked by a modern supermarket. But packaging requirements are made still more complex when products are destined for more harsh conditions of handling and storage than exist in air conditioned supermarkets. These range from package survival through military or emergency air drops to resistance of the package to moisture and mold deterioration under tropical jungle conditions. Fortunately very few packages must combine all of the above indicated properties.

TYPES OF CONTAINERS

Primary and Secondary Containers

The terms primary and secondary containers have been used. Some foods are provided with efficient primary containers by nature, such as nuts, oranges, eggs, and the like. In packaging these, we generally need only a secondary outer box, wrap, or drum to hold units together and give gross protection. Other foods such as milk powder, dried eggs, and fruit concentrates often will be filled into primary containers such as plastic liners which are then packaged within protective cartons or drums. In this case the secondary container provided by the carton or drum greatly minimizes the requirements that must be met by the primary container. Except in special instances, secondary containers are not designed to be highly impervious to water vapor and other gases, especially at zones of sealing, dependence for this being placed upon the primary container. Since primary containers by definition are those which come in direct contact with the food, the food scientist generally will be far more concerned with them than with secondary containers.

Degree of Rigidity

Reference also has been made to flexible and rigid containers. Between these extremes are several types of plastic milk bottles, squeeze bottles for mustard and ketchup, and tooth paste type tubes for food pastes, more popular in European merchandising. The flexible pouches for certain rations carried by the foot soldier not only present less of a hazard to bodily bruises but are lighter in weight and often easier to get rid of than rigid cans. So long as the customer continues to squeeze bread and other products as measures of quality, the flexible wrapper serves this desire among its other attributes. One application of nonrigid foils is in the single service pouches of ketchup and like condiments, which also serve as handy sanitary dispensers. The many types and thicknesses of food packaging plastics are particularly versatile in providing controllable rigidity for a growing range of food applications. This is also true of metal foils and foil-containing laminates.

Preformed and In-Line Forming

Containers may be preformed, that is fabricated as in the case of cans and glass jars at the factory; or containers may be in-line formed, such as assembly from roll stock or flat blanks just ahead of the filling operation in the food handling line. Today most flexible containers whether from paper, foil, or plastic are in-line formed, resulting in great savings in handling labor, container transportation costs, and warehouse storage space.

Preforming is illustrated by the can-making machine of Fig. 293, which generally is located in a can manufacturing facility distant from the food plant. In such a case, cylindrical cans with bottoms attached are shipped with separate can lids (Fig. 294). The lids are seamed onto the cans after the can filling step. The handling problems and expense are obvious in this type of operation. For this reason many large food companies set up can-making facilities in a building close by the can-filling line, and cans are continuously conveyed between the buildings. The same problems exist with preformed glass bottles.

In contrast, flexible foils, papers, plastic films, and laminates in the form of rollstock lend themselves to an endless number of in-line high speed package forming, filling, and sealing operations (previous Fig. 48). Common techniques employed with particulate foods are indicated in Fig. 295. Related methods package the widest variety of liquid and solid foods, from individual portions of jam and single slices of American cheese

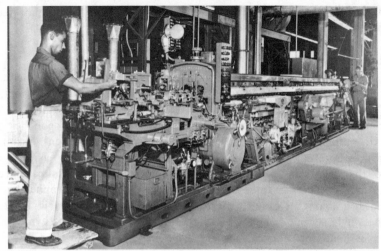

Courtesy of American Can Co.

FIG. 293.   AUTOMATIC BODY FORMING MACHINE WHICH FABRICATES CAN
CYLINDERS FROM FLAT METAL SHEETS

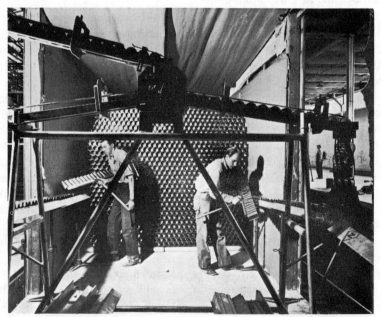

Courtesy of American Can Co.

FIG. 294.   BOXCAR LOADING OF SANITARY CANS FOR SHIPMENT TO FOOD
PROCESSOR

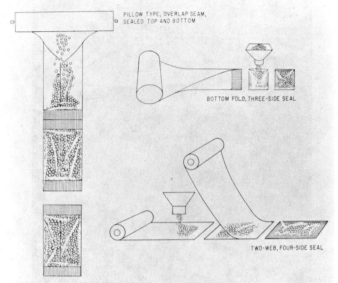

PILLOW TYPE, OVERLAP SEAM, SEALED TOP AND BOTTOM

BOTTOM FOLD, THREE-SIDE SEAL

TWO-WEB, FOUR-SIDE SEAL

Courtesy of Modern Packaging

FIG. 295. TECHNIQUES FOR PRODUCING BASIC POUCH PACKAGE CONSTRUCTIONS

to the multipacks of sausage products made skin-tight by vacuum forming. A device for packaging franks within buns in Cellophane for the vending trade, typical of a host of specialized machines for continuous in-line packaging, is seen in Fig. 296.

One of the earliest types of in-line packaging operations was the milk cartoning system which assembled cartons from coated fiber flats, filled them, and sealed the cartons. This is still one of the most important in-line packaging processes (previous Fig. 47). Some of the more advanced concepts for packaging milk and other liquids in plastic bottles, previously mentioned in Chap. 5, calls for the in-line conversion of thermoplastic resins from powder or pellet form into bottles by high temperature blow molding techniques, which at the same time heat-sterilize the containers. The automatically filled containers are then heat-sealed, again taking advantage of the thermofusing properties of the plastic. The comparative economics of such systems will largely determine their future.

Hermetic Closure

Two conditions of the greatest significance in packaging are hermetic and nonhermetic closure. The term hermetic means a container which is absolutely impermeable to gases and vapors throughout its entirety, in-

Courtesy of Modern Packaging

FIG. 296.   IN-LINE PACKAGING OF ROLL AND FRANK FOR VENDING
TRADE

cluding its seams. Such a container, so long as it remains intact, will automatically be impervious to bacteria, yeasts, molds, and dirt from dust and other sources since all of these agents are considerably larger than gas or water vapor molecules. On the other hand, a container which prevents entry of microorganisms, in many instances will be nonhermetic. A container that is hermetic not only will protect the product from moisture gain or loss, and from oxygen pickup from the atmosphere, but is essential for strict vacuum and pressure packaging.

The most common hermetic containers are rigid metal cans and glass bottles, although faulty closures can make them nonhermetic. With very rare exceptions flexible packages are not truly hermetic for one or more of the following reasons. First, the thin flexible films, even when they do not contain minute pinholes, generally are not completely gas and water vapor impermeable although the rates of gas and water vapor transfer may be exceptionally slow; second, the seals are generally good but imperfect; and third, even where film materials may be gas- and water-vapor-tight, such as certain gages of aluminum foil, flexing of packages and pouches leads to minute pin holes and crease holes.

The hermetic property of the sanitary tin can (Fig. 297) is a remarkable

ARCHITECTURE OF THE ENAMELED SANITARY TIN CAN

THE DOUBLE SEAM

The curl on the can end containing sealing compound and the flange on the can body are indexed and rolled flat, forming five folds of metal. Sealing compound between folds gives an air-tight seal.

THE SIDE SEAM

The edges of the can body are first hooked and then bumped or flattened together. Then final sealing is accomplished by soldering the outside of the side seam.

THE NOTCH

If side seam were extended to can end, four folds of metal would have to be included in the double seam. Body blank is notched, however, so that only a double layer of metal extends into the double seam. This permits tighter sealing.

THE TIN PLATE

This cross-section shows the relative thicknesses of component layers of tin plate. Steel is large segment; first layer on either surface is tin-iron alloy, second is tin. Inside surface is enamel coating.

Courtesy of American Can Co.

FIG. 297. CONSTRUCTION FEATURES OF THE SANITARY TIN CAN

engineering achievement when one considers that cans are manufactured and later sealed at speeds of 1,000 units per minute and defective cans are fewer than one in many thousands. The hermetic property of steel is extended to the seals by five folds of metal at the double seam can ends. Between these folds is an organic sealing compound to ensure gas-tightness. The side seam of the can has four folds of metal further protected by outside soldering of the seam. The outside of the can is protected from rust pitting by a thin layer of tin over the base plate steel. The inside of the can is protected against rusting, pitting, or reaction with the food by a thin layer of tin, or baked-on enamel, or both. These thin layers of tin are responsible for the designation "tin can," although the major metal is far less expensive steel. Recent departures from tin plate and the above construction features are to be found in tin-free steel and new can-making techniques involving thermoplastic adhesive-bonded seams and forge-welded seams for can bodies.

Hermetic rigid aluminum containers can be formed today without side seams or bottom end seams (Fig. 298). The only seam then to make hermetic is the top end double seam, which may be closed on regular tin can sealing equipment.

Courtesy of Food Processing-Marketing

FIG. 298.   EXTRUDED AND DRAWN ALUMINUM CANS MAY BE MADE
WITHOUT SIDE OR BOTTOM SEAMS

Glass containers are hermetic provided the lids are tight (Fig. 299). Lids will have inside rings of rubber or cork. Many glass containers are vacuum packed and the tightness of the cover will be augmented by the differential of atmospheric pressure pushing down on the cover. Crimping of the covers, as in the case of pop bottle caps which operate against

From Wright (1963)

FIG. 299. VARIOUS TYPES OF HERMETIC CLOSURES WITH EX-
CEPTION OF CREAM BOTTLE CAP

positive internal pressure, also can make a gas-tight hermetic seal. But bottles fail more often than cans in becoming nonhermetic.

PACKAGING MATERIALS

Metals

The "tin can" is a container made of steel with only a thin coating of tin, which may represent no more than about one quarter of one percent of the weight of the can. In some cases even this thin coating may be replaced with a nonmetallic lacquer. Tin is not completely resistant to corrosion but its rate of reaction with many food materials is considerably slower than that of steel. The effectiveness of a tin coating depends upon its thickness which may vary from about 20 to 80 millionths of an inch, the uniformity of this thickness, the method of applying the tin which today primarily involves electrolytic plating, the composition of the underlying steel base plate, the type of food, and other factors (Fig. 300). Actually certain canned vegetables including tomato products owe their characteristic flavors to a small amount of dissolved tin, without which these products would have an unfamiliar taste. On the other hand, where tin reacts unfavorably with a particular food the tin itself may be lacquer coated.

Because tin does corrode with time the nature of the base plate steel is of major importance, and various steels are used depending upon the product to be canned. Indicated in Table 73 are specifications for five types of base steels used in food canning. The classes of foods requiring these

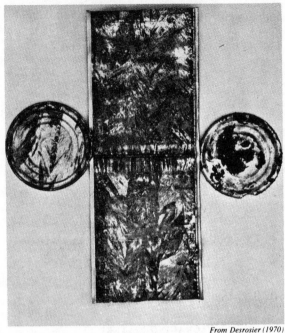

From Desrosier (1970)

FIG. 300. DETINNING OF INNER SURFACE OF SANITARY CAN AS MAY OCCUR WITH ACID FOODS

different steels are seen in Table 74. Thus, Type L plate is used with the most highly corrosive foods which are generally acidic. At the other extreme will be found mildly corrosive or noncorrosive low acid foods and dry products which may use type MR or MC steel.

TABLE 73

CHEMICAL SPECIFICATIONS FOR BASE STEELS[1,2]

Element	Type L	Type MS	Type MR	Type MC	Beer End Stock
			Percentage Permitted		
Manganese	0.25–0.60	0.25–0.60	0.25–0.60	0.25–0.60	0.25–0.70
Carbon	0.12 max	0.12 max	0.12 max	0.12 max	0.15 max
Phosphorus	0.015 max	0.015 max	0.02 max	0.07–0.11	0.10–0.15
Sulfur	0.05 max	0.05 max	0.05 max	0.05 max	0.05 max
Silicon	0.01 max	0.01 max	0.01 max	0.01 max	0.01 max
Copper	0.06 max	0.10–0.20	0.20 max	0.20 max	0.20 max
Nickel	0.04 max	0.04 max	No limitations specified		
Chromium	0.06 max	0.06 max	No limitations specified		
Molybdenum	0.05 max	0.05 max	No limitations specified		
Arsenic	0.02 max	0.02 max	No limitations specified		

[1] Adapted from R. R. Hartwell (1956).
[2] From Ellis (1963).

TABLE 74

GENERAL CLASSES OF FOOD PRODUCTS AND TYPES OF STEEL BASE REQUIRED[1]

Class of Foods	Characteristics	Typical Examples	Steel Base Required
Most strongly corrosive	highly or moderately acid products, including dark colored fruits and pickles	apple juice berries prunes cherries pickles	type L
	acidified vegetables	sauerkraut	type MS
Moderately corrosive	mildly acid fruit products	apricots figs grapefruit peaches	type MR
Mildly corrosive	low acid products	peas corn meats fish	type MR or MC
Noncorrosive	mostly dry and nonprocessed products	dehydrated soups frozen foods shortening nuts	type MR or MC

[1] From Ellis (1963).

Prior mention was made of tin-free steel. The newer tin-free steel is made electrochemically passive by means other than tinning. This may involve coating the base plate steel with layers of chromium followed by chromium oxide that are much thinner than the layer of tin but equally protective. The chromium oxide layer is further covered with an organic coating that is compatible with the food. Such tin-free steel has permitted new can making techniques involving thermoplastic adhesive-bonded seams and forge-welded seams in place of the hooked-and-soldered side seam for can bodies. Advantages are narrower and flatter seams, cost savings from use of less steel, and greater can surface for lithography. While cost savings per can are small, multiplied by billions they become substantial to the user. Tin-free steel is now finding wide use in canning beer and carbonated soft drinks.

The strength of the steel plate is another important consideration, especially in larger size cans which must withstand the pressure stresses of retorting, vacuum canning, and other processes. Can strength is determined by the temper given the steel, the thickness of the plate, the size and geometry of the can, and certain construction features such as horizontal ribbing to increase rigidity. The user of cans will find it necessary to consult frequently with the manufacturer on specific applications, since metal containers like all other materials of packaging are undergoing constant change. A newer use of steel in food packaging has been the introduction of steel foil. One problem experienced with these thin foils has been the hazard of sharp edges, and their future is yet to be determined.

Aluminum as a packaging metal has among its attributes lightness of weight, low level of atmospheric corrosion, and ease of shaping. However, along with ease of shaping is a lower order of structural strength than steel at the same gage thickness. Further, aluminum is difficult to solder, which adds to the problems of sealing weaker aluminum seams. On the other hand, the lower structural strength and softness of aluminum have been responsible for substantial recent gains in the use of aluminum for the fabrication of easy-open can lids. Common types use a ring riveted to the lid which is scored for easy open property. Scored aluminum pulls apart with less force than comparably scored steel. This feature also has scored aluminum lids being sealed to steel can bodies in great numbers. When this is done special care must be taken that there is an unbroken enamel coating between the two metals in contact, otherwise bimetallic reactions can occur which can be harmful to the contained food. Aluminum in contact with air forms an aluminum oxide film which is responsible for its resistance to atmospheric corrosion. However, in relative absence of oxygen, as within most food-containing cans, this aluminum oxide film gradually becomes depleted and the underlying aluminum metal is then no longer highly resistant to corrosion. This can be overcome with enamel coatings much as in the protection of steel and tin.

TABLE 75

GENERAL TYPES OF CAN COATINGS[1]

Coating	Typical Uses	Type
Fruit enamel	dark colored berries, cherries and other fruits requiring protection from metallic salts.	oleoresinous
C-enamel	corn, peas, and other sulfur-bearing products, including some sea foods.	oleoresinous with suspended zinc oxide pigment.
Citrus enamel	citrus products and concentrates.	modified oleoresinous
Seafood enamel	fish products and meat spreads.	phenolic
Meat enamels	meat and various specialty products.	modified epons with aluminum pigment.
Milk enamel	milk, eggs, and other dairy products.	epons
Beverage can enamel (non-carbonated beverages)	vegetable juices; red fruit juices; highly corrosive fruits; non-carbonated beverages.	two-coat system with oleoresinous type base coat and vinyl top coat.
Beer can enamel	beer and carbonated beverages.	two-coat system with oleoresinous or polybutadiene type base coat and vinyl top coat.

[1] From Ellis (1963).

Common organic coatings of FDA approved materials and their uses are indicated in Table 75. The coatings not only protect the metals from corrosion by food constituents but also protect the foods from metal contamination, which can produce a host of color and flavor reactions depending upon the specific food. Particularly common are dark colored sulfides of iron and tin produced in low acid foods that liberate sulfur compounds when heat processed, and bleaching of red plant pigments in contact with unprotected steel, tin, and aluminum.

Glass

As related to food packaging, glass is chemically inert, although the usual problems of corrosion and reactivity of metal closures will of course apply. The principal limitation of glass is its susceptibility to breakage, which may be from internal pressure, impact, or thermal shock, all of which can be greatly minimized by proper matching of the container to its intended use and intelligent handling practices. Here consultation with the manufacturer cannot be overstressed.

Forming of glass containers from a carefully controlled mixture of sand, soda ash, limestone, and other materials made molten by heating to about 2800° F is seen in Fig. 301. After forming, the containers are sent through curing (annealing) ovens to impart toughness or temper to the glass. Apart from influences of chemical composition, optimum shaping of the container, times and temperatures of forming, annealing, and cooling of jars and bottles, and other production practices, the breakage properties of glass containers can be minimized by proper choice of container thickness, and coating treatments.

The heavier a jar or bottle for a given volume capacity the less likely it is to break from internal pressure. The heavier jar, however, is more susceptible to both thermal shock and impact breakage. Greater thermal shock breakage of the heavier jar is due to wider temperature differences which cause uneven stresses between the outer and inner surfaces of the thicker glass. Greater impact breakage susceptibility of the heavier jar is due to less resiliency of its thicker wall.

Coatings of various types can markedly reduce each of these types of breakage. These coatings, commonly of special waxes and silicones, impart lubricity to the outside of the glass. As a result, impact breakage is lessened by bottles and jars glancing off one another rather than sustaining direct hits when they are in contact in high speed filling lines. Further, after coming from the annealing ovens the glass surfaces, virtually free of abrasions, quickly acquire minute scratches in normal handling. These scratches then provide the weak points where many of the subsequent internal pressure and thermal shock breaks originate. Surface coating after annealing protects glass surfaces from many of these scratches.

From Wright (1963)

FIG. 301. FORMING GLASS CONTAINERS TO BE CONVEYED
THROUGH ANNEALING OVENS

Surface coating also improves the high gloss appearance of glass containers, and is said to decrease the noise from glass to glass contact at filling lines, probably due to the increased rate of glancing blows rather than direct impacts.

With regard to thermal shock, it is good practice to minimize temperature differences between the inside and outside of glass containers wherever possible. Some manufacturers will recommend that a temperature difference of 80° F between the inside and outside not be exceeded. This requires slow warming of bottles before being used for a hot fill, and partial cooling before such containers are placed under refrigeration.

Papers

As primary containers few paper products are not treated, coated, or laminated to improve their protective properties. Paper from wood pulp and reprocessed waste paper will be bleached and coated or impregnated with such materials as waxes, resins, lacquers, plastics, and laminations of aluminum to improve water vapor and gas impermeability, flexibility, tear resistance, burst strength, wet strength, grease resistance, sealability, appearance, printability, etc. A few papers are made highly porous to be absorbent, such as paper meat and poultry trays.

Kraft paper is the brown unbleached heavy duty paper commonly used for bags and for wrapping. It is seldom used as a primary container. Acid treatment of paper pulp modifies the cellulose and gives rise to water and oil resistant parchments of considerable wet strength. Glassine-type papers are characterized by long wood pulp fibers which impart increased physical strength.

Where paper comes in contact with food its chemical purity and the nontoxicity of its coatings must meet FDA standards. Additionally, the microbiological condition of paper products is rigidly specified by food manufacturers and in certain food ordinances. Thus, the Grade A Pasteurized Milk Ordinance of the U.S. Public Health Service states that paper for milk cartons and caps be made from sanitary virgin pulp, and contain no more than 250 colonies per gram of disintegrated stock by a standard bacteriological test.

Plastics

Among the more important plastics of food packaging are regenerated cellulose (Cellophane), cellulose acetate, polyamid (Nylon), rubber hydrochloride (Pliofilm), polyester resin (Mylar, Scotch-Pak, Videne), polyethylene resin, polypropylene resin, polystyrene resin, polyvinylidene chloride (Saran, Cryovac), and vinyl chloride. Important properties of these plastics when made into flexible films are indicated in Tables 76 through 78. Study of the tables will reveal many of the relative strengths and weaknesses of these materials for specific food applications, and special uses of some of these plastics will be mentioned later on. But this does not even begin to convey the many forms that these materials can exist in, depending upon such variables in their manufacture as identity and mixture of polymers, degree of polymerization and molecular weight, spatial polymer orientation, use of plasticizers (softeners) and other chemicals, method of forming such as casting, extrusion or calendering, etc.

One of the newer classes of plastic materials referred to as copolymers illustrates what can be done with mixtures of the basic units from which plastics are built. The term copolymer refers to a mixture of chemical

TABLE 76

GENERAL CHARACTERISTICS OF PACKAGING FILMS[1,7]

Film Material	Thickness In.	Max Width, In.	Yield– 0.001-In. Thickness, Sq In./Lb	Clarity	Specific Gravity, at 73°F
Cellophane-plain	0.0008–0.0016[6]	...	20,000[6]	transparent[2] or colored	1.40–1.50[3]
NC coated	0.0009–0.0017	60	11,500–21,000	transparent	1.40–1.50
Saran coated[4]	0.002–0.0014	46	19,500	transparent	1.44
Polyethylene coated[4]	0.002 or more	60	11,800 (2 mil combination)	transparent to translucent	1.20
Cellulose acetate	0.0005–0.010	40–60	21,000–22,000	transparent or colored	1.28–1.31
Polyethylene low density	0.0004–0.010	480	30,000	transparent to translucent	0.910–0.925
medium density	0.0004 or more	480	29,500	...	0.926–0.940
high density	0.0004–0.010	60	29,000	...	0.941–0.965
Polyester (Mylar, Scotchpak, Videne)	0.00025–0.0075	50–55	20,000	transparent or opaque	1.38–1.39
Polypropylene	0.0005 or more	60	30,900–31,300	...	0.885–0.90
Polystyrene (oriented)	0.00075–0.020	43–60	26,100	...	1.05–1.06
Rubber hydro-chloride (Pliofilm)	0.0004–0.0025	60	25,000	transparent to opaque	1.11
Vinylidene Cryovac	0.0008–0.003	...	16,700	...	1.64
Saran	0.0005–0.010	40–54	16,000–23,000	transparent to opaque or colored	1.20–1.68
Vinyl chloride	0.001–0.010	54–84	20,000–23,000	transparent to opaque or colored	1.20–1.45
Nylon 6[5]	0.0005–0.01	60	24,000	transparent or colored	1.12

[1] All values by permission Mod. Plastic Ency. Issue for 1962, unless otherwise noted.
[2] By permission Mod. Packaging Ency. 1958. Copyright 1957 by Packaging Catalog Corp., 770 Lexington Ave., New York 21.
[3] Stone and Reinhart (1954).
[4] Test data assume coated side toward product.
[5] Miscellaneous sources.
[6] Miller (1959).
[7] From Ball (1963).

TABLE 76 (Continued)

GENERAL CHARACTERISTICS OF PACKAGING FILMS [1,7]

	Limit Conditions				
		Normal Performance			Flammability,
Film Material	Max Temp, °F	Min. Temp, °F	Sunlight	Ageing[2]	Temperature of Combustion, °F
Cellophane-plain	300	...	no effect	...	155–216[2]
NC coated	300	about 0	no effect	...	slow burning
Saran coated[4]	180	about 0	...	...	same as newsprint
Polyethylene coated[4]	180		excellent	good	slow burning
Cellulose acetate	150–220	brittle at 0	good	excellent	slow burning
Polyethylene low density	200	−50	fair to good	excellent	slow burning
medium density	220	−60	fair to good	...	slow burning
high density	250	−70	fair to good	...	slow burning
Polyester (Mylar, Scotchpak, Videne)	300	−80	moderate	excellent	slow burning
Polypropylene	190–220	−60	fair to excellent	...	slow burning
Polystyrene (oriented)	175–220	−60	good to fair	...	slow burning
Rubber hydrochloride (Pliofilm)	180–205	−20	fair	good in dark	self extinguishing
Vinylidene Cryovac	softens 270	depends on plasticizer	excellent to good	excellent below 76°	self extinguishing
Saran	150–220 (dry) 300 (wet)	−25 to −50	excellent to good	excellent below 76°	self extinguishing
Vinyl chloride	150–200	good depends on plasticizer	good	excellent	self extinguishing
Nylon 6[5]	400	−80	...	...	...

species in the resin from which films and other forms can be fabricated. If the plastic resin contains just one chemical species, such as polyethylene, it is said to be a homopolymer of polyethylene. If the resin contains a mixture of chemical species such as polyethylene and vinyl acetate, chemically joined, we have the copolymer polyethylene-vinyl acetate, also referred to as ethylene-vinyl acetate. Other copolymers include propylene-ethylene,

ethylene-acrylic acid, ethylene-ethyl acrylate, vinyl chloride-propylene, ethylene-vinyl alcohol, etc. The many variations possible make copolymers an important class of plastics to extend the range of useful food packaging applications.

Another new class of plastic materials, the ionomers, further illustrates how properties of plastics can be modified. Many polymers used for packaging are held together by covalent bonds linking carbon, hydrogen, or oxygen atoms. Ionic bonds generally are stronger than covalent bonds. It is possible to manufacture plastics such as polyethylene with either covalent

TABLE 77

PERMEABILITY AND CHEMICAL PROPERTIES OF PACKAGING FILM[1,7]

Film Material	Gas Transmission[2] cc/100 Sq In./24 Hr 72°F 1 Mil			Water Vapor Transfer Gm/100 Sq In/24 hr 76 cm Mercury 100°F 90% RH, 1 Mil	Water Adsorption in 24 Hr Immersion Test, % 1 Mil
	Oxygen	Nitrogen	Carbon Dioxide		
Cellophane-plain	low (dry); variable (moist)[3]			6.86–12.8[3]	44.7–114.8[3]
NC coated	very low (dry); variable (moist)			1.4–2.7	45–115
Saran coated[4]	very low			1.2	...
Polyethylene coated[4]		low		1.2	...
Cellulose Acetate	100–140	25–40	500–800	160	3.6–6.8
Polyethylene					
low density	500	200	1350	1.4	0–0.8
medium density	240[2]	...	500[2]	0.7	nil
high density	100–150	50–60	300–400	0.3	nil
Polyester (Mylar, Scotchpak, Videne)	5–10	0.50	7.30	1.0–3.0	0.5
Polypropylene	200–300	3–100	700–800	1.2	0.005 or less
Polystyrene (oriented)	200–300	40–100	500–1000	4.0–8.0	0.04–0.06
Rubber hydrochloride. (Pliofilm)	38–3,250[2a]	...	288–13,500[2a]	0.5–15.0	5.0
Vinylidene					
Cryovac	0.1–0.2	0.025	0.30	1.0–1.4	negligible
Saran	0.1–0.2	0.025	0.30	0.1–0.3	negligible
Vinyl chloride	100 (est)	25–50 (est)	500 (est)	3.5–13.0[1]	negligible
Nylon 6[5]	1.0	...	2.0	8.1	...

[a] Relative humidity, 0%.
[1] All values by permission Mod. Plastics Ency. Issue for 1962, unless otherwise noted.
[2] Data courtesy Mod. Plastics, 1961 all values unless otherwise noted.
[3] Stone and Reinhart (1954).

or ionic bonds. Plastics held together by ionic bonds are called ionomers. The stronger bonds can impart such improved functional properties as greater oil, grease, and solvent resistance, and higher melt strength. The range of applications for ionomers is just beginning to be explored.

Laminates

We have said that flexible packages, with very rare exceptions, are not truly hermetic although they may be excellent barriers against microorganisms and dirt. Fortunately, not all foods need absolute hermetic protection. Various flexible materials such as papers, plastic films, and thin metal foils have different properties with respect to water vapor

TABLE 77 (Continued)

		Resistance To		
Acids	Alkalies	Greases and Oils	Organic Solvents	Water
poor to strong acids[6]	poor to strong alkalies[6]	impermeable[5]	insoluble	moderate
poor to strong acids	poor to strong alkalies	impermeable	coating attached	moderate
excellent except H_2SO_4 & HNO_3	good except ammonia	impermeable	. . .	. . .
excellent	excellent	like polyethylene	like polyethylene	
poor to strong acids	poor to strong alkalies	good	soluble except in hydrocarbons	good
excellent	excellent	may swell slightly on long immersion	good except hydrocarbon and chlorinated solvents	excellent
excellent	excellent	good	good	excellent
excellent	excellent	excellent	good	excellent
good	good	excellent	excellent	excellent
excellent	excellent	good	good	excellent
good	excellent	good	excellent to poor	excellent
good	good	excellent	good except in cyclic hydrocarbons chlorinated solvent	excellent
excellent	good except ammonia	excellent	good to excellent	excellent
excellent except H_2SO_4 and HNO_3	good except ammonia	excellent	good to excellent	excellent
good	good	moderate to good	poor to good	excellent
poor	excellent	excellent	excellent	excellent

[4] Test data assume coated side toward product.
[5] Miller (1959).
[6] By permission Mod. Packaging Ency. Issue 1960. Copyright 1959. Packaging Catalog Corp., New York.
[7] From Ball (1963).

TABLE 78

MECHANICAL PROPERTIES OF PACKAGING FILMS[1,6]

Film Material	Tensile Strength[2] 100 Psi	Elongation,[2] %	Tearing Strength,[2] Gm/Mil	Bursting Strength, 1 Mil Thick, Psi	Folding Endurance/ 1 Mil Thick, No. of Folds × 10[3]	Heat Sealing Range,[2] °F
Cellophane-plain	104–186[3]	14–36[3]	275–426[3]	...	...	...
NC coated	70–150	10–50	2–10	55–65[1]	Over 15[5]	200–300
Saran coated	70–130	25–50	2–15	...	...	225–350
Polyethylene coated	50 and over[1]	15–25[1]	16–50[1]	40–50[5]	Good[5]	230–300[1]
Cellulose acetate	54–139[1]	25–45[1]	2–25[1]	50–85[3]	0.25–0.4[1]	350–450
Polyethylene						
low density	13.5–25	200–800[1]	150–350	48[5]	Very high[5]	250–350
medium density	20–35	150–650[1]	50–300	...	...	240–350
high density	24–61	150–650[1]	15–300	...	...	275–350
Polyester (Mylar Scotchpak, Videne)	170–237	70–130	10–27[1]	45–50[3]	20[3]	275–400
Polypropylene	45–100	400–600	32–1750[1]	Very high[1]	...	325–400
Polystyrene (oriented)	80–120	3–20	20–30	23–60[1]	...	250–325
Rubber hydrochloride (Pliofilm)	35–50	200–800[1]	60–1600	Stretches[3]	10–1000[5]	250–350
Vinylidene						
Cryovac	60–120[1]	50–100[1]	15–20[1]	...	Over 500[5]	275–300
Saran	80–200	40–80	10–100[1]	20–40[3]	...	280–300
Vinyl chloride	30–110	5–250	30–1400[1]	25–40[5]	250[1]	200–350
Nylon 6[4]	138–170[4]	200[4]	50[4]	No burst[4]	...	400–450[4]

[1] Data by permission Mod. Plastics Ency. Issue for 1962.
[2] Data by permission Mod. Plastics, 1961 all values unless otherwise noted.
[3] Stone and Reinhart (1954).
[4] Miller, (1959).
[5] By permission Mod. Packaging Ency. Issue 1960. Copyright 1959 Packaging Catalog Corp., New York.
[6] From Ball (1963).

transmission, oxygen permeability, light transmission, burst strength, pin hole and crease hole sensitivity, etc., and so multilayers or laminates of these materials which combine the best features of each are used (Fig. 302, Table 79).

Commercial laminates containing up to as many as eight different layers are commonly custom designed for a particular product. In the case of a popular instant tea mix, for example, the laminate (progressing from the exterior of the package inward) contains a specific Cellophane that is printable, a layer of polyethylene that is a good moisture barrier and serves as an adhesive to the next layer, a treated paper which adds stiffness to the package, a casein adhesive for bonding to the next layer, an aluminum foil which is the prime gas barrier, and an innermost layer of polyethylene as an additional water vapor barrier and to provide the thermoplastic material for heat sealing the package's inner surfaces.

Laminations of different materials may be formed by various processes

Courtesy of U. S. Army Natick Laboratories

Fig. 302. Flexible Laminate Container for Military Ration

Table 79

WATER VAPOR TRANSMISSION OF ALUMINUM FOIL LAMINATES[1,3]

				WVTR
				Gm/100 Sq In./ 24 Hr; 100°F; 100% RH
	Thickness, In.			After Creasing[2]
Material	Foil	Laminant	Flat	
Al. foil laminated to moistureproof	0.00035	0.0009	0.00	...
Cellophane			0.01	0.03
			0.01	0.01
Al. foil laminated to cellulose acetate	0.00035	0.0012	0.02	0.07
Al. foil laminated to rubber hydrochloride	0.00035	0.0008	0.01	0.01
			0.01	...
Al. foil laminated to vinyl polymer	0.00035	0.0012	0.01	0.02
			0.02	0.01
Al. foil laminated with wax to 30-lb glassine	0.00035	...	0.00	0.04
Al. foil BEIS-O	0.00035	...	0.07	0.42
Al. foil laminated to moistureproof Cellophane	0.001	0.0009	0.00	0.00
Al. foil laminated to vinyl polymer	0.001	0.0012	0.00	0.00
Al. foil laminated with wax to 35-lb glassine	0.001	...	0.00	0.02
Al. foil BEIS-O	0.001	...	0.00	0.40

[1]Alcoa aluminum foil—its properties and uses (1953). Each value is the average of measurements on 2 or 3 test pieces.
[2]"Creasing" means creased with 4 equidistant parallel folds and then with 4 more folds at right angles to the first.
[3]From Ball (1963).

including bonding with a wet adhesive, dry bonding of layers with a thermo-plastic adhesive, hot melt laminating where one or both layers exhibit thermoplastic properties, and special extrusion techniques. One of these, called coextrusion, simultaneously forces two or more molten plastics through adjacent flat dies in a manner that ensures laminar flow and pro-duces a multilayer film on cooling. Such structured plastic films may be complete in themselves or be further bonded to papers or metal foils to produce more complex laminates.

Edible Films

It is sometimes desirable to contain or protect a food system within an edible coating, which becomes a kind of package. One type of edible film is the natural casing surrounding frankfurters and sausages. Another type was mentioned in relation to confectionery products, namely con-fectioners glaze or a thin layer of the corn protein zein.

There are many cases where food materials must be protected from loss of volatiles or reaction with other food ingredients when they are stored in intimate mixture. The technique of spray drying various flavoring materials as emulsions with gelatin, gum arabic, or other edible materials to form a thin protective coating around each particle (microencapsula-tion) is one such practice. The coating of raisins with starches to prevent them from moistening a packaged breakfast cereal, and the coating of nuts with monoglyceride derivatives to protect them from oxidative rancidity are additional examples.

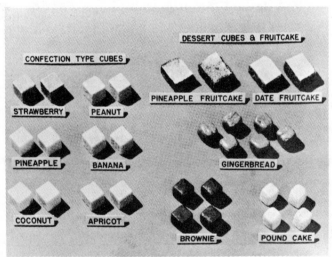

Courtesy of U. S. Army Natick Laboratories

FIG. 303. BITE-SIZE DESSERTS FOR SPACE FEEDING ARE COATED WITH EDIBLE FILM

Space foods provide another opportunity for the use of edible coatings (Fig. 303). Here the coatings of high melting point emulsions, gelatin, and related materials provide the double function of protection against moisture and oxygen pickup by the bite-size dehydrated and compressed cubes, as well as preventing them from crumbling at time of consumption and contaminating the spacecraft with floating debris.

Food materials such as amylose starch and the proteins zein and casein when solubilized can be cast to give sheets of edible films upon drying. These films may then be used to fabricate small packets to hold other food ingredients. One application of such films has been to package baking ingredients which could then be added directly to the mixing bowl as an intact packet. Upon addition of water the edible film dissolves and releases the packaged ingredients.

An edible film may be thought of as a primary package or as part of the food itself. In either case it requires an additional outer wrapping to protect it from dust and dirt.

PACKAGE TESTING

Many test procedures exist to quantitatively measure the protective properties of packaging materials and entire containers. Reference to the foregoing tables of this chapter indicates the nature of several of these tests.

Mechanical properties of packaging films such as tensile strength, elongation, tearing strength, bursting strength, etc. are determined on specially designed instruments that precisely measure the forces required to produce these effects.

Water vapor transmission rates are measured by sealing sheets and films across the opening of a vessel which contains a weighed quantity of a desiccant material. The vessel is then placed in an atmosphere of controlled temperature and humidity. Periodic weighings of the desiccant to determine water pickup give a measure of water vapor transfer in terms of grams per 100 sq in. of film per 24 hr under the defined conditions of temperature, humidity, and atmospheric pressure.

Total gas transfer rates can be measured by sealing a similar vessel with the film to be tested, pulling a vacuum on the vessel which also is fitted with a pressure gage, and noting the loss of vacuum with time. Gas transfer is expressed in terms of cubic centimeters per 100 sq in. of film per 24 hr under defined conditions of temperature, humidity, and pressure on both sides of the film. Transfer rates of specific gases can be measured with special electrodes fitted into the sealed vessel or by gas chromatographic analysis of the vessel contents. Leakage of air into vacuum packed food cans can be determined by puncturing the can with a needle through an air-tight seal which connects the can to a vacuum gage. Loss of initial vacuum by gain of air registers directly on the gage. Leakage of air into nitrogen flushed cans that are at atmospheric pressure can be measured by puncturing the can through an air-tight seal and drawing the can's head-space gas past an oxygen sensing electrode or into a gas chromatograph chamber.

Resistance of packaging films to acids, alkalies, and other solvents can be quantitatively measured by incubating the films in the solvent under controlled conditions and then determining either the leachings into the solvent or changes in the physical properties of the recovered films by some of the methods already mentioned. Resistance of tinned or lacquered cans to acid can be estimated in terms of dissolved underlying iron in the acid test solution, which gives a color reaction that may be measured spectrophotometrically. Resistance of metal cans to acid also can be established in terms of the rate at which hydrogen is given off by the corroding metal.

These are but a few of the approaches to package material testing. But in the final analysis, while such data permit intelligent initial screening of suitable packaging materials for a particular food application, the final package is best evaluated in actual or simulated use tests. This is especially so when the food will receive additional processing such as retorting, freezing, etc. in the final package.

Actual use tests consist of sending limited numbers of food-filled packages through the processing, shipping, warehousing, and merchandising chain where they will be exposed to naturally occurring vibrations, humidities, temperatures, and handling abuses. Such packages are then recovered for analysis. Simulated use tests involve machines and devices for producing physical stresses, and incubation cabinets where packages can be subjected to various temperature and humidity cycles comparable to what the packaged food will subsequently experience in trade channels. Simulated use test conditions can often be intensified to arrive more quickly at a judgement of package performance.

SPECIAL FEATURE PACKAGES

Having considered the general requirements and functions of containers it is interesting to look at a few kinds of packages that are designed to have special features.

In Fig. 304 the "boil-in-bag" package can be seen, which appears to be simple but in many ways is quite remarkable. In addition to being protective to the food against microorganisms and dirt, and sufficiently protective against moisture and gas transfer although not hermetic, it also is impermeable to grease, nontoxic, compatible with the food, transparent, can be evacuated and heat-sealed under vacuum, attractive,

Courtesy of Film and Allied Products Div., 3M Co.

FIG. 304. BOIL-IN-BAG TYPE PACKAGE

tamperproof yet easy to open and dispose of, light in weight, short on storage space requirement, and low in cost. But this is not all. Its material and seals withstand freezing temperatures and the expansion of foods frozen within it. It then survives frozen storage and the extreme shock of being taken from the home or restaurant freezer and plunged into boiling water for cooking. In boiling, the bag does not burst from internally expanding steam or allow boiling water to get in to dilute the food. All of this is made possible by the exceptional properties of polyester films (Mylar, Scotch-Pak, Videne), including high tensile strength and stability over a range of temperatures from $-80°$ to $300°F$ (Tables 76 through 78).

Figure 305 shows a very different kind of container, namely the fiberboard or foil-fiberboard refrigerated biscuit can. It is opened by peeling off the label and striking the spirally scored fiberboard cylinder on a table edge to unwind the cylinder which releases the biscuit dough without damage. Additionally subtle is the venting property that may be designed into certain types of this container. Refrigerated doughs containing baking powder slowly release carbon dioxide during slight self-leavening in refrigerated storage. The wall of the container may be manufactured with very small perforations or means for equivalent porosity to allow this gas to escape. Otherwise the container might explode.

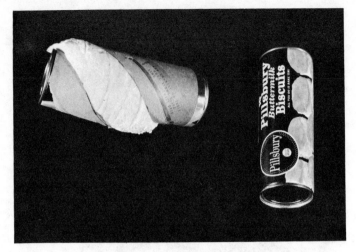

FIG. 305.   REFRIGERATED BISCUIT CONTAINER PROVIDES FOR GAS
ESCAPE

From Ball (1963)

FIG. 306.   SHRINK-PACKAGED CUT HAM

The popular plastic shrink package is seen in Fig. 306. It protects the food against contamination and yet lets the housewife see the meat. In addition it keeps moisture in the meat from drying out. It is made to fit skin-tight by first drawing a vacuum on the bagged item, twisting the bag and tying a knot or sealing with a metal clip, and then passing the package through a mild heat tunnel or immersing it in hot water to shrink the plastic. Commonly the plastic is a polyethylene film where the product can tolerate or is favored by a moderate oxygen transfer rate. The polyethylene film is specially treated during manufacture to produce a biaxial orientation of its molecules. This contributes to uniform shrinkage in all directions upon heating to about 180° F. Cryovac "Type L" film is such a polyethylene. Oriented polypropylene and certain other plastic films also have shrink properties. The shrink property is particularly useful in packaging poultry to be frozen. Here the skin-tight fit excludes pockets of air around the irregularly shaped bird and minimizes voids where water vapor can migrate to the package surface and result in freezer burn to the skin below. Another practical application of the shrink property is widely used in the packaging of fragile vegetables and fruits to keep these items from becoming damaged. Here several individual items may be packed in a paper tray overwrapped with the shrinkable plastic. When shrunk this type of package firmly holds the items in place preventing bruising from loose movement. This differs somewhat from the skin-tight packages described above since it does not usually employ vacuum prior to the shrinking step.

The aerosol container, most popularly used to dispense whipped cream and related products is seen in Fig. 307. There are many types of aerosol

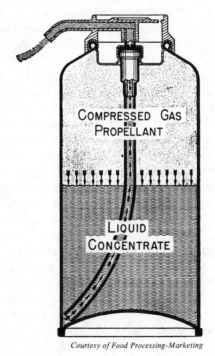

Courtesy of Food Processing-Marketing

FIG. 307.   ONE TYPE OF AEROSOL CONTAINER FOR FOOD

cans. In addition to providing near sterile conditions within the can and a hermetic closure, this can contains the food or a food concentrate, compressed gas, a tube for conducting the food under pressure to the dispensing valve, and the self-closing valve which releases food only on demand. In addition, the valve and other components can be designed to dispense the food in the form of a liquid, a spray, a semisolid extrusion, or a foam as in the case of whipped cream. In this latter case the cream is not actually whipped in the can but is held as a liquid. The gas that forces it up and out of the can also is in solution in the liquid, and on escape of the cream from the can the gas expands and in doing so whips the cream into a foam. Commonly used gases are nitrous oxide or a mixture of nitrous oxide and a food approved "Freon." These cans must be constructed to withstand an internal pressure of about 100 psi, and also to maintain food contents in sanitary condition even though their valves are opened and shut repeatedly.

One of the most exciting developments now in progress in the field of packaging is the gradual evolution of improved rigid plastic bottles that approach the barrier properties of glass and have the clarity of glass but further possess special features not shared by glass. Three limitations of glass include its heavy weight, breakage property, and difficulty of disposal by means other than grinding. Clear plastic bottles are now available that have essentially half the weight of glass (some are even lighter), do not break when dropped 50 ft onto concrete, when shattered break into only a few irregular pieces which are not likely to cut, and can be incinerated easily with the production of no toxic, corrosive, or noxious compounds beyond those found in burning household or municipal trash. The breakage advantages are not only gained at the consumer level but can reduce costs throughout production and shipping channels. Bottle breakage is a frequent cause of complete disruption of filling line operations. Resistance to breakage also permits use of lighter, less expensive corregated shipping containers. Besides shipping cost savings, with one type of bottle developed for carbonated soft drinks, the consumer 8-pack in the plastic bottle is $2\frac{1}{2}$ lb lighter than with glass. The properties of plastic bottles, as with plastic films, depend upon the type of plastic, bottle thickness, and method of fabrication. Clear rigid bottles of polyvinyl chloride have been found suitable for the bottling of fresh orange juice that does not require long-term storage. Polyvinyl chloride and polypropylene copolymer bottles are being used to bottle edible oils and maple syrup. A special requirement for the bottling of carbonated beverages is a very low permeation rate of carbon dioxide under pressure. Until very recently none of the available plastics could satisfy this requirement. Soda pop bottles made from plastics of the acrylonitrile family were test marketed in 1970–1971 with excellent results. Unlike soda pop, most beer is pasteurized in the bottle at temperatures from about 140° to 150°F. At present these newer plastics cannot be used at these temperatures but some beer manufactures are trying the plastic bottles with cold pasteurized beer.

Special packaging problems have always confronted the military. In addition to packaging for protection the package often has been called upon to simplify preparation and consumption of the food under adverse circumstances. Thus, one type of military food container is designed with a chemical system isolated from the food which can be made to undergo a rapid exothermic reaction upon opening the can for self-heating. It is also possible to design a self-cooling container that might be based upon the rapid expansion and release of a compressed refrigerant gas. Such containers presently would be too expensive for general commercial use. Space flight requirements put other demands upon containers. The elongated bag type indicated in Fig. 308 has a constricted neck for squirting water into the bag from an astronaut's water gun, a tough flexible plastic construction to permit reconstitution of the food in the bag by kneading and squeezing, the same squeeze property for conveying food to the mouth without the need for utensils, and an attached germicidal tablet to be added to the bag after the food is consumed to prevent subsequent development of spoilage odors.

Advances in packaging take many directions. One that is growing in importance as larger quantities of food must be moved over greater

Courtesy of U. S. Army Natick Laboratories

FIG. 308. SOME SPACE FOOD CONTAINERS WITH TOTAL CONTENTS OF TWO-MAN MEAL

Courtesy of Modern Packaging

FIG. 309.   TESTING TEN TON CONTAINERS FOR SHIP-TO-SHORE TRANSPOR-
TATION

distances is packaging for distribution. This usually involves consolidation
of large numbers of small unit packages into massive secondary or
tertiary containers. The containers in Fig. 309 being evaluated for ship-
to-shore transportation purposes weigh ten tons each. Related commercial
handling methods involving ship-to-rail, truck-to-air, and other combinations are becoming more sophisticated and important daily. The newer
methods are not simply obvious extensions of previous trucking and
railroad practices but represent a systems approach to integrating and
optimizing packaging, loading, transporting, and unloading practices for
greatest efficiency. This involves improved palletizing and stacking
techniques which often do away with intermediate size cartons, drums,
and sacks, and put new demands on unit package sizes and shapes for
maximum utilization of cargo container space. In many instances the
newer packing methods also shift unit package requirements from
abrasion, tearing, or puncture resistance to greater emphasis upon
compression and stacking strength. Major food companies are becoming
increasingly involved in how these advanced modes of containerization
and distribution will affect future package needs and their contents.

ADDITIONAL CONSIDERATIONS

Psychology of Design

The package designer knows that the message conveyed by the package
is often the most important single factor that determines a product's sale

or rejection. Among details to be considered are the package's color and symbolism. In one's own country errors are less likely to be made, but when packages are designed for distribution in a less familiar region special care must be taken and the services of a consultant often employed. Pitfalls are many. Purple is an unlucky color to the Chinese and white connotes mourning. The cherry blossom is a favored symbol of the Japanese but the chrysanthemum which connotes royalty in Japan is to be avoided on package labels. Further examples applying to Asian markets are seen in Table 79A. One of the more subtle examples of regional psychology recently reported was experienced in Japan where a U.S.-designed tunafish can pictured a tuna with nose turned down toward the water. When the product did not sell it was learned that to the Japanese a tuna with nose turned down meant a fish that was dead. When the picture of the tuna was modified sales increased.

TABLE 79A

COLOR AND SYMBOLISM IN PACKAGING FOR ASIAN MARKETS

Country	Color	Connotation	Symbol	Connotation
China	white	mourning (avoid)	tigers, lions, & dragons	strength (use)
Hong Kong	blue	unpopular (avoid)	tigers, lions, & dragons	strength (use)
India	green & orange	good (use)	cows	sacred to Hindus (avoid)
Japan	gold, silver, white, & purple	luxury & high quality (use)	cherry blossom	beauty (use)
	black	use for print only, prefer gay, bright colors.	chrysanthemum	royalty (avoid)
Malaysia (Population is mixed Malay, Indian, Chinese)	yellow	royalty (avoid)	cows	sacred to Hindus (avoid)
	gold	longevity (use)	pigs	unclean to Moslems (avoid)
	green	Islamic religion (avoid)		
Pakistan	green & orange	good (use)	pigs	unclean to Moslems (avoid)
Singapore	red, red & gold, red & white	prosperity and happiness (use)	tortoises	dirt, evil (avoid)
	red & yellow	Communist	snakes	poison (avoid)
	yellow	avoid	pigs & cows	same as for India & Pakistan (avoid)
Taiwan	black	avoid	elephants	strength (use)
Thailand			elephants	national emblem (avoid)
Tahiti	red, green, gold, silver, and other bright colors.	use		
Arab & Moslem States	white	avoid	animals	avoid
			pigs	religious pollution (avoid)
			Star of David	political (avoid)

Courtesy of Hygrade Products Co., New Zealand.

Environmental Issues

It has been estimated that in the United States 100 billion pounds of packaging waste is generated each year. This results in large measure from the major swing to convenience packaging, including disposable and non-returnable packaging. While this form of waste represents but a small fraction of total solid waste from all sources it is a major contributor to visible litter and has come under sharp attack from environmentalists and legislators. It is unlikely that the consumer will be willing to give up many of the present packaging conveniences, and a major swing back to returnable bottles, which would alleviate only part of the problem, is improbable. Some proposals suggest a tax on container materials that are not readily biodegradable. This would include glass, metals, and many plastics.

Innovation in plastics technology holds promise of yielding more plastics that incinerate cleanly. Plastics that can be recycled is another possibility but the economics of gathering and sorting plastic containers from other trash may limit the feasibility of this approach. Admirable progress is presently being made in the recycling of both steel and aluminum containers. Over 200 steel can collection stations have been set up by major steel companies and more are planned. Some municipalities mine steel cans from dumps using magnetic separating equipment before or after garbage incineration and then sell the recovered steel scrap. Major aluminum companies are broadening their interest in reclamation and recycling. Aluminum has greater scrap value than other materials found in solid waste— $200 a ton compared with $20 for steel and $15 for glass. Collectors bringing aluminum cans to Alcoa reclamation centers are receiving 10¢ per lb for the cans. The Reynolds Metals Co. is operating a number of mobile recycling units in the form of 40-ft truck trailers that carry a magnetic separator, electronic scale, and can shredder. The mobile units buy aluminum cans from the public and prepare them for smelting plants.

Because of lower economic value and certain other considerations glass recycling is not always feasible. One of the largest markets for salvaged glass is in conventional glassmaking where crushed waste glass can supply about 30% of the raw materials needed to make new bottles. But such waste glass must be free of food, metal, and other forms of contamination and needs to be color sorted. Where costs for these handling operations are prohibitive crushed glass of lesser purity can be absorbed by the construction industries for the making of glass bricks and for admixture with asphalt to pave roads. After incineration to form clinker, waste glass also is suitable as an undersurface for road construction. With or without crushing and incineration waste glass can provide useful landfill.

Over half of all packaging is presently done in paper and paperboard. Paper is easily recycled to produce fiber or is burned as fuel. Recycled fibers are used in the manufacture of cartons, boxes, newspaper, and other paper goods. However, more must be learned about recycling of paper and elimination of toxic contaminants that can find their way into paper goods not made from virgin pulp. Recent findings of polychlorinated biphenyls in cardboard food containers emphasize this point. Presently about 20% of the U.S. production of paper is recycled. More economic means of separating paper from other waste materials are being researched to increase this figure.

Some food companies and manufacturers of packaging materials have said that waste and litter from packaging is a problem to be solved at the consumer end rather than at the production end. But certainly innovations that make packaging materials more easy to degrade or recycle are to be encouraged. Development and use of such materials require input by the food scientist.

BIBLIOGRAPHY

ALTHEN, P. C. 1965. The aluminum can. Food Technol. *19*, 784–786, 788.

ANON. 1953. Alcoa Aluminum Foil—Its Properties and Uses. Aluminum Co. of America, Pittsburgh.

ANON. 1970. Glass Containers. Glass Container Manuf. Inst., New York.

ANON. 1972. Modern Packaging Encyclopedia Issue 1972. McGraw-Hill, New York.

ANON. 1972. Modern Plastics Encyclopedia Issue 1972. McGraw-Hill, New York.

BALL, C. O. 1963. Flexible packaging in food processing. *In* Food Processing Operations, Vol. 2. M. A. Joslyn, and J. L. Heid (Editors). Avi Publishing Co., Westport, Conn.

BRICKMAN, C. L. 1957. Evaluating the packaging requirements of a product. Package Eng. *2*, No. 7, 19.

BRODY, A. L. 1970. Flexible Packaging of Foods. CRC Press, Cleveland.

BRODY, A. L. 1971. Food canning in rigid and flexible packages. Critical Rev. Food Technol. 187–243. CRC Press, Cleveland.

BURTON, L. V. 1964. Protective packaging progress. *In* Food Processing Operations, Vol. 3. M. A. Joslyn, and J. L. Heid (Editors). Avi Publishing Co., Westport, Conn.

CAN MANUFACTURERS INSTITUTE. 1960. The History of the Metal Can and its 150 Years of Service to Man. Can Manufactures Inst., Washington, D.C.

CANNON, H. 1969. The tin-free steel revolution. Packaging Inst. Profess. Spring, 1969.

CARMAN, J. F., BOLTON, C. P., and SAUTIER, P. M. 1960. Measuring gas transmission. Mod. Packaging *33*, No. 9, 127–130.

CURTIS, E. A. 1962. Simple methods and good judgement help you predict shelf life. Package Eng. *7*, No. 5, 45–47.

DESROSIER, N. W. 1970. The Technology of Food Preservation, 3rd Edition. Avi Publishing Co., Westport, Conn.

ELLIS, R. F. 1963. Metal containers for food. *In* Food Processing Operations, Vol. 2. M. A. Joslyn, and J. L. Heid (Editors). Avi Publishing Co., Westport, Conn.

FRUEHLING, D. F. 1969. What's ahead for metal cans. Food Eng. *41*, No. 8, 117–118.

GRIFFIN, R. C., JR., and SACHAROW, S. 1972. Principles of Package Development. Avi Publishing Co., Westport, Conn.

HANNIGAN, K. J. 1971. The packaging scene—a time of change. Food Eng. *43*, No. 3, 53–56.

HARTWELL, R. R. 1956. Choice of containers for various products. Proc. 3rd Intern. Congr. Canned Foods, Rome-Parma, Italy.

KVALLE, O., and DALHOFF, E. 1963. Determination of the equilibrium relative humidity of foods. Food Technol. *17*, 659–661.

MEHRLICH, F. P., and SIU, R. G. H. 1966. Military and space operations. *In* Protecting Our Food—The Yearbook of Agriculture 1966. U.S. Dept. Agr.

MILLER, B. M. 1959. Nylon 6, now a packaging film. Package Eng. *4*, No. 3, 62–64, 78.

OSWIN, C. R. 1962. Emballistics: The science of package life prediction. Brit. Packer *12*, No. 12, 2–5.

PACKAGING INSTITUTE. 1961. Glossary of Packaging Terms, 3rd Edition. Packaging Institute, New York.

PAINE, F. A. 1962. Fundamentals of Packaging. Blackie & Son, London.

PETERSON, M. S. 1958. Looking at physical principles that explain packaging tests. Package Eng. *3*, No. 4, 36–51.

PHILLIPS, C. J. 1960. Glass—Its Industrial Applications. Reinhold Publishing Corp., New York.

RUBINATE, F. J. 1961. Flexible packages for heat processed foods. *In* Proc. 13th Res. Conf. Am. Meat Inst. Found. Chicago.

SACHAROW, S. 1969. Packaging materials for frozen foods. Frozen Foods *22*, No. 5, 29–40.

SACHAROW, S. 1971. Packaging machines, what type for your product. Food Eng. *43*, No. 3, 70–74, 77–78, 81.

SACHAROW, S., and GRIFFIN, R. C., JR. 1970. Food Packaging. Avi Publishing Co., Westport, Conn.

SALWIN, H. 1963. Moisture levels required for stability in dehydrated foods. Food Technol. *17*, 1114–1123.

STONE, M. C., and REINHART, F. W. 1954. Properties of plastic films. Mod. Plastics *31*, No. 10, 203–208.

U.S. DEPT. HEALTH, EDUCATION, AND WELFARE. 1965. Grade "A" Pasteurized Milk Ordinance of the U.S. Public Health Service. Public Health Serv. Publ. *229*, Washington, D.C.

WAECHTER, C. J. 1971. Plastic bottles for soft drinks and beer. Food Prod. Develop. *5*, No. 6, 74–75, 77.

WRIGHT, F. H. 1963. Glass containers. *In* Food Processing Operations, Vol. 2. M. A. Joslyn, and J. L. Heid (Editors). Avi Publishing Co., Westport, Conn.

CHAPTER 22

Water and Waste

INTRODUCTION

Life on earth and man's activities depend upon the continuous circulation of the earth's water. This movement of water from the oceans, lakes, and streams as water vapor to the atmosphere, its condensation and precipitation back to the earth's surface, its flow over the land and return to the ocean, its penetration into the ground and use by plants which return part of the water to the atmosphere through transpiration, and its subsurface return to the sea is known as the hydrologic cycle or water cycle. (Fig. 310). Man and animals enter this cycle as users of water and producers of waste in many forms.

It has been estimated that industrial uses of water in the United States amounted to about 70 billion gallons per day in 1950, about 175 billion gallons per day in 1970, and will reach some 250 billion gallons per day by 1980. The present industrial rate of more than 175 billion gallons per day slightly exceeds the quantity of water used for irrigation and represents approximately seven times the amount used for domestic purposes. Nearly all of this water becomes contaminated in one way or another, requires purification by nature or by man, and is then reused. The water we drink has a history of reuse, and if it could be traced, a given molecule may well have experienced passage through a domestic animal, partial purification enroute to the sea, further purification in a potable water treatment plant, reuse as cooling water in a canning plant or a paper mill, repurification on passage through a municipal sewage handling system, and so on repeatedly. Municipal sewage is over 99% water. Industrial wastes, including wastes from food production and processing, are highly variable in composition but commonly are of this same order of magnitude with respect to water content. It thus may be said that one man's waste ultimately becomes another's water.

The food production and processing industries are concerned particularly with three broad aspects of water technology, namely its microbiological purity and safety, its chemical impurities which affect suitability in processing, and its contamination load after use. Contamination load has always been important since it affects the difficulty and cost of disposing of waste water. It has taken on increasing importance in recent years since antipollution laws prohibit many of the former practices of waste water disposal. Further, the contamination loads of larger food plant waste waters fre-

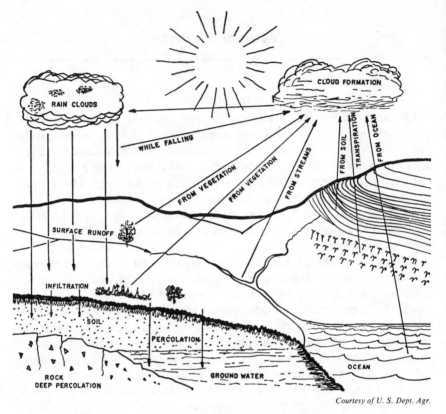

Courtesy of U. S. Dept. Agr.

FIG. 310. THE HYDROLOGIC CYCLE

quently exceed the purification capacity of municipal sewage plants. Where such is the case, food plants are being forced to adopt their own waste treatment systems if they are to be permitted to operate under a growing complexity of regulations by federal, interstate, state, and municipal agencies.

The availability of sufficient and suitable water together with means for disposal of plant wastes always have been prime factors in determining food plant locations. Enforcement of antipollution laws is now challenging the economic feasibility of many existing food production and processing operations. In some cases what was formerly considered a waste may now have to be further converted to a useful by-product as a more economical means for its disposal. In the past the food scientist had been concerned more with the purity and chemical composition of water as it affected processing and food properties. Problems of waste disposal were left mostly to the sanitary engineer. Now the food scientist and the sanitary engineer are being called upon to work closer together since the increasing problems in handling food wastes are having direct effects upon acceptable methods of food processing and disposition of the less desirable fractions of food raw materials.

PROPERTIES AND REQUIREMENTS OF PROCESSING WATERS

Water entering a food processing plant should meet U. S. Public Health Standards for potable (drinking) water. In addition to the chemical standards for such water (Table 80), this water must be free from contamination with sewage, pathogenic organisms, and organisms of intestinal origin. Standards call for such water to contain less than 2.2 coliform organisms (statisitcal value) per 100 ml. Coliform organisms of the type assayed are not pathogenic in themselves but serve as a sensitive index of possible sewage contamination, which if present could harbor many kinds of human pathogens. Such water from municipal supplies or from private

TABLE 80

U. S. PUBLIC HEALTH SERVICE DRINKING WATER STANDARDS[1]

Characteristic	Limit Not to be Exceeded[2]	Cause for Rejection
Physical		
color	15 units	. . .
taste	Unobjectionable	. . .
threshold odor number	3	. . .
turbidity	5 units	. . .
Chemical	(Milligrams per Liter)	
alkyl benzene sulfonate	0.5	. . .
arsenic	0.01	0.05
barium	. . .	1.0
cadmium	. . .	0.01
chloride	250	. . .
chromium (hexavalent)	. . .	0.05
copper	1	. . .
carbon chloroform extract[3]	0.2	. . .
cyanide	0.01	0.2
fluoride[4]	0.7–1.2	1.4–2.4
iron	0.3	. . .
lead	. . .	0.05
manganese	0.05	. . .
nitrate	45	. . .
phenols	0.001	. . .
selenium	. . .	0.01
silver	. . .	0.05
sulfate	250	. . .
total dissolved solids	500	. . .
zinc	5	. . .

[1]From Standard Methods for the Examination of Water and Wastewater, 13th Edition, 1971.
[2]When more suitable supplies can be made available.
[3]Organic contaminants.
[4]The concentration of fluoride should be between 0.6 and 1.7 mg/liter, depending on the listed annual average maximum daily air temperatures.

wells meeting U. S. Public Health Standards for drinking purposes, as pointed out in earlier chapters, may still not be suitable for certain food processing uses. On the other hand, this same water may be used as a heat exchange medium to condense vapors from an evaporator, to heat canned food in a retort, or to prechill orange concentrate enroute to a freezer. It then may still be quite suitable for subsequent plant reuse without further purification, for cleaning or conveying fruits and vegetables, or for plant clean-up purposes. Such reuse of water within the plant cuts down on the water bill, minimizes the volume of plant waste water that is discharged, and represents efficient operation.

Water Hardness

Among the soluble materials that potable water may possess, calcium and magnesium ions are of major importance. These ions form precipitates with bicarbonates in the water upon heating and with sulfates and chlorides when water is evaporated from solution. Hardness causes scale on equipment which acts as an insulating layer against efficient heat transfer, may eventually clog pipes and foul valves, produces deposits which harbor bacteria and add to the difficulty of equipment cleanup, and may affect food products directly. The hardness of waters may be expressed quantitatively in terms of ppm of calcium, ppm of calcium carbonate, grains per gallon of calcium carbonate, or equivalent values for magnesium (Table 81).

TABLE 81

RANGE OF THE HARDNESS OF WATER[1]

Degree of Hardness	Expressed as Calcium Carbonate Ppm	Gr per Gal.	Expressed as Calcium, Ppm
Soft	Less than 50	Less than 2.9	Less than 20
Slightly Hard	50–100	2.9–5.9	20–40
Hard	100–200	5.9–11.8	40–80
Very Hard	Above 200	Above 11.8	Above 80

Note: One grain of calcium carbonate per U. S. gal. is equivalent to 17.1 ppm; 100 ppm of calcium carbonate is equivalent to 40 ppm of calcium. In reference to magnesium carbonate, 100 ppm of carbonate is equivalent to 24 ppm of magnesium.
[1] From Bigelow and Stevenson (1923).

The firming effect of calcium ions on certain fruits and vegetables has already been cited (Chap. 18). This may be used to advantage under controlled conditions, but in excessive amounts the calcium from hard water can cause various textural defects. Thus, 200 ppm of hardness as calcium carbonate in the brine of canned peas may lead to excessive toughening. Certain varieties of beans are more sensitive in this regard. Another type of problem from water hardness occurs when such water is used as boiler-feed water. Here the continued evaporation of water as steam leaves behind a growing layer of scale which not only reduces boiler efficiency but tends to contaminate steam generated in the boiler. Such steam can become alkaline and corrosive to aluminum and tin cans.

There are various ways to soften water, depending particularly upon the nature of the hardness. In these cases water hardness must be looked upon as one kind of contamination and the softening treatment as a form of purification. When calcium or magnesium exist in water as the bicarbonates we have a condition known as temporary hardness since these salts can be easily precipitated from the water by heating prior to use. Chemical treatments involving the addition of hydrated lime are also effective in softening such waters. Hardness caused by sulfates and chlorides of magnesium or calcium, referred to as permanent hardness, is not removed by the above treatments but can be removed by ion exchange techniques. Here the hard water is passed over special ion exchange resins or similar materials which contain sodium or hydrogen as loosely bound cations. The resin, having a greater affinity for calcium and magnesium than for its bound sodium or hydrogen, exchanges these ions by taking calcium and magnesium from the water and giving up its sodium or hydrogen to the water. The water is thus softened.

Other Impurities

Water meeting health standards for drinking may be unsatisfactory for plant use from any of several other causes. A detectable taste or odor of chlorine from tap water is not uncommon. This may be due to overchlorination (satisfactory chlorination will leave residual chlorine of the order of one part per million or less), but more commonly is due to the presence of traces of phenol in the water which reacts with chlorine and gives a strong medicinal odor. This can frequently be removed by filtration of water through a bed of carbon or adsorbent clay. The amount of chlorine to produce a sterile or nearly sterile water is quite variable depending upon other substances present in the water. This will be enlarged upon further on.

Off-flavors and -odors may also be due to decomposition of organic matter in water by nonpathogenic bacteria since drinking water and the pipes through which it passes are seldom sterile. When water contains sulfates and reducing types of bacteria, production of sulfide odors may occur. While temporary improvement with respect to odor removal may be possible by filtering through carbon, the underlying cause of the problem can be more difficult to eliminate and may require pipeline sanitation or repair to eliminate pockets of microbial concentration.

Drinking water may be slightly off-color. Iron salts in water upon oxidation produce red-brown ferric hydroxides. Similarly manganese hydroxides are gray-black in color. Suspended colloidal matter of either organic or inorganic origin can produce excessive turbidity. Mineral impurities often can be effectively removed by in-plant ion exchange treatments, and color by carbon and clay adsorbents. Colloidal impurities may be flocculated with alum (aluminum and potassium sulfates) and the precipitate removed by filtration or centrifugation.

Municipal and well waters from different locations will vary in acidity and pH. It is not uncommon for certain hard waters to have a pH of about 8.5 or for acidic waters to have a pH as low as 5. This is generally easily corrected by in-plant water softening or direct neutralization.

Occasionally well waters and municipal waters entering a plant will be contaminated with moderate numbers of proteolytic or lipolytic food spoilage organisms. Such waters have caused problems when used in direct contact with foods, as in the washing of cheese curds and butter granules. Waters so contaminated may be in-plant chlorinated or treated with ultraviolet light, and many food processors have installed automatic chlorinators and ultraviolet systems for routine continuous treatment of water for such uses.

Chlorination

In addition to chlorination of water for the purpose of rendering it safe from a health standpoint, the food processor often further chlorinates water in the plant to use as a disinfectant in processing. Whether water is rendered bacteriologically pure at the municipal treatment plant or subsequently made to have disinfectant properties for special uses, effective chlorination must take into account the different chlorine demands of various waters before a germicidal effect can be achieved.

Materials may be present in water which react with chlorine and inactivate it before the chlorine can exert its germicidal effect. Hydrogen sulfide and organic impurities are particularly objectionable in this regard. Only after these interfering substances are satisfied in terms of their chlorine demands can residual free chlorine have a significant killing or inhibitory effect upon microorganisms. This gives rise to the concept of break-point chlorination illustrated in Fig. 311. If a water contains no interfering substances then the level of residual chlorine in the water is directly proportional to the amount added. Such a water is said to have zero chlorine demand. Waters higher in organic materials and other interfering substances will begin to show a residual chlorine level only after all of their chlorine demand is satisfied. The point where this occurs is known as the break-point for that particular water. Additional chlorine can then be added beyond the break-point to achieve any desired level of residual chlorine.

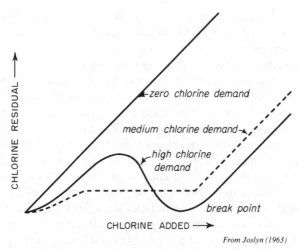

FIG. 311. CHLORINE DEMAND CHARACTERISTICS OF WATER

For drinking purposes a residual chlorine level in excess of about 0.4 ppm is seldom required. Tables and conveyors for food products may need frequent or continuous rinsing with water containing about 5 ppm of residual chlorine to maintain sanitary operation. Water used for general food plant clean-up may require a residual chlorine level of 25 ppm since much of this chlorine will be used up in satisfying the chlorine demand of soil before it can have disinfecting properties. Chlorine for chlorination may be discharged into the water from a cylinder of the gas or the chlorine may be derived from hypochlorite preparations.

PROPERTIES OF WASTE WATERS

Since food plant waste waters may contain such varied materials as meat and bone scrap, animal or fish entrails and excreta, blood and dairy wastes, pulp and peels of vegetable origin, spent coffee grounds and distillery "slop," soils and detergents from washings, etc., obviously their compositions and contamination loads will vary greatly. Nevertheless, food plant waste waters can be grouped somewhat according to the nature of their impurities and pollution potentials, and these of course determine what methods will be suitable for their treatment. It is convenient to consider waste waters according to the physical, chemical, and biological natures of their impurities.

Physical Nature of Impurities

Materials in food waste waters will vary in size from coarse floating or sinking solids down to colloidally suspended matter which will neither settle nor rise on undisturbed standing. Beyond this size limit are substances in true solution. Water-insoluble liquids such as oils and certain solvents also will be present.

Gross particulates generally must be removed before plant waste waters are sent on to treatment plants or dumped. Many treatment plants will not accept sizable solids since they contribute substantially to pollution load and may easily be the cause of exceeding the capacity of the plant in which the water is treated. Floating solids also are prohibited from discharge into most streams and lakes because of their high pollution potential and unesthetic appearance. Grinding to smaller size is not a solution. Such materials are generally easily removed at the food plant and treated separately, as will be described later on. After removal of gross particulates, colloidal and dissolved impurities may still constitute a greater pollution load in waste waters than will be acceptable to many municipal sewage treatment plants, or be permissible for discharge into streams, and so further treatment by the food plant is often required.

Chemical Nature of Impurities

Colloidal and dissolved impurities in waste waters may be characterized in terms of organic and inorganic materials. Organic impurities are further differentiated according to their ratios of nitrogenous constituents to carbohydrate materials. Meat, poultry, and seafood wastes are highest in this ratio. Many vegetable wastes will be intermediate. Fruit wastes generally will be higher in carbohydrate materials and lower in nitrogenous constituents. This becomes significant in terms of the end products of microbial degradation of these wastes both in treatment plants and when discharged onto land or into bodies of water. Wastes rich in nitrogen contribute this important element to sewage microorganisms which need it for growth and continued activity and so may stimulate the decomposition process. Municipal sewage treatment plants generally are designed to receive wastes rich in nitrogen. A high carbohydrate-low nitrogen waste may upset the pH and metabolic activities of decomposition bacteria and so has to be supplemented with nitrogenous material before it can be handled in such a treatment plant.

High and low pH wastes can be particularly damaging to fish and other stream life as well as to essential microorganisms in sewage treatment plants if the dilution factor is not sufficiently great. Food plant wastes usually require neutralization by simple addition of acids or alkalies to within a pH range of 6 to 9 before they may be discharged to sewage treatment plants or natural waters.

In the past, synthetic detergents and surface active chemicals which tend to foam have caused operating problems in sewage treatment plants and unsightly conditions in streams. The problem was related to the persistence of these foams and froths which were only slowly broken down by the action of microorganisms. This problem has now been largely overcome by a major shift on the part of detergent manufacturers to the production of readily biodegradable detergent types. Froths from such materials are quickly dissipated in sewage plants and streams.

Food plant wastes generally are not as corrosive as the wastes from many chemical and mining operations, but may be more odorous. Offensive odors frequently will require additional treatment of these wastes; less odorous wastes of otherwise acceptable pollution load may be dumped.

Biological Nature of Impurities

Food plant wastes are largely organic in character and are decomposed in treatment plants and in nature by biological degradation. This degradation is mostly by aerobic microorganisms which require large quantities of oxygen to completely oxidize carbohydrates and other organic materials to carbon dioxide and water, and to convert nitrogenous residues to their highest state of oxidation which is nitrate. To the extent that these oxidations are incomplete and leave intermediate products such as alcohols, acids, amines, and ammonia, waste decomposition may be said to be incomplete. These intermediates generally are odorous, may be toxic in themselves to plant and fish life, and in any event will undergo further degradation in nature. When this occurs in streams and lakes it often does so at the expense of fish life due to consumption of oxygen.

Biological Oxygen Demand

Perhaps the most significant property of organic wastes is their capacity to consume oxygen in the course of microbial decomposition. This constitutes a major pollution characteristic of the particular waste. To the extent that wastes are oxidized in waste treatment plants this biological oxygen demand (BOD) is diminished. When the BOD of waste discharged into a stream is excessive, microorganism depletion of the stream's oxygen to satisfy this BOD causes fish suffocation, death of the fish's natural food supplies, and a general upset of the stream's ecology. Biological oxygen demand of a waste can be measured quantitatively, as can the BOD of stream or lake water at any given time which is a most important index of its level of pollution.

The BOD test measures the quantity of oxygen in ppm (or milligrams per liter) required by aerobic microorganisms to stabilize waste or polluted water under specific conditions which generally include incubation at 68°F for five days. Another useful test is the chemical oxygen demand (COD) test, which has the advantage of indicating the oxygen demand of organic materials in a few hours by treatment with a strong chemical oxidizing agent such as potassium dichromate. The BOD and COD tests both measure oxygen demand, but because of different interfering substances and other factors results of the two tests do not always correlate. Both tests are fully described in "Standard Methods for the Examination of Water and Wastewater," 13th Edition, 1971.

The BOD and other values of various food processing wastes are given in Table 82. Generally the higher the BOD value the more difficult and costly

TABLE 82

VOLUME, BOD, AND SUSPENDED SOLIDS OF SOME FOOD PROCESSING WASTES[4]

Commodity	Volume in Gal. per Case	5-Day BOD, Ppm	Suspended Solids, Ppm
Apples		1,700–5,500	300–600
Apricots	57–80	200–1,000	260
Asparagus	70	20–100	30–180
Beans, baked	35	900–1,440	220
Beans, green or wax	26–44	160–600	60–150
Beans, kidney	18–22	1,030–2,500	140
Beans, limas, dried	17–22	1,740–2,880	160–600
Beans, limas, fresh	50–257	190–450	420
Beets	27–70	1,580–7,600	740–2,220
Carrots	23	520–3,030	1,830
Citrus	1,000[1]	1,000–5,000	1,200
Corn, cream style	24–29	620–2,900	300–670
Corn, whole kernel	25–70	1,120–6,300	300–4,000
Cherries, sour	12–40	700–2,100	20–600
Cranberries	4	2,250	100
Grapefruit	5–56	310–2,000	170–280
Meat packing house	2,000–8,000	600–1,600	400–720
Milk processing industry	3–5[2]	20–650	30–363
Mushrooms	6,600[1]	80–850	50–240
Peaches	1,300–2,600[1]	1,350–2,240	600
Peas	14–75	380–4,700	270–400
Peppers		600–1,220	
Potato chips	4,000[1]	730–1,800	800–2,000
Potatoes, sweet	82	1,500–5,600	400–2,500
Potatoes, white		200–2,900	990–1,180
Poultry packing industry	1 1/2[3]	725–1,148	769–1,752
Pumpkin	20–50	1,500–11,000	785–1,960
Sauerkraut	3–18	1,400–6,300	60–630
Spinach	160	280–730	90–580
Squash	20	4,000–11,000	3,000
Tomatoes	3–100	180–4,000	140–2,000

[1] Per ton.
[2] Per gallon of milk.
[3] Per chicken.
[4] From Casten (1964).

are waste treatment and disposal practices. Sewage and waste treatment plants can be rated in terms of their BOD removing capacity. Antipollution regulations virtually always are written to include maximum permissible BOD loadings into natural waters. These maximum loadings differ widely in accordance with the volume, flow, and other characteristics of the body of water.

On rare occasions food plant wastes have become contaminated with highly toxic materials such as pesticides and disinfectants. The need to keep these out of streams is obvious. Such wastes and waste waters, however, also should not be sent on to sewage treatment plants without prior warning and permission for such action since the toxic substances may be sufficiently concentrated to kill the plant's normal microbial flora essential to sewage and waste treatment. When this is the case the waste may have to be diluted substantially, sent on to the treatment plant a little at a time which is equivalent to the same thing, or possibly tanked and trucked to a remote dumping ground.

WASTE WATER TREATMENT

The final treatments applied to potable water for special food processing uses generally are not applicable to food plant waste waters because of the complex compositions of wastes in spent waters and the high concentrations in which these may occur. Such "polishing treatments" as water softening, ion exchange, and carbon filtration generally are not applied to waste waters. Rather, treatments are chosen for removal of gross particulates, coagulable colloidal matter, and reduction of BOD sufficient for ultimate discharge onto land or into streams.

The extent to which pollution load must be decreased before waste water leaves a food plant is highly variable, especially from one location to another. It depends upon many factors which include: (1) will the waste water be discharged to a municipal sewage or commercial waste treatment plant, and if so what is the maximum pollution load this plant can treat; (2) what will be the cost for such treatment and can it be done more economically by the food plant itself; and (3) what dumping privileges does the food plant have and what pollution laws exist and apply. Because the answers to these questions are so varied, all degrees of waste water purification are currently being performed with food plant and outside facilities.

Primary Treatment

Gross particulates generally are removed at the food processing plant by screening through vibrating sieves. Smaller particles may be removed by filtering or centrifuging. Minute particles may be allowed to settle or rise in large tanks. Scum and oil are readily skimmed from such tanks, and settled solids are concentrated for removal and subsequent treatment by pumping the supernatant liquid away. Colloidal materials commonly are coagulated or flocculated with the aid of alum which promotes settling. These primary treatments may remove some 50% of the waste water's

BOD and perhaps 75% of total solids, depending upon the nature of the waste.

Secondary Treatment

Secondary treatment often is performed by large food plants in plant-site facilities similar to those of municipal sewage installations. In other cases the partially treated waste waters are sewered and discharged to the municipal stations. Secondary treatment commonly involves the use of trickling filters, activated sludge tanks, and ponds of various types.

Trickling Filters.—These are of several designs but have as their purpose the bringing together of waste water and waste digesting bacteria under highly aerobic conditions. Commonly the trickling filter will consist of a bed of crushed rock or other material of large surface area in contact with air or through which air is blown. Waste water trickling through the crushed rock soon develops a highly aerobic microbiological growth around the rocks, or this may be initially established by seeding with an appropriate sewage culture. One such type of trickling filter is seen in Fig. 312. Oxidation of organic materials passing through several trickling

Courtesy of Dorr-Oliver, Inc.

FIG. 312. TRICKLING FILTER

filters in series can often reduce the BOD of incoming waters by factors of 90 or 95%.

Activated Sludge Tanks.—These are essentially large aeration tanks in which air is bubbled through waste water. The tanks soon develop a highly aerobic flocculent microbial growth which continues to be nourished by the incoming waste (Fig. 313). Where wastes may be low in nitrogen or phosphorus needed by the microorganisms these may be added in the form of sewage or other supplements. Waste water may be continuously added and removed from such tanks, providing a residence time of several hours as required to achieve a substantial decrease in the water's BOD.

Courtesy of Dorr-Oliver, Inc.

FIG. 313.   ACTIVATED SLUDGE PROCESS

Ponds and Lagoons.—Waters from trickling filters and activated sludge tanks frequently are pumped to concrete tanks or man-made ponds and lagoons. These must be shallow (of the order of 3 to 6 ft) to maintain an aerobic condition (Fig. 314). These ponds serve further microbiological decrease of remaining BOD as well as additional opportunity for settling of traces of solids. Water from ponds and lagoons usually is sufficiently low in BOD for approved discharge into lakes and rivers. Many municipalities further require that such water be lightly chlorinated to ensure its freedom from pathogens and to reduce coliform counts before such discharge. Frequently such water without chlorination is used to advantage, as are some waters from trickling filters and activated sludge tanks, for land irrigation.

Where a food plant has produced such waters and is without convenient means for their disposal it may choose to discharge these waters into sewer lines for further handling by a municipal plant. Municipal plants are

FIG. 314.   LAGOONS RECEIVING TREATED WASTE WATER

always situated for easy disposal of treated waste waters. As above, they
will be chlorinated for disposal into waterways or used for irrigation.
Except under conditions of emergency, municipal plants virtually never
route treated waste waters to be purified directly into potable water supplies. Plants that produce drinking water draw their supplies from protected reservoirs or unpolluted streams and purify it in accordance with
rigid standards for potable water.

SOLID WASTE UPGRADING AND TREATMENT

Under favorable economic conditions very few materials emerging from
a food production or processing plant must retain the lowly status of a
waste. Where economically feasible, almost every known "waste" material
can be upgraded. Fruit and vegetable skins, pulp, and pits can be pressed
to further remove water and be converted into compost for improving
soils. Cacao bean hulls are sold as a high priced ornamental mulch. Dried
spent coffee grounds have been used to dress tennis courts. Packing house
scraps have been ground, rendered, and dried into animal feeds. Entrails
have been similarly treated or shipped "wet" to mink farms. Spray and
drum dried blood meal is an important component of feeds. Inedible
portions of fish are steamed, ground, and dehydrated to yield fish meal
for animal consumption. The liquid pressed from such fish during processing (fish "stick" water) is concentrated and may be dried with the ground
fish or dried separately. Fish stick water obtained under sanitary conditions

of human food production is currently being desalted prior to spray drying into a high quality protein for human consumption. Poultry feathers may be collected, cleaned, and further processed for pillow stuffing. Animal hides are made into edible gelatin.

Dairy "wastes" such as cheese whey and buttermilk (from the churn) should be more correctly called by-products. Both are especially rich in valuable nutrients and are produced under highly sanitary conditions. Considerable whey and buttermilk is concentrated and drum or spray dried for animal feed and as ingredients in manufactured human foods including baked goods, confectionery, and sausage products. Unfortunately far greater quantities, which are truly enormous in the case of whey, are sewered. Double losses result from the throw-away of valuable nutrients and the subsequent cost of waste treatment. In some cases this is economically justifiable, especially when whey must be hauled great distances from a cheese plant to a dehydration plant and the market for the dried product is limited. Much research has been aimed at modifying whey and finding new food uses for it to remedy this situation, however there have been many problems. Dried wheys from acid coagulated cheese (such as cottage) are highly acidic and can be consumed by livestock in only limited quantities. If whey is neutralized with alkali then an undesirably high level of salts is produced. Even when not neutralized whey is too high in salts for direct consumption in large amounts. Acid and salts can be removed from whey by various ion exchange and desalting methods but costs of these further treatments are not always justified. Acid wheys as well as sweet wheys from rennet coagulated cheese (such as Cheddar) are all high in lactose. Lactose can be laxative when consumed in large amounts. These problems are not insurmountable, in fact many of them disappear when whey is blended with other food materials as a supplement. Similar type problems are encountered and have been overcome with many food wastes and by-products. The whey disposal problem, however, is outstanding in terms of the enormous quantities of whey produced, its high BOD value, its relatively low level of solids, and the marginal economic value of these solids without further costly upgrading. Meanwhile tighter antipollution laws threaten the existence of numerous cheesemaking plants if alternatives to whey dumping are not found.

Some materials cannot be economically upgraded to fit into an existing market structure. These too may still have some value. Corn cobs, nut shells, coffee grounds, and contaminated fats and oils commonly are burned as fuel to generate steam in food plants. Fruit and vegetable wastes have been used as a source of fermentable carbohydrate for growing feed yeast and for the recovery of alcohol. Some wastes are plowed into the ground as fill. When none of these uses are feasible then waste may be burned as garbage or sometimes hauled to sea. Sludges and residues remaining after waste water and sewage treatment, have been dried and sold as fertilizer or used wet for this purpose. When there is no outlet for this they may be trucked away and dumped. Sometimes they are incinerated leaving only a small amount of ash to dispose of.

LOWERING DISCHARGE VOLUMES

There are many alternatives to conventional processing operations that can substantially lower the volumes of waste waters currently being discharged from food plants. Reuse of water for less demanding operations within the plant has already been mentioned. Tighter antipollution laws are forcing a variety of innovative processing changes.

It is possible to peel certain fruits and vegetables by a "dry caustic" method in which concentrated sodium hydroxide combined with vigorous mechanical action replaces large volumes of dilute caustic solution to loosen the skins. In the case of potatoes about $\frac{1}{4}$ as much water, and in the case of peaches about $\frac{1}{15}$ as much water is required with the dry caustic method. Further, BOD of the water per pound of potato or peach peeled by the dry caustic method is only about $\frac{1}{3}$ that generated by the more conventional method. Dry caustic peeling is presently being studied for pears, apricots, and other fruits and vegetables.

Another operation that contaminates large quantities of water is conventional hot water blanching of vegetables. A newer method receiving study exposes diced vegetables in a monolayer to live steam for about 30 sec followed by a 60 sec or longer holding time for heat equilibration and enzyme inactivation. The blanched dice may next be cooled with chilled air. In addition to use of less water, less solids are dissolved from the vegetable dice which reduces the BOD level in the effluent, and texture of the vegetables after freezing, thawing, and cooking are reported to be improved.

The olive industry generates large quantities of processing brine of approximately 8% salt. Rather than dump the brine after olive storage, methods for recovering the salt for reuse are under study. One method uses evaporation to crystallize the salt. The crystallized salt slurry of about 58% solids contains about 6% of organic matter which must be eliminated before the salt can be reused. This is accomplished by incineration of the slurry at 1200°F, which leaves only a trace of carbon. The decontaminated salt can be stored for reuse the next season, when it is dissolved, adjusted in pH and filtered to remove the carbon. In addition to a potential saving in salt costs, a pollution problem is avoided.

Studies by the U.S. Dept. of Agr. indicate the feasibility of trailer-mounted tomato preprocessing units that complete all but the last steps of processing in the field. Tomato pulp, skin, stems, leaves, and other waste material are separated in the field area with wash waters going to irrigation ditches and solid wastes spread over the land. Juice alone is returned to the central processing plant. In similar fashion the ideal solution to much of the wastes generated by the seafood industry is butchering and disposal of fish wastes at sea, which is facilitated by greater use of floating fish processing factories.

Frequently waste water discharge volumes can be reduced by very simple changes in a food plant's routine operations. An ice cream manufacturer might better return rinsings from the freezer to the mix preparation vat for reconstituting dry mix ingredients. This not only decreases waste load but recovers food solids of economic value. The segregation of waste streams is often sound; it frequently is better to recover a concentrated high BOD waste such as blood or offal and handle it separately than to allow it to contaminate large volumes of more dilute waste water. The purchasing of certain preprocessed ingredients often can reduce waste loads needing treatment. These and related practices are not new but are becoming increasingly important to pollution control.

THE FUTURE

Waste disposal has always meant problems and expense to food producers and processors. With the passing of the years these problems generally have grown more severe. In the United States, the population is increasing and large numbers of people are moving from the cities to suburbs close by areas of food production and processing. The ability of any geographical area to absorb wastes is limited and frequently exceeded when controls are not intelligently administered.

Tables of equivalents have been developed to show the contribution of wastes from various sources. The waste from one cow is equivalent to that from 16.4 humans, and a poultry farm of 200,000 birds, not uncommon today, may produce a waste disposal problem equivalent to a city of 20,000. A sizable meat packing plant or cannery during peak season can easily exceed this. Conflicts of interest are common. Polluted waters have seriously hurt the oyster industry of the East Coast. The duck industry of Long Island, New York, is threatened with extinction if their contribution to pollution in this highly populated area cannot be significantly diminished. A twenty million dollar per year poultry industry in Southeastern New York State is in the heart of a sixty million dollar resort industry which is objecting to foul odors. This type of thing in many areas of the country is daily becoming more of a problem.

In the past it was considered reasonably safe to dump wastes into the ocean. Growing evidence that the ocean's capacity to absorb wastes also is finite is resulting in increasing legislation to protect both the deep oceans and the shores. The U.S. Council on Environmental Quality has recommended legislation to prohibit most and regulate all ocean dumping. The establishment of an international body to study and hopefully control the problem of ocean pollution also has been proposed. Forceful international protests have prevented the dumping of lethal chemicals in the past. All ocean dumping is now coming under increasing attack.

Future discharges into U.S. inland waters will be greatly affected by a recent interpretation of an old law, the Refuse Act of 1899. This law prohibits discharges, except in liquid form from public streets and sewers, into any U.S. navigable waters or their tributaries without a permit from the Army Corps of Engineers. In 1971 a program requiring all industrial dischargers to apply for permits was initiated. Permits to be granted require information on effluent pH, temperature, color, odor, electrical conductance, chemical composition, and biological characteristics. This information must be supplied by the industrial discharger. Appropriate state and interstate agencies must certify that a discharge meets permitted standards before a permit will be issued by the Army Corps of Engineers. The Environmental Protection Agency, which also reviews permits, is developing guidelines for acceptable effluents from different industry categories. The food industry is included.

For most food-related wastes adequate methods of control exist but they often are costly. Yet there is no question that they will have to be employed to a still greater extent in the future. The problem is everybody's since it affects the air we breathe, the water we drink, and the price we will have to pay for food.

BIBLIOGRAPHY

AMERICAN PUBLIC HEALTH ASSOCIATION. 1971. Standard Methods for the Examination of Water and Wastewater, 13th Edition. Am. Public Health Assoc., Washington, D.C.

ANON. 1969. Animal Waste Management. Cornell Univ. Conf. Agr. Waste Management. Cornell Univ., Ithaca, N.Y.

ANON. 1969. Cleaning Our Environment—The Chemical Basis for Action. Am. Chem. Soc., Washington, D.C.

BABBITT, H. E., DOLAND, J. J., and CLEASBY, J. L. 1962. Water Supply Engineering, 6th Edition. McGraw-Hill Book Co., New York.

BAIER, W. E. 1955. Citrus by-products and derivatives—an introductory survey. Food Technol. 9, 78–80.

BERNSTEIN, S. 1960. The utilization and value of brewery by-products. Paper presented at 1st Tech. Session, Master Brewer's Assoc. Am., 73rd Anniv. Conv., Los Angeles.

BIGELOW, W. D., and STEVENSON, A. E. 1923. The effect of hard water in canning vegetables. Natl. Canners Assoc. Bull. 20-L.

BLAINE, R. K. 1965. Fermentation products. In Industrial Wastewater Control. C. F. Gurnham (Editor). Academic Press, New York, London.

BORUFF, C. E. 1947. Recovery of fermentation residues as feeds. Ind. Eng. Chem. 39, 602–607.

CASTEN, J. W. 1964. Utilization and disposal of liquid and solid residues. In Food Processing Operations, Vol. 3. M. A. Joslyn, and J. L. Heid (Editors). Avi Publishing Co., Westport, Conn.

CULP, R. L., and CULP, G. L. 1971. Advanced Wastewater Treatment. Van Nostrand Reinhold Co., New York.

ECKENFELDER, W. W., JR., and O'CONNER, D. J. 1961. Biological Waste Treatment. Pergamon Press, Elmsford, N.Y.

FOOD ENGINEERING. 1971. Special Report: Pollution Control. Food Eng. *43*, No. 8, 47–64.

GAINEY, P. L., and LORD, T. H. 1952. Microbiology of Water and Sewage. Prentice-Hall Co., Englewood Cliffs, N.J.

GREENFIELD, R. E. 1965. Starch and starch products. *In* Industrial Wastewater Control. C. F. Gurnham (Editor). Academic Press, New York.

GRIFFIN, A. E. 1945. Break-point chlorination. Tech. Publ. *213*. Wallace and Tiernan Co., Newark, N.J.

GURNHAM, C. F., (Editor). 1965. Industrial Wastewater Control. Academic Press, New York.

JAMES, G. V. 1971. Water Treatment. CRC Press, Cleveland.

INGLETT, G. E. (Editor) 1973. Symposium: Processing Agricultural and Municipal Wastes. Avi Publishing Co., Westport, Conn.

JENSEN, L. T. 1965. Sugar. *In* Industrial Wastewater Control. C. F. Gurnham (Editor). Academic Press, New York.

JOHNSON, A. S. 1965. Meat. *In* Industrial Wastewater Control. C. F. Gurnham (Editor). Academic Press, New York.

JOSLYN, M. A. 1963. Water in food processing. *In* Food Processing Operations, Vol. 1. M. A. Joslyn, and J. L. Heid (Editors). Avi Publishing Co., Westport, Conn.

KOSIKOWSKI, F. V. 1967. Greater utilization of whey powder for human consumption and nutrition. J. Dairy Sci. *50*, No. 8, 1343–1345.

LEVIN, E. 1961. Fish Flour. VioBin Corp., Monticello, Ill.

MARSH, G. L. 1943. Recovery of tartrates from winery wastes. Proc. Inst. Food Technologists 183–195.

MATZ, S. A. 1965. Water in Foods. Avi Publishing Co., Westport, Conn.

McDONALD, M. 1971. Paper Recycling and the Use of Chemicals 1971. Noyes Data Corp., Park Ridge, N.J.

MERCER, W. A. 1965. Canned foods. *In* Industrial Wastewater Control. C. F. Gurnham (Editor). Academic Press, New York.

MERCER, W. A., and SOMERS, I. I. 1957. Chlorine in food plant sanitation. *In* Advances in Food Research, Vol. 7. Academic Press, New York.

MERCER, W. A., and YORK, G. K. 1953. Re-use of water in canning. Natl. Canners Assoc. Inform. Letter *1426*, 74–78.

MURRAY, R. V., and PETERSON, G. T. 1951. Water for canning. Continental Can Co. Res. Div. Bull. *22*, 1–27.

NOLTE, A. J., VON LOESECKE, H. W., and PULLEY, G. N. 1942. Feed yeast and industrial alcohol from citrus waste press juice. Ind. Eng. Chem. *34*, 670–673.

NORDELL, E. 1961. Water Treatment for Industrial and Other Uses. Reinhold Publishing Corp., New York.

PAZAR, C. 1971. Wastewater Cleanup Equipment 1971. Pollution Control Handbook *2*. Noyes Data Corp., Park Ridge, N.J.

SITTIG, M. 1968. Air Pollution Control Processes and Equipment 1968. Noyes Data Corp., Park Ridge, N.J.

SLAVIN, J. W., and PETERS, J. A. 1965. Fish and fish products. *In* Industrial Wastewater Control. C. F. Gurnham (Editor). Academic Press, New York.

VIGSTEDT, C. R. 1965. Poultry and eggs. *In* Industrial Wastewater Control. C. F. Gurnham (Editor). Academic Press, New York.

WATSON, C. W., JR. 1965. Dairy products. *In* Industrial Wastewater Control. C. F. Gurnham (Editor). Academic Press, New York.

CHAPTER 23

Food Additives, Wholesomeness, and Consumer Protection

INTRODUCTION

With respect to its food supply, the public must be protected on all matters related to health and economic deception. This encompasses such far reaching concepts as safety, purity, wholesomeness, and honest value. Because in a highly complex society the individual consumer is not in a position and usually does not have the specialized knowledge to protect himself, the responsibility rests on the food industry and on government. Industry and government must cooperate in the role of providing protection, and they do. Quite commonly today industry standards pertaining to food quality, wholesomeness, and accurate representation of food products are higher than minimum government regulations. This is because in addition to public-mindedness industry must protect its valuable brand names in order to survive and to compete effectively. The damaging publicity that a food company can get as a result of a single food poisoning outbreak, the detection of a harmful chemical in their product, or exposure of a dishonest practice can often be sufficient to put it out of business. What is more, the food industry looks to government to set high standards and to enforce these standards, in order to protect itself against unethical competition. A special kind of wholesomeness of fundamental importance has to do with nutritional quality. This will be considered separately in Chap. 24.

FOOD ADDITIVES

Recent years have seen an intensification of focus upon the safety of our food supply, particularly with respect to intentional and unintentional chemical additives including pesticides. Arguments have been offered abundantly, both defending and attacking the liberal use of functional chemicals, and still continue. It must also be said that few issues of major influence upon general well being are as little understood by a large segment of the consuming public, or are as capable of evoking emotional response from the truly misinformed, as is the issue of food additives. On the other hand, no area related to public health has ever received more thorough scientific study as the basis for conscientious and conservative legislative policy, although much remains to be learned from continued research.

622

There may have been a time when adding chemicals to foods was not necessary and not practiced, but one would have to go quite far back into human history to find it. Prehistoric man added chemicals to foods when he smoked meat. The later practices of salting fish and flesh, of fermenting plant and animal substances, and of improving the palatability of insipid diets with spices are other examples of introducing chemicals. Today, chemicals added to foods are as much a part of our modern lives as high speed transportation, and can be regulated to be perhaps even safer. Such regulation, however, depends upon unending scientific investigation, careful interpretation of data, and changes in legislative policy as additional knowledge becomes available.

Why Food Additives

No highly developed society could exist today without food additives. Food additives immediately become necessary when areas of food production are separated from areas of population concentration and the food must be stored or transported under conditions that can affect spoilage. These food additives are preservative in character. A wide variety of chemicals added to foods are not primarily preservative, but are added for functional properties associated with food color, flavor, and texture. Still other additives are incorporated as nutritional supplements and as processing aids in manufacturing the thousands of products that we have become accustomed to, and that customers demand. There is scarcely a quality attribute that foods may possess for which a useful chemical additive has not been developed. Many of these additives and their functions have been referred to in the preceding chapters.

In his book *The Technology of Food Preservation,* Desrosier calls attention to the list of varied uses for chemical additives commonly employed in food processing and manufacture and compiled by the U.S. Food and Drug Administration. These include acidifying, alkalizing, anticaking, antidrying, antifoaming, antihardening, antispattering, antisticking, bleaching, buffering, chillproofing, clarifying, color retaining, coloring, conditioning (dough), creaming, curing, dispersing, dissolving, drying, emulsifying, enhancing flavor, enriching, firming, flavoring, foam producing, glazing, leavening, lining food containers, maturing (flour), neutralizing, peeling, plasticizing, preserving (including antioxidants), pressure dispensing, refining, replacing air in food packages, sequestering unwanted metal ions, stabilizing, sterilizing, supplementing nutrients, sweetening, texturizing, thickening, water-proofing, water-retaining, and whipping.

Many of these functions of food additives would not be required if the majority of our foods were prepared in the home from basic food raw materials somehow acquired and held without spoilage. This of course is not the case in the United States and in other advanced countries of the world where most of what is eaten is consumed in the form of convenience foods. We may not always recognize convenience foods as such because we have become so accustomed to them and take them for granted. Nevertheless, a can of peas is a convenience food since it requires just warming but no shelling of the peas. A can of vegetable soup is still more of a convenience food since the various vegetables have been cut, blended, supplemented with spices, and so on. Similarly flour is a convenience food to anyone who otherwise would have to mill their own grain, as is still common in certain parts of the world. However, a prepared cake mix is far more of a convenience food than is flour, and over the past 20 or so years the cake mix has become more complete and more convenient. When cake mixes first appeared the housewife generally had to add fresh milk and fresh eggs at the time of preparation. Then dried milk was incorporated and special emulsifiers shortened beating time. Today, there are cake mix types that require only the addition of water, mixing, and baking, and some of the newer cheese cake and chiffon mixes have even done away with the baking step. The ultimate in convenience is the completely baked and iced frozen cakes or their unfrozen manufactured counterparts, which can be of excellent quality and have largely replaced home baking.

Convenience foods of many different types are now offered. Convenience foods are simply foods which have had various degrees of their preparation labor moved from the household or restaurant back to the food processor or manufacturer. This trend has moved at an accelerating rate through the past decade and will continue to do so on the strength of increased knowledge of food science and technology that can support quality product development. There also will be more convenience foods in the future because as technological development continues there is greater accent upon speed and efficiency. This includes speed of food preparation in the restaurant, industrial and school cafeteria, hospital, airliner, military installation, and in the home. Further, the number of skilled cooks and other commercial food preparation personnel is steadily decreasing as more young people are seeking higher prestige career positions. The homemaker too is spending far less time in the kitchen and more in part time work or community affairs, and welcomes the savings in time and effort that convenience foods make possible. The convenience food revolution would not be possible without food additives.

And food additives can find their way into foods in trace amounts as a consequence of pesticide treatment of crops and drugs administered to livestock. Every effort is being made to minimize, and, where possible, virtually eliminate these and other unintentional residues from the foods we consume since many can be detrimental to human health. But pesticides and drugs properly used are essential to modern agriculture and no enlightened person would advocate their discontinued use because of the possibility of misuse. This of course is the crux in any discussion of the pros and cons of chemicals added to foods. Their use in many cases is essential and their proper use provides countless benefits; on the other hand their misuse must be rigidly controlled to protect the health and welfare of the consuming public. Today, there are regulatory bodies in all countries of the world to protect food supplies and to control the use of food additives, and because food is imported and exported methods for control are being strengthened on an international basis.

Definition of Food Additive

A useful definition of the term food additive has been very difficult to formulate, particularly since such a definition carries with it far reaching legal implications. A report of an Expert Committee on Food Additives made up by representatives of the Food and Agriculture Organization (FAO) and the World Health Organization (WHO) after Rome meetings in 1956, defined food additives as nonnutritive substances added *intentionally* to food, generally in small quantities to improve its appearance, flavor, texture, or storage properties. They did not consider in this catagory substances added primarily for their nutritive value, such as vitamins and minerals. But chemicals finding their way into foods also can be *nonintentional*. Pesticide residues are an example. Further examples are chemicals that may leach into foods from packaging materials or trace amounts of lubricants that can get into foods from processing machinery. The distinction between these two kinds of additives is most important. Intentional additives are substances purposely added to perform specific functions. Nonintentional or incidental additives are substances which have no intended function in the finished food but become part of the food product through some phase of production or subsequent handling. Since both kinds of additives in excessive amounts can be detrimental to health, the Food and Drug Administration of the United States in their regulations uses a more comprehensive definition of food additives in accordance with the thinking of the Food Protection Committee of the National Academy of Sciences—National Research Council.

The Food Protection Committee has defined a food additive as "a substance or a mixture of substances, other than a basic foodstuff, which is present in a food as a result of any aspect of production, processing, storage, or packaging. The term does not include chance contaminants." Such a definition encompasses intentional as well as incidental additives.

The legal definition that the FDA has used in recent years is more descriptive. Particularly significant is that it has exempted from classification as a food additive any material that had been granted prior sanction of use based on "known" safety. Thus, the FDA has been defining a food additive as: "any substance, the intended use of which results or may reasonably be expected to result, directly or indirectly, in its becoming a component of or otherwise affecting the characteristics of any food (including any substance intended for use in producing, manufacturing, packing, processing, preparing, treating, transporting or holding a food; and including any source of radiation intended for any such use), if such substance is not generally recognized, among experts qualified by scientific training and experience to evaluate its safety, as having been adequately shown through scientific procedures (or, in the case of substances used in food prior to January 1, 1958, through either scientific procedures or experience based on common use in food) to be safe under the conditions of its intended use."

The Food Additives Amendment of 1958

In keeping with the above definition, on September 6, 1958 the Federal Government enacted the Food Additives Amendment to the Federal Food, Drug, and Cosmetic Act of 1938. This amendment which went into effect shortly afterwards and covers both intentional and incidental additives completely altered the government's method of regulating the use of additives in foods, and put sharp teeth in the Food and Drug Administration's power to protect the health and welfare of the food consuming public. The current law states that no additive can be used in foods unless and until the Food and Drug Administration is convinced by thorough scientific evidence that such additive is safe at the intended level of use in the intended food application.

GRAS vs. NonGRAS Substances.—As indicated in the above legal definition for a food additive, exempted from the requirement of proving safety were materials which either by prior scientific evaluation, or from experience based on long time common usage in food, were generally recognized as being safe by acknowledged experts. These "generally recognized as safe" substances have been referred to by the abbreviation GRAS, and lists of GRAS materials covering approximately 600 such substances have been published and are periodically revised. Typical GRAS substances include the common spices, natural seasonings, and numerous flavoring materials; baking powder chemicals such as sodium bicarbonate and monocalcium phosphate; fruit and beverage acids such as citric acid, malic acid, and phosphoric acid; gums such as agar-agar and gum karaya; emulsifiers such as fatty acid monoglycerides and diglycerides; and many, many more. But substances presently on the GRAS list are not immune to removal should new toxicological findings produce evidence disproving or even seriously challenging their safety. In such a case a substance removed from the GRAS list may be placed under more rigid control of its use, or even prohibited from further use if warranted. Thus, in 1971 a comprehensive review of present GRAS list items was initiated by the FDA to determine eligibility for continued GRAS status in light of new scientific knowledge and the expanded consumption of some GRAS substances in recent years.

In the case of nonGRAS substances, approval by the FDA is granted upon submission of scientific data clearly showing that the intended chemical is harmless in the intended food application at the intended use level. This is done by petition to the FDA. The FDA then sets limits with respect to the kinds of foods in which the additive may be used and the maximum concentrations that may be employed. Commonly, a food additive may be permitted at a level of say 100 ppm in one food, only 25 ppm in another food, and be prohibited from use in a third food. At present, over 2,400 nonGRAS food additives may be used in foods within the limits that have been deemed safe by the FDA. In addition to new listings being approved, the FDA also has the right to delist an approved additive should new data throw doubt upon its safety. All changes in food additive status are published in the Federal Register. Presently a number of previously approved nonGRAS substances are under renewed investigation.

Burden of Proof.—Prior to the 1958 Food Additives Amendment, the FDA certainly exercised control over chemicals in foods, but the burden of proof that an additive was unsafe was on the FDA and they had to establish that such was the case before they could prohibit its use. This could take years in certain cases, and in the meantime a harmful substance might be consumed by millions of people. With the new amendment the burden of proof of safety of a new chemical substance lies with the organization that wishes to market or use the chemical. This can require a period of testing of several years since the FDA usually requires that a new additive undergo at least a two-year feeding test in two species of animals to reveal long term as well as acute effects. In some cases, feeding tests of seven years duration have been required as well as limited tests in human subjects. Other chemicals may be cleared rapidly where data on related substances are applicable. In extreme cases proof of safety of an additive may well exceed a cost of a million dollars, which of course tends to provide a conservative influence of its own. This work generally is not done by food companies, or even by manufacturers of food chemicals or other materials that may impart incidental additives to foods, but is contracted out to specialized toxicology laboratories (Fig. 315).

Courtesy of Food and Drug Research Laboratories, Inc.

FIG. 315. ANIMAL FEEDING TESTS COMMONLY INVOLVE RATS
AND A SECOND NON-RODENT SPECIES

The Food Additives Amendment of 1958 excludes some classes of chemical additives such as pesticides on raw agricultural commodities and food colors. These are specifically covered by the 1954 Miller Pesticide Amendment and the 1960 Color Additives Amendment, which we will further refer to shortly. The Food Additives Amendment, however, does cover foods that have been subjected to ionizing radiation since such treatment can induce chemical changes that could possibly be harmful. In this case, the FDA approves the foods that may be irradiated, the irradiation sources, and sets limits on the maximum permitted irradiation dosage as discussed in Chap. 11.

Removes Older Restrictions.—While the Food Additives Amendment of 1958 might appear to have worked a hardship against food producers who must use food additives, this is not really the case. No reputable food producer would want to use an unsafe chemical, nor risk his reputation on the possibility that one of his products might constitute a health hazard. But in addition, rather than a hardship, the Food Additives Amendment actually may permit the use of chemicals that were prohibited earlier on unscientific grounds. Prior to the amendment the law prohibited chemicals in foods that were considered to have "poisonous properties" at any level. The difficulty here was to decide what constituted a poison.

Virtually every substance known can be a poison to humans if taken in large enough amounts. This is true of caffeine in coffee, alcohol in beverages, oxalic acid in rhubarb and spinach, common salt, carbon dioxide, oxygen, and even water. Iodine in large amounts certainly is a poison but in small amounts prevents goiter.

The 1958 Food Additives Amendment does away with the arbitrary and incorrect designation of substances as poisons and nonpoisons. It recognizes that substances which may have poisonous properties in excessive amounts may be quite harmless and useful in smaller quantities and sets usage levels accordingly. It fully recognizes that some materials may have dangerous cumulative effects when ingested over a long period of time, and that a level of an additive permitted in a food such as bread eaten every day may have to be lower than the level of the same additive permitted in a food consumed far less frequently. This recognition, and the establishment of legal tolerances for all approved additives where upper limits of use are warranted, has removed the guesswork in the use of additives and contributed to confidence on the part of the user.

The Cancer Issue.—The 1958 Food Additives Amendment contains a highly controversial clause known as the "Cancer Clause" or the "Delaney Clause." This states that no additive may be permitted in food if the material at any level can produce cancer when fed to man or animals, or can be shown carcinogenic by any other appropriate test. The problem in this case is that some rather harmless and common substances may possibly induce cancer in one animal or another under special conditions that have nothing to do with normal food consumption. Further, what constitutes "other appropriate tests"? Cancers have been induced in test animals by the rubbing of numerous substances onto animal tissues. The simple act of rubbing itself, as with a glass rod, has been effective in some cases. Materials from charred meat and burned fat have also been implicated. The causes of cancer, especially over a long term period, are not yet well understood and this issue, part of the present law, has not yet been fully resolved. In the meantime, there are many who believe that the spirit of the Delaney Clause should be extended to cover food additives that may have possible mutagenic or teratogenic effects. Here the findings from animal studies carried through several generations can be exceptionally difficult to interpret in terms of their applicability to man.

Additional Additive Requirements.—There are several requirements for a food additive beyond proof of safety with respect to health; these include the following:

(1) That in the case of an intentional additive the additive does indeed perform its useful function.

(2) That the additive is not put into food to deceive the customer, or to cover up the use of faulty ingredients or faulty manufacturing practices.

(3) That the additive does not cause a substantial reduction in the food's nutritional value.

(4) That the additive is not used to obtain an effect that could be obtained by otherwise good manufacturing practices.

(5) That a method of analysis exists with which to police the use of the
additive in foods or its incidental occurrence in foods (e.g., trace quantities of permitted migratory chemicals from packaging materials).

Any one of these requirements if not met could cause rejection by the
FDA of a proposed food additive.

The Miller Pesticide Amendment of 1954

This covers chemical fertilizers, herbicides, and pesticides used in or on
raw agricultural commodities. Among other features, in a fashion quite
like the 1958 Food Additives Amendment, it provides for approval and
the establishment of safe tolerances for some 2,000 pesticide chemicals.

As this amendment to the Federal Food, Drug, and Cosmetic Act was
written it states that certain pesticides can be used only if they leave
absolutely no residue on or in the treated commodity. This has been the
cause for another hotly debated issue.

The problem with any zero tolerance requirement is the virtual im-
possibility of guaranteeing zero concentration and the further problem
of proving zero. If an analytical method can be made sufficiently sensitive then there would be very few foods that would be absolutely free from
detectable levels of contamination. Analytical methods exist today that
can detect a few parts per billion of many chemicals. Lower levels of a
pesticide would be undetectable and would meet a zero tolerance requirement. However, a food meeting a zero tolerance requirement today
might be deemed adulterated at any time in the future if a more sensitive
method was found to detect still lower levels of pesticide. Precisely this
occurred in recent years with the application of newer chromatographic
and atomic absorption spectrophotometric methods of analysis (Fig. 316).
The law now recognizes the futility of the zero tolerance requirement and
is replacing it with finite negligible residue tolerances for pesticides and
similar chemicals. Because of the wide range effects pesticides can have on
the environment, various aspects of pesticide regulation recently have been
transferred from the U.S. Dept. of Agr. to the Environmental Protection
Agency, and new policies to reconcile the need to control pests with the
need to prevent contamination of food may be expected.

The Color Additives Amendment of 1960

This amendment defines color additives to include all dyes, pigments,
or other substances which can impart a color to food, whether these
are synthetic, extracted, or otherwise prepared. It further lists all
permitted color additives with tolerances where these apply. Like the
1958 Food Additives Amendment it includes the Delaney Clause. Uniform
compositional standards also have been established for color additives

FIG. 316. CHEMIST USING GAS CHROMATOGRAPHY TO DETECT PESTICIDE RESIDUES

and there is provision for certification of manufacturer's individual batches of color, through chemical testing by the FDA, to insure purity and safety. Like other food additives, an approved coloring material can be disapproved when new scientific evidence provides cause. Presently several color additives are receiving renewed scrutiny, with difficult toxicological questions being referred to the National Academy of Sciences—National Research Council for evaluation.

Food Chemicals Codex

The approval of a chemical as an acceptable food additive and the establishment of maximum use levels in specific applications can still fall short of providing the intended degree of protection if the chemical is of variable purity. In such a case an approved intentional additive can be the vehicle for introducing an objectionable incidental additive into food. The Food Chemicals Codex, prepared by the Food Protection Committee of the National Academy of Sciences—National Research Council, and first issued in 1966, was undertaken with this in mind. The Codex sets standards for purity of food chemicals in terms of maximum allowable trace contaminants and methods of analysis to establish these. The Codex, endorsed by the FDA, is particularly useful to the purchaser of food chemicals and has become a guide book to the manufacturer of food chemicals as has the U.S. Pharmacopeia in the case of drugs.

Broad Classes of Intentional Food Additives

In their 1965 Publication 1274, entitled *Chemicals Used In Food Processing,* the Food Protection Committee listed about 3,000 intentional food additives in twelve major groups. A few representative types from each group are indicated below.

Preservatives.—These include chemical preservatives against bacteria, yeasts, and molds such as sodium benzoate used in soft drinks and acidic foods, the sodium and calcium propionates used in breads and cakes as a mold inhibitor, sorbic acid used on cheese and in moist dog foods to control mold, and compounds of chlorine used as a germicidal wash for fruits and vegetables. The preservatives also include fumigants such as ethylene oxide and ethyl formate used to control microorganisms on spices, nuts, and dried fruits. Preservatives which control browning of fruits and vegetables caused by enzymes, such as sulfur dioxide, also are included.

Antioxidants.—These include the compounds used to prevent oxidation of fats. Without them potato chips, breakfast cereals, salted nuts, fat-containing dehydrated foods, crackers, and many other fatty foods could not be stored for any length of time on supermarket shelves without developing rancidity. Principal among these antioxidants are butylated hydroxyanisole (BHA), butylated hydroxytoluene (BHT), and propyl gallate. Nordihydroguaiaretic acid (NDGA), previously used as an antioxidant was removed from food use by the FDA in 1968. The antioxidants also include such diverse materials as ascorbic acid, stannous chloride, and tocopherols (vitamin E). Sulfur dioxide, listed as a preservative, is further listed as an antioxidant. Many other food chemicals also exhibit dual roles.

Sequestrants.—These are the chelating agents or sequestering compounds. They are also referred to as metal scavengers since they combine with trace metals such as iron and copper and remove them from solution. The trace metals are active catalysts of oxidation and also enter into many off-color reactions in foods. Their removal by chelating additives such as ethylenediamine tetraacetic acid (EDTA), polyphosphates, and citric acid prevents these defects.

Surface Active Agents.—These include the emulsifiers used to stabilize oil-in-water and water-in-oil mixtures, gas-in-liquid mixtures, and gas-in-solid mixtures. In addition to emulsifiers of natural origin such as lecithin, and emulsifiers that can be prepared synthetically such as mono- and diglycerides and their derivatives, other emulsifying agents include certain fatty acids and their derivatives, and bile acids such as are important in digestion. Among the surface active agents also are numerous defoaming compounds and detergent chemicals.

Stabilizers, Thickeners.—Included here are the gums, starches, dextrins, protein derivatives, and other additives that stabilize and thicken foods by combining with water to add viscosity and to form gels. Gravies, pie fillings, cake toppings, chocolate milk drinks, jellies, puddings, and salad dressings are among the many foods that contain such stabilizers and thickeners as gum arabic, carboxymethyl cellulose (CMC), carrageenan, pectin, amylose, hydrolyzed vegetable proteins, gelatin, and others.

Bleaching and Maturing Agents, Starch Modifiers.—Freshly milled flour has a yellowish tint and suboptimum functional baking qualities. Both the color and baking properties improve slowly in normal storage. These improvements can be obtained more rapidly and with better control through the use of certain oxidizing agents. Benzoyl peroxide is an oxidizing agent which bleaches the yellow color. Oxides of nitrogen, chlorine dioxide, and other chlorine compounds both bleach color and mature the flour.

Oxidizing agents such as hydrogen peroxide also are used to whiten the color of milk for certain kinds of cheese manufacture and to bleach tripe. Bromate and iodate oxidizing agents are also used to condition bread doughs for optimum baking performance. Starch modifiers include compounds such as sodium hypochlorite which oxidize starches to a higher degree of water solubility.

Buffers, Acids, Alkalies.—As pH adjusting and controlling chemicals these additives affect an endless number of food properties many of which have been previously described. The acids in particular may be derived from natural sources such as fruits, and from fermentation, or they may be chemically synthesized. Like any pure chemical compound, whether the additive is from natural or synthetic sources, its properties and degree of wholesomeness are identical.

Food Colors.—Colors are added to thousands of food items, not as a means of deception but to give the public the appetizing and attractive qualities they desire. Colors of synthetic origin, such as the certified coal tar dyes, extend the range of coloring applications that can be satisfied with the natural coloring agents of which extract of annatto, caramel, carotene, and saffron are examples. Synthetic colors generally excel in coloring power, color uniformity, color stability, and lower cost. Further, in many cases natural coloring materials do not exist for a desired hue. Maraschino cherries, hard candies, carbonated beverages, and gelatin desserts are among items colored with certified coal tar dyes. Food colors also include carbon black to give blackness, and titanium dioxide to intensify whiteness.

Nonnutritive and Special Dietary Sweeteners.—Until 1969 these chiefly included saccharin compounds and the cyclamates of sodium, calcium, magnesium, and potassium. In 1969 cyclamates were banned from the U.S. food supply, leaving saccharin as the only major artificial sweetener available for food use. Early in 1972 the FDA further limited the use of saccharin to restrict saccharin intake from foods to one gram per day for a 155-lb person. This act was taken following evidence that rats develop bladder tumors when fed extremely high levels of the artificial sweetener. The biggest users of nonnutritive sweeteners are the low calorie soft drink manufacturers. But they also are essential to the manufacture of low calorie liquid foods, and dietetic forms of canned fruit, frozen desserts, salad dressings, gelatin desserts, and some baked goods. These nonsugar sweeteners in addition to helping control weight, also have made it possible for diabetics to enjoy several foods they otherwise would not be able to eat. There are new nonnutritive sweeteners being studied which have sweetness ranges from 10 to 3,000 times that of sucrose.

Nutrient Supplements.—Principal among these are the vitamins and minerals added as supplements and enrichment mixtures to a number of products. Major examples are vitamin D added to milk; B vitamins, iron, and calcium added to cereal products; iodine added to salt; vitamin A added to margarine, cheeses made from bleached milks, and dietary infant formulas; and vitamin C added to fruit juices and fruit-flavored desserts.

Several amino acids also are listed in this group. The amino acid lysine has received considerable study since it is the only essential amino acid absent from the protein of wheat flour in sufficeint amount to prevent wheat flour from being a nutritionally complete protein source. To date, lysine supplementation of wheat flour and white bread is not permitted in the United States (except in specialty bread and cereal mixes) on the grounds that the average consumer gets sufficient lysine from other foods in a normal diet.

Flavoring Agents.—These include both natural and synthetic flavoring materials. Some of the natural flavoring substances include spices, herbs, essential oils, and plant extractives. Typical of the synthetic flavor additives are benzaldehyde (cherry), ethyl butyrate (pineapple), methyl anthranilate (grape), and methyl salicylate (wintergreen).

Currently there are over 1,100 different flavoring materials used in foods, making this the largest single group of food additives. Part of this is due to the ever increasing variety of different foods, including foods of international character. But the increasing use of added flavors also must be attributed to the need to replenish flavors lost, or partially lost, by various modern processing methods involving heating, concentrating, drying, and other food handling practices.

Among the flavor additives are also included the flavor enhancers or potentiators, which do not have flavor in themselves in the low levels used but intensify the flavor of other compounds present in foods. Monosodium glutamate, and the 5'-nucleotides (related to components found in nucleic acids) are examples of this kind of material.

Monosodium glutamate (MSG) came under intensive investigation in 1969 after it was reported that brain damage resulted when MSG was injected under the skin of young mice. Since MSG had been a common ingredient in baby foods this caused alarm and pressure to prohibit it from further use in this class of foods. Without FDA action the producers of baby foods promptly discontinued use of MSG. At the same time the FDA requested the National Academy of Sciences—National Research Council to further investigate the safety of MSG in the general food supply. The National Academy of Sciences—National Research Council report of 1970 concluded that the risk from MSG in baby foods is extremely small but recommended that it not be added to foods for babies since its benefits for babies are dubious. It further found no evidence of risk from MSG used in reasonable amounts in foods for older children and adults. This corroborated previous years of intensive study indicating the relative harmlessness of this compound. Presently MSG continues to be widely used in foods as a flavor enhancer, but past adverse publicity has left many consumers still uneasy about this additive.

Miscellaneous Additives.—There are a great number of food additives that provide functions other than those indicated above. Some of these include yeast foods (to promote growth of bakers' yeast) such as ammonium sulfate, firming agents (for fruits and vegetables) such as calcium chloride, anticaking agents (for salt and granular foods) such as calcium phosphate, antisticking agents such as hydrogenated sperm oil, clarifying agents (for wine) such as bentonite, solvents such as ethanol, acetone and hexane, machinery lubricants such as mineral oil, meat curing agents such as sodium nitrite and sodium nitrate (both of these currently are under renewed investigation with regard to safety), crystal inhibitors such as oxystearin, growth stimulants (used in malting barley) such as gibberellic acid, enzymes for a wide variety of uses, and many more.

MICROBIOLOGICAL CONSIDERATIONS

Regulation of chemical additives is but one kind of protection that must be exercised over our food supply. The past dozen or so years have seen particular concentration in this area. There is every reason to believe that in the years ahead there will be a similar probing and upgrading of the microbial safety of food materials, especially in relation to advanced processing and handling methods.

This is already well underway. The occurrence of *Salmonella* organisms in low numbers within a wide range of fresh and manufactured food products is well recognized, and until very recently was judged by many authorities to be the number one food-related health problem in the United States and other parts of the world. Currently *Clostridium perfringens* is reported to be the most common cause of U.S. foodborne disease outbreaks. Sanitation and processing techniques to largely eliminate *Salmonella* (such as the mandatory pasteurization of all eggs used for manufacturing purposes) are currently being stressed by the FDA in the United States and similar agencies in other countries. Food products found to contain *Salmonella* organisms are being confiscated. The true significance of staphylococcal food poisoning, botulism, mold toxins, and enteric virus infections of certain food products is continually being assessed, although it is generally acknowledged that our present food supply, at least in the United States, is more abundant, varied, and microbiologically safe than ever before in history. Nevertheless, there is growing concern from several quarters.

In 1964, the Food Protection Committee voiced such concern in the National Research Council Publication 1195 entitled *An Evaluation of Public Health Hazards from Microbial Contamination of Foods*. Presently the FDA is strengthening their departments of microbiology. Similarly, microbiologists are in greater demand by food processors than ever before, and this demand is expected to increase in the years ahead.

Such concern is warranted, not primarily because of relaxed diligence on the part of food manufacturers, but because of the increasing pace of technological change and innovation in the methods of food processing and distribution.

It must be appreciated that the subtle effects that changes in processing and handling may have on microbial selection and survival in foods often are not fully known at the time new processes and products are first introduced commercially. This is nothing new. It applied when canning and freezing were introduced, and certainly applies in this age of dielectric and microwave heating, pasteurization and sterilization by irradiation and microporous membrane filtration, preservation by various methods of freeze drying, use of high temperature-short time and ultra high temperature-short time methods, application of accelerated ageing and curing techniques, widespread use of an ever increasing number of packaging materials in conjunction with vacuum and inert gas atmospheres, and combinations of these and other innovations. To be sure, the vast majority of such food processing applications to date have provided benefits of new products, improved quality, and lower costs without known adverse effects upon food safety. But potential dangers must be equally appreciated, and new applications of technology investigated to a degree that provides maximum feasible assurance of microbial safety.

It is to be expected that the FDA will set far more rigorous requirements to be met in such testing in the future, and that the burden of proof will rest upon the processor much as has become the case with chemical additives. It is likely that the areas which will come under increased scrutiny will include the following five:

(1) Mishandling of precooked frozen, refrigerated, catered, and vended foods. It is necessary to emphasize the word mishandled, which is not the usual practice.

(2) Mildly processed foods, which can involve a number of the newer processing methods being practiced or considered.

(3) Newer packaging methods, especially those which alter gas atmospheres in the packaged food.

(4) The centralization of plant operations and large scale production of individual food products, which has the potential for both greater microbiological control, as well as exposure of a large segment of the population in the event of a single mishap.

(5) Microbiological methodology.

Mishandling of Precooked Frozen, Refrigerated, Catered, and Vended Foods

These foods make up a major portion of the current convenience food revolution both in and out of the home. Generally a hazardous potential is the result of departure from well understood principles, usually traceable to neglect during preparation, or mechanical failure of refrigeration equipment during transportation and storage. It is well to recall here a few simple principles that cannot be violated if food safety is to be assured. Freezing is not a sterilization process nor even a pasteurizing process. While total bacterial counts can be expected to be lowered during freezing of food, substantial numbers of many major pathogens that may be conveyed by food, if present, will survive freezing. This degree of survival will be greater, the quicker the freezing process. Thus the newer liquid nitrogen and carbon dioxide freezing processes offer even less in the way of microbial destruction than the slower freezing methods, which are only poorly bactericidal. Thus, frozen foods, whether precooked or not, must be safe before freezing if they are to be safe after freezing. In the case of precooked foods this obviously means prevention of contamination after cooking, and minimum time of holding between cooking and freezing since the cooking treatment seldom is sufficient to inactivate spores of *Clostridium botulinum* which are commonly present in small numbers in nonsterilized foods, but are no cause for alarm unless conditions are such as to permit germination, growth, and toxin formation.

After processing, frozen and refrigerated foods with few exceptions rely principally on a continuum of cold, uninterrupted through warehousing, transportation, and marketing if safety is to be assured—particularly in nonacid foods. The AFDOUS code for frozen food handling, calling for zero degrees Fahrenheit until the food reaches the consumer, is not yet a widely applied practice in the United States, and it is a disconcerting fact that tens of thousands of trucks and frozen food cabinets in current commercial use are not capable of maintaining the zero condition. Generally the pathogens common to food cannot grow below 40° F, and grow but very slowly in the range of 45° to 50° F. This temperature range in the case of frozen foods is seldom encountered, as it would represent complete breakdown of freezer facilities which would be quickly evident and corrected. However, in the case of refrigerated, catered, and vended foods this range must be considered with caution; particularly where precooked foods are held which will receive no subsequent cooking, or only reconstitution with minimal heat to bring them to serving temperature. The following facts are of significance. *Staphylococcus aureus* and certain *Salmonella* organisms can grow down to 44° F. *Clostridium botulinum* type E may grow at 38° F under appropriate conditions of anaerobiasis and freedom from chemical or other microbial antagonists. At the same time commercial and household refrigerators are often at temperatures somewhat above 44° F. Where precooked foods are marginally heated or reconstituted it is not uncommon for times and temperatures to be insufficient to guarantee destruction of pathogenic organisms or their toxins in food materials that may be protective to these agents. It is not uncommon in fast-food eating establishments to encounter deep fat reconstituted items that retain cold spots in their centers. Electronic ovens of the microwave type are not inherently unsafe, but different constituents of food absorb microwave energy at different rates; it is not uncommon for precooked food to emerge from such an oven unequally heated.

Seldom will departure from a single operating condition result in an unsafe food product. But when such a chain of events as unsanitary preparation practices, insufficient refrigeration, and marginal heating occurs, then a hazardous outcome can result. By no means do our current commercial practices provide absolute safeguards against such occurrences.

Mildly Processed Foods

When we come to this broad catagory, interrelationships are far more complex, subtle, and less well understood. Unquestionably many situations exist which are potentially dangerous, and some of them have occurred and provided classic examples of unfortunate sequences of events. One of the better known cases was the 1963 smoked fish botulism outbreak. Here mild heating and smoking was short of complete sterilization. The product was packaged under anaerobic conditions which were sufficient to prevent molds and other aerobic spoilage organisms from growing and giving warning of spoilage should poor refrigeration subsequently occur. Inadequate refrigeration did follow in some cases and botulinum toxin was produced. The product was of a kind not generally heated before consumption and several deaths resulted. We do not have to look far for processing conditions which have the potential to produce equally dangerous results.

Any processing condition which is effective in lowering total bacterial counts, but which is short of achieving complete sterilization can be expected to shift the normal microbial flora from what it otherwise would be. Time-honored processes that cause such shifts include fermentation and acidification, nitrate and nitrite additions to cured meat, salting and smoking, and pasteurization of milk. These treatments coupled with proven methods of subsequent handling of the products constitute no special dangers.

Far less certain, at our present state of knowledge, are minor variations of these proven techniques, and newer techniques being introduced and considered to replace them. There is a considerable tendency at the present time to produce blander foods to meet changing American tastes with respect to salting, smoking, and degree of acidity. Mildly smoked fish, less highly cured meats, and less acidic cottage cheese, as well as milder natural ripened cheeses are examples. To some extent these changes are offset by greater sanitary control during manufacture. However, lower salt levels generally make a food medium more favorable to the potential growth of staphylococci, as does lower acidity increase the likelihood of survival and growth of most human pathogens including clostridia. Mild heat or mild irradiation sufficient to reduce substantially total counts often is far less than is effective in destroying bacterial spores, among which some of the most resistant belong to the genus *Clostridium*. When such treatments substantially decrease the numbers of less resistant organisms such as the acid forming streptococci and lactobacilli, and the lipolytic and proteolytic members of such genera as *Pseudomonas, Achromobacter, Proteus,* and the molds, then clostridia find many foods more favorable substrates for growth. This is also true for many nonspore forming pathogens including members of the genera *Staphylococcus* and *Salmonella* that may survive the mild treatment or find their way into foods as contaminants following the treatment. Not only may these pathogens grow in the subsequently less competitive environment, but with a gross reduction in the normal spoilage flora, mishandling of the food frequently will not result in the familar spoilage patterns that warn consumers of potential danger.

Mild processing conditions capable of microbial selection are of many kinds. In addition to the above there is a great tendency toward milder heat treatments to better retain food texture, color, and flavor attributes. Not only have numerous high temperature-short time and ultra high temperature-short time regimens been introduced, but prior to restrictive action by the FDA in 1968, based on new toxicological data, irradiation sterilization which caused adverse affects on many foods had been giving way to irradiation pasteurization as a potential preservation process for seafoods, fruits and vegetables, cereal grains, and other commodities. To be sure, these practices are preceded by intensive investigation before they are proposed for commercial use. In the case of irradiation, no previous preservation method, including canning, had been so thoroughly studied prior to its introduction to use. Yet there still remains much that is not known about the microbiology as well as the toxicology of irradiated foods.

Yet less is known of the microbiology of other cold pasteurization techniques, including the use of microporous membrane filters. These are being successfully used for the cold pasteurization of beer, but beer contains bacteriostatic substances and has a pH that makes this medium quite unfavorable to the growth of pathogens. On the other hand similar membranes have been suggested as a possible means of pasteurizing milk and other foods, and this is a different matter. For one thing microporous membranes with sufficient permeability to permit feasible through-put rates may not remove viruses that could constitute a health hazard in a nonheated product.

It also should be reemphasized that such preservation methods as conventional canning have substantial safety factors built into their standard procedures. In the case of nonacid foods, for example, the heat treatment is selected to give a 12 log cycle decrease in the heat resistant spores of *Clostridium botulinum* or kill more resistant spore formers. A similar safety factor commonly was incorporated into radiation sterilization treatments in the petitions for FDA approval. Little generally is known about the quantitative relationships in food systems between intensity of treatment and death rates of bacteria when a new destructive method is proposed. Certain ultraviolet, X-ray, dielectric, and microwave processes that have been proposed in the past, and are being experimented with at the present time, fall into this category. To this must be added the engineering problems associated with today's requirements for automatic high speed processing. It is one thing to achieve an average effect, such as an average heat exposure of 300° F for 1 sec. It is quite another to assure that every particle of food experiences this exposure. The engineering of high temperature-short time systems for liquid foods has advanced to a high degree but the problems associated with laminar flow, product burn-on, changes in viscosity, and uniform heat transfer plague the development engineer. The situation becomes more complex where suspensions of particulates and solid foods are involved.

When dehydration is the method of preservation, the microbial safety of freeze-dried foods frequently is raised. This is because freeze drying is the most gentle commercial dehydration procedure with respect to the food as well as the microbial population. No drying method known today, capable of producing a food of high organoleptic and functional quality, produces a sterile product. In the case of freeze drying particularly, a high bacterial count in the frozen food prior to drying will be reflected in the dried food. In the dry state no microbial growth will occur, but upon reconstitution such food is perishable and must be held under appropriate conditions of refrigeration if not soon consumed. This also applies to foods dehydrated by other methods and constitutes no special health problem. In the case of freeze drying, however, it is easy to visualize a sequence of events that could produce a potential danger. Such a sequence could involve contamination of precooked food with pathogenic organisms before or after freezing, freeze drying, reconstitution with cool water, and holding without adequate refrigeration prior to consumption. Abuses in the preparation and use of precooked freeze-dried shrimp and similar products could thus lead to danger.

The more subtle aspects of population shifts and microbial selection also must be considered in the case of freeze drying. Several of the steps leading to the final product for consumption are capable of producing these population shifts. These include the freezing operation prior to drying, the dehydration step, packaged storage in the dry condition, and the reconstitution procedure. Generally, if present, pathogenic clostridia and staphylococci would survive these stresses better than many of the less resistant harmless types. With a total microbial count thus reduced substantially, conditions favoring subsequent microbial growth could result in selective advantage to organisms of public health significance.

When we speak of freeze drying today we are not talking about a single process. Numerous variations especially in the dehydration step are in use and are being proposed, particularly to lower the cost of the process. These include various heating cycles to speed rate of ice sublimation, use of conductive and radiant heating by infrared and other electromagnetic radiations of varying frequency, and use of gases with desirable heat conductivity properties in place of vacuum to speed drying. Recent work has shown that several of these variations can shift the normal flora to favor survival and growth of pathogenic types should these be present in the original food material. This is another example of an area where microbiological knowledge has not yet caught up to the pace of technological innovation.

Newer Packaging Methods

Potential dangers from imperfect closure or mechanical failure of the countless new plastic, foil, and laminated types of packages are of course always present, but the record of safety of these newer packages has been generally excellent. Another problem that may increase in importance, however, is related to the increasing use of easy open-reclosable type packages. The deplorable practice of some customers opening baby food jars in supermarkets, sampling the contents, and then replacing the reclosed container has occurred in the past and been largely eliminated by the switch to the clicking type tamperproof lids. This type of thing must be a consideration in the design of easy open containers in the future.

More subtle, however, are the potentials for changing microbial population balances by vacuum and inert gas packaging within materials that are impervious to moisture and gas transmission, or selectively alter headspace gas composition. In nonsterile moist products an anaerobic environment favors the selection of clostridia, although clostridia also are quite capable of subsurface growth within nonacid food pieces even in an aerobic package provided the oxygen level is sufficiently low. The selective permeability of certain films to oxygen, carbon dioxide, and water vapor can further alter the equilibrium composition of the atmosphere within a package. As previously discussed, this is used to advantage in meat packaging, where some films impermeable to the loss of water vapor, but permeable to the inward diffusion of oxygen from the atmosphere, result in longer retention of the red color of fresh meat. In other instances the color of food is protected by the exclusion of oxygen. Much is yet to be learned about the potentials for pathogen survival and growth under altered gas atmospheres, especially in new products that have not yet met the test of time.

Centralization of Plant Operations and Large Scale Production

It is obvious that this continually increasing trend has the potentials for greater microbiological quality control of our food supply on the one hand, and rapid widespread dissemination of a hazardous product should this quality control fail. The continued improvement in the wholesomeness of our food supply is strong evidence for the dominance of the former. However, in 1971 the seriousness of the latter was emphasized when some cans from two major U.S. soup manufacturers were found to contain botulism toxin. Recall of coded suspect cans by both companies followed rapidly. In the case of the larger manufacturer, recall of suspect product produced by one plant necessitated the checking of over 102,000 retail outlets in 16 states plus stores in 17 Latin American countries. To the credit of this manufacturer no single case of human botulism followed.

Microbiological Methodology

While it is beyond the scope of this book to consider microbiological testing procedures it is well to recognize that our most widely used bacteriological tests were evolved to measure the microbial condition of familiar products made by traditional methods. There is much evidence to show that many of these tests give variable results when applied to a food product other than the one for which the method was developed. The modifications of procedure required to recover *Salmonella* organisms from different foods is an example of this. Varying of processing techniques short of sterilization not only alters relative bacterial populations, but can produce different degrees of attenuation of the surviving organisms. Such organisms may or may not be quantitatively revealed by standard methods, and the usual interpretations of standard test results may possibly be misleading. It also is to be recognized that to date there have been developed few practical methods to test for the presence of contaminating viruses in foods.

Current Status

The overall microbiological quality and safety of the U.S. food supply is outstandingly good. It would be entirely wrong to draw the conclusion from the above considerations that we are headed for great trouble. Quite the contrary, innovation in the food industry has continuously improved the variety, low cost, and wholesomeness of our food supply and will continue to do so. At the same time, greater knowledge of the interrelationships between microbial populations and new methods of production and handling is needed to assure continued safety. The Department of Health, Education, and Welfare through its agencies which include the U.S. Public Health Service and the FDA promotes research and maintains intensive surveillance in this and related areas.

THE FEDERAL FOOD, DRUG, AND COSMETIC ACT

In the United States the earliest food protection laws were passed by individual states and the first federal laws were directed primarily at imported foods. With the beginning of the current century there developed an increasing activity in interstate commerce, and food products shipped across state lines created a need for an overriding unified federal law to protect consumers in one state from possible food manufacturing or handling abuses in another. The first major law of this kind was the Federal Food and Drug Act of 1906, also known as the Pure Food Law (Fig. 317). This law underwent major revision as the economy grew and more was learned about food and drug science in succeeding years. It was partially rewritten and enlarged to become adopted in 1938 as the Federal Food, Drug, and Cosmetic Act, which remains today the basic food law of the United States. Since 1938, the previously described Miller Pesticide Amendment of 1954, the Food Additives Amendment of 1958, and the Color Additives Amendment of 1960 have been the major amendments that have kept this law up to date. Additional amendments can be expected in the future.

The Federal Food, Drug, and Cosmetic Act of 1938 with its amendments is administered by the Secretary of Health, Education, and Welfare through the Food and Drug Administration. The FDA currently employs over 4,000 scientists, legal advisers, and inspectors with offices throughout the country. That part of the Federal Food, Drug, and Cosmetic Act which deals with foods and which may be called the "Federal Pure Food Law" has as its purpose, through the FDA, to ensure that foods entering interstate commerce are safe, pure, wholesome, sanitary, honestly packaged, and honestly labeled. The Federal Food, Drug, and Cosmetic Act is a comprehensive and precisely defined body of regulations. Its major aspects related to food have been excellently summarized by M. P.

Courtesy of U. S. Food and Drug Admin.

FIG. 317. DR. HARVEY W. WILEY, "FATHER OF THE PURE FOOD LAW OF 1906," IN HIS LABORATORY

Duffy in "Food Processing Operations," Vol. 2, Joslyn and Heid (1963). Several of the following numbered points on FDA function, and conditions constituting adulteration and misbranding, are derived from his discussion.

To carry out the provisions of the Federal Pure Food Law the FDA has the following major functions:

(1) works with industry in matters of interpretation of the Federal Pure Food Law; (2) helps industry in establishing control measures for product protection; (3) makes regulatory inspections of food plants; (4) examines food samples from interstate shipments; (5) issues and enforces regulations on food additives; (6) approves and certifies acceptable food colors; (7) issues and regulates pesticide residue tolerances; (8) examines imported foods for acceptability; (9) works with state and local food inspection agencies in an advisory capacity; (10) works with state and local agencies in times of disaster to detect and dispose of contaminated foods; and (11) sets up "standards of identity" for manufactured foods to promote honesty and value of products. For example, standards of identity define the allowable ingredients and compositions of macaroni products. If a product is sold as macaroni and doesn't meet its standard it is considered adulterated and misrepresented and the manufacturer is prosecuted.

In order for the Federal Pure Food Law to protect the public and ensure that foods are not adulterated, mislabeled, deceptive, falsely packaged, or falsely guaranteed, the law scrupulously defines these and other terms. For example, food is considered adulterated if any of the following (and still other conditions) exist:

(1) if the food contains poisons or other harmful substances at a detrimental concentration; (2) if the food contains filth, is decomposed, or is otherwise unfit; (3) if the food was prepared or handled under unsanitary conditions such that it *may* have become contaminated; (4) if the food is derived from a diseased animal; (5) if the food was subjected to radiation, other than where permitted; (6) if any valuable constituent of the food is omitted; (7) if any specified ingredient has been substituted by a nonspecified ingredients; (8) if inferiority is concealed; (9) if the food is increased in its bulk weight or reduced in its strength making it appear better than it is; and (10) if the food contains a coloring agent that is not approved or certified.

Similarly, the Federal Pure Food Law says that a food is misbranded if any of the following exist:

(1) if labeling is false or misleading; (2) it goes by the name of another food; (3) it is an imitation of another food, unless the label connotes it as an imitation; (4) its container is made, formed, or filled so as to be misleading; (5) it is packaged and the label fails to list the name and address of the manufacturer, packer, or distributor, and if the label fails to give a statement of net contents; (6) if the label fails to declare the common name of the product, and the names of each ingredient (exceptions are made for spices, flavorings, colors, and preservatives as part of the food—their presence must be indicated but specific names need not be given); further, foods that have standards of identity need not list individual ingredients; (7) the product is misbranded if information is not legible and easily understood; (8) if the food is represented as a food for which there is a standard of identity but the food does not conform; (9) if the food is represented to con-

form to a quality standard or to a fill of container and doesn't conform; and (10) if the food is represented for special dietary use but the label fails to give information concerning its dietary properties as required by law.

With regard to misrepresentation, even beyond the broad range of possible abuses intended to be covered by the above, new kinds of food products and changing merchandising methods require frequent revision and strengthening of protective regulations. To this end, in 1966 the Federal Packaging and Labeling Act was enacted. This has also been referred to as the Fair Packaging and Labeling Bill, and the Truth in Packaging Law. This Bill further defines in precise terms the kinds of information that must appear on the labels of food packages, the size of type and the positions on labels and packages that may be used to convey information, and the kinds of designations and terms that would be misleading to the consumer and are therefore forbidden.

Regarding matters of food sanitation and general wholesomeness, here too regulations and guidelines are being frequently updated. In 1967 the FDA published in the Federal Register proposed regulations that have since become known as "Good Manufacturing Practices." After appropriate revisions a Code of GMP's went into effect in 1969. This Code defines requirements for acceptable sanitary operation in food plants. Appendices are being issued periodically to cover specific GMP's expected of different segments of the food industry. In the case of GMP's for manufacturers of smoked fish, for example, specified along with sanitation requirements are temperatures to be used before, during, and after processing as well as salt content to be used. Here in addition to general sanitation the GMP's are directed to minimize the hazard from botulism.

To help administer the law FDA representatives are authorized to inspect any and all aspects of food production, manufacture, warehousing, transportation, and sale, so long as the product enters interstate commerce. Malpractice can result in confiscation of the food, closing down of the plant, and fines or imprisonment. With regard to imported foods, all items must meet the Federal Pure Food Law requirements. Further, no exports may violate the laws of the country for which the food is intended. Since the laws of another country may be less strict than our own and the food manufactured accordingly, the law also requires that all foods for export be labelled for export.

In recent years the FDA has come under frequent attack on the charge that food inspections lag while reports of contamination and other abuses are on the increase. This charge is not without foundation but it is unjust in its implication. In 1971, the FDA had only 210 inspectors on its staff to cover some 60,000 food processing plants and food storage facilities. Thus, on the average a food plant could be inspected less than once in six years. Needed are substantial increases in budgets and personnel.

ADDITIONAL FOOD LAWS

Besides the Food, Drug, and Cosmetic Act of 1938 and its amendments, there are additional federal laws covering certain specific foods and food related areas. Some of these predate the Food, Drug, and Cosmetic Act of 1938. Illustrative are the Federal Meat Inspection Act, the Federal Poultry Products Inspection Act, and the Federal Trade Commission Act.

Federal Meat Inspection Act of 1906

This provides for mandatory inspection of animals, slaughtering conditions, and meat processing facilities. It helps ensure that meat and products containing meat are clean, wholesome, unadulterated, free from disease, and properly represented. Such products are stamped "U.S. Inspected and Passed by Department of Agriculture." All meat and meat products must bear this stamp to be permitted shipment in interstate commerce. The law also applies to imported meats. Authority is with the Meat Inspection Division, Agricultural Marketing Service of the Department of Agriculture. This law was strengthened following Upton Sinclair's famous book of 1906 *The Jungle* which revealed unsanitary conditions in the Chicago meat packing industry of that time.

Federal standards for meat under this law have been mandatory only for products crossing state lines. State and city meat regulations have always operated in matters of intrastate activity. But this has very recently been changed. For some years there has been growing awareness that state and city inspection and enforcement practices are not always equal to federal requirements and in extreme cases may fail to adequately protect the public safety. To correct this, in December 1967, the Wholesome Meat Act was passed by Congress. Under this new law all state and city meat inspection regulations must be upgraded to at least meet federal standards. Existing meat plants that do not now come up to these standards are being given a limited period of time to make the required construction and other sanitary changes or they will be forced to close down.

Federal Poultry Products Inspection Act of 1957

This is essentially the same as the Meat Inspection Act but applies to poultry and poultry products. The new Wholesome Meat Act has been essentially paralleled to cover poultry by the Wholesome Poultry Products Act of 1968.

The Federal Trade Commission Act (Amended for Food in 1938)

This protects the public as well as the food industry against any kind of false advertising related to foods or their alleged properties. This extends to newspapers, radio, television, or any other advertising media.

Federal Grade Standards

These are primarily standards of quality to help producers, dealers, wholesalers, retailers, and consumers in marketing and purchasing of food products. Establishment of grade standards and inspection programs come under the authority of the Agricultural Marketing Service of the Department of Agriculture. The grade standards, which were discussed in previous chapters, are not aimed at health protection but rather at ensuring value received by labeling products according to uniform quality standards. Federal law does not require this type of grading. Inspection and grading service is on a voluntary basis and may be performed by Federal Inspectors for a fee upon request of food producers or marketers.

State and Municipal Laws

Every state and many cities in the United States have their own food laws in addition to being subject to federal regulations. This is important since food produced and consumed within a state and not entering interstate commerce generally is not subject to federal laws. In practice, these state and city laws commonly are adopted or patterned after the federal laws. In addition, where needed, special regulations have been created to protect health, ensure sanitary practices, and prevent economic deception at specific operating levels, including eating establishments.

NONGOVERNMENT AGENCIES

The food laws of our nation incorporate the best thinking of scientists and lawmakers from industry, education, and government. To deal with difficult problems of policy and scientific judgments certain nongovernmental agencies have been established in the United States. These are supported by government funds and private contributions and are staffed by senior scientists who are appointed because of their outstanding abilities and generally give of their services without pay. These agencies maintain liaison with government and scientific societies in matters of food and nutrition, promote needed research, interpret research findings and their broad implications, and advise government. Such agencies which contribute to the strengthening of our food laws include: the Food and Nutrition Board of the National Academy of Sciences—National Research Council, the Food Protection Committee of the Food and Nutrition Board, and the Nutrition Foundation.

In matters of international scope two very important agencies include: the World Health Organization of the United Nations (WHO), and the Food and Agriculture Organization of the United Nations (FAO). These are organized to increase and improve food resources, nutrition, and health throughout the world. More will be said about FAO activities in these pursuits in Chap. 25.

INTERNATIONAL FOOD STANDARDS—CODEX ALIMENTARIUS

The conditions that existed between the states at the turn of the century and required unified federal food laws to promote safety, wholesomeness, and fair practices in interstate food trade have now reached major importance on an international basis. The scope of world food trade and the importance of its regulation can be judged from the fact that prior to 1962 over 135 organizations and agencies other than governments were working on international food standards and related problems.

The need for unification in this effort has long been recognized, and in 1962 an international body operating under the auspices of the United Nations through FAO/WHO was established and designated as the Codex Alimentarius Commission. The object of this Commission is "to develop international and regional food standards, and publish them in a Codex Alimentarius—or food code." The Codex Alimentarius is to include standards for all of the principal foods, whether of raw material or processed character. Included are to be "provisions in respect of food hygiene, food additives, pesticide residues, contaminants, labeling and presentation, methods of analysis, and sampling." Besides safety and wholesomeness aspects, Codex Standards are aimed at overcoming misuse

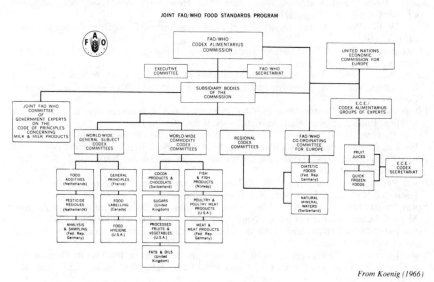

From Koenig (1966)

FIG. 318. COMMITTEES OF THE CODEX ALIMENTARIUS COMMISSION'S FOOD STANDARDS PROGRAM

of alleged food standards set up by some countries in the past, more to protect their products from the competition of imports than to protect the health of their citizens.

To carry out the work of the Codex Alimentarius Commission, various Codex Committees chaired by different countries and responsible for specific food areas have been established (Fig. 318). Participation in the program and acceptance of Codex Standards by individual countries is strictly voluntary. However, by 1966 a code of principles covering milk and milk products had been accepted by 66 countries. In 1971 Codex Alimentarius Standards for various fats and oils along with recommended test methods were released for acceptance or rejection by world governments. Presently several U.S. food standards of identity are being revised to bring them into agreement with proposals of the Codex Alimentarius and thus support the movement to international standards. The continuing work of the Commission, highly valuable to developing nations with as yet few food standards of their own, as well as to other countries whose standards may need updating, is another step towards protecting consumer health and facilitating world trade.

BIBLIOGRAPHY

ANON. 1956. Report of the joint FAO/WHO Expert Committee on Food Additives, First Session, Dec. 3–10, Rome, Italy.

ANON. 1961. Food Additives. What They Are, How They Are Used. Manufacturing Chemists Assoc., Washington, D.C.

CODY, W. F. 1969. Authoritative Effect of FDA Regulations. Food Drug Cosmetic Law J. 24, 195–209.

DESROSIER, N. W. 1970. The Technology of Food Preservation, 3rd Edition. Avi Publishing Co., Westport, Conn.

DUFFY, M. P. 1963. Federal and state regulation of processed foods. In Food Processing Operations, Vol. 2. M. A. Joslyn and J. L. Heid, (Editors). Avi Publishing Co., Westport, Conn.

FOOD PROTECTION COMMITTEE. 1959A. Principles and Procedures for Evaluating the Safety of Food Additives. Natl. Acad. Sci.—Natl. Res. Council Publ. 750.

FOOD PROTECTION COMMITTEE. 1959B. Problems in the Evaluation of Carcinogenic Hazards from Use of Food Additives. Natl. Acad. Sci.—Natl. Res. Council Publ. 749.

FOOD PROTECTION COMMITTEE. 1962. Radionuclides in Foods. Natl. Acad. Sci.—Natl. Res. Council Publ. 988.

FOOD PROTECTION COMMITTEE. 1963. New Developments and Problems in the Use of Pesticides. Natl. Acad. Sci.—Natl. Res. Council Publ. 1082.

FOOD PROTECTION COMMITTEE. 1964. An Evaluation of Public Health Hazards from Microbial Contamination of Foods. Natl. Acad. Sci.—Natl. Res. Council Publ. 1195.

FOOD PROTECTION COMMITTEE. 1965A. Chemicals Used in Food Processing. Natl. Acad. Sci.—Natl. Res. Council Publ. 1274.

FOOD PROTECTION COMMITTEE. 1965B. Some Considerations in the Use of Human Subjects in Safety Evaluation of Pesticides and Food Chemicals. Natl. Acad. Sci.—Natl. Res. Council Publ. 1270.

FOOD PROTECTION COMMITTEE. 1966A. The Food Chemicals Codex. Natl. Acad. Sci.—Natl. Res. Council.

FOOD PROTECTION COMMITTEE. 1966B. Toxicants Occurring Naturally in Foods. Natl. Acad. Sci.—Natl. Res. Council Publ. *1354*.

FOOD PROTECTION COMMITTEE. 1970. Evaluating the Safety of Food Chemicals. Natl. Acad. Sci.—Natl. Res. Council.

FREEDMAN, B. 1957. Sanitarian's Handbook, Theory and Administrative Practice. Peerless Publishing Co., New Orleans.

GASCOIGNE, C. E. 1971. Frozen Food Standards and Regulations—An Industry View. Food Technol. *25*, 522, 524, 526.

GUNDERSON, F. L., GUNDERSON, H. W., and FERGUSON, E. R., JR. 1963. Food Standards and Definitions in the United States—A Guidebook. Academic Press, New York.

HALL, R. L. 1971. GRAS Review and Food Additive Legislation. Food Technol. *25*, 466–470.

HAZLETON, L. W. 1962. What the food technologist should know about safety evaluation and toxicity testing. Food Technol. *16*, No. 4, 46–48.

HERRICK, A. D. 1947. Food Regulation and Compliance. Revere Publishing Co., New York.

KOENIG, N. 1966. Food standards for the world. *In* Protecting Our Food—The Yearbook of Agriculture 1966. U.S. Dept. Agr.

MCLAUGHLIN, F. E. 1966. The Food and Drug Administration. *In* Protecting Our Food—The Yearbook of Agriculture 1966. U.S. Dept. Agr.

NATENBERG, M. 1957. The Legacy of Doctor Wiley. Regent House, Chicago.

NATIONAL CANNERS ASSOCIATION. 1960. Modern Labels for Canned Foods. Natl. Canners Assoc., Washington, D. C.

PABLO, I. S., SINSKY, T. J., and SILVERMAN, G. L. 1967. Selection of microorganisms due to freeze-drying. Food Technol. *21*, 748–754.

POTTER, N. N. 1965. The AMFare automated restaurant system—sanitary aspects. N.Y. State Assoc. Milk Food Sanitarians, 39th Ann. Rept., 9–25.

POTTER, N. N. 1967. Newer food processing methods and microbial safety. N.Y. State Assoc. Milk Food Sanitarians, 41st Ann. Rept., 37–44.

SANDERS, H. J. 1966. Food additives. Part 1. Chem. Eng. News *44*, No. 42, 100–120; Part 2, No. 43, 108–128.

SANDERS, H. J. 1971. Food Additive Makers Face Intensified Attack. Chem. Eng. News *49*, No. 28, 16–20, 23.

WALKER, H. W. 1971. Good Manufacturing Practices—Review and Discussion. Food Technol. *25*, 518–520.

WODICKA, V. O. 1972. Wodicka Brings Message from FDA. Food Eng. *44*, No. 1, 58–61.

WORLD HEALTH ORGANIZATION. 1970. Specifications for the Identity and Purity of Food Additives and Their Toxicological Evaluation. WHO Tech. Rept. Ser. *445*. World Health Organ., Geneva.

ZIEMBA, J. V., and ALIKONIS, J. J. 1972. What's Happening with Food Additives. Food Eng. *44*, No. 1, 80–83, 85–86, 88.

CHAPTER 24

Improving Nutritional Quality: Nutritional Labeling

INTRODUCTION

The safety, quality, and honest representation of the U.S. food supply, always subject to scrutiny, criticism, and improvement, has come under especially heavy attack in recent years. In addition to the wide range of difficult and often controversial questions discussed in the previous chapter, safety, quality, and honest representation extend to the nutritional attributes of foods. At the time of this writing it is fair to say that no food-related issue is receiving more attention than the question of the nutritional quality of the U.S. food supply especially with respect to products that have been highly processed. Since the 1969 and 1971 White House Conferences on Food, Nutrition and Health, there has been a kind of nutritional awareness revolution in the making; and along with this an unprecedented amount of energy is being directed toward means of communicating meaningful nutritional information to increasingly sensitized consumers. Terms such as "empty calories" charged against breakfast cereals, and "bellywash" directed against juiceless fruit-type drinks have strongly aroused consumers. There is now increasing demand for nutritional product improvement and nutritional labeling, and in some cases this is strongly justified.

The complexities inherent in nutritional product improvement and nutritional labeling are remarkably diverse. It therefore is not surprising that opinions and recommendations currently being advanced by consumerists, consumers, food manufacturers and distributors, nutritionists, and governmental agencies frequently are not in agreement. In a sense the issue of nutritional product improvement and nutritional labeling is like the proverbial iceberg. What lies above the surface is readily apparent. The consumer has a right to the best nutritional quality that science and technology can economically provide, and a right to *know* the nutritional attributes of her food purchases. But hidden beneath these obvious rights are innumerable problems in providing substantive nutritional improvements and relevant consumer information that is accurate, comprehensible, and not misleading. Further, from the standpoint of the food industry, nutritional guidelines now being developed by government must be such as to prohibit unethical competitive merchandising practices, yet retain a climate conducive to nutritional product improvement through reformulation, enrichment, or fortification where real advantages can be gained.

652

Current efforts by governmental agencies to draft meaningful guidelines are being frustrated by many factors. In addition to numerous gaps in the state of present nutritional knowledge, these include political and economic considerations as well as the problems of educating the public in matters of nutritional relevance. Problems that must be faced by food processors with regard to raw material selection, manufacturing operations, and overall quality control to assure validity of nutritional label declarations are no less formidable. The nature of these problems must be understood by today's food scientist.

FOODS ARE CHANGING

One might ask, why has there developed an intensification of interest in nutrition in recent years? Have foods become less nutritious? Has the food industry become less ethical? Some answers can be given. If one refers back to Fig. 10 of Chap. 2 one sees how food was marketed in the early 1900's, and this still is essentially the way food is sold in many less technologically developed countries. Commodities were easily recognizable, and those consumers who understood that a varied diet of plant and animal products provided the necessities for health did not have difficulty in identifying such products when they were available. While this early type of marketing certainly did not guarantee a nutritionally adequate diet it stood in sharp contrast to today's supermarket with its thousands of different items, most of which are highly processed convenience foods often obscured in terms of their component ingredients.

Today more food preparations are appearing that contain meat analogues or meat substitutes. Fabricated meat structures from soybean and other proteins (previous Fig. 5, Chap. 1) can be interlaced with fats and other ingredients to provide the widest spectrum of nutrient composition. Without some kind of nutritional information or minimum standard that such products should meet, the consumer can't possibly know the nutritional attributes of the many products possible using this new technology.

An example from products belonging to the group sometimes designated as nondairy imitation milks is further informative. A large number of such products, generally formulated from vegetable oils, sugars, and proteins of dairy and other origin have appeared in recent years. While some of these products have been formulated to resemble milk in terms of amounts of protein, carbohydrate, and fat, others do not come close to milk's gross composition, and few even approach milk in terms of vitamin and mineral content. Thus, in one recent comprehensive study of 13 commercial nondairy imitation milks it was found that several of the samples contained less than 20% and some less than 10% of the riboflavin or thiamine content of cow's milk. The study further revealed gross deficiencies in levels of total protein, essential amino acids, calcium, and other nutrients for which milk is generally consumed. Alarmingly, 4 of the 13 samples contained less than 5% of the calcium present in cow's milk. Here certainly is a case for informative nutritional labeling, or some minimum standard of nutritional quality, since such products used in place of milk could lead to serious problems, especially among the young.

There presently are marketed numerous drinks that may or may not contain natural fruit juices in their formulation. The FDA and various states have set standards that include minimum contents of natural juices required in such products. Classifications of the FDA for orange juices and drinks have specified the following percentages of single-strength juice in the different products: orange juice—100%, orange juice drink—not less than 50% of orange juice present, orangeade—not less than 25%, orange drink—not less than 10%, orange soda—no juice required, imitation orange—no juice required. These classifications have been the target of much criticism on the grounds that they are not understood by the consumer and tend to misrepresent the real value of the products. Alternate designations for such products are being considered. Since orange juice commonly is consumed for its vitamin C content many believe that such products (as well as orange juice) should be required to display accurate information with respect to this vitamin on their labels.

One could cite numerous additional examples of foods that no longer resemble their generic counterparts in terms of nutritional attributes. This alone explains much of the current interest in nutrition and makes opposition to some form of nutritional labeling a very difficult position to defend.

INFORMATION NEEDED

The Food and Drug Administration, in cooperation with the National Research Council's Food and Nutrition Board and the food industry, has been gathering information as the basis for guidelines on nutritional labeling and fortification or enrichment practices for various classes of foods. These classes include minimally processed commodities, prepared meals, fabricated foods and analogs, breakfast cereals, and other important groups. Problems that are being given consideration include the following. What kinds of information should labels provide? Suggestions have ranged from mandatory fortification and complete listing of kinds and amounts of all essential nutrients in a given food, including trace minerals, to optional declaration of only the most important nutrients for which a food is a recognized major source. Should enrichment or fortification of major commodities be encouraged, and if so how much of which nutrients should be permitted in what commodity? Should fabricated foods be made nutritionally complete, and if so on what basis should vitamins and minerals be permitted? Obviously if a large number of foods are enriched to provide a substantial percentage of a nutrient's Recommended Dietary Allowance per serving, persons are likely to receive the nutrient in excess, which at best is wasteful, but more serious, may be physiologically harmful as with vitamin D, vitamin A, and iron. Some have suggested a food's caloric content as the base for nutrient supplementation levels on the logic that daily caloric intake is rather constant for an individual. Such a scheme would tend to promote balanced nutrition in proportion to the quantity of food consumed, but independent of dietary selection. Others have suggested that protein content of a food be included along with calories as a basis for permitted levels of added vitamins and minerals.

If protein is to be declared on labels as most agree it should, should the listing ultimately be of gross quantity, amino acid composition, or some other measure of protein quality? The consumer will draw confidence from figures designating gross quantity, but then will she appreciate the nutritional differences between various proteins, including animal and vegetable proteins in formulated products? Most will not. Nor will extensive lists of amino acids be readily comprehensible to her. Should iron be listed in terms of amount or physiological availability? In any event what analytical methods shall be deemed officially acceptable for purposes of quality control and inspection? What about changes in food standards of identity to allow nutrient additions where they are not presently permitted?

COMMUNICATION AND CONSUMER EDUCATION

As important as any of the above are the questions of communication and consumer education. Imposing lists of nutrients by themselves will prove confusing even to the moderately informed. It is becoming generally agreed that the purpose of nutritional labeling is to help the homemaker toward informed selection of nutritionally sound foods for balanced meal planning. Simplicity is to be favored over more specific data that would be required by a dietitian, and would be available to the dietitian from the manufacturer upon request. But then what is simple?

One possible kind of informative labeling wouldn't list nutrients but would simply list ingredients in the food. An example would be the listing of major ingredients and their percentages in a frozen or canned beef and vegetable stew. Brand X might then differ from Brand Y in containing 2% more beef, 3% more carrots, 6% less peas, 10% less potatoes, and 11% more water. But is the information really informative? The higher levels of beef and carrots, and the lower level of starchy potatoes in Brand X might be considered favorably by the consumer. But Brand X also has less protein-containing peas and more water. How should these be balanced? Such labeling would not only leave the average consumer in doubt but would give a trained nutritionist difficulty in deciding between the two products on nutritional grounds.

Additional simplified labeling schemes have been suggested and three have received thorough study to determine which would be most meaningful to all segments of the population.

The first of the three labeling schemes used percentages of the Recommended Dietary Allowances (see Table 8, Chap. 4) of the major nutrients actually present in a typical portion of a given food product. Here, still unresolved are questions arising from the fact that the Recommended Dietary Allowance values for various nutrients differ for children and adults.

The second system was similar to the first, but percentages were replaced by units. Thus, for example, a food portion containing 50% of a nutrient's Recommended Dietary Allowance listed 5 units, while another food containing 100% would list 10 units for that particular nutrient.

The third system used descriptive terms such as "fair," "good," "very good," or "excellent" corresponding to a list of important nutrients present in a serving of the food. Such a system would require FDA establishment of quantitative ranges for the important nutrients that correspond to the descriptive terms to prevent nonuniform use of terms by different manufacturers.

These labeling systems also included data on the actual amounts in grams of protein, carbohydrate, fat, and calories present in a portion of the food, and a general statement of the type "If you want more detailed information on the nutritional composition of the product write to . . ." and the address of the manufacturer.

These system proposals were considered for relative merits by food manufacturers, trade associations, advertising agencies, and were consumer tested. The study showed that some form of nutritional labeling was favored by the majority of consumers involved and that most consumers preferred a labeling scheme that utilized percentages of the Recommended Dietary Allowance for nutrients plus amount data for protein, carbohydrate, fat, and calories. These findings were incorporated into proposed rules for nutritional labeling that were published in the Federal Register on March 30, 1972. More will be said about these proposed rules shortly.

KNOWLEDGE GAPS

Quite apart from the problems of communication, a move to nutritional supplementation of foods and nutritional labeling immediately focuses attention upon present gaps in knowledge. The acquisition of nutritional data has not kept up with the rate of technological development of new food products and processes in recent years, and so a knowledge gap will have to be closed before there can be a major shift to nutritional product improvement and labeling.

Reference guides to food compositions, such as *Handbook 8* of the U.S. Dept. of Agr., will not be adequate for calculation of nutrient levels in a great many food products currently marketed. In many instances handbook values do not apply to new varieties of fruits and vegetables, or to changing geographic growing regions, harvest times, and degrees of maturity—all being influenced more and more by mechanical harvesting and special processing requirements. Nor do classical handbook values necessarily reflect nutrient changes from advanced storage methods, processing conditions, or reconstitution techniques. They do not contain data on manufactured proprietary products such as complex mixtures of ingredients, ethnic and snack foods, or food analogs. It may surprise some that one cannot now look up the nutrient composition of frozen pizza, fried egg rolls, canned soups, or various cake mixes and come away with reliable information. To be sure, nutrient compositions of many canned soups are listed in *Handbook 8* of the U.S. Dept. of Agr., but new formulations and changes in ingredients since its publication in 1963 limit accuracy. Further, many of the ethnic and regional foods for which data do not now exist are important items in the diets of poorly nourished poverty groups. Thus, the eating habits of American Indians, Mexican Americans, and certain Negro groups will have to receive special attention.

Handbook data also frequently fail to account for the food in the final form in which it will be eaten. Nutrient values for pork, chicken, or most other foods depend upon the cut, degree of trim, and extent of processing, including whether cooked at home or precooked and held on steam tables, as done with many institutional products.

The list of products for which nutritional data is presently inadequate is really quite formidable. An indication was given by Watt and Murphy in the June 1970 issue of *Food Technology*. Watt is the senior author of *Handbook 8* of the U.S. Dept. of Agr., entitled *Composition of Foods—Raw, Processed, Prepared*. Among various food groups inadequate nutritional data were cited in numerous specific areas.

Thus, in the past, the food industry generally was not concerned with quantitative data on the vitamin and mineral contents of raw or processed meat, poultry, or fish, and so new data will be required. This is especially true of meats other than beef, and for turkey in all its forms.

With regard to bread and other wheat products, data must be extended to cover breads made by the continuous mix method. Still less is known about the nutrient contents of sweet rolls, raised doughnuts, bagels, pretzels, pizzas, and farina. What losses are to be expected when different types of macaroni, spaghetti, and noodles are cooked and drained? Ingredients differ in cake, cookie, pie crust, muffin, and other convenience mixes. This includes differences in kinds and amounts of fats for shortening. Adequate data also are lacking on different kinds and forms of rice.

Among fruits and vegetables data are needed on new varieties of citrus fruits. Little is now available on the nutrient contents of varieties of avocados. Sweet potato varieties differ in vitamin A content, and are affected differently by storage. This also is true of carrots. New varieties of tomatoes have been introduced that are especially suited to mechanical harvesting. Their contents of vitamins C and A, and their sensitivities to processing losses need more study. New white potato varieties with high solids and nitrogen contents are being developed and will require investigation to determine nutrient changes during storage and processing. With regard to the considerable number of canned fruit and vegetable products, much of the nutritional data in the literature is based on intensive studies of the early 1940's. How have processing changes affected current products?

We know still less about a number of new products that have gained wide acceptance. Among these are coffee whiteners in liquid, powder, and frozen forms; dessert toppings; frozen desserts; canned puddings; dry roasted nuts; products containing soybean derivatives or freeze-dried components; snack foods; etc. The FDA already has indicated that for purposes of nutritional labeling not handbook values but direct analyses on specific products will generally be required. Certainly no less would be adequate where raw materials, formulations, and processing conditions rarely remain static.

Gaps in our knowledge go far beyond compositional data. We do not know enough about the influences of functional food additives on important nutrients. For example, what effects do chelating agents have on trace minerals, or phosphates upon calcium in processed foods? Methods of analysis will have to be improved or devised to yield rapid and accurate results despite interfering substances in complex formulations. If amino acid compositions are ever to be listed on labels then much research will be required on more reliable protein hydrolysis techniques, which yield variable results depending upon degree of completeness and severity. Basic studies involving animal feeding tests will be required if nutrient utilization information is ever to become part of nutritional labeling.

NEW RESPONSIBILITIES

Certainly nutritional labeling will place a whole new set of responsibilities upon industry. When a manufacturer lists a nutrient and its concentration on a product label he will be responsible for the accuracy of the declaration. Further, to be meaningful, the declaration surely will have to describe the food as close to the time of consumption as feasible, rather than the product's nutrient content as manufactured. Some tolerance with respect to amount will have to be allowed, but it is doubtful that more than perhaps a 20% discrepancy on the low side of a stated nutrient level will be permitted. Thus, nutrient labelers will have to maintain an active testing and quality control program to ensure nutritional values on final products in the marketplace.

Quality assurance programs will have to include controls over nutritional specifications of purchased ingredients, ingredient storage, all phases of processing, and product storage including warehousing, supermarket turnover, and expected holding time by the customer where feasible. Where a product is manufactured for wide range distribution, the possible effects of climate on storage stability of nutrients will have to be taken into account. These problems are not new to manufacturers of breakfast cereals and dietetic foods, but can add significantly to the production rigors of canners, freezers, and others choosing to use nutritional labeling.

Today readily available components of manufactured foods often are purchased on short notice to take advantage of changing prices. Functionally interchangeable ingredients also are substituted for one another as availability changes with season of the year. It also is common for a manufacturer to adjust processing temperatures and times to compensate for varying raw materials. Such practices will be more difficult with nutritional labeling, as will be application of any processing innovation that may affect the validity of label statements.

Manufacturers wishing to declare nutrient composition will face additional difficulties with regard to physical space on labels. This can be a greater problem with bottles and cans than with flat packages. Products that have standards of identity need not now list ingredient composition, which simplifies labeling. A separate question, but one that is directly related to label space, is whether food standards of identity ultimately will be changed to incorporate nutritional limits. Would nutritional labeling of standardized products for consumer information then become a subsequent requirement?

Certainly nutritional labeling will become a powerful factor in the competitive marketing of foods. This will force government to carefully consider equity in the granting of enrichment or fortification rights to various classes of products. For example, today certain vitamins can legally be added to margarine but not to butter. The butter industry considers this unfair, and there are many similar examples with other products. This type of inequity will become more important as consumers increasingly seek out the nutritional attributes of different products.

The nutritional value of certain foods has been subject to adjustment for many years. Vitamin D is added to milk, iodine to salt, and flour is enriched with thiamine, riboflavin, niacin, and iron for the making of bread. More recently some major manufacturers of crackers and snack foods have begun using enriched flour in their cookie, cracker, and snack food items. Several breakfast cereals have provided substantial quantities of vitamins and iron for years. But a great deal more is coming and research and development laboratories of major food companies are intensively working at nutrition. In fact, one of their current problems is to restrain their marketing divisions, many of which are pressing for the widest variety of nutritionally adjusted new products.

Government's role in providing and enforcing nutritional guidelines will not be an easy one. Government will be caught between various interest groups. Some of the current activities related to improving the nutritional quality of meals fed to school children illustrate this.

Public demands for nutritionally adequate breakfasts and lunches in federally subsidized school feeding programs have been intensified, especially since the White House Conferences on Food, Nutrition, and Health. The U.S. Dept. of Agr. has set criteria for fortified and extended foods that can be used in its school feeding programs. Criteria have been developed for three kinds of new products. One is a fortified baked product with a cream filling that should appeal to children. It can serve as a replacement for fruit or juice and bread or cereal in school breakfasts. This product with $1/2$ pt of milk will supply $1/4$ to $1/3$ of the Recommended Dietary Allowance for a 10- to 12-yr old child. Obviously fruit, juice, and cereal interests can be affected. A second product for school lunches is a protein-fortified, enriched, macaroni-type product that can nutritionally replace $1/2$ of the present 2-oz requirement for meat, poultry, cheese, or fish. The third type of product is meat extended with texturized vegetable protein up to a level of 30% of the product by weight. These will help schools provide nutrition at a cost that might otherwise be limiting. The meat and related industries can be affected in these latter two cases.

A large number of food companies already are supplying texturized soy protein or soy-extended meat products to schools. At least one major baking company has developed cream-filled fortified baked products that meet U.S. Dept. of Agr. criteria. At least two fortified macaroni-type products also have been developed for school feeding purposes. Here standards of identity were an obstacle to approval of this kind of product. Standards of identity for macaroni define ingredients that may be used in products recognized as macaroni. A new standard of identity was proposed for fortified macaroni by the Food and Drug Administration but it was met by objections from various interests in the macaroni industry. A similar situation has existed with fortified peanut butter, and many new and nutritionally exciting products will undoubtedly have to fight their way into commercial existence against regulations that were originally adopted to ensure food quality of another kind, as well as to protect specific commodity and food industry interests.

But a more general problem that government faces in this complex area of fortification, enrichment, and nutritional labeling is to devise rules to regulate what product claims a manufacturer may properly make on labels and in advertising. Here a special set of guidelines will be required. Today relatively few food products are promoted on the basis of nutrition. Along with fortification and nutritional labeling will come an increasing motivation to use statements such as "a balanced meal in a can," or "nutritionally equivalent to a steak dinner," or "complete nourishment for the athlete," and the like. Such statements, and still more subtle ones, will require much wisdom on the part of the FDA and the Federal Trade Commission for their regulation.

PROPOSED NUTRITIONAL LABELING RULES

As stated earlier, on March 30, 1972 the FDA published its proposed nutritional labeling rules in the Federal Register for reaction and comment. It is to be expected that these guidelines and criteria will undergo modification with time but provide the basis for future nutritional labeling regulation. Sections from these proposed rules are reproduced below:

The Commissioner has concluded, on the basis of the information available at the present time, that nutrition labeling should be based on the following general criteria:

1. Vitamins and minerals should be expressed as a proportion of the Recommended Daily Allowances (RDA) modified to provide a single RDA level for all ages and sexes.

2. The labeling should indicate the caloric content and the amounts of protein, carbohydrate, and fat in the product.

3. The nutrition content should be related to a portion or serving of the food expressed in common household terms or in easily identified units.

4. A complete listing of the seven important vitamins and minerals should appear on all products unless the product contains essentially none of these vitamins or minerals.

5. A listing of protein content should appear on all products unless the product contains no protein.

Listing protein in terms of both the amount present in the product and a percentage of the RDA offers consumers maximum information. Concern has been expressed that protein quality should be incorporated into this statement. Such a protein quality factor could be established by requiring that any protein with a quality less than that of casein must reduce the claimed contribution by the factor obtained by dividing 100 into the protein quality of the protein expressed as a percentage of the quality of casein as determined in standard protein evaluation tests and then multiplying the actual protein content by this factor. This calculation would give the amount of protein to be used in determining the percentage of RDA for the protein. A lower limit could also be set for any statement relating to protein quality; for example, no protein with a quality less than 50% of casein could be stated on the label in terms of the percentage of RDA. This approach offers maximum information but is complicated both for the manufacturer and for the consumer. Comment is particularly requested on this question.

The Commissioner also requests that comments be provided by interested groups and individuals on whether it would be most useful to consumers for protein, carbohydrate, and fat content to be stated by percentage, by weight, or by grams per portion.

The Commissioner is aware that there is variation in the natural nutrient content of food products. In developing a nutrition labeling system, it is therefore important that the manufacturer be permitted a sufficient tolerance so that he may provide useful nutrition information on the label without incurring excess costs for quality control which will result in a significant increase in prices to the consumer. However, consumers will expect that the nutrition labels will honestly represent the product. By using a percentage of the RDA expressed in increments of 5 to 10%, some of the variation in products can be accommodated. In addition, for the purposes of nutrition labeling, the statement will be considered in compliance if at least 80% of the product in the package meets or exceeds the claimed nutrient levels, and if no sample of the product will have a nutrient content less than 80% of the nutrient claim.

Finally, manufacturers frequently ask where to print nutrition labeling and other related information which is not required on the principal display panel. It is important that such information appear in a uniform location so that consumers will have it readily available. Uniformity in displaying such information will make it more easily found and read by consumers under normal conditions of purchase and use. For a number of years canners have utilized an information panel for serving sizes and other pertinent information concerning the contents of a can. Breakfast cereal manufacturers have primarily utilized one panel for nutrition information. An information panel, as well as the principal display panel, is a suitable location for nutrition information. The Commissioner therefore proposes to define the information panel as that part of the label immediately to the right of the principal display panel. If the package has alternate display panels the information panel may appear to the right of either. If the top of the container is the principal display panel, and there is no alternate principal display panel, the information panel is any part of the label adjacent to the top.

§ 1.16 Food; nutrition labeling.

(a) Nutrition information relating to a packaged food may be included on the label of the product provided that it conforms to the requirements of this section.

(b) All nutrient quantities including vitamins, minerals, calories, protein, fats, and carbohydrates shall be declared in relation to the average or usual serving expressed in common household measurements or in terms of a unit which is easily identified as an average or usual serving. The weight of the serving may also be expressed in grams. The declaration shall contain the following items:

(1) The heading shall be "Nutrition Information."

(2) A statement of the serving size shall be given.

(3) A statement of the caloric content per serving shall be expressed to the nearest 5-calorie increment.

(4) A statement of the number of grams of protein, fat, and available carbohydrates per serving shall be expressed to the nearest gram.

(5) A statement of the amounts per serving of the vitamins and minerals listed in

paragraph (c) of this section shall be expressed in percentages of the Recommended Dietary Allowances (RDA) as stated in paragraph (d) of this section. The percentages are expressed in 10-percent increments, except that 5-percent increments may be used up to the 20-percent level. Nutrients present in an amount comprising less than 5 percent of the RDA shall be considered insignificant and will be so listed under the RDA percentage. However, if a product does not contain at least 5 percent of the RDA for any of the vitamins or minerals listed in paragraph (c), the statement, "Contains no significant quantities of vitamins and minerals," may be used in place of the complete listing of the vitamins and minerals required in paragraph (c). The listing shall follow the order given in paragraph (c).

(6) A statement of the amount of protein present per serving shall be expressed as a percentage of the 65 gram RDA. The percentages are expressed in 10-percent increments, except that 5-percent increments may be used up to the 20-percent level. Protein present in an amount less than 5 percent of the RDA shall be considered insignificant. In such cases, the amount of protein will be represented either as 0 percent of the RDA or by the words "none" or "insignificant," whichever is appropriate. However, if a product contains no protein, the protein expressed as a percent of the RDA need not be listed.

(c) In the case of vitamins and minerals, the label declaration must contain information on vitamin A, vitamin C, thiamine, riboflavin, niacin, calcium, and iron and may contain information on any of the other vitamins and minerals listed in paragraph (d) of this section.

(d) For the purposes of nutrition labeling, the following daily amounts of vitamins and minerals are the standard Recommended Daily Allowances (RDA):

	(International Units)
Vitamin A	5,000
Vitamin D	400
Vitamin E	30
	(Milligrams)
Ascorbic acid (vitamin C)	60
Thiamine (vitamin B_1)	1.5
Riboflavin (vitamin B_2)	1.7
Niacin	20
Vitamin B_6	2
Folacin (folic acid)	0.4
Vitamin B_{12}	0.006
Biotin	0.3
Pantothenic acid	10
Calcium	1,000
Phosphorus	1,000
Iron	18
Iodine	0.15
Zinc	15
Magnesium	400
Copper	2

These nutrient levels have been adopted by the Food and Drug Administration from information in a report of the Food and Nutrition Board, National Academy of Sciences—National Research Council, *Recommended Dietary Allowances, Seventh Edition, 1968.*

(e) A statement may be included offering additional information upon written request to a specified address. Any such additional labeling shall comply with all the requirements of Part 1 and, if applicable, Part 125 of this chapter.

(f) The location of the nutrition information on the label shall be in compliance with § 1.8d.

At the present time the decision by a manufacturer to adopt nutritional labeling is voluntary, but there is pressure to ultimately make it mandatory for at least certain foods. The FDA also has stated that where manufacturers elect to use nutritional labeling they will have to conform to a single approved system. Nonuniform nutritional labeling that would result in consumer confusion will not be permitted. Guidelines to regulate nutrient additions to various classes of foods also will be forthcoming.

The consumer does indeed have a right to improved nutrition and the right to know. But to secure these rights added costs will have to be borne by the consumer. The benefits that can be derived from nutritional upgrading and nutritional labeling intelligently applied can outweigh the costs. It is doubtful that all foods warrant nutritional supplementation or nutritional labeling, and those that do surely do so to different extents.

In the years ahead the food manufacturer will have to become increasingly concerned about nutrition. What must not be permitted, however, is a nutritional arms race encouraged by overzealous consumerists and waged by insufficiently informed and prepared manufacturers eyeing a lucrative market. This would only serve to penalize the consumer and discredit the food industry.

BIBLIOGRAPHY

ANON. 1970. White House Conference on Food, Nutrition and Health—Final Report. U.S. Govt. Printing Office, Washington, D.C.

ANON. 1971. Philosophy and guidelines for nutritional standards for processed foods. Food Technol. 25, 36, 38.

BABCOCK, M. J. 1971. A proposed system for nutritive labeling. Food Technol. 25, 1160–1161.

CALL, D. L., and HAYES, M. G. 1970. Reactions of nutritionists to nutrient labeling of foods. Am. J. Clin. Nutr. 23, 1347–1352.

DEUTSCH, R. M. 1971. The Family Guide to Better Food and Better Health. Meredith Corp., Des Moines, Iowa.

FLECK, H., and MUNVES, E. 1969. Introduction to Nutrition. Macmillan Co., New York.

FOOD AND DRUG ADMINISTRATION, DEPT. OF HEALTH, EDUCATION AND WELFARE. 1972. Nutrition labeling—proposed criteria for food label information panel. Federal Register 37, No. 62, 6493–6497.

HARRIS, R. S., and VON LOESECKE, H. (Editors) 1960. Nutritional Evaluation of Food Processing. Reprinted in 1971 by Avi Publishing Co., Westport, Conn.

HOWARD, H. W. 1971. What useful purpose is served by quantitative ingredient labeling? Food Prod. Develop. 5, No. 4, 34, 36, 38.

KOSIKOWSKI, F. V. 1971. Nutritive and organoleptic characteristics of nondairy imitation milks. J. Food Sci. 36, 1021–1025.

LACHANCE, P. A.   1970.   Nutrification, a new nutritional concept for new types of foods. Food Technol. *24,* 724.
LACHANCE, P. A.   1971.   Innovation vs. nutrition as the criterion for product development. Food Technol. *25,* 615–617.
MCINTIRE, J. M.   1972.   Proposes nutritional guidelines for formulated meals—foods of the future. Food Technol. *26,* No. 4, 34, 36, 39, 42.
NAT. ACAD. SCI.—NAT. RES. COUNCIL.   1968.   Recommended Dietary Allowances. Natl. Res. Council Publ. *1694.*
POTTER, N. N.   1972.   Problems related to the nutritional labeling of food products. J. Milk Food Technol. *35,* No. 2, 107–111.
ROBINSON, C. H.   1967.   Proudfit-Robinson's Normal and Therapeutic Nutrition. Macmillan Co., New York.
U.S. DEPT. AGR.   1969.   Food for Us All, The Yearbook of Agriculture. U.S. Dept. Agr.
WATT, B. K., and MERRILL, A. L.   1963.   Composition of Foods—Raw, Processed, Prepared. U.S. Dept. Agr., Agr. Handbook *8.*
WATT, B. K., and MURPHY, E. W.   1970.   Tables of food composition: scope and needed research. Food Technol. *24,* 674–676, 678, 682–684.

CHAPTER 25

World Food Needs

INTRODUCTION

History and circumstance have been abundantly generous to a minority of the world's population. In the United States and a relatively few other countries such factors as suitable land, favorable climate, natural resources, and the application of science and technology under circumstances of advantageous marketing opportunity have produced a seemingly boundless food supply with respect to quantity and kind. But this is not the situation throughout most of the world. Contrasts are strikingly cruel, and from a position of plenty sometimes almost impossible to comprehend.

In their 1967 three-volume report, *The World Food Problem,* the Panel on World Food Supply of the President's Science Advisory Committee stated—

"We have been unable to devise any new or original statement of the world food problem. The subject has been treated so thoroughly in orations and editorials during the past two decades that both its size and significance tend to be obscured by rhetorical overkill." The report, however, continues . . . "The scale, severity, and duration of the world food problem is so great that a massive, long-range, innovative effort unprecedented in human history will be required to master it."

The above statement reflects the awareness and concern over world food shortages that were shared by all nations during the 1960's. While hunger and famine are as old as human experience, it was during this decade especially that the global significance of lagging food production at a time of exploding world population was brought into sobering focus.

Toward the end of the decade a new hope emerged, and the term "green revolution" was coined. Through the intensive cultivation of genetically improved varieties of wheat and rice enormous increases in yields of these grains were achieved in a number of countries. Some believe that this green revolution already has checked what only a very few years ago was feared to be the beginning of a world food crisis. Others, however, have stated that the recent substantial increases in grain yields, even if sustained, can provide only temporary relief from the hunger problem unless comparable gains are made in the production of many additional foods. Further, the technological changes responsible for the green revolution have not yet been adopted by many developing countries, may not be applicable in others, and already are causing serious economic and social problems where peasant farmers are being displaced by large land owners who can better afford the costs of technological change.

Notwithstanding the recent gains, the world food problem continues to be recognized today by leaders of government, industry, and enlightened citizens of all countries. A very substantial positive effort is now in progress but no one cognizant of the enormity of the challenge would say that more than a beginning has yet been made toward narrowing the gap between world food production and population rise. Thus, without minimizing the progress that has been made in some regions through the application of new technology, the Food and Agriculture Organization of the United Nations in their publication *The State of Food and Agriculture 1971* stated—

"But this is not yet a green revolution. Even in the most successful countries, mainly in the Far East, the increases in wheat and rice yields and output have not been matched by similar increases in the production of other foods. And in other regions intensive yield-raising programmes, with a few significant exceptions, are only at a very early stage, if they have been started at all. Perhaps the most telling indication of the precariousness of the food supply situation in much of the developing world is the large number of requests that FAO receives for emergency food relief, particularly from African countries. It is true that emergencies can always arise because of the fickleness of the weather. But many countries are still unable to cope even with what must be considered normal fluctuations in output."

PARAMETERS OF THE PROBLEM

While there have been considerable differences of opinion among experts with regard to the most productive approaches to the world food problem, and what priorities should be established in specific areas, some conclusions against which current and future action plans must be judged seem inescapable from data gathered largely by the Food and Agriculture Organization.

(1) The world's existing food supply, according to the best current sources of information, is inadequate for the present population. This would continue to be true even if it could somehow be equally distributed among the people of the world.

(2) Population in developing countries is currently increasing more rapidly than food production and so the overall shortage in these countries is becoming more acute.

(3) About 80% of the world's agriculturally productive land is already under cultivation; the remaining 20% is of poorer productivity. The food resources of the sea have as yet been only partially exploited, but great starving masses are isolated from the sea.

(4) Where population increase and starvation are greatest, agricultural yields from land and animals are lowest. This can be greatly improved through intensive application of technology, but where technology is needed most there is the least capital with which to obtain it.

(5) Developed countries do not have sufficient surpluses for export to feed all of the

hungry. Even if they did the problems of getting the food to areas of local need would preclude this as a feasible long range solution.

(6) Free enterprise with a profit-making incentive has proven to be the most effective boon to production, including food production. Technology, equipment, fertilizers, and pesticides are more important exports to less developed countries than food surpluses. Where they are needed most, the capital to purchase them is in shortest supply.

(7) Where hunger is most severe radical approaches would be expected to get quickest results. Yet these are the very regions where illiteracy, conservatism, and tradition frequently resist the acceptance of new methods.

(8) Where hunger is prevalent it exists in large cities as well as in villages. Education of villagers and farmers in food production can help a local region grow more food, but without simultaneous development of transportation, preservation, processing, and marketing systems no major long range improvement in the food situation can be made.

Unfortunately failure like success feeds upon itself and tends to become more extreme. The causes and factors contributing to starvation generally are interrelated so as to form a descending cycle in which poverty perpetuates illiteracy and poor health, which leads to low productivity, which in turn supports only more poverty. Currently there are about 3.7 billion people in the world with more than half of them ill fed, and in some areas up to 50% of newborn children fail to survive to school age due to inade-

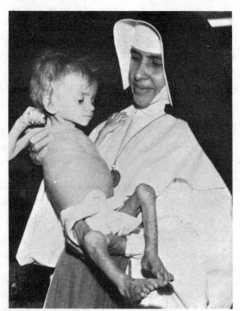

Courtesy of Senator G. S. McGovern

FIG. 319. A SCENE AT ALBERGUE SANTO ANTONIO HOSPITAL, BAHIA STATE, BRAZIL

THE "POPULATION EXPLOSION"

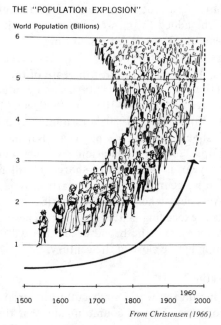

From Christensen (1966)

FIG. 320. THE "POPULATION EXPLOSION"

quate nutrition and its associated diseases (Fig. 319). At the present rate of growth world population is expected to well exceed 6 billion by the year 2000. Current rates of food production are not yet keeping pace. Fairly good estimates have been made regarding the extent to which food production and distribution must be increased if population growth is not curbed and mass starvation is to be prevented in the years ahead. But the problems are sufficiently complex so that no one can presently say with any degree of certainty whether projected goals can indeed be met. A closer look at the various aspects of the problem illustrates the interrelationships that exist and must not be lost sight of in developing aid programs most likely to be effective.

Population Trends

A graphic representation of the time-population increase curve from 1500 AD to the present, and projected to the year 2000 is given in Fig. 320. While it took about 230 yr for the world population of 1600 AD to double from approximately a half billion to 1 billion people, only 100 yr were required for population to double again by 1930. If the current rate of population expansion continues substantially unchecked then in about 30 yr the current 3.7 billion will essentially double. This will mean that in

the remarkably short period of the next third of a century as many new
hungry mouths will be added to the world's masses as it took all of man's
previous history to accumulate to the present time.

This can also be stated in terms of world average percentage increases in
population by years. Thus, while rates of increase of the order of 0.3% per
year characterized the 15th and 16th centuries and gradually rose to about
1.5% per year through the period 1950 to 1960, average world rate of
population increase from now to 1980 is estimated at 2.1% per year, and
from 1980 to 2000 should reach 2.6% per year. But this does not of itself
indicate the full impact of the population rise. The current average increase of 2.1% per year is not equally shared by all nations. The true
population explosion is occurring mainly in parts of Asia, Africa, the Near
East, and Latin America, where some countries are currently showing
population increases exceeding 3.3% per year. These are the areas of
greatest starvation today and the broad areas that will constitute 80% of
the world's population by the close of the century.

Population-Land Ratios

While this is going on the world's agriculturally productive acreage remains relatively constant. This of course means that the arable land per
person will be decreased proportionately. An interesting comparison can
be made by considering current and projected U.S. and world populations
in terms of this food-bearing land. Present U.S. population of 210 million
divided into this country's arable land gives a figure of approximately 2.2
acres per person. Present world population divided into current world arable land gives a corresponding figure of 1.1 acres per person. With land
remaining constant and U.S. and world populations expected to be approximately 350 million and 6.3 billion respectively by the year 2000, this
will result in approximately 1.3 arable acres per person in the United States
and only slightly over 0.5 acres per person for the world. Since little additional land will be made arable during this period it becomes evident that
the land must be made more productive.

Crop Yields

In keeping with the best current estimates that more than half the world
is ill-fed and that world population will essentially double by the end of the
century, it has been concluded by FAO and others that world productivity
of food must be increased 3- to 4-fold over essentially the next 3 decades to
prevent mass famine in the distressed areas. Where these increases are
most needed is evident from recent graphs on major crop yields (Fig. 321).
During the past decade wheat yields per acre in West Germany and France
ran some 5 to 7 times what they were in Tunisia and Brazil. Rice yields per

CURRENT WHEAT YIELDS IN SELECTED COUNTRIES RELATED TO UNITED KINGDOM'S HISTORICAL TREND

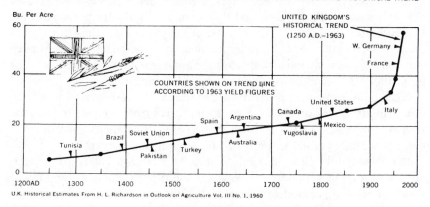

U.K. Historical Estimates From H. L. Richardson in Outlook on Agriculture Vol. III No. 1, 1960

CURRENT RICE YIELDS IN SELECTED COUNTRIES RELATED TO JAPAN'S HISTORICAL TREND

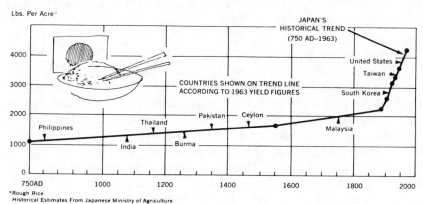

*Rough Rice
Historical Estimates From Japanese Ministry of Agriculture

CURRENT CORN YIELDS IN SELECTED COUNTRIES RELATED TO UNITED STATES' HISTORICAL TREND

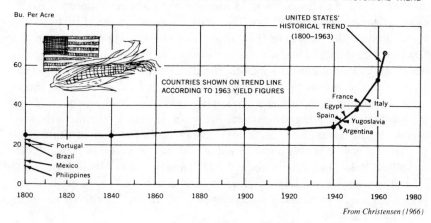

From Christensen (1966)

FIG. 321. RECENT CROP YIELDS IN VARIOUS COUNTRIES

acre in Japan and the United States averaged about three times greater than in India, the Philippines, and Pakistan. Yields of corn per acre in the United States ran some two times those of Egypt but more than three times those of Portugal or Brazil and approximately five times those of Mexico and the Philippines. Equally discouraging comparisons can be made for other important food crops. Since about 1968 the situation has improved appreciably with respect to yields of wheat and rice in several of these and other countries. However, many of the increases have been made from extremely low bases, and coupled with increased populations have thus far contributed only slightly to improving the overall food picture.

It is abundantly clear that major increases in crop yields are directly related to level of economic development and the possession of capital with which to purchase equipment, fertilizer, pesticides, and other technological devices of modern food production. Once again the poverty cycle appears and no one believes it can be broken in many of the less developed regions without major outside help.

Yields from Livestock

The quantity and quality of crop yields not only affect human nutrition but obviously also influence the state of well being of livestock and the yields of food that can be derived from them. Crop yields and animal feeding practices are not the only determinants of animal productivity but are major factors. In addition to being correlated with weight gains of animals and their further production of milk or eggs, improper feeding lowers resistance to disease. Thus the poverty cycle applies to man's animals as well as to himself. These factors aggravate productivity but the problem is still more basic since the efficiency of conversion of feedstuffs into flesh, milk, and eggs is a biological capacity of the animal or bird determined by its genetic history. In many of the more developed countries food producing animal and poultry strains are the products of over 200 years of controlled breeding. This is not at all the case in many of the less developed countries. Thus while a comparison of various livestock populations between agriculturally advanced nations may give a fairly good indication of the animal product contribution to the diet of a country, this is not a meaningful comparison when applied between advanced and developing countries. Striking differences between livestock productivities in various countries exist for all animal products. In the United States, for example, current average annual yield of milk per milking cow is over 8,000 lb while in Pakistan it is only about 1,000 lb and in parts of India a mere 500 lb. In the case of eggs, U.S. production level exceeds 200 eggs per bird per year while in some of the less developed countries it is believed to be no more than about 50.

Human Factors

Even where means can be made available to improve the nutritional status of a region or group there are often various kinds of barriers to overcome. Some of the proposed solutions to problems of hunger in specific regions have not always taken these barriers into account. Many have to do with custom, tradition, religion, or superstition.

On November 8, 1966 the following headline appeared in newspapers: "Worst Riots In 20 Years Hit India." These riots had to do with laws directed at the killing of some cattle. Presently the slaughter of cows is banned in much of India because the cow is sacred to orthodox Hindus. Hindu extremists demanded a total ban against slaughter of cows and threatened that unless this was enacted within two weeks there would be self-sacrifice by burning.

India has the greatest cattle density (including water buffalo) in the world for a similar size area. This amounts to some 250 million head of cattle, or one for every two persons. Not more than about 30% of the people of India eat meat of any kind. The cattle consume several times the total calories that are eaten by the human population. While much of this is not in competition with man because the sources of these calories are largely inedible by humans, there is nevertheless a considerable loss of potential food in not consuming more of the cattle. Further, resistance to elimination of the less productive animals results in a substantial drain upon total available livestock feed and forage that could otherwise be used more efficiently. The low milk productivity of the cattle as a whole also is rather resistant to change since cows that have dried up are not destroyed to be replaced with more productive animals. There is more to the total evaluation since transportation, work, and manure can be claimed from the cattle. However, only bulls are permitted to work, in keeping with the sacred status of the cows. The manure is commonly burned as fuel and has some land improvement value, although the latter is of no consequence in the case of animals roaming the cities. While these conditions persist, it has been estimated that 50 million Indian children may die of malnutrition in the next ten years. One must not make the mistake of judging another culture harshly or quickly. Nor are the problems of India to be solved in terms of livestock control alone. Human population control is unquestionably far more significant. But awareness of such barrier conditions is essential if programs are to be initiated that have a chance for success.

Even more fundamental than increasing crop or animal yields per acre in terms of pounds is to raise the levels of nutrients yielded per acre. In this regard crops differ, and not all animal conversions of grain are equally productive. Thus, for example, one bushel of grain consumed as such may supply a man with energy and protein adequate for about 23 days of sustenance. The same bushel of grain fed to cows and converted to milk would provide the man with energy for only about five days and protein for about 12 days. Similarly, the grain converted to pork or eggs would provide energy and protein in amounts far less than the grain consumed as such. This is because the animal or hen uses much of the potential nutrient of the grain to maintain its own body needs before it returns the excess in the form of useful food for man. Such relationships have been known for a long time, and in related fashion different crops are not equally efficient in their conversions of water, carbon dioxide, and soil constituents into animal or human food. Differences are further emphasized for a given plant or grain at the genetic variety level.

This appears to suggest that where food supply must be increased, and where climatic and land conditions permit, emphasis should be placed on growing the most productive plants and other food sources. Carried to a more extreme degree, attention is frequently called to the high conversion efficiency of nitrogen and carbon sources into nutritious proteins and carbohydrates by yeasts, bacteria, and algae. The food potential of plankton from the sea also is recognized. However, food habits and preferences are deeply rooted. They are passed from generation to generation and are difficult to change, even in the face of grave food shortages. There have been many instances where surpluses of one kind or another have been sent to villages only to have the unfamiliar food rejected. It has been pointed out by many experts that changes in eating habits could go a long way in improving the prospects of combating poor nutrition. On the other hand it is also well recognized that the human animal will most readily accept the foods indigenous to his area. Exports of wheat have been slow to be accepted by rice-eating populations. This can be changed through education, but the change is often slowest where illiteracy is greatest, which is precisely where hunger is most severe. From a practical standpoint, improvement of regional food yields from plants and animals traditionally accepted appears to offer the most promising results within a reasonable time.

Fertilizer

When one talks about improvement of crop yields one immediately thinks of fertilizer. Unfortunately, fertilizer like farm machinery and pesticide chemicals is not produced where it is most needed, and so currently much of it must be exported to less developed areas. This tends to raise the price of this high tonnage-low value commodity to the point where farmers in India and Africa must pay more for a pound of fertilizer than U.S. farmers. A further frustration with respect to fertilizer is that in the less developed areas, commonly the indigenous varieties of crops, which have not been improved by intensive breeding as they have in other parts of the world, are far less responsive to fertilizer than they are in many developed countries. This is generally true at any level of fertilizer application. Thus the Indian farmer who can least afford it must pay more for fertilizer which in turn gives him less of a result than the American farmer. Still more discouraging, he must pay with rupees from crops that sell for less than they do in the more developed nations.

Improved responsiveness to fertilizer requires the introduction of improved plant varieties and often changes in cultivation practices.This is what the green revolution is all about. But this too requires considerable reeducation and time. In the meantime it has been estimated that during recent years all of Latin America used little more fertilizer than Holland, and all of Africa employed about the same quantity as Italy.

Pesticides

With respect to pesticides a similar picture emerges. Cost limits use. In addition, imported pesticides generally were not developed for the specific pests and climatic conditions of unfamiliar regions. This has been especially true of tropical regions. Further, the effective application of pesticides often requires high pressure spraying equipment not generally found in the less developed areas.

Farm Machinery

As for heavy farm machinery again cost is a major deterrent. But even beyond cost the suitability of such machinery is presently limited by the characteristic small size of farms in most less developed areas. Such "farms" in many instances may constitute a very few acres or even less. Appropriate machines and tractors are being developed for these areas, but their use cannot be as efficient as that of machines on larger size farms. It also must not be overlooked that gasoline, oil, spare parts, and machine maintenance can become limiting factors in a remote region, as has happened many times in the past.

Transportation

The problem of transportation works two ways. Fertilizer must be applied at the local level. Thousand ton quantities of imported fertilizer cannot be efficiently moved inland on often primitive roads. The same problem applies to moving produce to highly populated areas of consumption. This latter situation has not always been appreciated in the past. Following the Italian-Ethiopean War of the 1930's, a mechanized tomato processing and canning plant was built in Ethiopia to take advantage of favorable tomato growing conditions. After building the plant, but not giving full consideration to the problems of road construction, it became evident that there was no way to move canned tomatoes from the plant except to fly them out. This was not economically feasible. Adequate roads have not yet been built, and the plant has never produced.

Current Status

Population and food production statistics in abundance have quantified the recent past and indicate that in most of the less developed countries food production and population trends have not yet been significantly altered, rather, food shortages continue to persist (Fig. 322). Current gross food supplies of various countries can be expressed in terms of available total Calories and protein (Table 83). Such figures have meaning when compared to recognized needs for normal body processes and health. It is difficult to generalize here since such needs vary widely depending upon different nationality's body weights, climates, occupations, individual's ages, sex, physiological state such as pregnancy or lactation, and so on. Nevertheless, considering populations in most developing regions, it may be said that gross inadequacy exists when per capita daily Calories drop below 2,000 and protein falls below 60 gm. But this is not the whole picture. In the case of proteins especially, quality can be as important as quantity. Quality is generally expressed in terms of protein of ani-

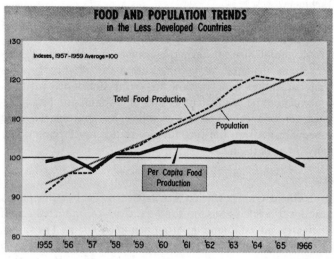

Courtesy of AID

FIG. 322.   FOOD AND POPULATION TRENDS IN THE LESS DEVELOPED
COUNTRIES

TABLE 83

FOOD SUPPLY OF VARIOUS NATIONS[1]

Country	Year	Per Capata Per Day		
		Calories	Total Protein Gm	Animal Protein Gm
United States	1969	3290	96.8	69.5
Mexico	1966	2620	66.3	14.2
Brazil	1968	2540	63.0	21.8
Equador	1966	1850	46.7	16.2
Japan	1969	2450	75.1	29.7
Pakistan	1969	2350	53.5	10.0
India	1969	1940	47.9	5.6
Philippines	1969	1990	51.6	20.0
Indonesia	1966	1750	38.2	5.2
Yemen	1966	1910	57.5	10.1
Ghana	1968	2070	43.0	7.3
Nigeria	1966	2160	58.6	5.1
Rwanda	1966	1900	57.0	3.6

[1] From FAO (1970B).

mal origin, of which much less than 20 gm per day is grossly insufficient. Since per capita availability of nutrients represent averages, actually the situation is worse than indicated because obviously segments of the population receive less than the average. Often worst affected by shortages is the group of children from weaning to five years old. Even beyond the grave mortality rate prior to school age in some areas, many children that do survive are permanently stunted both physically and mentally.

There are no simple answers nor quick solutions to the world food problem, and occasional headline-getting panacean schemes that fail to recognize many of the pertinent factors involved are to be deplored. Rather, most experts agree that widespread hunger will continue in several areas of the world before the trend can be reversed. But there is one very important positive factor: as never before the world has become increasingly aware of the problem and the means that must be taken to deal with it. This awareness has in large measure resulted from the extensive activities of the Food and Agriculture Organization of the United Nations.

THE FOOD AND AGRICULTURE ORGANIZATION

For the past quarter century FAO has been the most active and effective international force dedicated to the problems of world food needs. It is instructive to briefly examine its beginnings, objectives, and experiences toward these objectives.

The FAO was officially founded in 1945 as the first of the United Nations' special agencies. Its purpose in the broadest sense was the international handling of the problems of food and agriculture. These problems came into special focus at the close of World War II as a result of the war's disruption of industrial as well as agricultural economies, plus the emergence of several new nations without experience in government or modern agriculture. These new nations especially faced immediate prospects of food shortages, as did war torn countries with the problems of bringing neglected lands back to agricultural productivity.

When founded the entire FAO staff consisted of about 30 people including some seven professional men. While its staff and budget were small its aim was of great scope. This was stated as follows: "FAO will bring the findings of science to the workers in food and agriculture, forestry and fisheries everywhere; and it will bring the practical problems of these workers everywhere to the attention of the scientists. It will assemble, digest, and interpret information to serve as a basis for the formulation of policy, national and international. It can suggest action, but only through the activities of governments themselves can the objectives be finally won."

The first major undertaking of the FAO was in response to an urgent appeal from the Greek Government for help in getting its war wrecked agricultural economy going again. The FAO attack on the problem in 1946 set a pattern still typical of its operations. Recruiting from various national institutions it assembled a team that included experts in dairy, livestock raising, fisheries, fruit growing and packing, plant pathology, irrigation engineering, agricultural economics, home economics, and agricultural education. In Greece they found deserted and neglected farms, collapsed markets, destroyed transportation and service facilities, and widespread hunger. Their first proposals were for specific emergency measures to feed the children. At the Greek Government's request they then generated a comprehensive report for reconstruction. This included detailed plans for modernizing agriculture, expanding research and educational facilities, encouraging cooperatives, improving fisheries, supporting farmers with modernized processing plants, and harnessing water for irrigation and hydroelectric power. They further outlined needed changes in the fiscal system, civil service, and industrial development essential to support the agricultural reconstruction. Many of the proposals have since been carried out by the Greek Government with aid from the United States.

Since then FAO has grown substantially. Its new headquarters are in Rome and it is supported by over 100 member nations of the United Nations. Its experiences have clearly shown that progress in world feeding requires a total integrated approach of which the development and dissemination of technical and scientific information is only a part. This must be supported by the participation of experts working at the field level with farmers in their day to day problems. To accomplish this the substantial staff of FAO now includes several thousand experts from almost 100 nations working in as many countries and territories. This is further augmented by activities of FAO in advising governments on the effective disposition of aid and food surpluses, and in 1964 and 1965 by FAO entering into cooperation with the International Bank for Reconstruction and Development (World Bank) and the Inter-American Development Bank, to encourage and assist the flow of funds for agricultural and industrial development.

The work of FAO in the field is best grasped from some of their past projects. They have helped control plagues of locusts in North Africa. They have aided in stocking the streams and lakes of Haiti. In Liberia they have contributed to raising yields of swamp rice six-fold. In Tanzania, 1,000 small farmers were helped to plant tea in preference to other crops and thus increase their annual incomes 400%. They have instructed young farmers all over the world in the planting, growing, and harvesting of protein-rich plants. They have helped double the production of Iran's 20 million date palms. In Senegal, they assisted in setting up the first food canning plant in 1963. In less than one year the plant was producing 3,000 cans of meat and peanut sauce per day. In Burma, they helped establish a chain of rice storage centers spanning the country. They have provided assistance in the methods of catching anchoveta in Peru and in techniques of processing to convert them into a high protein, high quality palatable fish meal. They have helped set up 20 cooperative buying and marketing groups for fishermen and farmers in Columbia. They have instructed students in Bombay and other parts of the world in the operation of large scale food preparation equipment. They have sent nutritionists into India and other areas and instructed villagers in the values of local food materials. They have undertaken numerous modernization projects, especially in Asia, to combat problems of food transportation and preservation such as are underscored by the Indian fishermen of Fig. 323 painfully carrying their catch to market.

These are but a few of hundreds of such projects that FAO continues to be involved in. Throughout this work policy has been to enlist participation of local scientists, technicians, and labor and thereby always leave behind trained personnel to continue the work. FAO has defined hundreds of additional projects and needs and made them known to governments, universities, and industry, and they have awarded over 5,000 fellowships for study at universities, many of which were taken by technicians from developing countries. Two more contributions of FAO are of the greatest significance. They have determined quantitatively the magnitude of the world food problem in the face of exploding populations and their statistics have led to the important conclusion that the rate of world food production of the 1960's will have to be increased 3- to 4-fold to meet the needs of the doubled world population by the year 2000. Secondly, they

FIG. 323. FISHERMEN IN INDIA CARRYING THEIR CATCH TO MARKET

have been responsible for bringing to the attention of the world the importance of the problem. Governments and industry are now responding with increased imagination and energy.

AWARENESS AND AID PROGRAMS

Especially within the past 15 yr there has been a growing responsiveness to the world hunger condition by governments, international groups, the clergy, private industry, and individuals.

Food for Peace

The Food for Peace program was begun by the U.S. government in 1954 and expanded in 1960. The program has provided for the sale, trade, or donation of farm surpluses to needy nations. This program was carried out under Public Law 480 (the Agricultural Trade Development and Assistance Act of 1954). The Food for Peace program operated under four titles. Title I provided for the direct sale of U.S. agricultural commodities to friendly countries. Title II authorized government to government donations of farm products held in stock for famine and disaster relief, community development, school feeding, and other economic development purposes overseas. Title III provided for surplus commodity donations to needy peoples in foreign countries through American voluntary agencies and international organizations. Title IV provided for sale of commodities on credit repayable over an extended period. From 1954 to 1965 the total U.S. investment in this program amounted to approximately $25 billion. In recent years under Title II of Public Law 480 the United States also has been supporting the World Food Program. The World Food Program established in 1962 by the United Nations and FAO uses food in worldwide multilateral economic development, child feeding, and emergency situations.

A prime objective of the Food for Peace program was to make it possible for developing nations to move from aid to trade as they progressed economically. A number of countries, once large recipients of U.S. food aid, are now major cash buyers of American farm products. This is in keeping with the U.S. foreign policy goal of helping friendly countries move toward self reliance and economic independence. The Food for Peace program effectively used American food from 1954 through 1966. Its best features have since been incorporated into the current Food for Freedom program based on an amended version of Public Law 480. Two important features of the new Food for Freedom program include growing of crops to meet actual overseas needs rather than depending upon surpluses, and nutritional fortification of food supplements shipped as a donation, especially for children. Thus in 1967 more than 200 million pounds of a high protein supplement, blended of corn, soya, and milk powders plus vitamins and minerals, were shipped to 83 countries to complement incomplete diets. In 1970 over 330 million pounds of these high protein formulated foods were shipped overseas.

Freedom from Hunger Campaign

A landmark in focusing world attention on the challenge of hunger was the launching of the Freedom from Hunger Campaign by FAO in 1960. As stated by its originator, Dr. B. R. Sen, then Director-General of FAO, its purpose was "a vast educational and operational effort involving changes in the mental attitudes and social habits and customs of practically the entire human race." The Freedom from Hunger Campaign has intensively publicized available information on problems, needs, and possibilities of the hungry countries. It further has encouraged research into new methods of dealing with these problems and launched action in the form of specific projects many of which have been carried out at the field level, as described earlier.

International efforts to deal with poverty have created many United Nations special agencies, among them FAO, UNESCO, WHO, ILO, UNICEF, and others. But these organizations operate through their member governments or government institutions. The Freedom from

Hunger Campaign additionally called for the allegiance of nongovernmental organizations including religious groups, private foundations,
educational institutions, youth groups, private business, and individuals in
all countries in a coordinated strategy against hunger. The Campaign
further urged all nations to establish a Freedom from Hunger Foundation
to raise funds for the work to be done. The American Freedom from Hunger Foundation was named by the late President Kennedy in 1961.

There previously had been two surveys of the world's food situation, the
first published in 1946 and the Second World Food Survey published in
1952. Neither of these had anticipated the magnitude of the population explosion clearly evident by 1960. In this context, as part of the Freedom
from Hunger Campaign, the Third World Food Survey was undertaken
and later published in 1963. Besides presenting an overall picture of the
world's food needs it provided sharp comparisons between the developed
and less developed nations and established many of the food production
targets we accept today as crucial for the remainder of the century. In
his Christmas message of 1963, Pope Paul VI stated: "We knew that
hunger existed, but today it has been recognized. It now has been sci-
entifically proved to us that more than half the human race has not
enough food."

The mounting awareness of world food problems and international ded-
ication to positive action was dramatically revealed in an event of the
Freedom from Hunger Campaign designed by FAO to bring the pros-
perous and needy nations together in the common cause. This was the First
World Food Congress, held in Washington in 1963. Attended by 1,300
representatives of 107 countries and 65 nongovernmental organizations,
the assemblage of governmental officials, religious leaders, scientists, hu-
manitarians, industrialists, and observers from all walks of life constituted
a world parliament that confirmed hunger as a universal human responsibility. The Congress further provided for continued organized
planning and establishment of priorities with respect to use of resources
at present underutilized, and distribution of food surpluses for maximum
economic and social development. Many meetings of international scope
have since followed. Ushering in the 1970's was the Second World Food
Congress at The Hague, Netherlands, and the Third International
Congress of Food Science and Technology held in Washington. This latter
meeting, sponsored by the Institute of Food Technologists, also was
identified by the designation SOS/70. The letters SOS referred to Science
of Survival.

The Freedom from Hunger Campaign has awakened people throughout
the world and generated countless programs now continuing to go forward.
Literature has been disseminated worldwide. An International Stamp

Plan resulted in the issuing of special Freedom from Hunger stamps by more than 150 countries, which further spread awareness of the Campaign and yielded revenue toward its efforts. Artists and writers have publicized its goals. Religious leaders have presented the Campaign's message in sermons. Apart from the participation of governments, people of all nations have personally contributed funds and gifts and demonstrated in support of the Campaign's goals. Institutions such as the Ford Foundation and the Rockefeller Foundation have continued to give support. Teachers and professional associations have volunteered service. Educational institutions have established courses and scholarships in world food problems, and some have created branches in less developed countries. Technology centers have been established with help from FAO, governments, and the United Nations Special Fund. Fertilizer, pesticides, and machinery have been donated by industrial companies.

But for all that is presently being done, it is abundantly clear that the major contribution to helping developing nations help themselves can come only when industrial organizations of the developed nations become actively involved through investment in profitable ventures. It is a current major challenge to governments and banks to provide a favorable climate with minimum risk for this kind of activity.

Agency for International Development

In the United States, there is an agency of the Department of State which has as one of its principal functions to assist American industry in expanding overseas investment. This is the Agency for International Development, or AID. The services of AID take many forms in keeping with their view that "The United States itself has no better instrument for assisting development than its own private enterprise system with its reservoir of skills and investment capital."

AID maintains a "Businessmen's Information Service" which includes a "Catalog of Investment Information and Opportunities." The index of this catalog has already been supplied to over 50,000 organizations, firms, and individuals. It covers over 2,000 data and feasibility studies as well as current opportunities for joint ventures with developing country investors. These studies and survey reports relating needs to profitable ventures in every developing country of the world are directed at supplying equipment, building and operating processing plants, developing food distribution and marketing facilities, and so on. Many of these reports are so detailed that they provide blueprints for plant construction, lists of needed equipment with current market prices, utility requirements such as water, steam, and electricity, labor needs, etc. The reports then define feasible marketing outlets and prices that can be expected for products. Additionally they calculate the financial returns on investments that American firms could yield from such ventures.

In this type of activity AID is authorized to go still further. They will reimburse American firms for surveys the firms would wish to conduct on investment opportunities. They will provide financial guarantees for American firms investing in less developed areas against political and business risks. They will assist with financing of projects that promote international economic development. They will put American firms into contact with potential local partners in the developing countries for joint ventures. All of the above services are provided on a nonprofit basis to interested firms and individuals.

Participation of AID and the benefits it can offer American firms have attracted many to active interest and greater participation in overseas investment. Within very recent years top officers of some 30 major worldwide corporations formed an "Industry Steering Committee" to consider further opportunities in developing countries. As manufacturers of machinery, chemicals, fertilizers, containers, and as food processors and marketers these companies are in close liaison with AID and FAO and hold periodic meetings at FAO headquarters in Rome. AID also helped establish a volunteer corps of experienced American businessmen known as the International Executive Service Corps. In recent years over 2,600 experienced people have been available at modest rates to consult and assist small businesses in developing countries in such matters as market research, sales planning, buying techniques, product improvement, etc.

Quite apart from promoting American investment abroad, AID has contributed substantially to the goals of the Freedom from Hunger Campaign through its three-pronged assistance program in the broad areas of Agriculture and the War on Hunger, Health Improvement, and Education. The key to receiving assistance under the program is demonstration on the part of recipient nations of an earnest effort at self-help, a condition which past experience has shown is essential to make assistance programs aimed at development succeed. This AID program has represented a multibillion dollar investment of U.S. funds in recent years. The War on Hunger segment of the current program includes among its provisions the furnishing of American experts, commodities, and funds to increase agricultural productivity in developing countries through introduction of irrigation methods, better seeds, pesticides, fertilizer, improved farming methods, transportation, warehousing, distribution and marketing systems, etc. An important aspect of assistance also is concerned with financial and technical help in the area of birth control and family planning. This latter assistance will be entirely on a voluntary basis. Funds for disaster relief in any country also are provided. Plans with similar objectives also are being supported by many other nations.

THE GREEN REVOLUTION—A CHALLENGE

The term green revolution was first used in 1968 to describe enormous successive increases in the production of wheat and rice in India, Pakistan, the Philippines, and certain other countries following the planting of new hybrid varieties of seed.

The new "miracle" wheat seed culminated many years of breeding experiments by Japanese, American, and Mexican scientists, and in 1961 such strains as Pictic 62 and Penjama 62 were released by the laboratories of the Maize and Wheat Improvement Center, Chapingo, Mexico. Dr. Norman Borlaug, director of the wheat improvement program was awarded the 1970 Nobel Peace Prize for his contributions to this achievement. Similar successes with rice were achieved at the International Rice Research Institute in Los Baños, the Philippines. An outstanding rice variety IR-8 became available in 1965 and was planted in the Philippines and some other countries in 1966 with sensational results. These efforts received substantial financial assistance from the Rockefeller and Ford Foundations.

But the green revolution is not due to improved seed alone. The high yields possible from these improved varieties are realized only when large quantities of fertilizer and well-regulated supplies of water, generally through irrigation, also are provided. The costs of fertilizer, irrigation, and the large plots of land that can best exploit the potential yields from these miracle seeds have created new problems. In India, for example, small farms are rapidly being bought up by large land owners. Peasant farmers are thus being forced to leave the farms and seek employment in cities where there is now increasing joblessness. Further, increased grain yields in recent years have not necessarily reached the hungry millions in India and other countries. Much of the grain has been exported, making the large land owners richer at the expense of the needy. Additional problems arise from the lack of adequate grain storage and distribution facilities in India and other developing countries. These generally have not kept pace with the increased yields, and require great expenditures of capital before the promise of the green revolution can be widely fulfilled. It also is well recognized that the new varieties of rice and wheat are not as disease-resistant as some of the older types. This is especially significant where these new varieties have replaced a wide range of the older local types. Should new rust diseases emerge that are capable of infecting the principal wheat or rice hybrids now being planted, major disasters would result. This also is true with respect to changing insect pests, and has plant breeders concerned and occupied with the task of continued improvement of new varieties with broad spectrum disease resistance. Another problem with the new varieties of wheat and rice has been consumer resistance in some regions on the basis of cooking properties and taste.

As stressed by the FAO and other agricultural agencies, the green revolution has only just begun. Certainly one of its most positive effects has been to demonstrate what can be done in developing countries with available technology and capital under well managed programs. And this has provided new incentive for many countries at a time when it is much needed. But the growth of the green revolution and its influences upon social and political change are yet to be determined. The challenge certainly is not one for scientists alone.

SOME CONCLUSIONS

Much has been written on this subject and more will appear in the years ahead. A few things seem clear. We do not require any major scientific breakthroughs to markedly improve the world food situation now and in the future of the next few decades. Rather, we need to put to work effectively that which we now have and now know. The obstacles are not technological but rather organizational, administrative, and economic. New approaches to mass production of less conventional foods and proteins from algae, plankton, leaf extracts, microorganisms grown on petroleum fractions, and other sources are receiving considerable attention and are to be encouraged. But successes in some of these areas are still far off. Much can be done now toward at least doubling and possibly quadrupling food production with existing technology. Sometimes positive measures are ironically straightforward as in the case of Fig. 324. For many of us the outboard motor represents leisure and recreation. For this Ceylonese fisherman and his family it means more food, a better standard of living, and hope for the

Courtesy FAO

Fig. 324. One Means to a Better Life for a Ceylonese Fisherman

future. Certainly the wisdom and conscientious efforts of the highly developed nations in helping those less fortunate, while time remains, will determine the future for all.

BIBLIOGRAPHY

ANON. 1968. Strategy for the Conquest of Hunger—A Symposium. Rockefeller Foundation, New York.

ANON. 1971. Proceedings SOS/70. 3rd Intern. Congr. Food Sci. Technology. Inst. Food Technologists, Chicago.

BENDER, A. E., KIHLBERG, R., LÖFQVIST, B., and MUNCK, L. (Editors) 1968. Evaluation of Novel Protein Products. Pergamon Press, Oxford, England.

BORGSTROM, G. 1965. The Hungry Planet. Macmillan Co., New York; Collier-Macmillan, London.

BROWN, L. B. 1965. Increasing World Food Output—Problems and Prospects. U.S. Dept. Agr. Foreign Agr. Econ. Rept. 25.

CHRISTENSEN, R. P. 1966. Man's historic struggle for food. In Protecting Our Food—The Yearbook of Agriculture 1966. U.S. Dept. Agr.

DESROSIER, N. W. 1961. Attack on Starvation. Avi Publishing Co., Westport, Conn.

FOOD and AGRICULTURE ORGANIZATION. 1952. Second World Food Survey. FAO, United Nations, Rome, Italy.

FAO. 1963. Third World Food Survey. FAO, United Nations, Rome, Italy.

FAO. 1969. Manual on Food and Nutrition Policy. FAO Nutritional Studies 22. FAO, United Nations, Rome, Italy.

FAO. 1970A. Commodity Review and Outlook. FAO, United Nations, Rome, Italy.

FAO. 1970B. Production Yearbook. FAO, United Nations, Rome, Italy.

FAO. 1970C. The State of Food and Agriculture. FAO, United Nations, Rome, Italy.

GAYN, M. 1972. The dark side of the green revolution. In The 1972 World Book Year Book. Field Enterprises Educational Corp., Chicago.

ISENBERG, I. (Editor) 1969. The Developing Nations: Poverty and Progress. H. W. Wilson Co., New York.

KHARBAS, S. S., and SALUNKHE, D. K. 1972. World food and population problems: some possible solutions. Food Technol. 26, No. 4, 148–150, 152, 154, 156–159.

LAWRIE, R. A. (Editor) 1970. Proteins as Human Food. Avi Publishing Co., Westport, Conn.

LUNDEEN, G. A., and LUNDEEN, B. 1969. World Food Problems—Bibliography. Food Science Research Center, Fresno, Calif.

McGOVERN, G. S. 1964. War Against Want: America's Food for Peace Program. Walker & Co., New York.

MILNER, M. (Editor) 1969. Protein-Enriched Cereal Foods for World Needs. American Association of Cereal Chemists, St. Paul.

PARISER, E. R. 1971. The potential, the problems, and the status of using proteins of aquatic origin as human food. Food Technol. 25, No. 11, 88–90, 92, 94–96, 98, 100.

PRESIDENT's SCIENCE ADVISORY COMMITTEE. 1967. The World Food Problem, Vols. 1, 2, and 3. The White House, Washington, D.C.

REY, L. R. 1971. The role of industry in meeting the challenge of future food needs. Food Technol. 25, No. 1, 26–28, 30–32.

SCRIMSHAW, N. S. 1967. Ecological factors determining nutritional state and food use. In Alternatives for Balancing World Food Production Needs. Iowa State University Press, Ames.

UNITED NATIONS. 1969. Demographic Yearbook, 21st Issue. United Nations, New York.

U.S. DEPT. AGR. 1969. Food for Us All, The Yearbook of Agriculture. U.S. Dept. Agr.

VICKERY, J. R. 1971. Possible developments in the supply and utilization of food in the next 50 years. Food Technol. 25, No. 6, 55–60.

Index